Management Accounting for Healthcare Organizations
Fifth Edition

BRUCE R. NEUMANN, PhD
UNIVERSITY OF COLORADO AT DENVER

KEITH E. BOLES, PhD
UNIVERSITY OF MISSOURI

Healthcare Financial Management Association
and
Precept Press
Division of Bonus Books, Inc., Chicago

Library of Congress Catalog Card Number: 97-75989

International Standard Book Number: 0-944496-60-1

02   01   00   99   98   5   4   3   2   1

Healthcare Financial Management Association
Two Westbrook Corporate Center
Suite 700
Westchester, Illinois 60154

Precept Press
Division of Bonus Books, Inc.
160 East Illinois Street
Chicago, Illinois 60611

Printed in the United States of America

This edition is dedicated to the memory of

Professor James D. Suver, DMA, CMA, FHFMA (1932–1995), for his excellent contributions to the field of healthcare financial management.

About the authors

Bruce R. Neumann, Ph.D., is Professor of Accounting and Health Administration in the Graduate School of Business Administration, University of Colorado at Denver. Dr. Neumann is one of the founders of the University of Colorado's Executive Graduate Program in Health Administration. He also helped found HFMA's Executive Certificate Program in Health Care Financial Management. Dr. Neumann has also written instructional software for microcomputers in this area.

The author earned his doctorate at the University of Illinois, where his dissertation research pioneered the concept of peer grouping for hospital cost reimbursement and for performance evaluation. His undergraduate and master's degrees are from the University of Minnesota. Dr. Neumann has taught at Northwestern University, the State University of New York at Albany, Bond University (Queensland, Australia), and the University of Auckland (New Zealand). He has also served as a research associate at the Hospital Research & Educational Trust (Chicago) and the Health Services Management Unit (Manchester, England).

Dr. Neumann is author or coauthor of numerous articles as well as two texts on accounting. He designed and published a uniform chart of accounts for medical group practices, as well as a system for paying hospitals for prospective capital costs. He has also served on the board or as president of several community groups. Dr. Neumann's research interests include cost efficiency analyses, payment methods under Medicare and Medicaid, public policy analyses, and analyses of cost behavior patterns.

Keith E. Boles, Ph.D., is Associate Professor of Health Services Finance in the Health Services Management Program at the University of Missouri. Previously he was Assistant Professor of Finance at the University of Colorado at Colorado Springs, and Adjunct Assistant Professor of the Program in Health Services Administration at the University of Colorado at Denver. Dr. Boles is also on the faculty of the Executive Program in Managed Health Care Administration, a cooperative program between the University of Missouri Program in Health Services Management and the University of Missouri - Kansas City College of Business. He also serves on the faculty of the American College of Health Care Administrators.

Dr. Boles received his M.A. in Economics from Florida Atlantic University and his Ph.D. in Economics and Finance from the University of Arizona. His undergraduate degree was in accounting from the University of Illinois. Research activities include determination of indicators and predictors of financial distress, and development of risk management techniques. He is actively involved in projects with rural hospitals, nursing homes, and managed care organizations attempting to provide activities and changes necessary to ensure long-term survival of services in these areas.

Contents

Foreword

Management accounting is a discipline that is vital for healthcare leaders now and in the future. It is vital because the issues of increasing cost and limited access to healthcare services cause government representatives, business leaders, and the public to demand greater efficiency and effectiveness from healthcare providers. The discipline of management accounting provides to healthcare executives the tools they need to meet this challenge in the management of their organizations' resources.

This book provides the most comprehensive coverage of this topic for healthcare organizations. The authors describe the concepts of management accounting as applied to healthcare organizations and provide the techniques healthcare leaders need to make appropriate decisions.

This book assists healthcare executives in answering the myriad of questions concerning the business side of healthcare service delivery. The authors identify many of these questions at the beginning of each chapter and then provide the answers to these questions and many more in the pages that follow.

Healthcare financial managers and accounting students will have a special interest in this topic—and this book—because financial accounting is the basis for many management accounting techniques. Cost-benefit analysis, break-even analysis, and financial ratio analysis are but a few of the management accounting techniques that use financial accounting data.

Management accounting, however, is not just for financial managers and students. The techniques described in this book provide the basis for effective decision making in many disciplines. And effective decision making is the basis for the efficient and effective management of healthcare resources.

Of special interest to all healthcare executives is the chapter on total quality management (TQM). The TQM approach to management uses the techniques of management accounting to assist in the measurement of quality improvement, benchmarking, and management by fact. Most healthcare experts believe that TQM provides the paradigm to respond to the conflicting challenges of increasing cost and declining access to healthcare services—in other words, to do more with less.

By publishing this fifth edition of *Management Accounting for Healthcare Organizations,* the Healthcare Financial Management Association demonstrates its continuing commitment to provide students, healthcare financial managers, and other healthcare executives the tools they need for effective resource management. In an environment that expects more for less, these tools are vital.

Richard L. Clarke, FHFMA
President and CEO
Healthcare Financial Management Association
Westchester, Illinois

Preface

In this fifth edition, we have tried to continue the theme of the earlier editions in preparing a text that could meet the needs of two distinct users: practitioners experienced in the field of healthcare and newcomers just entering the field. Most academic programs would tend to fall in the latter category while continuing education programs would be closer to the former. The design of the text and the problems provide the flexibility to meet both needs. For example, the sequencing of the material in the chapters and the chapters themselves move from the basic concepts for the novice to the more sophisticated techniques for the senior manager. In a similar manner, the problems are sequenced from the easier concepts to the more difficult.

Because of the rapid change and increasing complexity of the healthcare financial management environment, this edition has been substantially rewritten to capture the impact of these changes on the management accounting function. For example, the impact of prospective pricing systems, the increase in capitated payments, the changes in capital payments for depreciation and interest, the use of a resource-based relative value system (RBRVS) for physician payment and the shift to total quality management (tqm) paradigm pose new challenges for the user of management accounting information. In addition, the increasing emphasis on alternative healthcare providers such as nursing homes, health maintenance organizations, and ambulatory care centers has required a more thorough coverage of the management accounting needs in nonhospital based settings. To meet these needs as effectively as possible, we have tried to provide conceptual frameworks which will be useful to a variety of financial management decisions in different types of providers.

The authors have field tested the chapters in this edition in traditional and nontraditional settings, and in standard graduate and executive program formats in several geographical locations. We are deeply indebted to all our students for their thoughtful insights and perseverance in reading through typos and incomplete sentences.

We are also indebted to the professionals at HFMA and Precept Press, who helped the authors through the process. In this revision we have corrected all of the errors of which we are aware. Your assistance in identifying future possible changes will be appreciated. A special thanks must go to the reviewers who provided many useful suggestions and clarifications of the field of practice which was necessary to appropriately apply many of the theoretical concepts. Richard L. Clarke, the President and CEO of HFMA, gracefully agreed to write the foreword to this edition to let all of us share in his views of the major challenges confronting the financial manager in the healthcare field today.

The authors would be remiss not to express a special sense of gratitude to our families who suffered through the deadlines and revisions. Their understanding of the tradeoffs was critical to the final product.

There are many individuals who have helped the authors during this revision and the earlier editions of this text. They have earned a share in whatever recognition and benefits that might be gained from this text. However, as all authors know, the authors alone must take full responsibility for the errors and omissions that may still remain.

CHAPTER 1

Introduction to management accounting

"Is there any chance that we will be able to at least break even this year?"

"Do we have sufficient information to be able to respond to this RFP from Acme Corporation to provide all the healthcare services for their employees?"

"How much does it cost us to lease this equipment, instead of buying it?"

"Our budget process really takes too long. Is there anything that can be done to speed up the process?"

"What can be done to make the departmental managers feel they will benefit if they improve the operations of their department?"

These are some of the questions which managers must answer that have a managerial accounting focus.

Introduction

What is management accounting? Management accounting is a discipline that focuses on the development, reporting, and use of accounting information that is useful for decision making. It is built primarily on a financial accounting base, but also includes the disciplines of economics, human behavior, and finance. Management accounting should provide information that will improve the efficiency and effectiveness of the use of economic resources. We will be using the concepts of efficiency and effectiveness as follows:

Efficiency means doing whatever we are doing in the best way possible, by either using the fewest amount of resources in the provision of appropriate health services, or getting the most health services out of the resources we are using.

Effectiveness means doing the right thing; we may be doing whatever we are doing extremely efficiently, but if we are not doing the right thing, we still have problems.

Another way to express the same concept is to focus on the difference between leaders and managers—"Managers do things right (efficiency). Leaders do the right things (effectiveness)."[1]

Management accounting is different from financial accounting in that it is future oriented. Financial accounting is used to report on what has happened in the past, (i.e., last year, last quarter, last week). Management accounting uses past information to focus on what will happen in the future. Financial accounting operates within a structure called GAAP (Generally Accepted Accounting Principles) that have evolved from the inputs of many authorities over the years and is continually being adapted to fit the needs of the users. The Financial Accounting Standards Board (FASB) or the Government Accounting Standards Board (GASB) have the primary responsibility for maintaining the currency of the accounting standards. A primary focus of GAAP is a reliance on standardization and verification. Since most external users (lenders, investors, regulators) depend on the financial statements for their assessment of the financial condition of the healthcare organization, the importance of having an independent auditor (CPA) attest that the financial statements were prepared in accordance with GAAP is understandable.

Healthcare is somewhat unique in that there are three distinct parties involved in most transactions: the provider, the consumer, and the payer, normally some form of insurance agent (the third party). Since the insurers provide many of the funds by which the healthcare providers are able to operate, these third parties are able to require additional forms of accounting information. The federal government through the Medicare program, the state government through the Medicaid program, and formal rate setting and reimbursement programs all mandate that specific quantitative information in a standardized report be provided. Finally, other major third party payers such as Blue Cross and Blue Shield also have required special reports. It appears the "golden rule" prevails in healthcare (i.e., "those that have the gold make the rules"). However, it must be remembered that these external reports are developed for a specific purpose, (i.e., meeting the needs, purpose, structure, and process of the third party payer) and may not be useful for internal decision making purposes.

Historically, the primary concern of healthcare organizations has been to meet the accounting requirements of the external providers of funds. This emphasis resulted in a lack of development of management accounting information. Although some of the information collected and developed for GAAP and third party accounting requirements are relevant to decision making, the majority is not. Management accounting requires additional information and generally a different format. Management

---

[1] Bennis, W.G., and B. Nanus, *Leaders: The Strategies for Taking Charge,* New York, Harper & Row, 1985.

accounting must be oriented toward decisions made by managers within the organization. The focus is internal and it is on decisions. Consequently, the information prepared for, and used by, internal decision makers must be relevant to that decision.

The purpose of this text is to develop the concepts and techniques that form the foundation of management accounting in healthcare organizations. Since accounting systems provide most of the quantitative information in a healthcare organization, it is important to understand the differences indicated above. However, it is equally important to recognize that different decisions require different types of information. For example, reports used to evaluate departments and individuals (performance reports) have different objectives than budget reports. Yet both are typically prepared from the same data base. In an effective internal information system the outputs of the management accounting process are usually unique and depend on the decision to be made.

The management control process

An example of an internal management function which relies heavily on management accounting information is the management control system. The management control process is concerned with both organizational effectiveness and efficiency. It is possible to be very effective but also very inefficient. The U.S. healthcare system is said to be effective (for most patients) yet inefficient in terms of resources consumed. In other words, if the objective is to prolong life there are vast amounts of resources to be used. However, just using the resources does not imply efficiency. The decision maker should always ask, "Is there another way to accomplish the same objective that is less costly in terms of resources utilized (i.e., substituting home healthcare or "step down" facilities instead of short-term, acute hospital intensive care beds)?"

Given current government interest in budget deficit reductions, there are some decision makers who feel the U.S. healthcare system has become overly concerned with efficiency and has lost sight of the effectiveness goal. It is important to recognize that both should be accomplished in a healthcare organization. *Exhibit 1–1* identifies the various stages in the management control process.

The management control process consists of several important steps. The establishment of objectives is necessary in order to determine the benchmark against which the outputs can be compared (effectiveness). The second step is to establish programs and products which are consistent with the established objectives. Once programs are determined which are believed to be consistent with the previously established objectives, it becomes necessary to determine the required resources (inputs) necessary to make the project or product operational. During this stage budgets are formulated and costs and revenues are estimated. During the

Exhibit 1–1
Management control process

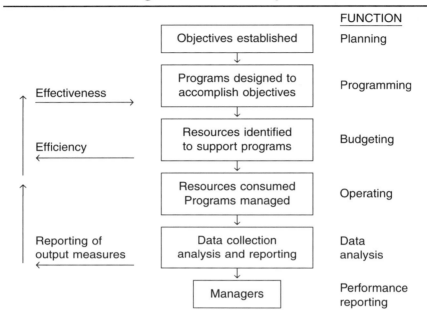

	FUNCTION
Objectives established	Planning
Programs designed to accomplish objectives	Programming
Resources identified to support programs	Budgeting
Resources consumed Programs managed	Operating
Data collection analysis and reporting	Data analysis
Managers	Performance reporting

Effectiveness

Efficiency

Reporting of output measures

process of implementation and operation of the project it is necessary to manage both the resources consumed and the project itself. This step requires that monitoring of the activities take place on a continual basis and that this data be analyzed and reported to the appropriate individuals. The feedback provided by the reporting mechanism should then provide valuable information with which to make any needed adjustments. It is important that management be involved at all stages in this process in order to ensure that their behavior will match the desired behavior.

A major problem occurs in the measurement of performance; we need to measure output. But what unit of measurement do we use? In the measurement of efficiency, an input/output relationship needs to be established, with outputs identified with the resources consumed. The measurement of inputs is fairly straightforward. We have the expense data for the inputs from the financial accounting system. However, the output is usually expressed in terms of DRGs (Diagnosis Related Groupings), patient days, lab tests, nursing hours worked, or meals served. Although these surrogate measures provide some indication of efficiency, they are not particularly useful for measuring effectiveness. To provide support for the measurement of effectiveness, these measures must be placed in an objective format, such as: we would like to admit a specific number of DRG 310, provide so many patient days, or pay for so many nursing hours. In the purest sense, when these output surrogates are used, we are implying the organization's objective is to provide employment for healthcare professionals as contrasted to an organizational objective of improving the health status of the individual or the community. Much work remains to be done in this area, but the researcher/designer must stay away from the "ease of collecting and availability of data syndrome" which has hampered efforts in the past. We must design measures which capture the real output of our objectives. Because of its importance in decision making, management accounting information should have an important role to play in the development of output measures.

Another major focus of management accounting is the assessment of behavioral responses to the performance reports. Ideally, a report on a department's performance should have some favorable impact on that department's decisions. If the department's costs are out of control some cost-reducing activity would ideally occur. If the department's performance level is acceptable, one would hope that a performance report would lead to the continuation of whatever activities contributed to the results achieved. In other words, if a manager has done something good, a report on that performance should help to induce similar behavior in the future. If unfavorable results are observed, performance reporting should lead to a change in decisions or managerial behavior that will help achieve better results in the future.

Unfortunately, the ideal results that are expected to occur as part of performance reporting do not always happen. Performance reports may be ignored. They may not be distributed on time to the right people. They may induce behavior in a direction opposite of that intended by top management. In such cases, performance reports may have no effect on decision behavior, or they may have negative effects. Ignoring or misusing performance reports may have deleterious consequences.

Research in this area suggests that management accounting must embrace the objective of goal congruence. That is, all parts of the management control system should lead to an increased congruence between organizational objectives and the objectives of individual managers and participants in the organization. Performance reporting can help the organization move toward a higher level of goal congruence. Research in this area suggests that increased participation in decision making will help to avoid the negative consequences of performance reports. Reports on a department's performance should avoid emphasizing noncontrollable costs. For example, nursing service supervisors cannot control the costs incurred in maintenance and dietary. Although these costs are a part of providing healthcare to the patient, they are not the responsibility of the nursing supervisor. Although the nursing service supervisor can often influence these costs and should be aware of them, all indirect or allocated costs should be separated from direct costs such as nursing salaries, etc. Performance reports should not include significant amounts of allocated costs that cannot be controlled by the responsible manager. In a similar manner, performance reports should reflect the impact of volume on the incurred costs. This concept of cost behavior is especially vital in healthcare organizations, where many of the costs are fixed, regardless of volume of services provided. Performance reports should reflect the relationship between managerial decisions and the behavior of costs.

Many of the ways to improve performance reporting and the behavioral impact of performance reporting are described in more detail in subsequent chapters of this book. Recognition of the potential behavioral impact is the first step to improving performance reporting. Alternative formats should be tested in the hospital or in the individual department. An effective manager will be aware of the potential behavioral impact of performance reporting and take action to avoid negative consequences.

Total financial requirements

A major problem in using financial accounting information for decision making is that the typical accounting system does not report the level of resources needed to meet the total financial requirements (TFR) of the organization. The total financial requirements of an organization include the following:

1. The costs of doing business.
2. The costs of staying in business.
3. The costs of changing business.
4. Returns to the suppliers of capital.

A financial accounting system does not capture the total financial requirements of an organization due to the fact that it is primarily based on historical events and does not recognize nonaccounting events. Total financial requirements by necessity are forward looking and therefore must include a consideration of future replacement costs, new technologies, growth, etc. Therefore, it is important to not only have a thorough understanding of the content and limitations of financial accounting, but also to recognize that the disciplines of economics and finance provide valuable inputs into the determination of total financial requirements. *Exhibit 1–2* illustrates the individual components of each category of TFR, each of which will now be discussed in greater detail.

The *costs of doing business* are captured adequately by a financial accounting system within the constraints of GAAP. However, the working capital requirements are not shown on the financial statements. Working capital provides the necessary funding to cover the timing difference between when the inputs used in the provision of services must be paid, and payment is received for those services. For a typical acute

Exhibit 1–2
Total financial requirements

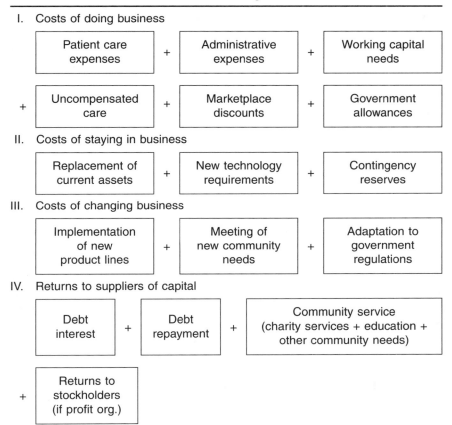

I.　Costs of doing business

| Patient care expenses | + | Administrative expenses | + | Working capital needs |

+ | Uncompensated care | + | Marketplace discounts | + | Government allowances |

II.　Costs of staying in business

| Replacement of current assets | + | New technology requirements | + | Contingency reserves |

III.　Costs of changing business

| Implementation of new product lines | + | Meeting of new community needs | + | Adaptation to government regulations |

IV.　Returns to suppliers of capital

| Debt interest | + | Debt repayment | + | Community service (charity services + education + other community needs) |

+ | Returns to stockholders (if profit org.) |

care hospital, this difference averages sixty to ninety days. The opposite is true for prepaid plans such as HMO's where payments are normally received before services are provided.

Information on the *costs of staying in business* is provided on a limited basis by the financial accounting system. For example, depreciation expense is reported in the financial statements, but depreciation expense is based on the acquisition cost of the original asset, not the current replacement cost which would include technological improvements that typically have been made in the healthcare asset. Merely funding (setting aside the cash) your depreciation expense will not guarantee you can replace the asset when it is obsolete or worn out. The healthcare manager must set aside enough funds to meet future needs, not just past expenditures. Similarly, due to the volatility of the healthcare environment, contingency reserves need to be available so the organization can react to unforeseen needs and errors in planning. The financial statements do not include these amounts.

The *costs of changing business* are seldom captured by the financial statements until the expenses have been incurred. New breakthroughs in healthcare technology, new community needs, government regulatory changes, and finally, opportunities such as the changes in Eastern Europe and the Soviet Union that can lead to international healthcare delivery systems require a manager to have resources on hand to respond quickly. Although subjective in nature, they are part of a manager's responsibilities.

The final category, *returns to suppliers of capital,* is also captured on a limited basis by the accounting statements. For example, interest expense and bad debt will be reported in expense accounts on the Statement of Revenue and Expense (net income). The repayment of debt principal will be reflected on the balance sheet and cash flow statement. Dividends to stockholders in investor-owned organizations will be captured in the cash flow statement. However, dividends to the community in the form of education, service, and free care are not recognized directly as expense items. They are typically buried in administrative or patient care costs, or show up as a footnote to the financial statements.

The identification of total financial requirements will show that operating with an accounting bottom line at breakeven, or zero net income, will not allow a healthcare organization to remain financially viable in the future. This is because accounting information is used and for the reasons stated above, not all economic costs are covered. Economic costs are based on the inflow of funds needed to maintain a financially viable healthcare organization in the future. It has been estimated that a bottom line of 10 to 15 percent of revenues will probably be needed to meet total financial requirements in the future. Healthcare organizations that do not meet this requirement will slowly decline while they are consuming resources built up through past efforts. Given the current accounting "bottom line" performance (2 to 4 percent) for most short-term, acute hospitals in this country, it would appear that the resource base for healthcare organizations is being consumed, and downsizing must occur in the future to match expectations with financial resources.

Overview of trends in health sector

The ever increasing proportion of national resources spent on the healthcare sector has led to concerns regarding the appropriate role of healthcare providers and the rate of annual growth in annual spending. As healthcare spending consumes a larger share of the nation's resources, it may supplant spending for other purposes, such as education, social programs, and growth of the infrastructure. Although there is no agreement about the portion of the nation's resources that should be devoted to healthcare, there is agreement that huge increases cannot be sustained.

Several factors are responsible for the rapid growth in healthcare spending. General inflation results in cost increases in non-medical items such as materials, non-medical supplies, and labor. Some of these factors also contribute to the growth in healthcare expenditures. A second factor is specific to the healthcare industry. This inflation occurs when firms must pay more for healthcare inputs, such as nurses or physical therapists who may be in short supply and demand higher wages. A third factor is the increase in population in the United States. As more people consume healthcare, total spending increases.

This last factor is primarily due to the expansion of private and public health insurance coverage and technology changes. Since 1960, both the number of individuals covered by health insurance and the benefits of the policies have expanded. In 1965 and 1966 many people were covered by Medicare and Medicaid, which increased access for the elderly and the poor. Similarly, the many health insurance policies and governmental programs have also expanded to cover more types of care.

Sources of payment for healthcare have also dramatically shifted in the past 30 years. Insurance as a source of payment for personal health services has increased from 1960 through 1993. Similarly, out-of-pocket spending has decreased. Payments by the government, often through Medicare and Medicaid, have increased. Private health insurers and government programs that pay for medical care are often called *third party payers*. The other two parties are the patient and the provider. Third party payers pay providers for the care they deliver to patients.

Insurance increases healthcare expenditures by increasing the demand and utilization of healthcare services. When third party payers pay medical bills, consumers tend to be less sensitive to the price of individual services. They often demand more services, as well as higher quality services. Since many employers pay medical care insurance premiums for their employees, individuals are further insulated from the price of healthcare services. The beneficiaries of governmental programs, such as Medicare and Medicaid, are also insulated from these prices.

Payment to providers for services have often been structured, through insurance coverage, in a way that stimulates increases in expenditures. From the mid-1960s, through the early 1980s, most third party payers paid providers on the basis of either charges or actual costs incurred. As a result, providers and consumers had few incentives to control utilization. Providers had no incentive to operate efficiently. The provider received more payment for providing more services as well as more expensive services. Efficiency was rewarded by decreased payments. Frequently, to attract patients, providers engaged in non-price competition by offering the latest technology, nicest surroundings, and other costly amenities. This type of payment, based on volume of services, is called *fee-for-service* payment.

New technology also contributes to the rise in healthcare expenditures. New, costly procedures, such as heart transplants and coronary artery bypass grafts, and new equipment, such as sophisticated magnetic imaging equipment, have been developed. Their use has spread rapidly. Often this results in duplication of services and excess capacity.

The escalation in healthcare costs has resulted in changes in the way that healthcare is purchased. The Federal government has a long history of trying to control healthcare cost increases, often by legislative control or by limiting eligibility to certain programs. For many years, private health insurance companies simply passed their cost increases on to individuals or employers by increasing health insurance premiums. During the last decade, most payers have cooperated to slow the escalation in healthcare expenditures.

Attempts to control spending have focused on regulation, new payment methods, and managing care. Early attempts to control spending were primarily regulatory. For example, certificate of need programs require review approval for capital expenditures. Other programs monitored and set payment rates within states or for certain designated programs (e.g. nursing homes). Changes in payment methods include:

1. placing limits on the annual rates of increase in fee-for-service payments;
2. switching from cost-based payments to establishing uniform payment rates for particular types of services, regardless of the cost;
3. paying discounted charges;
4. contracting with a limited number of providers selected on the basis of competitive bidding or quality criteria, e.g. "preferred providers."

Recently, payers have begun putting providers at financial risk. These methods involve uniform payments based upon the diagnosis of the patient, rather than on the basis of resources consumed. These financial incentives help control utilization of services. Often, managed care organizations pay a flat amount for the care of an enrolled member, on a monthly basis (per member per month), regardless of the utilization of services.

During the 1990s, *managed care organizations* have also become more involved in the coordination of a patient's medical care, controlling access to specialists and specialized services. This has become one of the most popular methods for trying to control the rapid increase in healthcare expenditures. *Figure 1–1* shows the growth in managed care which is expected to continue through the remainder of the decade. Managed care organizations coordinate care and control costs by:

1. coordinating a patient's medical care by a primary care physician;
2. requiring prior authorization for expensive or specialized care, such as surgical procedures;

Figure 1–1
How medically insured Americans' care is provided

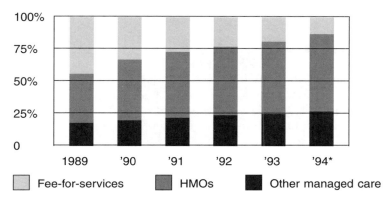

*Forecast
Source: Sanford C. Berstein & Co.
Source: *USJ,* August 26, 1994, p. 1.

3. paying primary care physicians a set amount (capitated amount) for each enrolled member regardless of the actual healthcare services that may be necessary or provided, also called "capitation;"
4. limiting patient's choice of physicians to a "pre-approved" roster who may have been selected based on quality, cost, price, or efficiency factors;
5. providing other financial incentives to providers and patients.

These methods, involving various financial and other incentives, often involve putting healthcare providers "at risk." They are at risk for financial loss if they do not control the healthcare cost or quantity of services provided to those enrolled in the managed care health plan. Although the practice of managed care is still evolving, there is some evidence of its success in controlling costs.

New organizations have emerged in the attempt to control healthcare costs. *Health maintenance organizations (HMO)* combine insurance and delivery of a broad range of comprehensive health services to an enrolled population. Members or enrollees pay a monthly fee or premium (per member per month, or *pmpm*) for access to services. *Preferred provider organizations (PPO)* link employer health benefit plans and health insurance carriers who contract to purchase healthcare services for covered beneficiaries from a selected group of participating providers (physicians or hospitals). Typically, participating providers in PPO's agree to abide by utilization limits or other controls that monitor and control access. They also agree to accept the PPO's reimbursement structure and payment levels. More than two-thirds of all hospitals have contracts with either an HMO or a PPO. More than one-third of all Medicaid participants are enrolled in managed care plans. Medicare participation in managed care plans is also increasing rapidly, more than doubling from about 6 percent in the early 1990s to more than 12 percent in 1996.[2] In summary, participation in various forms of managed care is growing throughout all sectors of the economy.

Historically, payers absorbed the risk of healthcare cost increases. If costs exceeded the premium revenues, payers were able to pass these losses and increased costs on to employers or individuals in the form of higher premiums. Recently, employers have demanded better cost control and lower rates of premium increases. Another recent change has been the transfer of risk to providers of healthcare services by changing the payment methods. Payers may make fixed payments for treatments regardless of the provider's cost; they may pay a fixed amount per enrollee who chooses to use a particular provider; or, payers may withhold a portion of the payment, "returning" it at the end of the year if specific utilization goals are met.

Providers and payers may be free-standing entities or part of complex multi-unit firms. Examples of free-standing organizations include unaffiliated hospitals, solo physicians, and community-based health plans. Increasingly, both providers and payers are consolidating in larger firms. The consolidations may occur through purchase or merger or through *alliances* where ownership does not change. This phenomenon has occurred among hospitals, physicians, insurance companies, and other healthcare organizations.

Larger firms may be *horizontally integrated,* when a firm is comprised of many similar units. Examples include multi-hospital systems, such as Columbia/HCA or Samaritan Health Services. Similarly, physician group practices can also be horizontally integrated by purchasing or merging across many physician groups, such as PhyCor. Horizontally integrated firms may own many nursing homes, such as Manor Care. They may also be *vertically integrated,* when they provide a continuum of care, such as when the same firm provides physician, hospital, nursing home, home health, preventive, and hospice care. Vertical integration of payer and provider firms is gaining in popularity. Examples include the development of an insurance or HMO division of a hospital or the purchase of an insurance firm by a hospital system. Integration may be accomplished through common ownership of all sub-units or through alliances with less formal involvement.

An additional factor that contributes to the rise in healthcare costs (per admission) and expenditures is the steady downward trend in occupancy rates. *Exhibit 1–3* illustrates this trend since 1989, when occupancy rates

---

[2] *Healthcare Trends Report.* (January 1997): 8–10.

Exhibit 1–3
Occupancy rates and staffed beds
at community hospitals, 1987–95

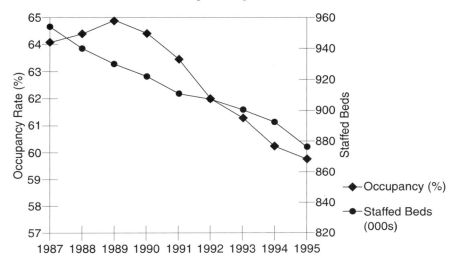

Source: Adapted from *Healthcare Trends Report* 10, no. 10 (October 1996): 10.

peaked at 64.9 percent. Since then, occupancy rates have declined by more than ten percentage points (to 59 percent in 1995). The paradox is that while declines in occupancy should contribute to cost reductions, they do not. After studying the fixed cost relationships in this text, you should have some further insight as to why this paradox exists. Even more interesting is the corollary decline in the number of staffed beds at community hospitals since 1987 (also shown in *Exhibit 1–3*). Such declines in beds and staffing should result in cost savings. As you study the cost behavior patterns in this text, you may gain insight into this conundrum.

Summary

The objective of this book is to improve managerial decision making. Management accounting should provide information that will improve the efficiency and effectiveness of the use of economic resources. Many issues and problems will be discussed that cannot be fully covered. Therefore, each chapter contains a list of recommended readings. As particular issues arise, the reader is advised to refer to as many of the recommended readings as necessary to develop an increased understanding about the concepts. Appendices at the end of each chapter contain related materials or excerpts from journal articles to provide additional insight into particular topics. In many cases, the problems in each chapter, along with their solutions, provide additional specific guidance for using the recommended techniques.

It is intended that this book will help the reader develop specific techniques that can be implemented in healthcare organizations. These techniques should lead to more relevant managerial accounting data. As the quality of information improves, the quality of decisions can improve. Whether it does is up to the decision maker. The mere presence of information will do nothing; it must be used in the decision process. If used correctly, it will help to improve managerial decisions. Generally, the cost of implementing any of these techniques will be minor compared to the benefit that can be obtained, but a benefit/cost analysis of any proposed change should be considered.

Questions and problems

1. Define management accounting.

2. What is the primary difference between management accounting and financial accounting?

3. Define the concept of efficiency in healthcare organizations.

4. Define the concept of effectiveness in a healthcare organization.

5. Can an overemphasis on effectiveness interfere with the efficiency objective? Explain.

6. Define the management control process for a healthcare organization.

7. Name several examples of surrogate output measures for a healthcare organization.

8. Why should healthcare administration be concerned with the format of the performance reports for their organizations?

9. Explain the concept of goal congruence in a healthcare organization.

10. Explain some of the difficulties that may occur when accounting statements prepared for external users are used for internal decision making.

11. Define total financial requirements for a healthcare provider.

Keywords: capitation; control; efficiency; effectiveness; fee-for-service; health maintenance organization; horizontal integration; managed care; managerial accounting; Medicaid; Medicare; not-for-profit firm; payer; performance reporting; preferred provider organization; third party payer; total financial requirements; vertical integration.

References

Abbey, Duane C., and L. Lamar Blount. "Assessing the Financial Implications of APGs." *Healthcare Financial Management* (October 1996): 50–55.

Anthony, Robert N., and David W. Young. *Management Control in Nonprofit Organizations.* Homewood, IL: Richard D. Irwin, 1988.

Boland, P. *Making Managed Healthcare Work: A Practical Guide to Strategies and Solutions.* New York: McGraw-Hill, 1991.

Broyles, Robert W., and Michael D. Rosko. *Fiscal Management of Healthcare Institutions.* Owing Mills, MD: National Health Publishing, 1990.

Bryce, Harrington J. *Financial & Strategic Management for Nonprofit Organizations.* Englewood Cliffs, NJ: Prentice Hall, 1987.

Cleverley, William O., ed. *Handbook of Health Care Accounting and Finance.* Rockville, MD: Aspen Publishers, 1989.

Cleverley, William O. "Improving Financial Performance: A Study of 50 Hospitals." *Hospital & Health Services Administration* (summer 1990).

Cleverley, William O., and Roger Harvey. "Profitability: Comparing Hospital Results with Other Industries." *Healthcare Financial Management* (March 1990).

Conrad, Douglas, Thomas Wickizer, Charles Maynard, Theodore Klastorin, Daniel Lessler, Austin Ross, Naomi Soderstrom, Sean Sullivan, Jeffrey Alexander, and Karen Travis. "Managing Care, Incentives and Information: An Exploratory Look Inside the 'Black Box' of Hospital Efficiency." *Health Services Research* 31, no. 3 (August 1996): 235–259.

"The Disturbing Trend of Not-For-Profit Hospital Conversions." *Public Citizen Health Research Group Health Letter* 12, no. 7 (1996): 1–7.

Fubini, Sylvia, ed. *Healthcare Trends Report* 11, no. 1 (January 1997).

Gapenski, L.C. *Understanding Health Care Financial Management.* Ann Arbor, MI: AUPHA Press/Health Administration Press, 1991.

Gapenski, L.C. *Healthcare Finance for the Non-Financial Manager.* Chicago: Probus Publishing, 1994.

Garner, Martha, ed. "Financial Reporting Issues." *Topics in Health Care Financing* 16, no. 4 (summer 1990): 1–85.

Granof, M., P. Bell, and B.R. Neumann. *Accounting for Managers and Investors.* 2d ed. Englewood Cliffs, NJ: Prentice Hall, 1993.

Hamburger, E., J. Finberg, and L. Alcantar. "The Pot of Gold: Monitoring Health Care Conversions Can Yield Billions of Dollars for Health Care." *Clearinghouse Review* (August–September 1995): 471–504.

Herkimer, Allen G., Jr. *Understanding Health Care Accounting.* Rockville, MD: Aspen Publishers, 1989.

Herzlinger, Regina E., and Denise Nitterhouse. *Financial Accounting and Managerial Control for Nonprofit Organizations.* Cincinnati, OH: Southwestern Publishing, 1991.

Ingram, Robert W., Russell J. Petersen, and Susan Work Martin. *Accounting and Financial Reporting for Governmental and Nonprofit Organizations.* New York: McGraw-Hill, 1991.

Lefton, Ray. "Aligning Incentives using Risk-Sharing Arrangements." *Healthcare Financial Management* (February 1997): 50–57.

Kongstvedt, P.R. *Essentials of Managed Care.* Gaithersburg, MD: Aspen Publishers, 1995.

Kovner, A.R., ed. *Jonas's Health Care Delivery in the United States.* 5th ed. New York: Springer Publishing, 1995.

Lee, P.R., and C.L. Estes, eds. *The Nation's Health.* 4th ed. Boston: Jones and Bartlett Publishers, 1994.

Managed Care Assembly, Medical Group Management Association. "Glossary of Terms Used in Managed Care." *Medical Group Management Journal* (September/ October 1995): 52–65.

Murray, Dennis, Bruce R. Neumann, and Pieter Elgers. *Using Financial Accounting: An Introduction.* Cincinnati, OH: South-Western College Publishing, 1997.

Neumann, Bruce R., Jan P. Clement, and Jean C. Cooper. *Financial Management: Concepts and Applications for Health Care Organizations.* Dubuque: Kendall/ Hunt, 1997.

Trahan, E.A., and L.J. Gitman. "Bridging the Theory-Practice Gap in Corporate Finance: A Survey of Chief Financial Officers." *The Quarterly Review of Economics and Finance* 35 (1995): 73–87.

Wacht, Richard F. *Financial Management in Nonprofit Organizations.* 2d ed. Atlanta, GA: Georgia State University Press, 1991.

West, Joan, Sandee Glickman, and Alan G. Seidner. "Investing: Reducing Risks to Enhance Returns." *Healthcare Financial Management* (September 1996): 48–51.

CHAPTER 2

Costs and managerial decision making

"What is the cost of this DRG, service, procedure, or test for pricing policies (or for reimbursement purposes)?"

"How much must the volume increase to break even on this service, test, or procedure?"

"Should we accept this discount offer from the HMO (or PPO)?"

"How can I measure the financial performance of this service, this manager, this hospital, or this physician?"

"What does it cost to provide all health services for this person?"

"Why does Medicare say it costs us only $456 for this procedure when our accountant says it costs $719?"

"Why can't the accountant give me the cost information I want? She always asks so many questions."

"Why are there a thousand different cost figures for the same procedure?"

"Is there any way we can assign costs so that our managers take the responsibility for their control?"

"How much of the cost will be saved if we decide not to offer this service?"

All of the above cost implications use accounting information as an input into the determination of cost. In this chapter we are going to discuss what cost means, how it is determined, and how it can be used in alternative types of decisions. A thorough understanding of these concepts will establish a solid foundation for grasping the material in later chapters.

Introduction

One of the most difficult concepts to grasp in healthcare decision making is how to use "cost" information effectively. In fact the term, cost, itself is difficult to define in a meaningful manner. Regardless, some of the most crucial decisions confronting healthcare managers today involve an understanding of cost information.

We often misuse the term "cost" when discussing with someone who has recently made a purchase, by asking, "What did that item cost?" What we are really trying to determine is the price of the item. This is contrasted to the value of the resources used in the production of the item, which is much closer to the concept of "cost" as used in this text.

The term "cost" in accounting theory has a very precise definition. It is the value assigned to an asset on the balance sheet. It becomes an expense when it is used in the provision of services and then appears in the income statement of investor-owned organizations (sometimes called Statement of Revenues and Expenses by tax exempt organizations). Therefore, while the typical question is asked: "What is the cost of this service?", the correct terminology would be "What is the expense of this service?" However, common usage of the term "cost" in everyday language makes it impossible to change to the more academically correct definition. As will be discussed later, this does not have to be a major issue if the decision maker recognizes that the term "costs" and "expenses" are the same when accounting costs are used in the decision. This is typically the case in today's environment. However, it should be recognized that 'economic' costs should be used in many decisions. This difference is more than semantic. For example, accounting costs are costs that have been determined in accordance with generally accepted accounting principles (GAAP). Economic costs are more inclusive and include a return to *all* the suppliers of capital to the organization and focus on cash flows. One way to resolve this difference is to include a positive operating profit in the determination of accounting costs for breakeven. Positive operating profit is defined as the amount required to keep the organization financially viable in the future. Economic costs consider the total financial requirements of the organization. Unfortunately, since this is rarely done, most decisions that use accounting costs in the determination of costs are understating what accountants call the *full costs* of the service. This concept is discussed in more detail in chapter 9.

Elements of accounting costs

The basic elements of accounting costs are materials, labor, and overhead costs. (Overhead costs are typically defined as the support and administrative costs.) The total accounting costs of offering a service or serving a department would include these costs. *Exhibit 2–1* illustrates this concept.

Total accounting costs would typically be included in the budget for the department or service. All of these costs must be covered if the organization is to achieve accounting breakeven.

Exhibit 2–1
Total accounting cost components

Total accounting cost components of intensive care service

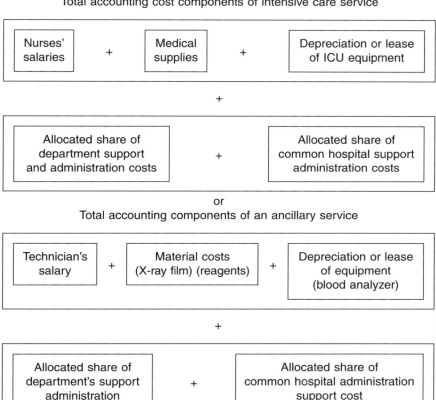

or
Total accounting components of an ancillary service

For many decisions, it is also necessary to determine the per service or unit cost. This is generally accomplished by use of the averaging technique where the total accounting costs of the service are divided by the level of activity as shown in *Exhibit 2–2*.

Exhibit 2–2
Per unit service cost determination

$$\text{Average or per Unit Service Costs} = \frac{\text{Total Costs}}{\text{Volume or Quantity of Activity}}$$

Exhibit 2–3
Sample activity bases for costing techniques

Department	(Macro)	(Micro)
Operating room	Surgical cases	Operating room minutes
Anesthesiology	Anesthesia cases	Anesthesia case minutes
Postoperative rooms	Postoperative cases	Post operating room minutes
Radiology	Exams	RVUs
Laboratory	Tests	RVUs
Physical therapy	Modalities	Treatment minutes
Isotopes	Treatments	RVUs
Blood bank	Transfusions	RVUs
Delivery room	Deliveries	Treatment minutes
Social service	Visits	Treatment hours or fractions of hours
Emergency room	Visits	Treatment minutes
Routine service	Patient days	Hours of care
Physician services	Charges	RBRVS
Ambulatory care	Visits	AVGs
Per procedure or per case	DRGs	Intensity of care or acuity levels

There is often more than one possible activity that could be used as the denominator in calculating the average or per service costs. Normally, this activity base is expected to be related to the incurrence of the total costs indicated in the numerator. The activity base selected will influence the average cost for the service being costed. Activity bases can be categorized as being either macro or micro in orientation. As indicated by examination of *Exhibit 2–3,* macro activity bases encompass more than one task or procedure, or are based on larger units of time than are micro activity bases. Micro activity bases require more extensive record keeping than do macro bases. There has been a marked increase in the use of micro activity bases in the determination of per unit costs to more accurately reflect the amount of care provided. The total costs of a particular department can also be influenced by the accounting system and allocation technique used. Therefore, total department costs are impacted to various degrees by the accounting system and allocation technique chosen. This will be discussed more thoroughly in chapter 9. However, it is useful to recognize that per unit costs can be influenced by the accounting methods used to determine total costs and the activity base selected.

Management accounting cost classifications

For decision making purposes, it is useful to group costs into three categories:

1. Responsibility
2. Volume
3. Capital Investment

Responsibility costs are the type of cost information used in performance evaluation. The determination of costs which are controllable within the responsibility domain of the person or department being evaluated is important in this category.

Volume-related costs are significantly influenced by changes in volume. Pricing decisions typically fall into this category along with average cost determination per unit of service. Fixed and variable cost concepts are crucial to this category.

Capital investment costs deal with decisions made today that heavily influence the future (i.e., a major equipment purchase or as a new joint venture). Marginal, incremental, and opportunity costs are key components in this category.

All of these categories will be discussed in greater detail in this and later chapters, but it is important to recognize that the type of decision being made will heavily influence the type of cost information needed.

Responsibility costs

As discussed earlier, this category focuses on assigning responsibility to some decision maker for the costs incurred in a department or for providing a service. In order to do this we need to segregate the total costs into direct and indirect categories. Direct costs are generally defined as those costs which can be specifically traced to, or identified with, a specific procedure or service. An example would be the salary and fringe benefits of the professional and support personnel who contribute directly to the providing of a service or the monitoring of the equipment in an intensive care unit. In most hospital or nursing home departments, this type of cost constitutes the major operating expense. Also included in the category of direct costs are materials such as lab supplies, special materials, etc., which are directly related to the providing of a service. It should be stressed that the concept of direct costs depends on the level of responsibility being discussed. All costs are direct costs to the total organization. This is not the case when discussing a specific department within the organization, or a specific service within the department, or for a specific procedure within a service within the department within the organization. For example: The CEO's salary is a direct cost to a health services organization, but is not a direct cost to any specific department within the organization. A departmental manager's salary is a direct cost to both the organization and the specific department, but is not a direct cost to any specific service provided within the department. The wages of a technician hired to perform only a specific service within the department are a direct cost to the organization, the department, and the service, but not necessarily to a specific procedure within the service.

The salaries of nursing personnel would be a direct cost to a nursing unit and also to the entire hospital. Basically, one major criterion in deciding whether an item is a direct cost or not is whether the cost would be eliminated if the service were no longer provided. For example, if the intensive care unit were closed, the staff costs would no longer be incurred, hence, these costs are direct costs of the intensive care unit. However, the CEO's salary would still have to be paid.

Indirect costs, on the other hand, are those costs which cannot be specifically traced to an individual service or procedure. Indirect costs will continue even if the particular service is no longer provided. Indirect costs include any cost that cannot be classified as a direct cost. Some examples are office supplies and equipment, rent, general insurance, and most management costs. Again, the definition of what is a direct or indirect cost depends upon the level of aggregation desired. Almost all costs could be considered direct at the organization level; however, at the individual department level there are fewer direct costs and many more indirect costs. *Exhibit 2–4* indicates some possible cost categories for a laboratory department.

The difference between direct and indirect costs is important to the CEO and to the department supervisor. There generally are no arguments that direct costs of providing a service should be included in charges for that service. However, there is no such clear relationship for indirect costs. How much of the cost of hospital administration is caused by the patient care procedure? There is no cause/effect relationship; therefore, some method of allocation must be used to calculate full cost. For example, the cost of utilities will probably not vary directly with the

Exhibit 2–4
Typical cost elements in a laboratory

Generally direct costs	Generally indirect costs
Individual supplies used for patient services	Secretaries' salaries Administration supplies
Laboratory personnel salaries	Administrator's salary Financial services
Equipment depreciation	Receptionist's salary Library expenses
Equipment repair	Rent General insurance Fund raising General depreciation

volume of service provided, yet it is a cost of providing service. One method used in the case of utilities is to allocate the total utility cost on the basis of the square footage of the space used to provide the service. This would mean that large, bulky equipment would receive more utility costs than smaller items, such as laser printers. The choice of an allocation base will naturally influence the allocated (indirect) portion of full costs.

As a general guideline, managers should only be held responsible for the costs they can control or significantly influence. This would indicate that the separation of total costs into direct and indirect is crucial for performance evaluation. It is also crucial that costs used in determining the full cost of a service must include both direct and indirect categories. The amounts should be determined by the best information available.

Cost/volume relationship

One key to the effective use of management accounting techniques is an understanding of how certain costs react to changes in volume. How does the number of admissions affect costs? If more laboratory tests are performed, how will costs change? The relationship of costs to volume is an important concept for managers to understand. If healthcare managers want to be able to predict changes in costs as the volume of service changes, they must understand cost/volume relationships and incorporate them into their decision models.

Conceptually, all costs can be divided into two categories: fixed and variable. Variable costs are those costs which vary directly and proportionately with volume. For example, if total costs associated with a certain procedure increase 10 percent with a 10 percent increase in volume, those costs would be classified as variable. Patient care supplies are examples of pure variable costs since they increase in proportion to the number of patients served. Fee for service activities in which the physicians are paid on a per procedure or visit basis are also variable costs to patient care.

Conversely, fixed costs are those costs that do not vary with volume. Most indirect costs such as rent, insurance or taxes, are examples of fixed costs. A good example of a fixed cost would be professional staff or supportive personnel who are paid on a salary basis. In other words, their salaries do not increase directly with the number of services provided. The word "fixed" should not imply that the costs cannot be changed, but rather that they do not change automatically as a result of volume. The salary of a nurse supervisor may be changed, but this change would be caused by a specific management decision, not automatically by an increase in volume of patients or services provided. *Exhibit 2–5* stresses the key characteristics of fixed and variable costs.

Exhibit 2–5
Volume related cost definitions

Fixed Costs (FC)—Do not vary directly with volume of activity (changed only by
management decisions).
Variable Costs (VC)—Vary directly with volume of activity; reflect resources
directly consumed if one unit of activity is provided.

It is sometimes easier to grasp the concept of fixed and variable costs by displaying their characteristics graphically. *Exhibit 2–6* for variable costs and *2–7* for fixed costs are examples of cost behavior.

Several assumptions are made in separating costs into fixed and variable categories. First, there is a finite range and a specific time frame associated with the categorization. For example, the level of fixed costs is a function of the range of volume of activity selected. A nurse supervisor could supervise five RNs on a shift. If additional volume of patients were expected and more than five RNs were needed for quality care standards, then another nurse supervisor must be hired. Therefore, the graphic portrayal of one level of fixed cost assumes that all resource constraints have been met for the ranges shown. In constructing a graphic portrayal of fixed cost for nurse supervisors, there would be a separate fixed cost graph for levels A, B, C, and D. *Exhibit 2–8* illustrates this relationship.

Exhibit 2–6
Total variable costs (TVC)
(no fixed costs)

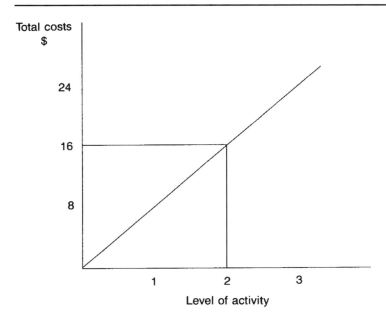

Level of activity

Exhibit 2–7
Total fixed costs (TFC)

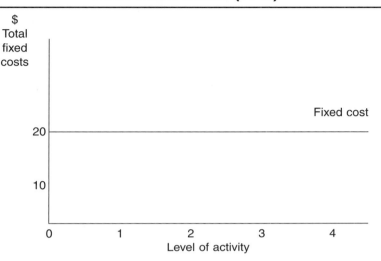

Exhibit 2–8
Ranges of fixed costs for nursing supervisors

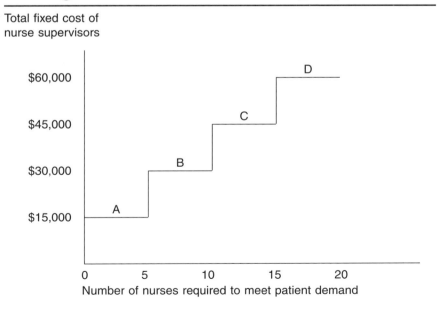

Some types of fixed costs cannot be changed as easily as discharging an employee. For example, an empty patient bed may not be staffed due to declining census. Staff would be sent home and the labor related costs would not be incurred. However, the capital related costs such as depreciation expense associated with the bed, building, and support equipment could not be changed in the short run. This is how the time dimension influences the level of fixed costs. In the long run, the bed, building, or equipment would not be replaced or it could be sold. This is why the statement can be made, that in the long run all costs are variable.

The identification of variable costs are also influenced by the level of activity and the time span of the analysis. A key assumption of variable cost behavior is that variable costs are linear—that is each unit costs the same as the one before. If each unit of supply costs $x, the variable costs for supplies for one patient day is $1x, for two patient days $2x, etc. This is captured by the slope of the variable cost curve in *Exhibit 2–6*. If we combine the graphs in *Exhibits 2–6* and *2–7*, we can construct a graph illustrating total costs for a specific activity as shown in *Exhibit 2–9*.

Exhibit 2–9
Total costs

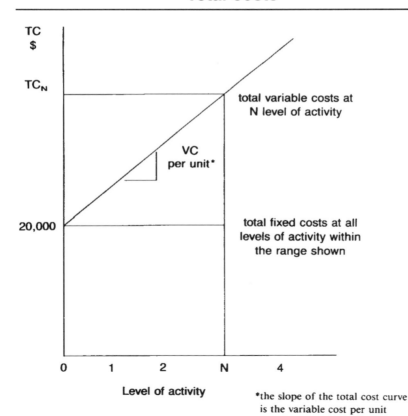

*the slope of the total cost curve is the variable cost per unit

So far, we have concentrated on total costs for a department, a service, or activity. Many decisions focus on the per unit costs for services and activity. In fact, most questions focus on "What does this procedure, service, etc., cost?" Although not specifically stated, the questioner usually wants to know the "full cost" amount. This brings into the discussion the concept of full costs and per unit costs. Full costs per unit mean the total cost of providing one unit of activity. This is obtained through the basic averaging technique; total costs divided by level of activity or $\frac{TC}{Q}$, where Q = level of activity completed (graphically, this would be portrayed as shown in *Exhibit 2–10*).

As is illustrated, there is a different total cost per unit at each level of activity. It is greater at Q_1 than Q_2, which is greater than at Q_N.

What causes the per unit costs to change? It is important to restate that the total cost (TC) of any level of activity consists of the total fixed (TFC) and total variable (TVC) costs. In order to get the full cost per unit, we

Exhibit 2–10
Per unit costs

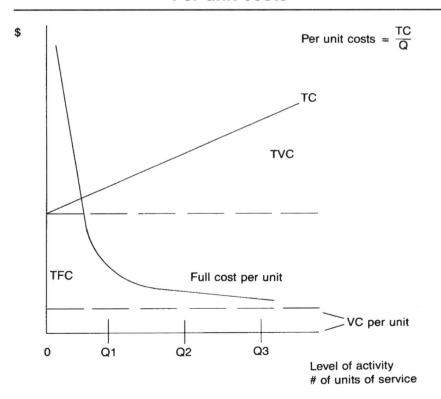

must divide the TFC and TVC (or TC) by the level of activity to calculate the average. *Exhibit 2–11* illustrates this concept.

As can be observed from the graphs in *Exhibit 2–11*, the standard definition of fixed and variable costs only refers to TFC and TVC. Total

Exhibit 2–11
Total and per unit cost behavior

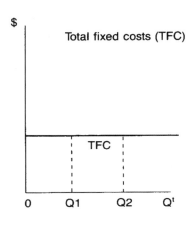

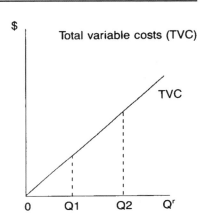

$$TC = TFC + TVC$$

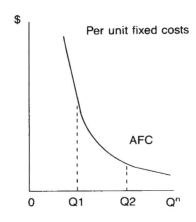

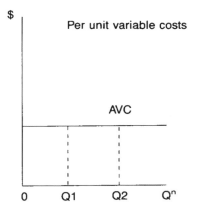

$$AC = \frac{TFC}{Q} + \frac{TVC}{Q}$$

fixed costs do not vary with changes in volume and total variable costs do. When per unit costs are determined, variable costs per unit are fixed and fixed costs per unit vary. Therefore, the only way full costs per unit can be calculated is to specify a level of activity, and the amount calculated will only be accurate at that level of activity. For example, let us assume a laboratory has a variable cost of $8 per visit and fixed costs of $200,000. The results shown in *Exhibit 2–12* would be obtained.

Exhibit 2–12
Full cost determination

(1) Estimated number of procedures	(2) Average variable cost	(3) Average fixed cost	(4) Full cost per procedure (2 + 3 = 4)
1,000	$8	$200	$208
2,000	8	100	108
3,000	8	67	75
4,000	8	50	58
5,000	8	40	48
6,000	8	33	41

In another example, consider the difficulty of determining the full costs of operating an emergency room. Most of the costs are usually fixed, with the exception of medical supplies and some record keeping. In a typical emergency room, the fixed costs probably approximate 90 percent of the total cost of this service. The estimate of the number of patients using the emergency room will be crucial in determining the cost per visit. Assume the following facts:

1. Total emergency room fixed cost is $60,000 per month.
2. Variable costs per unit are $1.
3. Estimated number of patient visits is 5,000.

The cost per patient visit would be:

$$\frac{60,000}{5,000} + \$1 = \$13$$

If the estimated number of patients to be seen is changed to 4,000, the cost becomes:

$$\frac{60,000}{4,000} + \$1 = \$16$$

When setting prices, it is generally more conservative to estimate volume on the low side. For example, in our previous problem, assume the patient volume is estimated to be 6,000 visits. Given this estimate, the cost per patient visit becomes:

$$\frac{60,000}{6,000} + \$1 = \$11$$

If charges are based on the high volume estimate (6,000 visits) and the low volume (4,000 visits) actually occurs, the hospital could run into financial difficulty by charging $11 when the costs are $16 per unit.

It is important to stress that direct and variable costs are not necessarily synonymous. Direct costs are those that can be traced to a single procedure or program. Variable costs are costs that vary with the change in volume of procedures. Most variable costs are also direct costs, but not all direct costs are variable.

For example, the laboratory materials used in a procedure are a variable cost because the costs increase proportionately with the number of procedures. The cost of these materials would also be a direct cost. The cost of the equipment used in the procedure would also be a direct cost, but it would not be a variable cost because the total cost of the machine is not affected by the number of procedures performed (unless it is leased on a units of service basis or the capacity of the equipment is exceeded). This would be called a direct fixed cost.

A determination of which costs are direct is very useful in assigning responsibility for cost control. At the same time, the separation of cost categories into fixed and variable is absolutely necessary to determine the full cost of a given number of procedures or services.

Estimating the variable and fixed cost components

The determination of the variable and fixed cost components can be accomplished by several methods. The most obvious one is direct inspection of the cost categories. For example, the chemicals used in a lab test, the film for an X-ray scan, and the fee charged for a physician's visit are all variable costs in relation to the volume of activity performed. It is also usually possible to separate the costs which are entirely fixed such as administrative salaries, plant depreciation, and housekeeping.

However, there will always be some costs which cannot intuitively be classified as clearly fixed or clearly variable. These "mixed" costs must be segregated into their fixed and variable components by statistical methods such as regression analysis, statistical sampling, and explanatory data analysis (see chapter 3). These techniques are especially necessary when only *total* data is available on costs and level of activity as shown in *Exhibit 2–13*.

Exhibit 2–13
Ward 3C—Nursing hours paid by month

Volume	Nursing hours	Total cost
July	2,200	$14,650
August	1,200	11,350
September	2,500	17,050
October	3,000	17,650
November	1,700	13,100
December	1,600	12,900

Nursing managers wanting to predict future costs would be interested in determining if there was a variable component to the cost of nursing in 3C as a function of nursing hours. A simple technique that approximates the regression analysis technique is called the high-low approach. In the high-low approach, the differences in total volume and total costs are determined and, based on the premise that between any two volumes only the variable costs would change, a variable cost per unit of activity can be calculated. Substituting the data from both the high and low volume into the basic cost equation (TC = TFC + TVC) and recognizing that TVC equals VC per unit times the quantity of units (TVC = $VC_u(Q)$), the fixed costs can also be determined. Using the data in *Exhibit 2–13* the following information can be calculated.

High volume	Low Volume	Difference
(Oct.) 3,000 hrs. −	(Aug.) 1,200 hrs. =	1,800 hrs.

Related total costs
(Oct.) $17,650   −   (Aug.) $11,350   = $6,300
Difference in total costs/difference in hours
= variable cost per hour
or
$6,300/1,800 = $3.50 variable cost per hour

The amount of total fixed costs (TFC) can be determined in the following manner:

Total costs = TFC + total variable costs
Total costs at volume of 3,000 hours = $17,650
Total variable costs = 3,000 × $3.50 = $10,500
Therefore: $17,650 = TFC + $10,500
TFC = $17,650 − $10,500 = $7,150
Therefore total costs = $7,150 + $3.50 (# of hours)

Using either the high or low volume total will yield the same fixed cost estimate. The reader should verify this assertion.

In this type of estimating, the high and low volume points are selected as representative totals of the entire distribution; this may not always be the case. A technique which offers a visual presentation of the cost behavior is called a scatter diagram. In a scatter diagram, the various volume/total cost relationships are plotted as shown in *Exhibit 2–14*. A straight line is visually fitted to the data points with the total fixed costs being indicated at the intersection of the curve and the y-axis.

Exhibit 2–14
Volume/total cost relationships

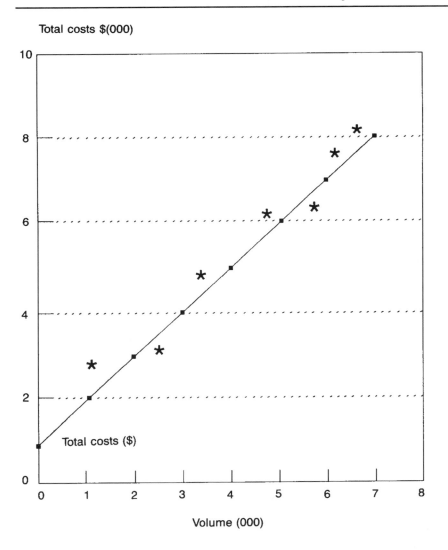

Total costs $(000)

Volume (000)

The total cost axis intercept can be estimated as $1,000 (*Exhibit 2–14*). Therefore, fixed costs are estimated at $1,000. Given this information, the variable costs can be determined using the same methodology as the high-low method. In this example, the variable costs are $1 per unit of service.

As one example of how the "real healthcare world" anticipates or uses the concept of variable costs, look back at the relationships shown in *Exhibit 1–3*. This data shows how the healthcare industry has adjusted staffing patterns to occupancy rates. Even though many managers in the 1980's thought that salaried staff (including nurses and physicians) should be treated as fixed costs, the data shows that managers adjusted their staffing patterns to reflect declines in occupancy; thereby treating what may have once been fixed costs as variable costs.

Differences in the terminology and application of fixed and variable costs exist in many healthcare organizations. The following debate, reported by Mistarz, illustrates these various views:[1]

> How much detail is needed in breaking down costs, and how far a hospital should go in constructing a matrix of costs, can be debated. But in order to break down costs to the procedure level, Truman Esmond, president of Truman, Esmond & Associates, advises that the hospital should first break down operations. For example, laboratories could be one unit, and they could be broken down into discrete subunits. Tests can be broken down, he says, because certain tests are for hematology, some are for chemistry, and others for nuclear medicine.
>
> "You may or may not be able to break these down into discrete sorting units in your laboratory," Esmond says, but the goal is to create discrete costing units not based on averaging. After breaking down operations into discrete units, he explains, the laboratory example can be broken into fixed and variable components. Costs are allocated to the laboratory, to radiology, and to other places. Ultimately, these costs are allocated to a procedure.
>
> Not all panel members agreed with the total methodology. Neil Bennett, vice-president and regional director, Pacific Southwest region, American Medical International, Inc. (AMI), stated that AMI "firmly does not use the term 'fixed.' That hospital is not fixed. That executive director is not fixed. Nothing is fixed."
>
> He explains that a laboratory manager may be regarded as a fixed cost at other hospitals. But that manager's responsibilities could be changed, and that person could become the manager of both laboratory and radiology departments. "So I don't have a fixed cost in the laboratory department," he says.

---

[1] Mistarz, Jo Ellen, "Cost Accounting: A Solution, but a Problem," *Hospitals,* October 1, 1984, pp. 96–101.

Regardless of variations in terminology and methodology, the need for a costing system remains. As Esmond explains "Basically, what we're talking about is modeling to develop the impact of change on the institution by changes in mix or volume. Hospitals really need to use a number of grids, or matrices, because the whole product-line format changes. At one point we may be talking about DRGs; at another, about physical organizations or subspecialties; and at still another, the major service categories."

Esmond comments that "in terms of where we are in costing, there's a possibility of going way overboard." But, he adds, many hospitals do not go far enough. "A focus on DRGs seems to be the only horizontal breakdown in most places. At many institutions, you see that not all patients are included in the matrix. Medicare patients are on the matrix, for example, and other patients are not. In some cases, we're still talking about DRGs, and in some cases it's general," he observes. What's appropriate depends upon the institution and its circumstances, he notes.

Five years ago, Esmond continues, the technology was not available. "Today, a hospital manager can ask, 'Why do I need this information? This system?' The choice involves what a hospital needs and what it wants a system for. Once it answers the questions, a match can be made with a system," he says.

Whether you agree with the opinion expressed above, the key point is the word "cost." Fixed cost, variable cost, etc., have different meanings to healthcare managers. It is very important that a common set of definitions be used in decision making in the organization.

Summary

Identification, measurement, and assignment for responsibility of cost is necessary in order for an organization to provide health services in a competitive market. There are numerous cost categories which must be examined and care must be taken when assigning responsibility for cost control. Departmental managers must agree with the cost definitions used to assign costs to their departments before they will be willing to be evaluated on the behavior of those costs.

Questions and problems

1. Are costs described in this chapter identical to revenues for a health services organization? Discuss.

2. Define each of the following as a direct or indirect cost of the operation of the health services organization's physical plant.

a. Supplies used for maintenance of facilities.
b. Supervisory salaries.
c. Costs of electrical power.
d. Costs of electrical power for the maintenance department.
e. Liability insurance premiums paid for any injuries by people coming to the health services organization.
f. A two-year lease for lawn maintenance equipment.
g. Maintenance on the physical facilities.
h. Depreciation on facilities.
i. Telephone expenses for the maintenance department.
j. Employer's share of social security taxes paid by the department.

3. Using the list above, determine whether these activities represent fixed or variable expenses.

4. Do variable costs per unit remain constant with changes in volume? Discuss.

5. Costs are fixed or variable only in relationship to a given time period. Discuss.

6. Do the providers of hospital care and third-party reimbursers use the same definition of costs? Discuss.

7. In many hospitals, a radiologist is contracted to provide services and receive a percentage of gross revenues. Would we classify this as a fixed or variable cost? As a direct or indirect expense? Discuss.

8. A group of doctors formed a group practice. In their efforts to determine a price to charge their patients they want to break all costs into fixed and variable costs. While they agree that rent represents a fixed cost, there is considerable debate about whether the power bill should be a fixed or variable expense. Discuss.

9. The present practice in hospitals and nursing homes is to define costs in terms of patient days. There is currently a growing movement toward the development of the concept of costs per case mix. Discuss the type of problems encountered in the use of these concepts.

10. Unit costs decrease as volume increases. Explain. Is this statement always true? Provide examples.

11. How can an analysis of each cost item be used to separate semi-variable costs into their fixed and variable elements?

12. The supervisor of the diagnostic radiology department furnished the following information concerning cost behavior in the department:

Volume	Total cost
5,000 procedures	$100,000
7,000 procedures	116,000

Determine the fixed and variable costs per procedure for the department.

13. The laboratory department had the following costs for the preceding six months:

	Jan.	Feb.	March	April	May	June
Total tests	2,000	2,800	2,600	3,000	2,400	2,600
Total costs	$8,000	$9,600	$9,300	$9,900	$8,700	$9,500

a. Estimate fixed and variable costs by the high-low method.
b. Estimate fixed and variable costs by drawing a scatter diagram.
c. If tests in a certain month are estimated to be 2,500 units, what is your estimate of total costs?

14. Determine the fixed portion of the semivariable expense for the first three months of 1990, using the high-low method. Information for the first three months of 1990 is:

Month	Direct labor hours	Semivariable expense
January 1990	32,000	$60,000
February 1990	31,000	$58,500
March 1990	34,000	$61,000

15. Community Hospital has an average occupancy of 80 percent per month based on 100 licensed beds. At this level of occupancy, the hospital's per diem costs are $120 per occupied bed per day, assuming a 30-day month. This per diem rate includes both a fixed and variable cost element. During the month of April, the occupancy rate was 70 percent and actual costs were:

Fixed costs	$180,000
Semivariable costs	102,000

a. Determine the variable cost per occupied bed per day.
b. Determine the total fixed costs for the month of April.
c. What would you have expected the total per diem costs to be for the 85 percent occupancy level?

16. The Chapel Hill Home Health Agency operates a semiskilled, hotel type facility for patients needing more than home, health type care

but less than the short-term, acute hospital type care. Custodial supply expense and admissions over the last six months were:

Month	Supply expense	Admissions
July	$12,000	175
August	8,250	110
September	7,500	65
October	9,750	125
November	10,750	150
December	13,500	200

a. Determine the cost formula for supply expense.
b. Estimate the supply expense for 250 admissions.

17. The number of X-rays taken and X-ray costs over the last twelve months in Beverley Hospital are given below:

Month	X-rays taken	X-ray costs
January	6,250	$28,000
February	7,000	29,000
March	5,000	23,000
April	4,250	20,000
May	4,500	22,000
June	3,000	17,000
July	3,750	18,000
August	5,500	24,000
September	5,750	26,000
October	6,100	27,000
November	6,350	28,500
December	6,200	28,000

a. Use the high-low method to determine the formula for X-ray costs.
b. What X-ray costs would you expect to be incurred during a month in which 4,600 X-rays were taken?
c. Prepare a scattergraph using the twelve months of data. Plot cost on the vertical axis and activity on the horizontal axis. Fit a regression line to your plotted points by visual inspection.
d. From the scattergraph, what is the approximate monthly fixed cost for X-rays? The approximate variable cost per X-ray taken?
e. Scrutinize the points on your graph, and explain why the high-low method would or would not yield an accurate cost formula in this situation.

18. Hospital Shared Services operates a fleet of delivery trucks in a large metropolitan area. A careful study by the company's cost analysts has determined that if a truck is driven 120,000 miles during a year, the

operating cost is 11.6 cents per mile. If a truck is driven only 70,000 miles during a year, the operating cost increases to 14.0 cents per mile.
a. Using the high-low method, determine the variable and fixed cost elements of the annual cost of truck operations.
b. Express the variable and fixed costs in the form Y = a + bX.
c. If a truck were driven 100,000 miles during a year, what total costs would you expect to be incurred?

19. Perkins Hospital experiences a considerable fluctuation in its utilities costs from month to month according to the number of machine-hours worked in its energy center. The company has plotted utilities costs at various levels of activity on a graph, and the plotted points indicate that total utilities cost is a mixed cost in the form Y = a + Bx. Machine-hours of activity and total utilities cost over the last six months are given below:

Month	Machine-hours	Total utilities cost
January	9,000	$14,000
February	12,000	17,000
March	16,000	20,000
April	21,000	23,000
May	18,000	21,000
June	14,000	19,000

Using graphs and the high-low method, determine the cost formula for utilities cost.

20. The data below have been taken from the cost records of the Atlanta Hospital. It relates to the cost of operating one department at various levels of activity:

Month	Units processed	Total cost
January	8,000	$14,000
February	4,500	10,000
March	7,000	12,500
April	9,000	15,500
May	3,750	10,000
June	6,000	12,500
July	3,000	8,500
August	5,000	11,500

a. Prepare a scattergraph by plotting the above data on a graph. Plot cost on the vertical axis and activity on the horizontal axis. Fit a regression line to your plotted points by visual inspection.
b. What is the approximate monthly fixed cost? The approximate variable cost per unit processed? Show computations.

21. Long-Term Corporation has a total of 2,000 rooms in its nationwide chain of nursing homes. On the average, 80 percent of the rooms are occupied each month. The company's operating costs are $7 per occupied room per day at this occupancy level, assuming a 30-day month. This $7 cost figure contains both variable and fixed cost elements. During October, the occupancy rate was only 65 percent. Some $316,000 in operating costs were incurred during this month.
    a. Determine the variable cost per occupied room per day.
    b. Determine the total fixed operating costs per month.
    c. Assume an occupancy rate of 70 percent. What total operating costs would you expect the company to incur?

22. University General is responsible for budgeting and controlling the fleet of ambulances owned by the city. Hospital administrators have determined that an ambulance driven 105,000 miles a year has an average operating cost for fuel, oil, and supervision of 11.4 cents per mile. If the ambulance is driven only 70,000 miles, the operating costs increase to 13.4 cents per mile. The budget analyst believes some of the costs are linear for the range of 50,000 to 120,000 miles. The next year's estimate of miles to be driven is 80,000. Determine the total budgeted costs for fuel, oil, and supervision for the prepared budget.

23. Draw a single graph that shows the following:
    a. Fixed costs at $30,000.
    b. Variable costs at $30.00 per visit.
    c. Total costs at 1,000, 2,000, 3,000, and 4,000 visits.
    d. Calculate cost per unit at 1,000, 2,000, 3,000, and 4,000 visits.

24. Prepare equations for fixed, variable, and total costs, using the data in the preceding problem.

25. Draw a graph that shows the following:
    a. Fixed costs at $35,000.
    b. Variable costs at $12.00 per visit.
    c. Total costs at 1,500, 2,500, 3,500, and 4,500 visits.
    d. Calculate cost per unit at 1,500, 2,500, 3,500, and 4,500 visits.

26. Prepare equations for fixed, variable, and total costs, using the data in the preceding problem.

27. Draw a graph that shows total variable costs that change under the following conditions:
    a. Variable costs at $10.00 per visit for 0–1,000 visits.
    b. Variable costs at $12.00 per visit for 1,001–3,000 visits.

28. Prepare equations for total variable costs, using the data in the preceding problem.

29. Draw a graph that shows total variable costs that change under the following conditions:
    a. Variable costs at $24.00 per visit for 0–2,000 visits.
    b. Variable costs at $18.00 per visit for 2,001–5,000 visits.

30. Prepare equations for total variable costs, using the data in the preceding problem.

31. Draw a single graph that shows fixed costs that change under the following conditions:
    a. Fixed costs of $200,000 for 0–2,500 visits.
    b. Fixed costs of $350,000 for 2,501–5,000 visits.
    c. Fixed costs of $450,000 for more than 5,000 visits.
    d. Calculate the fixed cost per unit at 1,000, 2,000, 3,000, 4,000, 5,000, 6,000, and 7,000 visits.

32. Prepare equations for fixed costs, using the data in the preceding problem.

33. Draw a single graph that shows fixed costs that change under the following conditions:
    a. Fixed costs of $125,000 for 0–1,000 visits.
    b. Fixed costs of $220,000 for 1,001–3,500 visits.
    c. Fixed costs of $300,000 for more than 3,500 visits.
    d. Calculate the fixed cost per unit at 1,000, 2,000, 3,000, 4,000, and 5,000 visits.

34. Prepare equations for fixed costs, using the data in the preceding problem.

35. Given the following data, use the High-Low Method to develop a Total Costs Equation:

Month	Costs	Activity level
March	$90,000	3,300 visits
April	70,000	2,400 visits
May	77,500	2,500 visits
June	82,000	3,000 visits
July	91,000	3,400 visits

36. With regard to the preceding problem:
    a. Draw a graph of the data.
    b. Show your Total Costs Equation on the same graph.
    c. Comment on how well the equation "fits" the data.
    d. How would you explain the non-representative points to other managers?
    e. Calculate the average activity level over the five months.
    f. Predict the total costs at this level of activity.

g. Enter this prediction on your graph and comment on how well the Total Costs Equation "fits" with your prediction.

h. Comment on how well the average activity level represents the entire data set.

37. Given the following data, use the High-Low Method to develop a Total Costs Equation:

Month	Costs	Activity level
April	$75,000	3,500 visits
May	52,000	2,300 visits
June	59,500	2,650 visits
July	63,500	3,100 visits
August	72,000	3,300 visits

38. With regard to the preceding problem:
    a. Draw a graph of the data.
    b. Show your Total Costs Equation on the same graph.
    c. Comment on how well the equation "fits" the data.
    d. How would you explain the non-representative points to other managers?
    e. Calculate the average activity level over the five months.
    f. Predict the total costs at this level of activity.
    g. Enter this prediction on your graph and comment on how well the Total Costs Equation "fits" with your prediction.
    h. Comment on how well the average activity level represents the entire data set.

39. Given the following data, use the High-Low Method to develop a Total Costs Equation:

Month	Costs	Activity level
March	$98,000	1,100 visits
April	64,000	2,200 visits
May	69,500	2,500 visits
June	76,000	3,000 visits
July	84,000	3,400 visits

Note: It is not obvious which months are the most representative.

40. With regard to the preceding problem:
    a. Draw a graph of the data.
    b. Show your Total Costs Equation on the same graph.
    c. Comment on how well the equation "fits" the data.
    d. How would you explain the non-representative points to other managers?
    e. Calculate the average activity level over the five months.

f. Predict the total costs at this level of activity.

g. Enter this prediction on your graph and comment on how well the Total Costs Equation "fits" with your prediction.

h. Comment on how well the average activity level represents the entire data set.

41. Given the following data, use the High-Low Method to develop a Total Costs Equation:

Month	Costs	Activity level
March	$87,000	3,500 visits
April	24,000	3,300 visits
May	67,500	2,850 visits
June	75,500	3,100 visits
July	65,000	2,500 visits

Note: It is not obvious which months are the most representative.

42. With regard to the preceding problem:

a. Draw a graph of the data.

b. Show your Total Costs Equation on the same graph.

c. Comment on how well the equation "fits" the data.

d. How would you explain the non-representative points to other managers?

e. Calculate the average activity level over the five months.

f. Predict the total costs at this level of activity.

g. Enter this prediction on your graph and comment on how well the Total Costs Equation "fits" with your prediction.

h. Comment on how well the average activity level represents the entire data set.

43. Data for the Radiology Department at Hot Springs Hospital are as follows:

Month	Number of X-rays	Department costs
January	6,250	$285,000
February	7,200	295,000
March	5,300	235,000
April	4,250	210,000
May	4,500	230,000
June	3,200	175,000
July	3,900	185,000
August	5,750	245,000
September	5,950	265,000
October	6,300	275,000
November	6,550	295,000
December	6,400	295,000

a. Draw a graph of the data.
b. Use the High-Low Method to develop a Total Costs Equation.
c. Show your Total Costs Equation on the same graph.
d. Comment on how well the equation "fits" the data.
e. How would you explain the non-representative points to other managers?
f. Calculate the average activity level over the 12 months.
g. Predict the total costs at this level of activity.
h. Enter this prediction on your graph and comment on how well the Total Costs Equation "fits" with your prediction.
i. Comment on how well the average activity level represents the entire data set.
j. Assume a 10 percent growth factor from December of the current year to January of the following year. Predict the total costs using your Total Costs Equation.
k. Enter this prediction on your graph and comment on how well the Total Costs Equation "fits" with your prediction.
l. Write a short memo to your superior explaining how this prediction might be used, and identify any reservations you may have regarding this prediction.

44. Data for the Pathology Department at Palm Resort Hospital are as follows:

Month	Number of tests	Department costs
January	4,150	$285,000
February	5,100	295,000
March	3,200	235,000
April	2,150	210,000
May	2,400	225,000
June	1,900	175,000
July	2,100	195,000
August	3,950	245,000
September	3,850	265,000
October	4,200	275,000
November	4,450	295,000
December	4,300	285,000

a. Draw a graph of the data.
b. Use the High-Low Method to develop a Total Costs Equation.
c. Show your Total Costs Equation on the same graph.
d. Comment on how well the equation "fits" the data.
e. How would you explain the non-representative points to other managers?
f. Calculate the average activity level over the twelve months.
g. Predict the total costs at this level of activity.

h. Enter this prediction on your graph and comment on how well the Total Costs Equation "fits" with your prediction.
i. Comment on how well the average activity level represents the entire data set.
j. Assume a 10 percent growth factor from December of the current year to January of the following year. Predict the total costs using your Total Costs Equation.
k. Enter this prediction on your graph and comment on how well the Total Costs Equation "fits" with your prediction.
l. Write a short memo to your superior explaining how this prediction might be used, and identify any reservations you may have regarding this prediction.

45. Data for the Laundry Department at Palm Shelter Hospital are as follows:

Month	Pounds of laundry	Department costs
January	205,000	$285,000
February	207,100	295,000
March	206,500	235,000
April	205,300	205,000
May	205,800	225,000
June	204,500	175,000
July	205,950	185,000
August	204,650	245,000
September	206,890	265,000
October	206,600	275,000
November	207,450	295,000
December	207,750	280,000

a. Draw a graph of the data.
b. Use the High-Low Method to develop a Total Costs Equation.
c. Show your Total Costs Equation on the same graph.
d. Comment on how well the equation "fits" the data.
e. How would you explain the non-representative points to other managers?
f. Calculate the average activity level over the five months.
g. Predict the total costs at this level of activity.
h. Enter this prediction on your graph and comment on how well the Total Costs Equation "fits" with your prediction.
i. Comment on how well the average activity level represents the entire data set.
j. Assume a 1 percent growth factor from December of the current year to January of the following year. Predict the total costs using your Total Costs Equation.

k. Enter this prediction on your graph and comment on how well the Total Costs Equation "fits" with your prediction.
l. Write a short memo to your superior explaining how this prediction might be used, and identify any reservations you may have regarding this prediction.

46. Data for the Medical Records Department at Palm Date Hospital are as follows:

Month	Number of records	Department costs
January	25,250	$275,000
February	26,100	285,000
March	24,400	225,000
April	23,350	215,000
May	24,450	225,000
June	22,980	165,000
July	23,345	185,000
August	24,950	235,000
September	24,876	255,000
October	25,345	265,000
November	25,567	285,000
December	25,300	275,000

a. Draw a graph of the data.
b. Use the High-Low Method to develop a Total Costs Equation.
c. Show your Total Costs Equation on the same graph.
d. Comment on how well the equation "fits" the data.
e. How would you explain the non-representative points to other managers?
f. Calculate the average activity level over the five months.
g. Predict the total costs at this level of activity.
h. Enter this prediction on your graph and comment on how well the Total Costs Equation "fits" with your prediction.
i. Comment on how well the average activity level represents the entire data set.
j. Assume a 5 percent growth factor from December of the current year to January of the following year. Predict the total costs using your Total Costs Equation.
k. Enter this prediction on your graph and comment on how well the Total Costs Equation "fits" with your prediction.
l. Write a short memo to your superior explaining how this prediction might be used, and identify any reservations you may have regarding this prediction.

47. Data for the Pathology Department at Palm Desert Hospital have become somewhat "scrambled" as a new computer system was installed.

Month	Number of tests	Department costs
January	1,050	$275,000
February	5,150	585,000
March	1,300	725,000
April	4,250	120,000
May	2,500	215,000
June	1,850	185,000
July	2,200	175,000
August	3,850	255,000
September	3,750	275,000
October	4,100	285,000
November	4,350	280,000
December	4,200	295,000

a. Draw a graph of the data.
b. Use the High-Low Method to develop a Total Costs Equation.
c. Show your Total Costs Equation on the same graph.
d. Comment on how well the equation "fits" the data.
e. How would you explain the non-representative points to other managers?
f. Calculate the average activity level over the five months.
g. Predict the total costs at this level of activity.
h. Enter this prediction on your graph and comment on how well the Total Costs Equation "fits" with your prediction.
i. Comment on how well the average activity level represents the entire data set.
j. Assume a 10 percent growth factor from December of the current year to January of the following year. Predict the total costs using your Total Costs Equation.
k. Enter this prediction on your graph and comment on how well the Total Costs Equation "fits" with your prediction.
l. Write a short memo to your superior explaining how this prediction might be used, and identify any reservations you may have regarding this prediction.

Keywords: accounting costs; cost; direct costs; economic costs; fixed costs; full costs; indirect costs; variable costs.

References

Granof, M., P. Bell, and B.R. Neumann. *Accounting for Managers and Investors.* 2d ed. Englewood Cliffs, NJ: Prentice Hall, 1993.

Hemeon, Frank E., III. "Productivity, Cost Accounting, and Information Systems." *Topics in Health Care Financing* 15, no. 3 (spring 1989): 55–67.

Herkimer, Allen G., Jr. *Understanding Hospital Financial Management.* Germantown, MD: Aspen Systems Corporation, 1989.

Kaplan, Robert S. "One Cost System Isn't Enough." *Harvard Business Review* (January–February 1988): 61–66.

Kolb, D.S., and J.L. Horowitz. "Managing the Transition to Capitation." *Healthcare Financial Management* (February 1995): 64–69.

Krueger, Deborah J., and Thomas A. Davidson. "Alternative Approaches to Cost Accounting." *Topics in Health Care Financing* 13, no. 4, (summer 1987): 1–9.

Murray, Dennis, Bruce R. Neumann, and Pieter Elgers. *Using Financial Accounting: An Introduction.* Cincinnati, OH: South-Western College Publishing, 1997.

Nackel, John G., George M.J. Kis, and Paul J. Fenaroli. *Cost Management for Hospitals.* Rockville, MD: Aspen Publishers, 1987.

Neumann, Bruce R., Jan P. Clement, and Jean C. Cooper. *Financial Management: Concepts and Applications for Health Care Organizations.* Dubuque: Kendall/Hunt, 1997.

Orloff, T.M., C.L. Littell, C. Clune, D. Klingman, and B. Preston. "Hospital Cost Accounting: Who's Doing What and Why." *Health Care Management Review* 15, no. 4 (1990): 73–78.

Seawell, L. Vann. *Introduction to Hospital Accounting.* 3rd ed. Healthcare Financial Management Association. Dubuque: Kendall/Hunt, 1992.

CHAPTER 3

Identification of cost behavior patterns

"I know I have some costs that vary with volume but I'm unsure how to identify them."

"How much would it cost to double the volume of procedures we do?"

"Why do they insist that the cost will increase only 5 percent if we increase the volume by 39 percent?"

"Is there any way we can predict what our department costs will be next year under different assumptions?"

"How much confidence can I place in the data analysis given to me by analysts predicting cost behavior in the future?"

"What factors will influence my choice of statistical approaches to analyze cost data?"

Introduction

This book emphasizes the concept that knowledge of cost behavior in healthcare organizations will usually improve the managerial decision making in such organizations. An increased understanding of cost behavior can improve the quality and effectiveness of management control in healthcare organizations. It can lead to improved efficiency and better cost control. At the highest level, managers who obtain and use information about the behavior of hospital costs can improve their efforts to achieve cost containment without sacrificing quality of care objectives.

Understanding cost behavior requires relating changes in costs to changes in some activity. Cost behavior relies on understanding the association or relation between costs and activities or services. In most cases, the activities, services or outputs are observable, often tangible, events. They can be objectively counted and recorded. Costs are recorded in the organization's information system according to the chart of accounts. They may be departmental costs, administrative costs, or patient costs.

A healthcare organization that is first attempting to develop information about cost behavior patterns may be required to revise its chart of accounts. Perhaps the existing cost data are so aggregated, or contain so many arbitrary overhead cost allocations, that no usable cost behavior patterns could possibly be identified. If so, the techniques described in this chapter must be preceded by the necessary revisions in the accounting system. Revising or refining the accounting system is beyond the scope of this book. The current chapter presumes that the cost data are accurately recorded in elemental units of direct and indirect costs. If the cost data are in a highly summarized format, or if they contain costs allocated from other departments or responsibility centers, any resulting cost behavior patterns must be used with extreme caution. For example, cost data that have passed through a stepdown cost allocation process may only reflect the allocation techniques rather than an underlying relationship with health services activities.

As indicated above, the purpose of identifying cost behavior relationships is to improve decision making. The primary improvement in decision making that can occur is to improve a manager's prediction of future costs. Prediction of future costs is relevant to planning and budgeting. Cost predictions are used in the determination of standard costs. Better cost predictions will also improve management control because they make the feedback comparison of actual costs to budgeted costs more meaningful. Better cost predictions make it possible to find out why deviations occurred; this can lead to making changes in operating policies and procedures. In other words, as the prediction of expected costs improves, so also do management planning and control. Knowledge of cost behavior patterns is essential to better cost prediction.

Cost prediction should be as accurate as feasible. Managers should spend time and money to improve cost predictions so that the extra benefit of better cost predictions approximates the extra costs of obtaining better information. This cost-benefit criterion is applied to the analysis of cost behavior. Managers should use the set of techniques described in this chapter to determine cost behavior patterns so that the analysis does not cost more than the benefits. The implicit question that must be asked about many of these techniques is: Will more accurate information change the decision I would have made with the information that is now available? If more accurate information will not reduce the risk or uncertainty, or if it will not change a recommended solution, the currently available information is probably sufficient. If not, additional techniques must be used to obtain more accurate cost predictions. Since more accurate cost predictions are a function of how much managers know about cost behavior patterns, the techniques described in this chapter can be used to identify the relevant cost behavior relationships. The remainder of the chapter describes different ways of identifying cost behavior patterns.

General guidelines

The purpose of cost behavior models is to identify and reflect the relationship between costs and activities in the hospital. The financial manager can never hope to uncover an exact and true relationship. If this relationship can be approximated or estimated with a low degree of error, the particular cost behavior pattern can be used with reasonable confidence.

As noted earlier, the basic goal is to be able to predict costs if the volume of activities are *known or planned*. A desirable state of affairs would be to identify a cause-and-effect relationship. If the manager knows the activities that cause the costs to occur, a cost behavior model that incorporates the causal variables is probably the most usable model that could be identified. However, causal relationships are not essential to the identification of cost behavior patterns. All a cost behavior model really has to accomplish is the accurate prediction of costs given a knowledge of the activities that will simultaneously occur. If a good long-term relationship can be shown between season of the year and administrative costs, that knowledge can be used to accurately predict future administrative costs. Many cost behavior patterns that are not causally related can be identified and used to good advantage by managers of healthcare organizations.

There are several important prerequisites to the identification of a cost behavior model. One obvious first step is to select the cost that is to be predicted. The cost that serves as the object of the cost behavior model is often called the dependent or *criterion variable*. The financial analyst wishes to predict costs that are dependent on some other activity or observable event. It may be called the criterion variable because the ultimate criterion of the goodness of the model depends on how well the actual costs match the predicted (criterion) costs.

The second step is to choose an action, or a set of actions or events, that will permit prediction of the dependent variable. The actions or events are called independent variables or *predictor variables* because they are used to predict the criterion or dependent variable. Most cost behavior models can be expressed in a form indicated by the following functional relationships:

$$\text{costs} = f \text{ (activities)};$$
$$\text{dependent variable} = f \text{ (independent variables)};$$
$$\text{criterion variable} = f \text{ (predictor variables)}.$$

If there is only one predictor variable, the cost behavior model is a univariate model. If there is more than one independent variable, the model is multivariate in dimension. Managers in healthcare organizations should try to identify a variety of possible predictor variables and select the set of predictor variables that provides the best cost behavior model. In other words, the starting point in identifying cost behavior models is to choose a cost to be predicted and a set of possible predictor variables. By refining the set of predictor variables, the cost behavior model can usually be successively improved. The optimal set of predictor variables is that set of independent variables that results in the best possible prediction of the cost.

Having identified the variables that will be used in the cost behavior model, the next step is to identify possible forms of the model. Cost behavior models are either linear or nonlinear. A linear cost behavior model can be expressed as a straight line. The equation for a straight line is usually of the form:

$$y = a + bx$$

In this case, "y" represents the criterion variable, "x" represents the predictor variable, and "a" and "b" are the coefficients of the model. A straight line can be graphed as shown in *Exhibit 3–1*. This graph shows

Exhibit 3–1
Graph of a straight line

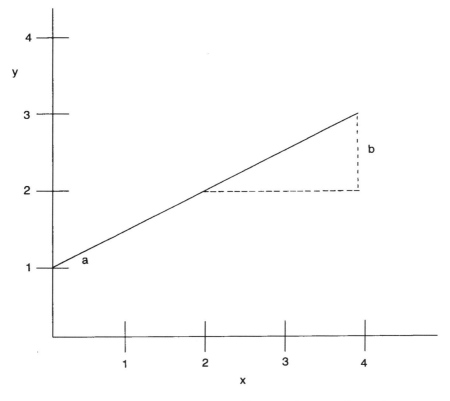

$$\text{Slope} = \frac{3 - 2}{4 - 2} = \frac{1}{2}$$

For every increase in x, y increases by half the increase in x.

that "a" is the intercept of the line on the "y" axis and "b" is the slope of the line. The slope can be intuitively thought of as "rise" over "run," or the difference in the "y" values for any two points divided by the difference in the "x" values for the same two points. The slope of the line in *Exhibit 3–1* is calculated as:

$$slope = \frac{y_2 - y_1}{x_2 - x_1} = \frac{rise}{run} = \frac{3-2}{4-2} = \frac{1}{2}$$

The slope can be interpreted as any increase in "x" of two units results in an associated increase in "y" of one unit. The criterion variable in this case increases half as fast as the predictor variable. A slope of 3.0 would indicate that every increase in "x" is accompanied by a corresponding threefold increase in "y." Similarly, an increase of 100 manhours (x) would be associated with a $300 increase in supply costs (y).

Nonlinear cost behavior models can also be expressed as univariate or as multivariate. A typical univariate nonlinear model would be the exponential model illustrated in *Exhibit 3–2*. However, univariate nonlinear

Exhibit 3–2
Graph of an exponential model

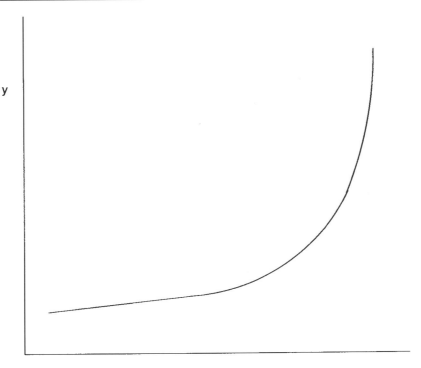

models have not been identified as useful or relevant to healthcare organizations. A set of linear multivariate models discussed in more detail later in this chapter is typically a better predictor of total costs. Note that any cost behavior model with more than two dimensions cannot be graphed on a flat surface; therefore, we will not attempt to graphically illustrate more complex models.

Another important step in the process of identifying cost behavior models in healthcare organizations is to evaluate the input data that will be used as the basis for the cost behavior model. The GIGO principle (garbage-in, garbage-out) can be a significant problem unless the healthcare financial manager takes time to evaluate and understand the input data. A scatter diagram of the input data is the single most important factor that can be used to evaluate the input data.

A scatter diagram is nothing more than a plot of the data. Usually the cost data are plotted against each of the potential predictor variables. For example, a scatter diagram of supply costs versus time is contrasted with a scatter diagram of supply costs versus surgical procedures in *Exhibit 3–3*. These relationships show that time will not be very useful in predicting supply costs, although season obviously has some effect.

Exhibit 3–3b illustrates a scatter diagram for a variable cost relationship that could be expressed simply as the equation of a straight line. In this case supply costs appear to have a definite linear relationship with surgical procedures. The techniques described later in this chapter will develop the specific methodologies for identifying this type of single predictor variable cost behavior model. On the other hand, the pattern of costs shown in *Exhibit 3–3a* would require a nonlinear cost behavior model. Without more data observation, it is hard to determine whether the cyclical (seasonal) patterns repeat themselves with enough regularity to justify pursuing the search for a relationship between supply costs and time.

Exhibit 3–3 illustrates the fact that one of the important contributions of a scatter diagram is to identify the form of alternative cost behavior models. Scatter diagrams help the manager discard unimportant predictor variables; they also help identify possible nonlinear relationships. Since one of the objectives of a cost behavior model is to make the best possible cost predictions at the lowest possible cost, the healthcare analyst is well advised to first pursue linear cost behavior models and to avoid nonlinear relationships unless they become absolutely necessary.

The second important contribution of a scatter diagram is to help identify the relevant range for the cost behavior model. The relevant range may be restricted to specific quantities of activities or to specific time periods. For example, very few hospitals would like to build cost behavior models for either 20 or 160 percent occupancy levels. However, some departments may have wide fluctuations in utilization, and a 40 percent utilization factor may be typical in those departments. Another example would be two hospitals that merged a year ago; very little of the data pertaining to the premerger period would be consistent with observations

Exhibit 3–3
Scatter diagrams of supply costs

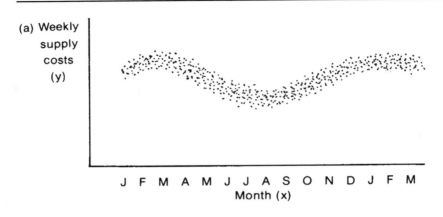

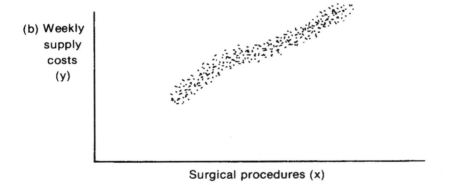

from the postmerger period. The point is that a scatter diagram can help isolate the relevant range of utilization that is expected to be most typical. It helps identify the activity levels that will serve as inputs to the identification of the cost behavior model.

Scatter diagrams also can be used to jointly identify a linear model over the relevant range. The scatter diagram in *Exhibit 3–4* illustrates two nonlinear segments and one linear segment. If the relevant range happens to coincide with the linear segment, the cost behavior model can be estimated with much greater reliability than if some model had to be identified that fit all three segments.

A final role that scatter diagrams have in the determination of cost behavior patterns is to help identify and eliminate erroneous or inconsistent data. In most cases, scatter diagrams will include several extreme

Exhibit 3–4
Linear and nonlinear scatter diagrams

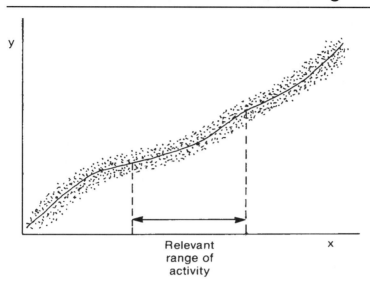

Relevant
range of
activity

observations; usually these extreme points are called outliers. *Exhibit 3–5* is an exact replica of *Exhibit 3–3b* except that several outliers have been added as asterisks.

Each of the three outliers in *Exhibit 3–5* must be investigated to determine if it is either the result of erroneous data or if it reflects some event

Exhibit 3–5
Scatter diagram with outliers

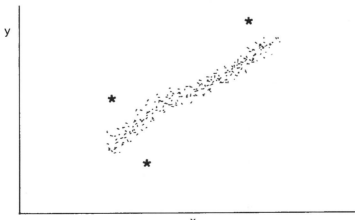

that will not be repeated (or expected to be repeated). If an outlier is a function of an identifiable error, the error should be corrected if at all possible. If the error cannot be corrected, the outlier should be discarded from the data base. If the outlier is a result of some nonrecurring event, it should also be eliminated. In some cases, outliers can be used to help predict what will happen under the same conditions that originally occurred. However, in most cases outliers that are due to random, nonrecurring events, or to events that are not part of the normal operations of the hospital (e.g., a strike, a boiler explosion or some other natural disaster), should be eliminated from the data base. Scatter diagrams should then be redrawn without the outliers.

In summary, the healthcare financial manager must be aware of several potential data problems that can affect cost behavior patterns. Scatter diagrams help identify the nature of the problem and permit the analyst to estimate the severity of the problem. A number of potential data problems are listed in *Exhibit 3–6.*

Exhibit 3–6
Potential data problems affecting
cost behavior patterns

1. Data not in the relevant range.

2. Data pertaining to time periods that reflect abnormal or nonrecurring operations.

3. Data stated in incompatible units; for example, pounds and ounces, kilowatts and kilowatt hours, quarts and liters, "paid" hours and "worked" hours, full-time equivalent employees, and "head count" employees, etc.

4. Cost data that have been grossly affected by changing rates of inflation. In this case, adjusted data should be considered.

5. Data that reflect clerical errors.

6. Data that reflect anomalies or other nonrecurring events.

7. Data that reflect significant cost allocations.

8. Data that are misclassified into the wrong accounts and/or the wrong departments.

9. Data that are misclassified according to cost behavior; for example, fixed costs classified as variable costs or vice versa. Another example would be fixed costs that have already been allocated on some basis (per hour, per patient, or per patient day) so that the costs now appear to be variable with some activity factor.

10. Data that have been recorded during start-up or transition phases. The learning curve effects on cost data must be anticipated, and cost behavior patterns should not be identified until any learning phenomena have stabilized.

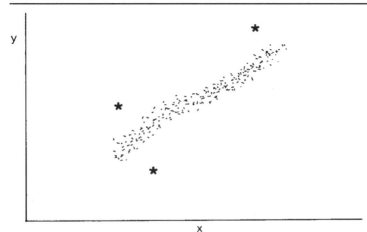

The final problem that complicates identification of cost behavior patterns is the need to make sure that appropriate techniques are being used. For example, visual methods should not be used if precision and accuracy are critical. Complex mathematical models should not be used if simpler models can provide acceptable results. In addition, the assumptions inherent in the model must be consistent with the data base. This last caveat pertains primarily to statistical techniques that can be used to identify cost behavior patterns. If the statistical assumptions or conditions of the data base are not met, the results may be so distorted as to be useless or deceiving. We will discuss these assumptions later in this chapter in conjunction with the statistical regression models.

Other types of nonlinear costs that may cause concern for healthcare financial managers are step-function costs. Step costs are usually fixed costs that have discrete increments, or steps, as activity increases. For example, each step may represent the employment of an additional employee. Alternatively, the steps may be salary increments as specified in union agreements. *Exhibit 3–7* illustrates three types of step-function costs.

In each of the cost behavior patterns illustrated in *Exhibit 3–7*, costs (y) jump to a different level for small change in activity (x). The step costs shown in *Exhibit 3–7b* can easily be approximated by a straight line because each step is of uniform height and width. The other two-step cost patterns are grossly incorrect cost predictions at many different levels of activity. The pattern shown in *Exhibit 3–7c* is an obvious candidate for a nonlinear relationship; the shape of that relationship could be easily determined. However, the step costs in *Exhibit 3–7a* are all fixed costs that cannot be approximated by a single cost equation. On the other hand, the step costs in both *3–7a* or *3–7c* can be conveniently expressed by a straight line, as long as the manager can operate within the volume of activity (relevant range) embodied by any single line segment. For example, if the manager can be reasonably sure that operations will be at the extreme right side of either *3–7a* or *3–7c,* the appropriate cost behavior pattern is simply a fixed cost. That fixed cost relationship will provide accurate cost predictions only if operations continue at the upper levels of (x) activity. As activities contract, other line segments will become relevant, and cost predictions must rely on different cost equations. The point to remember is that any cost behavior pattern is accurate and useful only within a limited relevant range of volume. As operations move outside of that relevant range, new cost behavior patterns may supersede the original cost equations.

Physical observation of cost behavior patterns

The next three sections of this chapter will describe different ways of identifying cost behavior patterns. The three techniques are physical observation, logical observation, and statistical analysis. No single tech-

Exhibit 3–7
Step-function costs

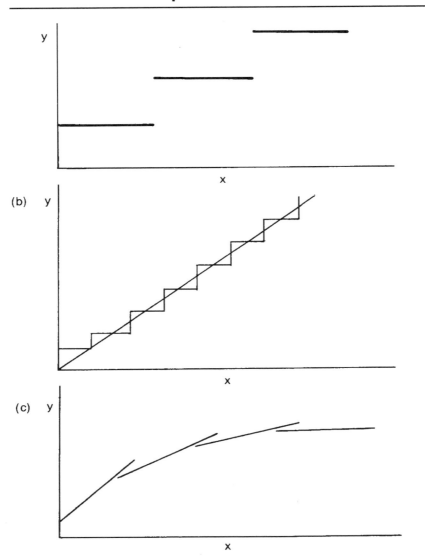

nique is suitable under all conditions. Rather, each technique should be used wherever it can lead to the best prediction of costs with the least effort. In addition, these techniques may be used in combination with each other where the results from one phase of the analysis can be used to confirm results from earlier phases. One of the three major ways to identify cost behavior patterns is to observe and measure the relationship of costs to activities. Physical observation is the most direct, and usually the most costly, way to identify cost behavior patterns. It is the technique best suited to identifying causal relationships because the accountant or engineer conducting the analysis can actually verify the direction of causality.

Physical observation can also be called the industrial engineering approach because it includes work measurement and time-and-motion studies. It is also normative in the sense the engineers search for the best possible way to accomplish each objective. The industrial engineering approach to cost behavior patterns may involve all the techniques noted below. However, the factor that differentiates it from these other techniques is that one of the initial steps is to physically monitor the existing process.

In healthcare organizations, physical monitoring may also take place at other sites. For example, the industrial engineering programs develop normative productivity standards for nursing, housekeeping, dietary, laundry, etc. These productivity standards, initially determined by physical observation, are continuously revised and updated as a result of ongoing monitoring in a few hospitals. After extensive testing of these normative standards, industrial engineers may generalize productivity standards to a variety of hospital and healthcare organizations. Different standards have been established for individual institutional sites and organization structures.

The physical observation technique is also used to identify and determine standard costs. It starts by reviewing the actual supplies, labor, and other overhead elements that are presently used to provide healthcare. Time-and-motion studies and other evaluations of people's capabilities and skills serve as inputs to the development of normative task specifications. Each task is first outlined in terms of its physical requirements (hours, skill levels, supplies, space, equipment, etc.). These physical requirements are then transformed into dollars by applying appropriate unit prices and costs. Expected units of output are then estimated, and the standard costs per unit of output are calculated for material, labor, and variable overhead by dividing the input cost data by the expected output. The resulting standard costs are then used for performance evaluation, which will be described in later chapters.

In all cases the physical observation approach should include discussions with the department head and responsible supervisors. They can help with the proper selection of time and persons to be observed; they are in a better position to judge when the resulting standards are reasonable.

In the event that the healthcare organization doesn't want to obtain standard cost data from the industrial engineering approach, it can halt the process at the point where flexible budget formulas can be established. That is, the input price data can be used to prepare flexible budget formulas that relate input costs to units of activity. These cost behavior relationships then serve as inputs to the planning and control process. The major disadvantage with the industrial engineering approach is that it cannot be applied where the service activities cannot be physically observed. The analyst must be able to trace the costs to input or output units of activity. If that link is not feasible, then physical observation and the industrial engineering approach are not applicable.

Logical knowledge of cost behavior patterns

The second approach to identifying cost behavior patterns relies on a logical knowledge of the operations of the healthcare organization. The manager or analyst applies expert judgment in determining a representative cost behavior pattern. The physician applies this type of logic in administering treatments to patients with observable disease conditions. A physician can usually make a preliminary diagnosis with knowledge of a set of symptoms and some background information about the patient's history. This preliminary diagnosis then leads to a set of recommended treatments.

The logical approach to identifying cost behavior patterns proceeds in an analogous fashion. The analyst, based on previous knowledge of similar operations, has some idea about how certain costs typically relate to activities or services. The analyst then estimates a cost behavior equation and confirms it with a small sample of information.

The small sample of confirmatory information can be derived by three different techniques. The analyst first identifies the appropriate variables and the relevant range over which the cost behavior relationship is expected to apply. One of these techniques is called account analysis. Account analysis then proceeds to examine the costs recorded in the organization's accounts. These costs are then classified, on the basis of the analyst's judgment, as fixed or variable costs. The cost behavior equation is judgmentally determined. In some cases, the costs cannot be fit into any known linear pattern, and the analyst must discard or ignore costs that cannot be classified on a linear basis.

The second way to confirm logical relationships with limited information is by using the high-low method. The high-low method reduces this subjectivity by identifying cost behavior patterns as a function of the highest cost and the lowest cost. The pair of data points with the most extreme costs, over the expected relevant range, becomes the basis for the predictive cost equation. These two points are then input to the rise-over-run calculation discussed earlier. For example, consider the data in *Exhibit 3–8*. The months with the highest cost and the lowest cost are the only basis for the cost behavior equation.

Exhibit 3–8
High-low method

Month	Supply cost (y)	Hours of activity (x)
1	$200	19
2	400	41
3	300	32
4	100	11
5	500	49

High-low cost behavior equation =

$$\frac{y_2 - y_1}{x_2 - x_1} = \frac{500 - 100}{49 - 11} = \frac{\$400}{38} = \$10.53 \text{ per hour}$$

The coefficient calculated by the high-low method is the slope of the line that connects these two points. It can be interpreted as predicting that supply costs will increase by $10.53 for each hour of activity. There is no information about whether this is a representative relationship. There is no statistical information on the relationship's goodness of fit for more than the original two data points. We shall investigate these issues in the next section on statistical techniques.

In any event, the high-low method relies on limited information. If that information is distorted or biased, the entire cost behavior relationship may be unusable. Consider the scatter diagram in *Exhibit 3–9*. The two points with the highest and lowest costs are completely atypical of the other data. The cost relationship, predicted from the two outlier points (*) in *Exhibit 3–9,* is completely different from the relationship that would have been predicted from the balance of the available observations. Perhaps, as outliers, they should have been eliminated from the data base. If the relevant range does not include such high (x) volumes, the outliers definitely should have been eliminated. Blind faith in the high-low method will rarely lead to acceptable cost behavior patterns. In all cases a scatter diagram should be used to assist in evaluating the results of the high-low method.

The third technique that can be used to confirm logical relationships is a derivative of the high-low method. It is called representative cost analysis or incremental cost analysis. In this case, two data points are selected that are *representative* of the expected cost behavior pattern with the prespecified relevant range. The two points are selected on the basis of how well they represent the typical cost behavior pattern. In other words, this technique is used to estimate the variable and fixed cost coefficients; using two subjectively determined data points. If the analyst is interested in both fixed and variable cost behavior patterns, the

Exhibit 3–9
Scatter diagram with extreme outliers

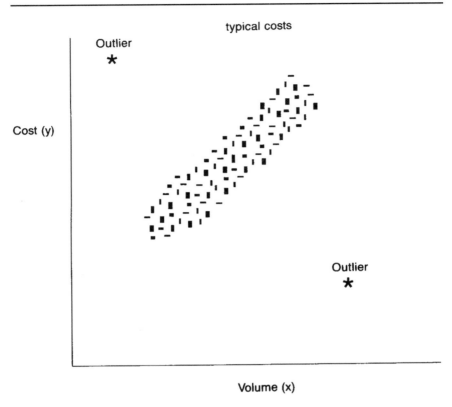

representative or incremental cost behavior technique gives slightly different but more useful results than the high-low method. However, it has all the other disadvantages of the high-low method except that the possibility of choosing two unrepresentative data points is minimized.

In summary, the logical approach to identifying cost behavior patterns relies on the manager's judgment. We recommend that these concepts be used to evaluate the results of either of the two techniques. Logic and managerial judgment can be used best to evaluate whether a particular cost behavior pattern is reasonable. Is it plausible? Does it reflect the way in which the department has been operated in the past? Are the results of these "quick and dirty" techniques consistent with the results derived from more elaborate cost behavior models? In our opinion, logical techniques serve as final tests of reasonability and plausibility. They should rarely be used as the sole means for identifying cost behavior patterns.

Statistical techniques for cost behavior identification

Statistical techniques should be an integral element of cost behavior identification. Statistical techniques are techniques that combine the scatter diagrams discussed earlier in the chapter with a statistical analysis of the dispersion shown in the data. Statistical techniques permit the analyst to obtain the best possible fit between the data and the cost behavior equation. In addition, they provide objective measures of the error that may be associated with the predicted costs. If the assumptions are met that permit statistical analysis, managers in healthcare organizations can use this powerful tool to complement other, more intuitive approaches.

When the appropriate assumptions hold, statistical techniques are superior to the other cost behavior identification techniques discussed earlier in this chapter. They are superior because of the objective estimates of potential error that are obtained and because the extent to which each of the statistical conditions (assumptions) is met can be tested. Furthermore, statistical techniques can be used where more than one predictor variable is required. The techniques discussed earlier in this chapter are only appropriate for univariate cost behavior models.

Statistical techniques rely on the premise that historical cost behavior patterns can be used to predict similar relationships in the future. There is nothing normative about the results of statistical analyses; nor is there necessarily anything logical about these results. Statistical models simply extrapolate historical patterns and apply them to some future period. To the extent that operating conditions are changing, or to the extent that the past does not serve as a valid predictor of the future, the benefits ascribed above to statistical techniques are reduced. In other words, statistical techniques are most valid when operating conditions are stable and when future costs are expected to be influenced by the same factors that affected costs in previous periods. The following sections describe a statistical approach based on regression analysis. Regression analysis is the most common statistical approach, and the next sections will help managers use and interpret regression of cost behavior models.

Regression analysis of cost behavior patterns

This section extends the discussion of cost behavior patterns through an extensive presentation of regression analysis. All the caveats and preliminary steps discussed earlier also apply to regression analysis. Linear and multiple regression (nonlinear) analyses represent the most typical statistical approaches to the identification of cost behavior patterns. Correlation analysis, discriminant analysis, cluster analysis, and principal components analysis are beyond the scope of this text. While a manual approach to regression calculations can be attempted, we recommend using computerized models whenever possible. Certain assumptions must be met in order to use regression analysis.

Least squares calculations (linear regression)

Assuming that the manager or analyst has used the techniques described earlier to identify any possible errors or inconsistencies in the data base, and assuming that a linear cost behavior relationship is to be tested, the next step is to use the least squares mathematical computations to obtain the coefficients of the line that best fits the observed data. The coefficients describe the computed cost behavior equation. The least squares method assures an objective, unbiased fit, and the calculations are relatively simple and straightforward. The least squares method will provide the information necessary to construct a univariate (one dependent variable) cost behavior equation of the form:

$$y = a + bx,$$

where y = criterion (dependent) variable
x = predictor (independent) variable
a = intercept or fixed cost
b = slope or variable cost

Assume that the departmental manager wants to investigate the relationship between supply costs and staff hours. The data for eight payroll periods are displayed and plotted in *Exhibit 3–10*. The scatter diagram in *Exhibit 3–10* illustrates how the "a" and "b" coefficients of an approximate linear relationship can be interpreted. These coefficients are approximate because the line was obtained by the visual fit method. Consequently, it may be biased, and there is no measure of error. The analyst or manager who wants to identify a more precise relationship would use the least squares method to obtain the best available cost behavior equation. Note that each of the data points in *Exhibit 3–10* is paired, and this association must be maintained throughout the calculation.

The least squares technique will result in a line that is the smallest (squared) distance from all the data points. The least squares (smallest squared distance) criterion has several desirable mathematical properties. *Exhibit 3–11* illustrates the final least squares regression line superimposed on the data points. No other linear relationship would result in a smaller sum of squared deviations. The fact that these are vertical deviations and that the regression line represents the best fit, statistically, will provide measures of the relative goodness of the fit and how much error is associated with the predicted costs. In other words, the least squares calculations result in desirable statistical properties that permit compari-

Exhibit 3–10
Departmental supply costs and patient days

Period	Supply costs (y)	Patient days (x)
1	$3,500	1,000
2	4,500	1,200
3	4,000	1,100
4	4,800	1,350
5	3,200	950
6	5,100	1,500
7	4,700	1,300
8	4,400	1,150

son with other alternative cost behavior equations. They also will provide an estimate of the potential error so that the manager can determine how much confidence to place in the cost predictions. This deviation can be expressed mathematically as:

$$\Sigma \, (y - y^1)^2, \text{ where}$$
$$y = \text{observed (cost) data, and}$$
$$y^1 = \text{predicted (cost) data}$$

The least squares calculation minimizes $\Sigma(y - y^1)^2$ by calculating the "a" and "b" coefficients from a set of normal equations. The normal equations are:

$$na + (\Sigma x)b = \Sigma y, \text{ and}$$
$$(\Sigma x)a + (\Sigma x^2)b = \Sigma xy$$

Exhibit 3–11
Illustration of least squares criterion

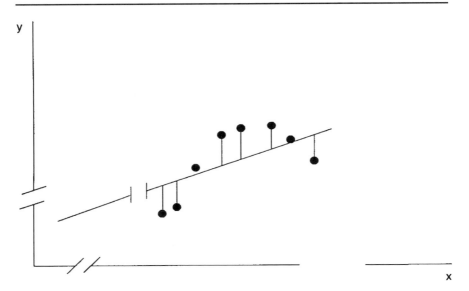

In this case, "n" is the number of data observations, and the summation expressions for the "x" and "y" values are calculated from the observed data. *Exhibit 3–12* illustrates these calculations.

The summations indicated in *Exhibit 3–12* are then substituted into the two normal equations. This results in two equations in two unknowns:

$$8a + 9,550b = 34,200$$
$$9,550a + 11,637,500b = 41,640,000$$

Exhibit 3–12
Least squares calculations

Period	Supply costs (y)	Patient days (x)	x^2	xy
1	$3,500	1,000	1,000,000	3,500,000
2	4,500	1,200	1,440,000	5,400,000
3	4,000	1,100	1,210,000	4,400,000
4	4,800	1,350	1,822,500	6,480,000
5	3,200	950	902,500	3,040,000
6	5,100	1,500	2,250,000	7,650,000
7	4,700	1,300	1,690,000	6,110,000
8	4,400	1,150	1,322,500	5,060,000
	Σy = 34,200	Σx = 9,550	Σx^2 = 11,637,500	Σxy = 41,640,000
	$\bar{y}$ = 4,275	$\bar{x}$ = 1,193.75		

These relationships can be solved by first solving for "a" and "b" and then substituting the obtained value in the other equation. For example:

$$8a + 9,550b = 34,200$$
$$8a = 34,200 - 9,550b$$
$$a = (34,200 - 9,550b) \div 8$$
$$a = 4,275 - 1,193.75b$$

Substituting the expression for "a" into the other equation permits calculation of the "b" coefficient:

$$9,550a + 11,637,500b = 41,640,000$$
$$9,550(4,275 - 1,193.75b) + 11,637,500b = 41,640,000$$
$$40,826,250 - 11,400,312.5b + 11,637,500b = 41,640,000$$
$$237,187.5b = 813,750$$
$$b = 3.4308$$

Replacing the calculated value for "b" into the expression for "a" results in:

$$a = 4,275 - 1,193.75b$$
$$a = 4,275 - 1,193.75(3.4308)$$
$$a = 4,275 - 4,095.5175$$
$$a = 179.4825$$

The resulting cost prediction equation is obtained by substituting the calculated values for each of the coefficients into the equation for a straight line:

$$y^1 = a + bx$$
$$y^1 = 179.483 + 3.4308x$$

If the manager now wants to prepare a flexible budget for supply costs at 1,000 hours of activity and at 1,600 hours of activity, the cost prediction equation can be used for those calculations. For example, the cost prediction equation could be used to predict supply costs of $3,610 at 1,000 patient days. At 1,600 patient days, predicted costs are almost $5,670. These calculations are summarized below:

$$y^1_{1000} = 179.483 + 3.4308 \, (1,000) = \$3,610.28$$
$$y^1_{1600} = 179.483 + 3.4308 \, (1,600) = \$5,668.76$$

The cost prediction equation can be used to predict supply costs at "y" activity level as long as it is within the relevant range of 1,000 to 1,600 patient days. These calculations can be performed easily with a computer spread sheet. Note that slightly different values for "a" and "b" may be obtained because of differences due to rounding. For example, the precise coefficients obtained with a computer for the data in *Exhibit 3–10* are:

$$a = 179.467 \text{ and } b = 3.4308$$

Since few of the original data points fit exactly on the regression line (*Exhibit 3–11*), it is important to have some measure of the dispersion around the regression line. Any cost behavior equation derived from real data represents an average relationship. The regression line calculated with the least squares computation only estimates costs relative to activities.

Measures of dispersion

Measures of dispersion provide information about the extent of possible errors in the predicted costs. If all the observed data points fit precisely on a single straight line, the hospital financial manager would be reasonably certain that next period's predicted costs would also fit on the same line. Since this happy coincidence rarely occurs, the analyst must allow for possible errors or deviations. The dispersion measures provide a statistical description of these deviations. They also permit calculation of a range of possible predicted costs in which the analyst can be reasonably confident that actual future costs will fit.

Another way of looking at dispersion is to ask how much of the total variation in the observed data can be attributed to chance. How much of the variation is due to a random relationship between the predictor variable and the criterion variable? The least squares regression model permits the analyst to separate the total variation into two components: the amount of variation that is random and the amount of variation that is due to a relationship that can be used to predict costs.

The average value ($\bar{y}$) of the criterion variable serves as a baseline for evaluating variation. In other words, if the only information that the analyst had to predict costs was $\bar{y}$, the prediction would be at the average level. *Exhibit 3–12* shows that $\bar{y}$ is at \$4,275 for the original data in *Exhibit 3–10*. In the absence of any other data, the best possible prediction of future costs would be the average costs \$4,275. However, the analyst also has all the information in *Exhibit 3–10* and has calculated the regression coefficients described above. How much better is the prediction based on the regression coefficients than a prediction based solely on the mean (average)? Least squares regression analysis is based on an implicit comparison between averages ($\bar{y}$) and predictions (y^1).

Exhibit 3–13 illustrates the two components of the total variation. The regression coefficient would provide a cost prediction of almost \$5,500 at 1,540 hours. Coincidentally, actual costs at 1,540 hours were slightly higher at \$5,700. The total variation (from the mean) of \$1,425 can be separated into the two components of that portion that is unexplained ($y - y^1 = 200$) and that portion that is explained by the regression ($y^1 - \bar{y} = 1,225$). These two components fully account for all the observed variation.

Exhibit 3–13
Two components of total variation

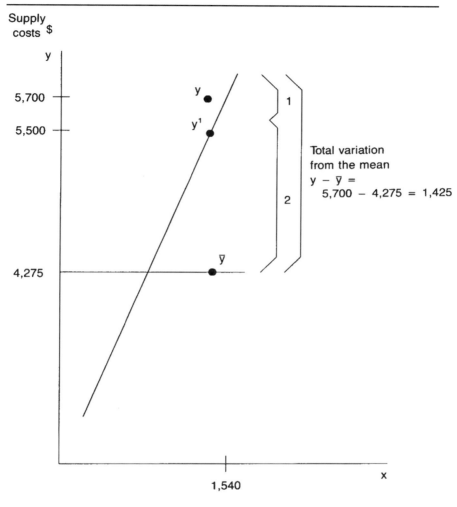

Patient days

y = *observed cost*
y^1 = *predicted cost* (179.467 + 3.4308[1,540])≈5,500
$\bar{y}$ = *average cost*
$y - y^1$ = *variation not explained by (x) activity* = 5,700 – 5,500 = 200 (1)
$y^1 - \bar{y}$ = *variation explained by (x) activity* = 5,500 – 4,275 = 1,225 (2)

Similar measurements of variation of dispersion can be calculated for all of the data points originally plotted in *Exhibit 3–10*. One summary measure of dispersion describes how close the regression line is to the actual data. Deviations from the mean are squared and summed. For example, the total deviation of \$1,425 ($y - \bar{y}$) is first squared and then added to all such deviations for the remainder of the actual data (see *Exhibit 3–11*):

$$\Sigma(y - \bar{y})^2 = (3,500 - 4,275)^2 + (4,500 - 4,275)^2 \ldots$$
$$(4,400 - 4,275)^2 = 3,035,000$$

These squared deviations represent the total sum of squares for the entire variation between actual costs and average costs. The squared deviations are then compared to the squared deviations that are explained by the regression line:

$$\Sigma(y^1 - \bar{y})^2 = (3,610.28 - 4,275)^2 + (4,296.44 - 4,275)^2 +$$
$$(4,124.90 - 4,275)^2 = 2,829,337.95$$

In similar fashion, the sum of the squared deviations that are not explained by the regression line are computed (see *Exhibit 3–14*):

$$\Sigma(y - y^1)^2 = (3,500 - 3,610.28)^2 + (4,500 - 4,296.44)^2$$
$$(4,400 - 4,124.90)^2 = 243,162.05$$

The computations necessary for dispersion analysis are usually a standard output of a computerized regression program. The separate computations for each month's data are added to determine the total explained and unexplained deviations. Again, if all the data fell on a single straight line, there would be no unexplained deviations ($[y - y^1]^2 = 0$). Since this result only occurs in textbooks the analyst then compares the sum of the unexplained deviations against the total deviations:

$$\frac{\Sigma(y - y^1)^2}{\Sigma(y - \bar{y})^2} = \frac{unexplained\ variation}{total\ variation} = \frac{243,162.05}{3,035,000} = 8.01\%$$

This calculation can be interpreted so that 8.01 percent of the total dispersion is due to random variation, random errors, or variables not included in the model. The remaining variation of 91.99 percent (100

Exhibit 3–14
Dispersion calculations

Period	$y - \bar{y}$	$(y - \bar{y})^2$	y^1	$y - y^1$	$(y - y^1)^2$
1	−775	600,625	3,610.28	−110.28	12,161.68
2	225	50,625	4,296.44	203.56	41,436.67
3	−275	75,625	3,953.36	46.64	2,175.29
4	525	275,625	4,811.06	−11.06	122.32
5	−1075	1,155,625	3,438.74	−238.74	56,996.79
6	825	680,625	5,325.68	−225.68	50,931.46
7	425	180,625	4,639.52	60.48	3,657.83
8	125	15,625	4,124.90	275.10	75,680.01
		$\Sigma(y - \bar{y})^2 = 3,035,000$			$\Sigma(y - y^1)^2 = 243,162.05$

percent – 8.01 percent) is due to the variation in costs that can be attributed to differences in staff hours.

A statistical measure of the explained variance is called the coefficient of determination (r^2). This measure is typically used as a measure of how well the regression line explains the total variance between actual costs and average costs. It is a summary measure of the "goodness of fit" of the regression. It is calculated as the complement of the total variation versus that portion not explained by the regression:

$$r^2 = 1 - \frac{unexplained\ variation}{total\ variation} = 1 - \frac{\Sigma(y - y^1)^2}{\Sigma(y - \bar{y})^2}$$

$$= 1 - \frac{243,162.05}{3,035,000} = 1 - .0801$$

$$= 100\% - 8.01\% = 91.99\%$$

Of the total variation (100 percent), almost 92 percent is explained or accounted for by the regression line. A coefficient of determination larger than 70 percent is usually considered to be quite acceptable.

The square root of the coefficient of determination ($\sqrt{r^2} = r$) is called the coefficient of correlation:

$$r = \pm \sqrt{1 - \frac{\Sigma(y - y^1)^2}{\Sigma(y - \bar{y})^2}}$$

where the ± is determined by the sign of the coefficient "b" in the regression equation. For the data above:

$$r = \sqrt{r^2} = + \sqrt{.9199} = .9591$$

The correlation coefficient indicates that patient days are positively, and highly, correlated with costs. The coefficient of correlation, a measure of the relationship between two variables, can vary between 0 and ± 1.0. A negative correlation coefficient indicates that a positive change in one variable is accompanied by a negative change in the other variable (or vice versa). Note also that the correlation coefficient provides no direct information about the degree of error attributed to the regression equation; only r^2 provides that information.

Another measure of dispersion is the standard error of the estimate (s_e). The standard error of the estimate is a measure of dispersion around the regression line. A measure of this dispersion will help the analyst evaluate the accuracy of the regression line as a basis for predicting costs. The standard error of the estimate indicates the degree of scatter of the actual costs around the regression line. It indicates the relative scatter in a scatter diagram. The standard error of the estimate is calculated as:

$$s_e = \sqrt{\frac{\Sigma(y - y^1)^2}{n - 2}}, where\ the\ size\ of\ the\ sample\ is\ 'n'.$$

For the data discussed above:

$$s_e = \sqrt{\frac{243,162.05}{8-2}} = \sqrt{40,527.01} = 201.31$$

A similar computation, particularly where pocket calculators are used to calculate the regression coefficients, is:

$$s_e = \sqrt{\frac{\Sigma y^2 - a\Sigma y - b\Sigma xy}{n-2}}$$

Using the data from *Exhibit 3–12* (where $\Sigma y^2 = 149,240,000$):

$$s_e = \sqrt{\frac{149,240,000 - 179.467(34,200) - 3.4308(41,640,000)}{8-2}}$$

$$= \sqrt{\frac{243,716}{6}} = \sqrt{40,619.33} = 201.54$$

Note that this answer, 201.54, is almost equivalent (except due to arithmetical rounding) to $s_e = 201.31$ obtained earlier.

The standard error of the estimate is useful because any regression equation calculated from actual data is only an estimate of the true regression equation that could be calculated from the entire population. In other words, any set of observed data is probably a sample from a much larger population. The healthcare financial manager usually does not have the resources to fully explore or obtain the entire population. Consequently, a sample is used to identify an estimated equation that can be used to predict costs. The standard error of the estimate can be used to identify boundaries or limits within which the predicted cost will actually occur on a certain percentage of trials. If several important statistical assumptions (discussed later in this chapter) that pertain to regression analysis are met, the number of standard errors of the estimate are related to probabilities as follows:

Number of standard errors	Probability
$1s_e$	67%
$2s_e$	94%
$3s_e$	99%

Therefore, at a level of 1,540 patient days, the analyst would estimate that supply cost would be around $5,462.90, or $179.467 + 3.4308(1,540)$, with a range of $\pm 2s_e$, or $2(201.543) = 403.09$. The analyst would predict that actual costs (at 1,540 days) would be between $5,059.81 and $5,865.99 with a 94 percent chance of being correct.

The lower the standard error for the estimate (s_e), the better the regression equation. In other words, a low standard error will permit the organization's financial manager to make more accurate predictions. If the standard error can be reduced, the prediction can be improved. Therefore, the standard error of the estimate describes the dispersion around the regression line and allows us to predict the relative dispersion of predicted costs.

The standard error of the estimate is a measure of dispersion for the entire regression equation. However, each of the coefficients in the regression equation also has an associated error rate or measure of dispersion. The standard errors of the regression coefficients help assess the relationship between a sample and the entire population. Remember that any cost prediction model is based on a sample of actual observations. The population of all observations is much larger and can never be fully determined. The financial manager is usually trying to assess whether the sample data accurately represents the population and whether they can be used to predict something about the population.

The standard errors of the regression coefficients are used to determine whether the regression coefficient is significant in terms of the unknown population parameter. In other words, by pure random coincidence, does a regression coefficient indicate some relationship between a predictor variable and a criterion variable, when, in fact, there is no such relationship in the population? Are the calculated coefficients a function of chance (random), or do they indicate a "real" relationship that is consistent with the relationships that occur within the real world (population)? The standard error, for each regression coefficient, is used to help answer these questions.

To do so, the analyst sets up an implicit hypothesis that the true regression coefficient in the population is really zero. If this hypothesis can be rejected on the basis of the sample data, the analyst has some assurance that a significant relationship exists. Each standard error of a regression coefficient is a measure of the sample error associated with that coefficient. Consequently, the standard error of a regression coefficient is related to the standard error of the estimate (described above). For example, the standard error (s_b) of the slope (b) coefficient is calculated as:

$$s_b = \frac{s_e}{\sqrt{\Sigma(x - \bar{x})^2}} = \frac{s_e}{\sqrt{\Sigma x^2 - \bar{x}\Sigma x}}$$

Either term may be used to compute the standard error of b (s_b), although the second expression is easier to compute. Note that in each expression, the denominator indicates the dispersion of the observed data around the mean. Therefore, the standard error of a regression coefficient helps measure the dispersion of the components of the regression equation, while the standard error of the estimate measures the dispersion of the entire equation. For the data in *Exhibit 3–12*, the standard error of b is calculated as:

$$s_b = \frac{201.54}{\sqrt{11,637,500 - (1,193.75)(9,550)}} = \frac{201.54}{\sqrt{237,187.5}}$$

$$= \frac{201.54}{487.019} = .4138$$

The standard error of the regression coefficient must be evaluated relative to the original coefficient. The analyst uses the standard error to determine whether the regression coefficient is due to random chance. To accomplish this objective, the standard error is used to compute the number of standard errors that the calculated coefficient is away from a "real" coefficient of zero. For example, the regression coefficient (b), calculated earlier, is 3.4308. This calculated value is more than 8(8.291 = 3.4308 ÷ .4138) standard error units away from a population coefficient equal to zero. This calculation of the number of standard errors away from a population coefficient equal to zero is called a t-value. The t-value is computed as:

$$t = \frac{regression\ coefficient}{standard\ error\ of\ the\ regression\ coefficient} = \frac{3.4308}{.4138} = 8.291$$

A t-value in excess of 2.0 is usually considered sufficient. In other words, the chances that a deviation as great as two standard errors could occur (randomly), with a population coefficient equal to zero, are about 5 percent. The chances that a t-value as great as eight standard errors could similarly occur are almost zero. One could refer to a table of t-values to make the exact computations (see *Exhibit 3–15*). These computations are illustrated below; the financial manager can usually be satisfied if the calculated t-value is at least 2.0.

The corresponding calculations for the intercept (a) of the regression equation are:

$$s_a = (s_e) \sqrt{\frac{1}{n} + \frac{\bar{x}^2}{\Sigma(x - \bar{x})^2}} = (s_e) \sqrt{\frac{1}{n} + \frac{\bar{x}^2}{\Sigma x^2 - \bar{x}\Sigma x}}$$

For the sample data in *Exhibit 3–14*, the resulting calculations are:

$$s_a = (.4138) \sqrt{\frac{1}{8} + \frac{(1,193.75)^2}{11,637,500 - (1,193.75)(9,550)}}$$

$$= (.4138) \sqrt{\frac{1}{8} + \frac{(1,193.75)^2}{237,187.5}} = (.4138) \sqrt{\frac{1}{8} + 6.0081}$$

$$= (.4138) \sqrt{6.1331} = .4138\ (2.4765) = 1.0248$$

Exhibit 3–15
Table of student's distribution (values of t)

Degrees of freedom (df)	*Level of significance*					
	.2	*.1*	*.05*	*.025*	*.01*	*.005*
1	1.376	3.078	6.314	12.706	31.821	63.657
2	1.061	1.886	2.910	4.303	6.965	9.925
3	.978	1.638	2.353	3.182	4.541	5.841
4	.941	1.533	2.132	2.776	3.747	4.604
5	.920	1.476	2.015	2.571	3.365	4.032
6	.906	1.440	1.943	2.447	3.143	3.707
7	.896	1.415	1.895	2.365	2.998	3.499
8	.889	1.397	1.860	2.306	2.896	3.355
9	.883	1.383	1.833	2.262	2.821	3.250
10	.879	1.372	1.812	2.228	2.764	3.169
11	.876	1.363	1.796	2.201	2.718	3.106
12	.873	1.356	1.782	2.179	2.681	3.055
13	.870	1.350	1.771	2.160	2.650	3.012
14	.868	1.345	1.761	2.145	2.624	2.977
15	.866	1.341	1.753	2.131	2.602	2.947
16	.865	1.337	1.746	2.120	2.583	2.921
17	.863	1.333	1.740	2.110	2.567	2.898
18	.862	1.330	1.734	2.101	2.552	2.878
19	.861	1.328	1.729	2.093	2.539	2.861
20	.860	1.325	1.725	2.086	2.528	2.845
21	.859	1.323	1.721	2.080	2.518	2.831
22	.858	1.321	1.717	2.074	2.508	2.819
23	.858	1.319	1.714	2.069	2.500	2.807
24	.857	1.318	1.711	2.064	2.492	2.797
25	.856	1.316	1.708	2.060	2.485	2.787
26	.856	1.315	1.706	2.056	2.479	2.779
27	.855	1.314	1.703	2.052	2.473	2.771
28	.855	1.313	1.701	2.048	2.467	2.763
29	.854	1.311	1.699	2.045	2.462	2.756
30	.854	1.310	1.697	2.042	2.457	2.750

The t-value for the intercept is then calculated by dividing the standard error of "a" into the original value of the intercept:

$$t_a = \frac{179.467}{1.0248} = 175.12$$

Such a high t-value means that the true intercept could equal zero only under the most unusual circumstances.

Note that similar computations are possible if there is more than one predictor variable. The higher the t-value, the more confidence the financial manager has in using the particular coefficient as a predictor variable.

A regression coefficient with a low t-value is a candidate for exclusion from the cost prediction model.

The standard error of a regression coefficient can also be used to evaluate the probability that the population parameter is within certain limits. These limits, called confidence intervals, are computed using the standard error of the regression coefficient. Values from a table of t-statistics are also used to compute the confidence limits as follows:

$$\text{confidence limit} = \text{regression coefficient} \pm (\text{t-value probability})(s_b)$$

The t-value for a particular probability is obtained from a table of t-statistics. For example, *Exhibit 3–15* illustrates one such table for many degrees of freedom. Degrees of freedom relate to the sample size of the original observations. A regression equation with one predictor variable and one criterion variable has $n - 2$ degrees of freedom (where n is the total number of observations). The associated probability depends on how much confidence the analyst desires. A probability of 1 percent indicates a much wider range, and lower confidence, than a probability of .5 percent. A probability of 10 percent is interpreted to mean that there is a 10 percent chance that the true population parameter could be outside the calculated confidence limits. There is a 90 percent chance that the population parameter is within the confidence limit calculation from t-values associated with a 10 percent probability.[1]

The confidence limits for the sample data (slope), with a probability of .01 and six degrees of freedom (8–2) are:[2]

$$\textit{confidence limits}_b = b \pm (t_{.01}) (s_b)$$
$$= 3.4308 \pm (3.143) (.4138)$$
$$= 3.4308 \pm 1.3006$$
$$= 2.1302 \textit{ and } 4.7314$$

Therefore, the 98 percent confidence limits are 2.1302 to 4.7314. The analyst is 98 percent confident that the population parameter for the slope (b) (variable costs) is between these values. A lower level of confidence will result in a narrower range of values. The higher the confidence and its associated probability, the farther apart are the extremes of the confidence limits. Note that these confidence limits do not include zero, and, again we are able to reject the hypothesis that the population parameter is equal to zero.

---

[1] Statistical purists might quibble with our choice of terminology in this section and assert, correctly, that 90 percent of the confidence limits calculated from representative sample data will include the population coefficient. We prefer the more intuitive statements of the probability of correctly estimating a coefficient that can be used for predictive purposes. In our judgment, financial managers are more concerned with reasonable predictive ability than statistical purity.

[2] The probability of .01 represents 1 percent on each side of a two-tailed distribution. Note that the t-statistics in *Exhibit 3–15* also represent a one-tailed distribution.

In summary, measures of dispersion can be used to determine:

1. how much of the variation in all the data is explained by the regression equation (r^2);
2. the relative dispersion around the regression line (s_e);
3. the standard errors of the regression coefficients (s_b and s_a);
4. the probability that the calculated coefficients of the regression line occurred by chance (t-values and confidence limits).

These different measures of dispersion are useful for determining the usability of the regression data. They improve the analyst's understanding of the relationship of hospital costs to activity and permit the financial manager to better predict costs. There are no precise guidelines governing the required accuracy of predicted costs. As the financial manager gains experience and confidence with the use of regression data, the trade-offs between different types of errors and dispersion will become more meaningful.

Statistical assumptions of regression analysis

A healthcare financial manager cannot blindly apply the statistical techniques that have been discussed. In many cases, the data may not be appropriate for regression analysis. A naive application of a computerized regression analysis may actually mislead the analyst. The results must be subjected to a careful analysis to determine that the underlying assumptions are satisfied. If not, the financial manager must search for other, more appropriate tools or perhaps reevaluate the data base using the techniques described. The brief survey of regression analysis in these chapters only qualifies the financial manager of a healthcare organization to better evaluate the usefulness of cost behavior models. If difficulties that may violate these statistical requirements are encountered, the assistance of a professional statistician may be necessary.

Six different assumptions underlying regression analysis can be tested and evaluated. They are:

1. stable relationships;
2. linear relationships;
3. homoscedasticity (uniform dispersion);
4. absence of serial correlation;
5. absence of multicollinearity;
6. normal distribution.

Testing of these regression assumptions is often called specification analysis. Specification analysis is used to determine that the calculated regression coefficients (a and b), which are based on a limited sample of observed data, are unbiased, efficient estimators of the "true" regression coefficients in the entire population. Fortunately, many computer programs provide data that permit relatively quick and easy specification analyses. Spreadsheet programs provide the standard error of the estimate and R^2 as standard output. Many of the detailed tests of serial correlation, normality, etc., are automatically available as part of the regression output of the more sophisticated software program. However, the manager's judgment is still required in specification analysis because it is rare that the results are completely consistent and unambiguous. Some of the statistical assumptions may not be as strong as others, and the analyst must carefully weigh the conflicting evidence.

The first assumption that must be evaluated is whether the relationship between the predictor variable(s) and the criterion variable is stable. Will the relationship persist? Are the historical data used to predict costs useful for predicting future costs? Because of the need for a continuing and stable relationship between the regression variables, regression analysis is most successfully applied to repetitive activities. Consequently, laboratories, dietary departments, and other ancillary departments are excellent candidates for determining cost behavior equations through regression analysis. If the first assumption or requirement is not met, there is probably little reason, outside of intellectual curiosity, to continue the regression analysis. For example, if the hospital or the department anticipates a merger or some other type of reorganization, the regression equation probably cannot be used directly to predict future costs. On the other hand, the historical data can be used to establish a baseline measure of what the costs would have been, hypothetically, in the absence of the organizational change.

The second assumption pertains to linearity within the relevant range. Simple regression attempts to fit a linear equation of the form:

$$y = a + bx, \text{ which can be restated as}$$
$$y = a + bx + u$$

The "u" term, called the disturbance or error term, indicates the deviation of the actual data from the regression line. Consequently, $u = y - y^1$ as discussed earlier in this chapter. The value of the error term is expected to be zero. Error arises from the fact that the regression equation is calculated from sample data because the entire population is not known and therefore not included in the regression calculations. Therefore, some error will occur. If the relationship is linear, the financial manager would expect the average error to be zero.

In the case of simple regression, linearity can be easily checked by evaluating a scatter diagram of the data as discussed earlier. This test should never be omitted. Of equal importance is the necessity of assessing the width of the relevant range. The relationship may be linear within the anticipated relevant range, while it may be nonlinear outside of that range

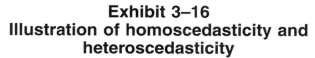

Exhibit 3–16
Illustration of homoscedasticity and heteroscedasticity

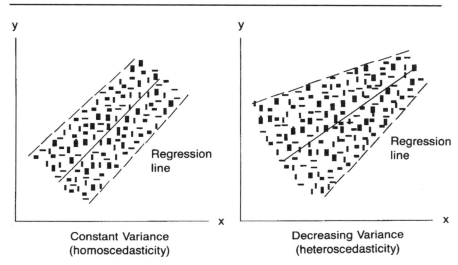

Constant Variance
(homoscedasticity)

Decreasing Variance
(heteroscedasticity)

(see *Exhibit 3–4*). If shifts in volume or activity are anticipated, the analyst must be careful about extrapolating the regression results outside the limits of the relevant range. In any event, both linearity and the relevant range must be simultaneously evaluated. A stable linear relationship within a reasonable relevant range of historical activity is a sound basis for pursuing the best cost behavior model. Note also that linearity does not usually apply to multiple regression analysis.

The third assumption that must be evaluated concerns homoscedasticity or constant variance. This condition requires that the standard deviation and variance be constant for all the error terms (u) of the observed data (x). Homoscedasticity indicates that data are uniformly dispersed around the regression line.[3] For example, *Exhibit 3–16* indicates constant variance in the first graph and decreasing variance in the second. Violation of the homoscedasticity assumption can be tested by calculating the standard deviation and variance for each quartile (or half) of the data base. If the standard deviations and variance from each partition of the data are not approximately equal, the constant variance assumption has been violated and there exists some pattern to the error.

If so, the analyst can place less confidence in the slope (b) coefficient of the regression line. In other words, the absence of homoscedasticity can

---

[3] The absence of homoscedasticity is called heteroscedasticity.

bias the "b" coefficient. This is likely to happen with typical cost data in healthcare organizations, and the financial manager must determine if the bias is significant enough to distort the cost predictions. Unfortunately, this is where judgment plays an important role; there is no rule that can indicate when the bias resulting from a violation of the homoscedasticity assumption will overwhelm the usefulness of the cost predictions.

The fourth statistical assumption that must be evaluated is whether serial correlation is present. This condition exists when any single disturbance term (u) is related to any other disturbance term. The error terms should be independent, and the size of one deviation or disturbance should not influence any other deviation. This condition is also called autocorrelation, and the analyst should test to determine whether the autocorrelation is significant.

This is, again, likely to happen with cost data from healthcare organizations. For example, cost increase may be variable with respect to increases in some activity level while decreases in the same activity may not lead to proportionate decreases in costs. For example, some costs are quite "sticky" or slow to decrease because managers are reluctant to fire people and close down departments (or beds) as volume declines. Many costs are related to time and to inflation over time, and the error terms of time-related costs are often serially correlated. Most computer programs permit the analyst to test for the degree of serial correlation. The Durbin-Watson statistic is often used to evaluate serial correlation; most analysts agree that a Durbin-Watson statistic around 2.0 indicates almost no serial correlation.

If the error terms are not independent, this can lead to several problems with statistical measures of dispersion. These problems include:

1. underestimation of the standard errors of the regression coefficients (s_a and s_b);
2. overestimation of the sampling variances of the regression coefficients;
3. greater dispersion among the predicted costs than would be ordinarily expected.

Simply stated, the standard errors will be underestimated and the variance of the coefficients (and the standard errors) will be overestimated because the deviations in the observed data (u) are not independent. There are just not enough independent observations in the data to permit valid and usable cost predictions.

The fifth assumption concerns the absence of multicollinearity. This condition pertains only to multiple regression, which is discussed in the last section. Multiple regression requires more than one predictor variable, and multicollinearity would indicate that these predictor variables are highly correlated. Multicollinear predictor variables lead to unreliable and unstable regression coefficients. The calculated coefficients are highly dependent on the sample observations, and the addition or deletion of a few observations will usually cause large shifts in the regression coefficients. The prediction of costs may still be quite feasible and valid, but the individual coefficients will provide unreliable evidence about the marginal effects of each separate predictor variable.

Fortunately, the presence of multicollinearity is relatively easy to observe. A correlation table can usually be obtained as part of any computerized regression program. The analyst should consider excluding a predictor variable if it is highly correlated with another predictor variable. The analyst's judgment is used to assess which variable is less important. The less important variables that are highly correlated with other, more important, variables should be excluded. Of course, separate analyses should be conducted with those excluded variables to confirm that they really are not important. Generally, correlation coefficients greater than .70 or .80 indicate variables that should be evaluated for inclusion in the regression equation.

The multicollinearity test is also consistent with the general objective of parsimony. The financial manager of a healthcare organization would like to use a regression equation that is as simple as possible and uses as few predictor variables as possible. Why monitor and collect twenty different variables when sufficient accuracy and reliability can be obtained with two or three variables? By eliminating some of the variables that are highly correlated with each other, the analyst is fully using all the information captured by the remaining variables. Redundant variables should always be eliminated, and a parsimonious model should be used for cost prediction purposes. The multicollinearity tests merely help achieve this objective; they can certainly be used to reduce what would otherwise be a multiple regression model into a simple regression model.

The final statistical assumption that must be evaluated concerns the distribution of points around the regression line. The statistical measures of dispersion discussed earlier in this chapter rely on a normal, or almost normal, distribution of the sample data around the regression line. This is exactly the same as testing whether the disturbance terms (u) are normally distributed. A normal distribution is a symmetrical bell-shaped curve. The error terms can actually be plotted to observe the shape of the distribution. The normality assumption is generally considered to be the least important statistical requirement; most analysts are satisfied if the distribution of the error terms is roughly symmetrical around a single mode (not bimodal or multiple modes).

Each statistical assumption described above must be successively tested and evaluated. The analyst, working together with the financial manager, must assess whether the statistical assumptions are met sufficiently to justify using the regression equation for cost prediction. In most cases, several of the statistical requirements will be strongly satisfied while others are only marginally satisfied. The financial manager of a healthcare organization must have some idea of the probable impact of any unsatisfied statistical requirements, and the manager will then be able to revise, probably downward, the level of confidence and assurance that may be placed in the results.

Possible misuse of regression analysis

This chapter has repeatedly emphasized the necessity for the financial manager to apply judgment and thought regarding the results of regression analysis. There are frequently alternative cost prediction models that all meet the statistical criteria described above. How does the manager or analyst choose between alternative predictor variables or between alternative cost prediction models? The best criterion for making this choice is to choose the cost prediction model that provides the best possible prediction at the lowest possible cost and with the minimum possible error. Three possible errors should be avoided:

1. measurement errors;
2. analytical error;
3. errors in judgment.

The total error of any cost prediction can be expressed as the sum of these three components. The total error should be minimized; therefore, it is generally good practice to minimize each component of the total error.

Measurement errors are errors in the data base. They include errors in data collection, coding and input, as well as errors of classification and definition. The techniques to avoid these errors were described previously. Analytical errors are errors of calculation. Not all computer programs yield the same results for equivalent input data. Specification errors are analytical errors. They were described in the preceding section of this chapter in terms of the statistical assumptions of regression analysis.

The most important and crucial error that is usually made in using regression analysis is error in judgment. A very important error in judgment is often due to omitted variables. The analyst must be aware of possible explanatory variables that would be useful and significant if included in the data base. These variables may be extremely important, but no one thought to collect or include them. Minor increments in data collection costs can often significantly improve cost prediction models. Unfortunately, there are no guides or signals to indicate when some significant variables have been omitted.

Another very crucial judgment error is introduced when the cost prediction is just not plausible. The relationships between the criterion variable (costs) and predictor variables must make "good economic sense." The predictor variables must be subject to managerial control, or else it is useless to identify the cost prediction model. Each of the predictor variables must also be logically defensible. There must be some reason why they were chosen.

The final error in judgment concerns the tests of "goodness of fit." Ideally, the cost behavior model that satisfies all of the above criteria will also be the one that best fits the observed data. The coefficient of determination (r^2) should be as high as possible. The t-values for the regression coefficient should exceed 2.0. The standard error of the estimate (s_e) should be low relative to the average predicted costs. The sign of the slope (b) coefficient should be consistent with the expected sign.

Exhibit 3–17
Illustration of a negative intercept

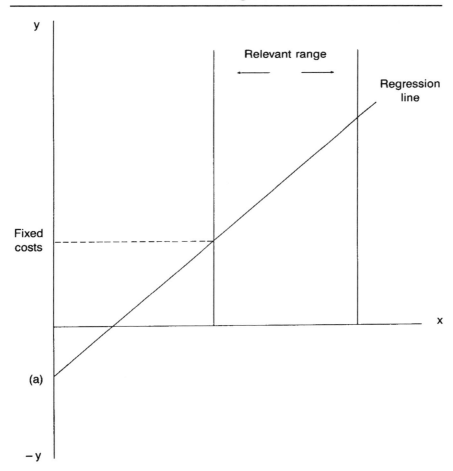

That is, if the plausible economic model has a positive sign, upward sloping to the right on *b,* then a calculated *b* with a negative sign would be sufficient cause to reevaluate alternative models. In any event, the financial manager cannot just choose that model that has the highest r^2. Blind faith in high r^2 has led many unwary analysts to nonsensical cost predictions.

Further thought concerns possible negative signs on the intercept (a) coefficient that might be obtained through regression analysis. Does a negative intercept indicate that the results are unusable? Does a negative intercept mean negative fixed costs? Not necessarily. The answers to these questions depend on the relevant range. *Exhibit 3–17* illustrates a regression line with a negative intercept (and positive slope). The fixed costs are certainly not negative within the relevant range. In fact, to obtain a more accurate estimate of fixed costs, the intersection of the (lower) relevant range and the regression must be extended to the vertical axis. The horizontal dotted line illustrates how the fixed costs would be read from a graph. Similar calculations could be made using the regression equation and the appropriate value of the criterion (x) variable.

Note also that a true variable cost, with no fixed component, should be expected to have an intercept (a) of almost zero. The intercept (a) should also have a very low t-value because the analyst would then be interested in accepting the hypothesis that the intercept was not significantly different from zero.

Summary

One of the preliminary steps, identified above as part of any cost behavior identification process, was to construct or obtain scatter diagrams of costs as a function of a variety of predictor variables. Once the manager has selected the most logical predictor variable, a line may be visually fit to the observed scatter diagram. The visual fit technique can actually be used to obtain a cost behavior equation. This course of action is not recommended because the results are so subjective and because, for a minor incremental cost, statistical techniques can be applied and a much more accurate equation can be obtained. As noted above, the visual fit technique assists in selecting (or rejecting) possible predictor variables. In other words, the visual fit technique is a cheap and expedient step that should be used before statistical techniques. Visual fit techniques help the analyst focus attention on promising cost behavior relationships and they help avoid wasting time and effort on analyses that have little hope of success.

This chapter also focused on the statistical methods that can be used to obtain estimates of cost behavior patterns. Regression models offer considerable help to the management team when applying the cost accounting techniques discussed in this book. Like all statistical tools, regression analysis cannot be applied blindly, especially when computer applications are used. The effective manager understands both the strength and weakness of the tools he/she uses.

Questions and problems

1. What is the advantage of understanding cost behavior in healthcare organizations?

2. How can management improve its decision making by knowing more about cost behavior patterns?

3. Why is the prediction of future costs important?

4. What criterion must first be applied when analyzing cost behavior?

5. Name five steps in the identification of a cost behavior model.

6. What is the difference between univariate and multivariate models?

7. Describe what a slope of two in a linear cost behavior model means.

8. Describe the usefulness of a scatter diagram.

9. Identify potential data problems affecting cost behavior patterns.

10. What are step costs? How can they be approximated?

11. Name three approaches to identifying cost behavior patterns.

12. What are the advantages and disadvantages of the industrial engineering approach to the identification of cost behavior patterns?

13. Can you think of any additional uses for the industrial engineering approach to the identification of cost behavior patterns?

14. List the assumptions underlying regression analysis.

15. What is the purpose of specification analysis?

16. Why is regression analysis most successfully applied to repetitive activities?

17. Identify how linearity of your data can be evaluated.

18. How can you test for homoscedasticity?

19. Why is it important to test for autocorrelation?

20. How would you evaluate a correlation coefficient of .785 determined through multiple regression? What should be done next?

21. How does the financial manager choose between various cost prediction models?

22. Identify the components of total error. What can the financial manager of a healthcare organization do about each type of error?

23. Why is the financial manager's judgment necessary in conducting regression analyses?

24. The following six monthly observations of healthcare costs are to be used as a basis for a budget formula. A scatter diagram indicates behavior in the form y = a + bx.

Month	Supply usage	Healthcare costs
January	800	$2,000
February	400	1,100
March	700	2,100
April	1,200	2,600
May	1,000	2,300
June	600	1,500

Using least squares, compute the variable and fixed costs for the budget equation.

25. The following observations of supply costs and patient level are to be used to develop a budget formula. A scatter diagram indicated the data fit to a linear equation.

Period	Patient level	Supply costs
1	1,100	$ 8,700
2	1,200	9,400
3	1,500	11,270
4	900	7,580
5	1,100	8,840

a. Determine a least squares regression equation.
b. Calculate the predicted supply costs given a level of 1) 1,300 patients and 2) 1,450 patients.

26. Metropolitan General Hospital has collected the following supply cost data from the prior four periods for the outpatient department. The departmental manager wants to investigate the relationship as a basis for future budgets.

Period	Supply costs	Patient level
1	$350	800
2	350	1,200
3	150	400
4	550	1,600

   a. Draw a scatter diagram.
   b. Using the high-low method, calculate the budget equation.
   c. Using least squares analysis, calculate the budget equation.
   d. Compute the coefficient of determination. (R^2)
   e. Compute the standard error of estimate.
   f. Calculate a 95 percent confidence limit for the slope of the regression line.

27. The healthcare departmental manager wishes to investigate the relationship between supply costs and service level. Below are the data for the last five periods.

Period	Service level	Supply costs
1	250	$2,600
2	210	2,150
3	230	2,500
4	200	2,100
5	260	2,700

   a. Draw a scatter diagram.
   b. Using least squares analysis, compute the equation of the line.
   c. Calculate the unexplained and explained portions of the total variation at a level of 230 patients.
   d. Calculate and explain the coefficient of determination. (R^2)
   e. Describe how well the service levels correlate with supply costs.
   f. Calculate and explain the standard error of estimate.
   g. Calculate a 99 percent confidence limit for the slope of the cost line.

28. An administrator at Hillside Health Center wants to prepare a budget for the outpatient department. Below are the supply costs and related patient levels for the past six quarters.

Quarter	Patient level	Supply cost
1	600	$1,300
2	900	2,000
3	800	1,400
4	1,100	2,500
5	1,200	2,700
6	1,000	2,100

a. Is a linear equation appropriate?
b. Calculate the regression equation, using least squares analysis.
c. Determine the explained and unexplained portions of the total variation at a level of 1,000 patients.
d. Calculate the coefficient of determination. (R^2)
e. Compute the standard error of estimate.
f. Determine a 95 percent confidence limit for the slope of the budget line.

29. In developing a budget formula, the following healthcare data for the last six months were collected. The least squares analysis will be used.

Total costs Σy	$3,600
Average costs $\bar{y}$	$ 600
Total usage Σx	900 units
Σx^2	3,240,000
Σxy	5,760,000

a. Determine the budget formula.
b. What are the fixed costs?
c. What are the variable costs?
d. Calculate total costs given a usage of 162 units.

30. A healthcare departmental manager has collected the data below for the last twelve months. He wants to determine a budget formula using least squares analysis.

Total costs Σy	$19,320
Average costs $\bar{y}$	$ 1,610
Total patients Σx	2,400
Average patients $\bar{x}$	200
$\Sigma(y - y^1)^2$ Unexplained variation	107,324
$\Sigma(y_2 - \bar{y})^2$ Total variation	1,393,818
Σx^2	484,000
Σxy	3,869,000

For the month of June that patient level was 130 with total costs of $1,580.

a. Determine the budget equation.
b. Calculate the explained and unexplained portions of the total variation at a level of 130 patients.
c. Calculate and explain the coefficient of determination.

Keywords: confidence limit; cost prediction; dependent variable; independent variable; least squares; linear; nonlinear; regression; scatter diagram.

References

Aczel, A.D. *Complete Business Statistics.* Homewood, IL: Irwin, 1989.

Borok, L.S. "The Use of Relational Databases in Health Care Information Systems." *Journal of Health Care Finance* (summer 1995): 6–12.

Bridges, M.J. and P. Jacobs. "Obtaining Estimates of Marginal Cost by DRG." *Healthcare Financial Management* 40, no. 10 (1986): 40–46.

Cooper, Robin, and Robert S. Kaplan. *The Design of Cost Management Systems: Text, Cases, and Readings.* Englewood Cliffs, NJ: Prentice Hall, 1991.

Friedman, L., F. Selto, B. Neumann, and J. Suver. "A Computer Simulation Model of Hospital Mergers." *Health Care Management Review* (summer 1980): 53–65.

Michela, William. "Defining and Analyzing Costs—A Statistical Approach." *Hospital Financial Management* (January 1975): 36–41.

Neumann, Bruce R., Jan P. Clement, and Jean C. Cooper. *Financial Management: Concepts and Applications for Health Care Organizations.* Dubuque: Kendall/Hunt, 1997.

Rowley, C. Stevenson. "Which Is Best to Find Cost Behavior?" *Hospital Financial Management* (April 1976): 18–28.

Ryan, J.B., and S.B. Clay. "Understanding the Law of Large Numbers." *Healthcare Financial Management* (October 1995): 22–24.

Suver, James D., and Bruce R. Neumann. "Resource Measurement by Health Care Providers." *Hospital & Health Services Administration* (September/October 1986): 44–52.

CHAPTER 4

Cost/volume/profit models

"How can it be that we will need to see 100,000 patients next year just to break even, but the most we can see is 95,000?"

"How many lab tests do we need to do in order to cover our costs?"

"Is it possible to reduce the number of procedures and still improve our financial performance?"

"I don't know how I am supposed to make a profit when over 50 percent of my patients are Medicare and Medicaid."

"I need to know how many patients I have to see to cover my costs and make a normal profit."

"As a nonprofit provider, my board tells me to set my charges to break even. How do I handle the patients that can't or don't pay?"

Introduction

In chapters 2 and 3 the focus was on understanding cost behavior. In this chapter we will introduce an equally important variable, revenue, and then use both of these factors (revenue and costs) in the development of cost/volume/profit (CVP) models which can be very useful to decision makers. CVP is sometimes closely identified with the concept of break-even analysis. However, breakeven analysis is just one aspect of CVP models and not an interesting economic one at that. Even nonprofits have to have a positive "bottom line" (or profit) if they want to survive in today's healthcare environment. It is, however, important to recognize whether your organization is operating above or below breakeven.

Revenue analysis

The term "Revenue" can be expressed as either the total revenues (TR) from all services provided by the healthcare environment, or as the price of a specific service, usually identified by the letter P. In healthcare, it is important to stress that the price of a service is usually called the rate or charge for the service. Revenue to an HMO refers to the premium. There-fore, P also means charge or rate or premium per unit of services or per capita. It is also important to stress that because of the discounts from charges that most healthcare providers must grant to third party payers such as Medicare, Medicaid, managed care plans, and also all large cus-tomers, the established charge is usually not collected. Therefore, the P must be adjusted for the discount if the CVP model is to be meaningful. This adjusted P will be identified as P* in the models used in this text.

Total revenue is usually a function of *P* times Quantity of services* provided at that price. P* and Q can represent a single service or a mix of P* and Q's weighted by their relative values. There is also the as-sumption in the revenue curve of the CVP model that the collected price (P*) is linear or the same for each unit for the relevant quantity range in the analysis. *Exhibit 4–1* illustrates the total revenue concept.

Exhibit 4–1
TR curve in a fee for service environment

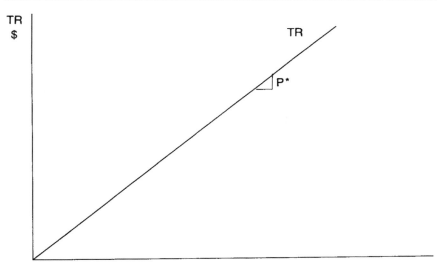

Q *# of services*	P* *Fee per service*	TR *Total Revenue*
0	25	0
1	25	25
2	25	50
3	25	75
4	25	100
5	25	125

It should be noted that P* is the slope of the TR curve.

Exhibit 4–2
Total revenue line in a managed care environment
(for a fixed number of enrollees)

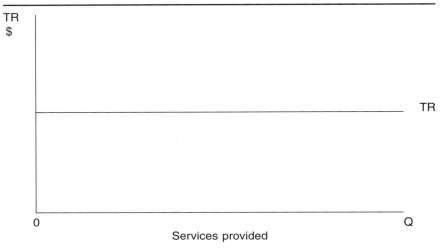

In a managed care or capitated environment, the total revenue received is not a function of the amount of service provided. It is a function of the number of members. For example, in most managed care contracts, a fixed fee per month is paid per member. An increase in the number of members would increase the total revenue but not the amount of services provided to each member. Therefore, since the number of members covered by the managed care contract are known before services are provided, the total revenue curve will be known in advance and can be shown as drawn in *Exhibit 4–2*.

The concepts behind the total revenue curve under both fee for service and managed care are fairly straightforward. However, the implications of each for management decision making are greatly different. These differences will be discussed in the next section.

Cost/volume/profit models

The total cost curve (developed in chapter 2) can now be combined with the total revenue curve developed in the previous section as illustrated in *Exhibit 4–3*.

As *Exhibit 4–3* illustrates, the more services provided, the greater the profit or the smaller the loss. If the objective is to maximize profits, the correct economic response would be to provide services until capacity constraints occur. In a managed care environment, a CVP model similar to *Exhibit 4–4* could be drawn.

Exhibit 4–3
Cost/volume/profit model
under a fee for service format

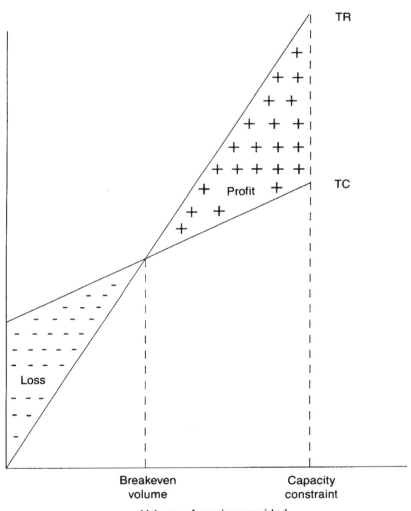

The total cost curve remains the same because the cost curves would not be impacted by a change in the revenue curve. The total revenue remains constant because once the number of members is known under the prepayment of the fixed fee per member approach, the only factor that does change as the amount of services provided increase is the profit. In this type of revenue-cost relationship, the profit is maximized when no services are provided and minimized (maximum loss) when services up to

Exhibit 4–4
Cost/volume/profit model under a capitated
method of payment

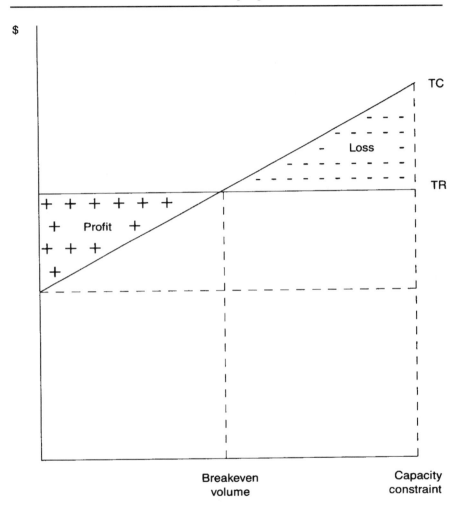

Volume of services provided

the capacity constraints are supplied. This relationship makes it easier to understand the remark made by some policy makers that capitated or managed care approaches cause a poor quality of service to be provided. At least the financial pressures push in that direction. However, it has also been said by some policy makers that the fee for service approach gives the economic incentive to provide more services than required for quality care. Perhaps the reasons for peer review of service provided is clear now. It serves as a safeguard against economic pressures that could influence the care provided under either model. The reader should also note that the capitated revenue model also fits the prospective payment system (PPS) used under the DRG system. A flat amount is paid per DRG regardless of the amount of services actually provided. The same concepts noted above apply equally to any form of fixed payment per test, service, etc.

Formula approaches to cost/volume/profit models

Cost/volume/profit models can be a very useful management tool in decision making. For example, how many patients do I have to see to cover my costs? How many lab tests do I have to perform, etc.? It is possible to estimate answers to these questions by using diagrams and financial statements. However, it is usually quicker and simpler to use mathematical (formula) approaches. In this chapter we will concentrate on the cost relationships (formulae) that may aid in decision making. Based on the cost behavior concepts developed in chapters 2 and 3, these relationships can be identified.

Definitions:

1. TC = total cost or expenses
2. Q = quantity of services or procedures
3. VC_T = total variable costs
4. VC_U = per unit variable cost
5. $VC_R = VC_T/TR_T$ = total variable costs as a percent of total revenue
6. P_U = charge or rate per individual service or procedure
7. P_U^* = charge or rate adjusted for discounts
8. FC_T = total fixed costs
9. FC_U = per unit fixed costs
10. M = excess of revenue over expenses (margin)
11. TR = total revenue (expressed in dollars)
12. TR^* = total revenue adjusted for discounts
13. $TR = (P_U) \times (Q)$ or $TR^* = (P_U^*) \times (Q)$
14. $VC_T = (VC_U) \times (Q)$ or $VC_U = (VC_T/Q)$
15. $TC = FC_T + VC_T$
16. $TR = TC + M$
17. $FC_U = (FC_T/Q)$
18. BE = breakeven where $M = O$ or $TR = TC$
19. BE_Q = breakeven point expressed in units of output rather than dollars

20. BE_R = breakeven point in terms of total revenue
21. CM_U = contribution margin per unit
22. CM_T = contribution margin total
23. CM_R = contribution margin expressed as a percentage of total revenue

The preceding definitions are important in understanding the basic cost and revenue relationships:

1. $TR^* = (FC_T) + (VC_T) + M$

This can also be expressed as:

2. $(P_U{}^*)(Q) = (FC_T) + (VC_U)(Q) + M$

The breakeven point is generally defined as the point where total revenues (TR) equal total costs (TC) or when profit (M) is zero. This point can be expressed in either dollars or units of service as shown in formulae 3 and 4 (below).

3. $BE_R = (FC_T)/(1 - VC_R)$ or (FC_T/CM_R)
4. $BE_Q = (FC_T)/(P_U{}^* - VC_U)$ or (FC_T/CM_U)

The problem shown in *Exhibit 4–5* illustrates the use of the cost formulae in a typical situation.

More examples of this type of problem will be demonstrated in the following pages. These basic relationships are important in effective use of many management accounting techniques which will be used extensively throughout the text.

Exhibit 4–5
Use of cost/volume/profit models to solve for excess of revenues over expense

Given: Q = 1,500 procedures performed
        $P_U{}^*$ = \$25 charge per procedure
        VC_U = \$5 variable cost per procedure
        FC_T = \$10,000 fixed cost for department

Using formulae 13, 14, 15, and 16 the following results would be obtained:
     13. $TR^* = (P_U{}^* \times Q)$ or (\$25 × 1,500) = \$37,500
     14. $VC_T = (VC_U \times Q)$ or (\$5 × 1,500) = \$7,500
     15. $TC = (FC_T + VC_T)$ or (\$10,000 + \$7,500) = \$17,500
     16. $TR = (TC + M)$ or \$37,500 = \$17,500 + \$20,000
               Therefore M = \$20,000

Contribution margin techniques

One of the many questions a manager has to answer is what will happen to a department's financial position if the volume of service is increased. Coupled with an understanding of cost behavior, a very effective management accounting tool is the concept of *contribution margin*. The contribution margin is the difference between the rate or fee charged after discounts for the service performed and the variable costs incurred in providing the service. For example, if the charge for a specific procedure is $20 and the variable costs associated with the service are $8, the contribution margin is $12. The contribution margin represents the resources available to pay for fixed expenses, working capital needs, and expansion of services among other needs. As *Exhibit 4–6* indicates, the formulae for determining the contribution margin is easy to grasp.

For example, assume 2,000 patients will be provided service during the next month. If the charge after discounts is $20 per patient, total revenues are $40,000. Assuming variable expenses are $8 per patient, total variable expenses are $16,000. This means $24,000 is available to cover other (fixed) expenses and profit requirements. These data are summarized in *Exhibit 4–7*.

From this understanding of the contribution margin concept, we can determine how many procedures are necessary to cover full costs. This type of analysis, typically called cost/volume/profit (CVP) analysis or breakeven analysis, further expands our knowledge of the decision variables that can be controlled by managers who are aware of the relationship between volume and costs.

For example, the manager may want to know what level of patient volume will just cover all of a department's costs. This point is called the breakeven point. Following the previous discussion of cost behavior and contribution margin, the breakeven point can be determined by dividing fixed costs by the contribution margin.

Exhibit 4–8 indicates that 20,000 patients are needed each month to be able to cover the total costs. This model can be developed further to cover any additional amounts needed to repay debt, meet profit objectives, or replace equipment. For example, assume that in the preceding situation we want to generate an additional $60,000 for debt repayment.

Exhibit 4–6
Contribution margin

Contribution margin per unit =
Price after discounts – Variable cost per unit

$$CM_U = P^* - VC_U$$

Exhibit 4–7
Contribution margin computation

Total revenue approach (after discounts)

Total revenues	$40,000	(2,000 × $20)
Total variable expenses	16,000	(2,000 × $ 8)
Total contribution margin (CM$_T$)	$24,000	(2,000 × $12)

Individual service approach (after discounts)

P^* = 20
VC_U = 8
CM_U = $12 per unit of service

CM_T = $24,000 = $12 × 2,000

Exhibit 4–8
Computation of breakeven point

Given: $20 Average revenue per patient visit after discount
        8 Average variable cost per patient visit

        $12 Contribution margin (CM$_U$) per patient visit

Total fixed costs (TFC): $240,000

$$BE_Q = \frac{TFC}{contribution\ margin} = \frac{\$240,000}{12} = 20,000\ patient\ visits$$

This can easily be proven by the following financial statement:

Total revenue	(20,000 × $20.00)	=	$400,000
Total variable costs	(20,000 × $8.00)	=	160,000
Total contribution margin	(20,000 × $12.00)	=	$240,000
Total fixed costs		=	240,000
Excess of revenue over expenses			$ 0

The only element of the model that changes is the level of additional revenue (cash) that must be generated to cover fixed requirements (*Exhibit 4–9*).

The same model can also be used to develop the price that must be charged if the number of procedures is known. It can also identify the variable cost relationship if the number of procedures and the price are known. For example, if only 15,000 patients can be seen, what price must be established to meet the cost objective of $300,000? In this case, we can substitute terms in the CVP equation as shown in *Exhibit 4–10*.

Exhibit 4–9
Volume required to cover additional requirements

Contribution margin per unit ($12) remains the same because price and variable costs did not change.

Fixed costs	$240,000
Additional funds required	60,000
Total funds required	$300,000

Substituting in the CVP model we obtain the following results:

$$\frac{\$300,000}{\$12} = 25,000 \text{ patient visits}$$

This can also be easily verified in the following income statement:

Total revenue	$ 500,000	($20 × 25,000)
Total variable costs	−200,000	($ 8 × 25,000)
Total contribution margin	$ 300,000	($12 × 25,000)
Total fixed costs	−240,000	
Net income	$ 60,000	

Exhibit 4–10
Computation of charges

Let CM_U = contribution margin per unit:

$$\frac{\$300,000}{CM_U} = 15,000 \text{ patient visits}$$

Solving this equation; $15,000 (CM_U) = \$300,000$

$$CM_U = \$20$$

With a required contribution margin of $20 and a variable cost per patient visit of $8, we can develop the required price which is equal to the sum of contribution margin and per visit variable cost:

$$P_U^* - VC_U = CM_U$$
$$P_U^* = CM_U + VC_U = 20 + 8 = 28$$

The following revenue and expense statement verifies that $28 is the price that satisfies the stated objectives.

Total revenues after discounts	($28 × 15,000)	$420,000
Total variable costs	($ 8 × 15,000)	120,000
Total contribution margin	($20 × 15,000)	$300,000
Total fixed costs		240,000
Excess of revenues over costs		$ 60,000

Exhibit 4–11
Computation of maximum variable costs

Maximum price	$33
TFC	$300,000
Maximum volume	10,000

What is the maximum level of variable costs that will permit the department to break even at maximum volume?

$$TR - (VC_U)(Q) = TFC$$
$$(33)(10,000) - VC_U(10,000) = 300,000$$
$$330,000 - 10,000\ VC_U = 300,000$$
$$30,000 = 10,000\ VC_U$$
$$\$3 = VC_U$$

In some cases, the variable cost relationships are not known. However, even under these circumstances, the maximum level of variable costs can be estimated using the breakeven model. Knowledge of this maximum would help managers determine the level of variable costs or efficiency factors in their own departments. *Exhibit 4–11* illustrates these concepts.

It is important to note that the figures calculated in the preceding examples are the number of dollars which need to be received, after discounts have been subtracted. To determine the full charge to be established, P* must be adjusted in the following manner:

P* = $33 (amount after discounts)
d = 40% (discounts from full charges)
P = full charge price

$$P = \frac{P*}{1 - d}$$

Using the data given above, the full charge to be established is:

$$P = \frac{33}{1 - .4}\ or\ \$55$$

This can be verified in the following manner:

Full price	$55
discount 40%	22
Price after discount	$33

Cost/volume/profit relationships under a cost-based reimbursement environment

Although the federal government no longer uses a cost-based approach to reimbursement, it is useful to understand the concept. In the preceding discussion, it was assumed that all patients paid charges at some negotiated amount or a prospective rate. Graphically this is shown in *Exhibit 4–12*.

In a cost-based reimbursement environment, the CVP model must be modified to show that the cost-based, third party payers will only pay costs above the breakeven point. This behavior is based on the practice of paying costs or charges, whichever is lower. Below the breakeven point, charges are lower than costs; the cost-based payer will reimburse on the basis of charges. In this case it is possible to have a loss, but impossible to make a profit.

If a hospital had 100 percent cost-based patients and was operating beyond breakeven, then the hospital would only recover its costs (as defined by the payer), and the model would appear as shown in *Exhibit 4–13*.

Exhibit 4–12
Cost/volume model
(no cost-based reimbursement)

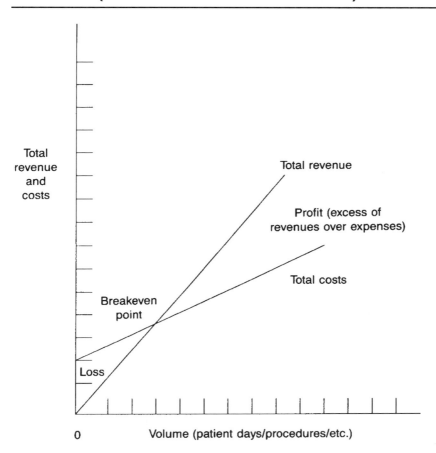

Exhibit 4–13
Cost/volume/profit model
under 100% cost-based reimbursement

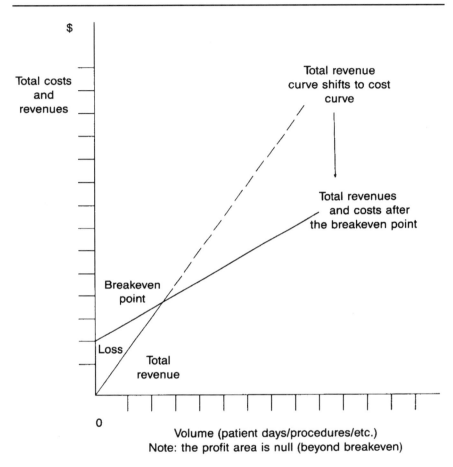

Volume (patient days/procedures/etc.)
Note: the profit area is null (beyond breakeven)

Since most hospitals have less than 100 percent cost-based patients, the CVP relationship for most hospitals is probably a line segment between the 100 percent charge-based and 100 percent cost-based reimbursement levels, as shown in *Exhibit 4–14*.

The practice of basing reimbursement on costs clearly has an impact on the financial position of the hospital and the ability to generate the funds needed to continue to provide quality healthcare. The use of CVP models very effectively demonstrates the impact of an increasing number of cost-based patients on the hospital's bottom line.

Exhibit 4–14
Cost/volume/profit model
under 50% cost-based reimbursement

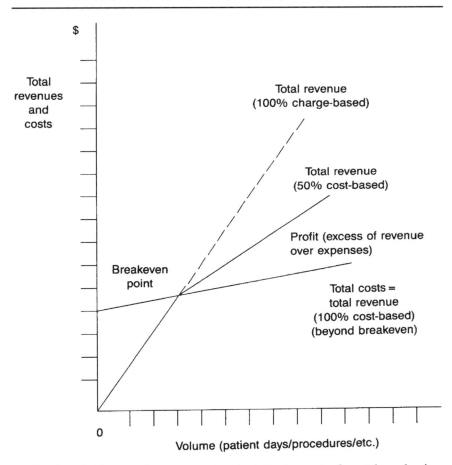

The inquisitive reader may notice that the impact of cost-based reimbursement on a nonprofit organization is very similar to the income tax placed on the profit organization. In the profit organization the amount of profit that management gets to retain must be reduced by the tax rate. The amount of profit the nonprofit organization gets to retain is reduced by the percent of cost-based reimbursement patients. Therefore, the two organizations would get to retain equal amounts of profit when the corporate tax rate is equal to the percent of cost-based patients (1 – tax rate) = (1 – cost-based %). This is graphically illustrated in *Exhibit 4–14* if the statement 50 percent cost-based is changed to 50 percent tax rate. Further discussion of this concept is left to the reader. Although the preceding analysis has concentrated on the concept of a single type of patient or service, it is recognized that most departments offer a number of procedures.

Multiproduct breakeven analysis incorporating changes in patient mix

Thus far, this chapter has assumed that there was only one primary source of patient revenue. However, there are at least four, and usually more, patient (payment) categories. For example, the following categories are usually found:

a. self-pay patients
b. private insurance
c. Medicare plans
d. Medicaid plans

Each of these plans would probably pay different proportionate amounts of the total patient charges. This complication is the same problem faced by industrial companies who produce or sell more than one product. Breakeven analysis can be utilized in these types of environments by using a *composite* contribution margin. For example, consider a hospital with the following cost structure and patient mix:

	Patient mix		*Reimbursement basis*
a)	self-pay	20%	total charges
b)	private insurance	25%	greater of total charges
			or DRG rates
c)	Medicare	30%	prospective rates (DRG)
d)	Medicaid	25%	reimbursable costs only

Cost structure			
Fixed costs	=	$800,000	
Required margin	=	200,000	
Daily charges	=	120	per patient day
Variable charges	=	40	per patient day (hospital out-of-pocket costs are assumed to be the same for each patient, regardless of the method of payment)

The following schedule indicates the amount expected to be received from each type of payer:

a)	self-pay	$120	
b)	private insurance	$120	
c)	Medicare	$110	(DRG - based rates)
d)	Medicaid	$100	(to the point where costs are greater than charges)

Given the above data, what level of total revenue must be achieved to break even? In order to determine this point, a composite contribution margin can be developed in the following manner:

Payer type	Patient mix	Contri- bution margin	Weighted contribution margin	Reimburse- ment rate	Weighted reimburse- ment rate
self-pay	20%	(120–40) = $80	$16	$120	$ 24
private insurance	25%	(120–40) = $80	$20	$120	$ 30
Medicare	30%	(110–40) = $70	$21	$110	$ 33
Medicaid	25%	(100–40) = $60	$15	$100	$ 25
		Composite contribution margin =	$72	Composite average daily charges =	$112

The composite contribution margin ratio is .6429 ($72/$112). Therefore, variable costs are 36 percent (rounded) because variable costs plus contribution margin sum to unity (one). Using the data in our original formula:

$$TR = \$800{,}000 + .36\ TR + \$200{,}000$$
$$TR - .36\ TR = \$1{,}000{,}000$$
$$TR = \$1{,}562{,}500$$

This projected level of total revenue can then be used to determine the number of patient days from each payer type.

The average number of patient days in each category is obtained by first determining the total number of expected patient days. The projected revenue ($1,562,500) must be divided by the composite average daily charges ($112).

$$\$1{,}562{,}500/\$112 = 13{,}951 \text{ patient days}$$

This relationship indicates an expected level of volume, in terms of patient days. The number of patient days in each category is determined by multiplying the projected volume (13,951) by the patient mix.

Method of payment	Patient mix	Patient days
self-pay	20%	2,790
private insurance	25%	3,488
Medicare	30%	4,185
Medicaid	25%	3,488
Total patient days =		13,951

The total revenue to be received from each payer source would be determined in the following manner:

Payer type	Payer rate	Patient days	Total revenue	% of total revenue
self-pay	$120	2,790	$ 334,821	21.4%
private insurance	$120	3,488	$ 418,527	26.8%
Medicare	$110	4,185	$ 460,379	29.5%
Medicaid	$100	3,488	$ 348,772	22.3%
		13,951	$1,562,500	100%

The preceding table highlights the impact of cost shifting from payers who do not pay full charges to those that do. The self-payer and private insurance payers with only 45 percent of the patient days must provide 48.2 percent of the total revenues. As Medicare and Medicaid payers further reduce their reimbursement levels, the required revenues to remain financially viable must come from other payers.

Multipayer breakeven applications

Using the multiproduct or multipayer breakeven concept from the preceding section, healthcare services management can determine if the forecasted revenue is realistic and, if not, take action to change cost patterns or patient mix to achieve the organization goals. In addition, the same techniques can be used at the end of an accounting period to determine why actual performance did or did not meet the budgeted goals. This technique is called variance analysis, and is discussed in chapter 6.

It should be obvious that any of the calculations illustrated above depend on the patient mix actually achieved. As patient mix changes, the breakeven level of revenue changes. The analysis can also be used to evaluate changes in the patient mix. For example, if the hospital were able to eliminate Medicare and Medicaid patients and obtain an adequate volume of self-pay and privately insured patients, what volume of patients is required to break even? Assume:

Method of payment	Patient mix	Contribution margin
self-pay	50%	$80
private insurance	50%	$80

The composite contribution margin is now $80 and the variable cost ratio is now 1/3 (40/120) and the breakeven volume of total revenue is obtained:

$$TR = \$800,000 + (40/120)TR + \$200,000$$
$$2/3\ TR = \$1,000,000$$
$$TR = \$1,500,000$$
$$\$1,500,000\ /\ 120 = 12,500 \text{ required patient days}$$

Using the projected level of total revenue ($1,500,000), the number of patient days in each category can be determined:

Method of payment	Patient mix	Revenue	Patient days
self-pay	50%	$ 750,000	6,250
private insurance	50%	750,000	6,250
		$1,500,000	12,500

This analysis shows that if the number of patients in each category (self-pay and privately insured) can be approximately doubled, the hospital can break even under these conditions. It also shows that, under these conditions, the hospital will be able to cover its fixed costs and required margin at a volume of 12,500 patient days.

These brief examples indicate that patient mix is a significant and crucial variable that cannot be ignored in cost/volume/profit analysis in the healthcare industry. Assumptions about patient mix are extremely critical in planning for the future. It would be very misleading to ignore the effects of a change in patient mix.

These methods would also permit the hospital to engage in separate breakeven calculations for each type of patient. A breakeven analysis for each type of patient would require knowledge of the fixed costs that could be attributed to each type of patient. The authors suspect that a proper analysis of this question would indicate that twice as many patients (or patient days) might be required to cover all related costs for patients covered by government reimbursement programs versus private (self-pay or privately insured) patients. This question should be investigated by the healthcare planner in determining the organization's commitment to serving all types of patients. The authors further suspect that organizations that have chosen to reject Medicare and Medicaid patients have performed analyses such as those outlined above.

In summary, patient mix must be included in the healthcare organization's planning models. It is essential to be able to identify and separate the effects of changes in patient mix. Managerial information that must be available includes composite contribution margins and composite average daily charges. This information should be incorporated into the cost/volume/profit model and used to estimate the effects of patient mix on the cost and volume of operations.

Summary

Cost/volume/profit techniques provide healthcare managers with the capability to determine the impact of changes in charges, volume of services, fixed and variable costs on meeting the financial requirements of the organization. A basic familiarity with these tools can offer considerable flexibility to the manager in testing various alternatives before the final decisions are made.

Questions and problems

1. Why do nonprofit organizations have to be concerned with decision making tools such as cost/volume/profit models.

2. What is "revenue" to a healthcare provider?

3. What is the difference between the TR curves in a "fee for service" and "managed care" environment?

4. Define "contribution margin."

5. Does an increase in the number of services provided in a "fee for service" environment always result in more profit to the organization?

6. Some noted economists have stated that this governments' reimbursement policies are effectively taxing the income of nonprofit providers. How can this be true if nonprofit organizations are exempt from paying federal income taxes?

7. There is considerable talk of placing a ceiling on patient charges which would limit charge increases to 9 percent a year. Assume this ceiling goes into effect and that your total costs increase by 10 percent per patient. Is it possible for the hospital to still be better off and have a higher fund flow than the previous year? Discuss.

8. Hospitals find that they are reimbursed at different rates for different types of patients. State and federal programs reimburse at one rate, Blue Cross reimburses at a different rate, and private insurance and self-paying patients pay another rate. How would this information be integrated into a cost/volume/profit analysis?

9. A clinic estimates that its breakeven point is 500 patients per month. What is the impact of a fall in patient volume on the breakeven point? On profits?

10. A clinic invests $1,500,000 a year in a positron emission tomography (PET). What effect will this have on the clinic's breakeven point in terms of patients?

11. The following are examples of cost/volume/profit graphs for three separate hospitals. Analyze each graph and answer the following

questions about them. All measures are in hundreds of thousands
(R = revenue).

Required:
a. Are the fixed costs in Hospital X considerably more than in
   Hospital Y? Explain.
b. Are the breakeven units smaller for Hospital Y than for Hospital
   Z? Explain.
c. If volume is at the 4,000 level, will Hospital X produce more profit
   than Hospital Z at the same level. Explain.

Problem 4–11

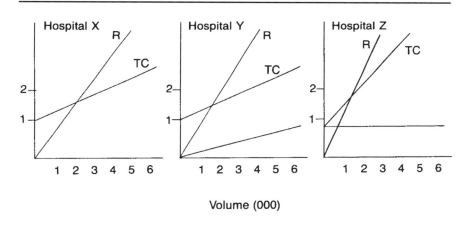

Volume (000)

12. Fill in the blanks for the four unrelated cases:

	Sales	Variable expense	Fixed expense	Total costs	Net profit	Contribution margin ratio
a.	$1,000	700	(1)	1,000	(2)	(3)
b.	$1,500	(4)	300	(5)	(6)	.30
c.	(7)	500	(8)	800	1,200	(9)
d.	$2,000	(10)	300	(11)	200	(12)

13. A radiologist has the following cost structure:

Fixed cost per period	$15,000
Variable cost per film	$25
Units processed per period (budget)	3,000
Charges per unit	$60

a. Calculate the breakeven point in units.
b. Calculate the profit or loss at the budget volume.
c. Compute the income which would result at the budget volume if both the variable cost per unit and the charge per unit increase by 20 percent.

14. Dr. Andersen started a health prevention clinic in 19X0. For this purpose he rented a building for $400 per month. He hired a receptionist, a clerk, and a nurse. In addition, an outside accountant was hired at $300 per month to do tax and bookkeeping work. The necessary furniture and equipment for the clinic were purchased with cash. Dr. Andersen has noticed that utility rates per unit and supply costs per unit have been fairly constant.

The clinic volume has increased between 19X0 and 19X3. Profits have more than doubled since 19X0. Dr. Andersen does not understand why his profits have increased faster than his volume.

See the following projected income statement for 19X4 prepared by the accountant.

Dr. Andersen Clinic
Project Income Statement
for the year ended Dec. 31, 19X4

Clinic Revenue (11,875 visits at $8.00)		$95,000
Cost of test performed	$28,500	
Wages & benefits of		
receptionist & clerk	$15,150	
Wages & benefits - Nurse	$10,300	
Rent	$4,800	
Accounting Services	$3,600	
Depreciation of Equipment	$5,000	
Depreciation of Furniture	$3,000	
Utilities	$2,325	
Supplies - Medical	$1,200	$73,875
Net Income before Taxes		$21,125
Income Taxes (30%)		$6,338
Net Income		$14,787

a. What is the breakeven point in terms of the number of visits that must take place?
b. Revenue is what dollar level at the breakeven point?
c. Dr. Andersen would like an after-tax net income of $20,000. What volume must be reached in order to obtain the desired income?

15. A hospital has total fixed costs of $750,000 and average variable costs of $50 per patient day. The hospital charges $100 per patient day.
   a. How many patient days are needed to break even?
   b. If the hospital has 75 beds, what occupancy rate would be required to break even?
   c. If the hospital estimates it will have 18,000 patient days, how much income would be generated?

16. A hospital has total fixed costs of $750,000 and average variable costs of $400 per admission. The hospital has 100 beds and estimates admissions to be 3,750. Medicare patients will represent half of the total admissions and are reimbursed for actual costs only.
   a. What is the total cost per year?
   b. What amount would Medicare patients be charged?
   c. The hospital wants to earn $200,000. What charges must non-Medicare patients pay?

17. Glass Laboratories Incorporated plans to organize a company to provide testing facilities to physicians. A marketing study has provided them with the following figures on price/volume relations.

Amount charged per test	Volume per month
$10	25,000
$15	15,000
$20	8,000

   Budgeted fixed costs per month are $100,000 and variable costs are budgeted at $3 per test.
   a. What is the breakeven point in units for each price?
   b. Which price would provide the highest income for the company?
   c. If variable costs actually turn out to be $4, would the decision made in "b" still represent the best decision?
   d. If fixed costs increase to $125,000, which decision would be the best?
   e. What other factors might be considered in the pricing decision process?

18. Memorial Hospital has a licensed bed capacity of 450 beds. An average occupancy rate of 90 percent is used for most cost estimations. At this level of occupancy, the hospital's operating costs are $16 per occupied bed per day, for a 30-day month. During March,

the occupancy rate was only 80 percent. The following costs were incurred during the month:

Fixed Operating Costs	$ 79,350
Mixed Operating Costs	$105,600

a. Determine the variable costs per occupied bed on a daily basis.
b. Determine the fixed operating costs per month.
c. Assume an occupancy rate of 86 percent. What are the estimated total costs?

19. Ely Memorial Hospital is planning to add a new birthing wing to its existing OB/GYN department. This wing is to simulate the environment of one's home. Ely Memorial prepared the following forecast concerning the new wing:

Revenue	$750,000
Revenue per Delivery	$1,500
Variable Cost	$400,000
Fixed Costs	$200,000

Further studies by an outside consulting firm found that revenue per delivery could be increased by 20 percent with an expected volume decrease of 10 percent. What would Ely Memorial Hospital's operating income be if these changes were used?

20. The pharmacy department of St. Mary's Hospital is expected to price its drugs to provide a 25 percent return above its actual costs. The department employs two pharmacists who are paid $20,000 each. The department also has several clerks whose total salaries equal $20,000. The department is allocated $25,000 for costs such as maintenance, depreciation, heating, and lighting. The department averages around 250,000 prescriptions a year with an average cost of $4 per prescription.
a. What price should be charged per prescription in order to obtain the necessary return?
b. What would the net income per year be?
c. Calculate the breakeven point in units.

21. Mount Mary Hospital operates several eye clinics around the state. Although many different procedures are performed at the clinics, the majority of revenue comes from routing eye examinations. Mount Mary is determining the feasibility of opening a new clinic in a rural

town. The following estimated revenues and expenses for the new clinic are available to Mount Mary:

Revenue per visit	$ 20.00
Cost per visit	$ 5.00
Physician professional fee	$ 5.00
Total variable costs	$ 10.00
Fixed expenses:	
Rent	$ 7,500
Salaries	$17,500
Total fixed costs	$25,000

a. What is the breakeven point in revenue and in units?
b. If the number of examinations (eye tests) performed is estimated to be 2,000, what would be the net income of loss to the clinic?
c. Determine the annual breakeven point in revenue and in units assuming that Mount Mary decides to discontinue the physician professional fee in favor of a fixed salary increase of $15,000.
d. Suppose the physicians earned $5 for every eye examination performed in excess of the breakeven number of units. Determine the clinic's net income (loss) if 3,500 tests are performed.

22. S.T. EmergiCenter specializes in emergency outpatient care and has experienced steady growth in revenue for the past five years. However, increased competition has led the administrators to believe that an aggressive advertising campaign will be necessary next year to maintain sufficient growth. The following data was presented to the administrator for the current year:

Revenue per visit	$25.00
Expected revenue 1990 (20,000 visits)	$500,000
Variable cost/visit	$13.75
Fixed costs	$135,000

The administrator has set the revenue target for next year at a level of $550,000 (22,000 visits).
a. What is the breakeven point in units for the current year?
b. The administration believes an additional selling expense of $11,250 for advertising next year will be necessary to attain the revenue target (all other costs constant). What will be the breakeven point in revenue for next year if the additional $11,250 is spent for advertising?
c. If the additional $11,250 is spent for advertising next year, what is the required revenue in dollars to equal the current year's after-tax net income? Assume a tax rate of 40 percent.

23. St. Elizabeth's Hospital is a general hospital; however, it rents space to separately owned entities rendering specialized services such as psychiatric and alcohol rehabilitation units. St. Elizabeth charged the following costs to the psychiatric unit for the year ending December 31, 1990.

	Patient days (variable)	Bed capacity (fixed)
Dietary	$ 300,000	$
Janitorial		35,000
Laundry	150,000	
Lab	225,000	
Pharmacy	225,000	
Repairs/maintenance		15,000
G & A		650,000
Rent		750,000
Billing and collections	150,000	
Totals	$1,050,000	$1,450,000

For the year ending December 31, 1990, the psychiatric department charged each patient an average of $300 per day and had a capacity of 30 beds and had revenue of $3,000,000 for 365 days.

The psychiatric unit operated at 100 percent capacity on 90 days during the year ending December 31, 1990. If it is estimated that during these 90 days, the demand exceeded 10 patients more than capacity. St. Elizabeth has an additional 10 beds available for rent for the year ending December 31, 1991. Such additional rent would increase psychiatry's fixed costs based on bed capacity.

a. Calculate the minimum number of patient days required for the psychiatric unit to break even for the year ending December 31, 1991, if the additional beds are not rented (use 1990 information).

b. Prepare a schedule of increase in revenues and increase in costs for the year ending December 31, 1991, in order to determine the net increase or decrease in earnings from the additional 10 beds if the psychiatric unit rents this extra capacity from St. Elizabeth's.

24. Paradise Hospital produces and sells highly technical services directed to the teenage market. A new product has come onto the market which the company is anxious to produce and sell. Enough capacity exists in the company's plant to produce 15,000 units each month. Variable costs to manufacture and sell one unit would be $1.60, and fixed costs would total $16,000 per month.

The marketing department predicts that demand for the product will exceed the 15,000 units which the company is able to produce. Additional production capacity can be rented from another company at a fixed cost of $3,500 per month. Variable costs in the rented facility would total $1.75 per unit, due to somewhat less efficient operations than in the main plant. The product will sell for $2.50 per unit.

a. What is the monthly breakeven point in units and dollar amount?

b. How many units must be sold in order to make a profit of $3,750 each month?

c. If the sales manager receives a bonus of 10 cents per unit sold in excess of the breakeven point, how many units must be sold each month in order to earn a return of 10 percent on the monthly investment in fixed costs?

25. The Bauer Aspirin Company manufactures a high quality aspirin product which is distributed throughout the western part of the United States. The company sells an average of 250,000 bottles of aspirin each month, with the following cost relationships:

	Per bottle
Selling Price	$0.50
Variable Cost	$0.15
Contribution Margin	$0.35
Fixed Monthly Cost:	
Building Rental	$12,250
Equipment Depreciation	$ 8,000
Salaries	$20,000
Advertising	$25,000
Other Fixed Cost	$15,250
Total Fixed Costs	$80,500

a. Prepare a contribution-type income statement showing the company's monthly profits. Include total, per units, and percent columns.

b. What is the monthly breakeven point in bottles of aspirin? In total sales dollars?

c. Suppose that the company would like to earn a monthly profit of $10,500. How many bottles of aspirin would have to be sold?

d. If the building rental were doubled, what would be the monthly breakeven point in bottles of aspirin? In total sales dollars?

e. Refer to the original data. If sales persons are given a 2-cent bonus commission for each bottle sold over the breakeven point, what would the company's net income be if 260,000 bottles were sold? Use the incremental approach.

f. Refer to the original data. The president is confident that an additional $5,000 in advertising each month would generate a 10 percent increase in sales. Would you recommend the increased advertising? (Use the incremental approach.) Would your answer be the same if the contribution margin was 15 cents per bottle rather than 35 cents? Explain.

26. Looking at the information for Oakridge Clinic given below:
    a. What must revenue be to achieve a net income of $5,500 after taxes?
    b. By what percentage must revenue increase over 1990 to achieve net income of $20,000 before taxes?

Oakridge Clinic		
12/31/90 Income statement		
Revenue		$40,000
Operating variable cost		$15,000
Operating contribution margin		$25,000
General variable cost		$10,000
Net contribution margin		$15,000
Operating fixed cost	$5,000	
General fixed cost	$5,000	$10,000
Net income before taxes		$ 5,000
Taxes		$ 2,500
Net income		$ 2,500

27. The pharmacy at XYZ Health Services currently has three different prescriptions that can be sold for a certain ailment. The selling price and cost data by product are as follows:

Product	A	B	C
Selling price	$20	$10	$ 5
Variable costs	8	3	3
Contribution margin	$12	$ 7	$ 2
Contribution margin %	60	70	40
Percentage of total sales dollar mix	40	40	20

Below are the income statements for two recent months for the pharmacy (000 omitted).

Sales	$80	$60
Costs	$60	$52
Income	$20	$ 8

a. Using the income statement for the two months provided, find fixed and variable costs as a percentage of sale dollar.
b. Determine the breakeven point in dollar sales.
c. Which product is more profitable per unit sold?
d. Which product is most profitable per dollar of sales?
e. What sales dollars are needed to earn $35,000 per month, and how many units of each product will be sold at the figure if the usual mix is maintained?
f. In the month following the two given above, sales were $100,000 with a mix of 40 percent A, 30 percent B, and 30 percent C. What is the income?

28. Consider a hospital with the following data:

Patient mix		Reimbursement basis (per patient day)
Self-pay	25%	$150 (total charges)
Private insurance	20%	$150 (total charges)
Medicare	25%	$110 (lower of cost or charges)
Medicaid	30%	$100 (allowable costs)
Fixed costs		$20,000,000
Other necessary costs		$5,000,000
Daily charges		$150 per patient day
Variable costs		$60 per patient day

Given this data, what level of total revenue must be achieved to operate at breakeven?

29. Discuss the difference between breakeven quantity (BEQ) and the point of equality (in dollars).

30. The income statement for Dr. Lonely Heart's private medical practice is summarized as follows:

Net revenue	
(8,000 patient visits)	$240,000
Expenses	
(including $40,000 fixed expenses)	$125,000
Profit	$115,000

Dr. Heart believes that adding a nurse practitioner to her medical team would increase patient volume and patient revenues. The nurse practitioner would increase expenses by $55,000 ($35,000 in salary and fringe benefits and $20,000 in additional equipment and overhead).

a. How many patients (on average) must be seen to add the nurse practitioner and realize the same profit as before?

b. Dr. Heart wants to increase her profit by $30,000 by adding the nurse practitioner. How many patients would have to be seen to achieve this increase? State any necessary assumptions.

c. Graphically represent the situations in a and b.

31. The Community Health Center offers a weekly hypertension clinic. Clients receive information on diet and exercise and a personal hypertension evaluation. The clinic is currently being funded through a Federal grant, which is going to be cut in the next fiscal year. The directors are examining cost-volume data before trying to locate another source of funding.

Fixed Monthly Expenses	
Depreciation Expense	$250/month
Space Rental, 2 locations ($4,000 center city,	
$2,500 shopping mall)	$6,500/year
Wages (3 RN's, 2 days per week)	$640/month
Travel Expense	$235/month
Variable Cost Per Client	$4

a. If the clinic is currently being reimbursed at $27 per client, what is the breakeven point in number of clients? In dollars?

b. What is the breakeven point in clients if the clinic only receives $22 per client?

c. The administrators are considering a plan to close the center at the shopping mall. Volume is expected to drop to 40 clients a month; all of the mall rental expenses will be eliminated, the nurses will work only 1 day a week, and travel expenses will be cut to $120 a month. If they receive the $22 per client as assumed in b, will they break even? Why or why not?

32. Dr. Cavitee, a dentist for the County Health Department, submitted the following costs for the first year of operations of a dental clinic:

Dentist's salary	$9,000 + 20% of gross receipts
Hygienists' and clerical salaries	$39,000
Other fixed costs	$20,000
Depreciation	$2,500
Utilities and supplies	$5/patient
Charges	$55/patient
Patients	2,400

Dr. Cavitee proposes to expand the dental clinic by adding another examining station (purchase of equipment would be $40,000; expected life: 8 years) and hiring a full-time X-ray technician ($79,000). Additional variable costs per patient would be $2. This would allow the clinic to see 21,000 more patients per year. Charges would remain the same.

a. Determine the breakeven point in new patient visits for the clinic as it is set up now.

b. How much did the patients' visits contribute as "profit" to the dental clinic during the first year? (This might also be called a contribution to overhead expenses for the entire health department.)

c. Determine the breakeven point in patient visits if Dr. Cavitee is able to implement the changes he wants to make.

d. Assuming the dental clinic implements the plan and sees an additional 2,000 patients over current volume, how much will the clinic contribute to the health department's overhead?

33. Lincoln Memorial Hospital is a small community hospital with three departments: Medical-Surgical, Pediatrics, and Obstetrics. Each department is billed for some services based on patient volume and for other services on a flat rate based on number of beds. Below are the expenses charged to the Medical-Surgical Department in 19X8.

	Expenses based on patient-days	Expenses based on number of beds	Total
Meals	$ 65,420		
Laundry	32,000		
Pharmacy	85,220		
Laboratory	108,420		
Nursing	253,800	$ 85,280	
Maintenance/Janitorial	14,800	19,210	
Rent		196,420	
Other	8,045	22,640	
	$567,705	$323,550	$891,225

The Medical-Surgical Department has a bed capacity of 60 and did not expect to change this number for the coming year. During 19X8 each patient was charged, on average, $196 per day. The Department charged $2,915,600 in gross patient revenues. Lincoln Memorial is planning to contract with a management firm to supply all administrative services for the hospital in 19X9. The hospital will charge the departments for administrative expense on a patient-day basis or on the number of beds. The budgeting office is trying to determine whether to charge $450 per bed in each department (administrative) or $51.20 per patient-day.

a. How many patient-days were required in 19X8 to break even?

b. Assuming all expenses in the Medical-Surgical Department increase by 20 percent in 19X9 and charges increase to $225: What is the breakeven point in patient-days for 19X9 if the department is charged administrative services on a per-bed basis?

   c. What is the breakeven point if the department is charged per patient-day?

34. Apply Cost-Volume-Profit concepts to a radiology department, using the following data:

Monthly budgeted fixed costs (FC)	$245,000
Variable costs per X-ray (VCU)	$68
Budgeted revenues per X-ray (RU)	$215
Expected monthly X-ray volume (Q)	5,500

   a. Develop the Total Cost Equation at the expected monthly volume:

$$\text{Total Cost} = \text{Total Fixed Cost} + \text{Total Variable Cost}$$

$$\text{Total Cost} = \text{TFC} + (\text{VCU} \times \text{Q})$$

   b. Develop the Breakeven Equation:

$$\text{Total Revenue} = \text{Total Cost}$$

$$\text{Total Revenue} = \text{Total Fixed Cost} + \text{Total Variable Cost}$$

$$\text{RU} \times \text{Q} = \text{TFC} + \text{VCU} \times \text{Q}$$

   c. Determine the breakeven number of X-rays by solving the breakeven equation.

   d. Using per unit data, calculate the Contribution Margin Ratio and the Variable Cost Ratio. Show that they are complementary.

$$\text{Contribution Margin Ratio} = \frac{\text{Contribution Margin per Unit}}{\text{Revenue per Unit}}$$

$$\text{CMR} = \frac{\text{CMU}}{\text{RU}}$$

$$\text{Variable Cost Ratio} = \frac{\text{Variable Cost per Unit}}{\text{Revenue per Unit}}$$

$$\text{VCR} = \frac{\text{VCU}}{\text{RU}}$$

$$\text{Contribution Margin Ratio} + \text{Variable Cost Ratio} = 100\%$$

   e. Using dollars, at the expected monthly X-ray volume, calculate the Contribution Margin Ratio and Variable Cost Ratio. Show that they are complementary. Use the cost-volume-proft equation to develop the revenue and cost estimates:

$$\text{Total Revenue} = \text{Total Cost} + \text{Profit}$$

$$\text{Revenue per Unit} \times \text{Quantity} = \text{Total Fixed Cost} + (\text{Variable Cost per Unit} \times \text{Quantity}) + \text{Profit}$$

$$\text{RU} \times \text{Q} = \text{TFC} + (\text{VCU} \times \text{Q}) + \text{Profit}$$

Contribution margin, at the expected monthly X-ray volume, is:

$$\text{Contribution Margin} = \text{Total Revenue} - \text{Variable Costs}$$

$$\text{Contribution Margin Ratio} = \frac{\text{Contribution Margin}}{\text{Total Revenue}}$$

$$\text{Variable Cost Ratio} = \frac{\text{Variable Costs}}{\text{Total Revenue}}$$

$$\text{Contribution Margin Ratio} + \text{Variable Cost Ratio} = 100\%$$

f. Determine the target profit at the expected monthly X-ray volume. Use the cost-volume-profit equation to develop the revenue and cost estimates:

$$\text{Total Revenue} = \text{Total Cost} + \text{Profit}$$

$$\text{Revenue per Unit} \times \text{Quantity} = \text{Total Fixed Cost} + (\text{Variable Cost per Unit} \times \text{Quantity}) + \text{Profit}$$

$$\text{RU} \times \text{Q} = \text{TFC} + (\text{VCU} \times \text{Q}) + \text{Profit}$$

g. Using the information in the preceding step, prepare a simple income statement, using contribution margins.
h. Calculate the breakeven activity, stated in X-ray units, using a different method than in step c above. Do the two answers agree?

$$\text{Breakeven level of Activity} = \frac{\text{Fixed Cost} + \text{Desired Profit}}{\text{Contribution Margin per Unit}}$$

$$\text{BEQ} = \frac{\text{Fixed Cost} + \text{Desired Profit}}{\text{Contribution Margin per Unit}}$$

$$\text{BEQ} = \frac{\text{FC} + \text{P}}{\text{CMU}}$$

i. Calculate the point of equality, in dollars. Verify your answer by multiplying the BEQ by the price per unit (RU).

$$\text{Point of equality (in dollars)} = \frac{\text{Fixed Cost} + \text{Desired Profit}}{\text{Contribution Margin Ratio}}$$

$$\text{Point of equality} = \frac{\text{FC} + \text{P}}{\text{CMR}}$$

35. As an application of Cost-Volume-Profit Concepts to a laboratory department using the following data:

Monthly budgeted fixed costs (FC)	$535,000
Variable costs per test (VCU)	$44
Budgeted revenues per test (RU)	$180
Expected monthly volume of tests (Q)	36,500

a. Develop the Total Cost Equation at the expected monthly volume:

$$\text{Total Cost} = \text{Total Fixed Cost} + \text{Total Variable Cost}$$

$$\text{Total Cost} = \text{TFC} + (\text{VCU} \times \text{Q})$$

b. Develop the Breakeven Equation:

$$\text{Total Revenue} = \text{Total Cost}$$

$$\text{Total Revenue} = \text{Total Fixed Cost} + \text{Total Variable Cost}$$

$$\text{RU} \times \text{Q} = \text{TFC} + \text{VCU} \times \text{Q}$$

c. Determine the breakeven number of X-rays by solving the break-even equation.
d. Using per unit data, calculate the Contribution Margin Ratio and the Variable Cost Ratio. Show that they are complementary.

$$\text{Contribution Margin Ratio} = \frac{\text{Contribution Margin per Unit}}{\text{Revenue per Unit}}$$

$$\text{CMR} = \frac{\text{CMU}}{\text{RU}}$$

$$\text{Variable Cost Ratio} = \frac{\text{Variable Cost per Unit}}{\text{Revenue per Unit}}$$

$$\text{VCR} = \frac{\text{VCU}}{\text{RU}}$$

$$\text{Contribution Margin Ratio} + \text{Variable Cost Ratio} = 100\%$$

e. Using dollars, at the expected monthly X-ray volume, calculate the Contribution Margin Ratio and Variable Cost Ratio. Show that they are complementary. Use the cost-volume-profit equation to develop the revenue and cost estimates:

$$\text{Total Revenue} = \text{Total Cost} + \text{Profit}$$

$$\text{Revenue per Unit} \times \text{Quantity} = \text{Total Fixed Cost} + (\text{Variable Cost per Unit} \times \text{Quantity}) + \text{Profit}$$

$$\text{RU} \times \text{Q} = \text{TFC} + (\text{VCU} \times \text{Q}) + \text{Profit}$$

Contribution margin, at the expected monthly X-ray volume, is:

$$\text{Contribution Margin} = \text{Total Revenue} - \text{Variable Costs}$$

$$\text{Contribution Margin Ratio} = \frac{\text{Contribution Margin}}{\text{Total Revenue}}$$

$$\text{Variable Cost Ratio} = \frac{\text{Variable Costs}}{\text{Total Revenue}}$$

$$\text{Contribution Margin Ratio} + \text{Variable Cost Ratio} = 100\%$$

f. Determine the target profit at the expected monthly X-ray volume. Use the cost-volume-profit equation to develop the revenue and cost estimates:

$$\text{Total Revenue} = \text{Total Cost} + \text{Profit}$$

$$\text{Revenue per Unit} \times \text{Quantity} = \text{Total Fixed Cost} + (\text{Variable Cost per Unit} \times \text{Quantity}) + \text{Profit}$$

$$\text{RU} \times \text{Q} = \text{TFC} + (\text{VCU} \times \text{Q}) + \text{Profit}$$

g. Using the information in the preceding step, prepare a simple income statement, using contribution margins.

h. Calculate breakeven stated in X-ray units, using a different method than in step c above. Do the two answers agree?

$$\text{Breakeven level of Activity} = \frac{\text{Fixed Cost} + \text{Desired Profit}}{\text{Contribution Margin per Unit}}$$

$$\text{BEQ} = \frac{\text{Fixed Cost} + \text{Desired Profit}}{\text{Contribution Margin per Unit}}$$

$$\text{BEQ} = \frac{\text{FC} + \text{P}}{\text{CMU}}$$

i. Calculate the point of equality, in dollars. Verify your answer by multiplying the BEQ by the price per unit (RU).

$$\text{Point of equality (in dollars)} = \frac{\text{Fixed Cost} + \text{Desired Profit}}{\text{Contribution Margin Ratio}}$$

$$\text{Point of equality} = \frac{\text{FC} + \text{P}}{\text{CMR}}$$

36. Apply Cost-Volume-Profit concepts to a laboratory department using the following data:

Monthly budgeted fixed costs (FC)	$254,000
Variable costs per test (VCU)	$127
Budgeted revenues per test (RU)	$235
Expected monthly volume of tests (Q)	9,250

a. Develop the Total Costs Equation at the expected monthly volume.

b. Use this data in the Breakeven Equation.

c. Determine the breakeven number of tests by solving the Breakeven Equation.

d. Using per unit data, calculate the Contribution Margin Ratio and the Variable Cost Ratio. Show that they are complementary.

e. Using dollars of revenue, at the expected monthly level of activity, calculate the Contribution Margin Ratio and Variable Cost Ratio. Show that they are complementary. Use the cost-volume-profit equation to develop the revenue and cost estimates.

    f. Determine the target profit at the expected monthly volume. Use the cost-volume-profit equation to develop the revenue and cost estimates.

    g. Using the information in the preceding step, prepare a simple income statement, using contribution margins.

    h. Calculate breakeven stated in units, using a different method than in step c above. Do the two answers agree?

    i. Calculate the point of equality (in dollars). Verify your answer by multiplying the BEQ by the price per unit (RU).

37. Apply Cost-Volume-Profit concepts to a laboratory department using the following data to answer these questions:

Monthly budgeted fixed costs (FC)	$175,000
Variable costs per test (VCU)	$62.50
Budgeted revenues per test (RU)	$135.00
Expected monthly volume of tests (Q)	8,650

    a. Develop the Total Costs equation at the expected monthly volume.

    b. Use this data in the Breakeven Equation.

    c. Determine the breakeven number of tests by solving the Breakeven Equation.

    d. Using per unit data, calculate the Contribution Margin Ratio and the Variable Cost Ratio. Show that they are complementary.

    e. Using dollars of revenue, at the expected monthly level of activity, calculate the Contribution Margin Ratio and Variable Cost Ratio. Show that they are complementary. Use the cost-volume-profit equation to develop the revenue and cost estimates.

    f. Determine the target profit at the expected monthly volume. Use the cost-volume-profit equation to develop the revenue and cost estimates.

    g. Using the information in the preceding step, prepare a simple income statement, using contribution margins.

    h. Calculate breakeven stated in units, using a different method than in step c above. Do the two answers agree?

    i. Calculate the point of equality (in dollars). Verify your answer by multiplying the BEQ by the price per unit (RU).

38. Midwest Urgent Care Centers, Inc. is planning for the next fiscal year. Its staff projects the following visit types, prices, and product mix for a particular facility.

Visit	Percent of total visits	Avg. payment per visit	Variable cost/visit	Total fixed costs
Short	60%	$50	$35	$150,000
Intermediate	10	70	45	70,000
Long	20	90	65	135,000
Seriously Long	10	145	90	140,000
	100%			$495,000

In addition, the staff projects $266,000 fixed costs that are indirect with respect to the visits. Assume that the marginal tax rate is 30 percent and that the particular facility must realize $85,000 in profit.

a. How many visits must be produced for this facility to achieve its goals?

b. How many of each type of visit must be produced?

c. Before presenting your results to top management, describe and test an alternative scenario to decrease the number of visits needed.

39. A physician group practice is negotiating with an HMO. If the group practice accepts the contract, all of its revenues and all of its patients will be members of the HMO. The following annual information has been supplied for 6,000 visits.

Revenue per Member per Month	$ 33
Physician Salaries	350,000
Nursing Salaries	200,000
Office Staff Salaries	45,000
Office Supplies	25,000
Building and Equipment Leases	25,000
Utilities	6,500
Miscellaneous	13,600
Profit Goal	50,000
Medical Supplies	$ 15 per visit

All salaries include fringe benefits.

Assume that 40 percent of the nursing and miscellaneous expenses are variable. Also assume that each member is expected to make .75 visits to the group each year. (Therefore, to convert the visit data to cost per member month, multiply the cost per visit by .75 and divide by 12.)

a. Determine the number of member months required to breakeven. EXCLUDE TAXES.

b. Convert the member months to covered lives.

40. A physician group practice is negotiating with an HMO. If the group practice accepts the contract, all of its revenues and all of its patients will be members of the HMO. The following annual information has been supplied for 7,000 visits.

Revenue per Member per Month	$ 37
Physician Salaries	375,000
Nursing Salaries	215,000
Office Staff Salaries	65,000
Office Supplies	35,000
Building and Equipment Leases	30,000
Utilities	7,500
Miscellaneous	11,600
Profit goal	60,000
Medical Supplies	$ 13 per visit

All salaries include fringe benefits.

Assume that 50 percent of the nursing and miscellaneous expenses are variable. Also assume that each member is expected to make one visit to the group each year. (Therefore, to convert the visit data to cost per member month, multiply the cost per visit by 1.0 and divide by 12.)
a. Determine the number of member months required to breakeven. EXCLUDE TAXES.
b. Convert the member months to covered lives.

41. Insurance firm XYZ contracts with medical providers for services. It provides the following data:

Variable	Quantity	Fixed or variable cost
Revenue pmpm	$135	NA
Member Months	60,000	NA
Administrative Costs pmpm	$15	FC
Medical Expenses pmpm	$65	VC
Other Professional Expenses pmpm	$12	VC
Outside Referral Expenses pmpm	$15	VC
Emergency and Out of Area Expenses pmpm	$3	VC

a. What is the BEQ in member months?

42. Use the following projections to estimate the BEQ for the newly formed Integrated Health Systems (you must decide which items are fixed and which are variable costs):

Revenue pmpm	$145
Member Months	55,000
Administrative Costs pmpm	$16
Medical Expenses pmpm	$67
Other Professional Expenses pmpm	$13
Outside Referral Expenses pmpm	$16
Emergency and Out of Area Expenses pmpm	$2.20

a. What is the BEQ in member months?

43. An ambulatory surgery center has just received its reimbursement rates from its payors for the upcoming year. Medicare, Medicaid, and Blue Cross all group outpatient surgical procedures into categories. Assume that each payor uses the following three categories for reimbursement purposes.
   a. Determine the overall breakeven quantity of cases required to breakeven.
   b. Determine the quantity of cases in each category required to breakeven.
   c. If a study reveals that the number of cases required to breakeven is unlikely, list the actions that you, as manager, could take.

Category	Percent of cases	Payor	Net rate	Variable cost	Fixed costs
I.	10	Medicare	$1100	$550	
	10	Medicaid	850	550	
	4	Blue Cross	850	550	$150,000
	9	Other	1150	550	
II.	5	Medicare	$ 790	$460	
	13	Medicaid	610	460	
	7	Blue Cross	820	460	$ 50,000
	11	Other	710	460	
III.	2	Medicare	$1100	$770	
	10	Medicaid	900	770	
	9	Blue Cross	1350	770	$160,000
	10	Other	1450	770	

Joint Fixed Costs: $200,000*
Some direct fixed costs can be assigned to each category. *Additional fixed costs of the center cannot be easily allocated to each category.

44. The following fixed and variable costs per RVU have been estimated using two alternative RVU scales for lab procedures.

	Estimates for	
	Scale 1	Scale 2
Intercept	$160,000	$110,000
Significance	0.25	0.10
Independent Variable	$1.35	$1.60
Significance	0.68	0.002
Adjusted R^2	0.15	0.45

Assume the price per RVU is $2.60.

Determine the quantity of RVU's that the lab must produce to break-even.

45. Dr. Nightingale's Outpatient Clinic (NOC) performs three kinds of procedures. The expected mix, unit variable costs, and reimbursement rates for each procedure are presented below. All payers use the same rate based on the complexity of the procedure. Total fixed costs for NOC for the year are expected to be $575,000.

Procedure	Expected mix	Unit variable cost	Reimbursement rate
I	0.45	$1,600	$2,500
II	0.35	$2,350	$3,100
III	0.20	$3,100	$4,100

a. How many procedures must be performed for NOC to breakeven?
b. How many of each procedure level must be performed for NOC to breakeven?
c. If the managers of NOC wanted to earn $200,000 in after tax profits, how many total procedures would have to be performed? Assume a tax rate of 30 percent.
d. Suppose that market competition precludes achieving the total number of procedures identified in part c. Briefly, explain the actions you could take.
e. Using the information from part c, if the planning department estimated that only 700 procedures would be demanded by patients in the market area, how would that new information affect earnings after taxes?

Keywords: breakeven; breakeven revenue; contribution margin; contribution margin ratio; CVP; quantity; total cost; total revenues breakeven.

References

Andrianos, James, and Mark Dykan. "Using Cost Accounting Data to Improve Clinical Value." *Healthcare Financial Management* (May 1996): 44–48.

Awasthi, V.N., and L. Eldenburg. "Providing Cost Data to Physicians Helps Contain Costs." *Healthcare Financial Management* (April 1996): 40–42.

Baker, J.J. "Activity-Based Costing for Integrated Delivery Systems." *Journal of Health Care Finance* (winter 1995): 57–61.

Bender, A. Douglas. "Budget Model Can Aid Group Practice Planning." *HFM* (December 1991): 50–59.

Canby, J.B., IV. "Applying Activity-Based Costing to Healthcare Settings." *Healthcare Financial Management* (February 1995): 50–56.

Carpenter, C.E., L.C. Weitzel, N.E. Johnson, and D.B. Nash. "Cost Accounting Supports Clinical Evaluations." *Healthcare Financial Management* (April 1994): 40–44.

Cook, D. "Strategic Plan Creates a Blueprint for Budgeting." *Healthcare Financial Management* (May 1990): 21–27.

Feuerstein, T., and C.A. Anderson. *Budgeting and Cost Management for Medical Groups.* Englewood, CO: Center for Research in Ambulatory Health Care Administration, 1990.

Herkimer, Allen G., Jr. *Understanding Hospital Financial Management.* Germantown, MD: Aspen Systems Corporation, 1989.

Kerschner, M.I., and J.M. Rooney. "Utilizing Cost Accounting Information for Budgeting." *Topics in Health Care Financing* 13, no. 4 (1987): 56–66.

Kolman, Herman A. "Determining a Contribution Margin for DRG Profitability." *Healthcare Financial Management* (April 1984): 108–110.

Mays, Janet, and Gus Gordon. "Developing a Cost Accounting System for a Physician Group Practice." *Healthcare Financial Management* (October 1996): 73–79.

Neumann, Bruce R., Jan P. Clement, and Jean C. Cooper. *Financial Management: Concepts and Applications for Health Care Organizations.* Dubuque: Kendall/Hunt, 1997.

Ramsey, R.H. "Activity-Based Costing for Hospitals." *Hospital & Health Services Administration* (fall 1994): 385–396.

CHAPTER 5

Budgeting, reporting, and responsibility centers

"There is a negative budget variance in the pharmacy. The manager says she has no control over the costs which caused the variance. Is she correct?"

"Why in the world does it take us six months to develop our budget? By the time it is completed, isn't it already outdated?"

"My supervisor is always after me to spend less than my budget; but if I do, I get less next year."

"They tell me it is my budget, yet I never am asked to participate in the planning process."

"Why is it we are making a profit yet can't pay our suppliers on time?"

Introduction

In previous chapters, we developed a foundation for understanding cost behavior. In this chapter we will develop the technical and behavioral aspects of the budgeting process and its relationship to the planning function. It is generally recognized by most experienced managers that a properly prepared budget can be a vital tool in the effective control of hospital operations. Because of the service orientation of most healthcare providers and the lack of an overall output measurement similar to a profit margin for nonprofit organizations, the budget may be one of the most valuable tools the administration has to monitor costs. A thorough understanding of the budget process and its strengths and weaknesses is an important part of a manager's job. Typically, the planning function should establish the foundation for the preparation of the budget, therefore it will be discussed next.

The planning function

Planning for the future is a vital function of the management process. Typically the manager will be helped by several committees composed of members of the staff and the trustees. Regardless of the organization entities involved, the planning function should consider two major areas: 1) environmental factors and 2) decision factors.

Environmental factors cannot usually be changed by the provider in the short run. This includes consideration of the economic, social, and political forces which will affect the future of the healthcare provider. Examples of such forces are future population mix (both in absolute numbers and composition), age factors, mobility, special health risk categories, etc. The number of competitive providers in the area, the types of equipment available, and community support are also vitally important in planning future operations. Finally, relationships with local health planning agencies and political leaders should be clearly assessed and analyzed in preparing plans for the future.

The decision factors are those specific goals, objectives, and programs that are selected by management. For example, decisions may be made on quality of care, type of services to be offered, and the composition of the medical staff.

Generally, the planning function for the decision factors can be separated into two related aspects: strategic and operational. The strategic aspect includes the process of deciding the future direction of the healthcare organization. It involves:

1. identifying the healthcare organization's mission;
2. setting goals and objectives;
3. identifying the resources available to the organization in the future;
4. defining programs to accomplish the goals and objectives within the constraints of available resources.

The operational aspect of the planning function deals primarily with the preparation of the budget. It consists of organizing the resources to accomplish the programs identified in the strategic planning process. Operational planning involves projecting financial resources needed for up to five years in the future. The first year of the projection would be the detailed operating budget, which will be discussed in the next section. The next two years would be summarized to capture the major aspects of the long-range plan. Any remaining years in the plan would be expressed in terms of overall financial objectives. The budgeting and planning process should be repeated each year to maintain a multiyear approach at all times. Typically, the operational planning process should be developed from the bottom up. However, the strategic function must be accomplished from the top down because it requires the special expertise and judgment of top managers and medical/clinical staff and provides guidance for operational planning.

A diagram of the budget and planning process is shown in *Exhibit 5–1*.

Exhibit 5–1
The planning and budgeting process

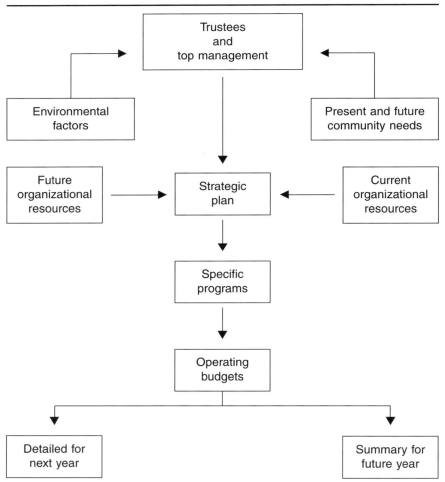

The budget process

The preparation of the operating budget requires the participation of all managers in the organization within the framework of an overall philosophy which reflects the organizational culture. For example, there is a major question that top managers must answer: *What do you want your budget process to accomplish*?

One approach is to *instill fear* in managers. Examples of this style would be a heavy handed, top down approach to the budget preparation and an insistence on strict compliance with the approved budget. Initiative is not encouraged.

The opposite approach is to use the budget to help the organization to become more *effective* and *efficient.* Effectiveness means the accomplishment of the organizational objectives. Efficiency is the relationship of resources consumed to outputs achieved.

In the remainder of this chapter, we will assume the latter approach is desired by management but the actual specifics of the organization and the environment may dictate which approach offers the best chance to succeed. In either case, the budgeting process should focus on the *outputs* to be achieved, not the *inputs* to be consumed.

What is a budget?

A completed budget results in a plan of operations for the coming year expressed in quantitative terms. This budget, if properly accomplished, *combines* and *coordinates* all the individual activities of the hospital into an approved statement of revenues and expenses for the coming year. In a sense, the preparation of the budget becomes the process of planning for the next fiscal period. When completed, the budget *communicates* the approved plans to supervisors responsible for carrying out specific functions. It *coordinates* activities of the organization and serves as a central device for *monitoring* expenditures. It can *motivate* managers and personnel at all levels, and finally it offers a *measurement* device against which actual performance subsequently can be compared. In states with commissions which are charged with approving rate structures, the negotiated budget becomes the focal point for the review and approval process.

In all cases, budgeting is a top management responsibility, and the effective preparation and utilization of the data should be a continuing concern.

The effective budget process will include procedures for monitoring changes in the assumptions under which the budget was prepared and procedures to allow changes as needed. A useful point of departure would be an analysis of past budget behavior. *Exhibit 5–2* illustrates these concepts.

Major parties in the budget process

An effective budget process requires the involvement of the following levels of management.

Exhibit 5–2
The budget revision cycle

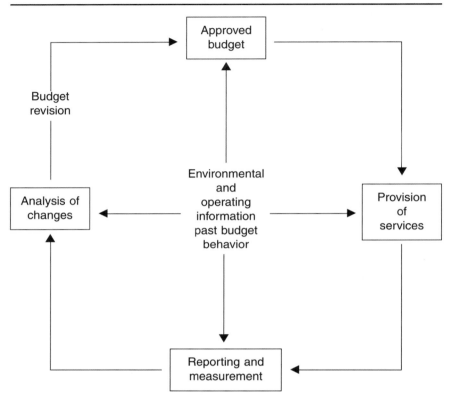

Level of Management	Responsibilities
Board of directors	Establishes initial guidelines and approves final budget monitoring of environmental changes and budget compliance.
Top management	Implements the approved budget, recommends changes as needed to meet environmental and operating changes, measures performance of managers.
Finance, accounting, MIS	Distributes approved guidelines and policies to line managers; maintains operating results and completes variance analysis at planned intervals; provides financial information to top management.

Departmental managers   Prepares initial budget estimates to finance based on guidelines; provides services to meet organizational objectives, reports information to finance department; recommends changes to approved budget as needed.

The budget timetable

To be effective, budget preparation should start well in advance of the implementation date. At least six months should be allowed in those states which require regulatory approval of the budgets for rate setting. In other cases, a minimum of at least three months should be established. This time constraint means that the most recent or current year figures can not always be incorporated into the budget. The decision to wait as long as possible before preparing the budget in the hope of including the most up-to-date figures will depend on the current healthcare environment, the budgetary experience of the supervisors, and the preference of top management. Generally, the need for sufficient time to prepare and review the budgets should outweigh the disadvantage of not having the last few months of actual data. The controller and his/her staff and the supervisors should be able to estimate sufficiently accurate cost data for budget preparation to begin. An example of a budget timetable is shown in *Exhibit 5–3*. This timetable should and will vary by healthcare organization. However, it is usually better to err on the side of too much time than too little.

Exhibit 5–3
The budget preparation timetable

Implementation date	Activity
7 months	Budget committee meets
6 months	Guidelines and instructions to operating supervisors
5 months	Initial budgets from operating departments
4 months	Controller review of initial budgets
3 months	Budget committee review with operating supervisors/Submission to regulatory agencies
2 months	Integration and review of final budgets/appeal process
1 month	Final budget approval/Submission to operating department
0	Operations started

An overview of the operating budget process

In most large, healthcare providers, an effective budget process requires input from and coordination between several departments. One way to achieve this is to establish a budget committee composed of a senior manager, the CFO, and the major department heads. This committee recommends to the CEO the general planning factors for the next fiscal period, reviews the submitted budgets, and resolves differences whenever possible.

The CFO takes the guidelines and activity levels approved by the CEO and disseminates them to the operating supervisors responsible for individual budget preparation. This information should include the planned level of operations for the coming year, this year's actual expenses, and any known increases in costs for salary, supplies, etc. In addition, it is useful to hold training sessions before actual budget preparation starts to clear up any misunderstanding of the formal budget documents and due dates.

In most cases a formal budget manual should be provided to the supervisors responsible for preparing departmental budgets. It should be recognized that many operating supervisors will have had little formal training in budget preparation. A budget manual should explain in considerable detail how the budgeting system works in the provider. It should include deadlines for completion of individual steps, the approval process, examples and instructions for completing the required forms, and the glossary. Many finance and accounting terms are foreign to personnel trained to provide healthcare. Thus, a ready reference source can prove to be invaluable during the budget preparation period.

The meetings and the budget manual can do much to minimize the frustrating budgeting experiences for many operating supervisors. The manual should be prepared with their needs in mind and above all, the controller and his/her staff should be available to assist the supervisors at all times.

The total budget concept

Although we have used the term budget in a unitary sense, a completed budget actually has several components. This master budget should consist of the following principal parts:

1. A statistical budget showing planned levels of patient days, ancillary services, and related activities.
2. A revenue budget based on the statistical budget, types of services to be offered, the payer mix, and reimbursement rates for each payer.

3. An expense budget based on the statistical budget and the resources needed to accomplish the activities. The operating budget should be expressed in terms of responsibility centers and the personnel responsible for accomplishing the objectives. A pro forma income statement should result from the data developed in steps 2 and 3.
4. A cash budget which shows the anticipated cash flows to meet requirements of the operating budget and the capital expenditure budget. A pro forma balance sheet and statement of cash flows would be prepared at this time.
5. A capital expenditure budget for the acquisition of capital assets for the fiscal period. The entire budget cycle is shown in *Exhibit 5–4.*

Budgetary techniques

In preparing the types of budgeting listed above, there are several budgeting techniques that can be used. Each of these have strengths and weaknesses and can be used in combination with each other. Traditionally, healthcare organizations have used an incremental approach. In the cost-based environment of the last twenty years, the incremental approach provided sufficient information and control for healthcare managers. It did not require a lot of training or involvement by clinical personnel. The switch to a prospective reimbursement focus in 1983 required many healthcare organizations to experiment with more sophisticated techniques in their attempt to involve more commitment to the process from clinical personnel. A zero based budgeting (ZBB) approach was briefly tried in the late seventies and early eighties. It attempted to merge incremental and program management concepts, but was generally unsuccessful. A more detailed approach to ZBB is given in *Appendix 5–1.*

Program budgeting is probably the most theoretically correct approach to use, but the difficulty in defining and costing outputs and assigning responsibility for results has inhibited the adoption of a program budgeting approach. Even in the heyday of PPBS (Planning Programming Budgeting System) in the mid-sixties, very few healthcare providers adopted this approach. PPBS was required to be used by all federal government agencies by President Johnson in 1965.

Standard cost budgeting has been touted as an effective way to achieve efficiency and cost control through detailed analysis of the service to be provided. This microcosting approach was introduced during the mid-1980s but the time required and other practical difficulties in costing the services hampered use of this approach. *Exhibit 5–5* presents an overview of the various techniques. (For a more detailed analysis of the techniques, refer to the bibliography at the end of the chapter.)

Exhibit 5–4
The operating budget cycle

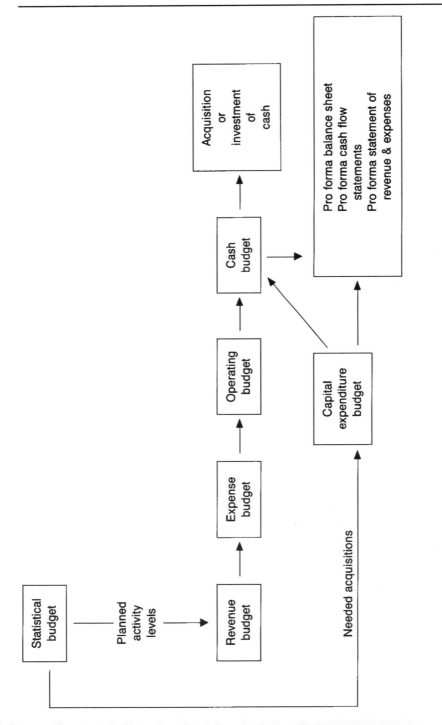

Exhibit 5–5
Budgeting techniques
Strengths and weaknesses

Technique	Incremental	Program	Zero-Base Budgeting	Standard-Cost Budgeting
Process	• Last year's actuals are starting point • Amounts added for inflation, new programs	• The outputs (programs) to be achieved are costed and benefits evaluated	• Activities to be completed are broken into small decision packages by supervisors and then ranked by management	• Requires development of what activities "should cost" for given output and quality levels using time and motion studies and detailed cost data
Strengths	• Budgeting is by responsibility center • Easy to do	• Focuses on outputs • Input/output comparisons	• Starts from zero each year • All dollars requested must be justified • Involvement of lower levels of management • Provides a priority ranking of activities proposed to be accomplished • Combines inputs with outputs	• Provides goals for supervisors to meet • Required involvement of supervisors, technicians, and financial personnel • Focuses on currently attainable efficiency
Weaknesses	• Assumes last year's amount was right • Subject to arbitrary shifts • Focus on inputs	• Does not align with responsibility centers • Difficult to assign responsibility when more than one cost center is involved	• Lengthy process • Lower level supervisors are not trained to complete decision packages • Impossible, from a practical point of view, to start from zero each year	• Reliable cost data typically not available • Lengthy process • Standards need to be updated frequently

Preparing the operating budget

The controller's organization and the responsibility center supervisors must work together to estimate the level of activity for the budget period. Generally, senior management will provide an estimate of the level of occupancy to be anticipated. This occupancy level can then be used by the individual supervisors to project the activity levels for their departments based on the most appropriate measurement. For example, nursing wards can use patient days and acuity levels to estimate required nursing hours. Ancillary departments can use tests, procedures, visits, etc. The important factor is to pick the statistical measure which most nearly approximates the factors which cause the incurrence of costs.

For example, some ancillary department supervisors may base their projections on an average number of tests per patient day. However, this type of projection may ignore a change in the patient mix or the addition of a new service. Care should be taken that projections reflect the new budget period, not just what happened in the past.

After statistical worksheets are prepared and approved, revenue and expense worksheets can be prepared. Statistical projections are critical to insure that the department's budgets are coordinated. Coordination problems could result, for example, if one department was planning on implementing a new test which required participation by another department which was not notified of the work load.

Preparing the revenue budget

The revenue projections for a healthcare provider must reflect the type of services provided for each patient payment category. For example, some patients will pay full charges, others will pay a negotiated charge, and the remainder may pay on a DRG basis or cost basis. The use of DRGs for reimbursement for Medicare patients, and in many states for Medicaid, makes the estimating of the type and volume of DRGs crucial to the revenue budget. Since payments for each DRG are now determined prospectively by the federal and state government, this has taken out some of the uncertainty on how much will be paid; however, the estimating of volume of each DRG by type of payer is not a minor task for most healthcare providers.

The amount of payment to be received for outpatient care provided to government patients is primarily a function of reasonable costs. There has been some shifting in outpatient charges for nongovernment patients to reflect the intensity of services provided. This refinement will add to the complexity of estimating revenue for the outpatient department, but it should be done as accurately as possible. The outpatient revenue may be a function of patient visits or it may be based on a categorization of visits by intensity of care received. Considerable research has been completed on switching outpatient services to a prospective basis such as ambulatory visit groups (AVGs). In the interim, maximum rates of reimbursement have been established for many commonly provided outpatient services such as renal dialysis and minor surgical procedures.

The development of a resource based relative value scale (RBRVS) for physician's services will also influence revenue projections for many healthcare providers. Finally, as of October 1, 1991, capital pass through costs such as depreciation and interest for prospective payment providers are included in the DRG rates. The amount to be paid is a function of the national average and hospital specific costs. Over a ten-year phase-in period, the hospital specific portion will be reduced until all PPS hospitals are paid the national rate.

In addition, many healthcare providers are entering into capitation rates with HMOs or other alternative health providers. This revenue can be considered fixed for the budget period as contrasted to the payment by DRG which will vary by the volume and type of DRG.

For some patients, the rate to be charged for each type of service will be determined by the previous year's charges, the state regulatory agencies, federal reimbursement regulations, and competitive conditions (i.e., what other hospitals in the area are charging). In the 1970s many providers typically estimated their expenses for the budget year, then established charges to cover these expenses. Before cost containment became an issue, this may have been acceptable, but in today's environment, it is not realistic or appropriate.

Some healthcare providers prepare the revenue and expense budgets at the same time. The revenue budget is projected first at last year's charges. These revenue projections are compared with the expense projections for the same volume of activity, and adjustments are made in both rates and expenses to meet cost containment objectives.

In other healthcare providers, revenues are projected first, and guidelines are then given to the department supervisors to help them establish their expenses. Under prospective pricing concepts, this may be the most logical manner in which to proceed if caps are to be placed on total authorized revenues. To summarize, revenue projections should be done at the departmental level based on: 1) type of service to be provided and 2) amount of payment to be received.

Preparing the expense budget

The labor hours worksheet and full-time equivalent (FTE) projections are very significant cost projections, as most provider departments are labor-intensive. The division between productive and nonproductive labor hours is an important management decision. Small changes can lead to significant labor cost-savings, but they can also create considerable employee unrest.

Once the total labor hour and FTE budgets are prepared, salary dollars can be computed on the basis of planned cost of living increases, merit raises, and implementation dates.

Other expense items such as supplies, maintenance, service contracts, etc., would be estimated to prepare the total department expense budget, which would be submitted to the reviewing authority.

Preparing the capital expenditure budget

Because of the large amounts of resources involved and the long-term commitment aspect of the decision, the capital expenditure budget is usually considered separately from the operating budget. However, the same information on planned activity levels is also required to make judgments about the capital expenditures. Capital expenditure decisions can be grouped according to their purpose, such as:

1. health and safety requirements;
2. cost reduction and replacement equipment;
3. expansion and improvement of existing services;
4. new services;
5. special requirements.

Capital budgeting requirements should include an economic analysis whenever possible in order to help in the evaluation of the project. It is recognized that political and nonquantifiable aspects of the project may overwhelm the economic aspects. However, it is always useful to obtain the best possible estimates of the economic impact of the project. Techniques for evaluating capital expenditure proposals will be discussed in greater detail in chapter 12.

Preparing the cash flow budget

After the operating and capital expenditure budgets have been completed and approved, the financial staff can review the cash position of the organization for the budget period. This usually can be done on a macro level by comparing total cash requirements and total cash receipts for the year. This macro review tests the overall feasibility of the master budget. However, it will not indicate when cash shortages may occur during the budget period. This is accomplished by preparing monthly cash inflow and outflow projections. Shortages can either be met by short-term borrowing or delaying certain capital expenditures. (For example the total cash budget for the period could be projected as shown in *Exhibit 5–6*.)

Management would have to decide on actions that could be taken to make up the estimated shortage indicated in *Exhibit 5–6*. This could involve postponing capital investments, reducing the deficit from operations by increasing charges or reducing expenses, delaying other cash outflows, or incurring more debt. For the short-term cash budget, the financial staff would prepare a more detailed statement as shown in *Exhibit 5–7*.

Exhibit 5–6
Determination of financial feasibility
of budget planning

Cash requirements		
Capital investments		$ 500,000
Repayment of debt		300,000
Third-party audit		50,000
Depreciation fund		200,000
Expansion reserve		100,000
Total requirements		$1,150,000
Cash available		
Excess of revenues over expenses (loss)	(100,000)	
Add back noncash expenses:		
Depreciation	300,000	
Total cash available from operations		$ 200,000
Endowment income		300,000
Donations		500,000
Investment income		50,000
Total cash available		$1,050,000
Anticipated cash shortage		$ 100,000

Exhibit 5–7
Monthly cash flow budget

	*August**
Beginning cash balance	$ 50,000
Cash receipts	
Patient service income	1,050,000
Misc. cash income	20,000
Other cash receipts	30,000
Total cash available	$1,150,000
Cash outflows	
Cash operating expenses	80,000
Accounts payable	850,000
Salaries	20,000
Other cash expenses	20,000
Debt repayment	100,000
Capital investment purchase	50,000
Total cash outflow	$1,120,000
Ending cash balance	$ 30,000†

*This format would be used for each month of the year.
†The ending balance becomes the beginning balance for the next month.

The completed cash budget becomes an integral part of the total budget process and can lead to revisions in the operating and capital budgets in order to meet overall hospital objectives. The ending cash balance provides information to the financial management staff on amounts that could be invested in short-term investments.

Summary of the budget process

1. The trustees establish goals and objectives for the institution for the coming budget period.
2. The budget committee establishes and the administrator approves budget guidelines for the budget period, including such factors as planned activity levels and salary guidelines.
3. The revenue budget is prepared by the controller's department and involved supervisors.
4. The initial expense budgets are prepared by the operating departments.
5. Initial review and negotiation take place between the controller and the operating staff.
6. The capital budget is prepared.
7. The cash budget is completed and coordinated with the operating and capital budgets.
8. The budget committee coordinates and reviews the budgets.
9. Final approval is given by the administrator, trustees, and the regulatory agencies (if required).
10. The approved budget is distributed to all department heads.

Performance measurement

Performance measurement is a vital part of the management function. It requires an information system which provides data by responsibility centers, by product lines, and by physician. Much of this information flows from the patient medical record, the charge sheets, and the accounting system. *Exhibit 5–8* illustrates the flow of information necessary to accomplish the performance measurement function in an organization.

An effective performance measurement system requires a responsibility accounting system, standards for performance, and variance analysis.

Responsibility accounting

The preceding section focused on some of the techniques that can be used to plan and control costs in a healthcare organization. However, it must be recognized that people, not methods or systems, actually make the decisions that achieve the desired results. In this section we will concentrate

Exhibit 5–8
Performance measurement

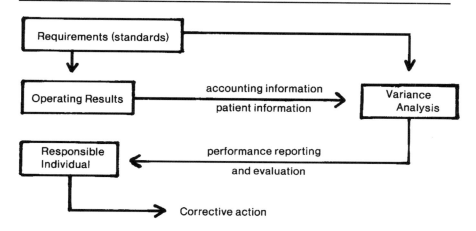

on fixing responsibility for cost incurrence. This fixing of responsibility generally falls under the heading of responsibility accounting.

Accounting information

Anthony and Reece characterize management accounting information as:

1. full cost accounting;
2. differential accounting;
3. responsibility accounting.[1]

Each of these categories is, of course, related to the others, but each is used for a different purpose. For example, the full cost of an item is usually identified as direct costs plus an allocated share of any indirect costs. In healthcare organizations indirect costs may comprise 50 percent or more of the full cost of services, and the allocation process is vital to rate setting and reimbursement decisions. In this case, full costs include elements from many different responsibility centers.

Differential accounting, also called incremental analysis, focuses on those costs that would be different if one alternative were selected over another. Costs that would not change under different alternatives are clearly not relevant to the decision process. In most cases, indirect costs do not change under different alternatives. Examples would include such decisions as whether to add a service to an existing department or whether

---

[1] Anthony, Robert N., and James S. Reece, *Accounting: Text & Case,* 8th ed., 1988, pp. 524–526.

to offer a reduced rate for a short-run increase in volume. Most capital investment decisions require differential accounting information.

The third type, responsibility accounting, collects and reports costs for various organization entities or levels. It is used to motivate, direct, and control the actions of managers. Behavioral considerations are much more important in responsibility accounting, where people's motivations and objectives are an important component of management control. The ability to affect future decisions is an important component of responsibility accounting.

Responsibility accounting requirements

Responsibility accounting is a vital part of the management control process in every organization. Anthony and Young define management control as the process by which managers insure that resources are obtained and used effectively and efficiently in the accomplishment of an organization's objectives.[2]

Effectiveness is the relationship between a department's outputs and its objectives. For example, an objective in a radiology department may be to report on the results of all "stat" tests in six hours. Accomplishing this objective would indicate effective behavior or effective results. A nursing station may establish an objective of completing all patient records within two hours after discharge. The degree to which this is accomplished could also be measured.

Efficiency, on the other hand, is defined as the relationship between inputs and outputs. In the radiology and nursing examples above, the amount of resources required to accomplish each objective would be a measure of efficiency. If three X-ray technicians are normally required to meet the objective, the budget would logically include resource costs for three (FTE) technicians. However, the actual number of FTEs required would depend upon the volume of procedures completed. The relationship between resources consumed and number of procedures completed would be a measure of efficiency.

A properly designed management control system will motivate managers to control their operations in such a manner as to satisfy both efficiency and effectiveness requirements. Managers must be able to balance both efficiency and effective behaviors so that neither is neglected.

Responsibility centers

A key aspect of a management control system is the concept of a responsibility center. A responsibility center is an organizational unit in which

---

[2] Anthony, Robert W., and David Young, *Management Control in Nonprofit Organizations,* 4th ed., Homewood, IL: Richard D. Irwin, Inc., 1988.

the manager has clearly defined areas of responsibility or activities over which he/she exercises some measure of control. A department supervisor or chief nurse who has both supervisory and budgetary control fits this definition. Responsibility centers are typically one of four types:

1. Cost center: An organizational entity in which the supervisor is responsible for the expenses that have been incurred. The output, however, is not measured because it is not feasible or practical from a cost viewpoint. Examples would be the accounting department or the maintenance department.
2. Revenue center: In a revenue center, managers are primarily held accountable for total revenues. In such centers, growth or volume is most important. Revenue or volume management may be appropriate in divestitures or cutback situations.
3. Profit center: In this type of center, the supervisor is held responsible for both expenses and revenues. Examples may include any department that provides patient care, e.g., laboratories, nursing wards, and pharmacies.
4. Investment center: This center is considered the final evolution in the responsibility center concept. The supervisor is held accountable for revenues, expenses, and the capital assets utilized to provide the services. Examples might include radiology departments and laboratories. From a theoretical point of view, any revenue center could easily be made into an investment center; however, from a practical point of view, only departments with a clearly defined asset base are feasible investment centers.

Establishing responsibility centers

A healthcare provider that wants to implement the responsibility center concept must meet two major requirements: a sound organizational structure that assigns responsibility clearly to specific individuals and an accounting system that supports the organization structure. Without these two factors, it is impossible to establish an effective responsibility center concept.

Organization

As stated above, individuals must be responsible for achieving the goals and objectives of the hospital if they are to be accomplished. These individuals need clearly defined areas of responsibility and authority. The organizational structure plays a vital role in establishing responsibilities and duties. If properly designed, the organizational structure becomes the basis for reporting operating data and evaluating results. At a minimum, the healthcare provider must be divided into manageable units designed to foster a coordinated effort to accomplish these objectives. There is not one type of structure that is better than others. Berman, Weeks, and Kukla illustrate several possible arrangements in their text on hospital financial management.[3]

Some healthcare providers perform well with poor organizational structures while others do poorly with sound organizational structures. The key features are, and will continue to be, the motivation of the personnel. Needless to say, it is a highly important area, and the reader is encouraged to review some of the suggested reference books in this area.

One important behavioral aspect of responsibility accounting must be recognized by managers in healthcare organizations. This is the concept of goal congruence. People have their own individual objectives. They also have professional objectives that are a function of their educational background and experience. Healthcare organizations certainly have objectives that encompass both professional objectives and patient care objectives. They also have a responsibility to evaluate and maintain fiscal solvency, financial viability, and long-run survival. Many of these objectives require a healthcare organization to be concerned about the control of both internal and external (societal) costs. In some cases, a conflict between an individual's personal and professional objectives and the organization's objectives may arise.

The goal congruence concept attempts to identify and minimize such conflicts. The basic premise is that accounting reports should show how an individual's objectives and the organization's objectives can be simultaneously accomplished. Research suggests that such conflicts do occur and that changes in accounting data and accounting reports can help to alleviate conflicts between organizational and individual objectives. If an individual can satisfy both his/her own objectives and those of the organization, there is a much higher probability that both will be better off in the long run. The concepts of responsibility accounting discussed in this chapter will lead to higher degrees of goal congruence.[4]

Cost definitions

Responsibility center procedures require further refinement of cost terminology. The fixed and variable cost definitions of chapter 2 take on another dimension, this time in terms of controllability. An item of cost can be considered controllable if its amount is significantly influenced by the actions of the supervisor. As one moves upward in the hospital management structure, costs become more and more controllable. When the

---

[3] Berman, Howard J., Lewis E. Weeks, and Steven F. Kukla, *The Financial Management of Hospitals,* 7th ed., Ann Arbor, MI: Health Administration Press, 1990, chapter 3.

[4] The goal congruence problem is also referred to as the agency problem in the financial management literature.

organization is viewed as a single entity, all costs must be considered controllable by the hospital administrator. Whether this is true will depend upon the range of authority and responsibility given to the administrator. It should be stressed that the concept of controllability does not mean absolute control. Few managers have absolute control of their costs; rather, controllability is a measure of significant influence over cost incurrence.

In chapter 2, we classified costs as either direct or indirect. Indirect costs are usually allocated to the responsibility center; therefore, they cannot be considered controllable by the supervisor. For example, the allocated share of hospital administration is an indirect and noncontrollable cost. On the other hand, all controllable costs are direct costs; however, not all direct costs are controllable, at least in the short run. For example, the depreciation on X-ray equipment is a direct cost of the radiology department; however, it is not a controllable cost. There is no way the supervisor can undo the decision to buy the equipment after it has been purchased. The preceding discussion highlights the "committed" cost concept. Committed costs are for decisions previously made. The depreciation referred to above, or a long-term contract with a radiologist, are committed costs in that the supervisor has little influence on their amounts after the decision to incur them has been made.

Variable costs can also be compared with controllable costs. Usually all variable costs are controllable. However, the amount of medicine or medical supplies used by a department may not be a cost controllable by the supervisor. Typically, the medical staff and health standards determine usage rates. In such cases, variable costs are not necessarily controllable.

Given the responsibility accounting associated with controllable costs, some supervisors may try to put as many costs into the noncontrollable area as possible. Higher level managers must be aware of this possibility. Effective management control requires identifying controllable costs at the lowest possible level in the organization hierarchy. In most cases, all costs can be made controllable by assigning different levels of responsibility and by turning indirect costs into direct costs. For example, utility expense is usually allocated to each department. The installation of meters could change the cost from indirect to direct and increase the controllability of some utility costs. This type of change requires a detailed analysis of the costs versus the benefits to be gained from the conversion program.

The reporting process

In order to effectively monitor progress towards objectives, periodic budget reports must be furnished to both operating supervisors and management. A typical approach to reporting for performance measurement is illustrated in *Exhibit 5–9*. This report focuses on a comparison of actual costs with the budgeted costs.

Exhibit 5–9

Departmental budget report for the month of February 199X

Cost Component	Current month			Year to date			Last yr YTD
	Actual	Budget	Variance	Actual	Budget	Variance	Actual
Salaries	$111,000	$105,000	$ 6,000 U (5.7%)	$ 803,000	$ 750,000	$53,000 U (4.7%)	$ 785,000
Supplies/materials	86,750	90,000	3,250 F (3.6%)	600,000	630,000	30,000 F (4.8%)	590,000
Insurance	20,000	20,000	0	140,000	140,000	0	110,000
Repairs/maint.	15,000	10,000	5,000 U (50%)	70,000	50,000	20,000 U (20%)	50,000
Depreciation							
Departmental overhead	100,000	100,000	0	700,000	700,000	0	600,000
Allocated general overhead	50,000	45,000	5,000 U (11%)	335,000	315,000	20,000 U (6%)	315,000
Totals	$382,750	$370,000	$12,750 U (3%)	$2,648,000	$2,585,000	$63,000 U (2%)	$2,450,000

Exhibit 5–10
Departmental budget report for the month of February 199X

Expense Component	Current month			Year to date			Last yr YTD
	Actual	Budget	Variance	Actual	Budget	Variance	Actual
Salaries	$111,000	$105,000	$ 6,000 U (5.7%)	$ 803,000	$ 750,000	$53,000 U (4.7%)	$ 785,000
Supplies/materials	86,750	90,000	3,250 F (3.6%)	600,000	630,000	30,000 F (4.8%)	590,000
Insurance	20,000	20,000	0	140,000	140,000	0	110,000
Repairs/maint.	15,000	10,000	5,000 U (50%)	70,000	50,000	20,000 U (20%)	50,000
Depreciation							
Departmental overhead	100,000	100,000	0	700,000	700,000	0	600,000
Total controllable expenses	332,750	325,000	7,750 U (2%)	2,313,000	2,270,000	43,000 U (2%)	2,135,000
Allocated general overhead	50,000	45,000	5,000 U (3%)	335,000	315,000	20,000 U (6%)	315,000
Totals	$382,750	$370,000	$12,750 U (3%)	$2,648,000	$2,585,000	$63,000 U (2%)	$2,450,000

The difficulty in measuring and motivating the responsible supervisor is that some of the costs reported in this type of report are not fully controlled by him/her. The allocated general overhead costs include a share of administrative, housekeeping, and other support areas. Clearly, the departmental supervisor has little control over the amount of these expenses. A more effective reporting format would require dividing the expenses into controllable and noncontrollable expenses. The key in this separation is the ability of the supervisor to directly control or influence the amount of the cost. Using this concept, a report similar to *Exhibit 5–10* could be presented.

This report highlights the costs the supervisor can control. However, additional information on the fixed and variable costs in the budget information on the volume of services provided can lead to further refinements in the measurement process. For example, in our departmental budget, let's assume that the fixed costs are insurance, depreciation, departmental overhead, and allocated general overhead. The salaries, supplies/materials, and repairs/maintenance vary with the number of patient visits. By varying the format of the report and adding the number of patient visits, we would be able to adjust the budget for changes in patient visits that differ from the budgeted number of visits. This *flexible budget concept* will be further developed in chapter 7 but for the purposes of this chapter the information will be presented in the format illustrated in *Exhibit 5–11*. Without additional information, the actual variances cannot be determined but clearly the difference in actual versus budgeted number of patient visits should have a major impact on the variable costs that should be incurred.

In the next section, a series of reports which can be used for performance measurement will be presented. Each of them is designed to stress certain performance measurement aspects. The responsible manager will use several of them to properly evaluate the performance of key individuals.

Alternative reporting formats

An alternative reporting format is illustrated in *Exhibit 5–12*. Its strength lies in its summary approach to presenting data by specific cost categories. In this report, standard costs are used to determine variances. Standard costs will be developed in chapter 6 but they are predetermined costs which should be incurred by the provider of the service. The inclusion of volume information is useful but without a breakout of the costs into fixed and variable categories, it would be difficult to evaluate cost performance.

In some cases, it may be desirable to review specific tests in greater detail. *Exhibit 5–13* illustrates this type of measurement with an emphasis on labor efficiency.

Exhibit 5–11
Departmental budget report for the month of February 199X

Cost Component	Current month			Year to date			Last yr YTD
	Actual	Budget*	Variance	Actual	Budget*	Variance	Actual
Variable Expenses							
Salaries	$111,000	$105,000	$ 6,000 U (5.7%)	$ 803,000	$ 750,000	$ 53,000 U (4.7%)	$ 785,000
Supplies/Materials	86,750	90,000	3,250 F (3.6%)	600,000	630,000	30,000 F (4.8%)	590,000
Repairs/Maint.	15,000	10,000	5,000 U (50%)	70,000	50,000	20,000 U (20%)	50,000
Total Variable Costs	$212,750	$205,000	$14,250	$1,473,000	$1,430,000	$103,000	$1,425,000
Fixed Expenses							
Departmental Overhead	100,000	100,000	0	700,000	700,000	0	600,000
Depreciation							
Insurance	20,000	20,000	0	140,000	140,000	0	110,000
Total Controllable Expenses	$120,000	$ 120,00	0	$ 840,000	$ 840,000	0	$ 710,000
Allocated General Overhead	50,000	45,000	5,000 U (11%)	335,000	315,000	20,000 U (6%)	315,000
TOTALS	$382,750	$370,000	$12,750 U (3%)	$2,648,000	$2,585,000	$ 63,000 U (2%)	$2,450,000

*the approved budget would be adjusted to reflect changes in actual volume of patient visits from the budgeted number based on the data below

Statistics	Current month			Year to date		
	Actual	Budget	Variance	Actual	Budget	Variance
Patient Visits	10,000	9,500	500 F (5%)	80,000	105,000	25,000 U (24%)

Exhibit 5–12
Department performance area: clinical laboratory

	Current Month			YTD		
Department	Standard	Actual	Variance (U or F)	Standard	Actual	Variance (U or F)
Chemistry: Volume	813,409	807,320	6,089 F	2,400,000	2,400,000	-0-
Labor	$137,354	114,263	23,091 F	528,145	518,145	10,000 F
Materials	$ 84,300	70,093	14,207 F	322,100	328,100	6,000 U
Indirect	$ 14,033	16,033	2,000 U	60,000	56,000	4,000 F
Total	235,687	200,389	35,298 F	910,245	902,245	8,000 F

Exhibit 5–13
Body scanning (cost center)
Labor efficiency report (period)

Number	Procedure, description, body scanning	Volume total	Labor standard (minutes)	Applied hours
0650	Head scan, ltd. (0–5 cuts)	3	20.00	1
0655	Head scan, comple. (6–12 cuts)	228	30.00	114
0660	Head scan, rutn. (13–19 cuts)	41	45.00	30.75
0665	Head scan, exten. (20–29 cuts)	4	60.00	4
0670	Head scan, ltd. (0–5 cuts)	3	35.00	1.75
0675	Head scan, comple. (6–12 cuts)	157	45.00	117.75
0680	Head scan, rutn. (13–19 cuts)	207	60.00	207
0685	Head scan, exten. (20–29 cuts)	3	75.00	3.75
6200	Body scan, ltd. (0–9 cuts)	37	30.00	18.5
6205	Body scan, comple. (10–19 cuts)	296	60.00	296
6210	Body scan, rutn. (20–41 cuts)	406	90.00	609
6215	Body scan, exten. (42–70 cuts)	53	120.00	106
6250	Body scan, ltd. (0–9 cuts)	18	45.00	13.5
6255	Body scan, comple. (10–19 cuts)	220	75.00	275
6260	Body scan, rutn. (20–41 cuts)	357	105.00	624.75
6265	Body scan, exten. (42–70 cuts)	1	135.00	2.25
	Total	2034	71.00	2425

Other hours: Supervision	1768
Total required worked hours	4193
Total worked hours	5304
Total paid hours	6240
Labor efficiency index	79.1%

Exhibit 5–14
Case performance

Description	DRG/MDC	Revenue	Cost	Contribution
Hernia	D379			
Expected		239,427	214,881	24,546
Actual		287,337	273,439	13,898
Variance		−47,910 F	−58,558 U	10,648 U
G.I. Disease	M7			
Expected		2,877,993	2,497,897	380,096
Actual		3,667,000	2,937,901	729,099
Variance		−789,007 F	−440,004 U	349,003 F
Hospital	All DRG/MDC			
Expected		189,789,040	189,697,088	91,952
Actual		184,066,322	179,239,113	4,827,209
Variance		5,722,718 U	10,457,975 F	4,735,257 F

Exhibit 5–15
Clinical service contribution

Clinical service	Discharges	Average cost	Average revenue	Average contribution	Net contribution
Gynecology	429	$2,918	$ 2,944	$ 26	$ 11,154
Medicine/general	1,047	3,142	3,313	171	179,037
Surgery/general	1,353	4,652	4,906	254	343,662
Cardiology	1,233	2,932	3,492	560	690,480
Hematology	410	4,014	4,340	326	133,660
Hemodialysis	34	4,084	4,177	93	3,162
Neurology	287	2,616	2,596	−20	−5,740
Pulmonary chest	97	2,790	3,167	377	36,569
Trauma/general	140	6,754	7,133	379	53,060
Ear/nose/throat	376	2,764	2,755	−9	−3,384
Opthalmology	2	2,561	2,118	443	−886
Orthopedics	594	3,375	3,443	68	40,392
Plastic surgery	259	3,387	3,357	−30	−7,770
Urology	306	3,542	3,628	86	26,316
Vascular surgery	810	8,660	10,845	2,185	1,769,050
Psychiatry	317	3,117	2,488	−629	−199,393
Totals	7,694				3,069,369

It is also possible to focus on the contribution margin for various cases or product/diagnosis output. *Exhibit 5–14* is an example of this approach. A more macro approach to contribution margin is illustrated in *Exhibit*

5–15. The focus on averages can be useful as long as the basis for computing the average costs and revenues is known. It is doubtful that psychiatry really loses this much money.

It is also possible to focus on the mix of services by DRGs, according to HCFA Weighting Factor ranking. This can be useful in evaluating potential changes in services offered. *Exhibit 5–16* presents an example of this report.

Exhibit 5–16
Cases by HCFA weight

Order	DRG	DRG Description	HFCA Wt.	Jan-Aug Number Dischg.
Top 5 cases by HCFA Weight:				
1	104	Cardiac Valve Procedure w/Pump & Cardiac Cath.	6.8527	3
2	302	Kidney Transplant	6.6322	2
3	106	Coronary Bypass w/Cardiac Cath.	5.2624	22
4	105	Cardiac Valve Procedure w/Pump & Cardiac Cath.	5.2308	13
5	108	Cardiothor. Procedure, except Valve & Coronary Bypass, w/Pump	4.3756	2
Median 5 cases by HCFA Weight:				
164	90	Simple Pneumonia & Pleurisy Age 18-68 w/o C.C.	0.9849	3
165	83	Major Chest Trauma Age = 70 and/or C.C.	0.9809	3
166	467	Other Factors Influencing Health Status	0.9799	12
167	300	Endocrine Disorders Age = 70 and/or C.C.	0.9731	12
168	93	Interstitial Lung Disease Age = 70 w/o C.C.	0.9724	5
Last 5 cases by HCFA Weight:				
328	40	Extraocular Procedures Except Orbit Age = 18	0.3977	3
329	410	Chemotherapy	0.3527	86
330	412	History of Malignancy with Endoscopy	0.3400	3
331	351	Sterilization, Male	0.2655	1
332	465	Aftercare with History of Malignancy as Secondary Dx.	0.2071	20

Adapted from MGMA presentation, March, 1984, Denver, Colorado.

Finally, it may be important to be able to monitor performance of specific physicians. *Exhibit 5–17* illustrates this type of report.

The reports in this chapter illustrate some of the variations possible to monitor performance measurement either by department, service, or individual. In all cases, each of them have specific strengths and weaknesses. They should be customized to fit the needs of decision makers in a particular institution. Many of the concepts discussed in later chapters will provide techniques that can be used to adapt the reports to provide better information to decision makers. That should be the primary goal of personnel involved in the reporting process.

Qualitative aspects of performance measurement

Although the material in this chapter emphasizes the cost aspect of management control and the reporting of cost information, it is equally important to define qualitative goals for performance measurement. At higher levels in the organization, qualitative goals become even more important in assessing performance because few cost items are directly controlled at this level. For example, a vice president may be responsible for many of the day-to-day financial operations of the healthcare provider but he/she does not actually control the operations. Rather, he/she has delegated that authority to lower-level supervisors. Yet, the requirement to measure performance still exists. Therefore, performance measurement standards need to be developed for the key areas of responsibility such as cash management, budgeting and financial reporting. *Appendix 5–2* provides a detailed example of performance standards at the vice president level.

Behavioral aspects of budgeting

No chapter on budgeting would be complete without considering the behavioral aspects of the budgeting process. People, not systems, incur costs. A manager would like the budget process to influence the responsible persons to take actions which are consistent with the goals of the hospital administration and to refrain from those actions which are not. To do this, the budget system must recognize the needs of the human beings involved. These needs can be grouped into material needs (monetary) and psychological (recognition and involvement). In most cases, material needs can be quickly identified and met to a large extent through the personnel policy. However, psychological needs are much more difficult to identify and satisfy. They can vary from person to person and within the same person at different times.

The budgeting system must be aware of and take into account the human element. Otherwise, even the best designed system is doomed to failure.

Exhibit 5-17
DRGs by physician

	Discharge Date	Length of Stay		Mean Chgs. VMH DRG[3]	Medicare Payment[4]	Actual Total Chgs.[5]	Difference Chgs. Payment
		DRG[1]	Actual[2]				
MD XXX							
DRG 1 Craniotomy							
Age Less than 18							
Except Trauma:							
National Los ___							
Patient #XX-XX-XX	7/15/83	35.0	30.0	21,500	17,500	18,500	-1,000
Patient #XX-XX-XX	8/01/83	35.0	32.0	21,500	17,500	19,100	-1,600
Patient #XX-XX-XX	8/04/83	35.0	34.0	21,500	17,500	22,700	-5,200
Total DRG 1		105.00	96.0	64,500	52,500	60,300	-7,800
Mean DRG 1		35.0	32.0	21,500	17,500	20,100	-2,600
Total MD XXX			32.0	64,500	60,300	60,300	

1 Average length of stay for all Patients w/specified DRG
2 Actual length of stay for Patient
3 Average charge for all Patients w/specified DRG
4 Medicare Case Mix WDEX multiplied by standard base reimbursement per Case Mix Unit
5 Actual charges for Patient

Adapted from MGMA presentation, March, 1984, Denver, Colorado.

Summary

The preparation and proper utilization of the budget can be an extremely effective management control tool for management. It can communicate to all levels of supervision the goals and objectives of top management and the resources that should be used to achieve these objectives. It also provides a yardstick for measuring performance in accomplishing these goals and objectives. The CEO must take an active role in the budget process if the maximum benefits are to be obtained.

Responsibility accounting offers an important advantage to the senior healthcare manager. By classifying costs as controllable or noncontrollable, he/she can motivate the department supervisor to take action on those costs he/she can control. In the total picture, all costs should be the responsibility of an individual who can influence their incurrence. If a cost is not the responsibility of an individual, in most cases, it will not be controlled effectively. The responsibility reporting format offers a significant improvement in the potential to control costs.

Questions and problems

1. Define the planning function for a healthcare organization.

2. Define the budgeting function for a healthcare organization.

3. What are the differences between the strategic and operational planning functions in a healthcare organization?

4. What environmental factors should be considered in designing a strategic plan for a healthcare organization?

5. Name the major budget components of the healthcare organization master budget.

6. Historically, in hospitals, the expense budget has been prepared before the revenue budget. Explain why this was so in the past, and the impact of this policy.

7. Discuss the budget timetable. Why is such a long time frame involved?

8. What are the major requirements of an effective budgeting process?

9. Explain the three types of management accounting information.

10. What is the management control process in a healthcare organization?

11. Define effectiveness and efficiency in a healthcare organization as it pertains to the management control process.

12. List and describe the four types of responsibility centers.

13. What are the two major requirements for establishing a responsibility center concept in a healthcare organization?

14. A manager has responsibility for both revenues and costs in her department. What type of responsibility center would be most appropriate in terms of motivation and control?

15. Explain the major differences between the normal revenue and expense statement for a revenue department and the responsibility center report.

16. It has been stated that all variable costs are usually direct costs but that all direct costs are not variable. Is this statement true or false, and why?

17. Describe and provide examples of a controllable fixed cost and a committed fixed cost.

18. Why would a healthcare organization prefer a revenue center to an investment center? When would a cost center be preferable?

19. What does the term "goal congruence" mean? How is it related to responsibility center accounting?

20. Give some examples of direct and indirect costs. Indicate the level in the organization where such costs are controllable.

21. How can the concept of contribution margin be used in performance reporting?

22. Describe the types of reports that would be required to evaluate a free-standing outpatient clinic with salaried physicians and minor surgical procedures being performed.

23. Congratulations! You have just been employed as the budget officer of Memorial Hospital. In outline form, list the steps you would take in fulfilling this responsibility. Give particular emphasis to the manner in which the accounting office may be of assistance to you.

24. You are discussing with your superior the advantages of a budgeting program for your organization. The administrator asks, "Why can't

we just continue to compare our monthly figures with last year's monthly figures instead of going through all this trouble to set up a budget?" In addition to responding to the specific question, present in outline form the benefits of a budgeting system.

25. Prepare an annual income and expense budget for the laboratory department of Community Managed Care (CMC) using the information supplied. The budget is for the period from July 1, 1990 through June 30, 1991. Indicate what you would do if, at the end of six months, the actual increase in the number of units of service for the department is only 50 percent of that anticipated in preparing the budget.
   a. CMC establishes charges for services at an amount that will approximate costs as nearly as possible. Total budgeted income for a department should be within range of $1,000 of total budgeted expenses. A relative value system is used in the laboratory department. During the fiscal year ended June 30, 1990, the average charge per unit was $1.02.
   b. Allowances, such as Blue Cross, Medicare, and bad debts, should be assumed to be 10 percent of gross income.
   c. In preparing the budget assume that the laboratory department will continue to grow at the same rate, as far as the number of relative units of service is concerned, as it has in the past two years.
   d. The two pathologists are guaranteed a base salary of $20,000 each, plus a pool of 10 percent of net revenue (gross charges less deductions) which is divided equally.
   e. The budget committee of CMC has instructed you to allow for a five percent salary increase for all eligible personnel except pathologists. These increases are to become effective for each employee on the first of the month following the anniversary of his/her employment date.
   f. Because of the increased workload, the budget committee has approved the addition of one new technologist to begin at the approved starting rate.
   g. Overtime, vacation and holiday relief, and on-call pay should be computed at 15 percent of the technologists' and aides' salaries.
   h. The indirect cost ratio for the laboratory department is 25 percent of direct expenses.
   i. The nonsalary direct expenses for the laboratory department in the year ended June 30, 1990 amounted to $50,000. It is expected that the 1990–91 nonsalary direct expenses will continue at approximately $0.25 per unit.

Community Managed Care	
Fiscal year	Units of service Laboratory
7/1/87–6/30/88	165,300
7/1/88–6/30/89	181,820
7/1/89–6/30/90	200,000

Community Managed Care Laboratory department			
Fiscal year	Gross charges	Deductions	Net charges
7/1/87–6/30/88	$175,218	$17,500	$157,718
7/1/88–6/30/89	$189,093	$18,900	$170,193
7/1/89–6/30/90	$204,000	$20,300	$183,700

Community Managed Care Schedule of selected wage range for the fiscal year ended 6/30/90		
Job code	Title	Range in dollars per month
23	Secretary	$325–450
44	Laboratory technologist	$375–525
67	Aides	$300–400

Community Managed Care Analysis of personnel—laboratory as of July 1, 1990				
Job code	Authorized position	Annual rate	Monthly rate	Employment date
01 Pathologist	J. Brown	$20,000	—	7/1/82
01 Pathologist	T. Smith	$20,000	—	9/1/81
23	J. Rocket	$ 4,800	$400	1/15/86
44	A. Dick	$ 6,120	$510	8/5/79
44	B. Searle	$ 6,000	$500	7/9/78
44	C. Noonan	$ 5,520	$460	9/14/83
44	O. White	$ 4,680	$390	12/13/86
67	N. Dupree	$ 4,560	$380	6/12/82
67	L. Jones	$ 4,080	$340	7/13/86

26. The Valley Community Hospital has completed its budget of operations for the new fiscal year (10/1/91 to 9/30/92) as shown in the summary statement *Exhibit A,* labeled "before rate adjustments." The statement shows an operating loss of $242,342 and a net loss of $177,942.

Exhibit A
The Valley Community Hospital
Actual for 12 months 9/30/91 compared with
projection for 12 month - 9/30/92
(before rate adjustments)

	9 month actual 3 month estimate 12 months 9/30/91	Projection 12 months 9/30/91	Variance increase amount
Patient days (excluding newborns)	66,029	69,000	2,971
Newborn days	3,870	3,870	
Operating income:			
Routine service— room and board	$3,152,616	$3,286,322	$133,706
Special— professional service	$2,970,628	$3,012,600	$ 41,972
Gross earnings from patient	$6,123,244	$6,298,922	$175,678
Deductions from earnings	$ 622,136	$ 639,985	($ 17,849)
Net earnings from patients	$5,501,108	$5,658,937	$157,829
Other income— auxiliary services	$ 98,286	$ 114,359	$ 16,073
Total operating revenues	$5,599,394	$5,773,296	$173,902
Total operating expenses	$5,467,750	$6,015,638	$547,888
Operating gain	$ 131,644	($ 242,342)	($373,986)
Supplementary income	$ 78,809	$ 64,400	($ 14,409)
Net gain	$ 210,453	($ 177,942)	($388,395)

Exhibit B

	Cash objectives
Capital budget	$173,974
Estimated due to Medicare for 9/30/89 & 9/30/90	$ 56,000
Estimated due to Blue Cross for 9/30/89 & 9/30/90 audit	$ 20,000
Bond amortizations:	
2/1/92 $43,000	
8/1/92 $44,000	
	$ 87,000
Property "A" note payment	$ 15,603
Property "B" note payment	$ 6,777
Cash transfer to building fund	$150,000
Total cash objectives for 1991–92	$509,354

The controller must make a recommendation to the executive committee in September 1991 regarding the hospital's cash objectives as indicated in *Exhibit B*. She must also do a cash flow analysis to see if these cash objectives can be met. The analysis shows that cash flow is substantially under the cash objectives. Therefore, a recommendation for both routine service and special service rate adjustments must be made to the executive committee for implementation on 10/1/91.

Part A:
Given below is information necessary for the controller to prepare the cash flow analysis:
1. Included in operating expenses for 9/30/92 is depreciation of $361,720.
2. The hospital was able to select an accelerated method of depreciation for non-government, cost-based patients. The amount for depreciation is $496,720 for the new fiscal year. Non-government, cost-based patients account for one-third of the total patient days.
3. The HMO contract with the hospital provides a 5 percent plus factor superimposed over the basic reimbursable cost of $2,040,000 for the fiscal year ended 9/30/92.
4. Inpatient accounts receivable for patients not under a reimbursement program is expected to affect cash flow. The utilization of the hospital for the fiscal year ending 9/30/92 will increase patient days and cause an increase of 5 percent in receivables. Only 20 percent of such receivables are not under a cost reimbursement program. The inpatient accounts receivable total, as of 9/30/91, is $850,000.
   a. Prepare a cash flow analysis and compare the results to the cash flow objective as shown in *Exhibit B*.

Part B:
Since your analysis shows a substantial variance between cash flow and cash objectives, you must proceed with the recommendation for rate adjustments. Again, the controller is given certain information to prepare such an analysis:
1. Projected patient days for 9/30/92 is 72,870, of which 3,870 is applicable to newborn. The room rate adjustment per day is $6 for both categories. Additional income from patient day utilization can be obtained from *Exhibit A*.
2. Special professional service rate adjustment is $5 per day. Additional income from patient day utilization can be obtained from *Exhibit A*.
3. The rate adjustments will have an effect on both inpatient and outpatient accounts receivable and will cause an increase of $50,000 and $20,000 respectively.
   a. Prepare a projected statement of operations as of 9/30/92 (after the rate adjustments have been in effect for one year), compar-

ing the 9/30/92 figures with the actual for 9/30/91 and showing variances in dollars.

b. Prepare a cash flow statement resulting from rate adjustments and compare the statement to the cash objectives for the coming year.

c. Will the rate adjustment, as proposed, meet all objectives of the hospital? Do you have any comments regarding either the proposed rate adjustments or the cash objectives of the hospital?

27. Mulberry Memorial Hospital (MMH) is a 250-bed hospital providing the usual range of hospital services. As an outside consultant, you have been asked to provide consulting services for the year. The initial task is to help in the preparation of the client's budget.

Part A:

Assume that, for a department providing three services, management has given you the following information:

Expected Volumes	
Service	Volume
A	100 units
B	200 units
C	300 units

Departmental Indirect (Fixed) Costs	
Department Supervisor	$4,200
Supplies	$ 325

Standard Cost per Resource Requirement	
Resource	Unit Cost
Labor	
Level 1	$ 8.00 per hour
Level 2	$10.00 per hour
Level 3	$12.00 per hour
Supplies	
Supply 1	$ 6.00 per unit
Supply 2	$ 1.50 per unit

	Standard Resource Requirement per Unit of Service				
	Labor Hours by Skill Level			Supply Items in Units	
Service	Level 1	Level 2	Level 3	Supply 1	Supply 2
A	0.0	1.0	2.0	0	2
B	1.0	2.0	0.0	2	1
C	2.0	3.0	2.0	1	0

a. Prepare a budget for this department, itemizing by expense category and fixed and variable cost.
b. Assume that indirect costs are allocated to procedures on the basis of direct labor hours. Assume further that there is no overhead allocated to this department. What is the total cost for each service?
c. Determine the standard labor cost per unit of service.
d. Determine the supply cost per unit of service.

Part B:

You have been notified by management that the hospital has been approached by Cottrell's, a local employer, to provide care to its employees at a flat rate of $1,300 per discharge. The following information is available:

Project Patient Load	
Case Type	Volume
C1	1,500
C2	3,000
C3	6,000
C4	4,500

	Standard Resource Consumption Profiles				
	Ancillary Services (units)			Nursing Services (days)	
Case Type	Lab	X-Ray	Pharm.	Surgical	Medical
C1	0	2	1	7	0
C2	3	4	0	0	6
C3	6	8	6	3	0
C4	0	2	3	0	5

Standard Cost per Resource Requirement	
Resource	Unit Cost
Labor	
Level 1	$10.00 per hour
Level 2	$ 8.00 per hour
Level 3	$ 6.00 per hour
Supplies	
Supply 1	$ 1.50 per unit
Supply 2	$ 2.00 per unit
Supply 3	$ 4.00 per unit

| | Standard Resource Requirement per Unit of Service | | | | | |
| | Hours of Labor by Skill Level | | | Supply of Items in Units | | |
Service	Level 1	Level 2	Level 3	Supply 1	Supply 2	Supply 3
Lab	0.0	2.0	1.5	0	3	4
X-Ray	2.0	0.0	3.0	1	0	2
Pharm.	6.0	6.0	0.0	3	2	1
Surgical	8.0	0.0	2.0	1	0	0
Medical	0.0	4.0	3.0	2	0	1

Based on the relevant information you have been asked to make a recommendation regarding acceptance or rejection of the proposal. Note any information which would be useful in making the recommendation. Regardless of your initial recommendation, what would be your recommendation if the projected patient load was adjusted as follows:

Case Type	Volume
C1	1,500
C2	3,000
C3	14,000
C4	4,500

Part C:

Following your completion of the preceding proposals from Cottrell, MMH provides you with the following budgets for its overhead departments, which consist of housekeeping, dietary, and laundry.

| | Budgeted Allocation Statistics | | | | |
Department	Cost	Basis	Sq. Ft.	Meals	Pounds
Housekeeping	$30,000	Sq. Ft.	200	20	200
Dietary	70,000	Meals	300	40	800
Laundry	80,000	Pounds	500	10	20
Lab	—	—	400	18	30
X-Ray	—	—	230	12	22
Pharmacy	—	—	170	15	280
Surgical	—	—	700	850	520
Medical	—	—	500	950	580
Total	—	—	3000	1915	2452

You have been told that the patient services and resources requirements used in calculating your recommendation for the Cottrell proposal comprise the hospital totals. In addition, you are to assume the following indirect (fixed) costs for the patient care departments:

Lab	$2,300
X-Ray	3,850
Pharmacy	1,275
Surgical	3,300
Medical	2,950

Using the information available, determine the amount of overhead allocated to each patient case department, and develop the budget for the entire hospital.

Part D:

It is now the end of the year and management has noted actual results differ significantly from budget. The actual operating results are as follows:

Actual Patient Load	
Case Type	Volume
C1	1,700
C2	2,850
C3	6,400
C4	5,800

	Actual Resource Consumption Profiles				
	Ancillary Services (units)			Nursing Services (days)	
Case Type	Lab	X-Ray	Pharm.	Surgical	Medical
C1	1.0	1.5	2.0	6.0	1.0
C2	2.0	6.0	0.0	0.0	8.0
C3	4.0	7.0	8.0	4.0	2.0
C4	1.5	1.0	2.0	2.0	6.0

	Actual Resource Usage per Unit of Service					
	Hours of Labor by Skill Level			Supply of Items, in Units		
Service	Level 1	Level 2	Level 3	Supply 1	Supply 2	Supply 3
Lab	0.5	2.5	1.0	0.0	2.0	4.0
X-Ray	3.0	0.0	2.0	2.0	1.0	3.0
Pharmacy	5.0	7.0	1.0	2.5	1.0	0.0
Surgical	7.0	1.0	1.0	2.0	0.5	1.5
Medical	0.0	2.0	4.0	3.0	2.0	0.0

Actual Cost per Resource Requirement	
Resource	Unit Cost
Labor:	
Level 1	$11.50 per hour
Level 2	$ 7.00 per hour
Level 3	$ 6.75 per hour
Supplies:	
Supply 1	$ 2.30 per unit
Supply 2	$ 1.80 per unit
Supply 3	$ 4.40 per unit

Management has asked you to provide the following variances from budgeted costs:

Treatment
Labor (Lab. Department)
    Rate
    Efficiency
Supplies (Surgical Department)
    Price
    Usage
Overhead (Total Only)*

*Note: Assume the following for overhead:

Standard OH case-type unit costs are allocated based on total direct resource consumptions.

Standard OH unit cost per case:
    C1 $ 9.40 per case
    C2 $ 7.28 per case
    C3 $18.00 per case
    C4 $ 8.01 per case
Actual overhead costs were $180,000, as budgeted.

28. Your goal is to develop a flexible budget for the nursing function and the laundry services department. This will be done for nursing services by developing a budget for only one nursing station.

    For laundry services a rate and amount budget will be developed which will be applied to the forecast level of operations to determine the expected level of expenses. Later, this same rate and amount budget will be used to prepare a control budget that will be used to pinpoint expenses that are out of line. The accounting department prepared the information in *Exhibits A* and *B* at your request.

Using the information provided in *Exhibits A* and *B,* develop budgets based on the planned volume of service for the laundry and nursing station 2N.

Exhibit A
Laundry Service Data

Laundry required by all departments except 2N for the coming week— 15,350 pounds.

Salaries for each of the following individuals are fixed expenses that remain constant for each month regardless of the level of operation:

Manager	$1,030
Clean Linen Room Manager	$ 700
Sewing Room Seamstress	$ 520
Line Porter	$ 450
Total	$2,700

The laundry is able to increase the size of the production work force as the number of pounds processed increases. As a result, production labor is a variable cost that varies directly with the number of pounds processed. Labor hourly rates and the times needed to process 100 pounds of laundry are shown in the table below:

Production Labor	Hourly Rate	Hours per 100 Pounds
Washroom	$4.30	.50
Flat Department	$4.30	1.50
Press Department	$4.00	.75

Maintenance on the laundry equipment is made up of a fixed cost of $50 per month for preventive maintenance, and additional maintenance is required at the rate of one hour of maintenance for every 10,000 pounds processed. One hour of maintenance costs $40.

Soap and other supplies are estimated to be $0.60 per 100 pounds, and are considered to be variable costs.

Exhibit B
Data for Nursing Station 2N

Daily personnel requirements for each shift at three levels of occupancy:

	Below 70% Occupancy	*70%–85% Occupancy*	*86%–100% Occupancy*
First Shift:			
Head Nurse	1	1	1
Registered Nurse	2	2	2
Licensed Practical Nurse	3	3	3
Aides	2	4	4
Second Shift:			
Registered Nurse	3	3	3
Licensed Practical Nurse	2	3	3
Aides	2	3	4
Third Shift:			
Registered Nurse	2	2	2
Licensed Practical Nurse	2	2	2
Aides	1	2	3

Supplies expense amounts to $0.25 per patient day with a fixed portion of $7 per week.

Laundry services are required at the rate of 10 pounds per patient day plus 150 pounds per week for items not related to the level of occupancy. The cost for laundry services is estimated to $0.16 per pound. There are 46 beds in 2N.

Forecasted occupancy levels for the coming week are as follows:

	Patient Days
Sunday	45
Monday	44
Tuesday	43
Wednesday	40
Thursday	33
Friday	25
Saturday	20
Total	250

Percentage of patients ordering meals on a specific day:

Breakfast	90%
Lunch	87%
Dinner	99%

Standard cost for meals:

Breakfast	$1.40
Lunch	$1.52
Dinner	$1.53

Keywords: budget; capital expenditure budget; cash flow budget; decision package; effectiveness; efficiency; expense budget; operating budget; responsibility accounting; revenue budget; statistical budget; timetable; zero base.

References

Block, L.F., and C.E. Press. "Product Line Development by DRG Builds Market Strength." *Healthcare Financial Management* 39, no. 12 (1985): 50–52.

Brandeau, M.L., and D.S. Hopkins. "A Patient Mix Model for Hospital Financial Planning." *Inquiry* 21, no. 1 (1984): 32–44.

Cook, D. "Strategic Plan Creates a Blueprint for Budgeting." *Healthcare Financial Management* (May 1990): 21–27.

Esmond, Truman H. *Budgeting for Effective Hospital Resource Management.* Chicago, IL: American Hospital Association, 1990.

Feuerstein, T. and C.A. Anderson. *Budgeting and Cost Management for Medical Groups.* Englewood, CO: Center for Research in Ambulatory Health Care Administration, 1990.

Horngren, Charles T., Srikant M. Datar, and George Foster. *Cost Accounting: A Managerial Emphasis.* 8th ed. New York, NY: Prentice-Hall, 1994.

Kolb, D.S., and J.L. Horowitz. "Managing the Transition to Capitation." *Healthcare Financial Management* (February 1995): 64–69.

Krueger, D., and T. Davidson. "Alternative Approaches to Cost Accounting." *Topics in Health Care Financing* 13, no. 4 (1987): 1–9.

Mays, Janet, and Gus Gordon. "Developing a Cost Accounting System for a Physician Group Practice." *Healthcare Financial Management* (October 1996): 73–79.

Neumann, Bruce R., Jan P. Clement, and Jean C. Cooper. *Financial Management: Concepts and Applications for Health Care Organizations.* Dubuque: Kendall/Hunt, 1997.

Schroeder, David H. "A Departmental Bottom-Line Perspective." *Health Care Management Review* 14, no. 1 (winter 1989): 25–40.

Steir, Margaret M., and Alan H. Rosenstein. "Scrutiny of Resource Use Can Increase Efficiency." *Healthcare Financial Management* (November 1990): 26–34.

Ward, D.L. "Operational Finance and Budgeting." in *The Managed Care Handbook.* 2d ed., edited by P.R. Kongstvedt. Gaithersburg, MD: Aspen Publishers, 1993.

Washburn, E.R. "Budgeting for a More Likely Future." *Medical Group Management Journal* (July/August 1995): 74–78.

APPENDIX 5-1

Zero base budgeting[1]

It is generally agreed upon by most practitioners and academicians that the proper design and use of the budget process is one of the most effective management tools. An effective budget process can be used to: 1) express the administrator's goals and objectives in a quantifiable manner; 2) serve as a communication and commitment device for the hospital staff; 3) act as a measurement tool and feedback loop for corrective action; 4) point out deficiencies in the current financial structure; and 5) forecast when shortages might occur.

For the budget to accomplish its function, there needs to be a well-designed process which can relate the resources committed to the outputs obtained. However, in most service organizations there are no clear input/output relationships similar to those found in manufacturing organizations. Most input resources fall in the category of managed costs. Many costs are discretionary and are set by management actions. It is uncertain how much costs will vary with changes in output. When this uncertainty is coupled directly with the difficulty in measuring both quantity and quality of outputs, a quandary exists. For example, if the number of nursing staff is reduced by 5 percent, will the quantity or quality or output also be reduced by 5 percent?

Despite these difficulties, hospital administrators do have to make decisions on the amount of resources to be committed to each area. Given the current emphasis on cost containment, better budgeting techniques are becoming more important to administrators and to hospital financial managers.

One tool is the zero base budgeting process. This concept requires that each activity be able to justify its budget request completely. It also requires that no level of expenditure be taken for granted. As Jimmy Carter, then governor of Georgia, explained zero base budgeting in his budget address on January 13, 1972: "Zero base budgeting requires every agency

---

[1] Adapted with permission from the quarterly journal of the American College of Hospital Administrators, *Hospital and Health Services Administration,* Vol. 24, No. 2, Spring 1979, pp. 42–62.

in the state government to identify each function it performs and the personnel and cost to the taxpayers for performing that function."[2] Or, expressed in a more concise manner. "Perhaps the essence of zero base budgeting is simply that an agency provides a defense of its budget request that makes no reference to the level of previous appropriations."[3]

Whether zero base budgeting was successfully applied in Georgia can be debated; there are conflicting reports.[4] However, it is important to stress that the concept of zero base budgeting is not new. It has its roots in incremental budgeting, program budgeting, and management by objectives. What is new is that it is recommended for all activities in an organization, particularly for the kinds of services that are usually found in hospitals.

Basically, zero base budgeting takes the program budgeting concept and applies it to a responsibility-oriented organizational structure. As such, program elements are transformed into organizational activities. The size of the program element (called decision package) depends upon which level in the organization structure is requested to participate in the zero base budgeting process. Basically, there are three key steps:

1. Develop decision packages.
2. Rank and prioritize them.
3. Allocate resources based on the priorities of the decision packages.

The design of the decision package is one of the most crucial elements in the budgeting process. Typically the first level of supervision in the hospital is responsible for preparing the decision package. This requires them to define their objectives and responsibilities and forces them to determine the costs of meeting objectives at various levels of effectiveness. The impact of this task can be traumatic, at best: or it can be totally dysfunctional if some guidelines are not formalized by top management. One approach would be to define specific levels of activity that should be calculated for each decision package. This could be some minimum budget level below the current budget figure at which the activity could not be reduced without ceasing to exist entirely, for example, 75 percent of the current budgeted amount. The next level of activity might indicate what could be achieved with the current budgeted amount. Another level

---

[2]Minmier, George S., and Roger H. Hermanson, "A Look at Zero Base Budgeting —The Georgia Experience," *Atlanta Economics Review*, July-August 1976, pp. 5–12.

[3]Merewitz, L., and S. Sosnick, *The Budgets' New Clothes* (Markheim Series), Rand McNally, 1971, chapter 5.

[4]Minmier, George S., "An Evaluation of the Zero-Base Budgeting System in Government Institutions," *Research Monograph No. 68,* Georgia State University: Publishing Services Division, School of Business Administration, 1975.

would be the amount of budget required to perform the current level of activity (adjusted for inflation). Finally, the highest level of activity should include a budget for any new activities to be performed. This might be limited to 125 percent of the current budgeted amount.

The preparation of this type of analysis requires considerable time, effort, and training. It is particularly difficult to identify relevant output measures. These are typically not identified in many hospital departments. Gross measurements, such as patient days, are not valid indicators of effectiveness or efficiency. Statistical indicators such as case mix, nurse experience or skill levels, or productivity norms, would probably be needed before realistic decision packages could be developed.

The ranking process

After the initial development of the decision packages, all of the supervisory levels must become involved in the ranking process. For example, the nursing supervisor would be required to give a priority ranking for all the decision packages submitted from team leaders or head nurses who have already assigned their priority rankings. In theory, each decision package should be ranked in order of decreasing benefits to the organization.

Peter Phyrr describes the ranking process as an answer to the questions: How much should we spend? Where (or for what) should we spend it?[5] Each manager should rank the packages that he/she prepared, and each supervisor would rank the decision packages of all his/her subordinates. This process would continue, through each level of the organization, until a final list of prioritized decision packages is obtained. A tree diagram, such as *Figure 1,* would result.

Most large hospitals would have to rank a considerable number of decision packages. The state of Georgia had more than 10,000. If an effective review and prioritizing is to be accomplished, sufficient time must be spent at each review level. For example, assuming 500 decision packages and 6 minutes for each decision package, it would require 50 hours to review the entire budget. Clearly, most large hospitals would have more than 500 decision packages and it is doubtful that a thorough analysis could be completed in 6 minutes.

There appears to be a great deal of benefit to be gained from minimizing the number of decision packages. One way of doing so would be to increase the size of the decision package. Yet there is a direct conflict between the size and the ability to complete and evaluate it. The larger the package, the more difficult it is to determine a direct input/output relationship. Clearly, there must be some trade-off between the size and the total number of packages.

---

[5] Phyrr, Peter, "Zero Base Budgeting," *Harvard Business Review*, November-December, 1970, pp. 111–121.

Figure 1
Ranking the decision process

(Not all hospital activity shown—for illustrative purposes only.)

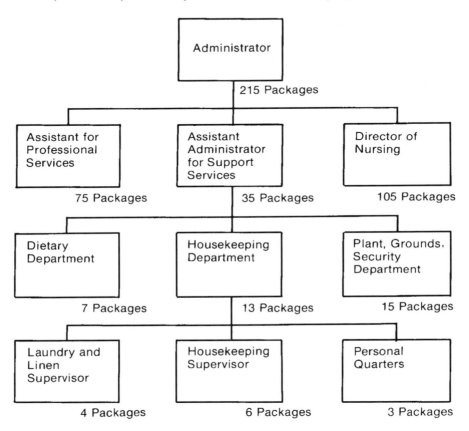

To reduce the time required to rank decision packages, a hospital can establish specific cut-off points for review. Each level of supervision could be required to only review the lower 40 percent of the decision packages. The top ranking packages would be automatically approved. It should be stressed that detailed data on each decision package would be available to the administrator; but the zero base budgeting system should not require that the top-level administrator review every one; there simply is not enough time to do an effective job.

This brief introduction to the zero base budgeting concept should indicate that the implementation of a complete package in a hospital would be a monumental task. However, there are considerable advantages to be gained from its techniques. It forces supervisors to think of their activities and resources. They must determine what can be accomplished for marginal levels of resource expenditures. In addition, they must rank their activities in terms of importance to the hospital or, at least, to their department.

Recommendations

To minimize the costs (and frustration) associated with zero base budgeting, it is recommended that the techniques be applied selectively to a few departments. The process can be gradually expanded to the entire organization. One local hospital selected their housekeeping and laundry departments as a first cut at zero base budgeting.

There are many benefits to a selective application. First, it minimizes the impact on the total organization. Secondly, managers can develop a reservoir of experience. Finally, the organization has the opportunity to gradually refine and improve its guidelines and instruction.

Regardless of which approach is used, there are several key steps which must precede implementation:

1. Top management must support it, especially in the initial steps and in the commitments to use decision packages in allocating resources.
2. Adequate instructions must be developed so that each supervisor knows what information is required and how it should be prepared.
3. Sufficient time must be allowed both for the design of decision packages and for review of each set of decision packages.
4. The accounting system must be able to provide the data required for the decision package.

Conclusion

The zero base budgeting process offers a management technique for the administrator and for all levels of health service management to get more fully involved in the budget process. It enables the administrator to make a more constructive allocation of resources. Zero base budgeting is not a panacea; it is a tool that requires careful preparation to be effective.

There are other alternatives that the administrator should consider. One is to adopt the "sunset law" concept and only review a department (or set of decision packages) in detail every few years. It is questionable that zero base budgeting must be an annual process to be utilized effectively and the basic similarities between the requirements of an in-depth sunset review and the zero base budgeting process make this a variable alternative.

Performance auditing is another alternative. It embodies an evaluation of managers and their results in improving the efficiency and effectiveness of an activity. Even though it does not include a ranking of activities, it does have the advantage of not requiring a change in the budget process or in the accounting system. Sunset reviews and performance auditing will offer many of the benefits of zero base budgeting at a lower cost and at a lower level of frustration.

Summary

The cost containment environment confronting most hospital administrators requires that all activities in a hospital be evaluated in a cost/benefit mode. Zero base budgeting is one way to accomplish this task. The administrator who desires to implement a zero base budget is encouraged to read the "Additional readings suggested by the authors" as the first step in implementing the process.

Keywords: decision package; zero base budget.

Additional readings suggested by the authors

Anderson, Donald N., "Zero-Base Budgeting—How to Get Rid of Corporate Crabgrass," *Management Review,* Vol. 65, October 1976, pp. 4–16.

Carbutt, Michael H., and George S. Minmier, "Incremental, Planned, Programmed and Zero-Base Budgeting," *Public Finance and Accountancy,* November 1974, pp. 350–357.

Granof, Michael H., and Dale A. Kinzel, "Zero-Based Budgeting: Modest Proposal for Reform," *Federal Accountant,* Vol. 23, December 1974, pp. 50–56.

Miller, Karla, "Zero Budgeting Works in Yonkers, N.Y.," *Government Executive,* January 1977, pp. 39–40.

Murray, T.J., "Tough Job of Zero Budgeting," *Duns,* Vol. 104, October 1974, pp. 70–72.

Phyrr, Peter A., "Zero Base Budgeting," MBA, April 1977, pp. 25–31.

———, *Zero Base Budgeting: A Practical Tool for Evaluating Expenses* (Systems and Controls for Financial Management Series), New York: Wiley-Interscience, 1973.

———, "Zero Base Budgeting: Where to Use it and How to Begin," *Advanced Management Journal,* Vol. 41, Summer 1976, pp. 4–14.

Singleton, David, Bruce A. Smith, and James R. Cleaveland, "Zero-Based Budgeting in Wilmington, Delaware," *Governmental Finance,* August 1976, pp. 20–29.

Stonich, Paul J., and William H. St. Eeves, "Zero-Based Planning and Budgeting for Utilities, *Public Utilities Fortnightly,* Vol. 98, No. 6, September 9, 1976, pp. 24–29.

Suver, James, and Ray Brown, "Where Does Zero-Base Budgeting Work?" *Harvard Business Review,* November-December 1977, pp. 76–84.

Sample Decision Packages

The following decision packages were developed as illustrations to show the diversity of approaches that can be used to design packages.

Sample Format

Package Name _____ Department _____

Management Review Level _____ (Organizational Level)

Prepared By _____ Approved By _____

Purpose of Activity:

Description of Activity:

Resources Required:

	Current Year	Budget Year	Change/%
Personnel (FTE)			
Salary			
Fringe			
Equipment			
Supplies			
Travel			
Other:			
Total $			

Activity Measurements

Effectiveness:

Efficiency:

Benefits of Approval:

Consequences of Nonapproval:

Incremental Package Numbers: Resources Required & Output Achieved
1.
2.
3.

Decision Package 1

Package Name: Financial Analysis   Department: Finance

Management Review Level _____ (Organizational Level)

Prepared By _____ Approved By _____

Purpose of Activity:

To provide the necessary financial reporting and analytical functions for a
large university medical center.

Description of Activity:

Responsible for the preparation and
distribution of:
—Monthly financial statements
—Annual financial reports
—Accounts receivable reconciliation
—Hospital administrative services
—Statistical charts

Performs accounts receivable analysis
and correction.

Responsible for performing special financial analyses at the request of the
state or administration.

Resources Required:

	Current Year	Budget Year	Change %
Personnel (FTE)	4	5	10.0
Salary	42,168	51,792	22.8
Fringe	4,428	5,438	22.8
Equipment			
Supplies	500	550	10.0
Travel			
Other			
Total	$47,096	57,780	

Activity Measurements

Effectiveness:

Employees have been averaging 200
hours of overtime per year per employee,
which is an indicator of inadequate staffing to fully assume assigned responsibilities. Effectiveness is impaired.

Efficiency:

Overall efficiency is decreased due to the
heavy overtime schedule. Accountants
borrowed from other sections which in-
terrupts daily activity and overall efficiency of the office.

Benefits of Approval:
—Provides the required manpower for effective timely financial reporting and
analysis in a rapidly growing institution.
—Provides the required manpower to meet increased demands of state and federal
governments as well as central administration.

Consequences of Nonapproval:
—Financial statements would be late, Executive Budget Office report would not meet
the deadline, and there would be little reconciliation of Accounts Receivable.
Overall effectiveness of the Finance Office would be curtailed because other
sections are picking up part of the workload.

Incremental Package Numbers:	Resources Required and Output Achieved
1) 3 FTEs instead of 4 FTEs for entire Finance Ofc. $28,872	75%
2) 2 FTEs instead of 4 FTEs for entire Finance Ofc. $19,248	50%
3) 1 FTE instead of 4 FTEs for entire Finance Ofc. $9,624	25%

Decision Package 2

Program Area:

Housekeeping

Activity:

Stripping, sealing, waxing of floors

Objective:

To provide technically correct floor protection to all of the necessary square footage to increase the lifetime of the floor and to provide an aesthetically pleasing environment.

Activity Description:

Specially trained floor care specialists, on year-round, regular basis, would strip, seal, and wax each appropriate square foot of floor in the institution at least once a year. High traffic areas would need more frequent attention.

Costs:

Personnel:	2 FTEs @ 6,760	$13,520
Supplies:	Stripper, sealer, wax for 90,000 sq. ft.	
	scrub and buff pads	2,300
Equipment:	No New Purchases Necessary	—
Total:		$15,820

Benefits:

Effective floor protection and aesthetic environment without decreasing the general cleaning standards presently adhered to. Shift to floor care specialists will not require more departmental FTEs, will provide other (fewer) sanitarians more time for general care, will place floor care responsibility on identifiable individuals, who will be responsible for use of floor care supplies and maintenance of expensive machinery. Presently 90,000 sq. ft. are waxed irregularly once a year. This program will allow 30,000 sq. ft. of high traffic area to be cared for twice yearly; 10,000 sq. ft. will be cared for 3 times yearly.

Alternatives: Same Result:

1. Contract to wax 30 + 30 + 10K = 130,000 sq. ft. yearly @ .15/sq. ft. = $19,500.

Alternatives: Different Effort Levels:

	Alternatives	Benefits	Resource	
1.	Care for	loss of 3rd	salaries (1.75 FTE)	11,830
	120,000 sq. ft.	waxing/yr.	supplies (.92 × 2300)	2,116
				13,946
2.	Care for	loss of 2nd &	salaries 1 FTE	6,760
	90,000 sq. ft.	3rd wax/yr.	supplies (.69 = 2300)	1,587
				8,347
3.	Do no floor	loss of all floor		-0-
	care activity	protection & aesthetics		

Decision Package 3

Program Area:

Materials Management

Activity:

Supplies and equipment management

Objective:

To manage the institution's inventory in an efficient and scientific manner to achieve the twin goals of cost reduction and stockout elimination.

Activity Description:

A trained inventory manager would, on an ongoing regular basis, establish and maintain supplies and equipment storerooms, a physical inventory record of all equipment and supplies on hand, optimum reorder points and quantities, and would monitor the actual flow and expense to user departments against the budgeted volume and dollar figures.

Costs:

Personnel	2 FTEs	1 manager	$11,000
		1 assistant	7,000
			$18,000
Supplies:	Stock control forms, etc.		1,000
Total:			$19,000

Benefits:

Shift to full-time inventory manager would continue to provide all the services presently rendered (partial storeroom mgt., partial equipment mgt., shipping & receiving) and would substitute trained inventory mgt. hours for presently unskilled hours trying to do that job. Those unskilled hours would be used more efficiently on tasks appropriate to the skill level because that person would be supervised by the inventory manager. For the same amount of budgeted expense, this program can expect to totally eliminate stock-out problems and reduce inventory carrying costs by 20% over the last year.

Alternative: Same Result

1. Replace present shipping and receiving clerk and hire a new trained inventory manager. Cost = $11,000, plus present supplies manager at 11,000. Total, $22,000.

Alternatives: Varying Effort Level:

	Alternatives	Benefit	Resource	
1.	Maintain present system	loss of inventory cost reduction	1.5 FTE	$12,000
2.	Eliminate part-time supplies mgt. function	loss of cost reduction & stockout elimination benefits	1 FTE	7,000

Decision Package 4

Program Area:

Department of Pediatrics

Activity:

Pediatrics Day Treatment Program

Objective:

To provide medical, educational, and psychological services on a daytime outpatient basis to asthma pediatric patients. These patients require special services which cannot be provided in an ordinary school situation.

Activity Description:

This is a pilot program which may be expanded into an ongoing activity of the hospital. The program would provide medical and psychological support services for five to six students in a classroom setting. The hospital would use psychiatrist, psychologist, nurse, social worker, and physician personnel to supply these support services.

Activity Benefit/Result:

This pilot program is intended to demonstrate the benefit of integrating psychological, medical, and educational services in the treatment of the asthmatic pediatric patient.

Resources (Minimum Level):

		Direct Expenses (12 mos.)
Salaries:	1 half-time psychologist	$10,500
	1 1/4-time psychiatrist	9,000
	1 half-time R.N.	6,000
	1 half-time psychiatric social worker II	14,000
Supplies:	School lunches for 5 children	1,500
	Supplies and expenses	2,500
		$43,500
Subtotal:	Employee benefits	11,912
	Indirect expense	16,142
Total		$71,554

Alternative Way of Accomplishing the Same Result: Comprehensive evaluation of each student

Complete psychological assessment	$400
Psychiatric evaluation	100
Parents psychological evaluation	90
Nursing evaluation	10
Physical evaluation	40
Total	$640

Performance standards* Vice President, Fiscal Affairs

Financial solvency

1. Cash management

   a. Responsible for monitoring the implementation of aggressive cash management strategies to maximize investment income.

   Performance is acceptable when monthly bank statements report that the average bank balance does not exceed the balance required to service the account.

   b. Responsible for monitoring funding of depreciation consistent with corporate policies.

   Performance is acceptable when the hospital's accounting records report that annual depreciation has been funded.

   c. Responsible for monitoring deposits of cash receipts on a timely basis.

   Performance is acceptable when daily cash receipts are deposited within twenty-four hours. The vice president monitors compliance weekly.

   d. Responsible for monitoring funding of accounts payable on a timely basis.

   Performance is acceptable when all discounted payables are paid on the tenth of each month, when all other vendors are paid on the twenty-fifth day of each month, when all scheduled payments are paid when due and when payrolls are funded when due.

   e. Responsible for providing adequate working capital.

   Performance is acceptable when the ratio of current assets to current liabilities is one and one-half to one as documented by the hospital's interim financial statements.

   f. Responsible for monitoring that inventory levels do not exceed needs.

   Performance is acceptable when inventories are turned over at least eight times a year as documented by issue reports.

---

* Adapted and reprinted by permission from Saint Joseph Hospital, Denver, Colorado.

g. Responsible for monitoring accounts receivable on a regular and ongoing basis.

Performance is acceptable when gross accounts receivable represent not more than forty-five days of revenues.

h. Responsible for reviewing and approving annual cost reports for Medicare and Medicaid.

Performance is acceptable when annual cost reports for Medicare and Medicaid are filed on a timely basis, and when final settlements do not exceed $250,000.

i. Responsible for negotiating Medicaid per diems annually.

Performance is acceptable when Medicaid per diem rates have been negotiated at the highest level under existing reimbursement formulas.

j. Responsible for reviewing and monitoring quarterly construction cash flow updates.

Performance is acceptable when quarterly construction cash flow updates have been presented to and reviewed by the president and the board of directors.

2. Financial reports

a. Responsible for the review of interim financial statements and written interpretations.

Performance is acceptable when interim financial statements are released on the fifteenth working day of each calendar month accompanied by an executive summary highlighting major events.

b. Responsible for reviewing and monitoring all departmental operating statements

Performance is acceptable when departmental operating statements have been reviewed on an ongoing basis and when the president has been informed of trends as well as areas for corrective action.

c. Responsible for reviewing and monitoring quarterly financial analyses.

Performance is acceptable when quarterly financial reviews are published and distributed by the fortieth working day following the end of each quarter, accompanied by an executive summary highlighting major financial events.

d. Responsible for reviewing and monitoring special financial reports such as productivity analyses, overtime reports, contract labor reports, etc.

Performance is acceptable when all special reports have been monitored, when the president has been made aware of trends and when recommendations have been made for corrective action wherever called for.

e. Responsible for reviewing and monitoring the approved capital expenditure forecast.

Performance is acceptable when quarterly comparative capital expenditure reports have been reviewed within forty-five days of the end of each quarter, and when the president has been advised of significant variances.

f. Responsible for reviewing the efficacy, practicability, and usefulness of all computerized statistical and financial reports.

Performance is acceptable when all computerized statistical and financial reports generated by computer information services have been reviewed for accuracy, efficacy, and usefulness, and when the president has been advised as to their use, add-on's, or elimination.

g. Responsible for reviewing all new applications for computerized statistical and financial information systems.

Performance is acceptable when all new applications for computerized statistical and financial information have been reviewed, and when the president has been advised of the recommendations relative to implementation.

h. Responsible for reviewing the annual audited financial statements prepared by the hospital's public accountants.

Performance is acceptable when the annual audited financial statements have been reviewed, and when the president has been advised of significant changes in financial position and reasons why.

i. Responsible for reviewing the recommendations prepared by the hospital's public accountants.

Performance is acceptable when the accountants' recommendations have been reviewed, and when the president and the board of directors have been advised of their implementation or lack thereof.

j. Responsible for reviewing and monitoring all statistical and financial reports that directly affect the performance of the departments under his/her administrative jurisdiction.

Performance is acceptable when all statistical and financial reports directly impacting performance of these departments have been reviewed and monitored, and when corrective action has been taken to remove deficiencies.

3. Budgets

a. Responsible for the preparation and review of the annual operating budget and three-year capital expenditure forecast.

Performance is acceptable when the annual operating budget and three-year capital expenditure forecast have been prepared and reviewed for completeness and accuracy, when the forecasts have been reviewed with vice presidents and their respective department directors and when the forecasts have been presented for approval to the president, governing bodies and other agencies as provided for by law.

b. Responsible for the review of all lead schedules relating to significant changes in categories of expense, departmental productivity, and FTEs as forecasted in the annual operating budget.

Performance is acceptable when all lead schedules have been reviewed, when the president has been advised of significant variances and their potential impact on the competitive status of the hospital in the community and when recommendations for corrective action have been submitted to the president.

4. Communication and education

   a. Responsible for keeping the president informed of significant internal and external events.

     Performance is acceptable when the president has been informed of significant internal or external events, their possible implications and the pros and cons of alternative solutions.

   b. Responsible for keeping the department directors under his/her administrative jurisdiction informed of significant internal and external events.

     Performance is acceptable when he/she meets with his/her department directors regularly and when he/she meets with employees of each of his/her departments at least quarterly.

   c. Responsible for attending meetings of the administrative council, the operations committee, the board of directors, Health Services Corporation, and finance committee of the hospital executive council.

     Performance is acceptable when meetings of the administrative council, the operations committee, etc., have been attended on a regular basis.

   d. Responsible for reviewing and approving the annual operations plan, as well as the performance standards of each of the directors and supervisors under his/her jurisdiction.

     Performance is acceptable when the annual operations plan, as well as the performance standards of each director, assistant director, and supervisor of departments under his/her administrative jurisdiction, have been reviewed, approved and submitted to the president on a timely basis.

   e. Responsible for the annual evaluation of department directors under his/her administrative jurisdiction.

     Performance is acceptable when the annual evaluation of departmental directors under his/her jurisdiction has been submitted to the president on a timely basis, in an approved format.

5. Public relations

   a. Responsible for monitoring and developing relationships with external agencies, including Blue Cross, Medicare, Department of Social Services, etc.

     Performance is acceptable when meetings of external agencies are attended regularly and when the president has been advised of significant developments that affect the hospital's financial position.

   b. Responsible for monitoring and developing relationship with the medical staff.

     Performance is acceptable when he/she regularly attends meetings of the executive committee.

c. Responsible for monitoring and developing relationships with the hospital executive committee.

Performance is acceptable when meetings of the hospital executive council are attended on a regular basis, and when he/she regularly interacts with members of the finance committee.

d. Responsible for monitoring and developing relationships with the hospital's public accountants.

Performance is acceptable when he/she interacts regularly with local and national representatives of the hospital's auditors.

6. Contracts

a. Responsible for the review and negotiation of all contracts and agreements underwritten by the hospital.

Performance is acceptable when all contracts and agreements have been reviewed on a timely basis and when the president has been advised of the accuracy and completeness of contracts, possible deficiencies, and alternative approaches.

CHAPTER 6

Flexible budgeting, standard costs, and variance analysis

"I know I spent more than my budget but my costs for fuel have more than doubled since the budget was approved."

"Since our budget was based on 60,000 visits, and we are providing more, does that mean we have to throw the whole budget out?"

"The manager of the laboratory is correct—he said that he has no control over volume, so his cost should have gone up—but should it have increased 100 percent?"

"How can we determine how much it should cost to perform a CT scan?"

"It is not my fault that personnel gave me more senior nurses than I requested. Senior RNs were not in my budget."

"Our volume is down 10 percent. I want every supervisor to cut their expenditures by 10 percent."

Introduction

In earlier chapters, we introduced the concepts of cost behavior, budgeting, and responsibility centers. An important use of these techniques is in performance measurement. Performance measurement requires the development of standards to compare with the actual costs incurred. In this chapter, we will focus on developing the relationship between cost behavior, standards, and performance measurement.

The flexible budget concept

In preparing a budget for a new operating period, most healthcare organizations forecast the most likely demand for services for the budget period. This forecasted or predicted demand is used in developing the revenue, expense, and cash flow budgets. This single volume approach is generally satisfactory for the planning process and for initially establishing a standard to measure performance. However, for performance measurement purposes, the initial budget will need to be adjusted for changes between the actual and predicted volume and the resulting impact on total variable costs.

In our discussion of fixed and variable costs in chapter 2, we developed the concept that total variable costs will change as the level of activity changes (TVC = VC_U × Q). The recognition of this relationship forms the basis for the management accounting technique called *flexible budgeting*. The flexible budget allows management to incorporate volume changes in the budgeted amounts to be used to compare with the actual costs incurred to more accurately evaluate the performance of the manager. *Exhibits 6–1* and *6–2* illustrate the impact of using a static budget approach (the planned budget is not adjusted for volume changes) and the flexible budget approach which adjusts the budget.

In these examples, the following data are used:

variable cost per unit	$ 5.00
total fixed costs	$10,000
planned number of procedures	5,000

The flexible budget formula for this example is:

$$TC = TFC + VC_U \times Q$$
$$\$35,000 = \$10,000 + \$5(5000)$$
($35,000 will be the static budget for this department when 5,000 procedures were estimated to be completed)

Given the information presented in *Exhibit 6–1*, did the supervisor do a good job if 4,000 procedures were completed? 5,000? 6,000? Using the static budget approach, the supervisor came in $4,500 under budget at 4,000 procedures, $500 under at 5,000, and $6,000 unfavorable at 6,000 procedures. Would you give a bonus if 4,000 or 5,000 procedures were completed or a poor cost performance rating if 6,000 were completed? In *Exhibit 6–2*, the same data is used in a flexible budget format.

How does this information influence your decision? In this analysis, the supervisor was successful in controlling costs at the planned volume while the flexible budget was exceeded at the other two volumes. Most supervisors recognize that costs should be reduced as volume declines. Conversely, costs should increase as volume increases. The question is

Exhibit 6–1
Static budget performance evaluation

Actual number of procedures	Actual costs	Planned budget (based on 5,000 procedures)	Variance
4,000	$30,500	$35,000	$4,500 F
5,000	34,500	35,000	500 F
6,000	41,000	35,000	6,000 U

Exhibit 6–2
Flexible budget variance analysis

Actual volume	Actual costs	Flexible budget	Variance
4,000	$30,500	$10,000 + $5(4,000) = $30,000	$ 500 U
5,000	34,500	10,000 + 5(5,000) = 35,000	500 F
6,000	41,000	10,000 + 5(6,000) = 40,000	1,000 U

Estimated number of procedures: 5,000
Cost function: $10,000 + $5 per procedure
Budget for 4,000 procedures is: $10,000 + $5(4,000) = $30,000
Budget for 5,000 procedures is: $10,000 + $5(5,000) = $35,000
Budget for 6,000 procedures is: $10,000 + $5(6,000) = $40,000

"by how much *should* the costs have changed as the volume changed?" The flexible budget answers this question. However, unless fixed and variable costs are determined during the budget process, the flexible budget concept cannot be used.

It is usually more effective and efficient to control expenditures before they occur rather than to affix blame after the fact. The development of a flexible budget during the planning process can help solve this management problem. For example, using the format developed in *Exhibit 6–3* the manager can easily forecast the impact of volume changes on total costs. A flexible budget formula is then effective for both planning and control.

Given these relationships, department supervisors can monitor their own spending patterns as volume changes.

Exhibit 6–3
Flexible budget—month of January 1980
Emergency room services
(based on number of patient visits)

Cost category	Budget formula		Jan. budget
	Fixed	Variable	(1,500 visits)
Salary expenses	$12,000	2.00	$15,000
Employee benefits	9,000	-0-	9,000
Professional fees	4,000	-0-	4,000
Drug expense	-0-	.70	1,050
General supplies	-0-	3.00	4,500
Repairs and maintenance	60	-0-	60
Telephone	18	-0-	18
Miscellaneous	-0-	1.00	1,500
TOTAL	$25,078	$6.70	$35,128

January budget based on 1,500 visits

Administrators and department managers may question the accuracy of fixed and variable cost components determined for individual services or departments. The more important concept is to recognize that fixed and variable costs exist and to make the best possible estimate of their relative amounts. Most short-term, acute hospitals have fixed costs in the 75 to 80 percent range because of the heavy investment in physical assets and most employees are on salaries. Other types of healthcare providers with a heavy volume of fee-for-service business could have significantly different proportions with variable costs constituting a much greater percentage than the typical short-term, acute hospital. The amounts will change by the type of organization and the philosophy of top management. The key is intelligent use of the concept in decision making.

Determining flexible budgets

Flexible budgets are computed from cost behavior equations that must be identified using any of the processes discussed in the earlier chapters. To be specific, a cost behavior equation must be identified for each cost category in a department, or a separate equation must be identified for the entire department as a unit. The cost behavior equation will indicate the portion of costs that are fixed, for some time period or range of services, and it will indicate the portion of costs that are variable. The general form of such an equation will be:

$$y = a + b (x) \text{ where } a = \text{intercept (est. fixed costs)}$$
$$b = \text{variable cost per unit}$$
$$x = \text{varying service levels}$$
$$y = \text{total costs}$$

Such an equation is usually created for each cost element, such as supplies, nursing salaries, administrative salaries, other overhead costs, etc. This equation is then used to determine the budgeted or estimated costs for each cost element, given the estimated fixed costs, the variable cost per unit, and the estimated service level for the next period. For example, if the equation for supply costs is:

$$y = 15,000 + 10.00 (x)$$

where x = number of lab tests, which are estimated to be at a level of 1,000 tests for next month. At 1,000 tests:

$$y = 15,000 + 10.00 (1,000) = 15,000 + 10,000 = 25,000$$

In this case, total costs for supplies would be estimated at $25,000. This amount would be included in the flexible budget for the next month.

These equations will be obtained through a combination of the high-low method, account analysis, expert opinion, regression analysis, and other cost behavior identification methods. These methods have been discussed in earlier chapters and will not be reviewed here. However, some further clarification about how to discern the flexible budget equation from historical data is now relevant.

If the budget analyst or department manager has historical data on several prior months' costs and activity data, a high-low analysis can be conducted on each pair of observations (i.e., January and February, February and March, etc.). The analyst should proceed as follows:

1. Identify any fixed costs that do not seem to change from one month to the next. All fixed costs will fit the equation form of $y = a$, or $y =$ estimated fixed costs for any month.
2. For all other costs, compute the average cost per unit of service (i.e., divide the monthly cost for each cost element by the units of service in that month). If the same ratio ("b" in the previous equations) is not obtained for each month, then that cost element is a mixed cost and a high-low analysis must be conducted for that cost element. If the average cost is the same for each month, then that average is the variable cost per unit (i.e., the "b" coefficient).
3. For all mixed costs, conduct a high-low analysis and derive a flexible budget equation of the form:

$$y = a + b\,(x).$$

Use this equation to forecast the costs for the estimated volume of services for the next period.

Exhibit 6–4 indicates how this sequence of cost determinations will usually occur in a flexible budgeting process. This set of steps should not be viewed as a rigid format, but rather as a set of steps that is generally appropriate and that may need to be modified in difficult or unusual circumstances.

In the final budget for March, the equations would not generally be separately shown. The flexible budget for March could include separate columns for actual costs for January and February and the forecasted costs for March, or it could include data for March of the prior year, total costs for the year-to-date, and budgeted costs for the year-to-date. Budget formats are selected by each organization, hopefully with input from department managers.

It is not our purpose to specify a "correct" format for the final budget report, but rather to indicate our experience regarding possible ways to construct and use flexible budgets. In most circumstances, a volume-driven budget is preferable to a static budget. The impact of volume changes is often ignored when costs are forecast or when budgets are derived or evaluated. The purpose of flexible budgeting is to include these impacts as they are appropriate and to make the impact of volume changes more prominent in the healthcare managers' budgeting and evaluation processes.

Exhibit 6–4
Development of the flexible budget

Month	January	February
Number of tests	1,000	1,500
Salaries	$40,000	$50,000
Utilities	1,000	1,400
Supplies	300	400
Indirect Materials	4,000	6,000
Depreciation	5,000	5,000
Payroll Taxes	6,000	7,500
TOTAL	$56,300	$70,300

Step 1.
   The only apparent fixed costs are depreciation costs which would be estimated at 5,000 per month (y = 5,000).

Step 2.
   Divide the remaining costs by the number of tests each month.

	January	February
Salaries	40.00	33.33
Utilities	1.00	.93
Supplies	.30	.27
Indirect Materials	4.00	4.00
Payroll Taxes	6.00	5.00

The only apparent variable costs are indirect materials which would be estimated at 4.00 per test [y = 4.00 (x)].

Step 3.
   Conduct high-low analysis on the remaining cost elements.

Salaries
$(50,000 - 40,000) / (1,500 - 1,000) = 20.00$
$50,000 = a + 20.00 (1,500) = a + 30,000$
therefore, a = 20,000 and the flexible budget
formula for Salaries is: y = 20,000 + 20.00 (x)

Utilities
$(1,400 - 1,000) / (1,500 - 1,000) = .80$
$1,400 = a + .80 (1,500) = a + 1,200$
therefore, a = 200 and the flexible budget
formula for Utilities is:
y = 200 + .80 (x)

Supplies
$(400 - 300) / (1,500 - 1,000) = .20$
$400 = a + .20 (1,500) = a + 300$
therefore, a = 100 and the flexible budget
formula for Supplies is:
y = 100 + .20 (x)

Indirect Materials   y = 4.00 (x) as determined in Step 2
Depreciation   y = 5,000 as determined in Step 1
Payroll Taxes $(7,500 - 6,000) / (1,500 - 1,000) = 3.00$
                      $7,500 = a + 3.00 (1,500) = a + 4,500$

therefore, a = 3,000 and the flexible budget formula for Payroll Taxes is:

$$y = 3,000 + 3.00 (x)$$

Step 4.

Estimate the level of services, in this case the number of tests, for the next month. The estimate is for 1,200 tests to be required in March.

Step 5.

Insert the estimated volume of services into each flexible budget formula and calculate the estimated costs for each cost element.

Salaries	$y =$	20,000 +	20.00 (1,200) =	44,000
Utilities	$y =$	200 +	.80 (1,200) =	1,160
Supplies	$y =$	100 +	.20 (1,200) =	340
Indirect Materials	$y =$	0 +	4.00 (1,200) =	4,800
Depreciation	$y =$	5,000 +	0 =	5,000
Payroll Taxes	$y =$	3,000 +	3.00 (1,200) =	6,600
Total		28,300 +	28 (1,200) =	61,900

Standard cost systems

In the development of a flexible budget, we were in effect using the concept of a standard cost although we did not label it as such (a budget is really a group of standards). Basically, a standard cost represents what a procedure or service *should* cost. It is a detailed estimate of the amount of resources required to provide a specific procedure, test, or service within professionally determined quality of care constraints and in an efficient manner.

The use of standard costs can provide several important benefits:

1. The development of standard costs is a vital part of the flexible budgeting process. Because they are carefully predetermined, future oriented costs, standard costs are the basic building blocks for preparing effective budgets.
2. Standard costs provide a basis for measuring management performance by permitting the comparison of the actual costs incurred with the planned standard costs. Information can then be obtained to explain differences between these two costs. Managers can determine why the differences occurred and whether corrective action is needed.
3. Standard costs can be useful in making future decisions where the analysis is dependent on cost estimates.
4. Standard costs provide a more rational and useful basis for inventory valuation. They can also simplify accounting systems and/or procedures, especially concerning inventory management. For example, inventory items can be carried or transferred within the organization at standard, not actual, cost. In high volume

areas such as pharmacy, this could simplify record keeping and billing to patients.

5. Standard costs can be very useful in establishing charges for procedures or services.

Development of standard costs

A standard cost is composed of two key factors: 1) the amount and type of resources required to provide the test, service, and/or procedure; and 2) the per unit cost of each of the resources. The amount and type of resources is properly a function of the clinical professional, who has the necessary clinical background and experience to insure that quality of care concerns are met. The determination of the cost of the service is influenced by management decisions such as equipment cost, salary schedules, and sources of capital. Management personnel have an obligation to provide the required resources in an effective and efficient manner. The development of standard costs requires a joint effort of the medical staff and management personnel. It is not properly the sole responsibility of the accounting department, even though they play an important role in the process. *Exhibit 6–5* indicates possible sources of data in establishing standards in a healthcare provider.

In developing the standard costs for a laboratory procedure, it is necessary to estimate the time required, by type of equipment, as well as the time it takes technicians to take the sample and read the results. The quantity of lab supplies and associated costs required would also be estimated. These labor and material costs are combined with overhead and administrative costs to determine the total cost, which then becomes the standard cost for the particular test. An example of these calculations is shown in *Exhibit 6–6*.

These calculations include as direct costs the variable costs of labor as well as the fixed cost of depreciation on the equipment used. Indirect

Exhibit 6–5
Source of standards

Cost determination
- External Authoritative Source such as professional associations or consultants
- Internal Industrial Engineering Staff
- Averages [Ratio of Cost to Charges (RCC), Relative Value Units (RVU)] per unit costs from accounting records and case-mix data

Resource use determination
- Medical staff
- Nursing staff
- Other allied health professionals
- Medical records
- Regulatory agencies

Exhibit 6–6
Standard cost for one lab procedure
Chemistry examination (Type A1)

Estimated direct technician's time	15 minutes	
Estimated direct lab materials		$ 2
Equipment use time	5 minutes	
Total department fixed overhead (excluding depreciation)		$100,000
Planned hourly salary of technician		$ 16
Monthly depreciation expense on equipment used in exam		$ 2,000
Estimated number of tests to be performed monthly on Equipment E1	10,000	
Estimated total number of procedures to be performed in lab during the month*	50,000	

The standard cost for the procedure Type A1 would be:

Direct labor** (15/60 × $16.00)=	$ 4.00
Direct materials =	2.00
Total direct variable costs	$ 6.00
Equipment charge (***depreciation $2,000/10,000) = total costs/total units=	.20
Total direct costs	$ 6.20
Fixed overhead costs $100,000/50,000 =	2.00
Chemistry procedure Type A1 standard direct costs	$ 8.20
Indirect general and administrative costs (40% of direct costs)	3.28
Total standard costs	$11.48

*Note that Equipment E1 is used for only 10,000 tests during the month while the laboratory performs a total of 50,000 procedures.
**Labor is considered a variable cost in standard costing in this example. However, it is not a true variable cost if the technician is paid on a salary basis as defined in chapter 2. The time is the variable factor.
***Depreciation may be calculated on the basis of time or the units processed.

costs, which would include the depreciation on the building and other general fixed assets, are not directly traceable to this particular test, but are also included in the total standard cost. Note that both the depreciation and the other overhead costs are fixed costs in this case. A standard cost includes both direct and indirect costs. In some cases, indirect costs may be omitted from the standard cost but this is not recommended because of the importance of determining the *full* cost of providing a service.

The information developed in *Exhibit 6–6* indicates the standard cost for performing a chemistry procedure Type A1 should be $11.48. Once this type of analysis has been completed, the resulting standard can be used in budgeting for the laboratory. When computations similar to that in *Exhibit 6–6* have been performed for all or most high volume or expensive procedures, the responsible supervisor has the information necessary to develop the appropriate flexible budget.

In establishing a budget for the laboratory, it is not necessary to include all indirect costs for performance measurement purposes. The indirect general and administrative costs of the healthcare organization are not under the control of the laboratory supervisor. Under responsibility accounting, therefore, they should not be included in the manager's performance evaluation.

It should be stressed at this point that budgets are the standards for approved projects or programs within the department during the budgetary period. Budgets reflect what future costs are expected to be incurred. However, it is customary to associate the term "standard" with *individual* services or procedures and the word "budget" with *total* department costs. We will follow that practice in this text, noting that a budget may or may not be based on standard costs for individual services (depending on whether or not the standard is based on "full" costs or only direct costs).

Standards can also be developed for diagnosis or case-mix systems such as DRGs. *Exhibit 6–7* illustrates an example of a standard cost approach for DRG 154.

Exhibit 6–7
Standard cost (e.g., DRG 154)
Stomach, esophagus, and duodenum procedures

Resources required:

Inpatient care	7 days
Radiology	3 diagnoses
Laboratory	3 procedures
Pharmacy	4 prescriptions
Medical	2 procedures

Resource cost:	*Per unit*	*Per DRG 154*
Inpatient	$210.30	$1,472.10
Radiology	41.00	123.00
Laboratory	10.50	31.50
Pharmacy	20.10	80.40
Medical	45.00	90.00
Other direct costs	$20 per patient day	140.00
	Direct costs subtotal	$1,937.00
Allocated indirect costs @ 45%		871.65
	Total cost	$2,808.65

To summarize, standard costs represent what a service "should cost" in an "effective" and "efficient" healthcare provider. They require: *estimated types of resources, estimated quantity of resources by type, and estimated cost per unit of resource.* The estimated cost per unit requires: *fixed and variable costs components, direct and indirect categories of costs, and an estimate of the volume of services to be provided.*

Types of cost standards

Given the importance of meeting standards and a supervisor's expectations, it is very important that the standards established reflect the objectives of the healthcare organization's management. For example, standards may reflect average performance based on past results, targeted performance level for expected operating conditions, or targeted performance level for optimum operating conditions. Each of these approaches have a different motivational impact on the organization.

In some healthcare organizations, the objective might be to have the standards reflect what the costs *should* be if everything were accomplished at maximum levels of efficiency. This type of standard represents an *ideal* standard; that is, all employees would work at maximum efficiency, equipment would never break down, and there would be no time delays in obtaining patients or resources. Clearly, this type of standard will generally be impossible to meet and sizeable variances will occur (a variance is the difference between standard and actual costs). The strength of an ideal standard (also called a theoretical standard) is that it sets a high standard example for employees to meet.

However, if a standard is clearly impossible to meet, employees may become disenchanted and lose their motivation to reach it. The *ideal* standard may be ignored, or employees may sabotage the whole performance reporting process in their attempts to "meet" or "beat" the budget.

A more realistic standard would be based on the degree of efficiency that the department is expected to achieve. This type of standard would make allowances for retesting and repeating of tests, slack time, and human limitations. Standards of this type are usually called *currently attainable standards.* They generally result in more meaningful variances than the ideal standard and are more useful in planning for employee/staffing and materials requirements. They result in more predictable cash flows and shorter turnaround times for reporting results.

Given the difficulty and time consumed in establishing accurate standards, some managers incorporate a long-term orientation (learning and/or startup factors are included) in the standard cost computation. For example, the rate of usage is normally expected to be low during the first year a new service such as the CAT scan is offered. A standard cost could be established, based on projected volume for the third or fourth year.

Thus, sizeable variances during the startup periods would be expected. However, these variances would be expected to decrease as the service reached projected usage rates. For management control purposes, effective variance analysis should not (and could not) be accomplished until the end of the startup period is reached.

In a situation where the expected level of services fluctuates widely over several budget periods, a projected long-run average volume of services could be used in establishing the standard cost. Such a standard, called a *normal* standard, minimizes the impact of volume changes on fixed cost allocations. The favorable and unfavorable variances would be expected to offset each other over several budget periods. Such variances are not controllable in the short-run, but would be monitored over several periods.

Standard cost systems and the control process

The financial accounting systems of all healthcare organizations collect actual costs; that is, as salaries are paid and supplies utilized, the actual costs are collected in the accounting records. Because most managers have less than perfect forecasting and estimating capabilities, the actual costs will usually differ from the planned (budgeted) costs. This difference is called a variance. If the actual costs are less than the budget, a favorable variance is normally said to have occurred. Conversely, actual costs higher than the budget are normally considered an unfavorable variance. However, care must be taken when interpreting variances. For example, actual costs less than budgeted may be unfavorable when inappropriate actions were taken to gain the reduction in costs: savings on marketing costs may not be construed as favorable if the result is a loss in market share, and declining revenues. Apparent savings in purchase costs can be achieved by reducing the quality of the purchased materials, which ultimately may result in excess wastage or inaccurate laboratory results and actually increase the total costs of the service. It is important to ensure that quality considerations are applied to all levels of operations and inputs.

The type and relative amount of the variances will influence how much attention should be devoted to a particular department. In order to recommend the corrective action to be taken, the possible causes for the variances need to be determined. Specifically, managers would like to know if the variances were caused by random, uncontrollable factors that may be exogenous to the organization or if the variances could be traced to a policy, procedures, or system breakdown. In all cases, a cost/benefit analysis of the corrective action needs to be calculated before variance analysis as a change agent can be effective. The primary purpose of variance analysis is to provide questions to be answered, not the answer itself.

A general approach to variance analysis

The initial step in performing variance analysis is to start with the approved budget. This budget was approved for a specific volume of input and/or output. If the approved budget is not to be adjusted for volume changes, then a straight comparison between budget and actual results determines the budget variance. In some healthcare organizations, this initial step represents their approach to variance analysis and is called static budget analysis. *Exhibit 6–8* illustrates this concept.

This simplistic approach does not provide meaningful information about the impact of any volume changes or external price increases of resources purchased (i.e., gasoline, energy prices), and can lead to inappropriate action if used in performance evaluation.

This lack of information can be partially alleviated by using the flexible budget concept introduced earlier in this chapter. By adjusting the budget for the impact of volume changes, the comparison with actuals becomes more meaningful. *Exhibit 6–9* illustrates this refinement.

The process of adjusting for volume changes the variance from $20,000 (favorable) to $10,000 (unfavorable) and provides a different assessment to management. If the $2 per test was a variable cost then $30,000 (15,000 × $2) should not have been incurred when the volume was reduced from 40,000 to 25,000 tests.

However, even the use of the flexible budget concept does not provide enough detailed information to adequately determine what corrective action is appropriate. Most healthcare supervisors are confronted with two major types of decisions in their attempts to control costs. One concerns the price to be paid for labor and material; the other relates to the quantities of these resources used. The question of who actually controls the price to be paid for the resources used needs to be answered. In some healthcare organizations, a purchasing agent is responsible for the prices paid and the materials ordered. In some healthcare organizations, department heads may not be able to control the salaries paid to their employees since this may be a function of hospital (or union) salary schedules. In other cases, the department manager may be responsible for placing purchase orders, controlling input prices and negotiating departmental wage levels.

Exhibit 6–8
Static budget variance analysis

Planned budget	–	Actual costs	=	Budget variance
Budget		*Actuals*		
$200,000	–	180,000	=	$20,000 F
	OR			
$200,000	–	210,000	=	$10,000 U

Exhibit 6–9
Flexible budget variance analysis

Given:	Actual costs	$180,000
	Fixed costs	$120,000
	Variable costs	$2 per test
	Planned volume	40,000 tests
	Planned budget	$120,000 + 40,000($2) = $200,000
	Actual volume	25,000 tests
	Flexible budget	$120,000 + 25,000($2) = $170,000

Variance calculations

	Planned budget	Actual		Variance
Static budget analysis	$200,000	$180,000	=	$20,000 F
	Adjusted budget			
Flexible budget analysis	$170,000	$180,000	=	$10,000 U

It seems clear that in order to properly evaluate the differences between the actual costs incurred and the standards established, some separation of the differential effects of price and quantity must be obtained. The remainder of this chapter will concentrate on developing such a model. Price changes and quantity changes are usually the most important factors that affect costs containment. If other factors are also important, a variance analysis model can be developed to reflect these factors.

The variance model

The healthcare manager is interested in the total variance that occurs in a specific department, that is, the difference between the actual costs and the budgeted costs. However, in order to determine if, and what, corrective action is needed, more information is required. *Exhibit 6–10* displays the basic calculation of the total variance for materials and supplies.

How does the manager evaluate the $1,400 variance? Who is responsible for the overspending? Is it the result of a change in price of the materials or were more materials used than planned? Answers to these questions must be obtained if the manager is to take effective action.

Exhibit 6–10
Flexible budget variance for Department A

Actual total material costs	$4,400	
Standard material costs for output achieved*	3,000	
Budget variance	$1,400	Unfavorable

*Based on standards developed during budget cycle.

In order to develop answers to these questions, a general framework for analysis must be developed which can be used for all variable costs such as materials, labor, and variable overhead. This model separates the total variance into price and quantity components, thereby providing more information to the manager. *Exhibit 6–11* depicts this general framework for the variable cost variance.

The major thrust of this framework is to separate the total budget variances into the amounts that were caused by price changes and those that were caused by using more or less than the amount of inputs planned to be used per unit. Given this framework, the $1,400 unfavorable variance in *Exhibit 6–10* can be broken down as illustrated in *Exhibit 6–12*.

The computations in *Exhibit 6–12* indicate that about $400 of the total variance of $1,400 can be explained by the increase in prices. If the Department A supervisor had no control over the prices paid for the materials, then he/she should not be held responsible for this variance. The remaining $1,000 unfavorable variance is a result of using more material than planned.

It should be stressed at this time that variance analysis does not give a definitive indication that the supervisor of Department A was inefficient

Exhibit 6–11
A general framework for variable cost variances

The price/wage variance is the variance which occurs when only the price is allowed to vary. Thus, for the given quantity (actual), the difference in cost due to the price change is determined by taking the difference between the standard price and the actual price.

The usage/efficiency variance is the variance which occurs due strictly to a change in quantity between what was actually used and what should have been used. The price is held constant. Thus, the standard price is multiplied by the difference between the standard quantity that should have been used and the actual quantity used.

The price variance* = $[(AQ_I) \times (AP)] - [(AQ_I) \times (SP)]$ or $AQ_I (AP - SP)$ where,

  AQ_I = actual quantity of input resources used
  AP = actual price paid per unit of resource
  SP = standard price per unit of input

The quantity** variance = $[(AQ_I) \times (SP)] - [(SQ_A) \times (SP)]$ or $SP(AQ_I - SQ_A)$ where,

  AQ_I = actual quantity of input resources used
  SQ_A = standard quantity of inputs that should be used for the actual units of output completed.

*This is called a price variance for materials, a wage or rate variance for labor, and a spending variance for variable overhead.
**This is called a quantity or usage variance for materials, and an efficiency variance for labor and variable overhead.

Exhibit 6–12
Calculating variable cost variances

Material budget planning factors for Department A

Budgeted price per gallon (SP) = $2.00
Standard allowance in gallons for each procedure (SQ_U) = .075

Actual price per gallon (AP) = $2.20
Actual gallons used (AQ_I) = 2,000
Actual total material costs
  (AC) = AP × AQ_I = ($2.20) × (2,000) = $4,400

Actual number of procedures completed = 20,000 (AQ_O)
Standard amount of gallons per procedure = .075 (SQ_U)
(SQ_A) Standard quantity for output achieved = (AQ_O) × (SQ_U)
SQ_A = 20,000 × .075 gal = 1,500 gallons

SC = Flexible budget for output achieved (20,000 procedures)
SC = (SQ_A) × (SP) = 1,500 × $2.00 = $3,000

AC − SC = Total variance
$4,400 − $3,000 = $1,400 Total variance

Price variance for Department A (materials)

(AQ_I × AP) − (AQ_I × SP) = Price Variance
(2,000 × $2.20) − (2,000 × $2.00) = $4,400 − $4,000 or 2,000 × $0.20 = $400
unfavorable price variance*

Quantity variance for Department A (materials)

(AQ_I × SP) − (SQ_A × SP) = Quantity variance
(2,000 × $2.00) − (1,500 × $2.00) = $4,000 − $3,000 = $1,000 unfavorable usage*
variance or 500 × $2.00 = $1,000

*The question as to when a variance is favorable or unfavorable is best answered by
 determining if the supervisor paid more or less than budgeted price and used more or less
 material than the standard allowed.

because of either the price or usage variances. For example, the standards
may have been in error, the materials may have been of an inferior quality,
or the procedure itself may have been changed. It does, however, separate
the causes of the variances, and management can decide whether to investigate further. In most cases the amount of the variance gives some indication of which variance should be investigated further. For example in
this case, the quantity variance is certainly more important than the price
variance. The manager must decide, as a result of subsequent investigation, whether a variance is controllable or not, and by whom.

To summarize the variances presented so far:

1. The price variance represents the difference between the actual
   price paid and the standard price allowed times the actual quantity used, or AQ_I(AP − SP).

2. The quantity variance represents the difference between the actual quantity used and the standard quantity that should have been used for the actual output obtained times the standard price, or $SP(AQ_I - SQ_A)$.
3. Separating the total variance into its price and quantity components provides more information to help the manager decide which variances to investigate further. Breaking the variances into components allows the manager to evaluate the relative importance of each variance.

The labor variance

The variance for labor can be explained using the framework developed for materials. For example, assume the operating results for labor costs in Department A were as indicated in *Exhibit 6–13*.

The total labor cost variance (*Exhibit 6–14*) can be analyzed using the formulas in *Exhibit 6–11*.

Some of the questions that could be asked of the Department A supervisor are: Why did the average wage rates change from $6.50 to $7.00, and why were 11,000 hours used instead of 10,000 that should have been used? Answers to these questions can determine if corrective action is needed to prevent future problems in this area.

Although the labor variances in the examples above were both unfavorable, it is also important to examine situations where one favorable variance offsets an unfavorable variance, especially when different supervisors are responsible for each component. For example, in Department A, let us assume that the wages to be paid are negotiated by the hospital personnel specialists while the supervisor of Department A is only responsible for the hours worked. Let us also assume that the same actual condi-

Exhibit 6–13
Labor costs for Department A

Actual labor hours used (AQ_I)	11,000 hours
Actual wage rate (AP)	$7.00 per hour
Total labor costs (AC)	$77,000
Standard hours allowed for 20,000 procedures accomplished, based on 30 minutes per procedure = 20,000 (.5 hours per procedure) = (SQ_A)	10,000 hours allowed
Standard wage rate (SP)	$6.50 per hour
Total standard labor costs (SC)	$65,000

Actual labor costs minus standard costs = $77,000 − $65,000 = $12,000 unfavorable labor variance

Exhibit 6–14
Labor rates and labor efficiency
variances for Department A

Labor rate variance	=	$AQ_I(AP - SP)$
	=	(11,000 hours)($7.00 – $6.50)
		(11,000 hours)($.50 per hour) = $5,500 U
Labor efficiency variance	=	$SP (AQ_I - SQ_A)$
	=	($6.50 per hour)(11,000 – 10,000)
	=	($6.50 per hour)(1,000 hours) = $6,500 U
Total labor cost variance	=	($5,500) + ($6,500) = $12,000 or
		$12,000 unfavorable labor variance*

*The question as to when a variance is favorable or unfavorable is best answered by determining if the supervisor paid more or less than the standard wage or used more or less hours than the standard.

tions prevailed as in *Exhibit 6–13* for the wage rates but the actual number of hours used changed. The new condition is presented in *Exhibit 6–15*.

In the example in *Exhibit 6–15,* the Department A supervisor was actually doing a superior job in meeting the standard hours, but the total variance approach would have hidden the full impact of his/her efforts. Questions as to why the average salary costs were higher should be directed to the personnel section. On the other hand, perhaps a more costly mix of RNs was used which could be the responsibility of the supervisor. Answers to these questions can result in more effective control of future costs.

Exhibit 6–15
Revised labor costs for Department A

Actual labor hours used	9,300
Actual wage rate	$ 7.00
Total labor costs	$65,100
Standard hours allowed for 20,000 procedures accomplished, based on 30 minutes per procedure (20,000 × .5) =	10,000 hours
Standard wage rate	$ 6.50
Total standard labor costs	$65,000
Unfavorable labor variance ($65,000 – $65,100)	$ 100

Revised labor rate and labor efficiency variances

Labor rate variance	=	$AQ_I(AP - SP)$
	=	9,300 ($6.50 – $7.00)
	=	$4,650 U
Labor efficiency variance	=	$SP (AQ_I - SQ_A)$
	=	$6.50 (10,000 – 9,300)
	=	$4,550 F
Total labor cost variance	=	$4,650U – $4,550 F = $100 U

Standard costs and the accounting system

In the healthcare environment, costs are allocated for two primary reasons: first, to measure departmental or supervisory effectiveness and efficiency (the management control problem identified in chapter 1), and second, to determine the costs of providing specific services for reimbursement purposes and for income determination.

Accounting systems should be designed to collect both costing and performance measurement information. Generally, accounting systems in healthcare organizations can provide satisfactory data for control purposes, but they are basically weak in product costing, especially for prospective reimbursement. In the next section, we will develop product costing concepts and how they can be applied to healthcare organizations.

Cost accounting techniques and product lines

Cost accounting systems are designed to facilitate the determination of the cost per unit of output. To accomplish this objective, the healthcare organization output or product line must be specified. However, there is not universal agreement on what the output of a healthcare provider should be. Is it a service such as a test, procedure, or inpatient day? Or should it be a function of a positive change in health status? Rather than enter this argument, assume that the output and resulting product line is a measurable activity. Rather than focus on the test, procedure, or inpatient day approach as the final output, consider them as subactivity measures which will be costed in order to determine the cost of the healthcare organization's output. This is in general agreement with the standard cost models developed earlier in this chapter.

Based on this simplification, the healthcare organization's product line is defined as one that can be measured by one of three possible methods: per diem, case/discharge, or case diagnosis. To select the most appropriate basis, we need to determine a set of criteria to evaluate each of these approaches. *Exhibit 6–16* presents a set of criteria which could be used.

Exhibit 6–16
Product line selection criteria

- Does it measure services provided?
- Can profitability be determined for individual cases?
- Does it facilitate cost monitoring and control?
- Does it facilitate resource use monitoring and control?
- Does it facilitate comparison with competitors?
- Does it facilitate budgeting and forecasting capabilities?

Exhibit 6–17 demonstrates how each of the proposed product lines meets the criteria established in *Exhibit 6–16*.

The analysis in *Exhibit 6–17* indicates that a case approach is preferable to per diem in providing information for managerial decision making. If a qualifier such as diagnosis is used, it permits collection of data which relates more effectively the consumption of resources to the specific product. For example, DRGs are currently used by many payers and providers as an output surrogate. The use of DRGs as a product has certain advantages. First, it provides a limited number of products as compared to the ICD–10 approach (490 to 10,000). They are clinically-based and provide a reasonably understood format. It is possible to compare DRG costs and resource consumption with other healthcare providers. Finally, it appears that more and more payers recognize the DRGs as a basis for payment.

DRGs also have several disadvantages. Perhaps most importantly, the data from which DRGs were developed were averages based on Medicare cost reports from a time frame when the data could be considered suspect at best. Resource use by DRG was based on past medical practice and service patterns; cost data depended on the ratio of costs to charges when revenue reimbursement maximization was the primary goal. Finally, DRGs

Exhibit 6–17
Evaluation of proposed product lines

Managerial decisions	Alternative product lines		
	Per diem	Case/discharge	Case diagnosis
1. Measure services provided	Average of all services	Average by discharge	Average by diagnosis
2. Profitability determination	Average revenue-average cost	Departmental profit	Departmental profit
3. Cost control and monitoring	Cost control by average/Cost shifting occurs	Departmental costs	Departmental costs
4. Monitoring resource use	Resource consumption based on average	Average use by number of discharge	Resources use by diagnosis
5. Competitive comparison	No allowance for case mix	No allowance for case mix	Comparison by specific diagnosis
6. Budget/ forecasting	Macro approach only (number of patient days)	Some micro potential	Micro potential

do not adequately reflect severity of illness within the DRG. Attempts are being made by HCFA to correct or minimize these differences.

Patient management categories (PMC) can also be used as a diagnosis based product line. PMCs capture more of the clinical specific information for each patient in contrast to the DRG because whereas patients can only be assigned to one DRG, multiple PMCs can be assigned to a patient. Finally, there are 852 clinically specific categories in the PMC contrasted to 477 DRGs. Because of this, the use of PMC requires less aggregation of data than a DRG.

Cost accounting techniques

The costing of healthcare services requires that cost information be collected in an appropriate and efficient manner. Two methods for costing are generally in use in healthcare organizations. They are:

- Process Costing
- Job Order Costing

Process costing is used when a department produces a series of homogeneous products (laboratory, radiology, housekeeping, laundry, and nursing services are representative departments). Costing of units of output is done on an averaging basis as illustrated in *Exhibit 6–18*.

Job order costing depends on accumulating individual costs by specific job. For example, the cost per patient stay is a classic example of job order costing. Costs are collected by services received. An example of a job order system is illustrated in *Exhibit 6–19*.

Most healthcare providers use both costing methods in their patient billing system. It is important to recognize when averages are involved, especially for nonhomogenous outputs. *Exhibit 6–20* presents an overview of the hybrid cost system in use in a typical healthcare provider.

Since process costing is primarily an averaging technique, close monitoring by management and an understanding of cost behavior is vital to controlling costs and quality parameters.

Exhibit 6–18
Process costing

Total Costs	$20,000,000
Units of Outputs	5,000,000
Average Cost	$4.00

Each output would cost $4 regardless of the actual resources used for a specific output. For homogeneous products, this would not appear to cause serious distortions.

Exhibit 6–19
Job order costing DRG 101

Inpatient service charge (days × rate) = Amt.
Radiology (procedure × rate)   = Amt.
Laboratory (test × rate)   = Amt.
                                     Total cost

Each service is costed individually in terms of resources used.

Exhibit 6–20
The hybrid cost accounting system

Per diem/Discharge/Diagnosis/Visit   Requires
                                                                                job order
                                                                                costing

Healthcare organization departments

Nursing, Lab, X-ray, Drugs, etc.   Requires
                                                                                process
                                                                                costing

JOB ORDER COSTING TECHNIQUE

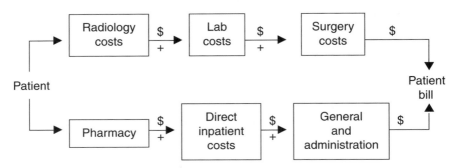

PROCESS COSTING TECHNIQUES
Example: Radiology Department

Labor	$100,000
Materials	$20,000
Overhead	$200,000
Total costs	$320,000
Number of tests	5,000 = $64 per test

Output measurement and standard cost

In the past, sufficient attention has not been paid to the difficult task of measuring hospital output, especially at the department level. This output measurement problem is closely identified with the setting of standards, both in terms of input and output costs. Measuring output is usually an important part of the rate-setting process for specific services. Output measures can also be used in evaluating individual performance for merit increases.

One of the more difficult aspects of output measurement is the determination of the physical unit to be used for each department. This unit should be a factor that accurately reflects the procedure or service being produced by the department. It should be subject to objective identification and should have identifiable cost elements. Fortunately, the increasing use of computers by most large- and medium-sized hospitals can alleviate many of the problems that may be encountered in establishing micromeasures of output for individual procedures and services. In smaller healthcare organizations with minimal access to computers, the use of macromeasures of output is preferred to the absence of any attempt to measure output. Since the volume of output is low and the mix of patients fairly constant, the use of macromeasures of output will generally provide sufficient information for managers to take appropriate corrective actions. However, any healthcare provider with a wide range of services should consider micromeasures of output.

Herkimer identifies the output of healthcare organizations as falling into two types: 1) gross or macro units of measurement and 2) weighted or micro units of measurement (see *Exhibit 6–21*).[1]

Most healthcare organizations have developed macromeasures of output. Unfortunately, they typically do not reflect the complexity or mix of the micro outputs for various departments. Weighted units of measurement are designed to allow for different complexities and mixes of procedures. They take into account the different amounts of labor, materials, and overhead required for the different procedures. Many professional societies have developed weighted units of measurement for their professional disciplines called relative value units. For example, the Resource Based Relative Value Scale (RBRVS) developed by HCFA to reimburse physicians is an example of a weighted value system. In his book, Herkimer presents detailed information on the methodology used by the College of American Pathologists and the Connecticut Hospital Association's Laboratory Cost Distribution Statistics.[2]

---

[1] Herkimer, Allen G., Jr., *Understanding Hospital Financial Management*, Germantown, MD: Aspen Systems Corporation, 1986, p. 93.

[2] Ibid, pp. 285–329.

Exhibit 6–21
Comparative study of healthcare departmental
gross service units and weighted production units*

Department	Gross production unit (Macro)	Weighted production unit (Micro)
Operating room	Surgical case	Person-minutes
Anesthesiology	Anesthesia case	Anesthesiology-minutes
Postoperative rooms	Postoperative case	Person-minutes
Radiology	Examinations	RVUs
Laboratory	Tests	RVUs
Physical therapy	Modalities	Person-minutes
Isotopes	Treatments	RVUs
Blood bank	Transfusions	RVUs
Delivery room	Deliveries	Person-minutes
Social service	Visits	Person-hours
Emergency room	Visits	Person-minutes
Nursing	Patient days	Hours of care
Nursery	Patient days	Hours of care

*Reprinted from *Understanding Hospital Financial Management* by Allen G. Herkimer, Jr., by permission of Aspen Systems Corporation, Germantown, MD, 1986, p. 93.

The calculation of standard costs requires the use of weighted or micromeasures of output in the management control process. Standard costs based on gross or macromeasures do not have sufficient precision to permit the identification of price and quantity variances or intensity of service. They do not allow managers to effectively assess the causes of the variances. In the management control process, this type of gross (macro) measure may be acceptable at the top management level, but not at the departmental level.

Summary

The establishment of standard costs is not an exact science. It requires input from several knowledgeable sources, including the department manager. In addition, several professional associations and independent groups publish averages on such items as costs, labor, and materials, which afford an opportunity to compare individual hospital standards with those from similar institutions. These comparisons and past experiences can be helpful; however, these data must be used with caution, as they probably contain inefficiencies and other undesirable characteristics. The

Exhibit 6–22
Key factors in developing standards

* Standards must correspond to department's primary patient care activity.

* They must consider mix of controllable and uncontrollable costs.

* They should be precise enough to meet management needs but not require extensive accounting systems.

* Standards should consider quality as well as time and quantity.

* Department personnel and management must accept standards.

* Standards must be periodically re-evaluated with respect to operational and organizational changes in department.

data must be modified to adjust for changing economic conditions, volume requirements, and technology. Effective standards must reflect what a procedure *should* cost, *not what it cost in the past. Exhibit 6–22* summarizes some of the key factors in developing standards.

Questions and problems

1. Explain the difference between flexible and static budgets.

2. If a hospital prepares a budget based on an estimate of 100,000 admissions, and only 80,000 admissions actually occur, what effect will this have on hospital costs?

3. Management prepared a fixed budget based on 10,000 admissions and arrived at total costs of $20,000,000 for the coming year. During the year, actual admissions came to 8,000 and costs totaled $18,500,000. Did management do a good job of containing costs for the year? Discuss.

4. St. Anthony's Hospital experienced wide variations in patient days from a low of 8,500 in December to a high of 13,000 days in July. Total costs at the lowest activity level were $39,275 and at the highest level were $53,900.
   a. What are the variable and fixed costs if fixed costs are constant?
   b. Prepare a flexible budget for these two months.
   c. Using the flexible budget developed, determine total costs at 10,000 patient days.
   d. Discuss how reliable these figures might be.

5. Define the concept of "standard costs."

6. What advantages can be gained from using a "standard cost" system?

7. What factors should be considered in developing a standard cost for an X-ray procedure?

8. Define three types of standard costs, and provide the pros and cons of each.

9. Define the term "variance" as it pertains to a standard cost system.

10. Explain the two types of output measurement for healthcare organizations.

11. Why are output measurements necessary for healthcare organizations?

12. The measurement of the output of healthcare organizations is important to the recognition of efficiency and effectiveness. List the pros and cons associated with each of the following output measures:
    a. cost per patient day
    b. cost per case
    c. cost per DRG
    d. cost per member per month (used by HMOs)
    e. cost per visit (used by physician groups)

13. Average cost per unit for a hospital is typically based on patient days, although increasingly the basis is per admission or per discharge. What would be the most appropriate measurement device to measure performance in the following departments?
    a. Dietary
    b. Laundry and Linen
    c. Accounting
    d. Pharmacy
    e. Medical School
    f. Operating Room

14. Explain the differences between process and job order costing systems, the need for each in a healthcare provider, and potential problems in using both.

15. University Hospital management personnel collected the following information to be used in establishing a standard cost for DRG 101:

Resources Required	
Inpatient Care	4 days
Radiology	5 diagnoses
Laboratory	4 tests
Surgical	2 procedures

Cost Information

Routine Care
Direct Costs $2,000,000
Indirect Costs $4,000,000
Total Estimated Days of Care 20,000 days

Radiology
Direct Costs
    Fixed $2,000,000
    Variable $10 per diagnosis
Indirect Costs $400,000
Estimated Number of Diagnoses 10,000

Laboratory
Direct Costs
    Fixed $400,000
    Variable $1 per test
Indirect Costs
    Fixed $600,000
    Variable $.50 per test
Estimated Number of Tests 20,000

Surgical
Direct Costs $500,000
Indirect Costs $5,000,000
Estimated Number of Procedures 5,000

a. Develop a standard cost model for DRG 101. Make any assumptions you need and identify them in your answer.
b. What would be the budget total cost associated with having 100 admissions under DRG 101?

16. Department A of a tax exempt clinic has a standard materials usage of three units per procedure. The standard cost of the materials is $4 per unit. Last month this department completed 1,500 procedures at

a cost of $27,000. Assuming the actual cost of materials was $4.50 per unit, calculate:
a. the total variance
b. the price variance
c. the quantity variance

17. A specialized hospital treats only one type of patient, with these planned results:

Services (10,000 units)	$80,000
Variable costs	32,000
Contribution margin	$48,000
Fixed costs	40,000
Net income	$ 8,000

Actual results were:

Services	$84,000
Variable costs	38,400
Contribution margin	$45,600
Fixed costs	40,000
Net income	$ 5,600

a. If 12,000 patients were served at a price of $7.00 per unit, what quantity and price variances would explain the change in net income?

18. The pharmacy department of Community HMO developed the following standards for manufacturing one unit of solution X:

Direct chemicals	7.5 ounces @ $1.50 per ounce
Direct labor	0.5 hours @ $6.00 per hour

During a recent period, 1,760 units were produced, 15,000 ounces of chemicals were purchased and used, at a cost of $1.25 per ounce, and 835 hours of direct labor time were used at a total labor cost of $5,177.
a. Compute the materials variances for the period.
b. Compute the labor variances for the period.

19. The radiology department at Suburban Hospital computed the following standard times for completing diagnostic procedures on the CT scanner:

Direct technician time	15 minutes per test
Direct technician rate	$24.00 per hour

During 1991, the department worked 7,750 hours to produce 30,000 procedures. The technician cost was $175,000.
a. Determine the total labor cost variance for the department.
b. Separate the total labor cost variance into rate and efficiency variances.

20. During 199X, the nursing department at Skilled Nursing Home completed 300,000 paid nursing hours for 75,000 patient days. During the budgeting process, the nursing supervisor had estimated that the nursing salary budget would be $2,500,000 and the 275,000 nursing hours would be needed for 80,000 planned patient days. Actual nursing salary costs were $2,700,000. Assuming the nursing hours in excess of 200,000 are considered variable, what are some possible reasons for the budget overrun?

21. The Wild West County Clinic provides a single service to its clients. The following data were available from the clinic records:

	Test material	Test labor
Standard quantity per test	3 pounds	?
Standard input price	$5 per pound	?

During a recent month, the clinic paid $55,650 for test materials, all of which were used in the completion of 3,200 tests, and worked 4,900 labor hours at a cost of $36,750. The following variance data are available:

Test materials quantity variance	$4,500 U
Total test labor variance	1,650 F
Total labor efficiency variance	800 U

a. Compute actual cost paid per pound of test material.
b. Compute the test materials price variance.
c. Compute the standard direct test labor rate per direct labor hour.
d. Compute the standard hours allowed for the tests completed during the period and the standard labor hour per test.

22. Assume the following types of services offered by the Mary Grace Gans Speech and Hearing Center for the next planning period:

	Percentage of total
Audiological examination	30
Pediatric audiological examination	20
Pure tone—air and bone	10
Speech evaluation	10
Speech therapy	15
Hearing therapy	10
Hearing and evaluation	5
Total	100%

Also assume the following cost structure for the center:

	Fee	Variable costs	Contribution margin
Audiological examination	$25	$ 5	$20
Pediatric audiological exam	20	5	15
Pure tone—air and bone	15	5	10
Speech evaluation	30	5	25
Speech therapy	15	3	12
Hearing therapy	30	10	20
Hearing and evaluation	24	10	14

a. Using the above data, construct a composite or weighted average contribution margin for the center.
b. Given the contribution margin developed in part a, determine the volume of procedures the speech and hearing center needs to meet its profit goals for the next budget year.

Estimated fixed costs	$240,000
Desired additional income	$100,000

c. The Mary Grace Gans Speech and Hearing Center reported the actual results in the following exhibit. Develop the departmental budget based on a contribution margin concept for the speech and hearing center based on the information contained in parts a and b, and the actual results. Assume that $140,000 of the estimated fixed costs are direct costs of the program and $100,000 are indirect.
d. Explain why the reported income was less than the desired objective. (Use data from parts a, b, and c, if needed.)

Actual results for the year 198X
for the Mary Grace Gans Speech and Hearing Center

	Total	Audio-logical examination	Pediatric audio. exam.	Pure tone	Speech eval.	Speech therapy	Hearing therapy	Hearing and evaluation
Number of procedures	19,500	5,500	4,200	2,100	2,300	2,700	1,500	1,200
Revenues (assume fees were as planned)	$436,300	$137,500	$84,000	$31,500	$69,000	$40,500	$45,000	$28,800
Variable costs	117,500	32,000	20,000	11,000	15,000	9,500	18,000	12,000
Contribution margin	318,800	105,500	64,000	20,500	54,000	31,000	27,000	16,800
Direct fixed costs	140,000	30,000	40,000	5,000	10,000	18,000	27,000	10,000
Program contribution	178,800	75,500	24,000	15,500	44,000	13,000	-0-	6,800
Indirect fixed costs	110,000							
Net income	$ 68,800							

23. The finance department at Memorial Hospital has devoted all its efforts to compiling the data needed for Blue Cross and Medicare reports, reports which were not particularly useful for management decisions because of the cost allocations made to satisfy the reporting requirements of these two agencies.

   You would like to change the emphasis in the accounting department from developing information for external reports to developing information for internal reports that lead to sound management decisions. If a good reporting system for internal purposes can be developed, Blue Cross and Medicare reports could be prepared from information in the accounting records. In this way, both external reporting information and internal accounting information that helps in planning and controlling the hospital's operations can be developed by the accounting system. You would like to establish a flexible budget system, but before you can even consider making the change, you must first analyze some of the expenses to determine which are fixed and which are variable.

   You have discovered that there has been no analysis of fixed and variable costs for any of the departments of the hospital. Such a classification of expenses is useful if costs are to be controlled—primarily because variable costs are controllable in the short run, and fixed costs are controllable over a longer time period. By separating expenses into fixed and variable, the use of a flexible budget and standard costs become feasible.

In addition to determining cost behavior patterns, you want to get a standard cost system installed as soon as possible because it is essential in pinpointing costs that are out of control. An effective standard cost system will enable the hospital managers to determine more quickly which costs are not in line with planned amounts. Standard costs can also be used to introduce the flexible budget process to the hospital.

a. The accounting department has collected the information below for the dietary department. From the information, you plan to develop a standard cost for the noon meal #16.

Cost Elements for the Dietary Department—
Standard prices for ingredients used in noon meal #16
(200 portions):

Item	Price	Unit	Quantity Per Meal
Meat	$2.40	Pound	4 ounces
Vegetable #1	1.92	Two-Pound Package	1 ounce
Vegetable #2	1.60	Five-Pound Package	4 ounces
Salad	0.64	Pound	2 ounces
Dessert	0.96	Pound	2 ounces
Coffee	8.00	Five-Pound Can	1 ounce
Bread	6.40	Twenty 1-pound loaves	2 ounces

Additional direct expenses incurred in preparing meal #16:

Electricity, steam, etc.	$0.075 estimated cost per meal served
Supplies	0.010 estimated cost per meal served
Maintenance expense	0.025 estimated cost per meal served

Two cooks spend four hours each to prepare meal #16. These two cooks work overlapping shifts, so half of each cook's shift is devoted to this meal. In addition, a cook's helper spends one and one-half hours preparing the salad; another cook's helper spends two hours helping to prepare the meal. Two cooks and two cooks' helpers are on duty every day to prepare the necessary meals each day.

The hourly wages of these employees are:

Cook	$8.00 per hour
Cook's helper	4.00 per hour

Keywords: efficiency variance; flexible budget; job order costing; price variance; process costing; quantity variance; standard cost; static budget; variance analysis.

References

Andrianos, James, and Mark Dykan. "Using Cost Accounting Data to Improve Clinical Value." *Healthcare Financial Management* (May 1996): 44–48.

Awasthi, V.N., and L. Eldenburg. "Providing Cost Data to Physicians Helps Contain Costs." *Healthcare Financial Management* (April 1996): 40–42.

Baker, J.J. "Activity-Based Costing for Integrated Delivery Systems." *Journal of Health Care Finance* (winter 1995): 57–61.

Canby J.B., IV. "Applying Activity-Based Costing to Healthcare Settings." *Healthcare Financial Management* (February 1995): 50–56.

Carpenter, C.E., L.C. Weitzel, N.E. Johnson, and D.B. Nash. "Cost Accounting Supports Clinical Evaluations." *Healthcare Financial Management* (April 1994): 40–44.

Church, L. "Positioning Hospital-Based Home Care Agencies for Managed Care." *Healthcare Financial Management* (February 1996): 29–32.

Dove, H.G., and T. Forthman. "Helping Financial Analysts Communicate Variance Analysis." *Healthcare Financial Management* (April 1995): 52–54.

Duncan, D.G., and C.S. Servais. "Preparing for the New Outpatient Reimbursement System." *Healthcare Financial Management* (February 1996): 42–49.

Fogel, L.A., and K. Gossman-Klim. "Getting Started with Subacute Care." *Healthcare Financial Management* (October 1995): 64–74.

Granof, M.H., P.W. Bell, and B.R. Neumann. *Accounting for Managers and Investors.* Englewood Cliffs, NJ: Prentice Hall, 1993.

Kolb, D.S., and J.L. Horowitz. "Managing the Transition to Capitation." *Healthcare Financial Management* (February 1995): 64–69.

Kothmann, W.L. "Is Subacute Care Feasible?" *Healthcare Financial Management* (October 1995): 60–63.

Krueger, D., and T. Davidson. "Alternative Approaches to Cost Accounting." *Topics in Health Care Financing* 13, no. 4 (1987): 1–9.

Mays, Janet, and Gus Gordon. "Developing a Cost Accounting System for a Physician Group Practice." *Healthcare Financial Management* (October 1996): 73–79.

Miller, T.R., and J.B. Ryan. "Analyzing Cost Variance in Capitated Contracts." *Healthcare Financial Management* (February 1995): 22–23.

Murray, M.J., and D.J. Anderson. "How Should Hospitals Relate to Medicare HMOs?" *Healthcare Financial Management* (January 1996): 40–46.

Neumann, Bruce R., Jan P. Clement, and Jean C. Cooper. *Financial Management: Concepts and Applications for Health Care Organizations.* Dubuque: Kendall/Hunt, 1997.

Orloff, T.M., et al. "Hospital Cost Accounting: Who's Doing What and Why." *Health Care Management Review* 15, no. 4 (1990): 73–78.

Ramsey, R.H. "Activity-Based Costing for Hospitals." *Hospital & Health Services Administration* (fall 1994): 385–396.

Richman, T. "Performance Measurement." *Harvard Busines Review* 73, no. 4 (1995): 10–11.

Rode, Dan. "Determining Indicators of Patient Financial Service Performance." *Healthcare Financial Management* (December 1991): 104–105.

Saliman, Soliman Y., and William Hughes. "DRG Payments and Net Contribution Variance Analysis." *Healthcare Financial Management* (October 1983): 78–86.

Schimmel, Victor E., C. Alley, and A.M. Heath. "Measuring Costs: Product Line Accounting vs. Ratio of Costs to Charges." *Healthcare Financial Management* 13, no. 4 (summer 1987): 76–86.

Shafer, Paul L., B.J. Frauenthal, and C. Tower. "Measuring Nursing Costs with Patient Acuity Data." *Topics in Health Care Financing* 13, no. 4 (summer 1987): 20–31.

Suver, James D., Edward E. Opperman, and Theodore Helmer. "Variance Analyst: Using Standards to Predict Recognized Nurse Staffing Patterns." *Healthcare Financial Management* (September 1984): 48–50.

Thorley Hill, N., and E. Loper Johns. "Adoption of Costing Systems by U.S. Hospitals." *Hospital & Health Services Administration* (winter 1994): 521–537.

Van Bodegraven, Art. "Developing and Using Standards for Working Performance." *Topics in Health Care Financing* 15, no. 3 (spring 1989): 13–26.

Young, David W. *Financial Control in Health Care: A Managerial Perspective.* Homewood, IL: Dow Jones-Irwin, 1984.

CHAPTER 7

Overhead control and variance analysis

"I don't know how they expect me to stay within my budget. I don't control over 50 percent of the costs."

"We closed our delivery wing yet I was told I had to increase my prices to cover increased overhead allocations. How can our overhead costs go up?"

"I believe they waste a lot of film in radiology. They are always asking the patients in my ward to return!"

"Who in the organization is responsible for the overhead expenditures?"

"Is there any way of keeping track of overhead variances?"

"How should we decide to allocate indirect costs to the various departments?"

"The department manager says she should not be held accountable for variances which come about because of allocated overhead."

Introduction

In chapter 6, the discussion of standard costs focused on direct labor and direct materials costs. Direct costs, costs that can be directly traced to a specific service or procedure, are usually the easiest to control because they occur at the departmental level. They also pose fewer problems in determining the full cost of a service or procedure. However, in most health services organizations, there are also indirect costs. The concept of indirect costs was introduced in chapter 2. As discussed in chapter 2, most indirect costs fall into what is typically called overhead costs. Overhead costs include the indirect administrative costs of patient care departments and other administrative and support services of the hospital such as information services, maintenance, housekeeping, etc. They cannot be traced directly to a service or procedure because 1) no clear relationship exists between the incurrence of the cost and the providing of the service, or 2) it is not cost effective to do so. An example of costs in the latter category are utility costs. Every use of electricity *could* be monitored by putting meters on each receptacle. This would transform the indirect cost of utilities into a direct cost to the service. However, the additional cost of installing meters would probably not be cost effective in terms of the additional management information obtained. Therefore, it is a management decision not to treat certain overhead costs as direct costs, even though such treatment would facilitate both management control and cost determination.

Types of overhead costs

While many healthcare organizations' overhead costs fall into the indirect category for cost determination purposes, i.e., the costs of housekeeping, laundry, dietary, maintenance, administration, etc., must be allocated to procedures or services in order to obtain the full cost of providing a given service or procedure. However, in terms of responsibility accounting and management control, there is a supervisor of each of those sections who is responsible for the direct costs incurred in those departments. It is important to stress that the direct and indirect cost categories are determined by the cost objective being pursued. A direct cost in a department for control purposes may be treated as an indirect cost for some other cost determination purpose, such as rate setting. In summary, overhead costs can be designated as either direct or indirect. It depends upon the purpose for which the cost information is being collected.

The level of responsibility also influences the determination of direct and indirect costs. For example, whether costs are direct or indirect can be visualized by considering them as an inverted pyramid (*Exhibit 7–1*). At the top of the pyramid is the hospital or organization. At this level all costs are direct and can be considered to be the responsibility of the administrator. At the departmental level there are both direct and indirect costs. Direct costs can be directly related to the function of the department, whether it is patient related or not. There are also indirect costs when considering the department level, since depreciation on the building is assumed to be continuous and independent of the individual departmental activities. Fire insurance and liability insurance are other categories of costs which are functions of the total organization and cannot be directly related to the activities of any single department. Thus, these costs are direct costs to the total organization, but cannot be controlled by individuals within any of the departments, except the chief executive officer (CEO). The CEO is responsible for the management of this cost, similar to all the other costs of the organization. However, each department will still be allocated a portion of these costs in the interest of full cost determination for charge setting or reimbursement purposes.

At the department level, direct costs are determined by the function of the department. Direct costs to the department would include all staff salaries and wages, supplies used in the provision of departmental ser-

Exhibit 7–1
The direct cost hierarchy for
control/responsibility decisions

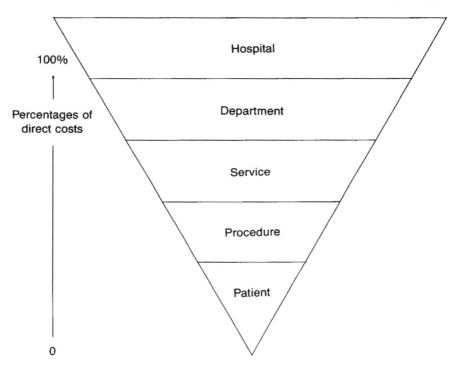

vices, etc. Indirect costs to the department will include depreciation, fire insurance, liability insurance, and organizational utilities expense.

Services within the department have direct costs associated with the supplies, and salaries, or wages of the technicians or professionals performing the service. Indirect costs to the service would include some portion of the supervisor's salary and departmental administrative costs, in addition to some portion of the indirect overhead costs allocated to the department.

Services can be made up of several different procedures. Direct costs to each procedure would include supplies plus clinician time and wages. Indirect costs would include costs allocated from the service level, departmental level, and organizational level. By the time the services and procedures are provided to the patient, there is a relatively small component of direct costs and a relatively larger component of indirect costs. However, care must be taken to understand the purpose of allocating all costs to the services which are eventually provided to the patient, as opposed to a determination and assignment of responsibility for cost control at each level within the organization.

Taking these factors into consideration results in the following decision rule: for cost control as many costs as possible should be made direct costs; for price setting purposes, full costs must be determined regardless of whether or not they are direct or indirect. A final caveat must be added to the decision rule for cost control: costs should be made direct as long as it remains cost effective to do so.

Allocation of overhead costs

If a healthcare organization is to remain financially viable, it must receive the full cost of maintaining the institution. Full costs should be defined as the total financial requirements of the organization as identified in chapter 1. These total financial requirements include both the direct and indirect costs. The direct costs, which are variable (such as labor and materials), are generally easy to trace to individual procedures. However, the full cost of providing a service must also include the overhead costs, which are not directly traceable to the specific service.

Overhead costs must be allocated to the individual service in order to determine the full costs of providing that service. The allocation process requires two inputs: the set of costs to be allocated and the selection of a volume base on which to allocate those costs. The accumulation of costs to be allocated is a function of the accounting system and the chart of accounts. The choice of the allocation base is much more difficult and subjective. For example, an allocation base could be patient days, square feet of space, pounds of laundry, number of personnel, etc. Despite the apparent subjectivity, it is generally agreed that the allocation process should be accomplished on a logical and rational basis as much as possible, with consistency from year to year an important goal.

Whenever possible, the choice of the allocation base should depend on some clear relationship between the activity and the incurrence of the cost. The relationship may be causal, that is, the particular activity causes the costs to change. Alternatively, the relationship may be correlational; the costs and activities may change in a known direction and in a known relationship. The base should be simple and easily understood whenever possible. However, it is also true in many cases that the choice is made on a purely subjective basis, i.e., whatever is most apparent, convenient and/ or feasible is selected. The allocation procedures discussed above typically fall into the area of cost allocation, which will be discussed in greater detail in chapter 9. However, the impact of the allocation base on full cost determination has forced many cost-based reimbursers to establish very detailed and restrictive policies for deciding what bases can be selected for allocating specific costs. When these external reimbursement policies are used for internal decision making, major inconsistencies and improper decisions can result. For example, an allocation of social service department costs to outpatient care may be proper to maximize reimbursement. However, in deciding whether to expand the outpatient clinic, this cost allocation could distort the incremental costs of that decision.

For management control, there is no need to allocate direct overhead costs because, by definition, these costs are traced directly to the department responsible for incurring the costs. For example, the direct cost associated with the plant maintenance department is the responsibility of the supervisor of that department. There can be both fixed and variable overhead costs in the plant maintenance department, but the determination of fixed and variable is usually related to the volume base selected. For example, the variable expenses of running emergency generators would be the gas and oil used. This would probably be a function of utilization (number of hours). The fixed expenses would be the cost of buying the generator and related equipment, prorated over the life of the generator through the use of depreciation formulas. Depreciation is the accounting process of allocating acquisition costs over a period of time. When the cost objective becomes the full cost determination of providing a specific service or procedure, a fair share of the full cost of the plant maintenance department must be allocated to the department that provides the service. *Exhibit 7–2* illustrates some typical allocation bases.

Exhibit 7–2
Schedule of allocation bases

Allocated costs	Allocation bases
Depreciation—buildings and fixed equipment	Square feet of area occupied
Depreciation—major movable equipment	1. Specific identification of expense by center through plant asset records 2. Square feet 3. Accumulated costs
Employee benefits	1. Specific identification of expense by center through detailed payroll records 2. Gross salaries and wages 3. Average number of employees
Administrative and fiscal services (a general cost center which usually should be broken down into several cost centers and be allocated on different bases)	1. Accumulated costs 2. Number of personnel
Admitting	Number of admissions
Plant operation and maintenance	1. Square feet of area occupied 2. Work orders *(cont.)*

Exhibit 7–2 (cont.)
Schedule of allocation bases

Allocated costs	Allocation bases
Purchasing	1. Costs of supplies and services used by each center 2. "Other" direct expenses
Laundry and linen	1. Pounds of soiled laundry processed 2. Pounds of processed laundry issued 3. Weighted pieces of laundry
Housekeeping	1. Hours of service 2. Square feet of area occupied
Net cost of meals sold	1. Number of meals served 2. Number of employees 3. Accumulated costs
Nursing service— administrative office	1. Hours of nursing service supervised 2. Estimated supervision time
Central services and supply	1. Amount of priced requisitions at retail 2. Special analyses of labor and supply usage
Pharmacy	1. Amount of priced requisitions 2. Special studies
Medical records	1. Estimated time spent on records 2. Number of patient days 3. Number of admissions
Social service	Estimated time spent in providing case work service for patients in each center
Diploma school of nursing	1. Number of patient days 2. Assigned hours of experience
Intern and resident service	Assigned hours of service
Patient accounting	Number of patient days

Source: *Cost Finding and Rate Setting for Hospitals,* copyright 1968 by the American Hospital Association.

Overhead rates

Once the allocation base is determined, the next step is to determine the rate of allocation per unit of the allocation base. This is necessary since most pricing decisions are based on the concept of full cost recovery. This would include all direct costs and a fair share of the overhead costs. It is generally expressed as follows:

$$\text{per unit cost} = \frac{\text{indirect overhead costs}}{\text{activity measure}} + \frac{\text{direct costs}}{\text{activity measure}}$$

Notice the similarity to the flexible budget formula in chapter 4. Since most prices or charges need to be determined before the services are provided, the per unit costs need to be estimated when costs serve as the basis for price setting. The change from a retrospective to a prospective pricing system by many third-party reimbursers has put added emphasis on better cost information in establishing or reviewing existing charges, since the healthcare provider is now at economic risk for inadequate rates. The assignment or allocation of overhead to specific products to determine a full per unit cost can be facilitated by the development of overhead rates.

A key decision in the development of overhead rates is the choice of an activity measure. The base or activity measure for developing overhead rates is typically more closely identified to the patient care activity than the allocation bases listed in *Exhibit 7–2*. The most common bases would be the number of procedures, services, or tests provided, the amount of labor or machine time used for the service, the amount of drugs or supplies used, or a weighted average approach such as relative value units (discussed in chapter 8). A key determinant in the decision on what base to use would be the availability of data. Rather than create a new data requirement, many providers use existing data such as labor hours, dollar amount of supplies, or equipment time. *Exhibit 7–3* summarizes the major steps in developing an overhead rate for a healthcare provider. *Exhibit 7–4* illustrates how the actual overhead rate would be determined.

Exhibit 7–3
Development of overhead rates

Steps:

1. Determine whether a macro or micro basis will be used. The key question here is whether to have a single overhead rate for all services provided by the healthcare organization or a micro basis which would have individual rates for each department.

2. Collect the costs of the organization which will be included in the overhead rate (usually the indirect costs) from the accounting system.

3. Determine the overhead rate as illustrated below.

Macrolevel (average basis)

$$\frac{\text{total overhead costs}}{\text{activity measures}} = \text{overhead rate}$$

Total overhead costs = All general and administrative costs of provider

Microlevel (dept. specific basis)

$$\frac{\text{dept. overhead costs}}{\text{activity measures}} = \text{dept. overhead rate}$$

Possible activity measures
- Units of service (i.e., patient days, procedures, tests)
- Surrogate measures (revenues, costs)

Exhibit 7–4
Determination of overhead rates

Data

Total overhead costs	=	$10,000,000
Total revenues	=	$20,000,000
Patient days	=	50,000
Routine service overhead costs	=	$ 4,000,000
Routine service revenues	=	$16,000,000
Relative value units	=	10,000

Macrolevel (average basis)

$$\frac{\text{total overhead costs}}{\text{patient days}} = \frac{\$10,000,000}{50,000} = \$200 \text{ per patient day}$$

$$\frac{\text{total overhead costs}}{\text{total revenues}} = \frac{\$10,000,000}{\$20,000,000} = \$.50 \text{ per revenue dollar}$$

$$\text{Relative value units} = \frac{\$10,000,000}{10,000} = \$1,000 \text{ per RVU}$$

Microlevel (dept. or specific basis)

$$\frac{\text{routine service overhead costs}}{\text{patient days}} = \frac{\$4,000,000}{50,000} = \$80 \text{ per patient day}$$

$$\frac{\text{routine service overhead costs}}{\text{routine service revenue}} = \frac{\$4,000,000}{\$16,000,000} = \frac{\$.25 \text{ per routine service}}{\text{revenue dollar}}$$

$$\frac{\text{routine service overhead costs}}{\text{relative value units}} = \frac{\$4,000,000}{10,000} = \$400 \text{ per RVU}$$

Actual overhead rates will match the budget rates in *Exhibit 7–4* only if the total overhead budget was expended as planned and if the actual units of service were the same as the budgeted units of service. However, this is a rare occurrence and variances from the plan usually occur. The reasons for the variances need to be investigated, the same as for the variable cost factors discussed in chapter 6.

Overhead costs, flexible budgeting, and the management control process

Overhead costs must be budgeted in the same manner as other costs in the institution. Although most overhead costs fall into the fixed cost category, the total amount to be spent (fixed and variable) must be determined and included in the approved budget. The amount budgeted for the variable overhead costs is, of course, dependent on the volume of services to be offered.

As discussed in chapters 5 and 6, flexible budgeting offers a considerable improvement over a static budget because 1) it is geared to a range of activities rather than to a single level of activity and 2) a budget can be constructed for the actual level of activity accomplished. That is, the supervisor can look at the actual level of activity and construct a flexible budget to determine what costs should have been incurred at each activity level.

In terms of management control, we now have the two facts necessary to evaluate the operating results of the period—the actual cost incurred and what cost should have been incurred from the flexible budget. The analysis of this variance, or difference between these two costs, can provide the manager with the information necessary to take corrective action. The remainder of this chapter concentrates on these concepts in overhead control.

Overhead costs

For variable cost variance analysis, the actual direct labor and direct material costs can usually be collected through payroll records and supply requisition sheets. These are the costs which are necessary for both retrospective reimbursement and budgetary control purposes. On the other hand, overhead costs are more difficult to trace to specific products or services because, by their very nature, they cannot be specifically identified with the particular output. For example, both department supervisors and administrative clerks are necessary inputs to a laboratory, and their salary costs are part of the cost of providing lab tests. Yet, how much of each person's salary "belongs" to each test? In the current retrospective reimbursement environment, this allocation is done by cost finding techniques at the end of an operating period using aggregate data by cost centers. It is difficult to control spending without sufficient detailed information, and it is clearly impossible to control expenditures after they have been expended. As discussed in the previous section in this chapter, an overhead rate can be developed to allocate the overhead costs that should be applied to each output. For example, with total budgeted overhead of $2,000,000 and an estimated volume of 1,000,000 tests, the overhead allocation rate would be $2 ($2,000,000/1,000,000 tests) per test.

Clearly, if the actual volume of output achieved is different from the estimated amount, a different overhead rate would be required to cover the budgeted overhead dollar amount. For variable costs this does not present a major problem, because total variable overhead costs should fluctuate with the changes in volume. However, fixed overhead costs per unit (of volume) would change, creating a volume variance which cannot be known in advance of providing the service. For example, if the $2,000,000 of budgeted overhead consisted of $1,500,000 fixed costs and

$500,000 variable for 1,000,000 tests, the overhead cost equation would be $1,500,000 + $.50Q ($500,000/1,000,000 tests) and as indicated above, the overhead budget for 1,000,000 tests would be $1,500,000 + $.50(1,000,000) or $2,000,000 with the per unit overhead rate being $2. If only 900,000 tests were actually completed, the overhead rate *should have* been [$1,500,000 + .50(900,000)] or $1,950,000/900,000 = $2.17 per unit of output. The $.17 (2.17 − 2.00) difference times the 100,000 units not sold or $17,000 would be the volume variance caused by not meeting the planned (budgeted) output.

Use of standard costs for control purposes

One way to improve management control of costs is to use standard costs. When each unit of service is provided, the department accounting system would be credited with the standard costs for labor, material, and overhead. The actual costs would still be collected but they would not be identified with specific products. The amounts in the standard cost accounts would be reconciled with the actual costs each month at the end of the accounting period. Variances could be calculated and explained as illustrated in chapter 5. In this case, standard costs would be used for performance evaluation and for interim financial statements.

In addition to improved control, using standard costs removes seasonal variations, unusual expenses, and volume effects from the cost calculations used for management control. If the department is performing at standard, this should be an acceptable goal for both the supervisor and the organization.

As discussed in the last chapter, the determination of standards for various services and procedures is a vital input into the flexible budgeting process explained in chapter 6. Using the predetermined individual standards, aggregate standards can be developed for each department to determine the budget for the given volume and mix of services or procedures to be performed during the budget period. The flexible budget adjusted for the actual volume achieved can be compared with the actual costs incurred, and suitable variance analyses can be performed. In the next section, a framework for calculating overhead variances will be developed to facilitate the understanding of the difference between variable and fixed overhead variances.

Overhead variance analysis

Most overhead costs have both fixed and variable components. The variable overhead costs are similar to the labor and material components discussed earlier except they are not traced directly to the services provided. Even though they are variable, they are also indirect because the

Exhibit 7–5
Variable overhead costs* for
Radiology Department B

Indirect labor	$.10 per film
Maintenance	.05 per film
Misc. supplies	.12 per film
Total variable overhead per film	$.27 per film

*Based on number of films.
(Variable overhead costs are those costs that vary with volume changes in the base selected; in this example, the amount of film used.)

cost to trace them to a specific service is not cost effective. Small medical supplies typically fall into this category.

The basic framework for variable overhead variance analysis is similar to the techniques developed in chapter 6 for labor and materials. As a review, let's look at the following variable overhead problem. The standards established for the variable overhead costs are as shown in *Exhibit 7–5*. Determination of these costs would be part of the flexible budgeting process.

The allocation base selected for Radiology Department B is the number of X-ray films processed. Let's assume 5,800 films were processed last month. The actual variable overhead costs incurred were $1,740. What should the costs of processing 5,800 films have been? This can be determined by using the budget data in *Exhibit 7–5* and multiplying the number of films by the cost per film (5,800 × $.27) = $1,566.

The variance of $1,740 – $1,566, or $174, needs to be explained. If all the films were good, we could explain the $174 as a spending variance; the department spent more than it should have. However, let's introduce the concept of efficiency into Radiology Department B. For example, assume out of the 5,800 films processed, only 5,000 were usable for diagnostic purposes since only the usable tests will be billed to the patients. The standard costs are now 5,000 × $.27 = $1,350 and the total variance is $390 (1,740 – 1,350). We now can complete the variance framework introduced in chapter 6. Remember how the two variances are calculated: spending variance = actual cost $(AQ_I \times AP)$ – budgeted costs $(AQ_I \times SP)$, and the efficiency or quantity variance = budgeted costs $(AQ_I \times SP)$ – standard costs $(SQ_A \times SP)$.[1] In terms of Radiology Department B, the variance components are:

Spending variance $= 5,800(.30 - .27)$ =	$174 U
Efficiency variance $= .27(5,800 - 5,000)$ =	216 U
Total	$390 U

---

[1] The variances could also be expressed as $AQ_I(AP - SP)$ and $SP(AQ_I - SQ_A)$.

The total variable cost variance achieved by Radiology Department B would be $390, composed of a price variance and a quantity variance as determined above.

This example stresses the similarity between variable overhead variances and the variance for the materials and labor. Variable overhead variances are calculated in the same manner as for any variable costs. In *Exhibit 7–5*, no fixed costs were given. Therefore, only variable overhead cost variances could be calculated. Also, it should be noted that film was used as the allocation basis. This would be a rational basis for Radiology. In many cases, direct labor hours are used to allocate the variable overhead expenses. An example of this approach will be demonstrated later in this chapter.

The inclusion of fixed costs into the analysis poses different types of problems. Fixed overhead costs include depreciation on equipment, supervisors' salaries and clerical costs. Fixed costs, by definition, do not vary with volume levels. In the flexible budgeting process, fixed costs were shown as a static amount and variable costs as a function of volume. This can be expressed as a linear equation ($y = a + bx$), where a = fixed costs, b = variable cost per unit basis and x = volume (units). If we assume the fixed costs in Radiology Department B were $6,000 for one month, the flexible budget total for this department would be $7,566 = $6,000 + .27(5,800). Let's assume the actual overhead costs for Radiology Department B were $8,000 ($6,260 fixed and $1,740 variable).

The manager would like to have more information to evaluate the operating results since the budget was only $7,260, [$6,000 + $.27(6,000) = $7,260], based on an estimated 6,000 films to be processed. In Radiology Department B the actual fixed costs were $6,260. Because by definition fixed costs do not vary with volume, and the fixed overhead budget for the department was $6,000, the spending variance for fixed overhead was $260 ($6,000 – $6,260) unfavorable.[2] When the fixed overhead spending variance is combined with the variable overhead variances computed earlier, the report in *Exhibit 7–6* could be made to the manager. Note that the flexible budget total of $7,566 is not valid in this analysis because it is based on 5,800 total films and only 5,000 good films were achieved.

In most hospitals, the variance information presented in *Exhibit 7–6* would be sufficient for the manager to evaluate the performance of the supervisor of Radiology Department B. However, there is another variance that must be determined if management is to properly control the financial results of Radiology Department B. During the budget process, management had planned on completing an output of 6,000 films. The fixed overhead for the department was to be recovered through an

---

[2] In some textbooks this might be called the fixed overhead budget variance.

Exhibit 7–6
Analysis of spending and efficiency variances
for Radiology Department B

	Budgeted costs based on good films achieved $7,350*	Total variance to be explained: $650 unfavorable
Actual costs: $8,000		
Spending variance (variable overhead)	$174 U	5800 (.27 – .30)
Efficiency variance (variable overhead)	216 U	.27 (5,800 – 5,000)
Spending variance (fixed overhead)	260 U	(6,000 – 6,260)
Total variance	$650 U	

*$6,000 + .27 (5,000) = $7,350

overhead charge to be added to each good film completed. The overhead cost calculations follow:

Variable overhead costs	$ .27 per film
Fixed overhead rate	1.00 per film*
	$1.27 overhead cost/film**

$$\frac{\text{*\$6,000 (total fixed overhead cost)}}{6,000 \text{ (budgeted number of films to be processed)}} = \$1.00 \text{ fixed overhead rate per film}$$

**This would be considered the standard overhead cost per film or the standard overhead rate per film. The direct labor and materials plus other allocated costs would be added to this amount to develop total standard costs.

Therefore, each time an acceptable film was processed, Radiology Department B would be credited with $1.27 for overhead costs. Given the actual results for the month of March, Radiology Department B would be credited with the overhead rate per film ($1.27) multiplied by the number of good films (5,000), or $6,350. The actual costs were $8,000; therefore, Radiology Department B would show an unfavorable variance of $1,650 ($8,000 – $6,350). What caused the difference between the variance computed in *Exhibit 7–6* and the $1,650 unfavorable variance computed above? The additional $1,000 of variance ($1,650 – $650 from *Exhibit 7–6*) can be explained by reviewing how the $1.27 rate was determined.

It was initially estimated that 6,000 films would be processed by Radiology Department B. Dividing the fixed overhead costs ($6,000) by the 6,000 estimated volume resulted in a fixed overhead rate of $1.00 per film. However, only 5,000 films were processed. The difference (1,000) between the 6,000 estimated and the 5,000 obtained times the $1.00 fixed overhead rate equals the $1,000 unfavorable variance achieved. This variance, typically called the volume variance, is caused by calculating and

Exhibit 7–7
Summary of variances for Radiology Department B

(1) Actual costs incurred $	(2) Flexible budget* (based on input of 5,800 films)	(3) Flexible budget** (based on output of 5,000 films)	(4) Standard overhead applied to output (5,000 × $1.27)
$8,000	$7,566	$7,350	$6,350

$$(1) \qquad\qquad (4)$$

Total variance to be explained = actual costs − amount recovered
$$\$8{,}000 - \$6{,}350 = \$1{,}650$$

Detailed Variances (see below for computations)

Variable overhead spending variance	174U
Variable overhead efficiency variance	216U
Fixed overhead spending variance	260U
Volume variance	1,000U
Total variance	1,650U

Variable overhead spending variance = $AQ_l(AP - SP)$ = 5,800 × (.30 − .27) = $174U

Variable overhead efficiency variance = $SP(AQ_l - SQ_A)$ = .27 × (5,800 − 5,000) = $216U

Fixed overhead spending variance = actual fixed overhead − budgeted fixed overhead, or 6,260 − 6,000 = $260U

Fixed overhead volume variance = standard fixed overhead rate × (planned volume − actual "good" volume or output) = $1.00 per unit (6,000 − 5,000) = $1,000U. The volume variance also may be computed as the fixed overhead budget minus the standard fixed overhead allowed = $6,000 − (5,000 × $1.00) = $1,000U.

* The flexible budget for inputs used would be $6,000 + .27(5,800) or $7,566
** The flexible budget for good outputs would be $6,000 + .27 (5,000) or $7,350

- The difference between actuals and the flexible budget for inputs (#2) ($8,000 − $7,566 or $134) represents the total of the spending variances ($174 for variable and $260 for fixed overhead or $434).
- The difference between the flexible budget for inputs (#2) and the flexible budget for outputs (#3) ($7,566 − $7,350 or $216) is the variable overhead efficiency variance.
- The difference between the flexible budget for outputs (#3) and the standard overhead applied (#4) is the volume variance ($7,350 − $6,350 or $1,000).
- The difference between the actual costs incurred (#1) and the standard overhead applied to the output (#4) ($8,000 − $6,350 or $1,650) is the total overhead variance.
- The difference between actual costs (#1) and the flexible budget for output (#3) ($8,000 − $7,350 or $650) is typically called the budget overhead variance which combines the spending and efficiency variances but does not include volume variances.

establishing rates at an estimated volume. Unless the actual volume is the same as the estimated volume, there will always be a volume variance. The volume variance may not be controllable by the department manager and should rarely enter the performance evaluation process. The volume variance can be used to explain why planned charges may be insufficient to cover all costs. The volume variance may also be called the "denominator activity" variance by some authors. *Exhibit 7–7* summarizes the variance for Radiology Department B.

A sample problem

The concept of variance analysis was discussed in some detail earlier in this chapter and in the previous chapters. This section describes how variance analysis can be integrated into the planning and control process. The variance analysis, although typically supervised by the controller or vice president for finance, should be understandable to each supervisor. A useful way of accomplishing this is to develop a series of reports based on the flexible budget concept using our framework for analysis.

Before the operating period starts, the supervisor and the budget personnel should develop the necessary inputs to complete the flexible budget. A flexible budget for laboratory services is shown in *Exhibit 7–8.*

Exhibit 7–8
Flexible budget for laboratory services

	Fixed costs	*Standard variable costs*	*Budget**
Direct labor (per test)	-0-	$2.00	$60,000
Direct materials (per test)	-0-	.60	18,000
Variable overhead (per test)			
Indirect labor	$ 1,500	.05	3,000
Miscellaneous supplies	1,800	.09	4,500
Fixed overhead			
Department supervisor	3,000	-0-	3,000
Automatic equipment lease costs	6,000	-0-	6,000
	$12,300	$2.74	$94,500

Flexible budget formula = $12,300 + ($2.74)(number of tests) =
$12,300 + $2.74(30,000) = $94,500

*Estimated volume of tests = 30,000 per month

Development of standard overhead rate

Variable overhead rate	$.14 per test
Fixed overhead rate (12,300/30,000)*	.41 per test
Total overhead rate	$.55 per test

The supervisor can use the information contained in *Exhibit 7–8* to monitor the costs as they are incurred relative to the volume of tests completed. He/she does not have to wait until the end of the budget period to take corrective action. Periodic performance reports can be used to describe the actual costs and budgeted cost using the flexible budget. These performance reports, provided to both the supervisor and administrator, can be based on the variance analysis framework developed earlier in this chapter. For example, assume the actual costs for the laboratory for one month are as shown in *Exhibit 7–9*.

Top management will typically compare the actual costs incurred with the approved budget for the period. Comparing the actual costs with the planned budget totals would indicate an unfavorable variance of $9,982, which should be investigated. But is this the most relevant variance that could be calculated? In the analysis of *Exhibit 7–9*, the manager is being evaluated on the basis of a budget for 30,000 good tests. However, the manager should have incurred costs for only 29,000 tests. Of these, only 28,500 were acceptable tests. As explained earlier, a flexible budget can perform an important role in performance measurement but the flexible budget approach does not provide sufficient information to fully explain all variances.

Using the flexible budget formula developed in *Exhibit 7–8*, flexible budget costs are ($12,300 + 2.74x), where x = number of tests.

Actual costs	$104,482
Flexible budget costs [$12,300 + $2.74(28,500)]	90,390
Total variance from flexible budget	$ 14,092

However, this is not the total variance that occurred. Because 30,000 tests were budgeted, the fixed overhead costs of $12,300 were planned to

Exhibit 7–9
Actual laboratory costs

Number of tests completed	29,000
Number of satisfactory tests	28,500
Actual direct labor	$ 65,291
Actual direct materials	19,591
Actual variable overhead	7,100
Actual fixed overhead	12,500
Total actual costs	$104,482
Planned budget from *Exhibit 7–8* (based on 30,000 tests)	94,500
Total variance from original budget	$ 9,982 U

be recovered by adding $.41 to each completed test ($12,300/30,000). When only 28,500 tests were completed, only $11,685 (28,500 × $.41) in fixed overhead costs were charged to patients. The difference $615 ($12,300 − $11,685) is the volume variance developed earlier in this chapter. This variance, although generally not useful for performance measurement at the department level, must be considered by top management in meeting financial requirements.[3]

In *Exhibit 7–10,* a detailed variance analysis is completed and *Exhibit 7–11* lists a summary of all variances.

Exhibit 7–10
Calculation of variances for laboratory services

	(1) Actual costs incurred	(2) Flexible budget based on inputs	(3) Flexible budget based on outputs	(4) Standard costs applied to outputs
Labor	$ 65,291	$58,000	$57,000	$57,000
Material	$ 19,591	$17,400	$17,100	$17,100
Variable overhead	$ 7,100	$ 4,060	$ 3,990	$ 3,990
Fixed overhead	$ 12,500	$12,300	$12,300	$11,685
	$104,482	$91,760	$90,390	$89,775

(actual costs in Column 1 come from *Exhibit 7–8*)
Calculations:

	Calculations for Column 2 $AQ_I \times SP$	Calculations for Column 3 $(SQ_A \times SP)$	Calculations for Column 4 $SQ_A \times SP$
Labor	29,000 × $2 = $58,000	28,500 × $2 = $57,000	28,500 × $2 = $57,000 (each good test received $2 in labor costs)
Material	29,000 × .6 = $17,400	28,500 × .6 = $17,100	28,500 × .6 = $17,100 (each good test received .60 in material costs)
Variable overhead	29,000 × .14 = $4,060	28,500 × .14 = $3,990	28,500 × .14 = $3,990 (each good test received .14 in variable overhead costs)
Fixed overhead	$12,300 The budget for fixed overhead does not change with volume.	$12,300 The budget for fixed overhead does not change with volume.	28,500 × .41 = $11,685 (each good test received the planned overhead rate of .41 per test) *(cont.)*

---

[3] If department level supervisors are responsible for meeting budgeted outputs, they can also be held responsible for the total variance of $14,707, ($14,092 + $615).

Exhibit 7–10 (cont.)
Calculation of variances for laboratory services

Labor rate variance is the difference between Column 1 and Column 2.
65,291 − 58,000 = $7,291 U

Labor efficiency variance is the difference between Column 2 and Column 3.
58,000 − 57,000 = 1,000 U

Labor volume variance or the difference between Column 3 and Column 4 will always be zero because total standard variable costs change automatically with changes in volume.

Material price variance is the difference between Column 1 and Column 2 or $19,591 − $17,400 = $2,191 U.

Material usage variance is the difference between Column 2 and Column 3 or $17,400 − $17,100 = $300 U.

Material volume variance or the difference between Column 3 and Column 4 is zero for the same reason as stated under labor volume variance.

Variable overhead spending variance is the difference between Column 1 and Column 2
$7,100 − $4,060 = $3,040 U.

Variable overhead efficiency variance is the difference between Column 3 and Column 4
or $4,060 − $3,990 = $70 U.

There is no variable overhead volume variance for the reasons stated above.

- The fixed overhead spending variance is the difference between Columns 1 and 2 or $12,500 − $12,300 = $200 U.
- There is no efficiency variance for fixed overhead as Columns 2 and 3 indicate. Since the budget for fixed costs does not change with changes in volume, the budget for inputs and outputs will be the same.
- The fixed overhead volume variance is the difference between budgeted fixed costs (Columns 2 and 3) and the amount of fixed overhead applied to the output Column 4 or $12,300 − $11,685 = $615 U. This is also the same as the difference between budgeted output of 30,000 tests and actual output of 28,500 tests times the overhead rate or 1,500 × .41 = $615.

As noted in the discussion above, there are various stages in developing a complete variance analysis. The final step is to explain the difference between the planned budget of $94,500 and the actual costs of $104,482. As the analysis indicates, the initial variance of $9,982 unfavorable understated the actual variance of $14,707 unfavorable.

The difference between these variances of $4,725 can be explained in the following manner. The original budget was based on a volume of 30,000 tests and only 28,500 were actually good. The original budget

Exhibit 7–11
Summary of variances for laboratory department

Rate variance	65,291	– (29,000 × 2.00)	=	$ 7,291	U
Efficiency variance	(29,000 × 2.00)	– (29,500 × 2.00)	=	1,000	U
Price variance	19,591	– (29,000 × .60)	=	2,191	U
Usage variance	(29,000 × .60)	– (29,500 × .60)	=	300	U
Variable overhead					
spending variance	7,100	– (29,000 × .14)	=	3,040	U
Variable overhead					
efficiency variance	(29,000 × .14)	– (29,500 × .14)	=	70	U
Fixed overhead					
spending variance	(12,500	– 12,300)	=	200	U
Fixed overhead					
volume variance	(12,300)	– (28,500 × .41)	=	615	U
Total variance				$14,707	

included the variable costs for the 1,500 tests not completed or $4,110 (1,500 × 2.74). In addition, $615 (1,500 × .41) of fixed overhead was not charged to the 1,500 tests not completed as planned. The $4,110 and $615 equals the unexplained variance of $4,725.

It would seem the detailed variances shown in *Exhibits 7–10* and *7–11* and the summary in *7–12* provide a clearer picture of why the actual costs differed from the budgeted costs. Whether correction is needed depends on the reasons for the variances. However, the supervisor and the administrator now have a better idea of what questions to ask or what areas to explore in greater detail.

Exhibit 7–12
Summary of variances

Actual costs	$104,482	
Standard costs allocated to tests		
(from Column 4, *Exhibit 7–10*)	89,775	
Total variance to be explained	$ 14,707	
Total wage rate and price spending variances		
(from Column 1 – Column 2, *Exhibit 7–10 or 7–11*)	$ 12,722	U
Total efficiency and usage variances		
(from Column 2 – Column 3, *Exhibit 7–10 or 7–11*)	$ 1,370	U
Volume variance (from Column 3 – Column 4, *Exhibit*		
7–10 or 7–11)	$ 615	U
Total variances	$ 14,707	

Summary

Overhead costs pose a special challenge to the organization management. Because of the difficulty in relating this type of cost to specific outputs, an allocation process must be designed to arrive at the full costs of providing a given service. The allocation is a function of the total costs incurred and the volume of output achieved. Variances can be caused by changes in many different factors. It is important for managers to recognize responsibility and assign accountability for costs where this is possible. It is equally important to recognize those areas where care must be taken in the assignment of responsibility, such as the case of volume variances. In order for managers to take corrective action, they need the type of information contained in the variance analyses described in this chapter.

The appendix to this chapter carries the concept of variance analysis another step, and considers the implications of other factors for creating variances between actual and budgeted costs. Other factors which need to be considered include payer mix, patient mix, acuity mix, and DRG mix.

Questions and problems

1. Define indirect costs for a healthcare organization. Give examples.

2. Define overhead costs for a healthcare organization. Give examples.

3. Why must indirect costs be allocated in a healthcare organization?

4. List and describe the two primary inputs necessary for the allocation process in a healthcare organization.

5. List the criteria for selecting a proper base for allocating indirect costs in a healthcare organization.

6. For the following cost elements, select the proper allocation base and state your reasons for selecting that base.

Depreciation	Dietary—cafeteria
Employee benefits	Inpatient—cafeteria
Fiscal services	Nursing administration
Administrative services	Central services
Plant operations	Pharmacy
Plant maintenance	Medical records
Laundry and linen	Social services
Housekeeping	Central purchasing

7. Explain the difference between fixed and variable overhead costs.

8. Define the volume variance for a healthcare organization.

9. Name and describe the three individual variances that can be computed from overhead costs.

10. Given the data on nursing administration indirect costs, develop the overhead rates for the hospital as required based on a planned volume of 800 admissions. You should develop a fixed and variable component if possible. Calculate:
   a. the overhead rate per admission at the planned level of activity (800 admissions)
   b. an overhead rate based on the entire range of activity (0–1,000)
   c. an overhead rate based on the relevant range of activity (600–1,000)

Nursing Administration Indirect Costs

Admissions	0	200	400	600	800	1,000
Occupancy	0%	20%	40%	60%	80%	100%
Supervision	$2,000	$3,000	$3,000	$3,500	$3,500	$3,500
Clerical	300	400	500	600	700	800
Supplies	60	120	180	240	300	360
Education	200	200	200	200	200	200
	$2,560	$3,720	$3,880	$4,540	$4,700	$4,860

11. Selected operating information on four different operating care centers for the year 19XX is given below:

	A	B	C	D
Full-capacity direct labor hours	9,000	16,000	14,000	11,500
Budgeted direct labor-hours*	6,000	15,000	14,000	9,000
Actual direct labor-hours	6,000	15,500	13,500	9,250
Standard hours allowed	6,500	14,000	14,000	8,600
(based on actual output achieved and budgeted standards)				
*based on planned output				

For each of the four centers, state whether the provider would have:
   1. no volume variance
   2. a favorable volume variance
   3. an unfavorable volume variance

12. The dietary service of Memorial Hospital established the following standard cost per breakfast served:

Raw food costs	6 ounces at $0.08 per oz. =	$0.48
Labor	12 minutes at $0.06 per min. =	0.72
Variable overhead		0.18
Fixed overhead		0.25
Total standard cost		$1.63

During January, 7,000 ounces of raw food was purchased at a cost of $563.50, and total labor costs were $712.48. One thousand breakfasts were served during the month, which required 6,220 ounces of food and 11,680 minutes of labor. Normally they expect to serve 1,100 breakfasts. Actual total overhead for the month was $450.
a. Compute all possible variances.

13. Ellen Townsend, associate administrator of St. Joseph's Nursing Home, was concerned about the overhead costs of her billing department. The total variable-overhead budget variance was $4,000 unfavorable, while the fixed overhead spending variance was computed to be $2,000, also unfavorable. Actual overhead costs were $168,500, with $110,000 being fixed. Other available information indicates the standard variable cost per billing was $0.05, and the standard productivity per clerk was 10 billings per hour.
   If the variable overhead spending variance was determined to be $2,000 favorable, compute:
a. actual hours of output
b. standard hours allowed for output achieved
c. variable overhead efficiency variance

14. Beth Butler, controller of the Total Health Center, was reviewing the results of last year's operations to prepare the operations performance report for the administrator, Jeff Elland. The Total Health Center provides medical and psychiatric services to persons recovering from drug and alcohol abuse. A standard cost system had been derived and used by the center in budgeting and controlling costs. For example, the standard costs per unit based on 60,000 patient days were:

Materials—1 pound at	$ 2.00
Direct nursing labor	
(1.6 hours at $4 per hour)	6.40
Variable overhead costs	3.00
Fixed cost per patient day	2.00
Total standard costs	$13.40

The variable overhead cost per unit was calculated from the following annual overhead cost budget for the 60,000 patient days volume.

Indirect labor		
30,000 hours at $4 per hour		$120,000
Supplies—medical		
60,000 units at $.50 per unit		30,000
Allocated variable service costs		30,000
Total variable overhead costs		$180,000

The actual costs for the Total Health Center for March, when 5,000 patient days were achieved, were:

Materials	5,300 lbs. at $2.00 per lb.	$10,600
Direct nursing labor	8,200 hrs. at $4.10 per hr.	33,620
Indirect labor	2,400 hrs. at $4.10 per hr.	9,840
Supplies—medical	6,000 units at $.55 per unit	3,300
Allocated variable		
service department costs		3,200
Fixed costs		11,000
Total actual costs		$71,560

a. Calculate all possible variances from the data presented.
b. Prepare a report to the administrator which highlights the information in ways that will be useful in evaluating the performance of Total Health Center.

15. The Free Standing Laboratory prepares pharmaceutical supplies for several private practices in Central City. These tests are usually accomplished in standard batches of 5,000 units. The standard cost for a batch is:

Raw materials	200 lbs. at $0.04 per lb.	$ 8.00
Direct labor	4 hours at $5.15 per hour	20.60
Overhead (including		
variable overhead of $4.50)		10.00
Total standard cost per batch		$38.60

Data for December are:

Planned production	240 batches
Actual production	250 batches
Cost of raw materials purchased (55,000 lbs)	$2,310.50
Cost of raw materials used (51,250 lbs)	2,152.50
Direct labor cost (998 hours)	5,189.60
Actual overhead cost	2,560.00
Budgeted fixed overhead cost	1,320.00

a. Compute all possible variances.

16. The radiology department of St. Louis Hospital has requested that an analysis be made of their overhead costs for the month of May. The standards as developed by the controller are as follows:

	Standard cost per test	Standard cost per DLH
Variable overhead	$5.00	$2.50
Fixed overhead	2.00	1.00
Total overhead per test	$7.00	$3.50

It takes two direct labor hours at standard to complete one test. In May, 1,600 tests were made, and actual total overhead was $12,000; 3,100 actual direct labor hours were used.

The flexible monthly overhead cost budget on a direct labor basis is:

Standard direct labor hours	Budgeted overhead
1,000	$ 5,500
2,000	8,000
3,000 (budgeted DLH)	10,500
4,000	13,000
5,000	15,500

a. Calculate the flexible budget formula.
b. Calculate the overhead variances.
c. Calculate the overhead variances assuming actual fixed overhead was $3,000.

17. Freedom Hospital plans to discontinue a department with a contribution to overhead of $117,000, and allocated overhead of $141,000 of which $123,000 cannot be eliminated. What would be the effect of this discontinuance on Freedom's operating margin?

18. The following information is available on the single service offered by Emergency Medical Supplies Company for the month of March:

	Materials used	Direct labor	Variable overhead
Total standard cost	$260	$1,900	$950
Actual costs incurred	276	?	985
Materials quantity variance	$ 20 favorable		

The following additional information is available for March production:

Number of units produced	100
Actual direct labor hours	410
Standard overhead rate per hour	$2.50
Standard price of one pound of materials	$0.40
Overhead is based on direct labor hours	
Difference between standard and actual	
cost per unit produced—March	$1.19 unfavorable

a. What is the standard cost of a single unit of service?
b. What was the actual cost of a unit of service produced during March?
c. How many pounds of material are required at standard per unit of service?
d. What was the materials price variance for March?
e. What was the labor rate variance?
f. What was the labor efficiency variance?
g. What was the overhead spending variance?
h. What was the overhead efficiency variance?

19. Fair Weight, Inc., produces testing instruments for laboratories. The company uses standards to control its costs. The labor standards which have been set for one very popular instrument are:

Direct labor time per instrument	15 minutes
Direct labor rate per hour	$5.20

During 19X1, the company worked 7,750 hours in order to produce 30,000 of these instruments. The direct labor cost amounted to $39,525.
a. What direct labor cost should have been incurred in the manufacture of the 30,000 instruments? By how much does the cost differ from the cost that was incurred?
b. Break down the difference in cost in terms of a labor rate variance and a labor efficiency variance.
c. For each direct labor hour worked, the company expects to incur $5 in variable overhead costs. This rate was experienced in 19X1. What effect did the efficiency (or inefficiency) of labor have on the variable overhead costs in 19X1?

20. General Laboratory flexible budget (in condensed form) is given below:

	Cost formula per DLH	Direct labor hours (DLH)		
		@8,000	@9,000	@10,000
Variable overhead costs	$ 1.05	$ 8,400	$ 9,450	$10,500
Fixed overhead costs		24,800	24,800	24,800
Total overhead costs		$33,200	$34,250	$35,300

The following information is available:

For 19X1, a standard activity of 8,000 direct labor hours was chosen to compute the predetermined overhead rate:
  Overhead rate: $33,200/8,000 DLH = $4.15
  Variable element: $8,400/8,000 DLH = $1.05
  Fixed element: $24,800/8,000 DLH = $3.10
In working 8,000 standard direct labor hours, the company should produce 3,200 units of output.
During 19X1, the company's actual operating results were:

Number of output units	3,500
Actual direct labor hours	8,500
Actual variable overhead costs	$ 9,860
Actual fixed overhead costs	$25,100

a. What were the standard hours allowed for the output of 19X1?
b. Compute the variable overhead spending and efficiency variances, and the fixed overhead budget and volume variances for 19X1.

21. Dietary costs at Memorial Hospital can be divided into two categories: labor costs and supply costs. Labor costs are considered 100 percent variable and are related to the number of meals served. Analysis of labor costs identifies two factors: the average hourly rate paid per manhour and the number of manhours per meal served. The following labor budget formula is used: dietary labor costs = meals served × (manhours per meal served) × (rate per manhour).

Supply costs are divided into two groups: food and all other. Food costs are 100 percent variable relative to the number of meals served. All other costs are considered fixed. Therefore the following budget formula is used for supply costs: supply costs = (meals served × food cost per meal) + fixed costs.

The following dietary worksheet identifies all the factors used to analyze the budget variances for April.

The following narrative was provided by the department manager:

"A general summary indicates that productivity is not as high as was anticipated; however, this is more than offset by the lower pay rates and lesser volumes than were expected. This creates an overall favorable labor cost variance. Food costs, although partially offset by lower volumes are so much higher than planned that there is an overall unfavorable variance in this department."

Data for April Dietary Department:

	Actual	Budget
Volume of meals served	19,476	21,250
Labor hours per meal served	.28	.26
Rate of pay per labor hour	$3.60	$3.79
Meals wasted	0	0
Fixed costs per meal	$0.96	$0.73
Fixed costs	$2,191	$3,425

a. Evaluate the variance analysis used in the dietary department.
b. Revise the analysis provided by the department manager as appropriate.

22. Memorial Hospital would like to evaluate DRG 101 and institute a standard cost approach for budgeting and planning purposes. The following data were collected for the DRG from hospital operations:

Costs:
    Operating room direct costs
        Fixed costs = $13,000
        Variable costs = $3.00 per operating room minute
    Radiology direct costs
        Fixed costs = $4,000,000
        Variable costs = $1.00 per relative value unit
    Laboratory direct costs
        Fixed costs = $2,000,000
        Variable costs = $0.50 per lab test
    Pharmacy direct costs
        Fixed costs = $800,000
        Variable costs = $3.00 per prescription
    Inpatient routine costs
        Fixed costs = $25,000,000
        Variable costs = $2.00 per patient day
    Indirect costs
        Fixed costs = $5,000,000
        Variable costs = $3.00 per DRG
    Medical procedures costs
        Fixed costs = $1,000,000
        Variable costs = $25.00 per medical procedure
    All other direct costs
        Fixed costs = $5,000,000
        Variable costs = $3.00 per DRG

Resources required for DRG 101:

4 medical procedures
10 inpatient days
3 lab tests
4 pharmacy prescriptions
2 radiology RVUs

Miscellaneous data:

Total DRGs for the year	100,000
Total medical procedures	10,000
Total laboratory tests	20,000
Total radiology relative value units	20,000
Total patient days	116,800
Total pharmacy prescriptions	20,000
DRG 101 admissions	2,500

Make any assumptions you need to complete the standard cost computation.

a. Develop a standard cost for DRG 101 using a direct cost format.

b. Develop a standard cost for DRG 101 using a full cost format.

23. Saint Mary's Hospital has an estimated patient mix and reimbursement basis as follows:

	Mix	Reimbursement
Self-pay	25%	$140 per patient day
Private insurance	40%	140 per patient day
Medicare	15%	120 per patient day
Medicaid	20%	130 per patient day
Fixed costs	$85,000	
Variable costs	$20 per patient day	

a. Calculate the breakeven point in terms of revenue.

b. Calculate the required number of patient days for breakeven.

c. Calculate the mix variance assuming the following actual mix of patient days (Note: no other variances can be computed from the data given).

Self-pay	189
Private insurance	301
Medicare	120
Medicaid	150
Total	760 patient days

24. Hillside Hospital estimated its patient mix to be:

	Planned mix	Actual mix	Planned contribution margin	Actual contribution margin
Self-pay	3,150	3,000	$203	$200
Private insurance	2,625	2,500	197	200
Medicare	1,575	1,500	181	180
Medicaid	3,150	3,000	163	170

a. Calculate the price variances.
b. Calculate the quantity variances.

25. Harborside Clinic estimated its volume for the next month at 5,150 units of activity. Harborside expects a mix of 30 percent inpatient, 25 percent outpatient, and 45 percent emergency services. Charges are $140 per patient day to inpatient, $110 for outpatient services, and $80 per unit for emergency. Actual results are:

	Mix	Contribution margin
Inpatient	1,530	$112
Outpatient	1,275	93
Emergency	2,295	57

Assume variable costs of $20.
a. Calculate the price variances.
b. Calculate the quantity variances.

26. Saint George Hospital projected its patient mix for the next month to be as follows:

	Mix	Charges
Inpatient	25%	$170
Outpatient	20%	145
Ambulance	25%	70
X-ray	30%	80

Fixed costs are estimated to be $73,000 with variable costs of $30.
a. Compute the breakeven volume and the planned number of patients in each category.

b. Compute the mix variance from the actual patient mix given below:

	Mix
Inpatient	212 patient days
Outpatient	169 patient days
Ambulatory	228 patient days
X-ray	259 patient days

27. The Sun Valley Health Care Center offers three services with the following projected patient mix:

Nursing care	120 patients per week
X-ray and lab test	1,350 patients per week
First aid classes	530 patients per week

Nursing care charges are $70 per week with variable costs of $15 per patient week. Lab fees are $25 per patient with variable costs of $10 per patient. Class charges are $10 per patient with variable costs of $2 per patient. Fixed costs = $1,310 per week.

a. What is the mix variance if the actual patient mix is:

Nursing care	109 patients per week
X-ray and lab tests	1,431 patients per week
First aid classes	460 patients per week

28. Valley Center Hospital has reimbursed rates of $210 per patient day from Medicare, $195 per patient day from Medicaid, and $225 per patient day from self-pay or private insurance companies. Fixed costs are estimated at $884,000 with variable costs of $25 per patient day.

a. Calculate the patient days required to operate at breakeven if projected patient mix is 20% for self-pay, 40% for private insurance, 15% for Medicare, and 25% for Medicaid.

b. Find the price, quantity, and mix variances with actual results as follows:

	Patient days	Contribution margin
Self-pay	901	$197
Private insurance	1,842	201
Medicare	688	200
Medicaid	1,165	208

29. A nonprofit clinic provides four types of services in the following proportions:

Service A	25%
Service B	40%
Service C	25%
Service D	10%

It is estimated that the clinic will serve 2,540 people next month. Planned charges are $55 per person, with variable costs of $5 per person and fixed costs of $90,000. Actual results are:

Service A	658 people
Service B	1,024 people
Service C	605 people
Service D	348 people
Total	2,635 people
Actual contribution margin = $45	

a. Calculate the contribution margin variance.
b. Calculate the patient quantity variances.

30. Assume the same facts as in question 29, except that the planned contribution margin (CM) and actual results are as follows:

	Planned CM	*Actual people served*
Service A	$50	607
Service B	45	1,072
Service C	40	612
Service D	50	246

a. Calculate the variances in the contribution margin.

31. The Lakeview Memorial Hospital has the following projected patient mix:

Self-pay	15%
Private insurance	30
Medicare	20
Medicaid	35

The reimbursement rate is $180 per patient day for both Medicare and Medicaid, and $190 per patient day for self-pay and private insurance.

Fixed costs	$840,000
Daily charges	$190 per patient day
Variable costs	$30 per patient day

a. Find the total revenue required to operate at breakeven.
b. Find the patient days required to operate at breakeven.
c. Assume the Lakeview Memorial Hospital is expecting to break-even. Assuming that actual results were as follows:

	Patient days	Contribution margin
Self-pay	910	$157
Private insurance	1,610	163
Medicare	1,050	148
Medicaid	1,720	145

Find the price, quantity, and mix variances.

32. Paradise Hospital's flexible budget is given below:

Overhead costs	Cost formula per patient day	Number of patient days 10,000	11,000	12,000
Maintenance	$1.15	$11,500	$12,650	$13,800
Indirect material	0.80	8,000	8,800	9,600
Professional development	0.50	5,000	5,500	6,000
Total	$2.45	$24,500	$26,950	$29,400

During a recent period the company provided 11,400 patient days. The overhead costs incurred were:

Maintenance	$11,200
Indirect materials	9,750
Professional development	7,300

The patient days budgeted for the period had been 12,000.
a. Prepare a performance report for the period. Indicate whether variances are favorable or unfavorable.
b. Discuss the significance of the variances. Might some variances be the result of others? Explain.

33. Memorial Medical Corporation has hospitals in Seattle and Dallas. The hospital in Dallas is a children's hospital while the facility in Seattle specializes in sports medicine (sports injuries). The following revenues and costs were budgeted for the year ending December 31, 1991. (Estimated revenue of $200 per day.)

	Total	Seattle	Dallas
Revenue	$3,000,000	$1,100,000	$1,900,000
Variable costs:			
Lab	750,000	275,000	475,000
Dietary	805,000	330,000	475,000
Billings and collections	505,000	220,000	285,000
Fixed overhead costs	800,000	350,000	450,000
Fixed regional promotion costs	100,000	50,000	50,000
Allocated home office costs	150,000	55,000	95,000
Total costs	$3,110,000	$1,280,000	$1,830,000
Operating income (loss)	(110,000)	(180,000)	70,000

Due to the budget operating loss of the Seattle facility, Memorial Medical Corporation is considering the possibility of closing it down. If this alternative is chosen, all but $100,000 of the fixed overhead costs would be eliminated. (Any proceeds from sale of any assets would exceed book value and exactly cover all termination costs.)

The home office costs referred to are fixed and allocated on patient days. Fixed regional promotional costs are discretionary advertising costs.

Memorial Medical Center is considering the following alternatives:
1. The prime location and excellent facilities offered by the Seattle location can allow Memorial Medical Center to lease the facility to another hospital specializing in sports medicine. The lease agreement would call for a fixed payment of $75 per patient day. Fixed overhead costs would remain the same, while promotional costs would be reduced by 50 percent. It is believed that 5,500 patient days are attainable.
2. Close the Seattle facility and expand the operation at the Dallas hospital to attain the budgeted total patient days. This alternative would increase Dallas' fixed regional promotional costs by $50,000.
3. Expand Seattle's operation from the budgeted 5,500 patient days to 8,000. This would increase promotional costs by $50,000.
   a. Compute the number of patient days required by the Seattle facility to cover its fixed overhead costs and fixed regional promotional costs (without considering the effects of implementing plans 1, 2, or 3).
   b. Prepare a schedule by hospital, and in total, computing budgeted contribution margin and operating income resulting from the implementation of each of the following plans:
      1) Plan 1
      2) Plan 2
      3) Plan 3

Keywords: allocation; composite contribution margin; fixed overhead; overhead; overhead allocation base; overhead rate; overhead variance; patient mix variance; payer mix variance; variable overhead.

References

Andrianos, James, and Mark Dykan. "Using Cost Accounting Data to Improve Clinical Value." *Healthcare Financial Management* (May 1996): 44–48.

Anthony, Robert N., and David W. Young. *Management Control in Nonprofit Organizations.* 4th ed. Homewood, IL: Richard D. Irwin, 1988.

Anthony, Robert N., and James S. Reece. *Accounting: Text & Cases.* 8th ed. Homewood, IL: Richard D. Irwin, 1988.

Awasthi, V.N., and L. Eldenburg. "Providing Cost Data to Physicians Helps Contain Costs." *Healthcare Financial Management* (April 1996): 40–42.

Berlin, M.F. "Using Cost Accounting in a Medical Group Practice." *Medical Group Management Journal* 42, no. 3 (May–June 1995): 22–32.

Canby, J.B., IV. "Applying Activity-Based Costing to Healthcare Settings." *Healthcare Financial Management* (February 1995): 50–56.

Chart of Accounts for Hospitals. Chicago, IL: American Hospital Association, 1976.

Cleverley, W.O. "Product Costing for Health Care Firms." *Health Care Management Review* 12, no. 4 (1987): 39–48.

Hill, N.T. "Adoption of Costing Systems by U.S. Hospitals." *Hospital and Health Services Administration* 39, no. 4 (winter 1994): 521–537.

Horngren, Charles T., George Foster, and Srikant M. Datar. *Cost Accounting: A Managerial Emphasis.* Englewood Cliffs: Prentice Hall, 1994.

Karpiel, M.S. "Using Patient Classification Systems to Identify Ambulatory Care Costs." *Healthcare Financial Management* (November 1994): 31–37.

Mays, Janet, and Gus Gordon. "Developing a Cost Accounting System for a Physician Group Practice." *Healthcare Financial Management* (October 1996): 73–79.

Miller, Thomas R., and J. Bruce Ryan. "Analyzing Cost Variance in Capitated Contracts." *Healthcare Financial Management* (February 1995): 22–23.

Neumann, Bruce R., Jan P. Clement, and Jean C. Cooper. *Financial Management: Concepts and Applications for Health Care Organizations.* Dubuque: Kendall/Hunt, 1997.

Ramsey, R.H. "Activity-Based Costing for Hospitals." *Hospital & Health Services Administration* (fall 1994): 385–396.

Ryan, J. B., and S.B. Clay. "Understanding the Law of Large Numbers." *Healthcare Financial Management* (October 1995): 22–24.

Schimmel, V.E., C. Alley, and A.M. Heath. "Measuring Costs: Product Line Accounting Versus Ratio of Cost to Charges." *Topics in Health Care Finance* 13, no. 4 (1987): 76–86.

Patient mix and variance analysis

Introduction

In chapter 4, we discussed how to use the well-known management accounting technique of "breakeven analysis" to help accomplish better planning and budgeting for hospitals and other healthcare organizations. This appendix extends the concepts of cost behavior analysis to the management control process of determining why actual results differ from the planned budget.

Background and description of the problem

Breakeven analysis, or cost/volume/profit analysis as it is commonly called, depends on the ability to determine cost behavior patterns and to segregate costs that vary with some index of activity, such as volume. For an entire hospital, the contribution margin is the difference between patient revenues and the variable cost of treating the patient. For example, assume that a patient's daily charge is $1,200 and variable costs of treating that patient are $400. In this case, the contribution margin is $800. The contribution margin is available to cover fixed costs (including nonreimbursable costs) and to provide funds needed to remain a financially viable healthcare provider.

In the following analyses, the concept of contribution margin will be used because the difference between reimbursement rates and variable costs seems to clearly indicate the effects of important decision variables. However, the same type of variance analysis could be done based on total reimbursement rates and total costs (fixed and variable).

Given the relationship between revenues and variable costs, the role of breakeven analysis can be clearly shown. The breakeven point in a hospital is assumed to be that level of charges or patient days that allows the hospital to cover all fixed costs and all nonreimbursable costs, provide funds for the future and, in a proprietary hospital, earn a return on investment. The hospital will breakeven at the level of activity where the contribution margin equals the total of these required costs.

For example, consider a hospital with the following data:

Patient mix		Reimbursement basis per patient day
Self-pay	20%	$1,200 (total charges)
Private insurance	25%	1,200 (total charges)
Medicare	30%	1,100 (cost or charges whichever is lower)
Medicaid	25%	1,000 (reimbursable costs only)
Fixed costs	= $8,000,000	
Required margin	= $2,000,000	
Daily charges	= $1,200	per patient day
Variable costs	= $ 400	per patient day (these costs are assumed to be the same for each patient, regardless of the method of payment)

Given the above data, what level of total revenue must be achieved to operate at breakeven? In order to determine this point, a composite contribution margin is developed in *Exhibit 1*.

The composite contribution margin ratio is .64($720/$1,120). Therefore, the composite average variable cost ratio is 36 percent because the variable cost plus the contribution margin must equal unity.

The breakeven level of revenue is calculated in the following manner:

$$TR = \$8,000,000 + .36TR + 2,000,000$$
$$TR - .36TR = \$10,000,000$$
$$TR = \$15,625,000$$

Exhibit 1
Composite contribution margin

Method of payment	Patient mix	×	Contribution margin	=	Weighted contribution margin	Reimbursement rate	Weighted reimbursement rate
Self-pay	20%		(1200 – 400) = $800		$160	$1200	$ 240
Private insurance	25%		(1200 – 400) = $800		200	1200	300
Medicare	30%		(1100 – 400) = $700		210	1100	330
Medicaid	25%		(1000 – 400) = $600		150	1000	250
Composite contribution margin =					$720		
Composite average daily adjusted rate =							$1120

The average number of patient days in each category is obtained by first determining the total number of expected patient days ($15,625,000/ $1,120 = 13,951 patient days). The quantity of expected patient days indicates an expected level of volume that is necessary to operate at break-even and cover all identified costs. The number of patient days in each patient category is determined by multiplying the projected volume (13,951) by the patient mix as shown in *Exhibit 2*.

Exhibit 2
Patient days by payer mix

Method of payment	Patient mix	Patient days
Self-pay	20%	2,790
Private insurance	25%	3,488
Medicare	30%	4,185
Medicaid	25%	3,488
Total patient days required to breakeven		13,951

Given the calculations in the preceding paragraphs, a budget could be developed for the coming operating period which would incorporate these assumptions regarding patient mix and expected cost behavior patterns. If these assumptions hold, there would be no differences between the planned level of operation and the actual results achieved, and, therefore, no need for variance analysis. However, under most actual conditions, some variances could be expected.

In order to take corrective action and allow for better planning in future periods, hospital administrators and managers need to be able to determine what caused the actual results to differ from the plan.

Applications

A. In the example discussed above, a composite contribution margin was developed from a planned patient mix and a planned cost behavior. With the composite contribution margin and planned fixed costs, the number of patient days was determined. Assume that during the period of operation the planned number of patient days (13,951) was achieved (this assumption is relaxed later), yet the hospital had a deficit contribution margin of $166,950 as shown in *Exhibit 4*. What caused this deficit? Two reasons typically are responsible—the mix of patients may have varied from the plan and/or the contribution margin may have differed from the plan.

For ease in following the analysis, the data from the planning phase are recapitulated in *Exhibit 3*.

Exhibit 3
Planning data

	Planned mix (Patient days)		Planned contribution margin	Weighted contribution margin
Self-pay	20%	2,790	$800	$160
Private insurance	25%	3,488	800	200
Medicare	30%	4,185	700	210
Medicaid	25%	3,488	600	150

Total patient days   13,951
Composite average contribution margin $720
Planned total contribution margin = $10,044,720 =
  (patient days)(planned contribution margin)
  ($13,951)   ($720)

Assume the actual results were as shown in *Exhibit 4*.

Exhibit 4
Actual results

	Actual mix %	Patient days	Actual contribution margin rate	Actual contribution margin
Self-pay	18.6%	2,600	$780	$2,028,000
Private insurance	24.7%	3,450	820	2,829,000
Medicare	30.9%	4,310	690	2,973,900
Medicaid	25.8%	3,591	570	2,046,870
Total days		13,951		$9,877,770

Total variance in contribution margin = $9,877,770 − $10,044,720 = $166,950

Hospital managers need to be able to identify why the variance ($166,950) in contribution margin occurred. What controllable or uncontrollable variables produced this unfavorable variance? A patient mix variance and a contribution margin rate variance can be developed from the above data.

The patient mix variances and the contribution margin rate variances (*Exhibits 5* and *6*) indicate that the deficit contribution margin was caused both by a change in patient mix and by a difference in the contribution margin rates per patient day. However, it highlights the fact that a significant portion of the total variance ($166,950) was caused by a reduction in the contribution margin rates of $133,830. Further analysis should be made to find out why either the reimbursement rate and charges or variable costs (or both) differ from the planned amounts. In addition, the

Exhibit 5
Variance due to patient mix differences

	Difference in patient days (actual-planned)	×	Expected contribution margin rate difference	=	Variance in contribution margins due to patient mix
Self-pay	(2,600 − 2,790) = −190		(800 − 720) = 80		$15,200 U
Private insurance	(3,450 − 3,488) = −38		(800 − 720) = 80		3,040 U
Medicare	(4,310 − 4,185) = 125		(700 − 720) = −20		2,500 U
Medicaid	(3,591 − 3,488) = 103		(600 − 720) = −120		12,360 U
Total mix variance					$33,100 U

Exhibit 6
Variance due to contribution margin rate differences

	Actual patient days	×	Difference in contribution margins (actual-budget)	=	Variance in contribution margin rates
Self-pay	2,600		(780 − 800) = −20		$ 52,000 U
Private insurance	3,450		(820 − 800) = 20		69,000 F
Medicare	4,310		(690 − 700) = −10		43,100 U
Medicaid	3,591		(570 − 600) = −30		107,730 U
Total contribution margin rate allowance					$133,830 U

patient mix variance indicates that net contribution margins have decreased in all (four) patient classes. Decreases in contribution margins from self-pay and private insurance patients resulted from a decrease in the number of patient days in those classes. Patient days did increase in both Medicare and Medicaid classes, however, this had a negative effect on contribution margin because of the shift from patients with above-average contribution margins to patients providing below-average margins.

B. The earlier constraint that the actual patient days were equal to planned patient days can now be relaxed. If, for example, the hospital achieved only 13,551 days, with a total contribution margin of $9,591,770 instead of the planned 13,951 patient days and $10,044,700 of contribution margin, the deficit contribution margin is now $452,930. A quantity variance (400 days)($720.00 per day) = $288,000 is added to the analysis indicated above. All three variances are recalculated in *Exhibits 7, 8,* and *9*. Given that the actual distribution of patient days is:

Exhibit 7
Variance due to patient quantity differences

	Difference in patient days (actual-planned)	×	Budgeted composite-contribution margin	=	Variance in contribution margins due to quantity differences
Self-pay	2,500 − 2,790 = −290		720		$208,800 U
Private insurance	3,350 − 3,488 = −138		720		99,360 U
Medicare	4,210 − 4,185 = 25		720		18,000 F
Medicaid	3,419 − 3,488 = 3		720		2,160 F
Total quantity variance					$288,000 U

Exhibit 8
Variance due to patient mix differences

	Difference in patient days	×	Expected contribution margin rate difference	=	Variance in contribution margins due to patient days
Self-pay	−290		80		$23,200 U
Private insurance	−138		80		11,040 U
Medicare	25		−20		500 U
Medicaid	3		−120		360 U
Total mix variance					$35,100 U

Exhibit 9
Variance due to contribution margin rate differences

	Actual patient days	×	Difference in contribution margins (actual-budget)	=	Variance in contribution margin rates
Self-pay	2,500		(780 − 800) = −20		$ 50,000 U
Private insurance	3,350		(820 − 800) = 20		67,000 F
Medicare	4,210		(690 − 700) = −10		42,100 U
Medicaid	3,491		(570 − 600) = −30		104,730 U
Total contribution margin rate variance					$129,830 U

	Actual patient days
Self-pay	2,500
Private insurance	3,350
Medicare	4,210
Medicaid	3,491
Total patient days	13,551

The total variance would consist of the following components:

Total quantity variance (*Exhibit 7*)	$288,000 U
Total mix variance (*Exhibit 8*)	35,100 U
Total rate variance (*Exhibit 9*)	129,830 U
Total contribution margin variance	$452,930 U

It is important to note that other quantity and mix variances can also be calculated. There is no unanimity regarding the theoretical, correct calculation of mix variances. The authors feel that the quantity and mix variance illustrated above will provide the most useful information to hospital managers regarding shifts in types of patients.

The analyses of variance presented above permit organization management to determine which areas of operation need further attention. These analyses direct him/her to analyze further why the variances in rate and quantity occurred. The unfavorable variances, by themselves, are only an indicator that some change may need to be made. On the other hand, the manager may find that certain exogenous effects may be resulting in the identified variances. The organization may have little control over some of these variables. In any event, isolating the effects of both controllable and uncontrollable variables will permit the manager of healthcare organizations to devote his/her attention and energy in areas where significant positive changes in contribution margin may be attained. Furthermore, the analyses outlined above do provide additional data for planning and for improving budgeting and motivation within the organization.

Variance analysis for a state medicaid program

This section summarizes the variance analyses used by a state agency to monitor the effects of utilization changes on total program costs. The actual FY86 data are a "standard," and variance analysis techniques are used to analyze the changes in costs of outpatient pharmacy services from one year to the next. Realistically, this type of analysis is believed to be useful for monitoring components of the Medicaid program. Linear regression techniques are used to develop estimates for the budget request to the legislature, but are not used to analyze cost changes from year to year.

The variance analysis performed is based on the data in *Exhibit 10* on the following assumptions:

> TC = R × U × P where:
> R = Number of unduplicated Medicaid recipients
> U = Units of service (days) per recipient (average)
> P = Price per unit of service (average)

Thus, the change in the total cost of a specific component of the Medicaid program, such as outpatient pharmacy services, is a function of the change in the utilization of services by each recipient and the change in the price of each unit of service.

The variance analysis for outpatient pharmacy services is shown in *Exhibit 11*. The total variance in outpatient pharmacy costs in 1990 is an increase of $1,512,224, noted as an unfavorable (U) variance. This total is broken down first into a price and a quantity variance, and the quantity variance is further broken down into a utilization rate variance (services per recipient) and a usage variance (recipients). Thus, the net increase in cost of $1,512,224 is explained by: 1) an increase in price per unit of service that accounted for a $358,917 increase in total cost; 2) an increase in the number of services consumed by each recipient which accounted for a $1,726,784 increase in total cost; and 3) a decrease in the number of recipients which accounted for a $573,006 decrease in total cost.

Once the variances are isolated, the next and most important step is to analyze the reason(s) for the variances. In the case of the price variance, the most obvious reason for an increase is inflation. The rate of increase observed between FY89 and FY90 was 4.9 percent. Nationally, the rate of increase in the medical care component of the CPI (1975–1976) was 9.5 percent. Due to the rural nature of the state and the number of small hospitals in it, the absolute increases in costs that show up in the Medicaid program reimbursement statistics are probably less than the national average. However, in any given year, the percentage increase may be greater.

Exhibit 10
Outpatient pharmacy services

	FY87	FY88	FY89	Projected FY90	Actual FY90
Recipients	8,604	9,727	8,323	8,756	7,546
Units of service	49,267	56,108	49,022	52,064	58,236
Total cost	$4,328,962	$5,757,866	$6,139,005	$7,305,968	$7,651,229
Units/recipient*	5.73	5.77	5.89	5.95	7.72
Price/unit*	$87.87	$102.62	$125.22	$140.44	$131.38

*Averages derived from the first lines of data.

Exhibit 11
Outpatient pharmacy services

$7,651,229 TC - FY90
6,139,005 TC - FY89

$1,512,224 Total variance to be explained*

AQ × AP	AQ × SP	SQ × SP
(58,236 × $131.38)	(58,236 × $125.22)	(49,022 × $125.22)
= $7,651,229	= $7,292,312	= $6,139,005

Price	Quantity	Total
$358,917 U	$1,153,307 U	$1,512,224 U

AQ × AU	AQ × SU	SQ × SU
(7,546 × 7.72) = 58,236	(7,546 × 5.89) = 44,446	(8,323 × 5.89) = 49,022

Utilization Rate	Usage	Total
13,790 U	4,576 F	9,214 U

13,790 × $125.22 =	$1,726,784 U	= Utilization rate variance
(4,576) × $125.22 =	(573,006) F	= Usage variance
	358,917 U	= Price variance
	$1,512,695	= Total variance explained*

*Differences due to rounding

The usage variance is difficult to explain. Why did fewer people utilize outpatient pharmacy services in FY90? One possibility is that the number of people on AFDC (welfare) decreased in FY90, as it did in FY89. This seems to correlate with the historical trend data for recipients presented in *Exhibit 10*. A tightening of eligibility requirements could also play a major role here.

Because the utilization rate variance is the most significant factor in the increase in total costs, it demands the most attention. It is also the most difficult to analyze. Possible explanations are that Medicaid patients with multiple diagnoses may have required more pharmacy services. It is also possible that persons eligible for Medicaid are becoming more aware of the program and of their right to use it, and are therefore using it more fully. Still another possibility is that there is no real incentive to control utilization, since the state reimburses fully for pharmacy prescriptions with no copayment.

Essentially, the total variance can be divided into several variances. With this type of information, the administrator is better able to fix responsibility, ask relevant questions, and take corrective action if needed.

Although this appendix focused on the variances associated with method of payment, the same analyses could easily be applied to patient care categories. The underlying objective of any variance analysis should be to obtain better information for decision making. These techniques can be adapted to a wide variety of managerial decisions.

Summary

In most organizations, actual results will differ from the planned budget. The healthcare manager needs to know not only what the amount of differences were, but, perhaps more importantly, why these differences occurred. Analytical techniques, such as variance analysis, are helpful in identifying the causes of these differences.

CHAPTER 8

Pricing strategies

"We have just been approached by an HMO wanting to know how much we are willing to discount from our published charges to get their business. What should we do?"

"We have made an offer to Acme Incorporated to provide physical examinations to all of their employees every six months, for $150 per employee. We charge $300 to do it in the office. How can we make money at that rate?"

"If our full costs are $250 to do a scan, how in the world can we keep doing them when we only receive $150?"

Introduction

Since the procompetitive environment started, the role of pricing decisions in healthcare management has received increased emphasis. Prospective pricing for hospitals, and its adaptation into outpatient services, physicians, long-term care, and home health services, pricing decisions and strategies in healthcare take on a more important meaning. At the same time, published charges of healthcare organizations have less meaning. Published charges may be compared to the sticker price on an automobile. It becomes the basis for negotiation about what amount the customer will pay. This is due to the fact that very few purchasers pay charges. Every major payer is seeking a discount from the published charges.

Determination of an appropriate price to charge for services has confounded decision makers and economists for decades. There was general agreement that the long-run pricing decisions should be based on the recovery of full cost, if the organization was to remain financially viable. However, this concept was not particularly useful in making pricing decisions. As explained below and in earlier chapters, the type of decision being made would influence the type of cost information needed. With the advent of a competitive market for health services, pricing policy required a different focus on what costs were relevant to the decision. In order to further understand the difficulties to be encountered, we need to enumerate several different concepts of price determination:

1. Full-cost pricing
2. Cost/volume/profit pricing
3. Marginal-cost pricing
4. Competitive pricing
5. Profit maximization pricing
6. Actuarial pricing
7. All-inclusive pricing
8. Transfer pricing
9. Other pricing methods

Full-cost pricing

In order to remain financially viable over the long run, every organization must recover the full costs of providing the service. The full cost of a specific service, test, procedure, visit, examination, case, discharge, etc., includes the variable costs plus a "fair" share of all fixed costs. In this respect all full-cost models involve some subjectivity in allocation and averaging techniques ("fairness" is subject to interpretation and negotiation). The allocation techniques will be discussed in greater detail in chapter 9.

In chapter 3 total costs were defined as total fixed costs plus total variable costs.

$$TC = TFC + TVC$$

To obtain full costs on a per unit basis, all terms in the equation need to be divided through by the activity being costed, or:

$$\text{Full Cost per Unit} = \frac{TC}{Q} = \frac{TFC}{Q} + \frac{TVC}{Q}$$

and, since $TVC = VC_U \times Q$, the formula for full costs per unit is

$$\frac{TC}{Q} = \frac{TFC}{Q} + VC_U$$

The choice of the appropriate activity to be costed is just as important as the determination of the total costs. There are many activity bases which can be used in determining full costs per unit. For example, in *Exhibit 8–1*, the type of procedure or service will help dictate the activity base to be selected.

For purposes of illustration, assume we wish to determine the full cost of providing dialysis services at a free standing kidney dialysis clinic. The full cost would be determined as follows:

TFC = $10,000,000
TVC = $ 5,000,000 (includes both direct and indirect variable costs)
TC = TFC + TVC = $10,000,000 + $5,000,000 = $15,000,000

Exhibit 8–1
Sample of activity bases

Service/procedure	Macrobase	Microbase
Routine inpatient cost per patient	Patient day	Nursing hours of care
Surgery cost	Surgical procedure	Surgical time
Laboratory cost	Laboratory procedure	Relative value unit Technicians' time Supplies cost

Remember, however, that in order to determine a total variable cost, both the per unit variable cost and a projected number of units of activity must be determined. The activity in this case is a kidney dialysis, and the projected volume is 100,000. The variable cost per dialysis treatment is calculated to be $50. Given the volume of 100,000 sessions, an average cost per session (full cost) can now be determined.

$$AC = \frac{TC}{Q} = \frac{TFC}{Q} + \frac{TVC}{Q} = \frac{TFC}{Q} + \frac{VC_U \times Q}{Q}$$

$$= \frac{\$10,000,000}{100,000} + \frac{\$5,000,000}{100,000} = \$100 + \$50 = \$150$$

If all payers paid full costs, and full costs included the necessary margin to provide for nonaccounting costs, contingencies, asset replacement (i.e., total financial requirements as defined in chapter 1), the $150 charge would be sufficient for the continued financial viability of the organization. If total financial requirements (usually considered to be economic costs) were not included in the costs above, an additional amount would be needed to change the accounting costs to economic costs. This margin would be added to the $150 cost determined above. In the following example, we will assume that all economic costs are included in the $150 (i.e., a $150 charge would meet the total financial requirements of the healthcare organization). However, as discussed earlier, very few payers are willing to pay full charges as determined above. Therefore, the major unanswered question is—when all payers do not pay the full costs of providing health services, what should be charged to the various types of payers for each kidney dialysis service performed?

The answer will depend to some extent on how much flexibility can be achieved in price setting. For instance, if we are the only dialysis clinic in town, we can take a total financial requirements approach. That is, from the 100,000 dialysis sessions, a total revenue of $15,000,000 must be generated. By forecasting the different types of payers, and the amount each will be paying, we can establish what the "price" should be. Assume the following payer mix:

Payer	Amount Paid	Treatment Volume
Medicaid	$ 90	20,000
Medicare	$100	30,000
HMO, PPO	90% of charges	25,000
Commercial insurance	100% of charges	25,000
		100,000 treatments

Given the above information, the charges would be determined as follows:

Total financial requirements			$15,000,000
Medicaid	$90 × 20,000 treatments	=	$ 1,800,000
Medicare	$100 × 30,000 treatments	=	$ 3,000,000
	Total recovered from prospective payers		$ 4,800,000
	Revenues remaining to be recovered		$10,200,000
	Dialysis treatments remaining		50,000

If all the remaining payers paid their fair share, the price per payer would be $204 ($10,200,000/50,000). However, the discount from charge payers will only pay 90 percent of charges. Therefore, the per unit charge to the full-cost payers must be determined. This can be calculated as follows:

$$.5(.9C + C) = \$204$$

Where C = charge per full-cost payer

$$.45C + .5C = \$204$$
$$C = \$214.74$$

The discount payers would pay .9($214.74)	=	$193.26
The discount payers total share	=	25,000 × $193.26
	=	$4,831,500
The full charges payers pay	=	25,000 × $214.74
	=	$5,368,500
Discount payers	=	$4,831,500
Full charge payers	=	$5,368,500
Total revenues		$10,200,000

A summary of the charges to each payer are:

Medicaid prospective rate	=	$ 90
Medicare prospective rate	=	$100
Discount rate	=	$193.26
Full charge payers	=	$214.74

The impact of the government not paying their share of total financial requirements can be illustrated in the following manner:

Revenues needed (TFR)	= $15,000,000
Average cost per treatment	= $150

The fair share not paid by the government payer is $1,200,000 (20,000 × ($150–$90)) plus $1,500,000 (30,000 × ($150 – $100)) for a total of $2,700,000. This is the cost shifting amount which many nongovernment payers feel is unfair. This amount must be shifted to the remaining payers. The average share per nongovernment payer is $54 ($2,700,000/50,000), providing an average price of $204 ($150 + $54) as determined previously. Because the discount payers will not pay the average price, the remaining charges must be established high enough to cover both the cost shifting by the government based payers, and the cost shifting by the discount payers. As illustrated above, the charges of $193.26 for discount payers and $214.40 for charge payers were calculated.

However, it should be noted that if a payer insists on a percentage discount from charges, they will always end up paying a part of their discount because the charges must be set high enough to cover all discounts granted. For example, if the two remaining payer classes paid the same amounts, each would pay $10,200,000/50,000 = $204. In this case, each class of payers' share is $5,100,000. However, since the discount payers (HMO/PPO/etc.) only pay 90 percent of charges they would pay a price of $183.60 (90 percent of $204). At this price, the discount payers would contribute a total of $4,590,000. This would leave a total required contribution from the charge paying payers of $5,610,000, resulting in a charge of $224.40 ($5,610,000/25,000). However, this would mean that the discount payers would pay $201.96 (90 percent of $224.40), which is higher than the $183.60 calculated as 90 percent of the average charge of $204. How do we respond to this seeming contradiction? If the discount payers pay $183.60, the full charge paying payers must make up the difference between the $204 average charge and the discount of $20.40, resulting in a charge of $224.40 ($204 + $20.40). This charge, however, increases the amount that the discount payers would pay ($201.96), since it is being based on charges to the charge paying payers, thereby providing more funds than required ($10,659,000 instead of $10,200,000). The full charge must be reduced, which will also reduce the discounted charge, until the total financial requirements from these payers is met. The final prices determined for charge payers ($214.74) and discount payers ($193.27) indicate that a theoretical 10 percent discount from charges (where average charges are $204), results in a real discount of about 5.26 percent (($204–$193.27)/$204), but a 10 percent discount from the higher charge of $214.74. This indicates why a negotiated 10 percent discount from charges cannot possibly result in a 10 percent reduction in expenditures by the payer (see *Exhibit 8–2* for calculations).

To add another complicating factor, the charge-based payers will undoubtedly include some patients who are unable to pay. Therefore, the charge must be increased to allow for this nonrecovery of costs. If the estimated bad debts are 10 percent per charge-based payer, then the charge must be increased to $238.60 ($214.74/.9). Since charges are now increased the discount price based on charges will also increase to $214.74 ($238.60/.9). This reasoning, however, results in more revenues being received than are required. Thus, the charge to charge paying payers must be reduced, until once again, total financial requirements are collected. In the process, the discount payers also end up paying for a portion of the bad debt expense. This can be seen by the fact that the appropriate charge becomes $226.67 and discounted charge becomes $204. Because of the percentages chosen for this example, the discount payers end up paying

Exhibit 8–2
Summary of pricing with cost shifting

Payment by Medicaid: 20,000 × $90 = $1,800,000	Cost for Medicaid: 20,000 × $150 = $3,000,000	Shift amount: $1,200,000
Payment by Medicare: 30,000 × $100 = $3,000,000	Cost for Medicare: 30,000 × $150 = $4,500,000	$1,500,000
	Total cost shifted from Medicare and Medicaid	$2,700,000

Adjusted cost to remaining payers:
  (50,000 × $150) + $2,700,000 = $7,500,000 + $2,700,000 = $10,200,000

Adjusted average cost to discount and full charge payers:
  $10,200,000/50,000 = $204

Charge to remaining payers: $226.67*

Payment by discount payers:
  25,000 × (90% of $226.67) = 25,000 × $204 = $5,100,000

Payment by charge-based payers:

25,000 × $226.67 =	$5,666,750	
Less bad debts (10%) =	566,675	
Net amount received from charge payers	$5,100,075	difference due to rounding $5,100,000

* [25,000 × (.9C)] + [(25,000 × C)] − (.1) × (25,000C)] = $10,200,000
22,500C + 22,500C = $10,200,000
45,000C = $10,200,000
C = $226.67

the actual costs of service provided to their beneficiaries, while the charge-based payers pay costs plus a share of those who do not pay. As payers become more adept at understanding and collecting cost information, they have become more insistent about paying only the "true cost" of providing care to their beneficiaries. To this extent they are becoming less willing to share a portion of the costs of those who do not pay their bills. A summary of the previous discussion is shown in *Exhibit 8–2*.

We now have a complete price list indicating the receipts by type of payer, with a 10 percent discount from charges for HMO and PPO, and a 10 percent bad debt portion from the charge paying payers.

Medicaid	$90	20,000 procedures	$1,800,000
Medicare	$100	30,000 procedures	$3,000,000
HMO/PPO	$204	25,000 procedures	$5,100,000
Commercial Ins.	$226.67	25,000 procedures	$5,666,750
Bad debt at 10% (rounded)			(566,750)
Total revenues			$15,000,000

As mentioned above, charges to charge based and discount from charge payers are not based on full cost since certain payers are not willing to pay full costs. This results in *cost shifting* from one class of payers to another class of payers, usually from high-volume purchasers such as Medicare and Medicaid agencies to self-insured and commercial insurance payers. The latter two payers are becoming less and less willing to assume the burden of the subsidies demanded by the government payers. In effect, discounts from charges have the same impact as a *hidden tax* on full-cost payers.

Cost/volume/profit models

As discussed in earlier chapters, the price to be established for specific products can be established through the use of cost/volume/profit models. The basic model, as previously developed, is:

$$P * Q = TFC + (VC_U * Q) + \text{desired margin}$$

The total fixed costs and desired margin must be allocated to the item being priced by the model. For example, given the following data:

Quantity of services	20,000
Total fixed cost	$300,000
Variable cost per unit	$ 10
Desired margin	$ 60,000

Now substitute these figures into the cost/volume/profit model:

$$
\begin{aligned}
P * 20{,}000 &= \$300{,}000 + \$10 * 20{,}000 + \$60{,}000 \\
20{,}000P &= \$560{,}000 \\
P &= \$28
\end{aligned}
$$

Thus, if estimates regarding the volume of services, fixed cost, and variable cost are correct, a price of $28 must be received to cover all costs and receive the desired margin. Changes in any of the estimates would require a recalculation of the required price. That a $28 price will cover the required costs and margin can be illustrated in the following abbreviated income statement.

Income Statement	
XYZ Health Services	
Total revenues ($28 × 20,000 units)	$560,000
Operating expenses:	
Fixed costs: $300,000 ($15 per unit)	
Variable costs: $200,000 ($10 per unit)	
Total operating expenses: ($25 per unit)	$500,000
Net income or margin ($3 per unit)	$ 60,000

The cost/volume/profit model is easily programmed into existing microcomputer spreadsheet software such as Lotus 1-2-3, Quattro-Pro, Minitab, and Microsoft Excel. Several possible scenarios on costs and volume could be used to determine the impact on the price to be charged. It should also be noted that the price determined in this fashion is the amount that must be received by the organization after any allowances for discounts, charity provisions, or bad debts. For example, if we expect to collect only 80 percent of total revenues, due to a 20 percent bad debt and charity care projection, the $28 price must be increased to $35 ($28/ (1−.2)). Adjustments must be made in the price to be charged in order to provide for the receipt of the desired amount. Adjustments must also be made for any discounts offered to an HMO. For example, assume we have negotiated an 11 percent discount with an HMO for the service used in the previous example. In this case, charges must be set as follows:

$$
gross\ price = \frac{net\ price}{1 - discount\ percentage} = \frac{\$35}{(1 - .11)} = \$39.33
$$

Another way of implementing the cost/volume/profit model for pricing purposes is to use a target contribution margin ratio. The target contribution margin is used to compute a target variable cost ratio which is then divided into the actual or standard variable cost per unit. The result is a target price which can be used to examine whether fixed costs will be covered at the target price according to the following steps:

Contribution margin pricing example
Assume Target CMR = 40%

Procedure	Variable cost per unit	1-CMR	Target price = VC/(1-CMR)
1	$120	0.60	$200
2	$240	0.60	$400
3	$300	0.60	$500

Procedure	Projected volume	Projected revenue	Projected variable cost	Projected contribution margin
1	100	$ 20,000	$ 12,000	$ 8,000
2	200	$ 80,000	$ 48,000	32,000
3	300	$150,000	$ 90,000	60,000
	Totals	$250,000	$150,000	$100,000

Marginal-cost pricing

Economists often talk about price being equal to the marginal cost in a competitive setting. The term marginal cost refers to the cost of providing one more unit of service, which in our case, is equal to variable cost per unit (VC_U). If we are already providing 20,000 units of the service in the previous example, in order to provide one more unit of service, it would cost only an additional $10 (the variable cost) to provide. Some entities, including Medicaid, will argue that the price they should pay should be only the marginal cost of providing one more unit, rather than the full cost, as presented in the first two pricing examples. In a competitive market, an argument could be made that a short-run price could be negotiated all the way down to slightly above $10, since any amount above the variable cost will contribute toward covering the fixed cost and the desired margin. In our previous example if we were unwilling to accept less than $39.33 we might lose the business altogether. Of course, we could not accept less than an average amount of $39.33 from all of our clients, or we would not remain financially viable for the long run. Government buyers and other discount purchasers have distorted the charges based on cost concept due to their shifting of costs to the remaining charge-based payers. However, it is an important fact that not all purchasers can buy at a marginal rate in the long run. As more purchasers demand discounts, the concept of a discount has become meaningless as charges are raised to cover the discounts.

The accounting profession has reacted to the decreasing relevance of a "charge" figure for healthcare services (especially hospital charges).[1] The format for the income statement for hospitals has been changed so that the first line is referred to as "Net Revenues," and includes only those sums which are expected to be received. This differs from the previous format where the first line of the income statement was "Gross Revenues," which was the value of all services provided, regardless of who the payer was. Previously, the second line was a deduction from revenues which accounted for the contractual allowances of the federal government, charity care provisions, and bad debt. After deductions were subtracted, the figure of net income was derived. This is now the beginning point for statements of revenue and expenses. Readers interested in the handling of contractual allowances, bad debt, and charity care in the financial statements should consult the *Audit and Accounting Guide: Health Care Organizations, 1996.*

Competitive pricing

Competitive pricing simply means that at certain times, in certain markets, the only important information for the setting of prices is what the competition is charging. Of course, consideration must be given to the long-term implications of such pricing strategies, but competitive prices cannot be ignored. Active competition tends to lower price to the short-run, marginal cost. This price cannot be maintained indefinitely and eventually leads to the exit of weaker firms from the market, leaving firms with more staying power, who then raise prices to a sustainable level.

With the removal of the lower of cost or charges, and introduction of prospective payment systems for payment to government buyers, healthcare providers have been free to price their services to meet market prices or community needs. Several key factors are important in developing the new pricing strategies. First, any price must at least cover variable or out-of-pocket costs if the organization is not to be worse off financially by offering the service. This method of pricing is typically called a marginal-cost approach to price setting. Secondly, marginal-cost pricing strategies are for short-run pricing only. The short-run time frame is difficult to define exactly. It depends on the financial resources of the provider, the needs of the community, and the nature of the competition. A definition of what is short run and what is long run depends on the time frame of the decision being made. In the long run, there are no fixed costs because even fixed assets must be replaced. Since the economic life of different assets vary widely, the definition of short run and long run is influenced heavily by the purpose for which the cost information is being used. As illustrated in *Exhibit 8–3*, there are three potential costs for the test. The

---

[1] *Audit and Accounting Guide: Health Care Organizations, 1996.* New York: AICPA, 1996.

Exhibit 8–3
A competitive pricing model

Given:

Variable costs = $15 per test
Estimated number of procedures = 5,000
Direct fixed costs = $20,000 per month
($20,000/5000) = $4 per unit
Allocated indirect administrative costs
= $30,000 per month
= $6 per unit

$$\frac{\text{Short-run competitive price}}{\text{Short-run competitive price} > \$15}$$

$$\frac{\text{Market penetration/phase-out competitive price}}{\text{Direct cost price} > \$4 + \$15 = \$19}$$

$$\frac{\text{Stable/mature market price}}{\text{Full cost price} > \$6 + \$4 + \$15 = \$25}$$

short-run pricing strategy would only require that, at a minimum, the variable costs be covered. In a phase-out decision, only the direct costs, at a minimum, would need to be covered until the test is dropped. If the test was to be continued to be offered, then full costs would be the minimum price. These uses of cost data are an expansion of the techniques introduced in chapters 2 and 4.

As illustrated, the use of competitive pricing models requires that the manager have access to variable and fixed cost information, direct and indirect allocations, and a reliable estimate of the number of procedures to be accomplished. Many accounting systems in use by healthcare providers today do not routinely provide these types of data without management requiring the breakout. In other cases, costs that appear to be variable are really fixed costs that the allocation techniques used by the accounting system present in a variable format. Allocation techniques will be presented in detail in chapter 9. Managers must be aware of this confusion and ask appropriate questions.

Profit-maximization pricing

Profit-maximization pricing strategies are generally considered only in markets where there is one firm with no competitors, and pricing decisions are being driven by the profit motive rather than other objectives generally associated with tax exempt or public organizations. In this case, price is set at that level which will maximize the total profits, which economists have shown results in prices higher than would be permissible when competition exists. This situation has historically been referred to as a monopoly, and although many hospitals have historically operated in monopoly situations, it is not commonly believed that they took unfair advantage of that position. This would be inconsistent with the mission and objectives of most healthcare providers. (It is commonly believed by some economists that their monopoly position encouraged inefficiency, which resulted in prices being higher than under a more competitive environment.) References for research studies testing the existence of these inefficiencies are listed at the end of this chapter.

Actuarial pricing

The advent of managed care, resulting in an organization which provides both insurance and health delivery functions, has increased the importance of actuarial functions to these organizations. Actuarial pricing means that actuarial information is used to determine expected utilization rates of health services by a defined group of individuals. The individuals have characteristics of age, socio-economic, education, income level, occupation, etc., which make it more or less likely that they will utilize specific health services. Data has been collected by actuaries which makes it possible to determine with a fairly high degree of accuracy the number of physician visits, hospitalizations, catastrophic illnesses, on-the-job accidents, etc. that the defined group of individuals will require. The utilization can be translated into an expected cost for the provision of those services, which can then be converted into a total financial requirement for the group of individuals and then used to determine prices.

Actuarial pricing might be considered to be a variation of the full-cost methodology where the unit of measurement is the set of health services expected to be provided to any individual in a group. Each individual in the group is theoretically charged the same amount. However, variations in charges per individual do exist and is dependent on the existence of different grouping categories. For example, the HMO Act of 1976 required HMOs to use what is called "community rating," and required that all enrollees be charged the same amount. Another methodology, called "experience rating" permits the HMO to categorize individuals according to a variety of cohort characteristics (age, sex, occupation, economic status, etc.). Variations on these exist and can be explored more thoroughly by referring to one or more of the references included at the end of this chapter. *Exhibit 8–4* provides a sample of the methodology by which the number of dialysis procedures can be estimated.

All-inclusive pricing

A method similar to full-cost pricing can be applied to a more comprehensive measure of output. In many organizations, outputs such as ser-

Exhibit 8–4
Actuarial pricing model

Given:
  Number of enrollees = 5,000,000

<table>
<tr><td colspan="5" align="center">Sex and age distribution</td></tr>
<tr><td></td><td colspan="4" align="center">Age</td></tr>
<tr><td>Sex</td><td>0–17</td><td>18–55</td><td>55+</td><td>Total</td></tr>
<tr><td>Male</td><td>400,000 (20%)</td><td>1,100,000 (55%)</td><td>500,000 (25%)</td><td>2,000,000 (40%)</td></tr>
<tr><td>utilization</td><td>2,000 (0.5%)</td><td>44,000 (4%)</td><td>25,000 (5%)</td><td>71,000</td></tr>
<tr><td>Female</td><td>500,000 (16.7%)</td><td>1,800,000 (60%)</td><td>700,000 (23%)</td><td>3,000,000 (60%)</td></tr>
<tr><td>utilization</td><td>1,500 (.3%)</td><td>18,000 (1%)</td><td>9,500 (1.4%)</td><td>29,000</td></tr>
<tr><td></td><td>Total enrollees</td><td></td><td></td><td>5,000,000</td></tr>
<tr><td></td><td>Total procedures</td><td></td><td></td><td>100,000</td></tr>
</table>

vices, procedures, or tests are priced on an all-inclusive basis. This method of pricing fits the government's current approach to pricing by DRGs. Diagnosis related groupings (DRGs) provide a mechanism by which the Health Care Financing Administration (HCFA) reimburses hospitals for Medicare beneficiaries a predetermined amount based on the individual's diagnosis. This prospective, all-inclusive amount is independent of individual hospital costs, thereby providing an incentive for the hospitals to try to control Medicare Part A costs. It also facilitates the development and identification of the output of the healthcare organization. For example, prior to the Tax Equity and Fiscal Responsibility Act of 1982 (TEFRA) the primary output of most healthcare organizations was expressed in terms of patient days. Reimbursement in this case was on a per diem basis. With TEFRA the government mandated a per case approach to pricing. A case-mix measure was developed similar to the approach to DRGs demonstrated in *Exhibit 8–5*. This case-mix measure was mandated by the Social Security Amendments of 1983. The case-mix index was designed to measure differences in the intensity of care provided by specific institutions. A hospital which specialized in the more costly procedures would have a higher index.

Using the case-mix index established in *Exhibit 8–5*, a reimbursement by discharge or diagnosis could be determined for each hospital. For example, if the average cost per discharge for all hospitals was $1,865.54, then a hospital with a case-mix index of .89 would receive an average of $1,660.33 (.89 × $1,865.54). If a diagnosis system such as DRGs were used, a similar approach could be used. Given DRG 86 and average cost of $2,350, Hospital A would receive $2,091.50 (.89 × $2,350).

As illustrated above, the identification of the hospital's output as either a case by discharge or a case by diagnosis necessitated an all-inclusive

Exhibit 8–5
Calculation of Medicare case-mix index

Hospital	Proportion of Medicare discharges by DRG (percent)					Total (percent)	DRG weighted expected cost per case	Case-mix index
	DRG 1	DRG 2	DRG 3	DRG 4	DRG 5			
A	2.5	27.3	10.5	41.5	18.2	100.0	$1,660.40	0.8897
B	21.0	0.9	30.1	2.0	46.0	100.0	$2,401.30	1.2867
C	40.6	5.0	2.3	47.2	4.9	100.0	$1,346.30	0.7214
D	5.1	18.4	62.5	10.0	4.0	100.0	$2,990.70	1.6026
E	30.4	65.0	1.0	1.6	2.0	100.0	$ 929.00	0.4978

Average proportion for all hospitals

	19.9	23.3	21.3	20.5	15.0	100.0	$1,866.20	
DRG cost weight	$1,000	$800	$4,100	$1,500	$2,000			

Notes:
1. All proportions adjusted to make these 5 DRGs hypothetically represent all Medicare DRGs.
2. DRG expected cost per case calculated as follows: (for Hospital A)
   .025(1000) + .273(800) + .105(4100) + .415(1500) + .182(2000) = $1,660.40
3. Case-mix index calculated as follows: (for Hospital A)
   $1,660.40 divided by $1,866.20 = .8900

Source: Ernst and Young, "The Revised DRG's: Their Importance in Medicare Payments to Hospitals," 1983, p.7.

pricing model which focused on the total resources required to achieve a specific output diagnosis. However, it did not dictate which technique must be used to price individual services. Each DRG had a desired number of services, tests, or procedures associated with providing a quality output. The total costs of the DRG would be the accumulated cost of the specific services, etc. The costs of specific services would be determined by any of the earlier methods. Since total reimbursement was fixed by DRG, the government as the major third party was not concerned about the costing and allocation techniques used by the provider. In fact, except for quality issues, the prospective payer was not concerned about the type or amount of services that were offered to the patient. That was the care giver's responsibility. Since the cost incentives were now to utilize as few services as possible, the payer felt the need to establish quality review mechanisms to guard against under utilization as contrasted to over utilization under a cost-based or charge-based system.

However, this freedom offered the provider the opportunity to control pricing and profit margins to other purchasers of the services. Under the cost-based method of reimbursement used by the government in purchasing services prior to 1983, most healthcare providers were unable to lower prices to meet the competition. The lower of cost or charges for government patients insured that rates were always set higher than costs to government payers and costs to government clients were determined through cost finding methods mandated by the Health Care Financing Administration (HCFA).

Recently, attempts have been made to develop a prospective payment mechanism for the long-term care industry. Since long-term care services and resource use are more closely related to specific types of services than to specific diagnoses, a reimbursement mechanism based on diagnosis is not appropriate. New York has in place a resource utilization grouping system (RUGS), which groups patients according to scores on the activities of daily living (ADL) surveys. In this system, each patient's rate would depend on the average cost of caring for patients requiring the same type of services. Patients from groups with higher ADL scores (and thereby having higher average costs) would also have greater reimbursement.

The most recent attempt at the application of a prospective payment mechanism is for physicians. The method developed and applied by HCFA is called the resource based relative value scale (RBRVS). The RBRVS developed by the Harvard researchers for HCFA grouped the inputs necessary to provide physician services into three categories:[2]

1. Physician work
2. Practice expenses
3. Opportunity costs

Physician work includes all services furnished to the patient from preservice through past service. Practice costs include the physical place, equipment, supplies, and administrative resources necessary to provide the service to the clinic. Opportunity costs include income foregone from practice while completing postgraduate training. This category was not included in the RBRVS adopted by HCFA for Medicare patients.

The absolute values assigned to each physician's service were then expressed in relationship to each other, resulting in the relative value scale. The development of the RBRVS was designed to eliminate the income differentials of physicians which have been developed over time due to the difference in payment for procedures as opposed to the cognitive skills. Under the RBRVS, payments are greatly increased for cognitive skills and dramatically decreased for the performance of procedures. The impact will be a narrowing of physician income dispersion across specialties. RBRVS would restrict pricing flexibility only. It does not address the volume issues which, like the quality concerns expressed above, must be addressed by other means. The setting of expenditure

---

[2] For an in-depth discussion of the Medicare RBRVS, see Grimaldi, Paul L., "RBRVS: How New Physician Fee Schedule Will Work," *Health Care Financial Management*, Vol. 45, No. 9, September 1991, p. 58.

targets (ET) was the initial proposal to meet this need. While the DRGs were designed to control Medicare Part A expenditures, the RBRVS is designed to place constraints on Medicare Part B expenditures.

In many organizations, outputs such as services, procedures, tests, etc., are priced on an all-inclusive basis. This method of pricing fits the government's current approach to pricing by DRGs and RBRVS. It also facilitates the development and identification of the output of the healthcare organization. For example, prior to the Tax Equity and Fiscal Responsibility Act of 1982 (TEFRA), the primary output of most healthcare organizations was expressed in terms of patient days (a macromeasure). Under TEFRA, a per diem basis of pricing was developed. Consistent with this approach, all patients paid the same per diem regardless of the amount of service provided.

The concept of an all-inclusive payment mechanism means that the payment is fixed, regardless of the resources used in providing the service. The use of an inclusive payment approach effectively shifts the risk to the provider to control the amount of resources used to provide the service. The risk is highest when the purchaser (payer) also has the power to establish rates to be paid as contrasted to when the provider can establish a rate high enough to provide a safety margin for uncertainty. One result of this process has been the unbundling of services. This is the term given to the process of separating various functions of health delivery into separate corporations or other entities, in order to permit their services to be billed separately and not be included in the all-inclusive rate.

Transfer pricing

Different components of a healthcare organization often provide services or products to other components of the same organization. It is necessary to place a value on this service or product. The process of placing a value on services or products provided within an organization is called "transfer pricing." The following material is derived from Garrison.[3] A more complete discussion can be found in that text or other managerial accounting texts.

There are four general approaches to the setting of prices for intra-organizational products:

   a. full cost
   b. variable cost
   c. competitive or market price
   d. negotiated

---

[3] Garrison, Ray M., *Managerial Accounting*, 6th ed., Homewood, IL: Irwin, 1990.

The issue of setting transfer prices has become more important as healthcare organizations have developed strategies for improving cash flows through diversification activities, or the selling of excess capacity in various departments to outside entities (laboratory, dietary, radiological, pharmaceutical, etc.). These services are also provided to other centers within the organization. In the process of placing a value on the services provided externally, a question arises as to the value of the same service provided internally, and deriving a method of providing for an efficient operation. Situations might exist where the organization should purchase their laboratory services from another organization rather than supplying it to itself. The method used to establish an appropriate transfer price will be dependent on the objective of the organization in establishing a transfer price.

a. The *full cost* method of transfer pricing recognizes the total accumulated costs of the services being provided. The primary argument against the use of full cost is that it provides no incentive for cost control. However, this method is commonly used because it is simple to use and very convenient. If this is the method of choice, then standard costs should be used instead of actual costs in order to provide incentives for efficiency.

b. The use of *variable cost* as a transfer price recognizes the actual incremental costs associated with providing any service. The same arguments that were used for full cost can be used here with the same suggested solutions. The advantage of variable cost as opposed to full cost as a method of transfer pricing is that variable costs may provide for the most efficient utilization of resources in the short run, since fixed costs are ignored. Any service which brings in revenues greater than variable costs (in the short run) is a profitable enterprise.

c. Many arguments can be made for the use of *competitive* or *market* pricing. The primary argument is that it provides a measure of what the service or product would cost if purchased from an outside vendor. In previous years, and in many locations at the present, there are no alternative suppliers of those services which have traditionally been supplied internally. However, competition and changing reimbursement methodologies have encouraged the unbundling of services, and the associated free-standing provision of many of these same services (laboratory, dialysis, pharmacy, radiology, dietary, etc.).

The primary advantage of competitive or market pricing is that it permits a valid comparison of costs to the purchasing department between purchasing the service internally versus externally. If the service cannot be provided internally at the same or lower "cost" as the external provider, then perhaps the service should not be provided in-house. On the other hand, this method provides an incentive for the service to be provided more efficiently in-house.

A major factor which has been ignored in this discussion has been the quality and timeliness of the service being provided. Outside purchase of services provide a loss of control in both quality and timing. This loss of control must be weighed against any potential cost advantages of outside purchasing.

d. A *negotiated* price is most realistic in cases where outside purchase of services is not an option, or where a competitive price might be available, but due to economies in administration and marketing (among other possibilities), the market price overstates an appropriate transfer price.

The issue of transfer pricing is extremely important to healthcare organizations. All organizations must make decisions as to the size of the various support units relative to one another. Due to technology, demographic changes, patient-mix shifts, planning errors, etc., excess capacity or capacity constraints may exist within one or more support centers. Transfer pricing provides a mechanism for decision making regarding expansion, purchase of services from outside vendors, the sale of excess capacity to outside purchasers, and the evaluation of the efficiency and effectiveness of support centers.

Other pricing techniques

The cost/volume/profit models are very useful when pricing clearly identifiable services, procedures, tests, etc. However, where a large number of individual items must be priced or where specific cost data cannot be determined, management may find it helpful to use a variety of approaches. In this section, three of the most common methods will be discussed.

In some departments, it is difficult to identify specific costs with individual patients, procedures, or outputs. All users of the service place a demand on the capacity of the department. The charge for this service is usually a function of the amount of capacity used by the specific service or patient, or an average resource consumed approach.

For example, in operating rooms, most costs are fixed and do not vary measurably with the type of procedure performed. The operating room has a certain capacity in terms of time, hours, minutes, etc. It seems reasonable that costs for the operating room should be based on the amount of time used. The time method involves estimating the types of surgical procedures to be provided, the standard amount of time by surgical procedure, and the total costs of the operating room. *Exhibit 8–6* illustrates the time method.

Data presented in *Exhibit 8–6* must be estimated by the budget process, collected from the medical staff or medical records. The standard charge per minute is calculated by dividing total operating room costs by the estimated units of time that can be billed for:

$$\frac{total\ operating\ room\ costs}{estimated\ total\ minutes} = \frac{\$4,000,000}{40,000} = \$100$$

The second method to be discussed is called the relative value unit (RVU). For some services, such as laboratory and radiology, a basic standard of activity has been developed by clinical personnel to price the services offered by the department. This basic standard of activity is called a relative value unit. Each specific service is expressed in terms of RVUs based on the complexity of the resources needed and the amount of time involved in relationship to a basic standard. The standard cost per RVU can be developed on a microbasis by using estimates of the individual resources needed such as clinical time, equipment, materials, and an allocation of overhead. A more macro approach to costing would be to determine the total financial requirements of the department and divide this amount by the weighted number of services to be provided. The resulting number is the average cost per RVU. This approach is illustrated in *Exhibit 8–7*. Under this approach, the cost of each service is determined by multiplying the relative value of each service by the average cost per RVU.

RVUs provide the opportunity for managers to monitor changes in the intensity of services provided. Many institutions are now starting to price nursing care in this manner to reflect the shift in the more seriously ill patients staying shorter periods in the hospital while the minimal care patient is now being seen on an outpatient basis. The resource based relative value scale (RBRVS) implemented to pay physicians for their

Exhibit 8–6
Time method of allocation

Surgical procedure	Standard time (minutes)	Standard charge per minute*	Standard charge
101	20	$100	$2,000
102	30	$100	$3,000
103	45	$100	$4,500
104	60	$100	$6,000

$$*Standard\ charge\ per\ minute = \frac{total\ financial\ requirements\ for\ the\ operating\ room}{total\ number\ of\ operating\ minutes\ to\ be\ completed}$$

$$= \frac{\$3,600,000}{36,000} = \$100$$

Exhibit 8–7
Relative value computation

Service	Relative value weights per service	Number of procedures	Number of RVUs	Average cost per RVU*	Charge per specific service
1	1.1	328	361	$3.41	$3.75
2	2.0	946	1,892	3.41	6.82
3	3.5	1,000	3,500	3.41	11.94
4	.8	841	673	3.41	2.73
-	—	—	—	—	—
-	—	—	—	—	—
-	—	—	—	—	—
N	.9	944	850	3.41	3.07
Total		511,973	1,016,506		

$$\text{*Average cost per relative value} = \frac{\text{total financial requirements}}{\text{total weighted services}} = \frac{\$3,466,322}{1,016,506} = \$3.41$$

services to Medicare patients was developed using a similar concept, where the type of resources used and a cost of these resources were determined through an analysis of thousands of Medicare patient records and each procedure performed by a physician was assigned a value.

The last method presented in this section is the surcharge approach. This approach is quite useful in pricing items which are easily itemized, such as pharmacy items and medical supplies. It is based on the concept that the total costs of the service department must be charged to the individual receiving the service. It is a straight forward method which assumes the total costs of the department are influenced by the activity base selected; i.e., cost of drugs or medical supplies, number of prescriptions, etc. Using the cost of drugs as an example, the surcharge would be determined in the following manner:

Total cost of drugs for coming year = $1,100,000
Total cost of pharmacy = $2,200,000

$$\text{surcharge percentage} = \frac{\text{total costs to be recovered}}{\text{total costs of drugs used}}$$

$$= \frac{\$2,200,000}{\$1,100,000} = 200 \text{ percent}$$

This means that whatever the drug costs, the bill will be doubled (200 percent) in order to recover the full department costs. If the drug cost to patient Y equals $750, the patient will be billed for $1,500 ($750 × 200 percent).

The pharmacy often also uses a surcharge based on the number of prescriptions. If the above drug costs had arisen from a total of 100,000 prescriptions being filled, the surcharge would amount to:

$$surcharge\ amount = \frac{costs\ to\ be\ recovered\ from\ surcharge}{total\ number\ of\ prescriptions}$$

$$= \frac{\$1,100,000}{100,000}$$

$$= \$11\ per\ prescription$$

For the above patient Y, the drug cost of $750 may have arisen from the filling of 50 separate prescriptions. The surcharge for these prescriptions would then be equal to $550 (50 × $11) giving a total drug bill of $1,300.

What pricing method should be used?

The choice of pricing technique to be used depends on the data available and the desires of management. In today's environment, the price that must be established is heavily influenced by competitive conditions and is essentially a market-based approach. In other cases, the price is determined by the third-party reimburser, either by fiat (Medicare, Medicaid) or by negotiation (Blue Cross, HMOs, PPOs, self-insured employers, etc.). Under all types of payers, it is vital to have the best data available on the cost of providing the service to determine if the service should be offered at all.

Summary

The changing healthcare environment and a shift to prospective fixed methods of reimbursement have presented an opportunity for healthcare providers to price their products selectively. This ability to meet price competition also means that the management must understand the various pricing strategies and assess the implications of using an average full-cost approach to many specific services. The focus should be on pricing services in such a manner as to maximize total revenues, considering market demands and community requirements.

Questions and problems

1. Discuss the impact on a healthcare provider's pricing strategies of the switch to a prospective pricing system by major payers.

2. What is the role of full costs relative to pricing strategies?

3. Cost-based payers stress that they are paying the full cost of services provided to their clients. Evaluate this statement in terms of its impact on other payers.

4. Define, compare, and contrast the alternative pricing strategies which can be followed by a healthcare provider.

5. Government and other payers insist that they are being "prudent" buyers by paying on a prospective basis. Evaluate this statement in terms of its impact on (a) healthcare providers; (b) other payers.

6. Define case-mix index, and explain (a) its role in payment strategies by government payers, and (b) its role in pricing strategies by healthcare providers.

7. Answer the following questions in terms of pricing in a competitive healthcare market.
   a. "Full cost can be viewed as a safety platform. If a healthcare organization always prices at or above full costs, it will never have to worry about losing money." Discuss this statement.
   b. Why is there more than one correct method of setting prices?

8. Why are "overhead rates" developed for procedure/service costing purposes?

9. Discuss what pricing strategy might be appropriate for a healthcare provider under the following circumstances. Assume that competition is in place or anticipated, and that you are a major player in the market.
   a. Meeting competition from a newly opened multispecialty group practice.
   b. Meeting competition from a newly opened solo-physician practice.
   c. Meeting competition from a free-standing unit owned by:
      1. local investors
      2. joint venture or medical practice
      3. major investor-owned healthcare chain
      4. religious organization

10. Is there ever an instance when marginal-cost pricing is a feasible option?

11. Why is there more than one correct method of setting prices?

12. University Hospital would like to establish a charge for the outpatient clinic which would recover all costs and contribute $120,000 for the year to the financial resources. The following data was established by the assistant controller of the cost behavior for the next year.

Variable costs per visit	$ 4.05
Direct fixed expenses	$100,000 per quarter
Allocated university overhead	$150,000 per quarter
Estimated number of visits	50,000 per quarter

a. Compute the charge which would meet the hospital's objectives.
b. What other data would you like to have to develop the charge structure?

13. The administrator of G.M. Frank Family Planning Center currently charges $20 per visit, which was set to recover full costs. A recent change in state law will allow healthcare providers similar to G.M. Frank to add an amount up to 15 percent of their costs to recover free care and bad debts. The financial vice president was reviewing the cost data from this year to prepare new rates for next year. The following information was available:

Variable costs were established at 10 percent of full costs based on this year's volume and are expected to remain the same for next year. Fixed costs are expected to be $162,000 for next year. Free care, bad debt, and allowances are set at 10 percent of gross revenue. Estimated volume for next year is 10,000 visits.

a. Determine the charge that could be proposed for next year and still fall within the 15 percent limitation of the state regulation.

14. The administrator of the speech and hearing center estimated the following costs for services in the department:

Service	Variable cost per service	Direct fixed
Audiological examination	$ 5	$ 30,000
Pediatric audiological evaluation	5	40,000
Pure tone—air and bone	5	5,000
Speech evaluation	3	18,000
Hearing therapy	10	27,000
Hearing and evaluation	10	10,000
Indirect fixed costs (to include administration costs, utilities, etc.)		100,000
Desired profit margin		100,000

The total volume of tests is estimated to be 25,000. The individual volumes are: audiological examination, 3,000; pediatric audiological evaluation, 4,000; pure tone—air and bone, 5,000; speech evaluation, 3,000; hearing therapy, 9,000; hearing and evaluation, 1,000.

a. Determine the fee schedule for these services based on the cost data above. The fee should cover all costs plus the desired profit margin.

15. The administrator of Memorial Hospital is planning to add a new 15-bed pediatric unit to the hospital. Currently, the hospital has 400 beds and the new pediatric center will be treated as a separate cost center. You have been asked to determine the routine service charge for the new unit. The following estimates for the new unit were collected by the assistant controller to help in your computations.

	500 Patient days	625 Patient days
Total direct cost:		
Salaries	$48,000	$55,000
Supplies and other expenses	3,000	3,500
Total allocated costs:		
Laundry and linen	2,800	3,500
Housekeeping	4,800	6,000
Dietary	12,000	15,000
Central service	840	1,050
Pharmacy	80	100
Medical records	1,920	2,400

It is not anticipated that the new unit will add significantly to the costs of other service departments.
a. Determine what charge you would recommend, and state any assumptions you feel are necessary to make in arriving at your decision.

16. Hampton Outpatient Clinic budgeted revenue from flu vaccinations at $20 per shot. Fixed costs total $5 per unit based on 4,000 shots, and remain unchanged within a relevant range of 1,500 shots to 6,500 shots. Variable costs are $10 per shot. After revenue was budgeted at $70,000, the clinic received a request from the local school district for flu vaccinations of its 1,000 students at a reasonable cost. If Hampton Clinic wants to increase operating income by $2,000, what should Hampton charge for the additional shots?

17. Fox Creek Hospital has variable costs of $840 for every arthroscope it performs. Fixed costs total $750,000, allocated on the basis of the number of arthroscopes performed. Revenue is calculated by adding a 10 percent markup to cost. How much should Fox Creek charge for an arthroscope based on a budgeted 7,500 arthroscopes?

18. The Colorado Clinic wants to establish a rate schedule for a series of laboratory tests that will be given to patients on a routine basis. The

administrator would like to know the cost of each test individually and the cost of the entire series. She estimated that approximately 1,500 women would need the series which consists of 3 tests, U, V, and R. Test U consists of 2 procedures; Test V, 3 procedures; and Test R, 4 procedures. The accountant estimated the following cost information.

Test U 2 Procedures	Cost per procedure
Preprinted forms	$0.15
Glassware breakage	0.10
Supplies	0.19
Reagents	0.23

Test V 3 Procedures	Cost per procedure
Disposable syringes	$5.00
Preprinted forms	0.15
Glassware breakage	0.10
Sterile bandages	0.05
Supplies	0.19
Reagents	0.25

Test R 4 Procedures	Cost per procedure
Preprinted forms	$0.15
Glassware breakage	0.12
Supplies	0.19
Reagents	0.22

In addition, the following costs were to be directly attributable to the individual tests.

Test U	Cost per quarter
Administration	$ 5,500
Maintenance, utilities, janitorial	7,200
Depreciation	3,180
Salaries	11,120

Test V	Cost per quarter
Administration	$ 6,500
Maintenance, utilities, janitorial	7,200
Depreciation	4,280
Salaries	11,120

Test R	Cost per quarter
Administration	$ 5,500
Maintenance, utilities, janitorial	7,200
Depreciation	3,180
Salaries	11,120

The administrator believed that each test's price should be set high enough to return 10 percent on allocated fixed costs. He also estimated that allowances for free care, bad debts, and discounts to HMOs would equal 15 percent of the billed amount.

19.

Medical Center Memo

To: Board of Trustees

From: Scott T. James
           Senior Vice President, Finance

Re: Discussion of Pricing Policies

The Medical Center currently maintains a pricing strategy based on all services generating sufficient gross revenues to cover their total operating costs. However, the hospital violates this policy whenever the service is an effective loss leader (profits from other related services offset the loss generated from providing the requested service), or the community has targeted the price for comparison and all hospitals are charging less than the true cost (e.g., room rates).

In order to make up for the effect of those services priced below cost, the hospital has several departments with high profit margins. The choice of departments and services for high profit margins is based on the percentage of cost payers using the service, the availability of third-party coverage, and the relative lack of price comparison data for the service.

Under the current pricing strategy, the hospital has departments where each dollar of revenue costs $2.06 to generate and other departments where a dollar of revenue costs as little as $0.27.

As a result of the recently enacted prospective payment system (PPS) for Medicaid, a hospital may, for the first time, ignore cost-payer percentages in its pricing strategies without adversely impacting overall profitability. Under PPS the Medicaid policy of paying the lower of cost or charges will not be applied to individual services. Accordingly, the percentage of cost-payer utilization will no longer directly affect the net cash generated from each dollar of price increase applied to a specific department.

Given the additional latitude provided by PPS, we are seeking Board direction in the following areas:

1. What is the Board's perspective on the hospital utilizing market-penetration pricing as a competitive tool?
2. What emphasis should be placed on each service's profitability in service-mix decisions?

3. Should the hospital make service-mix and/or pricing decisions based on a minimum return on sales criteria?
4. What criteria should be used to identify loss leaders? Should a maximum loss as a percentage of revenue be established?
5. Should the hospital take advantage of unique services and other, difficult to duplicate services, and price these services with very high profit margins?

Based on the results of the Board's input and future discussions with various Board committees, a pricing strategy will be developed and presented to the Board for implementation with the fiscal year budget.

Keywords: actuarial pricing; all-inclusive pricing; competitive pricing; CVP pricing; full-cost pricing; marginal-cost pricing; profit-maximization pricing; transfer pricing.

References

Abbey, Duane C., and L. Lamar Blount. "Assessing the Financial Implications of APGs." *Healthcare Financial Management* (October 1996): 50–55.

AICPA. *Audit and Accounting Guide: Health Care Organizations, 1996.* New York: AICPA, 1996.

Anderson, Gerard F., Earl P. Steinberg, Neil R. Powe, Shlomi Antebi, Jeffrey Whittle, Susan Horn, and Robert Herbert. "Setting Payment Rates for Capitated Systems: A Comparison of Various Alternatives." *Inquiry* 27 (fall 1990): 225–233.

Barber, Robert L., Walter J. Jones, and James A. Johnson. "Capitating Physician Group Practices." *Healthcare Financial Management* (July 1996): 46–49.

Boland, P. *Making Managed Healthcare Work: A Practical Guide to Strategies and Solutions.* New York: McGraw Hill, 1991.

Brewster, A.C., R.C. Bradbury, and C.M. Jacobs. "Measuring the Effect of Illness Severity on Revenue under DRG's." *Healthcare Financial Management* 39, no. 7 (1985): 52–60.

Burik, David. "The Changing Role of Hospital Prices: A Framework for Pricing in a Competitive Environment." *Health Care Management Review* 8, no. 2 (spring 1983): 65–71.

Conrad, Douglas, Thomas Wickizer, Charles Maynard, Theodore Klastorin, Daniel Lessler, Austin Ross, Naomi Soderstrom, Sean Sullivan, Jeffrey Alexander, and Karen Travis. "Managing Care, Incentives and Information: An Exploratory Look Inside the 'Black Box' of Hospital Efficiency." *Health Services Research* 31, no. 3 (August 1996): 235–259.

Coyne, J.S. "Is Your Organization Ready to Share Financial Risk with HMOs?" *Healthcare Financial Management* (August 1994): 31.

de Mars Martin, Pamela, and Frank J. Boyer. "Product Line Costing: Developing a Consistent Method for Costing Hospital Services." *Healthcare Financial Management* (February 1985): 30–37.

Eastaugh, S.R., and J.A. Eastaugh. "Prospective Payment Systems: Steps to Quality, Efficiency, and Regionalization." *Health Care Management Review* 11, no. 4 (1986): 37–52.

Etinger, David A. "How PHOs Can Avoid Price-Fixing Charges." *Healthcare Financial Management* (July 1996): 72–76.

Farmer, Anne, and Mark E. Toso. "Using Cost Accounting Data to Develop Capitation Rates." *Topics in Health Care Financing* (fall 1994): 1–7.

Graham, J., ed. "Providers Not Picked by Price." *Modern Health Care* 16, no. 16 (1986): 23.

Grimaldi, Paul L. "New Healthcare Price Indexes Aid Financial Analysis." *Healthcare Financial Management* (October 1994): 64–70.

Grimaldi, Paul L. "New Capitation Scenarios for HMO Medicare Risk Contracting." *Healthcare Financial Management* (February 1997): 35–38.

Jacobs, Phillip, and Charles R. Franz. "Developing Pricing Policies by Diagnostic Grouping." *Healthcare Financial Management* (January 1985): 50–52.

Karpiel, Martin S. "Capitated Contracting for Emergency Services." *Healthcare Financial Management* (May 1996): 33–37.

Kelly, Margo P. "How Global Pricing Works." *Healthcare Financial Management* (December 1995): 18–20.

Kennedy, Kevin M. "Evaluating and Negotiating a Profitable Capitation Contract." *Healthcare Financial Management* (February 1997): 44–49.

Kleinman, Mitchell A., and Judith L. Horowitz. "Advanced Pricing Strategies for Hospitals in Contracting with Managed Care Organizations." *Topics in Health Care Financing* (fall 1994): 90–96.

Kolb, D.S. and J.L. Horowitz. "Managing the Transition to Capitation." *Healthcare Financial Management* (February 1995): 64–69.

Kongstvedt, P.R. *Essentials of Managed Care.* Gaithersburg, MD: Aspen Publishers, 1995.

Lefton, Ray. "Aligning Incentives Using Risk-Sharing Arrangements." *Healthcare Financial Management* (February 1997): 50–57.

Lewis, James B. "How to Evaluate Effects of Managed Care Contracts." *Healthcare Financial Management* (December 1990): 32–42.

Long, H.W., and J.B. Silvers. "Medicare Reimbursement Is Federal Taxation of Tax-Exempt Providers." *Health Care Management Reveiw* 1, no. 1 (1976): 9–23.

Managed Care Assembly, Medical Group Management Association. "Glossary of Terms Used in Managed Care." *Medical Group Management Journal* (September/October 1995): 52–65.

Neumann, Bruce R., Jan P. Clement, and Jean C. Cooper. *Financial Management: Concepts and Applications for Health Care Organizations.* Dubuque: Kendall/Hunt, 1997.

Pearson, J.A. "Paragon Pricing." *Management Accounting* 67, no. 12 (1986): 41–42.

Pickard, J. Greg, Robert A. Friedman, and Timothy J. Johnson. "Repricing Plan Yields Realistic Revenue Enhancement." *Healthcare Financial Management* (May 1991): 45–52.

Powell, W.W., ed. *The Nonprofit Sector: A Research Handbook.* New Haven: Yale University Press, 1987.

Reepmeyer, H. Thomas. "Market Forces Can Boost Quality, Contain Costs." *Healthcare Financial Management* (December 1991): 60–78.

Reif, R.A., P.A. Bickett, and D.E. Halberstadt. "Case Study: Analyzing the Market Using DRGs and MDCs." *Healthcare Financial Management* 39, no. 12 (1985): 44–47.

Ross, E. "Making Money with Proactive Pricing." *Harvard Business Review* 62, no. 6 (1984): 145–55.

Schroeder, David H. "Toward a Departmental Bottom-Line Perspective." *Topics in Health Care Financing* 14, no. 1 (winter 1989): 25–40.

Sear, Alan M. "Hospital Charges: Analysis and Comparison." *Topics in Health Care Financing* 14, no. 1 (winter 1989): 49–54.

Sulger, Jack F. "Establishing Reserves for Capitation Contracts." *Healthcare Financial Management* (July 1996): 52–58.

Suver, J.D., W.P. Jessee, and W.N. Zelman. "Financial Management and DRG's." *Hospital and Health Services Administration* 31, no. 1 (1986): 75–85.

CHAPTER 9

Cost determination

"The CFO says that if we can't generate $150 per scan, we are not covering the full cost. I know for a fact that it only costs $55 to perform one scan."

"We are allocated $750,000 from the administration department. Why should we be held responsible for covering their expenses?"

"Why is it that a pain pill has a price tag of $0.05 when it arrives at the pharmacy, but the hospital charges $3.05 for it? This sounds a little high."

Introduction

This chapter analyzes the alternative methods used for allocating overhead or indirect costs to departments or responsibility centers. This allocation of costs is necessary in order to determine the full costs of providing a service or product. We have previously discussed direct and indirect costs as the two categories of total costs. Both costs must be recovered if the organization is to remain financially viable for an extended period of time. In order for any firm (health services related or not) to survive, management must receive revenues equal to the total economic costs of providing the services. Since some of the departments of a healthcare organization are not able to charge directly for the services they provide, their costs must be allocated to departments which are able to charge for their services.

Some major payers such as Medicare and Medicaid have required specific allocation techniques be used to allocate indirect costs to their patients. The ratio of cost to charges (RCC) was developed by cost-based reimbursement payers to determine their fair share when detailed individual cost data were not available. It is a generally accepted principle by third party payers that consumers of goods and services should pay their fair share of the total cost of the resources used in providing that specific good or service. This is true in short-term, acute hospitals and other types of healthcare providers. Because of the subjectivity involved in the allocation process, there has been increasing concern over the lack of accountability for resource use in providing health services. Payers of health services are increasingly demanding that they only pay for the amount of services they use.

The growth of the managed care industry was aided by the attempt of the purchaser to fix the amount in advance they will pay for health services. There was concern over the impact of reimbursement maximization techniques and allocation methods on the established charges.

As discussed earlier, the appropriate costing of resources requires the use of allocation techniques, since many of the costs of an organization are not directly associated with a specific product or service. This allocation process was typically called cost finding in the early days of cost-based reimbursement and it focused more on a macro approach to costing of services. Recently, in using cost-allocation techniques, a micro approach (called cost accounting) has been emphasized to determine per unit costs. However, the objective has not changed. The basic objective of cost finding or cost allocation is to determine the full costs (direct plus allocated indirect costs) of each revenue producing center of an organization which can then be used to price the outputs of that department. Full costs include direct costs such as salary and supplies, and indirect costs such as administrative and general costs.

Specifically, the objectives of cost allocation are:[1]

1. to provide full cost information as a basis of establishing rates for proposed services and to assess the adequacy of existing rates;
2. to provide a full cost basis for reimbursement by third party payers;
3. to provide cost information for negotiating reimbursement contracts with contracting agencies;
4. to provide information for reports to hospital associations, governmental agencies, and other external groups;
5. the authors also believe that the allocation process should provide information to managers for decision making whenever full costs are needed, as long as the limitations of the techniques are known.

Full cost information is needed for rate setting. The development of full costs will require the use of allocation techniques to provide the necessary information. This full cost estimate can or should be compared to market driven competitive rates, negotiated rates from managed care plans and fixed reimbursement rates such as DRGs. It should be stressed that the type of allocation technique used should depend on the needs of management, and not only the requirements of third party payers.

---

[1] Adapted from "Cost Finding and Rate Setting for Hospitals," Chicago: American Hospital Association, 1968, p. 2.

Cost allocation for reimbursement purposes is often a periodic, after-the-fact procedure that is used to allocate costs from support centers to revenue producing centers. Cost allocation may also be used prospectively in estimating reimbursement rates at the beginning of a financial period (for prospective payments). To the extent that cost allocation has been used to maximize reimbursement from third party payers, the results are less valuable for the setting of goals and measuring progress toward those goals involved in cost containment.

Internal management reports for performance measurement will generally find allocated costs less useful because of the subjective nature of many allocations. As a general rule, managers should be evaluated on the basis of costs they can control or influence, which would typically fall into the direct cost category.

Because of the heavy influence of third party payers on revenue generation, the term "cost finding" is used in the first part of the chapter to designate cost allocations used primarily for reimbursement reports and calculations. Generally, cost finding may be defined "as a procedure in which unassigned expenses and the expenses of support departments are allocated to the revenue-producing departments of an organization for the purpose of determining the full costs of providing various . . . services to patients." [2] Later in the chapter, cost allocations will be discussed as they affect cost accounting, rate setting, and managerial decision making.

The American Hospital Association has defined cost finding as:[3]

"Apportionment or allocation of costs of the support centers to each other and to the revenue producing centers on the basis of the statistical data that measure the amount of service rendered by each center to other centers."

Cost finding is relatively limited in terms of timeliness, acceptable methodologies, and relevance to ongoing managerial decisions. Cost analysis or cost accounting is much broader in scope and not as constrained as cost finding. Cost finding provides only averaging information for determining cost per test or cost per procedure. In other words, cost finding is used primarily to establish average costs per unit of service and as a by-product, total departmental costs. The price of the outputs of the department would be determined by dividing the total costs by the number of units of the output. Because of the lack of specific costing of products, it is not particularly useful for identifying cost behavior patterns or cost

---

[2] Seawell, L. Vann, *Introduction to Hospital Accounting*, 2nd ed., Health Care Financial Management Association, 1977.

[3] *Cost Finding and Rate Setting for Hospitals*, Chicago: American Hospital Association, 1968, p. 1.

elements within departments. Cost accounting typically provides more useful information for decision making.

The cost allocation techniques discussed in this chapter are useful for hospitals and nursing homes when individual services can be billed separately. With HMOs, where reimbursement is aggregated based on historical and actuarial cost estimates, calculations on a member per month basis do not generally require a cost finding process. However, in cases where there are a multitude of benefit packages with characteristics which may have an impact on the extent to which overhead costs should be allocated to different packages, then cost allocation as explained later may become more useful.

The underlying assumption or philosophy of each of these objectives is that the patients who receive particular services should pay the fair costs associated with those services. As a minimum all patients should at least pay the direct costs of all services necessary for their treatments. Full costs (which include both direct and indirect costs) should be determined by healthcare financial managers and reported to other managers for setting rates, negotiating reimbursement arrangements and contracts, and reporting on healthcare costs to external organizations. This is the philosophy of equity in that all services and their associated costs should be assigned to the patients who have received the services.

Allocated costs are not the same as transfer prices. Transfer pricing techniques are used when products or services are transferred from one responsibility center to another. They are primarily useful in determining profit performance. They have serious behavioral and economic considerations, and therefore must be developed with care. Transfer prices were discussed in chapter 8.

Note that most healthcare organizations should strive for understandable and meaningful cost allocation techniques. Cost allocation should be standardized, to the extent possible, for managerial decision making. Given that external agencies may require specific formats for external reporting, internal managers still require that allocation information be presented in a meaningful format for their decision making. In all cases where alternative approaches are available, the benefit-cost criterion should prevail. Cost finding is usually an expensive and time-consuming process which should only be conducted when the benefits justify the efforts.

The results of cost allocation calculations become valuable in decision making to the extent that it can be determined whether or not a specific service is capable of supporting itself. One ready example is the emergency department, which often has been assumed to be a "loser" from a financial standpoint when all costs have been allocated. For internal management purposes, only the direct costs associated with the department should be used in the performance measurement of the supervisor. It is assumed that the supervisor can influence the amount of direct costs. For

reimbursement purposes, however, and for the billing of services provided, it is important to acknowledge the contribution of other cost centers
to the provision of emergency department services. One way of convinc-
ing the departmental manager that these costs are just as important as the
direct costs is to think about what costs would be incurred if the department were a free-standing entity. It would still have to purchase utilities,
insurance, marketing, etc. Thus, effective methods of allocating the indirect expenses to the final product is crucial to develop full costs.

Prerequisites for cost allocation

Several conditions must exist before cost allocation can be implemented
effectively:

1. an up-to-date organization chart separating revenue centers and
   support centers;
2. a chart of accounts that is consistent with the organization
   structure;
3. an accurate information system that is capable of providing:
   a. financial and cost data for each support and revenue center,
   b. statistical and other nonfinancial data for each cost and revenue center;
4. an appropriate cost allocation technique that will be practical and
   meaningful to the specific healthcare provider.

The organization structure is a key element of cost allocation. Cost
allocation should ideally be consistent with the locus of authority and responsibility in the organization. The organization structure is analogous to
a road map showing how costs are routed or transferred through different
cost centers until they reach the final revenue centers. Clear lines of
authority and responsibility are used to divide the organization into the
responsibility centers with which costs are associated. Each organization
must identify its own responsibility center. Revenue centers and support
centers must be clearly identified. Revenue centers are ultimately charged
with all the allowable costs of the general or service (cost) centers. Since
cause-effect relationships are important, the relationships between each
center must be known so that the services provided to other support and
revenue centers are clear. An example of one organization's categorization
of support and revenue centers is shown in *Exhibit 9–1*.

The second important prerequisite for cost allocation is that the accounting system have the capability to collect costs by responsibility
center. Many health service organizations have never taken the time or
effort to modify their accounting system to accurately reflect the current
responsibility structure. Failure to maintain consistency here can result in
inaccurate and deficient cost allocation results. An up-to-date and accu-

Exhibit 9–1
Sample revenue and support centers

Support centers	Revenue centers
Admitting	Nursing
Counseling	Laboratory
Billing	Operating Room
Collections	Physical Therapy
Housekeeping	Cardiology
Laundry	Pharmacy
Central Supply	Audiology
Telecommunication	Occupational Medicine
Utilities	Blood Bank
Quality Assurance	Ambulance
Public Relations	Emergency Room
Marketing	
Infection Control	
Medical Records	
Pastoral Care	
Social Services	
Information Services	

rate chart of accounts is the first step in collecting relevant data for the allocation process. Unless the chart of accounts reflects the authority and responsibility of cost center managers, costs may be charged to the wrong cost centers and thereby be erroneously distributed under any kind of cost allocation method.

The American Hospital Association (AHA), Medical Group Management Association (MGMA), Group Health Association of America (GHAA), and other health service associations have formulated standardized charts of accounts for their respective organizational forms. *Exhibit 9–2* represents the chart of accounts developed by the American Hospital Association for hospital accounting systems. This format provides the flexibility needed to meet the needs of most hospital based providers. The flexibility concept is very important since management styles and organizational units vary considerably even in the same type of healthcare provider. In the late 1970s, the Department of Health and Human Services tried to introduce a uniform reporting system which was based on a standard chart of accounts. It was unsuccessful due to political factors at the time and lack of agreement by the field on which way was best. In any event, a chart of accounts developed to fit the needs of the organization is necessary as a starting point for the individual healthcare organization's cost allocation calculations. Each institution can modify, by dividing the standard accounts into smaller elements, as illustrated in the AHA chart of accounts. Such modifications would increase the precision and usefulness of the cost allocation calculations.

Exhibit 9–2
AHA numerical coding system
Revenue accounts

First Digit	Second, Third, and Fourth Digits	Decimal Point	Fifth Digit	Sixth Digit	Decimal Point	Seventh, Eighth, and Ninth Digits
0 Not used		.	Inpatient acute		.	
1 } Balance sheet accounts		.	Inpatient long-term		.	
2		.	Outpatient emergency	Classification according to individual hospital requirements	.	Classification by functional units
3 } Routine & other professional service revenue	Classification by organizational units	.	Outpatient referred		.	
4		.	Outpatient clinic		.	
5 Other operating revenue & deductions from revenue		.	Day care		.	
6		.	Home health care		.	
7 Expense accounts		.	↑ Other classifications ↓		.	
8		.			.	
9 Nonoperating revenue		.			.	

Expense accounts

First Digit	Second, Third and Fourth Digits	Decimal Point	Fifth and Sixth Digits	Decimal Point	Seventh, Eighth, and Ninth Digits
0 Not used		.		.	
1 } Balance sheet accounts		.		.	
2		.		.	
3		.		.	
4 Revenue accounts	Classification by organizational units	.	Natural classification of expense	.	Classification by functional units
5		.		.	
6 } Nursing & other professional services expense		.		.	
7		.		.	
8 Other services expense		.		.	
9 Nonoperating expense		.		.	

Source: American Hospital Association.

The third prerequisite concerns the accuracy and adequacy of the organization's information system. The information system must be capable of minimizing errors in recording and classifying data. It must be able to correctly match direct costs with the cost center incurring those costs. This problem becomes challenging when organizations similar in structure to multiple-site HMOs are considered, due to the need for networking of geographically separated computers. The information requirements of cost containment and cost management needed to negotiate in the increasingly competitive healthcare market make this function one of the most important. Indeed, the title of an article says it all, "Whoever Has the Data, Wins the Game."[4] Revenues must also be correctly classified as to the source. Accrual accounting must be used to properly record inventories, receivables, and payables. Estimation of unpaid claims liabilities for prepaid health systems requires accurate prior information regarding experience with past unpaid claims liabilities. The information system must be capable of separating cash flows from accruals. In addition, the information must be capable of producing necessary reclassifications and adjustments required by the different regulatory and reimbursement agencies.

Another important aspect of the information system is the nonfinancial data. Cost allocation depends on knowing the quantity of services provided by or to other cost centers. The quantity of services shared by separate cost centers is usually represented by nonmonetary statistical data which portray the activity level of services in each cost center. Each cost center, especially support centers, should collect and maintain at least one statistical measure of the volume of service activity (output). These activity measures should be feasible to compile and should be meaningful measures of the most important services provided by that cost center. The distribution of services between centers can be measured on either an input resources factors or output activity basis. Input resources factors would include structural factors in the provision of health services, such as number of nurses, FTE employees, square footage, number of meals, etc. Output measures would include such items as patient days, discharges, patient visits, ambulatory visits, physician contacts, procedures performed, etc. The distinction between the two has an impact on the value of the cost determination process for evaluation and standard setting (associated with information about inputs) as opposed to using the information for negotiating and rate setting (where output information is required).

Care must be taken to ensure that the costs of collection do not exceed the benefits to be derived from the improvement in cost allocation which results. The statistical measures of activity should result in an equitable allocation of costs. They must be able to be applied consistently across different time periods.

---

[4]Traska, M.R., *Hospitals*, April 5, 1988, pp. 50–55.

Cost allocation techniques

As discussed earlier, cost allocation is the allocation of the costs of support centers to each other and to revenue generating centers. This allocation is used to determine the full cost of each revenue generating center. The following exhibit (*Exhibit 9–3*) illustrates a simplified model of how services flow between healthcare departments within a hospital or nursing home setting. Each of these flows of service could be used as a basis for cost allocation. The specific techniques explained later in this chapter use varying sets of these flows of services as the basis for cost allocation.

Each cost allocation method starts with the process of determining costs which are to be allocated. For example, Medicare and Medicaid specify that certain costs are peripheral to the provision of health services of Medicare and Medicaid beneficiaries, and are not authorized and cannot be included in the allocation of costs for Medicare and Medicaid. In some cases, the third parties may require specific costs to be classified differently than management.

After determination and classification of the costs to be allocated has been performed, there are four basic methods of cost allocation which could be used:

Exhibit 9–3
Conceptual model for healthcare services

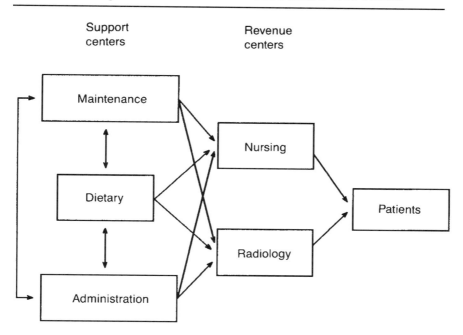

1. direct allocation
2. stepdown
3. double distribution
4. algebraic or reciprocal

These four methods differ primarily in the manner in which the costs are allocated between and from the support centers. They differ in terms of which flows are recognized as dominant. They are placed in order from the simplest to the most complex. In addition, this order also proceeds from the least correct to the most accurate cost representation.

Comprehensive example

The relationships provided in *Exhibit 9–3* will be used to demonstrate the different methods of cost allocation. It is assumed that the first two prerequisites for cost finding have been fulfilled, and provide realistic and accurate data. Information regarding the activity bases are included as *Exhibit 9–4*.

Activity bases: Maintenance expenses will be allocated to other departments based on the amount of square footage involved. Dietary expenses will be allocated based on the number of meals served. Administrative expenses will be allocated based on the number of full time equivalent (FTE) employees. Other bases could be used, as long as there appears to be a direct cause-effect or correlational relationship between resource utilization and the allocation or activity base chosen.

Direct apportionment

In the direct apportionment method, the costs of the support centers are allocated directly to revenue centers or to patient care centers. This method ignores the fact that most support centers also provide services to other support centers as well as the revenue centers. *Exhibit 9–5* illustrates

Exhibit 9–4
Illustrative data used for cost allocation example

Department	Direct costs	Square feet	Meals	FTEs	Admissions	Slides
Maintenance	$ 200,000	10,000	1,000	12		
Dietary	$ 400,000	30,000	900	10		
Administration	$ 300,000	20,000	1,000	10		
Nursing	$ 800,000	160,000	2,000	25	400	
Radiology	$ 300,000	40,000	1,000	8		900
Totals	$2,000,000	260,000	5,900	65		

Exhibit 9–5
Direct allocation method

Support centers   Revenue centers

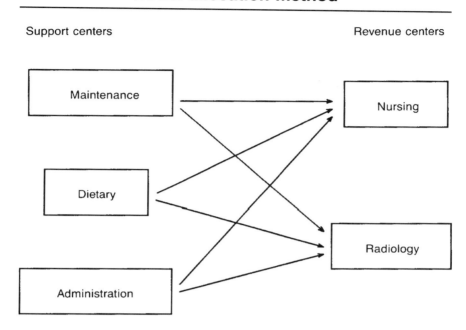

the flow of cost allocations when using the direct method. Costs of support centers are allocated directly to revenue centers, ignoring all of the services provided by the support centers to the other support centers (administration services provided to dietary and maintenance; dietary services provided to maintenance and administration; and maintenance services provided to dietary and administration).

The direct allocation method is the least accurate for cost determination. It is mainly indicated here for demonstration purposes, and to provide a starting point for comparison with the more appropriate methods to be presented. The Health Care Financing Administration (HCFA) does not permit the use of direct apportionment for cost reporting purposes, but does permit the remaining three methods.

Exhibit 9–6 provides the results of the application of the direct apportionment method to our example. Since the only relevant centers for allocation are the revenue centers, the allocation bases include only the data for those centers. Thus, for the allocation of maintenance expenses, a total of 200,000 square feet is used (160,000 + 40,000), with 80 percent (160,000/200,000) being allocated to nursing and 20 percent (40,000/200,000) allocated to radiology. The same process is followed for the direct allocation of dietary (67 percent to nursing and 33 percent to radiology) and administration (76 percent to nursing and 24 percent to radiology).

Exhibit 9-6
Direct method of cost allocation

Department	Direct Costs	Square Feet	Meals	FTEs	To: Nursing	To: Radiology	Nursing + Radiology
Support							
Maintenance[1]	($200,000)				$160,000	$40,000	$200,000
Dietary[2]	($400,000)				$266,667	$133,333	$400,000
Administration[3]	($300,000)				$227,273	$72,727	$300,000
Revenue							
Nursing	($800,000)	160,000	2,000	25	$800,000		$800,000
Radiology	($300,000)	40,000	1,000	8		$300,000	$300,000
TOTALS	($2,000,000)	200,000	3,000	33	$1,453,939	$546,061	$2,000,000
Per unit costs		$1.00	$133.33	$9,091			
Output measures:							
Admissions					400	900	
Slides							
Per admission					$3,635	$1,365	$5,000
Per slide						$607	$5,000
Nursing + Radiology per admission							

[1] Allocated on basis of square feet
[2] Allocated on basis of meals
[3] Allocated on basis of FTEs

Stepdown

The second allocation method to be explored is called the stepdown method. This technique secured its name by the "stairstep" appearance of the calculations as the costs were allocated from support center to support and revenue centers. This method compensates for one weakness of the direct apportionment method in that it is recognized that support centers do provide services to other support centers. *Exhibit 9–7* illustrates the complexity of using a stepdown approach. The first step in this process is to allocate the maintenance center costs to all other departments that have received maintenance services. The choice of using the maintenance support center is subjective and other support centers could have been selected. In a similar manner, the order of allocation of the remaining support centers is also subjective. After this has been done, the maintenance center is considered to be closed, and it has no further costs allocated to it. The second step in the process is to allocate dietary costs (which now include a portion of maintenance costs) to all the remaining departments (administration, nursing, and radiology). After this allocation has been performed, the dietary center is considered closed, in that it has no further costs allocated to it. The third step in this stepdown example is to allocate from the last remaining support center (administration) to the revenue departments (nursing and radiology). At this point, all the support

Exhibit 9–7
Stepdown allocation method

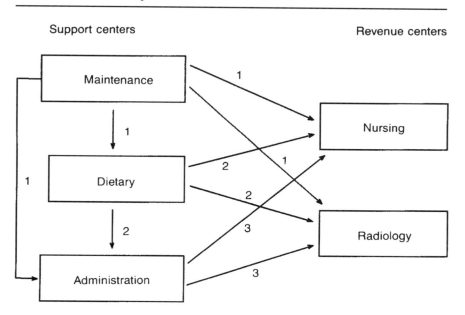

centers are considered closed since all costs have now been allocated to the revenue centers.

In summary, the stepdown method consists of the following steps:

1. Choose a starting point and an order of allocations.
2. Allocate the general administrative costs that are not already included in cost centers to both revenue and support centers where appropriate. Use an appropriate and reasonable allocation basis to allocate the general costs (such as bad debt, education, research).
3. Allocate the costs of the support centers to other support and revenue centers. This step is illustrated by the numbered steps (1, 2, and 3) in *Exhibit 9–7*. As a general rule, the costs of the center that provides the greatest amount of services to other centers, and receives the fewest services from other centers should be allocated first. The rationale for this is to minimize the impact of the fact that not all service interactions among support centers are recognized. For example, the maintenance department in our previous example received services from dietary and administration, but because it was allocated first, it did not receive any of these allocations. Another method which gets used to determine the order of the support centers in the allocation process is to order them from largest total costs to lowest.
4. Once all costs have been allocated from the first support center to all other centers (both revenue and support), that support center is closed — it has no further costs associated with it, and thus cannot receive any allocation of costs from other centers. It does not impact on the next allocation.
5. All costs are then allocated from the second support center to all remaining (those not yet closed) support centers and all revenue centers. This center is then closed.
6. Allocations continue from the third, fourth, etc., support center until all support centers have been closed. All costs have now been allocated to revenue centers.

In *Exhibit 9–8* we have performed the stepdown allocation process for our example. It is important to remember that the allocation percentage is based only on the nonclosed centers and the associated activity or allocation bases included in those centers. For example, for dietary there are only 4,000 meals included in the total, with 1,000 being served to administration, 2,000 to nursing, and 1,000 to radiology. Likewise, with administration the only FTEs to be included are those for nursing and radiology.

The stepdown method is an improvement over the direct apportionment method in that it recognizes that services are provided by support centers to other support centers, in addition to the revenue centers. However, the

Exhibit 9-8
Stepdown method of cost allocation

Department	Direct Costs	Square Feet	Meals	FTEs	To: Maintenance[1]	To: Dietary[2]	To: Admin.[3]	To: Nursing	To: Radiology	Nursing+ Radiology
SUPPORT										
Maintenance	($200,000)				(200,000)	$24,000	$16,000	$128,000	$32,000	$160,000
Dietary	($400,000)	30,000				($424,000)	$106,000	$212,000	$106,000	$318,000
Administration	($300,000)	20,000	1,000				($422,000)	$319,697	$102,303	$422,000
REVENUE										
Nursing	($800,000)	160,000	2,000	25				$800,000		$800,000
Radiology	($300,000)	40,000	1,000	8					$300,000	$300,000
Totals	($2,000,000)	250,000	4,000	33	$0	$0	$0	$1,459,697	$540,303	$2,000,000
Per unit costs		$0.80	$106.00	$12,788						
Output measures:										
Admissions								400		
Slides									900	
Per admission								$3,649	$1,351	$5,000
Per slide									$600	
Nursing + Radiology per admission										$5,000

[1] Allocated on basis of square feet
[2] Allocated on basis of meals
[3] Allocated on basis of FTEs

process does not recognize all the interrelationships between support centers, since the first center to be allocated does not receive support center allocations. The second center to be allocated from receives at most one allocation, the third receives at most two allocations, and so on. The next method to be discussed improves on this weaknesses.

Double or multiple distribution method

The double distribution method was designed to correct one of the major weaknesses of the stepdown method—failure to account fully for inter-departmental services. As described previously, centers are successively closed under the stepdown method. Under the double distribution method, each center remains "open" and costs can be reallocated to support centers. This method may use two iterations (allocations) at which time all support centers are "closed," or the iterations may continue successively until further allocations result in immaterial changes in the allocation amounts to each support center. In each case, the final allocation is made only to the revenue centers (as in the stepdown method).

The first allocation under the double distribution method is identical to the first step in the stepdown method (as indicated by step 1 in *Exhibits 9–7* and *9–9*). However, the maintenance center is not closed after this first allocation. The second allocation, as shown in *Exhibit 9–9*, includes an allocation of costs back to the maintenance center in addition to the other centers. The third step indicates that costs are allocated to both

Exhibit 9–9
Double distribution allocation method

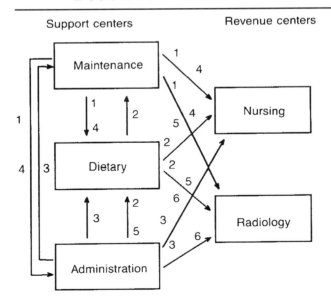

maintenance and dietary in addition to the revenue centers. This concludes the first "step" in the double distribution method. The second step in this method is identical to the stepdown method, and is denoted by steps 4, 5, and 6 in *Exhibit 9–9*. Costs are allocated from maintenance to all other centers and then maintenance is closed. Costs are then allocated from dietary to administration and the revenue centers, and then dietary is closed. Costs are finally allocated from administration to the revenue centers as the final step.

Unique approaches to the use of the double distribution method can be taken by different organizations, through the process of selectively excluding one or more departments, or basing the allocation on different service measures. A triple distribution method would simply leave all centers open until costs have been allocated from the support centers twice, then on the third pass, the stepdown method would be used. Each iteration would correspond to the patterns of service between centers. Consequently, each organization's approach to double or multiple distribution methods will be unique at the second or third stage of the allocation process. The application of the double distribution method to our example is provided in *Exhibit 9–10*.

Double, or multiple, distribution methods provide a better approximation of the full costs of the revenue centers. The results are more representative of actual patterns of activities and flows of services. This allocation method more precisely represents the interaction among the various centers. This becomes more true as more iterations are performed. Even though these allocation methods are gaining in popularity, they lack some objectivity. They are ambiguous about when to stop reallocating costs to support centers and with regard to the order of priority in which to consider the cost allocations. Any change in the order of precedence in the allocation, or a change in the stopping criteria, will change the final results— perhaps significantly. Historically, the rationale behind a specific allocation order and number of iterations was based on the objective of maximization of revenues. Therefore, reality has never been a major concern. In today's environment, allocation and full cost determination is valuable for the setting of charges and premiums, and provide required information to negotiate with HMOs, PPOs, regulators, hospitals, nursing homes, etc. Inaccurate cost determination can now have a major impact on the ability of a healthcare organization to remain competitive and financially viable. For these reasons, the next method is recommended as the most objective and accurate representation of all known patterns of services and activities.

Algebraic or reciprocal method

This method involves the simultaneous solution of a series of equations. These equations are mathematical representations of the known interrelationships between all centers. This results in the most complete allocation

Exhibit 9-10
Double distribution method of cost allocation

Department	Direct Costs	Square Feet	Meals	FTEs	To: Maintenance	To: Dietary	To: Admin.	To: Nursing	To: Radiology	Nursing+ Radiology
SUPPORT										
First allocation step:										
Maintenance	($200,000)	30,000	1,000	12		$24,000	$16,000	$128,000	$32,000	$160,000
Dietary	($400,000)	20,000	1,000	10	$84,800	($424,000)	$84,800	$169,600	$84,800	$254,400
Administration	($300,000)				$87,447	$72,873	($400,800)	$182,182	$58,298	$240,480
REVENUE										
Nursing	($800,000)	160,000	2,000	25				$800,000		$800,000
Radiology	($300,000)	40,000	1,000	8					$300,000	$300,000
Totals:		250,000	5,000	55	$172,247	$72,873	$0	$1,279,782	$475,098	$1,754,880
Per unit cost		$0.80	$84.80	$7,287						
Second allocation step:										
Maintenance					($172,247)	$20,670	$13,780	$110,238	$27,560	$137,798
Dietary		30,000				($93,542)	$23,386	$46,771	$23,386	$70,157
Administration		20,000	1,000				($37,165)	$28,156	$9,010	$37,165
Nursing		160,000	2,000	25						
Radiology		40,000	1,000	8						
Totals:		250,000	4,000	33						
Per unit cost		$0.69	$23.39	$1,126						
Totals	($2,000,000)	250,000	5,000	55	$0	$0	$0	$1,464,947	$535,053	$2,000,000
Per unit costs:										
Admissions								400	900	
Slides										
Per admission								$3,662	$1,338	$5,000
Per slide									$595	
Nursing + Radiology per admission										$5,000

of all costs. It is the most defensible method for regulatory and negotiation purposes. Unfortunately, it is also the most complex and it requires the aid of a computer. The multiple distribution approach is an approximation of the results that can be expected using the reciprocal method. Healthcare organizations that have access to computerized cost allocation methods should test several alternative approaches and choose the method best suited to their particular needs.

In order to utilize the reciprocal method it is necessary to state the relationships among the various departments in a mathematical formula. For example, using the centers provided in the exhibits in this chapter, it is necessary to know what fraction of services are provided by every center to every other center. This information is also required to use the direct allocation and double or multiple allocation methods.

From the information previously provided, the following mathematical relationships can be stated:

1. $M = \$200{,}000 + (1/5)D + (12/55)A$
2. $D = \$400{,}000 + (30/250)M + (10/55)A$
3. $A = \$300{,}000 + (20/250)M + (1/5)D$

Where: M = total costs of maintenance department after allocation
D = total costs of dietary center after allocation
A = total costs of administration center after allocation

These total cost equations use the proportions of services provided from *Exhibit 9–4*. They represent the total center's costs after recognizing the services each center provides to one another. After these costs are found, then direct apportionment to the revenue centers will provide an accurate full cost measure.

Linear algebra is then used to determine the cost allocations. The three equations in three unknowns are rearranged and expressed in matrix form, as follows:

1. $M - (1/5)D - (12/55)A = \$200{,}000$
2. $-(30/250)M + D - (10/55)A = \$400{,}000$
3. $-(20/250)M - (1/5)D + A = \$300{,}000$

This matrix arranges the coefficients associated with each center in vertical columns relative to each other. Separating these coefficients from the parameters (M,D,A) results in a coefficient matrix [C], a vector of unknowns [X] (which will become the total costs of each center after the allocations are performed), and a vector of constants [Y] (the direct costs of each center).

$$\begin{bmatrix} 1 & -(1/5) & -(12/55) \\ -(30/250) & 1 & -(10/55) \\ -(20/250) & -(1/5) & 1 \end{bmatrix} \begin{bmatrix} M \\ D \\ A \end{bmatrix} = \begin{bmatrix} 200{,}000 \\ 400{,}000 \\ 300{,}000 \end{bmatrix}$$

These matrices can then be expressed as:

$$[C][X] = [Y]$$

Since we want to obtain the values for the unknown costs in each support center (M,D,A) prior to the allocation to the revenue centers, we solve this equation for the unknowns, which are the X values.

$$[X] = [C^{-1}][Y]$$

Where $[C^{-1}]$ denotes the inverse of the coefficient matrix and is equivalent to dividing the vector of constants by the coefficient matrix. The inverse of [C] may be found by either manual, mechanical, or computerized techniques. As the number of support centers becomes larger than two or three, the more necessary it becomes to use computerized methods. The interested reader may refer to any standard reference on matrix algebra for assistance in the computations. The authors usually recommend a computerized approach to matrix inversion. The solution to this coefficient matrix was obtained using a spreadsheet. The results of this matrix inversion can be found using a spreadsheet program. For Quattro Pro, the commands are /TAI and for Lotus the commands are /DMI.

The results of the matrix inversion are placed into the original equation, permitting the solution of the problem:

$$
\begin{array}{ccc}
[X] = & [C^{-1}][Y] & \\
M = & \begin{bmatrix} 1.05426 & 0.26655 & 0.278485 \\ 0.147199 & 1.07495 & 0.227562 \\ 0.113782 & 0.236314 & 1.067790 \end{bmatrix} & \begin{bmatrix} 200,000 \\ 400,000 \\ 300,000 \end{bmatrix}
\end{array}
$$

Using the principles of matrix multiplication (first row of coefficients times column of direct costs, second row of coefficients times column of direct costs, etc.), we obtain the solution to the vector of unknowns (the multiplication can also be performed with the spreadsheet program (Quattro Pro /TAM; Lotus /DMM):

$$M = \$401{,}019$$
$$D = \$527{,}689$$
$$A = \$437{,}619$$

These are the values associated with total allocated costs of the support centers. These are really the costs that would have been charged to each center if the full share of all other support center costs had been charged to each support center. These results provide a simultaneous estimate of what these costs, before allocation to revenue centers, would be. Note that the sum of these costs are more than the original costs in the three support departments. For this reason, they are not "real" dollars or costs, but can be viewed as input costs in the cost allocation process. These costs must now be allocated to the revenue centers.

These costs are allocated to all centers—both support and revenue, using the allocation bases used in the first step of the double distribution method. This results in the distribution of costs shown in *Exhibit 9–11*.

The figures in *Exhibit 9–11* represent the costs that would have been charged to each support center if all the patterns (ratios) of services

Exhibit 9–11
Reciprocal method of cost allocation

	Mainten-ance	Dietary	Adminis-tration	Nursing	Radiology	Nursing+radiology
Mainten-ance	($401,019)	$ 48,122	$ 32,081	$ 256,652	$ 64,163	$ 320,815
Dietary	$105,538	($527,689)	105,538	$ 211,076	$105,538	$ 316,614
Adminis-tration	$ 95,481	$ 79,567	($437,619)	$ 198,918	$ 63,654	$ 262,572
Nursing				$ 800,000		$ 800,000
Radiology					$300,000	$ 300,000
Totals (rounded)				$1,466,646	$533,355	$2,000,001

provided had been simultaneously recognized in the accounts. The essence of the solution to the algebraic or reciprocal method is to obtain these "fictitious" costs using algebraic techniques. Once these costs are obtained, the solution is straightforward in that the original ratios of services provided are used to allocate or spread those costs to each of the affected centers. Note that the total allowable costs remaining in the support centers must sum to zero. Another way of stating this is to note that all costs allocated to the revenue centers sum to $2,000,000, the total amount of original costs. No allowable costs remain in the support centers, even though we have allocated the fictitious costs to these centers.

These results are more objective than the results obtained using the stepdown, direct, or double distribution methods because they are based on all the data. No assumptions about starting points or stopping points are made under the reciprocal method. All the interactive patterns of service that were originally identified are used as input data in the final allocation. For this reason, the reciprocal method is usually considered the most accurate of the four methods discussed in this chapter. Note also that some "straight line" adjustments may be needed as the last step in the reciprocal method. These adjustments are due to the numerous "rounding-off" calculations that are made throughout the process.

Exhibit 9–12 summarizes the results obtained under each of the different methods. Each method is described in percentage terms relative to the reciprocal method. The resulting percentage differences are minor. The double distribution method best approximates the results obtained under the reciprocal method. This is due to the fact that double distribution is closer to the reciprocal method than the others. A triple or quadruple distribution would come even closer to the result of the reciprocal method. Foyle[5] has suggested that in most cases, since the differences are

---

[5] Foyle, William R., "Evaluation of Methods of Cost Analysis," (unpublished manuscript), 1964.

Exhibit 9–12
Comparison of cost allocations per output measure

	Direct	Stepdown	Double distribution	Reciprocal
Nursing	$3,635	$3,649	$3,662	$3,667
Radiology	$607	$600	$595	$593
% Comparisons				
Nursing	99.13%	99.51%	99.86%	100.00%
Radiology	102.36%	101.18%	100.34%	100.00%

minor, other factors such as management decisions regarding utilization of space, employees and other resources may create wider differences in the results than just the different mathematical calculations.

A later paper by Howard[6] also compares the reciprocal method with the stepdown method. Howard's results show that for the six-month period of his test hospital's data, the differences in departmental costs varied by as much as 30 percent. He then compared the effect of different allocations on reimbursable costs and obtained a difference of only $517 (increase in reimbursement) under the reciprocal method. This was only a .05 percent increase in reimbursable costs. Not all cases result in such minor differences, however.

In any event, the management accountant in any healthcare organization must determine whether the added costs of any method are worth the expense and effort of using that method. Access to a computerized cost allocation program greatly simplifies the problems with any of these methods. However, the fees associated with such programs, or the costs of developing them, are not trivial. In all but the most complicated cases, a matrix inversion can be obtained through most computer programs, and the inverse of the coefficient matrix will facilitate the computations associated with the reciprocal method. The reciprocal method should not be ignored just because it looks more complicated. Given the matrix solution to the inverse, it is no more complicated than any of the other methods.

A major advantage of the reciprocal method is that the matrix inverse is relatively stable. As long as the pattern of service interactions does not drastically change, the same inverse of the coefficient matrix may be used repeatedly. This is an important simplification that should be recognized by healthcare organizations. In other words, once the expenses of obtaining the inverse have been incurred, they need not be incurred again until the patterns of service between departments change significantly. Consequently, the cost allocations will not change proportionately as these small

---

[6] Howard, Thomas P., "A Comparison of Two Methods of Cost Finding," *Proceedings of the Southwestern Regional Meeting, American Accounting Association,* Houston: American Accounting Association, 1979.

changes in service patterns occur. Of course, the allocation must be performed each period using the actual costs of that period.

Cost allocations for managers

The distinction between cost finding and cost allocation is primarily one of function. Cost finding is generally the term used when regulators, Medicare, Medicaid, Blue Cross/Shield, or other stakeholders require the determination of costs in a specific fashion or in a specific format. The Medicare cost reports and the associated allowable stepdowns for allocation methods are one obvious example. HMOs in every state are required to file the Annual Statement of Conditions and Affairs (nicknamed the Orange Blank). This provides for a standardized reporting form, and in the case of Medicare, provides a relatively consistent method of "cost finding." On the other hand, cost allocations for managerial purposes are guided by criteria of usefulness and relevance. Therefore, managers in healthcare organizations may choose appropriate cost allocation methods for each of the major types of decisions in their areas of responsibility.

For example, the reciprocal method may be used to allocate costs for setting rates in a particular clinic. The direct allocation method may be used to allocate costs from maintenance to revenue producing centers. Alternatively, the very same cost allocation methods may be used for both reimbursement purposes as for internal managerial decision making. The only difference is that for internal decisions, managers have flexibility in

Exhibit 9–13
Strengths and weaknesses of allocation methods

Method	Strengths	Weaknesses
Direct allocation	Simple	Does not recognize services provided by support services to other support services
Stepdown	Recognizes some of services provided between support centers	Dependent on center ordering; does not recognize all services provided between support centers
Double (multiple) distribution	Recognizes all services provided between support centers; approaches reciprocal method as more iterations used	Concludes with stepdown, so does not fully reflect all support center interrelationships
Reciprocal	Recognizes full impact of all support center interrelationships Most accurate	Mathematically complex

their choice of cost allocation methods and allocation bases, and the degree of complexity of the allocation method used.

The key point to remember in the choice between stepdown method and a reciprocal cost method is the extent to which managers want to avoid arbitrary allocation criteria, such as the order of precedence (which center is closed first, second, etc.), and the degree to which reciprocal services between centers is included. To recognize interactions between support centers a reciprocal method of cost allocation should be used for major managerial decisions.

Software has been developed which allocates costs to different patient groups (e.g., DRGs). Ideally, such software is based on either the double distribution method or reciprocal cost allocation methods. Use of less sophisticated methods does not utilize fully the computer's computational capabilities and does not offer the advantages noted previously.

Output costing

Healthcare providers and payers are interested in calculating the costs of their *outputs,* which usually take the form of products or services. As was discussed in the last chapter, they all must make *pricing* decisions. Generally, all providers will want to know if the market prices exceed their full costs. Both providers and payers need to *prepare budgets.* Furthermore, they must *evaluate performance* and *control costs.* All of these objectives require precise knowledge of costs. Most costing systems start with a determination of direct and indirect costs. The earlier part of the chapter has shown how to allocate indirect costs to departments or services. This section of the chapter shows how to use such allocated costs in determining what accountants call "full costs" or "fully absorbed costs" or "fully allocated costs."

For purposes of this chapter, healthcare outputs are produced by the organization's cost or revenue centers. A cost center is simply an organizational sub-unit where costs are the primary focus for budgeting and performance evaluation. It may be a department or the entire organization. A revenue center is a sub-unit of the organization for which both costs and revenues are monitored. As with a cost center, a revenue center may be defined as a department, such as a laboratory in the physician group practice, a product line division of a health maintenance organization, or the entire organization, depending on its size.

Direct and indirect costs are used to develop full cost information for pricing or negotiating payment rates for various outputs of healthcare firms. The outputs include individual services, groups of services, or, in the case of capitation costing, the availability of healthcare services during a time period. Since pricing and budgeting are both forward-looking, prospective decisions, our costing examples and discussion are framed around planned or projected costs.

Direct and indirect costs

To determine the full cost of an output, direct costs are added to some *proportionate share* of the indirect costs associated with that output. *Direct costs* are costs that are directly traceable to an output, sometimes called a "cost object." *Indirect costs* are costs that are not directly traceable, or not easily traceable, to an output or cost object. Indirect costs often benefit more than one cost object. Such expenses are often called *overhead.*

To determine direct and indirect costs associated with any output, the output must first be defined precisely. An output may be an individual service, such as a laboratory test, or the output may be a group of services delivered to a patient during an outpatient visit or an inpatient stay. Outputs may also be defined on an all-inclusive basis during the patient day or patient stay, or they may be itemized or listed in discrete terms. Once the output is defined, its *full cost* can be determined by identifying its direct costs and adding a share of indirect costs.

Identifying direct and indirect costs depends not only on the cost object, but also on the sophistication of the organization's information systems. In many cases, tracing direct costs to individual outputs may be difficult or very costly because of the number and variety of different outputs. For example, the direct costs for a specific laboratory test would include some supplies, but not all. It may be difficult to trace depreciation and labor expenses to a specific test; these would then be indirect costs. The extra costs necessary to trace many indirect costs, thereby transforming them into direct costs, may be too costly relative to the benefits provided. Therefore, some organizations may have access to direct cost information that may not be readily available to others.

General full costing model

A general model for determining the full cost of outputs for a cost or revenue center includes both direct costs and the share of indirect costs assigned to the output. Two kinds of indirect costs must be included. Some costs are indirect to the cost or revenue center as well as those that are direct to the center, but indirect to the output. Costs that are indirect to the revenue or cost center, such as general administrative costs, are allocated from other cost centers of the organization. Although the second type of indirect costs can be traced to the cost or revenue center, they cannot be easily traced to specific outputs. For example, salaries of supervisors in radiology are direct to the unit itself, but difficult to trace directly to specific X-rays. Thus, these costs are indirect to the output itself. Some indirect costs can become direct costs if the information system is modified or improved (or if estimates are used to determine how the indirect costs should be traced to the outputs).

In the majority of cases, cost and revenue centers produce more than one output. First, direct costs for each output are identified. Then, a share of indirect (overhead) costs from within the cost or revenue center is added to the direct costs. Shares of indirect costs allocated from other cost or revenue centers are also added to the center's outputs.

The general full costing model is based on costs from a cost or revenue center, such that:

> *Direct costs for each output* +
> Share of Center's *Indirect costs* assigned to each output +
>   (Direct to the Cost or Revenue Center)
> Share of *Indirect costs* allocated to the Center =
>   Full costs of output

Costing healthcare services

In this section, several methods for identifying direct costs are discussed. Then, indirect costs must be identified or assigned to healthcare services. Two methods for determining direct costs are discussed. The first method uses relative value units to help estimate the direct costs. The second method measures (traces) the direct costs. Next, two methods for assigning indirect costs to outputs are presented. They are based on (1) quantity of output or (2) relative value units. The direct and indirect costing methods may be combined in various combinations in order to determine an output's full cost.

Determining direct costs

Relative Value Units. As noted previously, it is difficult to trace costs directly to outputs. The difficulty is due to the number and variety of healthcare outputs produced, or it may be due to inadequate information systems. Therefore, it may be necessary to estimate direct costs.

One common method for estimating the direct cost of outputs is to determine the relative amount of resources or work necessary to produce each output, and then relative value units are assigned on the basis of relative proportions of resources consumed. *Relative value units (RVUs)* reflect the differences in resource usage necessary to produce one output relative to resources required to produce other outputs. A base value of one (or 100 percent) is assigned to one output and all other outputs are then compared to the base value. The differences are identified through empirical study. Relative value studies may be done internally or they may be adapted from studies done by others.

Exhibit 9–14 provides some examples of RVUs developed under the Medicare program. The case weights for Diagnosis Related Groups (DRGs) may also be viewed as relative value units. In addition, we provide examples of RVUs developed for the Resource Based Relative Value Scale

Exhibit 9–14
Examples of Relative Value Units (RVUs)

A. Case weights for selected Diagnosis Related Groups (DRGs)

DRG number	Title	Case weight for FY 1995
36	Retinal procedures	0.5989
64	Ear, nose, mouth, & throat malignancy	1.1419
78	Pulmonary embolism	1.4211
103	Heart transplant	13.5495
243	Medical back problems	0.7122
317	Admit for renal dialysis	0.5149
462	Rehabilitation	1.6623

B. RVUs for selected Resource Based Relative Value Scale (RB-RVS)

Procedure (CPT) code	Description	Total RVUs for 1994
11100	Biopsy of skin lesion	1.38
33860	Ascending aorta graft	72.93
50590	Fragmenting of kidney stone	20.93
67141	Treatment of retina	13.72
99295	Neonatal critical care	21.67
99354	Prolonged service, office	1.74

(RB-RVS) for physician reimbursement under Medicare. All of these examples illustrate the diversity and variety of RVUs associated with various healthcare services.

The example in *Exhibit 9–15* illustrates how relative value units are used to determine direct costs. In this case, total direct nursing costs are not routinely traced to the two different acuity levels of patient days. Therefore, the projected hours of nursing care per patient day, for each acuity level, are used to determine the relative resource usage as shown by the relative value units, for each of the two types of patient day outputs. As can be seen from *Exhibit 9–15,* an Acuity Level I patient day has a relative value of 1.0 while an Acuity Level II patient day has a relative value unit of 1.46.

After determining the RVUs associated with each Acuity Level patient day, the total number of relative value units is determined by multiplying the number of each output (days) by its associated RVUs. Then, total direct nursing care costs are divided by the sum of the RVUs (acuity weighted days) to determine the cost per RVU. Finally, the cost per RVU

Exhibit 9–15
Determining direct nursing costs under two patient acuity levels—using RVUs

I. Data

Acuity level	Patient days	Hours of nursing care	Number of RVUs	Total direct nursing care costs
I	6,575	5.20	1.00	—
II	1,895	7.60	1.46	—
				$830,000

II. Development RVUs—acuity level 2 relative to acuity level 1

$$\frac{7.60 \text{ hours}}{5.20 \text{ hours}} = 1.46 \text{ RVUs}$$

III. Determine the total number of RVUs

Acuity level	Patient days	Number of RVUs	Acuity weighted patient days (RVUs)
I	6,575	1.00	6,575
II	1,895	1.46	2,767
		Total	9,342

IV. Determine cost per RVU or weighted day

$$\frac{\$830,000}{9,342 \text{ RVUs}} = \$88.85 \text{ per RVU}$$

V. Determine cost per type of patient day

Level 1   1.00 RVU × ($88.85 per RVU) = $88.85 per day
Level 2   1.46 RVU × ($88.85 per RVU) = $129.72 per day

is multiplied by the RVUs for each output to determine the direct cost of each type of patient day.

Relative value units (RVUs) help identify direct costs. For the RVUs to be useful, the original determination of the RVUs must be quite accurate. Moreover, they should be updated periodically. Costing based upon RVUs is more expensive than under earlier approaches based on simple averages. Substantial time is required to calculate the original RVUs. Updating the RVUs is also costly.

Unfortunately, the direct costs produced using the RVU method may not be particularly useful for planning and budgeting or control purposes. Because fixed costs are likely to be averaged into the full cost estimates, the full cost obtained under the RVU method may not yield accurate estimates of total costs under different volumes. This defect plagues many costing methods and the cautious analyst must always be concerned about biases that may be created when full costs are determined at one particular level of output under conditions that may not persist at other volume levels.

Measurement of Direct Costs. To improve the accuracy of costing for health services, or outputs, some direct costs can be measured directly rather than being estimated (e.g., using relative value units). Some direct variable costs can be determined from available accounting records when an output is produced. Alternatively, special studies can be conducted (e.g. engineering studies, regression analyses, etc.). The goal here is to determine actual labor times per unit of output produced, supplies, and other materials used, as well as any traceable overhead costs necessary to produce the service. For example, a particular service may require two units of Input I, which costs $2.00 each, plus three hours of Labor Input III at $30 per hour. Therefore, the direct cost of this service is $94 ((2 × $2 = $4.00) + (3 × $30 = $90.00)).

Direct measurement is expensive to accomplish, and while it might appear to be more accurate, often it is less accurate and yields unstable, fluctuating results. Given the vagaries of human measurement error and changing prices and technologies, direct measurement is not the ideal basis on which to determine product costs. Direct measurements might be most appropriate for outputs that are costly or strategically important to the organization. As with all methods, the underlying records and the implementation of the costing methodology must be accurate if the results are to be useable and reliable. Reasonable amounts of spoilage, wastage, and other lost supplies and materials must also be included. Cost data must be updated as technology, patient mix, personnel, or abilities change.

Measuring direct costs can improve the usefulness of cost estimates used for planning purposes by better identifying variable and fixed costs. However, managers must respond consistently to both variable and fixed costs. In other words, managers must treat a variable cost as truly variable. They must make conscious decisions to increase or decrease fixed costs. For example, although the labor time required to produce an output may be identified as variable, it is not variable unless managers use only the amount needed to produce the required services. If, for example, staff members are not released when there is no work to do, labor costs are really fixed, not variable. Recall from our earlier discussion that a share of indirect costs also must be assigned to services or outputs. In the next section, we show how direct costs and indirect costs are combined to yield the full costs of healthcare services.

Assigning indirect costs

Quantity of Output. The most convenient way to assign indirect costs to outputs is by dividing the indirect costs by the quantity of outputs or services produced. In this way, each service is assigned an equal amount of indirect costs or overhead. We will call this the *averaging method of assigning indirect costs.*

Exhibit 9–16 illustrates the averaging method of assigning indirect costs to each of two radiology films. In this example, the direct variable cost has already been measured for each film. The direct costs in the radiology center that are indirect to each film are divided by the total volume of films (estimated). Additional costs allocated to the radiology center are also divided by the volume of output. Then, equal amounts of indirect costs (e.g., $12.50 and $20 per film) are added to the direct costs of each film to determine the full costs of each film (e.g., $35.50 or $44.50).

Assigning equal amounts of indirect costs to each output is inaccurate in most real-world situations. The only way the averaging method can be accurate is if the outputs are homogeneous in their resource requirements. For example, some services require more supervisory time than do other services. Therefore, an equal assignment of indirect costs will understate the cost of some outputs and overstate the cost of others.

As is true with direct costs, it is important not to confuse the fixed costs assigned to each output with variable costs. The total of the fixed costs does not increase when additional outputs are produced. Nor do total fixed costs decrease when fewer outputs are produced.

Relative Value Units. The assignment of indirect costs to outputs can be improved by reflecting significant differences in the resource requirements of outputs. One way to recognize such differences is to use Relative value units (RVUs) to determine how much indirect cost to add to the direct costs.

Exhibit 9–16
Assigning indirect costs to radiology films—averaging method

I. Data

	Volume (films)	Direct variable cost per film	Other indirect costs (indirect to each film)	Costs allocated to the laboratory (also indirect to each film)
Film A	9,000	$3	—	—
Film B	3,000	$12	—	—
Total	12,000	—	$150,000	$240,000

Cost Per Film = Direct Costs Per Film + Other Indirect Costs Per Film + Allocated Costs Per Film

II. Per unit cost of film A

$$\$3 \text{ per film} + \frac{\$150,000}{12,000 \text{ films}} + \frac{\$240,000}{12,000 \text{ films}} = \$35.50 \text{ per film}$$

III. Per unit cost of film B

$$\$12 \text{ per film} + \frac{\$150,000}{12,000 \text{ films}} + \frac{\$240,000}{12,000 \text{ films}} = \$44.50 \text{ per film}$$

Exhibit 9–17 uses the same radiology example as in *Exhibit 9–16* in order to assign indirect costs on the basis of RVUs, which were determined using a prior study. As before, when using RVUs to determine direct costs, it is necessary to determine the total number of RVUs expected to be produced during the time period. The number of films is, then, multiplied by its associated number of RVUs. The total RVUs are summed and divided into the indirect costs to determine the indirect cost per RVU. Then, for each type of film, the indirect cost per RVU is multiplied by the number of RVUs used to prepare each film. This indirect cost amount is added to the film's direct cost to determine its full cost.

Using RVUs can dramatically improve the accuracy of determining the cost of healthcare services. We have shown indirect costs can be assigned on the basis of RVUs. However, these procedures do increase the cost of determining the full cost of healthcare services. As noted above, the careful analyst must not confuse the fixed costs assigned to each output with variable costs. That is, even though the costs per unit of output may be treated in the organization's accounting system as variable costs, the indirect costs described in this section do contain significant fixed components. Remember that total fixed costs are constant for various levels of output within the relevant range.

Exhibit 9–17
Assigning indirect costs to radiology films— relative value method

I. Data

	Volume (films)	Direct variable costs per film	Relative value units per film	RVUs generated
Film A	9,000	$3	2	18,000
Film B	3,000	$12	3	9,000
			Total RVUs	27,000

Other Radiology Costs = $150,000
Allocated Indirect Costs = $240,000

Cost Per Film = Direct Variable Costs Per Film + Indirect Costs Per RVU

II. Determine the indirect cost per RVU

$$\frac{\$150,000}{27,000 \text{ RVUs}} + \frac{\$240,000}{27,000 \text{ RVUs}} = \$14.44 \text{ per RVU}$$

III. Determine cost of film A

$3 per film + ($14.44 per RVU × 2 RVUs) = $31.88 per film

IV. Determine cost of film B

$12 per film + ($14.44 per RVU × 3 RVUs) = $55.32 per film

Costing service capacity

The definition of a healthcare service or output may not always refer to an individual service provided to an identified patient. Within fully integrated delivery systems, and, increasingly, for most healthcare providers, the output or service may be represented by the *capacity* to provide specified services for enrolled members during a specified time period, usually a month. The cost of this capacity to provide services is relevant for payers, such as health maintenance organizations (HMOs), that enroll subscribers under their health plans. It is also relevant for providers who accept fixed payments *(capitated payments)* from payers or employers under an agreement to provide the capability (or capacity) to provide specified services to a group of members enrolled in a health plan. The cost of making these services available is determined on an average cost per member per month *(pmpm)* basis. A *member month* is defined as one member enrolled in a health plan for one month. The cost per member per month is also called a capitation rate.

In this section, we calculate the average (full) cost per member per month. As before, indirect costs are added to the direct costs of the healthcare services or outputs. Two methods can be used to identify direct costs. The first is the *budgetary method* because it is based on a prospective budget of expected costs. It is used by providers or payers who deliver healthcare services directly to patients. The second method is the *fee-for-service method* because the services are purchased on an individualized basis. It is useful for organizations that do not deliver the services, but are merely purchasers or intermediaries. Instead, these organizations contract with other providers to deliver healthcare services. They pay providers for each service delivered on a fee-for-service basis. An example would be a health maintenance organization (HMO) that contracts with physicians, hospitals, physical therapists, etc. to provide services to its enrollees. Alternatively, a physician group practice could use this method to establish subcontracts with other providers for services not provided within the group.

For both costing methods, the cost of the service capacity is determined by the expected cost of services expected to be used. To determine these costs, the analyst must precisely identify the package of eligible services and their expected use. Expected use depends upon many factors, including the enrolled members' demographic characteristics and the services included in the health plan or benefit package. Furthermore, the incentives and controls that affect physician behaviors and referral patterns will have a major impact on expected use. Past utilization data may be examined to identify future trends. Changes in coverage or benefits will also affect future utilization rates. Given the complexity and importance of these projections, actuarial assistance may be necessary to project expected use.

Budgetary method

Under the budgetary method, expected use is expressed in terms of the components of services expected to be used. The expected complement of physicians, nurses, laboratory and radiology technicians, support staff, and other personnel are determined (stated in full-time equivalent, *FTE,* terms). Then, the direct costs of each of the components are summed. These direct costs are divided by the total number of member months expected during the year to determine the cost per member per month (pmpm).

The necessary calculations under the budgetary method, using a radiology example for an enrolled population of 160,000 is shown in *Exhibit 9–18.* Direct costs include physician costs (salaries and benefits), other staff (salaries and benefits), supplies, and other overhead. In this example, expected use data under the health plan requires one physician for every

Exhibit 9–18
Budgetary method for determining average cost per member per month for ophthalmology office services for 100,000 covered lives*

Physicians	Covered lives per physician	Number of physicians	Annual cost per physician	Total cost per year	Average cost per member per month**
Radiologists	40,000	4	$200,000	$ 800,000	$0.417

Other staff	Personnel per physician	Total number of staff	Annual cost per staff member		
Registered nurses	1	4	$ 40,000	$ 160,000	$0.083
Nursing assistants	1.50	6	$ 25,000	$ 150,000	$0.078
Receptionists	0.50	2	$ 24,000	$ 48,000	$0.025
Fiscal and administrative	0.75	3	$ 36,000	$ 108,000	$0.056
Other	0.50	2	$ 20,000	$ 40,000	$0.020
			Staff Sub-total	$ 506,000	$0.263

	Visits per member per year	Average cost per visit		
Supplies	0.30	$30	$1,440,000	$0.750
Depreciation, interest, utilities, etc.			$ 255,000	$0.133
Total capitation rate				$1.563

* The number of member months per year is 1,920,000 (160,000 members × 12 months).
** Average cost per member per month equals total annual cost ÷ number of member months.

40,000 covered lives (enrollees). Similar requirements for other staff are also listed. In each case, the annual cost is first determined and then divided by the total number of expected member months. In this case, 160,000 enrollees for 12 months amounts to 1,920,000 member months. Average supply costs per visit are determined from prior data and multiplied by the number of visits expected per year. Each member is expected to average 0.30 visits to the radiologist each year. Then, the total costs for the year are calculated and, again, averaged over the number of expected member months.

In addition to the direct costs, indirect costs for building and equipment depreciation, interest expenses, utilities, and other overhead costs are shown. They are divided by the expected number of member months. Finally, the average cost per member per month is determined. This can be called the *capitation rate*. This rate can be determined by summing each component, or by summing the total annual costs and dividing by the number of expected member months. Both methods should be used as a mathematical check on this important calculation.

This method of costing requires accurate forecasts of expected use and the costs of resources necessary to provide care to the enrolled members. One crucial, but common, error is to treat average costs per member per month as a variable cost. Fixed costs are typical components of both direct and indirect costs. For example, physician and support staff salaries are fixed costs if they are paid as a weekly or monthly salary, even if fewer patients were seen. In addition, many indirect overhead costs, such as the depreciation expense, are fixed. Therefore, the average cost per member per month should not be used as a variable cost to project total costs whenever the number of member months is significantly different from the original quantities used to calculate the original average cost per member per month. In other words, once the pmpm cost is determined, it can only be used for time periods with similar numbers of enrolled members who exhibit similar patterns of healthcare utilization.

Fee-for-service method

The *fee-for-service* method relies on many of the same calculations as the budgetary method described above. The cost per member per month is determined by multiplying the expected use of each service by the average cost of each service. Again, these average costs are added and then divided by the number of member months to determine the expected direct cost per member per month. Similarly, the indirect cost is divided by the number of member months and added to the direct costs. The key point is that an average cost for each service must be determined, either using the budgetary method or the fee-for-service method, under which costs must be obtained from external negotiations with other providers.

The fee-for-service method is merely a computational tool for calculating the pmpm rates necessary for paying and contracting decisions involving a variety of healthcare providers.

For example, HMOs that purchase services from other providers, rather than acting as a producer of services, may use this method to determine their expected costs under fee-for-service payment schemes with a variety of providers. The providers' pmpm costs are used to calculate the premiums (monthly payment rates) for the HMO's enrolled members. Similarly, providers who contract with payers to provide a package of services, some of which they produce and some of which they do not produce, may use this method in contracting with other providers. Both providers and payers will use these pmpm rates as the basis for contracting and negotiating decisions with employers, purchasers, and other payers and providers. They will also use these expected pmpm costs to negotiate flat rates or other discounted rates, where the fee-for-service pmpm costs become a benchmark basis for further negotiations and price reductions.

As shown earlier under the budgetary method, expected use must be determined. This is often stated in terms of expected use of each eligible service in the benefit package per 1000 members. This utilization forecast is multiplied by the average cost per unit of service. This average cost is derived from internal cost data under the budgetary method, or it is obtained from general external market data or from rates negotiated with providers. These rates may be stated in terms of discounted charges, all-inclusive per diem rates, or other payment rates. Sources of such rate data include negotiations with other providers, professional associations or regional data bases, or HCFA data from Federal cost reports. The fee-for-service method can incorporate data from a variety of sources that are based on proposed or expected prices or rates from other providers.

The cost per member per month is determined by averaging the individual costs of each service calculated according to the following formula:

$$\frac{\text{Annual Use per } 1000 \times \text{Average Cost per Unit}}{12 \times 1000 \text{ Members}} = \text{Cost Per Member Per Month}$$

For example, the cost of inpatient and outpatient surgeries would be separately determined and then added to other service costs to obtain the gross cost pmpm. Any deductions for co-payments or co-insurance amounts must then be deducted from the gross cost in order to obtain the net cost pmpm. The key under the fee-for-service method is to multiply the annual utilization data per 1000 members by the average cost per service. Then that amount is divided by 12,000 (1000 members × 12 months) to determine the gross cost pmpm. Expected co-payment and co-insurance amounts are subtracted to yield the net cost per member per month (pmpm). As under the budgetary method, these individual service costs (pmpm) are added across all services to obtain the overall capitation rate on a pmpm basis.

In contrast to the budgetary method, the fee-for-service method does provide an average variable cost per member per month. As the payer or provider enrolls each new member, the total expected medical costs increase by an amount equal to the average cost per member per month multiplied by 12 months. Because this is a contracted rate of payment for each service purchased, the fee-for-service method can be used to determine total direct costs of care as the number of enrollees (member months) increases.

Healthcare cost drivers

After calculating the average cost of healthcare services, the results are used for various planning and control decisions. Knowing the direct and indirect costs of a healthcare service helps, but is not sufficient, to control its cost. Throughout this book we have shown that fixed and variable cost information is needed for planning and controlling costs. Although fixed and variable cost information is important in projecting costs, it is not sufficient. To control costs, as well as to evaluate performance, costs must be identified as controllable and noncontrollable. Further, knowing how costs are driven, that is, what causes costs to occur, is an essential part of planning and controlling costs.

To accomplish these objectives managers must identify the *cost drivers* which influence controllable costs. Cost drivers affect cost behavior in hospitals. They also affect the cost behavior of other types of healthcare providers. Each cost driver may influence costs by itself as well as in combination with other cost drivers. Cost drivers may include any of the following factors:

- case mix
- patient utilization preferences
- population demographics
- socioeconomic characteristics
- patient volume
- input prices
- input efficiency
- resource utilization patterns
- fixed costs
- other descriptors of physician and medical practice patterns

As the patients' *case-mix* changes, resources per case and input prices are likely to change. In contrast, as the volume of patients increases, fixed costs are spread over more patients, thereby reducing the average cost per case. Many key players, including managers, physicians, and insurers exert control over case mix and patient volumes. Physicians control admission, treatment, and discharge decisions. Insurers control the flow of patients to certain facilities as they exercise their "gate-keeper" and utilization review functions. *Utilization patterns,* are influenced by the primary care physician, as well as by specialists and the insurer's review mechanisms, which must approve use of services. Of course, patients also have strong preferences for access to convenient, high-quality healthcare services.

Population demographics and socioeconomic characteristics of the enrolled population are related to health status, case mix, and the type of services that are needed. For example, elderly enrollees require access to different services than do younger enrollees. Further, an insurer may experience *adverse selection* if its enrollees are sicker than expected.

These characteristics and the *volume* or number of enrollees are influenced by the insurer's marketing and enrollment efforts, as well as by the willingness of primary care physicians to participate in the health plan. The characteristics are also influenced by the enrollees' income, their preference for managed care vs. other types of health plans, etc. Increasing the volume of enrollees, stated in terms of number of covered lives, is one way to exert control over the average cost per member per month. Some members have high costs, while others have low costs; however, many members' costs per month are well within the high and low levels. When the number of enrollees is low, any extreme case, high or low, will have undue influence on the average cost pmpm. In contrast, with a large number of enrollees, a few extreme cases will not have a large influence on the average cost per member per month.

Using more resources for each case clearly increases ("drives") costs, as does decreasing *input efficiency* in delivering services. Senior managers exert influence on length of stay by working with clinicians to develop treatment protocols and guidelines for lengths of stay for particular types of cases. Managers of clinical services, along with key clinical staff members, can influence the length of stay through efficient clinical management, which includes performing tests and other procedures in a timely and efficient manner. Similarly, clinical staff and managers of clinical services, such as in the laboratory, can control the supplies used for each test by purchasing high quality inputs, setting standards, and performing each test efficiently. Insurers have an impact on the patient's length of stay, as well as on the types of tests and procedures that are approved. Control over *input prices* paid to hospitals and specialists depends on their ability to negotiate with suppliers and other providers. However, if payments are adjusted for severity of illness, then the population demographics and socioeconomic characteristics of the enrolled population will have a large influence on input prices.

Resource utilization patterns that indicate how healthcare services are delivered are controlled by providers; they are also influenced by the needs of the enrolled population. They are also affected by appropriate treatment protocols and by avoiding preventable errors and oversights.

Finally, high *fixed costs* will increase costs because they are indirect costs added to each output. Both managers and clinicians exert control over building and equipment costs. Physicians demand certain equipment to produce services, but managers evaluate the financial feasibility of acquiring and using equipment and facilities.

Summary

This chapter has described the four typical approaches to cost allocation in healthcare organizations. Each method is useful in its own right and may be appropriate in specific cases. The reciprocal method is often more complicated, but it is more objective. It is also more accurate because it uses fully all the available data for the services provided between centers. No information on the proportions of services provided between centers is ignored under the reciprocal method. It is the method that is recommended where the most accuracy and objectivity are required and where the expertise for its implementation is available. The ready accessibility to spreadsheet programs make the reciprocal method available to even the smallest organizations.

A final caveat must be added relative to the subject of cost finding and cost allocation. Care must be taken to recognize situations when full cost information should be used and when it should not be used. Full cost is valuable when examining total financial requirements and when attempting to justify levels of payment and reimbursement. Full cost should not be used in the decision to add a new service or seeking a use for vacant space, since this is an incremental cost decision. Full costs are also not useful for performance measurement purposes. Direct costs are usually more appropriate. The chapter on capital investment (chapter 12) decision making discusses this issue in more depth. Likewise, in a competitive situation, full cost may provide a beginning point for price negotiations, but marginal cost may become more important.

The management accountant must take great care not to overemphasize allocated costs. Cost data must be used for the intended purposes. Allocated costs are not relevant to every situation where they might be applied. Caution, diligence, and imagination are required.

Costing healthcare outputs and services involves estimating the direct cost per member per month (pmpm) and adding a *share* of the organization's indirect costs, which are not readily traceable to specific outputs. The resulting full costs are useful in setting prices or in negotiating payment rates. The availability of full cost information also permits managers to compare costs and prices.

In this chapter, we have identified two common methods of determining direct and indirect costs. Each method has strengths and weaknesses with regard to accuracy and implementation costs. For example, measuring direct costs yields the most accurate results, but is also the most costly to implement. Less costly, but less accurate, methods are likely to be used for determining the costs of low volume or low priced services.

Full costs are *estimates* that reflect many accounting decisions, as well as the methods that have been used to obtain the estimates. The estimates may change when alternative accounting methods are used. Full costs also depend on the quality of input data. Proper application of accounting methods and high quality data permit healthcare organizations to improve the accuracy and usefulness of cost data.

Managers should remember that these costs are average costs. Since many healthcare costs are fixed, as volume changes, full costs also change. Similarly, this average cost cannot simply be multiplied by a new volume to derive total costs. Managers and analysts should not ignore the constancy or stickiness of fixed costs within the relevant range.

Simply knowing the average cost of services is not enough to be competitive in today's healthcare environment. Payers and providers also must be able to control costs. Fixed and variable costs, which are important in projecting costs, are also not sufficient for controlling costs. For cost control and performance evaluation, managers must identify controllable and noncontrollable costs. Providers and payers can also identify cost drivers, which will assist in leading to activities and actions which will help control costs.

Questions and problems

1. Define cost finding in terms of reimbursement regulations.

2. Discuss the major weaknesses of most cost-finding techniques.

3. What are the prerequisites for effective cost-finding analysis?

4. Refer to Medicare regulations to identify the cost allocation methods that are currently acceptable. Which do they prefer? Why? How would you choose between alternative allocation methods?

5. What are the advantages and disadvantages of the reciprocal method?

6. How does the chart of accounts reflect the allocation of costs from nonrevenue departments (service centers) to revenue producing departments?

7. a. Using the given data, allocate the $600,000 of costs in the housekeeping, laundry, and plant departments to the two revenue-producing centers, using the direct and stepdown methods. What are the resulting total costs in the nursing and laboratory departments under each method?

b. Set up the cost equations for each department that would be needed for the reciprocal method.

Rearrange the equations so that the coefficient (C) matrix, the unknown matrix (X), and the constant matrix (Y) are apparent.

What is the (C) matrix?

If the inverse of this (C) matrix is assumed to be the same as the inverse derived by the computer in the section on matrix algebra calculations, calculate the reciprocal cost allocations for the nursing and laboratory departments.

c. Optional: Invert the (C) matrix, and use the inverse in the reciprocal allocation method.

	Cost data				
	House-keeping	*Laundry*	*Plant*	*Nursing*	*Laboratory*
Direct costs	$300,000	$100,000	$200,000	$1,000,000	$600,000
Statistics:					
Square feet		20,000	10,000	180,000	50,000
Pounds—wet laundry	20,000		5,000	170,000	10,000
FTEs	10	5		30	10

8. a. Given the following data, allocate the $400,000 of costs in housekeeping and laundry to the revenue centers using the direct, step-down, and reciprocal methods. What are the resulting total costs in the nursing and laboratory centers after the respective allocations?

b. What difference would it make in part (a) if FTEs were used as the allocation base under each method?

	Cost data				
	Cost centers		*Support centers*		
	House-keeping	*Laundry*	*Nursing*	*Lab*	*Totals*
Direct costs	$300,000	$100,000	$1,000,000	$600,000	$2,000,000
Statistics:					
Square feet		20,000	180,000	50,000	250,000
Pounds— wet laundry	20,000		170,000	10,000	200,000
FTEs	10	5	30	10	55

9. The Sugarloaf Mountain Hospital (SMH) was given thirty-five acres of forest land near a growing suburb of Denver. Since the hospital had been operating out of movable trailers (converted horse vans), the

administration and staff enthusiastically planned their new facility. Unfortunately, at the time of construction, there was no access to electric power or utilities. Consequently, the physical plant included:
a. a water pumping and filtration system with access to a nearby spring-fed mountain lake;
b. a coal-fired boiler to generate steam for heating;
c. an electric generating facility.

Each of these three service departments must rely on the products of other departments. Eighty percent of the water is used to produce steam, 10 percent is used for other auxiliary services (housekeeping), and 10 percent for direct patient care. Ninety percent of the steam is used for producing electricity, and 10 percent is used for auxiliary services. Thirty percent of the electricity is used by the water plant, 30 percent for direct patient care, and 40 percent for other auxiliary services. Variable and fixed costs can be traced to each department as follows:

	Fixed	*Variable*	*Total*
Water	$30,000	$ 3,000	$33,000
Steam	20,000	12,000	32,000
Electricity	25,000	6,000	31,000
Totals	$75,000	$21,000	$96,000

a. How should these costs be allocated using the reciprocal method? What are the full costs in each department?
b. If electricity were made available at 3 cents per KWH, should the current SMH purchase electricity or continue to generate it? The current volume of electricity is 900,000 KWH. The electricity department manager recommends rejecting the offer because the variable costs of producing electricity are only .67 cents per KWH. What should SMH do? Why?

10. The following data pertain to the departmental costs of a hospital. Allocate the service costs to nursing and lab using the direct method.

				Data		
	House-keeping	*Laundry*	*Nursing*	*Laboratory*	*Total*	
Direct costs	$200,000	$110,000	$510,000	$600,000	$1,420,000	
Housekeeping proportion		4,000	8,000	12,000	24,000	Labor
		16.67%	33.33%	50.00%		hours
Laundry proportion	24,000		12,000	36,000	72,000	Pieces
	33.33%		16.67%	50.00%		

11. Use the data in problem 10 to calculate allocations using the step-down method.

12. Use the data in problem 10 to allocate costs using the double distribution method.

13. Use the data in problem 10 to allocate costs based on the reciprocal method.

14. The financial manager of Greenacres is considering adopting the reciprocal method of cost allocation. Greenacres presently uses the direct method. Given the data below, calculate the reciprocal allocation and discuss its advantages.

	Direct costs before allocation	Allocated total costs direct method
Housekeeping	$125,400	
Laundry	110,000	
Nursing	694,800	$833,812
Laboratory	450,000	546,388

Fifteen percent of housekeeping services are provided to the laundry department, 40 percent to nursing, and 45 percent to laboratory.

Forty-five percent of laundry services are provided to housekeeping, 40 percent to nursing, and 15 percent to laboratory.

15. The Triangle Hospice has three service departments: grounds and maintenance, general administration, and laundry. The costs of these departments are allocated by the step method, using the bases and in the order shown:

Ground and maintenance:
    Fixed costs—allocated on a basis of square feet of space occupied.
General administration:
    Variable costs—allocated on a basis of number of actual employees.
    Fixed costs—allocated 20 percent to laundry, 14 percent to the grief center, 36 percent to food services, and 30 percent to lodging.
Laundry:
    Variable costs—allocated on a basis of number of items processed.
    Fixed costs—allocated on a basis of peak period needs for items processed.

Cost and operating data for all departments in the hospice for a recent month are presented in the following table:

	Grounds and Maintenance	General Administration	Laundry	Grief Center	Food Services	Lodging	Total
Variable costs	-0-	$ 915	$13,725	-0-	$ 48,000	$ 36,450	$ 99,090
Fixed costs	$17,500	12,150	18,975	$28,500	64,000	81,000	222,125
Total overhead costs	$17,500	$13,065	$32,700	$28,500	$112,000	$117,450	$321,215
Square feet of space	2,000	2,500	3,750	15,000	6,250	97,500	127,000
Number of employees	9	5	10	5	25	21	75
Laundry items processed	—	—	—	1,000	5,250	40,000	46,250
Peak period needs—items processed	—	—	—	1,500	6,500	42,000	50,000

Evaluate these allocation results. How might they be changed?

16. Cape of Good Hope Hospital provides three types of services in its clinic. Direct nursing costs total $197,000. Use the following data to determine the full cost of each type of clinic visit.

Service	Patient visits	Relative weight
Subacute	3,000	0.85
Acute I	2,500	1.0
Acute II	400	1.7
	5,900	

17. A state health cost commission has cited your hospital's cost per patient day for cardiac care as being well above the hospital's peer group norms. You argue that patients require more critical care so they spend more time in the cardiac care unit than in other facilities. Therefore, it is the CCU's costs that cause average cost per patient day to exceed the norms. To prove your point, you must determine the cost of days in the CCU, cardiac transition, and medical/surgery units. Total costs for all cardiac care services are $7,650,900.

Unit	Average daily supplies cost	Average daily nursing hours	Average nursing hourly wage	Average patient intensity level	Patient days
CCU	$400	8.0	$21	4	1,900
Cardiac Transition	300	6.0	19	2	2,600
Medical/Surgery	200	3.5	17	1	3,700

18. HMO Associates have offered a contract to purchase hospital services for 7,000 enrolled members from Class Hospitals, Inc. (CHI). CHI plans to purchase services as needed from other hospitals in the region. The capitation rate HMO Associates has set is $60 per member per month. CHI has gathered the following data regarding expected utilization and costs.

Service	Expected utilization per 1,000 members	Average payment rate ($)	Copay
Inpatient:			
Medical-Surgical	202 days	$1,369	
Maternity	59 days	1,595	
ICU/CCU	33 days	2,357	
Emergency Room	152 visits	295	$40
Outpatient	352 visits	345	20
Extended Care	20 days	209	20

a. Evaluate the contract and the proposed rate pmpm.
b. If CHI decides the capitation rate is too low, what actions could be taken to affect this situation?

19. Your CFO, in an HMO, wants to determine full cost information that will affect pricing of its contracts. Three types of contracts are being considered: (1) employee only, (2) family, and (3) employee and children. You find that the third type of contract uses 2.4 times as many resources as the first and that the second is 1.6 times as resource intensive as the first. Projected costs are $1,690,000. Determine the full cost of each type of contract using the following data.

Contract type	Expected volume	Direct variable Cost per contract
A	600	$ 50
B	2,500	150
C	1,500	130

Keywords: activity base; budgetary method; capitation rate; chart of accounts; cost allocation; cost driver; direct allocation; direct costs; double distribution; fee-for-service method; full costs; indirect costs; member month; overhead costs; per member per month (pmpm); reciprocal method; relative value units (RVUs); revenue center; stepdown; support center.

References

Awasthi, V.N., and L. Eldenburg. "Providing Cost Data to Physicians Helps Contain Costs." *Healthcare Financial Management* (April 1996): 40–42.

Baker, J.J. "Activity-Based Costing for Integrated Delivery Systems." *Journal of Health Care Finance* (winter 1995): 57–61.

Berlin, M.F. "Using Cost Accounting in a Medical Group Practice." *Medical Group Management Journal* 42, no. 3 (May–June 1995): 22–32.

Canby, J.B., IV. "Applying Activity-Based Costing to Healthcare Settings." *Healthcare Financial Management* (February 1995): 50–56.

Carpenter, C.E., L.C. Weitzel, N.E. Johnson, and D.B. Nash. "Cost Accounting Supports Clinical Evaluations." *Healthcare Financial Management* (April 1994): 40–44.

Cleverley, William O. "Product Costing for Health Care Firms." *Health Care Management Review* 12, no. 4 (fall 1987): 39–48.

Helmi, Medhat A., and Murat N. Tanju. "Activity-Based Costing May Reduce Costs, Aid Planning." *Healthcare Financial Management* (November 1991): 95–96.

Hill, N.T. "Adoption of Costing Systems by U.S. Hospitals." *Hospital and Health Services Administration* 39, no. 4 (winter 1994): 521–537.

Hogan, Andrew J., and Ronald Marshall. "How to Improve Allocation of Support Service Costs." *Healthcare Financial Management* (February 1990): 42–52.

Horngren, Charles T., George Foster, and Srikant M. Datar. *Cost Accounting: A Managerial Emphasis.* Englewood Cliffs: Prentice Hall, 1994.

Karpiel, Martin. "Using Patient Classification Systems to Identify Ambulatory Care Costs." *Healthcare Financial Management* (November 1994): 31–37.

Lindner, Carl A. "Using the Micro to Accurately Allocate a Hospital's Departmental Overhead." *Healthcare Financial Management* (February 1986): 56–61.

Miller, Thomas R., and J. Bruce Ryan. "Analyzing Cost Variance in Capitated Contracts." *Healthcare Financial Management* (February 1995): 22–23.

Neumann, Bruce R., Jan P. Clement, and Jean C. Cooper. *Financial Management: Concepts and Applications for Health Care Organizations.* Dubuque: Kendall/Hunt, 1997.

Ramsey, R.H. "Activity-Based Costing for Hospitals." *Hospital & Health Services Administration* (fall 1994): 385–396.

Schimmel, V.E., C. Alley, and A.M. Heath. "Measuring Costs: Product Line Accounting Versus Ratio of Cost to Charges." *Topics in Health Care Finance* 13, no. 4 (1987): 76–86.

CHAPTER 10

Materials management and control

"The CFO has just informed me that we have forty-five days worth of inventory on hand. I wonder what the cost implications of this are? How does it impact on the quality of care in our organization?"

"Acme Pharmaceutical's just informed us that they could give us a 15 percent discount if we could increase our order size to $150,000. Should we do it?"

"We have $1,250,000 worth of inventory. If we could somehow invest that money in the bank we could probably earn at least 8 percent. That would amount to $100,000. Is there any way we can free up the cash for investment?"

"A company has just contacted us to see if we want to take advantage of group purchasing techniques. How will this help us in terms of quality and dollars?"

Introduction

As can be seen from the above situations, inventory and materials management have many different aspects, and most have cost and quality implications. Over the past few years, the management of materials within the healthcare organization has been increasingly subsumed under the finance function. Since 1982 the percentage of hospitals reporting that individuals responsible for materials management report to finance has increased from 22 to 36 percent. This change is the result of the increasing emphasis on cost containment and a recognition that materials make up a significant portion of healthcare costs. The materials management function has the potential to improve cash flows, gain economies of scale, improve efficiency, and improve quality of care.

Materials management is defined more broadly than inventory management. Materials management is usually defined as the management and control of goods, services, and equipment from acquisition to disposition. This definition and concept requires the explicit recognition of the system involved in the materials decision of the organization, and that the decision has an impact on all of the parties involved in the total process of manufacturing and acquiring the material, in addition to the user of the item. Although the major emphasis of this chapter will be on inventory management, it should be recognized that total materials management decision involves more than inventory management.

Inventory items most commonly appearing in the healthcare field can be divided primarily into two major categories: patient care and administration. Patient care inventory categories include: medical supplies, surgical supplies, drugs, medicines, linens, uniforms, garments, food, infusion pumps, etc., while administration categories would include: housekeeping supplies, office supplies, maintenance supplies, and stationery and forms. These items represent a large investment on the part of the organization, and, like other assets, should be monitored and managed in an efficient manner. For most healthcare organizations, the amount of investment in inventory is considered an area that should be reduced as much as possible since excess inventory levels are a nonproductive use of resources. As this chapter will stress, better management and control of inventories can result in considerable savings. Even if inventory costs seem insignificant in comparison with labor costs, the total resources consumed annually represent a sizeable portion of total operating costs.

The objective of inventory management is to minimize the total cost associated with managing inventory while maintaining sufficient amounts and variety so that needed items of appropriate quantity and quality are available when needed. In addition to saving money, better inventory control can have a significant impact on the quality of healthcare services provided. Reducing stockouts or providing the right kinds of supplies at the proper time and place can result in better patient care and a more efficient organization. It should also be noted that inventory control techniques are an important element of internal control, which is concerned with both safeguarding physical assets and effectively using them. As inventory control is improved, so also is internal control strengthened.

The techniques presented in this chapter are used for more than cost containment. They are also important ingredients in improving the quality of patient care and the efficiency and effectiveness of the healthcare services delivery system.

The inventory control techniques discussed in this chapter can be applied to any kind of inventory item. For example, inventory control models can be adapted equally to cash balances, linen supplies, or food supplies. Accounts receivable also lend themselves to these techniques. For purposes of clarity, most of the examples used in this chapter deal with supplies of nonfinancial items.

Inventory definition

The definition of inventory has been universally accepted to include those items which are necessary for the providing of healthcare services during the normal operating cycle of twelve months. Items which are expected to have a useful life of longer than twelve months are generally defined as capital expenditures and are evaluated according to procedures presented in chapter 12. In this chapter we will concentrate on the control of items which are not considered capital expenditures. Most organizations establish a dollar amount on the value of items to be considered as capital expenditures items and go through the capital budgeting process. For accounting classification, the time factor of one operating cycle or twelve months usually takes precedence on how such items are classified in the financial statements. For example, item X may have a cost of $100,000 but is expected to be used during the next ten months. Since it does not meet the twelve month limit it would normally be expensed in the financial statements. However, the number of dollars involved makes this a significant item which should be evaluated as a capital budget item. Item Y (a software program) may have an expected useful life of three years, thereby qualifying it as a capital budget expenditure. However, it may only cost $400 and would normally be expensed during the first year of use.

Effective control of assets and sensible application of accounting principles require managers to establish balanced materials management policies.

Objectives of inventory management

There are many different objectives of inventory management. The priority of each will be influenced by the nature of the organization and the managers. For example, a partial list of objectives developed by supervisors of central supply departments would include the following:

1. to have necessary supplies available whenever and wherever needed;
2. to utilize storage space effectively;
3. to decide which items to hold in inventory and which items to purchase on an as-needed basis;
4. to stock enough supplies to meet demand within the inventory supplier's delivery time frame;
5. to provide an efficient schedule detailing when to place orders and how much to order.

There are many other factors which should be considered. However, an important objective of healthcare services managers should be to minimize the total costs of materials management, while maintaining an acceptable level of quality of care. A decision rule that managers could follow would be to add up the costs associated with a variety of inventory management alternatives (all promising equal quality) and to adopt that set of alternatives that has the lowest total costs. It is of little value to minimize one type of inventory cost if that action increases another type of cost. A decision rule that minimizes average purchase costs (per unit) may result in significantly larger storage and handling costs. Consequently, the emphasis must be on total costs. Managers must search for a set of control techniques that minimizes those total costs. However, the general rule that minimizes total costs for a given level of quality is the correct criterion in almost all circumstances. This decision will result in an appropriate balancing of the objectives presented above.

Some of the other objectives of inventory management concerns the question of why to have inventories at all. Inventory control techniques stress zero or minimum levels of investment in inventory (e.g., just-in-time, on demand, off-site, and stockless models). Inventory is considered to be a nonproductive asset in that it does not provide healthcare services. It is only when the inventory is placed into service that it becomes necessary and useful. Given this fact, an objective of financial management should be to minimize the investment in inventory. There are several reasons why this does not mean maintaining a zero balance of inventory.

Uncertainty is the primary reason for holding inventories. There are three major components of uncertainty. One reason for holding inventories deals with timing. It is impossible, in any healthcare organization, to exactly match the timing of receipt of supplies with the demand for supplies. No manager can order with such precision that physical deliveries will be made at the exact time that the materials are needed. Even if all the internal problems of inventory management were solved, the healthcare manager could not insure the timely delivery and/or receipt of those items already ordered with promised dates of delivery. Timeliness is mainly concerned with external factors that prevent or hinder timely deliveries and receipt of materials and supplies. In larger urban areas it is becoming more common for suppliers to guarantee that certain supplies can be delivered within a defined time period in exchange for a slightly higher per unit cost. However, if the organization determines that a single supplier will provide all their needs, the per unit cost might actually be decreased. Appropriate benefit-cost analysis applied to this situation may result in a much smaller inventory on hand than had previously been thought possible.

The second major uncertainty factor affecting inventories is related to discontinuities between the needs of the patient, and the quantities of materials and supplies necessary to meet these needs. It may be possible to predict with complete certainty the number of patient visits or admissions, while the acuity level of these patients may not be as anticipated. If a maternity department knew that demand for its services on a given day would be ten normal deliveries, it could still not forecast exactly the quantities of necessary materials and supplies. There is no perfect match between patients and the materials needed to provide services to those patients. These discontinuities require inventories to help smooth out the uneven flows of supplies needed by patients or patient services.

The uncertainty of patient arrivals or demands is another reason for maintaining adequate inventories. This has to do with both the numbers and timing of patient arrivals. Demand uncertainties prevent forecasting the exact number of patients who will need services, resulting in some of the discontinuities noted above. Demand uncertainty requires that the organization maintain a buffer between patient needs and the health services that it provides. Because of these related factors, it should be obvious that the health institution must maintain adequate supplies of backup materials. In order to minimize total inventory costs, it must also attempt to forecast patient loads, patient services and supplier responses in order to mitigate the effects of uncertainty (demand, discontinuity, and timing). To the extent that these factors cannot be predicted, inventory management and control functions become even more important. These uncertainties vary greatly depending on the type of organization involved. Hospitals tend to have greater uncertainties than do long-term care facilities, health maintenance organizations, or preferred provider organizations. Likewise, within health maintenance organizations there will be greatly differing inventory management problems involved with a staff model HMO as opposed to an IPA model. A staff model HMO must maintain all the inventory items that a medical group practice must maintain, while an IPA model has no inventory under the patient care category. Alternatively, an IPA model HMO might wish to act as the materials manager for the IPA physicians, thereby reducing their (the IPA physicians) materials expenses.

Physical control of inventory

Although the major thrust of this chapter is on concepts and techniques to estimate the cost of various inventory management models, it is important to stress that none of these models take the place of periodic physical counts of items in inventory. These physical inventory counts are typically done at the end of an accounting cycle but interim physical counts can be very effective in determining actual shortages, obsolescence, and out-dated items. Validation of the effectiveness of the current database and internal control system requires more than just using the data records.

Costs associated with inventory management

There are three groups of costs associated with the management of inventory. The first group consists of the cost of ordering inventory, the second group represents the cost of holding inventory, and the third group accounts for the costs of not holding sufficient inventory. Examples of costs associated with each group follows.

Costs of ordering inventory include:

1. administrative and clerical costs associated with performing the ordering function;
2. transportation costs associated with delivery of inventory items. These costs are generally a function of the amount of paperwork involved in the process, and the physical bulk of the items, and are not related to the value of the items being purchased. It takes the same amount of paperwork to place an order for a box of paper clips as it does a box of surgical gloves. A standard amount is usually established per order.

Costs of holding inventory include:

1. cost of storage space (this is more significant for hospitals, staff model HMOs, and nursing homes since there are often multiple storage sites) is a function of the physical characteristics of the item, and not its value;
2. handling costs which are associated with moving inventory from storage area to storage area, or from storage to usage area;
3. insurance costs, consisting of fire, theft, and liability associated with the inventory itself and the management of the inventory, and depending on the type of organization, there may also be some property taxes associated with inventory on hand;
4. risk costs in deterioration and obsolescence costs—as more inventory is held, and more different storage sites utilized, the likelihood of items being forgotten, stolen, or otherwise not utilized, increases;
5. lost interest or opportunity cost of funds invested in inventory, which obviously becomes more significant as amounts invested in inventory increases, is also dependent on the rate of interest, but also includes the fact that the funds could be used for other purposes.

Costs of not holding sufficient inventory include:

1. schedule disruptions and reduced quality of care;
2. inefficiency in service delivery, by having deliveries of many small orders;
3. additional transportation charges (for special orders, etc.);
4. the value of lost discounts by not ordering larger amounts.

The impact on quality of patient care of running out of a critical patient care item has tended to influence a policy of "never running out of anything." However, not all items in inventory are critical patient care items and carrying excess inventory does incur the holding costs explained above. Safety stock procedures are established to safeguard against stockout of critical items, therefore the holding costs of the safety stock represent the costs of not having sufficient inventory.

Representative values for some of the costs discussed are presented in *Exhibit 10–1*. Some of the costs associated with materials management are more closely related to value of the item than to physical bulk, while ordering costs are determined by the amount of paperwork which must be handled. This may or may not be related to the value of the item.

To summarize, costs are a critical element in the management of inventory and the selection of the most appropriate techniques to be used. However, before the costs can be determined, three basic questions must be answered. These questions are discussed in the next section.

Inventory control techniques

There are three basic questions that must be answered in designing an inventory control system and the selection of appropriate management techniques:

1. Classification: What kinds of materials and supplies are most susceptible to control techniques?
2. Order point (OP): When should supplies be reordered?
3. Order quantity (OQ): How many supplies should be ordered each time an order is placed?

Exhibit 10–1
Typical inventory costs

Ordering costs (typically considered a fixed amount per order):	
Administration	
Transportation	
Holding costs (as a percentage of purchase price):	
Capital costs	15.0%
Insurance and taxes	1.5%
Storage space costs	.5%
	17.0%
Risk costs (as a percentage of purchase price):	
Obsolescence	2.0%
Damage	.5%
Loss/theft	5.0%
	7.5%
Costs of not holding sufficient inventory:	
Holding cost of safety stock	7.0%

These three inventory management questions—what, when, and how many—form the basis for a well-managed inventory control system. Each concept must be dealt with sequentially. Once the inventory control system is designed, only periodic evaluations are necessary to see that it is functioning properly.

Classification: Which inventories should be controlled?

The most prevalent classification system is the ABC stratification plan. Inventory items are classified into three (or more) categories so that control techniques can be concentrated where they will be most effective. It makes little sense to design elaborate control mechanisms to monitor the use of bandages or gauze pads. On the other hand, some supply items cost hundreds or even thousands of dollars. Those items should be placed under the tightest control possible. The principle that the manager must use to decide which item to control is a subjective balancing of the costs of control versus the potential costs if an item is not closely controlled.

The ABC stratification plan can be used to help make these assessments. The following relationships between the number of items in inventory and the dollar value of the inventory are applicable to many organizations. For example, if an organization has 3,000 items in inventory, it may find that only 300 (10 percent) of these items account for 70 percent of the total value of the inventory. Under this approach, the A category would include the relatively expensive items used in small quantities (which account for 70 percent of the value). The B category might comprise 600 items that represent 20 percent of the inventory value. The C category would then include the remaining 2,100 items (70 percent) that represents 10 percent of the total inventory value.

Although dollar value or total cost is certainly important, other classification criteria can be used to establish the stratification plan. Other factors include:

1. frequency of use;
2. total usage during the year;
3. rate of obsolescence;
4. the critical requirement for an item (e.g., Could a stockout create serious patient care problems?).

Each of these factors must be subjectively assessed in establishing the classification plan. The real value of any ABC stratification plan is that different inventory categories can be controlled and evaluated differently. That is why using the ABC stratification approach is the first step in improving inventory control procedures.

Order point (OP)

The second item listed under inventory control questions is the order point. The order point is that point in time when an order should be placed, and is determined by the amount of inventory on hand and the time lapse between when the need is recognized and the materials are received in the patient care center. What signals should be used to initiate the next order? If orders could be placed and supplies received instantaneously, there would be no need to be concerned about order points. Since there is usually some delay between the time an order is placed and the time the items are received, inventory control must include a time interval. This time interval is called lead time or the lead-time interval. Lead time is determined by the amount of time necessary to:

1. recognize the need to place an order;
2. prepare the purchase order;
3. send the order;
4. receive the order;
5. check the items for correct quantity and quality;
6. put the items in place, ready to use.

Different types of organizations will have greatly varying lead times according to several factors:

1. type of organization—hospital, nursing home, HMO, PPO, home health agency, visiting nurse association, etc.;
2. geographic location—proximity to suppliers, transportation network;
3. size of organization—market clout and order size will determine the extent to which the organization can place demands on the suppliers. Larger organizations may wish to purchase or develop their own transportation system in order to ensure more predictable delivery schedules. Likewise, consortia of smaller organizations have gained purchasing power through their combined market size.

As materials are used in the process of providing healthcare and/or the process of managing the paperwork, inventory levels are depleted. When the next order is received, inventory levels rise once again. This pattern is illustrated in *Exhibit 10–2* assuming that usage of the inventory item is entirely predictable and stable over time. It also assumes that delivery time is entirely dependable and predictable.

Assume that an order (OQ) had just been received at the beginning of the first week (time = 0). The inventory level at the time the order came in was zero, and the amount ordered (OQ = Order Quantity) brought the

Exhibit 10–2
Inventory usage with one-week lead time

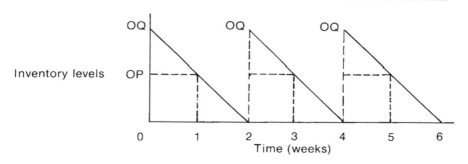

inventory level from zero to the highest point (OQ) at the beginning of the time period. As the supplies are used, the inventory quantity declines and, assuming a one-week lead time, a new order must be placed every other week (OP = Order Point), starting with week 1, and repeated at weeks 3, 5, 7, etc. Once the order is placed, the inventory levels continue to decline toward zero until the new order is received, reaching zero at the same time the next order is received. This pattern continues to be repeated as long as usage is constant and there are no changes in lead time.

The very simplistic assumptions used in the above ideal model may not hold in most organizations due to random uncertainties, uneven demand for healthcare services, and unpredictable delivery schedules (weather, strikes, etc.). Therefore, an additional buffer or safety stock must be acquired in order to cover those circumstances in which usage occurs at a faster (or slower) than normal rate. The safety stock for any item is usually estimated from historical data adjusted for current and future expected changes. If the usage during the lead-time interval (one week in this case) is 100 units and the maximum usage observed during any single week is 150, a safety stock of 50 units would insure that stockouts would be held to a minimum. That is, the safety stock is equal to the maximum usage minus the usage during the lead-time interval. This relationship is shown in *Exhibit 10–3.*

With a usage pattern, the safety stock never drops below 50 units. In the event that it were reduced, the next period's order point could occur sooner during the week, and the order quantity would be correspondingly increased to make up any deficit in the safety stock. For example, assume the quantity is 200, and 10 units of safety stock are consumed while the order is being processed by the buyer. The next order would be placed for 210 units. (The order quantity is equal to the normal order quantity (200) plus the desired safety stock (50) less the actual safety stock (40).)

Conceptually, the order point is a function of two factors: usage during the lead time, and the safety stock.

Exhibit 10–3
Inventory usage with one-week lead time and safety stock

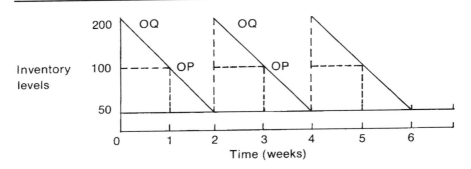

The order point (OP) can be computed as:

OP = (usage during lead time) + (safety stock) or
OP = (average daily use)(lead-time interval) + (safety stock)

Note that safety stocks must be subjectively determined as a function of the maximum levels of demand and of the acceptability of stockouts that may occur. If stockouts for a particular item would require shutting down operations, the safety stock must be large enough to satisfy any conceivable demand. If a stockout would only require deferring some activities, or if it would mean an hour's delay in some noncritical activity, then safety stocks can be correspondingly reduced.

In any event, the general rule should be to calculate the order point (OP) based on the relationships described above. These order points should be viewed as tentative and modified according to actual experience (stockouts or excess inventory). The healthcare financial manager can use historical demand, relative to known inventory quantities, to evaluate the effects of alternative inventory management policies. Successive adjustments, by a trial and error series of approximations, will often result in an appropriate order point.

Order quantity (OQ)

Once the financial manager knows the point (OP) at which an inventory order must be placed, the next problem is to determine the optimal size of the order. The optimal order quantity (OQ) is also known as the economic order quantity (EOQ) because it is determined by the combination of order point and order quantity which minimizes the total cost of managing the inventory. As the order quantity is increased, there will be fewer orders placed, thereby reducing the clerical, transportation, and other costs associated with the ordering process. However, as fewer orders are placed, and larger quantities are received from each shipment, the average investment in inventory and the physical quantity of the inventory is increased, thereby increasing the holding costs. This is the tradeoff which must be considered when determining the economic order quantity, and the order point. This concept is illustrated in *Exhibit 10–4.*

Management of inventory costs

The management of inventory costs requires that managers minimize the total costs (TC) of the inventory. Total costs consist of ordering costs and holding costs. Algebraically these relationships can be shown in the following manner:

$$TC = \text{(average inventory quantity)(holding cost per unit)} +$$
$$\text{(total number of orders placed)(average cost per order)}$$
$$= (AQ \times HC) + (NO \times AC)$$

Where: AQ = average inventory quantity
        HC = holding cost per unit
        NO = number of orders
        AC = average cost per order

A typical pattern of costs for holding costs and ordering costs is shown in *Exhibit 10–4.* Note that the pattern of costs show that ordering costs decrease as inventory increases and holding costs are increased. This general pattern will hold for most healthcare organizations. The key is to identify the ordering quantities that minimize the total cost of the inventory. This minimum point can be determined in several different ways. The easiest is by creating a table.

Assume that we estimate that the annual demand or usage of an inventory item is 100,000 units, an average purchase price of $20, the cost of placing one order is $3.60, the holding costs per unit of item in inventory is $5 per unit (25 percent of $20). *Exhibit 10–5* illustrates one approach to calculating holding costs (ordering costs are assumed to be

Exhibit 10–4
Inventory holding and ordering cost

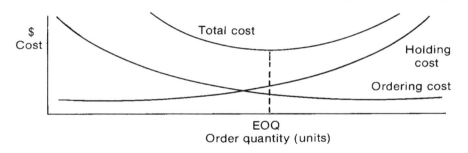

Exhibit 10–5
Inventory cost calculation
Purchase price equals $20 per unit

	Percent	Dollar cost
Ordering costs:		
Administration		$3.60 per order
Transportation		
Holding costs (as a percent of purchase price):		
Capital cost	15.00%	$3.00
Insurance and taxes	1.50%	$0.30
Storage space costs	0.50%	$0.10
		$3.40
Obsolescence	2.50%	$0.50
Damage	0.50%	$0.10
Loss/theft	5.00%	$1.00
		$1.60
Total holding costs	25.00%	$5.00 per unit

related to the amount of paperwork involved, and is a constant amount per order).

A table can now be created using these figures in order to compare the relative costs of different order quantities, as indicated in *Exhibit 10–6*.

The order size that has the least total cost is 400 units given the discrete number of potential order amounts. Note that total inventory management costs do not vary greatly as the order quantity changes. In actual practice,

Exhibit 10–6
Costs associated with alternative order quantities

Annual demand =   100,000 units
Cost/order (AC) = $3.60
Holding cost (HC) = $5.00
Price = $20.00

Order size	300	400	500	600	1,000
Number of orders per year	333	250	200	167	100
Average inventory (units)	150	200	250	300	500
Total ordering costs	$1,200	$ 900	$ 720	$ 600	$ 360
Total holding costs	$ 750	$1,000	$1,250	$1,500	$2,500
Total inventory costs	$1,950	$1,900	$1,970	$2,100	$2,860

total inventory costs are not usually sensitive to small changes in the input data. This statement can be interpreted to mean that minor errors in estimating any of the input costs will not significantly distort the results. The healthcare financial manager is really more interested in a range of acceptable economic order quantities than in the precise numerical estimate of a single EOQ.

A more precise EOQ ordering quantity can be determined through the use of the basic EOQ model. The results of this process provides the following equation:

$$EOQ = \sqrt{\frac{2\ (Annual\ Demand)\ (Cost\ per\ Order)}{Holding\ Cost\ per\ Unit}}$$

By putting the values provided in *Exhibit 10–6* into the above formula:

$$EOQ = \sqrt{\frac{2\ (100,000)(\$3.60)}{\$5.00}} = 379\ units$$

The objective in any inventory control or inventory management policy must be to find the best possible solution. If the calculated EOQ is within 5 percent to 10 percent of the optimal EOQ that truly minimizes all inventory costs, the financial manager has probably done better than if judgment alone had prevailed. In other words, an attempt can be made to bracket the minimum inventory costs, and an EOQ can be selected that is convenient and within that range.

Purchase price discounts

In the event that purchase prices vary according to quantity ordered, the simplest procedure is to adjust the calculations outlined in *Exhibit 10–6* to include the foregone discount associated with each particular order quantity. This is done in *Exhibit 10–7*. For example, if a $0.20 per unit discount could be obtained by ordering 1,000 units or more, then the first two columns in *Exhibit 10–6* must include the additional costs of the discount foregone by ordering fewer than 1,000 units. An order quantity of 1,000 or more units will result in an annual savings of $20,000 ($0.20 × 100,000). An order quantity of fewer than 1,000 units must, therefore, include an opportunity cost of the $20,000 discount foregone by not purchasing at least 1,000 units. In this case, 1,000 units became the economic ordering quantity.

There are some cases where the number of units is not as important as the dollar value of the items being ordered in determining the discount to be offered. An approximation of the EOQ can still be calculated by using a table similar to that presented in *Exhibit 10–6,* and including the purchase price per unit times the number of units and calculating the amount of the desired cost. In that case, several different order quantities can be tested to find the order quantity that reflects the minimum total costs.

Exhibit 10–7
Costs associated with alternative
order quantities with discount

Annual demand =   100,000 units
Cost/order (AC) = $3.60
Holding cost (HC) = $5.00
Price per unit = $20.00, Up to 1,000 Units
Price per unit = $19.80, 1,000 Units and beyond
Annual discount = $20,000 ($.20 × 100,000)

Order size	300	400	500	600	1,000
Number of orders per year	333	250	200	167	100
Average inventory (units)	150	200	250	300	500
Total ordering costs	$ 1,200	$ 900	$ 720	$ 600	$ 360
Total holding costs	$ 750	$ 1,000	$ 1,250	$ 1,500	$2,500
Total ordering + holding costs	$ 1,950	$ 1,900	$ 1,970	$ 2,100	$2,860
Foregone discount	$20,000	$20,000	$20,000	$20,000	0
Total inventory costs	$21,950	$21,900	$21,970	$22,100	$2,860

It must be stressed that the final consideration affecting ordering quantities is that reductions in purchase price must be balanced against changes in other inventory costs. A quantity discount will usually result in fewer orders and lower ordering costs. Fewer orders will result in larger inventory balances and greater holding costs. In summary, the EOQ model approach provides a method to determine whether a potential inventory price reduction is advantageous to the firm in terms of cost. The provider of health services that can justify and document its evaluations of these alternative cost factors will have no problem demonstrating that it is a "prudent buyer." One of the major myths that can be demolished on the basis of inventory control policies is that purchase price reductions must be automatically accepted under the "prudent buyer" concept. The truly prudent buyer can show that all of the costs of inventory management have been evaluated and that the particular decisions that have been made are the best possible decisions under the circumstances, the cheapest purchase price may not yield the lowest total inventory costs.

Probabilistic and uncertainty models

The previous discussions have assumed that demand, usage rates, lead times, and other factors were all stable and predictable. However, in reality, all of these factor values are only estimates. As a consequence of this uncertainty, actual inventory holdings will vary up and down depending on current situations. This is especially important in cases where shortages of the inventory item would place a constraint on the activities of the organization. Creation of a safety stock is one way to account for these uncertainties.

However, there are several other methods which can be used to handle uncertainty in the management of inventories. For example, a payoff matrix using expected values can be used to identify the policy with the lowest expected costs. A payoff matrix that incorporates probabilities is shown in *Exhibit 10–8*.

This approach requires estimating the cost (per unit) of being understocked (out of stock) and relating it to the storage costs of units that are in stock. For example, given the assumptions provided in *Exhibit 10–8*, if the order quantity is 17 and actual demand is 19, there will be a stock-out of 2 units. Since the cost per unit of being out of stock is $50, the total payoff for this situation is $100. Alternatively, when the order quantity is 19 and the actual demand is 16, there is an excess quantity of 3 units. This can be considered to be a safety stock, but there is a cost associated with having excess units, amounting to $2 per unit. Therefore, the payoff amount is equal to $6 (the cost associated with ordering 19 when the actual demand is 16). (Although this method uses what is called a "payoff" matrix, the figures are actually costs which need to be minimized.)

A payoff matrix that incorporates probabilities is shown in *Exhibit 10–9*. This approach adds a probability function to the various levels of

Exhibit 10–8
Payoff matrix for alternative order quantities

Assume: Cost of being out of stock = $50 per unit
          Storage costs = $2 per unit
          Lead time = 0 days

Alternative demand levels
15
16
17
18
19
20

			Actual demand			
Order quantity	15	16	17	18	19	20
15	$ 0	$50	$100	$150	$200	$250
16	2	0	50	100	150	200
17	4	2	0	50	100	150
18	6	4	2	0	50	100
19	8	6	4	2	0	50
20	10	8	6	4	2	0

Exhibit 10–9
Expected value of payoff matrix for alternative order quantities

	Actual demand						
	15	16	17	18	19	20	
Probability of demand	10%	20%	30%	30%	5%	5%	
Order quantity							Totals
15	$ 0	1.00	30.00	45.00	10.00	12.50	98.50
16	.20	0	15.00	30.00	7.50	10.00	62.70
17	.40	.40	0	15.00	5.00	7.50	28.30
18	.60	.80	.60	0	2.50	5.00	9.50
19	.80	1.20	1.20	.60	0	2.50	6.30
20	1.00	1.60	1.80	1.20	.10	0	5.70

demand. Using these data, an expected value of the payoff matrix is calculated. It is determined that the lowest-cost order quantity is 20 units, because the stockout costs are so much higher than the storage costs for items on the shelf.

The values appearing in this matrix are calculated by multiplying the amount appearing in the payoff matrix (*Exhibit 10–9*) by the probability that cost will be incurred. For example, the cost associated with having an order quantity of 15 and an actual demand of 17 is $100. Since there is a 30 percent chance of demand actually being 17, the expected value for this component of the matrix is $30. In order to determine the expected value associated with an order quantity of 15, the values appearing in *Exhibit 10–9* must be added across, and are provided in the column labeled "Totals." The order quantity which should be chosen, then, is that quantity which has the lowest expected value of the payoff matrix, which occurs with an order quantity of 20.

The Monte Carlo technique permits the analyst to simulate the effects of alternative inventory control policies and procedures, allowing evaluation of the effects of alternative order points and order quantities. The optimal points may be indicated by analytical procedures as noted above, while simulation then incorporates probabilities and random events to determine if the optimal solutions are feasible and realistic. Though the term "Monte Carlo" is generally associated with gambling, its use in this context refers to the uncertain or random nature of an inventory control system that will be evaluated using simulation techniques.

This model does not explicitly incorporate holding costs and ordering costs. It does show how and under what circumstances stockouts occur. The financial manager must then assess the costs associated with different stockout patterns and choose the policy that will result in the optimal inventory quantities and stockouts at the lowest possible cost. The advantage of a Monte Carlo simulation model is that it can be done easily by hand, or it can be converted to a computerized simulation model. In the latter case, a huge number of alternative inventory policies can be tested and a wide range of acceptable policies can be identified—at a relatively low cost.

The authors recommend using a single point estimate of demand and lead time if the relative dispersion around the point estimate is low. Alternatively, if the variance is high, a probabilistic model should be used. In other words, if the level of uncertainty is high, a model that emphasizes probabilities is preferred over a model that incorporates different cost elements. If the uncertainty is low, then the relative costs become more important to the decision, and an inventory control model that emphasizes cost is preferred.

An example

Suppose that a healthcare organization's management intuitively feels that its ad hoc approach to the management of inventory control has led to substantial diseconomies. For purposes of illustrating the use of Monte Carlo simulation, the example will be concerned with only one item in an outpatient care clinic's inventory. The management would like to determine (a) the optimal (or at least near optimal) inventory policy and (b) the extent to which deviations from this policy will result in increases in total inventory costs.

Investigation revealed that the pattern of daily demand was random and unstable, making application of the economic order quantity model inappropriate for this particular problem. Further investigation, however, disclosed that the pattern of daily demand did conform to a fairly stable probability distribution, with no detectable seasonal or secular shifts. The probability distribution of daily demand, based on historical observation, is shown in columns (1) and (2) of *Exhibit 10–10*. Notice that the distribution is not symmetric; it is skewed in the direction of high daily demand. Thus, for this example, the use of an optimization model based on the assumption of daily demand being normally distributed would not be appropriate. The organization's management also found that the lead time from placement of an order to receiving delivery varied randomly, but followed the probability distribution given in columns (4) and (5) in *Exhibit 10–10*. These historical data did not seem to fit the assumptions of any of the better known inventory policy optimization models.

This information—probability distributions of daily demand and lead time culled from old requisition and purchase orders—is sufficient for some preliminary investigations of alternative inventory policies. An inventory policy is specified by two parameters: the order point and the order quantity. That is, inventory policy will indicate at what level of existing inventory an order should be placed and the number of units that should be specified in that order.

Exhibit 10–10
Data for inventory policy example

(1) Daily demand	(2) Probability	(3) Random numbers	(4) Lag time	(5) Probability	(6) Random numbers
5 units	.08	00–07	3 days	.15	00–14
6	.13	08–20	4	.40	15–54
7	.15	21–35	5	.25	55–79
8	.18	36–53	6	.20	80–99
				1.00	
9	.17	54–70			
10	.12	71–82			
11	.08	83–90			
12	.06	91–96			
13	.03	97–99			
	1.00				

A meeting of the organization's top administrators was called to discuss the problem of formulating an inventory policy. Someone suggested a policy of ordering forty units whenever the inventory at the end of the day is thirty-five units or less. There were some murmurings of disagreement, with varied opinions as to whether the order should be greater or less than the levels first suggested. After considerable discussion, it was agreed to evaluate the policy suggested [denoted by (35,40)].

They quickly agreed that it could be an expensive lesson if they followed the (35,40) policy for a year's time and it turned out to be a very inefficient policy. Given the availability of dependable data on daily demand and lead times, however, they decided that simulation would be an appropriate technique for quickly and inexpensively evaluating the suggested (35,40) inventory policy.

For the purpose of performing the simulation, the two-digit random numbers given in column (3) were assigned to various levels of daily demand and the random numbers in column (6) were assigned to alternative lead times. Notice that from a long sequence of two-digit random numbers, each with equal probabilities of being selected, a random number in the range 00 to 07 should occur about 8 percent of the time; a random number in the range 08 to 20 should occur about 13 percent of the time, and so on. Thus, the random numbers are assigned in such a way that the occurrence of random numbers should conform to the probability distribution of daily demand. Similarly, random numbers are assigned to lead times so as to conform to the associated probability distribution.

The experience of 45 days under the (35,40) policy is simulated in *Exhibit 10–11*. A series of 2-digit random numbers, used to indicate units of daily demand, is given in column (2). The inventory at the beginning

Exhibit 10–11
Simulation for inventory policy example

(1) Day	(2) Random number	(3) Beginning inventory	(4) Daily demand	(5) Ending inventory	(6) Random number	(7) Lag time	(8) Order quantity
1	71	70	10	60			
2	39	60	8	52			
3	28	52	7	45			
4	63	45	9	36			
5	10	36	6	30	20	4 days	45
6	24	30	7	23			
7	87	23	44	12			
8	24	12	7	5			
9	53	5	8	0			
10	47	45	8	37			
11	70	37	9	28	27	4 days	47
12	33	28	7	21			
13	54	21	9	18			
14	75	18	10	8			
15	39	8	8	0			
16	43	47	8	39			
17	42	39	8	31	93	6 days	44
18	55	31	9	22			
19	45	22	8	14			
20	10	14	6	8			
21	32	8	7	1			
22	83	1	11	0			
23	57	0	9	0			
24	72	44	10	34	99	6 days	41
25	52	34	8	26			
26	61	26	9	17			
27	58	17	9	8			
28	08	8	6	2			
29	51	2	8	0			
30	00	0	5	0			
31	91	41	12	29	15	4 days	46
32	90	29	11	18			
33	01	18	5	13			
34	75	13	10	3			
35	18	3	6	0			
36	74	46	10	36			
37	51	36	8	28	91	6 days	47
38	68	28	9	19			
39	24	19	7	12			
40	82	12	10	2			
41	88	2	11	0			
42	41	0	8	0			
43	99	0	13	0			
44	66	47	9	36			
45	93	36	12	24	84	6 days	51

of day 1 is arbitrarily assigned to be 70 units. From *Exhibit 10–11* it is seen that the random number 71 represents daily demand of 10 units (column 4). The inventory at the end of day 1 is 60 units (indicated in column 5). The random number for day 2 corresponds to a daily demand of 8 units, giving an ending inventory of 52 units. By the end of day 5, the inventory level is down to 30 units, below the order point 35 units.

At the end of day 5, an order is made to replenish the inventory. Strict adherence to the inventory policy would call for ordering 40 units. It has generally been found, however, that a preferable policy is to order the specified order quantity plus enough additional units to bring the inventory up to the order point. Following this convention, an order for 45 units is placed at the end of day 5. The random number of 20 in column (6) corresponds to a lead time of 4 days. This means that delivery will be received at the end of day 9. Notice that the demand in day 9 exceeds the beginning inventory, resulting in unsatisfied demand.

The next step would be to evaluate the results of the simulation. For this purpose, management would have to estimate ordering costs, inventory carrying costs, and the costs of unsatisfied demand. These estimated costs would then be applied to the inventory experience depicted in *Exhibit 10–11* to get the total cost of the (35,40) inventory policy.

Exhibit 10–11 indicates that stockouts occur at days 9, 22, 23, 29, 30, 35, 41, 42, and 43. These frequent stockouts indicate that the order point should be raised. There were 7 orders placed during the 45 days experience. Unless inventory carrying costs are high relative to ordering costs, it probably would be advisable to also increase the order quantity. Thus, a new simulation could be performed using an inventory policy of, perhaps, (50,60). This policy could be simulated and evaluated and, based on the results, might be modified further and a new policy specified. Repeated refinement of the inventory policy would continue until management determines the inventory policy that best meets its needs.

It should be recognized that the use of Monte Carlo simulation to determine a healthcare organization's inventory policy yields only an approximate solution (so that an exact solution obtained by analytical evaluation is preferable when possible). Nevertheless, the approximation should be excellent if the number of computer assisted simulated trials is large and the model is valid. Moreover, the use of simulation allows the analyst to work with a more complex and flexible model.

This example assumed uniform demand throughout the period. With little additional effort, seasonal variations can be introduced into the demand pattern to make the model more realistic. The analysis of the simulation results can be modified to allow for an occasional rush shipment of an important item. The analysis might show that the expense of periodic emergency orders (so long as quality of patient care is not threatened) could be more than offset by the savings resulting from carrying small inventories. These examples illustrate the great flexibility available through the use of simulation.

Monte Carlo simulation does not eliminate the need to develop a model which depicts the operation of the system under study. The analytical solution is no longer a constraint and inventory control models can be developed without concern for their mathematical solvability.

It should be emphasized that while the model developed still needs to be a complete and realistic representation of all important aspects of the system under study, it need only represent the essential aspects of the system. Being overly realistic means spending a great deal of effort and computer time to obtain very small improvements in the overall results. Moreover, the mass of trivial implications may obscure significant results.

Not all inventory decisions need a Monte Carlo simulation solution; only models with a degree of uncertainty need to be simulated. Without a random aspect to the model, all samples (or trials) would yield the same outcome.

Zero inventory and stockless systems

The latest developments in inventory management suggest that most inventory control problems can be shifted to suppliers who are asked to provide the capability for daily or hourly deliveries. This method is called Just-In-Time (JIT) inventory management. Such a system is feasible and economically justified only where repetitive and stable services are being provided or for high cost items. In such cases, a limited number of suppliers are given annual contracts with appropriate definitions of expected performance. These techniques are most prevalent in high-tech electronics manufacturing, but they are being gradually incorporated into larger healthcare delivery systems. For example, multi-institutions or networked facilities may use a central warehouse with on-demand delivery capabilities so that on-site inventories are almost zero. Such procedures permit centralized inventory control so that materials management functions become highly specialized and more complex than indicated in this chapter.

Summary

Inventory control is an important function for hospitals, long-term care facilities, staff model health maintenance organizations, visiting nurse associations, and most other forms of healthcare provider. In many healthcare organizations, the major inventory control technique is to take a physical count at the end of each accounting period. The use of EOQ models and optimal order points puts the focus on controlling costs before they occur. Emphasis on proper inventory control can foster the development of a cost containment philosophy within the healthcare organization. EOQs and optimal order points are tools that can be used to improve cost containment efforts. The financial manager must select that set of tools that improves decisions in a particular healthcare organization.

Questions and problems

1. Why are inventories necessary in a healthcare organization?

2. What are the objectives of an effective materials management system?

3. What are the three fundamental concepts of inventory control?

4. What are the ordering costs associated with inventory management?

5. What are the carrying costs associated with inventory management?

6. Define lead time, safety stock, and order point.

7. Define economic order quantity as it pertains to a healthcare organization.

8. How can group purchasing agreements and quantity discounts be used in an EOQ determination?

9. How can uncertainty over future demand, lead times, prices, etc., be incorporated in an effective inventory management system?

10. The Memorial Hospital of Teller County estimated the demand for X-ray films for the coming year to be 36,500 with average daily usage to be 100 films. The purchase price of the film is estimated to be $2. The ordering costs are $20 per order, and carrying costs are estimated to be $0.40 per film per year. The lead time is 10 days, and the maximum daily usage last year was 150 films.
    a. Compute the economic order quantity.
    b. Compute the reorder point.
    c. Compute the safety stock.

11. As controller of Memorial Clinic, you have been asked by the administrator to review the buying practices of the purchasing department. You find that the objective of this department has been to keep as small a quantity of each item on hand as possible, thus achieving the highest possible inventory turnover.
    After extensive study, you determine that the average cost of processing an order is $9.50. This figure includes preparation of the requisition, issuance of the purchase order, processing and payment of the invoice, receipt of the merchandise, and so on. You also determine that the average cost of carrying inventory is 6 percent of the value of the inventory on hand.
    a. Explain what is meant by economic order quantity.

b. Illustrate the determination of the EOQ for the following nonperishable items:

Item A:	Annual usage = $30,000 Price quoted allows a 1/2 percent (.005) discount on purchases of $5,000 or more at one time.
Item B:	Annual usage = $800 Price = net
Item C:	Annual usage = $8,000 Price quoted allows a 1 percent discount on purchases of $5,000 or more at one time.

12. At the present time, purchasing at the Eastern Medical Center is decentralized. The purchasing department handles all departmental orders for items which are used by two or more departments. Other departments may order individual products themselves. These departments are radiology, pharmacy, pathology services, food services, plant operations, and housekeeping. The departments initiate their own orders and maintain their own inventories. The purchasing department uses the following techniques to monitor its own performance. It attempts to turn the total inventory twelve times a year. It has a standardized committee that approves purchases of medical/surgical supplies. (Pharmacy also has a standardization committee for pharmaceutical items.)

All purchasing is done on a competitive basis except for proprietary items and some miscellaneous items. Contracts are awarded on the basis of price and service. Two principal group purchasing arrangements are presently being used. One is a shared service arrangement with Methodist in Omaha; the second is the Hospital Purchasing Council based in Des Moines. At the present time, the purchasing department is investigating a prime vendor arrangement with American Hospital Supply.

a. Evaluate the current inventory ordering and control procedures.

b. What changes would you recommend?

13. The following information is available to Brookfield Hospital pertaining to lab item #12:

Annual usage	20,000 units
Working days per year	365
Safety stock	400 units
Normal lead time (working days)	15
Ordering costs	$0.50
Holding costs	$0.75

a. Determine the order point.

b. Determine the economic order quantity.

14. As controller of Melbrook Hospital, you have been asked by the administrator to compute a safety level of inventory that minimizes total costs. The following information is available to you:

Probability of a stockout	.25	.10	.04
Expected usage provided for (reorder point)	380	380	380
Safety stock:			
0 units	50	90	130
50 units	0	40	80
90 units	0	0	80
130 units	0	0	0

The above figures are to be interpreted as meaning that there is a 25 percent chance of a stockout shortage of 50 units when the safety stock is 0 units, a 10 percent chance of stockout shortage of 90 units when the safety stock is 0 units, etc.

Stockout costs	$1.20 per unit
Carrying costs	$1.00 per unit
Annual demand	8,000 units
EOQ	575

15. Shelby Cancer Research Clinic invented an injection to be used on cancer patients. It costs the clinic $85 to produce one injection (including $10 of fixed factory overhead). Setup costs for one injection are $125. Since the injections are only effective for a short period of time, units are inspected at a cost of $1.50 per unit before they are delivered to customers. The clinic carries insurance of the injections at a cost of $0.50 per injection (based on an average cost of inventory on hand). The rate of return required on investment in the inventory is 15 percent. Assuming an annual demand for 57,500 units, what is the economic order quantity?

16. The controller of General Hospital has given you the following information and wants you to determine the safety stock and order point for inventory item X (assume units of item X will be required evenly throughout the year).

Annual usage	16,425 units
Working days per year	365
Normal lead time (working days)	35
Maximum lead time (working days)	50

17. The Washington Clinic has hired you to control inventory levels of a very expensive drug that it has been using for the past year. You are given the following information:
   a. Cost of placing an order is $10.
   b. The company's average (before tax) cost of capital is 12 percent.
   c. Obsolescence and deterioration are 1 percent of average inventory per year.
   d. Insurance and taxes on inventory are 5 percent of average inventory.
   e. The storage space available in the pharmacy can accommodate 4,000 units.
   f. Additional space can be acquired at $0.75 per unit.
   g. The clinic is open 52 weeks a year, 5 days a week.
   h. A safety stock of 100 units is recommended by management.
   i. It takes 2 weeks from the time of order to the date of delivery.
   j. Per review of the clinic's records, usage can fluctuate from as low as 25 to as high as 70 per day.
   k. The anticipated annual demand is 13,000 units.
   In addition to the preceding information, you obtain the following data from the purchasing department concerning bulk purchases:

| | Invoice cost | | Freight cost | |
Quantity purchased	Unit cost	Total cost	Unit cost	Total cost
500	$100	$ 50,000	$2.00	$ 1,000
1,000	100	100,000	2.00	2,000
2,000	98	196,000	2.00	4,000
3,000	98	294,000	1.80	5,400
4,000	98	392,000	1.80	7,200
5,000	95	475,000	1.75	8,750
6,000	95	570,000	1.70	10,200
6,500	95	617,500	1.70	11,050
13,000	90	1,170,000	1.50	19,500

Assume that the maximum inventory to be computed for excess storage space is computed as follows:

(order point – minimum usage) + standard quantity

   a. What order size would you recommend, in order to minimize costs?

18. Selected information relating to an inventory item carried by the Santos Hospital is given below:

Economic order quantity	700 units
Maximum weekly usage	60 units
Lead time	4 weeks
Average weekly usage	50 units

Santos Hospital is trying to determine the proper safety stock to carry on this inventory item, and the proper reorder point.

a. Assume that no safety stock is carried. What is the reorder point?

b. Assume that a full safety stock is to be carried:
   1. What would be the size of the safety stock (units)?
   2. What would be the reorder point?

19. The Magnetic Research Corporation uses 15,000 ingots of Klypton each year. The Klypton is purchased from a supplier in another state, according to the following price schedule:

Ingots	Per ingot
500	$30.00
1,000	29.90
1,500	29.85
2,000	29.80
2,500	29.75

The Magnetic Research Corporation sends its own truck to the supplier's plant to pick up the ingots. The truck's capacity is 2,500 ingots per trip. The company has been getting a full load of ingots each trip, making 6 trips each year. The cost of making one round trip to the supplier's plant is $500. The paperwork associated with each trip is $30.

The supplier requires that all purchases be made in round 500-ingot lots. The company's cost analysts estimate that the cost of storing one ingot for one year is $10.

a. By use of the tabulation approach to EOQ, compute the volume in which the corporation should be purchasing its ingots. Treat the savings arising from quantity discounts as a reduction in total annual trucking and storage costs.

b. Compute the annual cost savings that will be realized if the corporation purchases in the volume which you have determined above, as compared to its present purchase policy.

20. You have been asked by the administrator to review the buying practices of the purchasing department. The objective of this department has been to keep as small a quantity of each item on hand as possible, thus achieving the highest possible inventory turnover.

After an extensive study, you find that the average cost of processing an order is $7.80. This includes preparation of the requisition, issuance of the purchase order, processing and payment of the invoice, receipt of the merchandise, etc. You have also learned that the average cost of carrying inventory is 6 percent of the value of the inventory on hand.

The purchasing department furnishes the following information on three nonperishable items:

Item A: Annual usage = $20,000 (cost)
Average cost = $10 per unit
Terms: ½ percent (.005) discount on purchases of $5,000 or more at one time

Item B: Annual usage = $600 (cost)
Average cost = $5 per unit
Terms: Net

Item C: Annual usage = 1,000 units
Average cost = $6 per unit
Terms: 1 percent discount on purchases of $5,000 or more at one time

---

As an aid in making purchasing decisions, you decide to develop a framework that can be used for future ordering quantities based on the examples given. This framework should also be used to calculate the EOQ of each item.

Keywords: economic order quantity; holding costs; inventory; just-in-time; order point; order quantity; ordering costs; stockout; total quality improvement.

References

Archer, Stephen H., and Charles A. D'Ambrosio. *The Theory of Business Finance.* 3rd ed. New York, NY: MacMillan, 1983.

Brigham, Eugene F., and Louis C. Gapenski. *Financial Management Theory and Practice.* New York, NY: The Dryden Press, 1988.

Czarnecki, M.T. "Benchmarking Can Add Up for Healthcare Accounting." *Healthcare Financial Management* (September 1994): 62–67.

Eastaugh, S.R. "Differential Cost Analysis: Judging a PPO's Feasibility." *Healthcare Financial Management* 40, no. 5 (1986): 44–51.

Kowalski, Jamie C. "Inventory To Go: Can Stockless Deliver Efficiency?" *Healthcare Financial Management* (November 1991): 20–23.

———. "Materials Management Crucial to Overall Efficiency." *Healthcare Financial Management* (January 1991): 40–44.

Seidner, Alan G., and William O. Cleverley. *Cash and Investment Management for the Health Care Industry.* Rockville, MD: Aspen Publishers, 1990.

Siebold, Paul T. "Purchasing Comes Into Its Own." *Healthcare Financial Management* (November 1991): 24–34.

CHAPTER 11

Financial statement analysis

"I'm sorry. But I just don't see how we can extend you any more credit at this time. You have too much debt in your financial structure. If only your bottom line was stronger."

Bank Loan Officer

"This is a good time to invest in the Acme Healthcare Supply Company. Their financial statements indicate that they are one of the strongest companies in the industry. The trends are all positive."

Stock Analyst

"Our liquidity position must be improved before we can approach the bond market for funds to finance our expansion."

CEO of Healthcare Provider

"The shakeout in the HMO business is continuing. An inability to increase premiums and reduce healthcare expenses as a percentage of premium income is hurting the weaker ones."

Industry Analyst

Each of these hypothetical quotations demonstrates the importance of a strong financial position to the well-being of a corporation. They also indicate the extent to which information collected and analyzed from the financial statements provides guidance for various decision makers. The tendency to compare the hospitals based on their financial statements fostered the growth of national comparative data services, such as the Center for Healthcare Industry Performance Studies (CHIPS), which publishes an annual *Almanac of Hospital Financial and Operating Indicators* that has proven invaluable for comparative analysis purposes. In a similar fashion, the Medical Group Management Association (MGMA) has published statistics for medical groups to provide comparative data based on group size, type, and geographic location. The growth of the managed care industry (HMOs, PPOs, etc.) and alternative healthcare providers is requiring new comparative data to evaluate the financial viability of these types of providers. Finally, increased interest in the long-term care industry is focusing attention on the financial statements of nursing homes and other providers of geriatric services.

Decreasing profit margins, along with the risk of reduced bond ratings, gives added emphasis to assessments of financial condition. The changes in payment for physicians and other alternative healthcare providers add additional uncertainty in assessing the financial risk associated with the healthcare industry. All stakeholders are becoming more concerned about the financial status of the providers and the extent to which they are able to meet their obligations.

Because of this standardized format and the requirement to use generally accepted accounting principles (GAAP), the financial statements are the primary source of information on the financial condition of most healthcare providers. This allows the comparison of one organization with another or with external standards published by professional associations. For example, one organization may be compared with another, one hospital with another, one nursing home with another, one HMO with another. Care must be taken when making these comparisons, however, to ensure that similar organizations are being compared; staff model HMOs of a given size may be legitimately compared with other staff model HMOs of a similar size, while comparison with IPA model HMOs may not be appropriate.

The same caution must be taken with national standards. The concept of peer grouping—establishing homogeneous comparison groups—is becoming more and more prevalent on a state, regional, and national basis for reimbursement and policy decisions. All such groupings and combinations, however, should be used with caution by the individual providers in assessing their own financial status.

This chapter concentrates on the use of ratios as comparative measures of performance. It presumes that valid and homogeneous data bases exist so that resulting ratio calculations are meaningful and useful performance indicators. It also presumes that a well developed accounting system exists for compiling the financial statements.

The use of ratios to assess financial strengths and weaknesses is not a new development. In 1974, Marc Choate[1] was one of the first researchers to apply ratio analysis comparisons to unrelated hospital organizations. He developed consolidated financial statements, prepared on a uniform basis, for several hospitals. Choate then compared each of the hospital ratios to a very rough industry norm. His research was invaluable in establishing the use of financial ratios to compare healthcare organizations.

For examples of how ratio analysis can assist the financial manager and other stakeholders, one needs only to look at the research studies that have

---

[1] Choate, Mark G., "Financial Ratio Analysis," *Hospital Progress*, January 1974, pp. 49–57, 67.

attempted to predict bankruptcy using ratio comparisons. Many different studies have been performed using different sets of ratios to predict (ex post) bankruptcies in industrial companies, railroads, airlines, etc. Cannedy, Pointer, and Ruchlin (1973) applied a series of multivariate statistical tests to a group of bankrupt hospitals and found that several factors could be used to explain or predict bankruptcy:

1. hospital size and ownership;
2. total costs;
3. utilization.

This study followed the general research form of comparing a group of four bankrupt hospitals with a group of four closely matched surviving hospitals. Four different ratios were identified that were able to correctly separate and identify the failed hospitals from the nonfailed hospitals:

1. cash flow to total debt;
2. total assets to FTE personnel;
3. payroll expenses to FTE personnel;
4. occupancy (utilization) ratios.

The concept was that if the various stakeholders in health service organizations could monitor a variety of complementary ratios, they would be able to identify when the organization was thriving or in danger of failing. Ratio comparisons could provide an early warning system for financial distress, which, when used appropriately, could be used to take corrective action or in the worst case, to plan for a well-structured, organized demise. The efficient manager should be monitoring ratios that can help identify potential problems.

More recently, Bill Cleverley, of Ohio State University, and developer of HFMA's Financial Analysis Service (FAS), published a wide range of articles dealing with the use of ratio analysis in decision making. Several of these are listed at the end of the chapter.

Industry data sources

Another key factor in the use of comparative financial analysis is the availability of industry data. For example, HFMA started the Financial Analysis Service (FAS) in 1979 to which healthcare organizations can subscribe. This service has been replaced by CHIPS' annual *Almanac*. Subscribers send their audited financial statements to CHIPS, in addition to other pertinent information, and receive comparative data on many financial and operating ratios. The ratios are categorized by upper, median, and lower quartile values for national, regional, geographic (urban, rural), ownership, and bed-size categories. CHIPS' data bases include a 400-

hospital constant sample size of data, as well as national data derived from Medicare cost reports. *Appendix 11–1* illustrates the type of information that is available from CHIPS. In a similar fashion, MGMA provides timely, comparative data to its members. For group practices, the Medical Group Management Association (MGMA) publishes *The Cost and Production Survey Report,* which presents summary statistics of medical specialty groups, showing the effect of size, managed care, and geographic region. Examples of MGMA reports are also included in *Appendix 11–3.* The Reference section of this chapter includes a list of sources of comparative external data.

Financial statement analysis

Financial statement analysis refers to the use of data from financial statements to make better decisions. Financial statements can provide valuable information, in a fairly consistent fashion, over time and across different organizations. The three basic financial statements are: balance sheet, income statement, and statement of cash flows. They are typically prepared in accordance with generally accepted accounting principles (GAAP).

Each financial statement has a unique set of characteristics. For example, the balance sheet is basically a financial "picture" of the firm at a specific point in time. It lists the assets and liabilities of the organization in a standard format.

In assessing the amounts shown on the balance sheet, it is important to know that the value of the balance sheet assets is determined at the time they become assets of the organization. This reflects the historical cost basis required under GAAP. Only a few assets are valued at current market values. A sample balance sheet is illustrated in *Exhibit 11–1.*

In the most recent *Audit and Accounting Guide: Health Care Organizations, 1996,* the accounting profession has redefined various balance sheet concepts and disclosure requirements for non-profit healthcare organizations. The difference between assets and liabilities should be shown as "net assets," though some organizations may continue to use the term "equity." Separate amounts should be shown for three classes of net assets: (a) permanently restricted net assets, (b) temporarily restricted net assets, and (c) unrestricted net assets. Such restrictions are based on the existence or absence of restrictions imposed by donors or other funding sources. Details of such restrictions will be shown in the financial statements or the notes. Government organizations may report all three classes as components of fund balances, or they may show unrestricted (general) and restricted fund balances.

While balance sheets may look more complicated under these new provisions, most analysts will be well-served by concentrating on the total amount of net assets. Such amounts may be compared across years (or other time periods) and across comparable organizations. In some cases,

Exhibit 11–1
Sample Hospital
Balance sheet

	Dec 31 19X9	Dec 31 19X8
Assets		
Current assets:		
Cash and cash equivalents	$ 1,322,324	$ 1,070,600
Accounts receivable		
(Less allowance for uncollectable accounts of		
$2,300,000 in 19X9 and $1,700,000 in 19X8)	$ 24,645,297	$ 14,092,527
Inventories	$ 2,549,676	$ 2,045,715
Prepaid expenses	$ 1,789,162	$ 1,807,197
Assets limited as to use	$ 2,100,000	$ 2,300,000
Total current assets	$ 32,406,459	$ 21,316,039
Assets limited as to use		
Internally designated for capital acquisition	$ 14,378,162	$ 20,577,341
By trustee—liability self-insurance-investments	$ 2,413,303	$ 3,692,205
By trustee—sinking fund-investments	$ 2,844,759	3,351,136
Total	$ 19,636,224	$ 27,620,682
Less current portion	($ 2,100,000)	(2,300,000)
Total assets limited as to use	$ 17,536,224	$ 25,320,682
Other assets:		
Unamortized bond financing	$ 3,151,894	$ 2,939,807
Less accumulated amortization	($ 1,371,000)	($ 1,247,000)
	$ 1,780,894	$ 1,692,807
Property and equipment	$118,701,947	$108,172,908
Less accumulated depreciation	($ 44,304,068)	($ 41,549,193)
	$ 74,397,879	$ 66,623,715
Total other assets	$ 76,178,773	$ 68,316,522
Total assets	$126,121,456	$114,953,243
Liabilities and Net Assets		
Current liabilities:		
Accounts payable and accrued expenses	$ 8,727,583	$ 3,769,078
Salaries, wages, and withholdings	$ 7,248,562	$ 5,893,249
Notes payable	$ 1,177,061	$ 10,000
Current maturities of long-term debt	$ 2,100,000	$ 2,300,000
Total current liabilities	$ 19,253,206	$ 11,972,327
Long-term debt, less current portion	$ 15,100,000	$ 17,200,000
Net assets, unrestricted	$ 91,768,250	$ 85,780,916
Total liabilities and net assets	$126,121,456	$114,953,243
Total beds	529	529

net assets of a non-profit organization must be compared and analyzed relative to the equity amounts reported for a particular investor-owned organization. In rare instances, where the relative amounts and composition of net assets are changing drastically, due to financial catastrophe or re-organization, then the analyst will need to fully understand all of the details associated with the components of net assets. Otherwise, just use the sub-totals shown as net assets in the ratio analyses described in this chapter.

The income statement shows the results of operations over a period of time. Revenues received and the expenses incurred to provide the revenues are netted against each other with the differences being net income or the famous "bottom line." Income statements can be prepared for any length of time (monthly, quarterly, etc.), but the typical time frame is one year. The balance sheet is related to the income statement, in that there would be a balance sheet prepared for the beginning and the ending dates of the income statement. The net income from the income statement would be reflected in the owner's equity section of the balance sheet as an addition or reduction, respectively, based on a positive or negative net income (net loss).

Income statements prepared in accordance with GAAP must use the accrual basis of accounting. Under the accrual concept the focus is on when the revenues are earned with the expenses accrued on a matching basis; not when the cash is received or paid out. A sample income statement is shown in *Exhibit 11–2*.

The AICPA's *Audit and Accounting Guide: Health Care Organizations, 1996* also clarifies the distinction between performance indicators on the income statement and other transactions that may be non-recurring or of such special nature that they should not be combined with the results of normal operations. The statement of operations for non-profit healthcare organizations should include a performance indicator, which we have referred to above as the "bottom line," that reports the results of operations. This is such an important indicator that it is included in many of the ratios described later in this chapter. The performance indicator may be called "revenues over expenses," "revenues and gains over expenses and losses," "operating income," "unrestricted net assets," or another similar label. We use the term "excess of revenues over expenses" as the primary performance indicator.

The following items, which usually represent changes in net assets, should be reported separately from the primary performance indicator:

- transactions with owners (acting as owners)
- equity transfers (with related organizations that may be controlled by or under common control of the reporting entity
- restricted contributions
- contributions of long-lived assets

Exhibit 11–2
Sample Hospital
Statement of Operations
for the year Jan 1 thru Dec 31

	19X9	19X8
Unrestricted revenues, gains, and other support:		
Net patient service revenue	$147,651,713	$132,376,986
Other operating revenue	1,907,390	1,878,059
Total revenues, gains, and other support	149,559,103	134,255,045
Operating Expenses		
Salaries and wages	71,188,228	65,662,968
Employee benefits	11,520,087	9,300,574
Physician and other professional fees	3,893,032	3,364,884
Supplies	24,285,494	22,810,454
Repairs and maintenance	2,249,573	2,136,898
Utilities	2,302,258	2,218,834
Insurance	2,869,367	2,644,094
Provision for bad debts	1,955,000	1,530,000
Interest	1,277,678	1,404,279
Depreciation	8,495,806	7,706,048
Other	8,832,262	7,142,982
Total operating expenses	138,868,785	125,921,993
Operating income	10,690,318	8,333,052
Investment income	1,317,182	1,401,179
Increase in unrestricted net assets	$ 12,007,500	$ 9,734,231

- assets released from donor restrictions
- unrealized gains and losses on investments
- investment returns on restricted assets
- other items that must be separately reported under GAAP (such as extraordinary items, effects of discontinued operations, or the cumulative effect of accounting changes)

Other changes in accrual accounting requirements affecting the income statement include the requirement that patient service revenue be reported after deducting (*net* of) provisions for contractual and other adjustments. Patient service revenue does *not* include charity care. Information about charity care should be shown in the notes. Significant revenue earned through capitation contracts and other arrangements must be shown separately in the statement of operations.

The major difference that will affect our analysis of the income statement is the inclusion of investment income as a separate category of income, shown below expenses on the income statement. Alternatively, some non-profit healthcare organizations might include such investment income in the unrestricted revenue section in the top section of the income statement. Where such differences occur, the revenue sections will not be directly comparable, unless the analyst makes an adjustment to include such investment income as part of revenues in all cases. In other words, the analyst must make sure that comparable disclosures and definitions have been used in all of the financial statements. In general, we assume and prefer that investment income that is of a normal and recurring nature should be reported as part of unrestricted revenues in the top section of the income statement.

A third financial statement that is required by GAAP is the statement of cash flows. This statement uses data from the balance sheet and income statement to provide information on determining the cash flow of the organization resulting from providing services, investing decisions, and financing decisions for the time frame covered by the financial statements.

The statement of cash flows is an important indicator of financial solvency. This statement separates the effects of normal operating activities from financing and investing activities. In other words, the effects of three major strategies and determinants of fiscal success are separated and shown in terms of their cash flow impact. This statement has only recently been required in external financial statements, but its impact will be significant for the analyst and the manager.

The statement of cash flows often appears in a variety of formats, depending on the methods that have been used to prepare the statement. These methods are called the direct or indirect method. Regardless of method used, the most important liquidity indicator on the statement of cash flows is the first subtotal shown, which is usually called cash provided by operating activities. Changes in this subtotal are an important indicator of continuing liquidity.

Since the cash flow statement may be prepared under either the direct or indirect method, analysts must be able to extract the most useful information from either format. While the direct method *(Exhibit 11–3A)* is more useful and easier to understand, common practice is to use the indirect method. For our purposes, we will focus on the first major subtotal shown on the statement of cash flows, which is almost always called "cash provided by operating activities" (CPOA). This important subtotal is identical under either reporting method, as is the remainder of the cash flow statement following this subtotal. We illustrate the first section of the indirct method in *Exhibit 11–3B*. Note that *Exhibits 11–3A* and *11–3B* both show the same "net cash provided by operating activities" of $16,577,474 (year 19x9). By focusing on the cash provided by operating activities (CPOA), the analyst can best understand and analyze the important trends in operating activities that affect cash flows. The analyst will, thereby, avoid most of the accounting intricacies and

Exhibit 11–3A
Sample Hospital
Statement of cash flows (direct method)
for the year Jan 1 thru Dec 31

	19X9	19X8
Cash flows from operating activities:		
Cash received from patients and third-party payers	$ 138,890,327	$ 131,705,045
Cash paid to employees & suppliers	(121,500,142)	(110,566,928)
Interest received	52,170	37,901
Receipts from other operating activities	1,776,797	1,771,010
Malpractice settlements paid	(1,364,000)	(1,742,000)
Interest paid	(1,277,678)	(1,404,279)
Net cash provided by operating activities	$ 16,577,474	$ 19,800,749
Cash flows from investing activities:		
Additions to property and equipment, net	($ 16,269,970)	($ 14,578,694)
Donations restricted for purchase of hospice supplies	38,410	38,289
Computer software acquired	(442,396)	(718,037)
Transfer of assets limited as to use	7,984,458	4,845,403
Net cash used in investing activities	($ 8,689,498)	($ 10,413,039)
Financing activities:		
Payments on long-term debt	($ 2,300,000)	($ 2,300,000)
Transfers to affiliates	(5,356,252)	(6,558,673)
Capitalization of bond financing costs	(80,968)	
Net cash used in financing activities	($ 7,636,252)	($ 8,858,673)
Net increase in cash and cash equivalents	$ 251,724	$ 529,037
Cash and cash equivalents, beginning of year	$ 1,070,600	$ 541,563
Cash and cash equivalents, end of year	$ 1,322,324	$ 1,070,600

banalities that differentiate the two reporting methods. The user need not be confused by these differences in methods as the important subtotals are the same under either method.

Other subtotals are also calculated for investing and financing activities. Financing activities include the proceeds from new debt or new issues of capital stock, cash used to repay debt, cash used to acquire the organization's own capital stock, and other sources or uses of capital resources. Investing activities include the purchase or sale of fixed assets, the purchase or sale of other long-term investments, and interest and dividends

Exhibit 11–3B
Sample Hospital
(Partial) Statement of cash flows (indirect method)
for the year Jan 1 thru Dec 31

	19X9	19X8
Cash flows from operating activities:		
Change in net assets	$12,007,500	$ 9,734,231
Depreciation and amortization	$ 8,996,891	$ 8,158,438
Increase (decrease) in accrual for professional liability expense	($ 803,292)	$ 573,765
Decrease (increase) in inventories, prepaid expenses, & other current assets	($ 485,926)	$ 6,559,225
Decrease (increase) in patient accounts receivable	($12,507,770)	($ 5,573,550)
Provision for bad debts	$ 1,955,000	$ 1,530,000
Increase (decrease) in accounts payable, accrued expenses, and the accrual for salaries, wages, and related withholdings	$ 6,313,818	($ 1,191,360)
Increase in notes payable	$ 1,167,061	$ 10,000
Increase in other assets	($ 65,808)	
Net cash provided by operating activities	$16,577,474	$19,800,749

that may have been earned on long-term investments. Some healthcare providers will, undoubtedly, adopt their own classification criteria for certain transactions to be included in each category. Regardless of these definitional issues, it is the trends in each category, in the three subtotals that are important indicators of liquidity. A sample cash flow statement is shown in *Exhibit 11–3A*.

Many non-profit organizations will also include a fourth financial statement called a Statement of Changes in Net Assets. Some organizations will include information about changes in net assets at the bottom of the Statement of Operations (income statement). This information is essentially a reconciliation of the net assets at the beginning of the year and the end of the year. It shows the significant changes and transactions that affect net assets. Only rarely will this information be germane to the financial analyses described in this text. The information needed for computing the ratios described in this chapter can generally be found in the other three statements or the notes. Therefore, we do not illustrate or discuss further the Statement of Changes in Net Assets.

Types of ratio comparisons

In order to evaluate the financial statements of a healthcare provider, some type of criterion must be established. One possible criterion might be comparing a specific ratio of one provider with the same ratio of another firm in the same industry, at the same point in time. When data permits, the comparison of a specific ratio from one provider, with the same ratio from a large number of providers in the same industry should be made. This use of industry standards provides a benchmark to evaluate the ratios of a specific provider in terms of industry wide conditions. It does not say whether the industry as a whole is financially solvent or in distress. Whether a specific ratio is favorable or unfavorable depends on the circumstances of the provider being evaluated. However, industry wide standards can be the starting reference for analysis.

A second type of evaluation, which provides valuable information, is determining the trend in the ratio values. For example, a provider might decide that the average collection period of 45 days is within an acceptable range. However, comparing this figure with the average collection period from previous time periods might lead management to examine why the value has increased from 25 days two years ago, to 32 days last year, and now to 45 days, which would usually be considered a negative trend. This trend might indicate that unless some action is taken, the days may continue to increase, which would indicate increasing amounts of capital are being invested in accounts receivables. Increasing days could be a sign of problems in the payer mix or credit problems which would require management attention.

On the other hand, with an HMO, an increasing collection period might mean that a greater proportion of total enrollees is made up of federal employees or large companies (which are notorious for slow payment). An increasing ratio under these conditions may not be unfavorable. Time series analysis permits the comparison of a financial indicator with the same financial indicator (for the same provider) at different points in time. In this way trends can be identified for management action.

Another caution must be noted before calculating ratios that use balance sheet data. The financial manager must be aware of significant changes in the structure of the balance sheet from the beginning of the year to the end of the year. If a merger has been consummated, if a large debt issue has been floated, or if other changes in financing or operating policies have occurred, the ending balance sheet is likely to be drastically different from the beginning of the year. The financial manager must assess whether an average from two balance sheets must be taken before calculating the necessary ratios. In some cases, an average or a weighted average (based on months) may be required. If the differences are immaterial, the end-of-year balance sheet may be the best indicator of future expectations. If so, no adjustments or averages are required. To illustrate the calculation of various ratios in this chapter, the assumption is made that no averages are required. Consequently, the ending balance sheet data are used to calculate the ratios.

Users of ratio analysis

There are many parties interested in the financial performance of health-care organizations. Interested parties have been referred to as stakeholders, in that their own interest is related to that of the healthcare organization. For example, stakeholders include: bankers, boards of directors, bond-holders, employees, employers, hospitals, insurance companies, invest-ment analysts, management, owners, physicians, regulators, researchers, stockbrokers, suppliers, and any other firm or individual who has an inter-est in the organization.

The type of financial information a stakeholder is interested in receiv-ing depends on the type of relationship that the party has with the organi-zation. For instance, a provider which provides supplies to a staff model HMO is concerned primarily with the short-term ability of the HMO to pay their bills. On the other hand, stockholders in an organization are concerned with the long-term ability of the provider to earn profits and grow sufficiently to earn at least their required rate of return. The orien-tation of banks will depend on whether they are suppliers of short-term funds, or long-term loans. If the bank provides a short-term line of credit, they would be concerned about short-term ability to generate cash. If the bank had provided a ten-year loan, the focus would be on profitability and long-term ability to generate sufficient cash to repay the principal and short-term cash to pay the interest. Regulators are primarily concerned with the ability of the provider to deliver the services they promised to their defined beneficiaries. This requires that the firm be able to pay their bills and stay in existence. This is especially true in the case of HMOs—if an HMO goes bankrupt, who pays for the healthcare services already provided to enrollees? However, it should be stressed that payers (Medi-care, employers, etc.) are not only concerned with the financial solvency of the firm, but also with the quality of services provided and with the efficiency with which the services are provided. Different management reports are required for this type of information.

The varying needs of the stakeholders must all be met if the orga-nization is to provide quality health services, have the support of its em-ployees, meet the needs of the community, and secure necessary funding. Information must, therefore, be available to each of these groups in order to meet their diverse needs. The financial statements are the most com-mon (and often the only) source of financial information available that is provided on a timely basis in a consistent format.

Categories of financial indicators

Financial indicators are designed to provide different types of informa-tion, which, when taken together, provide a financial assessment of an organization—past, present, and future. The categories of financial indicators include:

1. Liquidity
2. Profitability
3. Capital structure
4. Activity/efficiency
5. Other

Liquidity

Liquidity indicators provide an indication of the ability of the firm to pay off their currently maturing liabilities with currently available resources. They provide information on how the firm is managing its current assets and liabilities. The inability to meet short-term liabilities can result in reduced capability to provide quality health services.

The primary liquidity indicators are:

1. Current Ratio: $\dfrac{current\ assets}{current\ liabilities}$

   The current ratio represents the number of times short-term obligations can be met from short-term assets. It indicates a margin of safety for short-term creditors. Normally, a value of less than one has been assumed to be an indicator of potential financial distress. As the value of this ratio increases, there is lesser risk of insolvency. However, if the value becomes too large, inefficiency in the use of current assets may exist since current resources are not being matched with current needs. A current ratio in excess of what is necessary to provide adequate liquidity indicates excess investments in current assets which typically earn less than long-term investments. What constitutes an adequate current ratio will be different from one type of provider to another. Comparisons must be made to the industry norms and to comparable data for organizations with similar size, services, financial structure, and political environment. For example, a county health department and a university teaching hospital may both operate with almost no current assets, because in one case, the county treasurer pays all the bills, and in the second, the university pays all the bills and manages all the cash. In this case, the current ratio could be almost zero. Current ratios in these cases indicate nothing about the healthcare organization's ability to pay its bills. Many HMOs are able to manage effectively with a low current ratio because of the prepaid nature and predictability of monthly cash flow.

2. Quick Ratio: $\dfrac{cash\ and\ cash\ equivalents + accounts\ receivable}{current\ liabilities}$

   The quick ratio indicator uses the most liquid of the current assets to indicate a shorter term liquidity position. The quick ratio is by definition going to be less than the current ratio, because inventory and other current assets are not included in the calculation. Since the amount of investment in inventory is relatively unimportant to IPA and group model HMOs, this indicator is generally not calculated for these types of healthcare organizations. When calculating this ratio it should be recognized that organizations have many different collection procedures, relative to that of other organizations, and thereby distort the quick ratio. Consequently, outdated accounts that have a low probability of being collected should be eliminated. For example, accounts receivable over 120 days typically have a low probability of being collected unless frequent contact is maintained with the debtor.

3. Days Cash on Hand: $\dfrac{cash\ and\ cash\ equivalents}{cash\ operating\ expense/365}$

The days cash on hand is a measure of solvency associated with liquidity. It directly measures the number of days which an organization could pay their cash operating expenses if none of the accounts receivable were collected. This indicator does provide a measure of the ability of the organization to meet short-term cash shortfalls. This is a dynamic measure that converts liquidity ratios to the minimal survival period. A ratio expressed in terms of days is often easier to understand and convert into operating decisions. The manager can quickly see how critical the decision needs are and what period of time is available before results must occur. This type of margin of safety is a very important managerial indicator.

Profitability ratios

One of the main themes of this text is that unrestricted net assets in a health services organization are necessary to continue providing quality healthcare. The total financial requirements of any viable and adaptive financial organization include funds for growth, new programs, working capital needs, and replacement of equipment. As shown in chapter 1, healthcare organizations can grow and survive only when revenues exceed expenses.

The equity section of a non-profit, tax-exempt organization consists of "restricted and unrestricted net assets." The corresponding term for an investor-owned, or proprietary, organization is called "owners' equity" or "shareholders' equity." The generic term for equity in any organization is "net assets," while many of the following ratios are presented in terms of a tax-exempt organization; investor-owned organizations may simply delete the term "unrestricted" *or* insert the term "shareholders' equity." Similarly, where the term "increase in unrestricted net assets" denotes an increase in net assets for a tax-exempt organization, the term "net income" represents an increase in owners' equity for investor-owned organizations. Therefore, the analyst can use net income to replace an increase in unrestricted net assets in many of the ratios described below.

Profitability indicators are measures of the extent to which the organization is using its financial and physical assets to generate a profit. Profit ratios can be expressed in many different ways depending on the amount of capital furnished by the stakeholders of the organization.

The most common examples of profitability indicators are:

1. Return on Net Assets: $\dfrac{increase\ in\ unrestricted\ net\ assets}{unrestricted\ net\ assets}$

The return on net assets (ratio) indicates the extent to which the fiduciary responsibility to the owners of the organization is being met. The numerator (increase in unrestricted net assets) shown on the statement of operations indicates the resources remaining after all expenses have been paid for the current operating period, while the denominator indicates the resources attributed to owners or community control. The term "ownership" in this case is appropriate for both investor-owned (the shareholder) and tax exempt organizations (the community), since a fiduciary responsibility exists in both cases. If the return on the net assets is not high enough, suppliers of capital will consider placing their resources in alternative investments. For tax exempt entities this indicator provides a measure of assurance to the community, religious order, or other exempt entity, that resources are being used in a fiscally sound manner. A low return on net assets can be increased by either increasing revenues or decreasing expenses, or by decreasing the amount of unrestricted net assets while maintaining the same level of revenues and expenses.

2. Return on Assets: $\dfrac{increase\ in\ unrestricted\ net\ assets}{total\ assets}$

This profitability measure indicates the extent to which the assets of the organization are being used to generate increases in unrestricted net assets. The return on assets ratio indicates how efficiently assets are being used in making resources available for future financial requirements. An increase in return on assets will result in an increase in the return on equity (for the same financing structure). The return on assets can be increased by either increasing net assets or decreasing the size of the organization's assets.

3. Operating Profit Margin: $\dfrac{operating\ income}{total\ revenues}$

Operating profit margin is based on the excess of revenues over expenses from the primary patient care operations of the organization. The operating profit margin indicates the percentage of each dollar of operating revenues that are available for future financial requirements. Operating profit margin can be improved by either increasing operating revenues or decreasing operating expenses. Operating revenues can be increased by either increasing charges (as long as volume does not decrease by any significant amount), increasing volume (through marketing or other activities), or by changing the payer mix to include a larger proportion of charge-based patients.

Generally accepted accounting principles require that only net revenues be shown on the income statement with bad debt expense being shown as an expense instead of a deduction from revenues. Charity care and other deductions from revenues can be shown in the footnotes to the financial statements as needed for adequate disclosure.

4. Profit Margin: $\dfrac{\textit{increase in unrestricted net assets}}{\textit{total revenues}}$

   $or \quad \dfrac{\textit{net income}}{\textit{total revenues}}$

The profit margin goes beyond the operating margin to include all other sources of income and expenses. This includes nonoperating revenues provided by other activities such as an apartment rental, interest income, and other unrelated business, etc. Other sources of income are becoming more important to health service organizations since cost containment efforts are placing increasing constraints on operating income.

5. Prefinancing Return on Assets: $\dfrac{\textit{increase in net assets} + \textit{interest} \,(1 - \textit{tax rate})}{\textit{total assets}}$

This ratio is indicative of the return on all assets, or on all sources of capital, before deducting interest (or other financing costs). Thus, it is an operating profitability measure ignoring the methods of financing. For a taxable entity interest must be shown "net of tax" effects. This ratio can be compared with the organization's average interest costs (interest expense ÷ long-term debt). In the event that average interest costs exceed this ratio, financial theory states that negative leverage exists. Negative leverage indicates that the community or the organization is borrowing funds and investing it at lower rates than the interest cost.

Capital structure

The capitalization ratios indicate how the healthcare organization's assets have been financed. They indicate the mix of internal and external sources of capital in the capital structure of the healthcare organization. Capital ratios are risk measures indicating the degree of flexibility an organization might have when desiring to raise capital. These ratios fall into two categories—composition and coverage. Composition ratios indicate the amount of financing which has been received from alternative forms of capital financing, while the coverage ratios indicate the extent to which cash flows and operating income are sufficient to meet the financial requirements of the capital sources. It is conventional financial management wisdom that current assets should be financed from current liabilities, and fixed assets should be financed with long-term or equity sources of capital. Long-term debt sources are expected to be repaid from net assets generated by the organization or by obtaining new capital. Large amounts of debt in a capital structure and a low profit margin can make it difficult to borrow if additional financing is needed.

Capital structure, or capital composition ratios indicate the relative proportions of financing from each source of capital financing. These ratios are derived from the vertical analysis of the right-hand side of the balance sheet. They indicate the percentages of debt financing from various sources and the percentages of financing from equity sources. They can be as complex or aggregative as is needed for the analysis. Our recommendation is to include at least five major categories of capital financing:

1. Current liabilities
2. Long-term debt
3. Deferred taxes and other deferred liabilities
4. Unrestricted net assets
5. Restricted net assets

Each of these sources of capital financing would be related to the total balance sheet resources or claims against resources. In other words, the capital composition ratios show the percentage that each of these five categories represent of the entire set of capital claims (right-hand side). An equivalent calculation would be to calculate each of these percentages as a percent of total assets (left-hand side). In fact, the second category above is exactly equivalent to the "Debt to Total Assets" ratio.

These capital composition ratios must sum to 100 percent because they include all capital sources on the balance sheet. If they do not sum to 100 percent, then an error of omission may have occurred in the event that some form of capital has been omitted. Alternatively, a calculation error may have occurred, such as using the incorrect denominator.

Other examples of commonly used capital ratios include:

1. Debt to Unrestricted Net Assets: $\dfrac{total\ debt}{unrestricted\ net\ assets}$

Total debt includes both short-term liabilities and long-term debt. It indicates the extent to which the assets of the organization are financed with borrowed money. Unrestricted net assets represent the amount of funding from the owners of the organization. It is equal to total assets minus total debt. The greater proportion of debt in the capital structure the greater the financial risk to the organization since debt suppliers of capital require interest and principal payments at stated intervals. If the required payments are not paid, the debt suppliers can force the organization into bankruptcy. Suppliers of equity capital do not have these same rights and in addition receive a return of their investment only after all debt suppliers are satisfied. While this ratio is often used by investment bankers, the more detailed information provided by the five capital composition ratios is more complete.

2. Unrestricted Net Assets to Total Assets: $\dfrac{\textit{unrestricted net assets}}{\textit{total assets}}$

$$or \quad \frac{\textit{shareholders' equity}}{\textit{total assets}}$$

This measure is based on the capital composition ratios calculated earlier. It shows the ratio of financing provided unrestricted net assets relative to the total amount needed to support all the assets. It can be calculated separately, or it can be obtained from the subtotals shown as part of the capital composition ratios. This ratio is useful in showing the portion of financing not provided by creditors. It is usually complementary to the next ratio shown below (number 3) as these two ratios must sum to 100 percent. Once one has been calculated, the other can be calculated by subtracting it from 100 percent. This ratio is also used in the "Dupont" ratios described later in this chapter. It can also be called a net assets financing ratio or an "equity multiplier."

3. Debt to Total Assets: $\dfrac{\textit{total debt}}{\textit{total assets}}$

This measure indicates the percentage of debt used to finance the assets of the organization. The higher the percentage, the more risk in becoming insolvent and the less flexibility in meeting future financial needs of the organization. Debt ratios above 50 percent are considered to be very risky for most healthcare providers. This 50 percent level would be equal to the 100 percent result calculated earlier for Ratio number 1. Because of the increased risk involved with higher debt levels, the interest rate paid to all suppliers of capital has become higher, resulting in increased costs of healthcare to the community. As shown above, the debt ratio is complementary to Ratio number 2.

4. Times Interest Earned: $\dfrac{\textit{increase in unrestricted net assets} + \textit{interest expense}}{\textit{interest expense}}$

$$or \quad \frac{\textit{net income} + \textit{interest expense}}{\textit{interest expense}}$$

This is the primary coverage ratio. It determines the number of times that the organization can pay its current interest expenses.

Since short-term liabilities are usually noninterest bearing debt, this is primarily a measure of the ability of the organization to pay the debt service on long-term liabilities. A ratio of 1.0 indicates that the firm is in a high-risk position since there is no safety margin in paying the interest expense. It is important to use this ratio to determine the extent to which revenues can decrease or expenses can increase before the organization is in danger of technical insolvency (an inability to pay their interest expense). The lower this ratio, the more difficult it will be for the organization to borrow funds should the need arise even when the organization may have a low debt to equity ratio. This convention points to the necessity of using more than one ratio to evaluate the financial position of any organization.

5. Fixed Charges Coverage:

$$\frac{cash\ provided\ by\ operating\ activities\ (CPOA)}{interest\ payments + principal\ payments + other\ fixed\ charges}$$

This ratio meets objectives similar to the previous ratio except it includes repayment of the loan principal amounts, and it is based on CPOA. Thus, it is a somewhat broader measure of risk than the times interest earned ratio. The denominator of this ratio should also include any other fixed financing expenses such as noncancelable lease payments, payments for debt retirement, sinking funds, etc. In particular, capitalized lease payments (discussed in chapter 12) must be included in the denominator of this ratio since leasing is basically another form of permanent financing.

6. Cash Flow to Total Debt: $\dfrac{cash\ provided\ by\ operating\ activities}{total\ debt}$

This ratio uses cash flow to examine the risk associated with debt financing. The focus of this ratio is on cash flows, not accounting flows of revenues and expenses. It measures the cash generated by operating activities relative to debt. Lenders will prefer a higher ratio.

7. Cash Return on Assets:

$$\frac{cash\ provided\ by\ operating\ activities + interest\ expense}{total\ assets}$$

Cash return on assets measures management's success in using the organization's assets to generate cash flows from operations. Since CPOA is used to "grow" and "sustain" the organization, a high ratio is desirable. Interest expense is added to CPOA in the numerator in order to neutralize the effects of different patterns of debt financing. This adjustment creates a "level playing field" similar to the adjustments made in the prefinancing return on assets ratio shown earlier. For a taxable entity, a similar adjustment must be made by multiplying the interest expense by a tax adjustment factor (1 – tax rate). Since interest payments are deducted in determining the CPOA, they must be added back.

8. Quality of Income: $\dfrac{\textit{cash provided by operating activities} + \textit{interest expense}}{\textit{increase in unrestricted net assets}}$

or $\dfrac{\textit{cash provided by operating activities} + \textit{interest expense}}{\textit{net income}}$

This ratio indicates how the operating results (revenues and expenses) have been realized in cash. Often this ratio exceeds 100 percent as depreciation has been deducted from the denominator, but not from the numerator. It is related to the following ratio which examines how revenues are realized in cash.

9. Quality of Revenue: $\dfrac{\textit{cash received from patients and providers}}{\textit{total revenues}}$

It is desirable to realize most, if not all, revenues in cash payments from patients and providers and other payers. This assures that the organization's revenue objectives have been met and that investments in accounts receivable are minimized. This ratio is particularly useful in identifying instances where particularly liberal or "soft" revenue recognition policies may have been adopted. In both cases, the quality of revenue ratio may decline over several years. This ratio also reflects the organization's ability to collect cash from its clients. Note that the numerator of this ratio is shown on the cash flow statement prepared under the direct method. However, under the indirect method, it must often be estimated.

Capital structure ratios are important to the evaluation of the financial risk position of any organization. Potential creditors and other stakeholders are concerned with the ability of the organization to repay its debt obligations. However, no single category of ratios may be calculated and evaluated independently of other related ratios. It is important to recognize that capitalization and the effectiveness of the capital structure must be evaluated in terms of the ratios in this chapter that relate to the ability to generate funds and meet financial obligations as they become due.

Activity/efficiency ratios

Activity ratios are often referred to as turnover ratios. These indicators measure the effectiveness of management in using the assets of the organization to provide services, generate revenues, and provide profits. They are often expressed as turnover ratios as they relate the amount of revenue generated as a function of the resources utilized to provide services. The effective manager will attempt to optimize turnover ratios. For example, high turnover ratios may indicate that sufficient resources are not available to provide quality service and shortages are occurring too often. Conversely, low turnover ratios may indicate that too many resources are tied up in particular assets. With higher turnover ratios, the average investment will be lower for a specific group of assets. From a financial standpoint, this indicates fewer resources are being used to generate the revenues.

To summarize, asset turnover ratios indicate the degree of utilization of the organization's assets to generate revenues. A high ratio indicates more revenues per dollar of assets and a higher degree of utilization. A low turnover ratio may indicate that the organization has overinvested in particular assets and has excess capacity.

Most managers find that turnover is one of the more significant factors that can be affected by managerial decisions. Asset turnover in hospitals, staff-model HMOs, or in any capital intensive organization, will probably be lower than corresponding ratios for labor intensive firms. In contrast, turnover ratios for public health departments, clinics, professional service departments or organizations, and IPA or group model HMOs will probably be quite high since the amount of investment in fixed assets is relatively low. Turnover is directly related to the capital intensity required to support the activity. It is the manager's responsibility to balance an increasing need for more capital inputs with the organization's objective of providing quality healthcare services at a reasonable cost.

The primary activity ratios are:

1. Total Asset Turnover: $\dfrac{total\ revenues}{total\ assets}$

   Total asset turnover indicates how many dollars of revenues are generated for each dollar of assets used to meet the healthcare organization's goals. Normally, the higher the ratio the more effective the organization is in using its assets. Low values may indicate over investment in assets, or an inability to generate revenues through utilization. Since current assets are included in this ratio, the composition of the assets is important. This ratio is more valuable for hospitals, long-term care organizations, and staff model health maintenance organizations, than for home health, IPA, and group model HMOs due to the nature of the organizations. Improvements in this ratio can occur through increasing revenues (while maintaining utilization), increasing the number of enrollees, or decreasing the amount of assets. Elimination of obsolete plant and equipment will also improve this ratio as the investment in assets is reduced, therefore the average age of the plant, discussed under "Other indicators," should be considered in the analysis.

2. Fixed Asset Turnover: $\dfrac{total\ revenues}{fixed\ assets}$

   This ratio differs from the total asset turnover in that now only fixed assets are considered. These are the assets which are most directly involved with providing the services which generate the revenues appearing in the numerator. A higher ratio is preferred to a lower one, and indicates a higher utilization rate of the fixed assets of the firm. Strategies for improving this ratio are the same as those discussed above relative to the total assets.

3. Days in Accounts Receivable: $\dfrac{accounts\ receivable}{total\ revenues/365}$

Days in accounts receivable provides a measure of efficiency in the collections function. For a hospital this indicator measures the number of days of services which have been billed but not yet collected. For an HMO this ratio indicates the number of days past the beginning of the month that have passed without receiving premiums due for the month, and is referred to as a premiums receivable ratio. This ratio can help identify problems with the clerical staff, follow-up past due bills, collection policies, payer mix, or it may be an indication of a credit policy which is too lax, either in specification or enforcement.

This ratio should be calculated separately for inpatient and outpatient components because the turnover rates and collection periods will usually differ markedly between these two major groups of patients. In addition, ratios should be calculated for each of the major payers:

1. Private pay
2. Medicare
3. Medicaid
4. Private insurance
5. Blue Cross/Shield
6. Other

Each of these payers can have unique processing requirements and payment schedules. Consequently, it is desirable to evaluate receivables from each major payer category separately.

4. Number of Days Inventory on Hand: $\dfrac{inventory}{supplies\ expense/365}$

The number of days inventory on hand indicates how long the organization could continue to provide health services if no additional shipments of inventory were received, or no replacement of supplies was made. A low value indicates an organization which may risk suffering out-of-stock situations as a result of transportation interruptions, weather problems, etc. Alternatively, a value which is too high may indicate a large investment in inventory (supplies) which could be better put to use elsewhere. Values outside of an acceptable range should raise a flag and be examined. Care must be taken to consider the composition of the inventory, since out-of-stock conditions might occur in a specific item when the number of days in total inventory on hand indicates little risk of a stockout position.

Other indicators

Other indicators, which do not logically fall into one of the other categories, include:

1. Average Age of Plant: $\dfrac{accumulated\ depreciation}{depreciation\ expense}$

   This is an important indicator of the financial age of the fixed assets of the organization. It provides important information regarding the ability of the organization to use the most recent technology, it provides information regarding the future need for capital resources for plant replacement, etc. The older the average age of plant, the greater will be the near term need for capital resources. Consideration must also be given to the impact of the average age of the plant on both the total asset turnover and the fixed asset turnover.

2. Price Level Adjusted Operating Margin:

   $$\dfrac{operating\ income + depreciation\ expense - (price\text{-}level\ adjusted\ depreciation\ expense)}{total\ revenues}$$

   This ratio is probably one of the most valuable in terms of evaluating the long-term profitability and viability of the organization. By adjusting depreciation expense according to inflation, an approximation to replacement costs is made, making the operating margin a more realistic figure. This ratio indicates "sustainable performance." Organizations which do not require a lot of capital equipment need not calculate this ratio, while hospitals, nursing homes, and staff model HMOs that own their hospitals find this a valuable addition to their set of evaluation indicators. An example of the methods used to calculate price-level adjusted depreciation expense is illustrated in *Appendix 11–4*.

3. Replacement Viability:

   $$\dfrac{resources\ available\ for\ plant\ replacement}{price\text{-}level\ adjusted\ accumulated\ depreciation \times (desired\ debt\text{-}asset\ ratio)}$$

   This indicator provides a measure of the number of dollars which the organization has available relative to the price-level adjusted plant replacement. Multiplication by the "desired" debt-asset ratio indicates that the organization's expectations regarding how required funds for plant replacement may be acquired through borrowed funds. This ratio should be adjusted to fit the individual organizational requirements and *desired* capital structure ratios. The figure in the numerator uses the amounts available in any funded depreciation accounts as the estimate of funds available for plant expansion or replacement.

Operating indicators or other performance indicators

Other performance ratios relate to average costs per unit of service or per unit of input factor. A unit of service refers to an output unit such as patient days, admissions, laboratory tests, member-months, visits, sessions, etc. An input factor refers to hours of labor service, numbers of full-time equivalent employees, pounds of laundry, surgical minutes, relative value units, costs per member per month (pmpm), resource utilization groups, etc. Average costs per unit of input factor are usually more easily attainable than costs per output unit of service. For example, the difficulties in using macro-measures such as patient days as the unit of output for hospitals is reflected in the failure to allow for intensity of care or services provided. Health planners and other regulatory agencies should be extremely cautious about evaluating the performance of health service organizations solely on the basis of measures which consider only aggregate output measures, which generally do not reflect intensity of care or services provided. Because of this, input factors are generally used by external agencies because they are easier to understand, and it is easier to demonstrate the effects of managerial decisions by using a set of input factor performance ratios. The differential effects of mix, volume, and prices are easier to separate for departments or responsibility centers if input factor performance ratios are used. However, it is important to stress that output measures must be developed to adequately evaluate management's performance in using resources to provide high-quality care. Product line measures will prove to be most useful in this regard.

Another problem that financial managers may encounter is how to select from the almost limitless set of input factor performance ratios that are available. The department level manager has a limited scope because he or she is usually concerned with only one or a few departments; however, many different input factor performance ratios can be regularly evaluated at the departmental level. At the upper levels of managerial responsibility and at the regulatory or governmental level, information overload can easily occur if all possible input factor performance rates are computed and reported. The problem is to limit one's search and review to input factor performance ratios that reflect the essential elements of organizational operations. Many ratios are redundant, and the financial manager usually has only enough time and energy to evaluate and utilize relevant, nonredundant information. Most managers develop an informal and intuitive heuristic to eliminate unnecessary input factor performance ratios. It is the purpose of this chapter to only indicate what some of those alternative ratios are. The essential point is that managers should use both judgment and prior results to eliminate unnecessary ratios.

Examples of input factor performance ratios are shown in *Exhibit 11–4*. This set of ratios is not meant to be exhaustive, and it should be noted that many departmental level ratios can be further segregated into fixed and

Exhibit 11–4
Examples of input performance ratios

The input factor ratios can be categorized into several groups:
a. Profitability
  1. Operating income per occupied bed
  2. Operating income per staffed bed
  3. Operating income per FTE nursing staff
b. Activity
  1. Occupied bed per FTE nursing staff
  2. Occupied bed per FTE LPN
  3. FTE RN per FTE LPN
  4. Lab tests per visit
c. Expense
  1. Salary expense per occupied bed
  2. Medical expense per member per month
  3. Administrative expense per member per month
  4. Laundry expense per pound
  5. Medical expense per member per month
  6. Administrative expense per member per month
d. Composition
  1. Salary expense to total operating expense
  2. Administrative expense to total operating expense
  3. Inpatient expense to total medical expense
  4. Outpatient expense to total medical expense
  5. Total assets per FTE employee

variable cost components. This separation is desirable whenever fixed costs are material in amount or significant to performance evaluation.

There are an infinite number of ratios that can be calculated. The ratios to be calculated should be considered in the context of the information to be gathered from the ratios' calculation and monitoring. Different sets of ratios have been developed for the analysis of different industries. *Appendix 11–1* contains an example of the ratios used by CHIPS; *Appendix 11–2* contains ratios developed for the evaluation of long-term care facilities; and *Appendix 11–3* includes indicators considered to be important in the evaluation of group practices and managed care organizations (primarily Health Maintenance Organizations).

Performance indicators for managed care organizations

The term "managed care" generally encompasses health maintenance organizations (HMOs), physician hospital organizations (PHOs), preferred provider organizations (PPOs), medical service organizations (MSOs), or any other capitated form of financing and/or delivering healthcare services. The list of possible options is continually expanding and the links between provider organizations will continue to evolve as alternative risk-sharing arrangements are designed. This section describes some of the basic terms associated with managed care and some of the primary financial indicators that must be evaluated for managed care organizations.

Managed care organizations receive premiums on a monthly or periodic basis from employers or individuals or other groups. The managed care organization generally pays the healthcare provider who provides care to an enrollee. Or, it may reimburse the enrollee directly. The managed care organization generally bears most of the risk associated with paying for services that are needed by enrollees. However, various incentive arrangements may be created that shift some of this risk to the enrollee or to the provider. Managed care organizations must earn a reasonable level of net income in order to survive and prosper. Consequently, many of the financial ratios described earlier that pertain to investor-owned organizations may also be used to evaluate managed care organizations.

Since managed care organizations bear much of the risk associated with the costs of healthcare provided to enrollees, some of the critical success factors that are important to managed care organizations include:

- insurance, risk assessment, and underwriting success
- marketing strategies (enrollment rates, retention rates, etc.)
- claims administration
- utilization review (preventive and acute services)
- contract negotiation
- referral networks (links to physicians)
- degree of reliance on capitation payments to providers
- degree of vertical and horizontal integration
- shift from inpatient to outpatient services
- accurate, timely, and useful information systems

Performance indicators could be designed in each of these areas. However, they are beyond the scope of this text. The most typical ratios and indicators that must be evaluated under managed care include the following:

1. Estimated costs per member per month *(pmpm)* under capitation:

   (expected enrollee visits per year) × *(cost per visit)* / 12

   Determining each factor in this equation is not easy and it relies on a variety of utilization and cost parameters. Physicians and payers each make their own estimates of expected utilization on an annual basis for the enrollees. Each would also estimate the cost per visit, using a variety of historical data from comparable providers and from the provider itself.

   Note that the cost drivers inherent in this relationship are very complex and involve annual salaries and other budget items necessary for providing healthcare services. They involve a variety of fixed and variable costs. They are dramatically impacted by the number of visits and other factors driving utilization (disease, prevention, etc.). They also involve payment rates negotiated between physicians, hospitals, and the managed care organization. In many cases, various maximums may limit the payments that are made, incentives will be created for certain desired referral patterns and prescribing behaviors, and "withholds" will be retained by the purchaser to ensure performance by the healthcare provider. In addition, various "risk pool" arrangements may be created such that a percentage of costs or a percentage of profits are split into predetermined portions for various parties to the transactions.

It is ironic to note that patients are often excluded from these risk pools, even though they most often have the biggest stake, and the most to lose, in a healthcare environment. The patients certainly bear most of the costs of learning how to work within the managed care network, which may involve additional waiting times, additional costs and risks associated with obtaining proper referrals, and the costs of evaluating multiple options under the intricate patterns of service relationships created within managed care networks.

In any event, the evaluation of a managed care organization must include an evaluation of how risk payments and incentives have been shared across a variety of participating interests. The nature of "withholds" and "holdbacks" must also be examined. Much of this data will not be reported in the typical financial statements, but can often be identified in the prospectus associated with an issue of capital stock or in other filings with governmental organizations (e.g., state insurance commissions, Medicare, etc.)

2. Utilization ratios (for enrollee groups, by type of service):

    Utilization rate per 1,000 members:

    inpatient discharges per year / number of member-months

    inpatient hospital days per year / number of member-months

    ambulatory visits (clinic, ER, etc.) per year / number of member-months

    These ratios are indicative of the range of utilization ratios that would be used in the numerator of the *pmpm* ratio described above (number 1). Trends in these utilization ratios will be one of the most important "early-warning" signals monitored by managers in managed care organizations.

3. Administrative (or non-physician) expense ratios:

    administrative expenses / total revenues

    or *administrative expenses / total expenses*

These ratios are used to monitor the administrative costs associated with managing the managed care organization. They can be categorized by type of contract or purchaser. Physician and other healthcare costs are excluded from the numerator.

Managed care organizations use several unique indicators of financial distress and solvency. These are in addition to the traditional indicators described above that are used by hospitals, nursing homes, and other healthcare organizations. The primary indicators are the administrative expense ratio, and the medical expense ratio, sometimes called the medical loss ratio. These ratios recognize that revenues can be used for only one of three purposes: medical expenses, administrative expenses, or profit. These ratios are calculated as follows:

Administrative Expense Ratio = administrative expenses / total revenues

Medical Expense Ratio = medical expenses / total revenues

Historically, managed care organizations want to keep the administrative expense ratio below 10 percent, although most fall into the 10 to 15 percent range. The medical expense ratio should be less than 80 percent. Whatever is left over after medical and administrative expenses is profit. The medical loss ratio for most managed care organizations has been increasing, primarily due to competition placing pressures on premiums. The administrative expense ratio is highly dependent on the managed care relationship with providers, with IPA models having the highest administrative expense ratios, and with staff models having the lowest administrative expense ratios.

The last area that should be mentioned is the difference in time periods used for managed care. Many of our previous ratios, discussed above, include terms for days cash on hand; average payment period and average collection period, expressed in days; and days inventory on hand. In managed care, the primary time period of emphasis is the month. Therefore, collection periods and payment periods are expressed as months. Likewise, any revenue and expense categories are expressed on a per member per month (pmpm) basis.

Premium Collection Period = premiums receivable / (total premium revenue/30)

Claim Payment Period = claims payable / (total medical expenses/30)

4. For a group practice or other physician-based provider, revenue per physician:

net revenues / number of FTE physicians

This ratio will indicate the revenue productivity of each physician (or full-time equivalent). It is useful in monitoring seasonal and annual trends in revenues associated with each physician provider.

A variety of other factors must also be monitored by managed care organizations. These include medical loss ratios, premiums receivable (which are much like other accounts receivable), claims payable timing and trends (which include many of the same issues as other accounts payable), claims payable period (how long after receiving services may a claim be submitted), and success indicators for various services and product lines. In this latter case, healthcare services are all becoming much more market-oriented, with a resultant interest in product line performance. Again, the scope of these product line ratios is beyond the scope of this chapter. Many more detailed examples of these ratios will be found in the appendices to this chapter. *(Appendix 11–1, 11–2, and 11–3).*

Comprehensive example

The financial statements for Sample Hospital are shown in *Exhibits 11–5 and 11–6.* Two years of data are given in order to provide for a comparison from one time period to the next. Examination of the individual ratio categories will proceed in the order in which they were presented in this chapter. Figures for 19x9 are calculated, while 19x8 figures are in parentheses.

In addition, a horizontal analysis and vertical analysis of each financial statement for Sample Hospital has also been presented. The vertical analysis indicates a percentage composition for each item in each column of the financial statement. For the balance sheet, the vertical analysis is based on total assets or total equities (either would give the same result). The ratios must sum to 100 percent in each column. For the income statement, the vertical analysis is based on net operating revenues.

The horizontal analysis is based on the percentage change from the earlier year to the next year (i.e., from 19x8 to 19x9). A horizontal analysis indicates the percentage increase from the base year to the next year. Negative percentages may be confusing in such comparisons. Also, when the base year number is quite small, the percentage of change will look inordinately large. Consequently, the horizontal analysis is often the least useful of these comparisons and is only used to spot changes that merit further investigation.

Liquidity indicators for Sample Hospital:

1. $Current\ Ratio = \dfrac{current\ assets}{current\ liabilities} = \dfrac{\$32,406,459}{\$19,253,206} = 1.68\ (1.78)$

2. $Quick\ Ratio = \dfrac{quick\ assets}{current\ liabilities} = \dfrac{\$25,967,621}{\$19,253,206} = 1.35\ (1.27)$

3. $Days\ Cash\ on\ Hand = \dfrac{cash + cash\ equivalents}{cash\ operating\ expense/365}$

$$= \dfrac{\$1,322,324}{\$351,830} = 3.76\ (3.35)$$

Exhibit 11–5A
Sample Hospital
Balance Sheet
Vertical analysis

	Dec 31, 19X9		Dec 31, 19X8	
Assets				
Current assets				
Cash and cash equivalents	$ 1,322,324	1.1%	$ 1,070,600	0.9%
Accounts receivable	24,645,297	19.5%	14,092,527	12.3%
(Less allowance for uncollectable accounts of $2,300,000 in 19X9 and $1,700,000 in 19X8)				
Inventories	2,549,676	2.0%	2,045,715	1.8%
Prepaid expenses	1,789,162	1.4%	1,807,197	1.5%
Assets limited as to use	2,100,000	1.7%	2,300,000	2.0%
Total current assets	32,406,459	25.7%	21,316,309	18.5%
Assets limited as to use				
Internally designated for capital acquisition	14,378,162	11.4%	20,577,341	17.9%
By trustee—self-insurance investments	2,413,303	1.9%	3,692,205	3.2%
By trustee—sinking-fund investments	2,844,759	2.3%	3,351,136	2.9%
Total	19,636,224	15.6%	27,620,682	24.0%
Less current portion	(2,100,000)	–1.7%	(2,300,000)	–2.0%
Total assets limited as to use	17,536,224	13.9%	25,320,682	22.0%
Other assets:				
Unamortized bond financing	3,151,894	2.5%	2,939,807	2.5%
Less accumulated amortization	(1,371,000)	–1.1%	(1,247,000)	–1.0%
	1,780,894	1.4%	1,692,807	1.5%
Property and equipment	118,701,947	94.1%	108,172,908	94.1%
Less accumulated depreciation	(44,304,068)	–35.1%	(41,549,193)	–36.1%
	74,397,879	59.0%	66,623,715	58.0%
Total other assets	76,178,773	60.4%	68,316,522	59.5%
Total assets	$126,121,456	100.0%	$114,953,243	100.0%
Liabilities and Net Assets				
Current liabilities				
Accounts payable and accrued expenses	$ 8,727,583	6.9%	$ 3,769,078	3.3%
Salaries, wages, and withholdings	7,248,562	5.8%	5,893,249	5.1%
Notes payable	1,177,061	0.9%	10,000	
Current maturities of long-term debt	2,100,000	1.7%	2,300,000	2.0%
Total current liabilities	19,253,206	15.3%	11,972,327	10.4%
Long-term debt, less current portion	15,100,000	12.0%	17,200,000	15.0%
Net assets, unrestricted	91,768,250	72.7%	85,780,916	74.6%
Total liabilities and net assets	$126,121,456	100.0%	$114,953,243	100.0%

Exhibit 11–5B
Sample Hospital
Balance Sheet
Horizontal analysis

	Dec 31, 19X9		Dec 31, 19X8
Assets			
Current assets:			
Cash and cash equivalents	$ 1,322,324	23.5%	$ 1,070,600
Accounts receivable	24,645,297	74.9%	14,092,527
(Less allowance for uncollectable accounts of $2,300,000 in 19X9 and $1,700,000 in 19X8)			
Inventories	2,549,676	24.6%	2,045,715
Prepaid expenses	1,789,162	−1.0%	1,807,197
Assets limited as to use	2,100,000	−8.7%	2,300,000
Total current assets	32,406,459	52.0%	21,316,039
Assets limited as to use			
Internally designated for capital acquisition	14,378,162	−30.1%	20,577,341
By trustee—self-insurance investments	2,413,303	−34.6%	3,692,205
By trustee—sinking-fund investments	2,844,759	−15.1%	3,351,136
Total	19,636,224	−28.9%	27,620,682
Less current portion	(2,100,000)	−8.7%	(2,300,000)
Total assets limited as to use	17,536,224	−30.7%	25,320,682
Other assets:			
Unamortized bond financing	3,151,894	7.2%	2,939,807
Less accumulated amortization	(1,371,000)	9.9%	(1,247,000)
	1,780,894	5.2%	1,692,807
Property and equipment	118,701,947	9.7%	108,172,908
Less accumulated depreciation	(44,304,068)	6.6%	(41,549,193)
	74,397,879	11.7%	66,623,715
Total other assets	76,178,773	11.5%	68,316,522
Total assets	$126,121,456	9.7%	$114,953,243
Liabilities and Net Assets			
Current liabilities:			
Accounts payable and accrued expenses	$ 8,727,583	131.6%	$ 3,769,078
Salaries, wages, and withholdings	7,248,562	23.0%	5,893,249
Notes payable	1,177,061	11770.6%	10,000
Current maturities of long-term debt	2,100,000	−8.7%	2,300,000
Total current liabilities	19,253,206	60.8%	11,972,327
Long-term debt, less current portion	15,100,000	−12.2%	17,200,000
Net assets, unrestricted	91,768,250	7.0%	85,780,916
Total liabilities and net assets	$126,121,456	9.7%	$114,953,243

Exhibit 11–6A
Sample Hospital
Statement of Operations
for the year Jan 1 thru Dec 31
Horizontal analysis

	19X9		19X8
Unrestricted revenues, gains, and other support:			
Net patient service revenue	147,651,713	11.5%	132,376,986
Other operating revenue	1,907,390	1.6%	1,878,059
Total revenues, gains, and other support	149,559,103	11.4%	134,255,045
Operating expenses			
Salaries and wages	71,188,228	8.4%	65,662,968
Employee benefits	11,520,087	23.9%	9,300,574
Physician and other professional fees	3,893,032	15.7%	3,364,884
Supplies	24,285,494	6.5%	22,810,454
Repairs and maintenance	2,249,573	5.3%	2,136,898
Utilities	2,302,258	3.8%	2,218,834
Insurance	2,869,367	8.5%	2,644,094
Provision for bad debts	1,955,000	35.3%	1,530,000
Interest	1,277,678	–9.0%	1,404,279
Depreciation	8,495,806	10.2%	7,706,048
Other	8,832,262	23.7%	7,142,982
Total operating expenses	138,868,785	10.4%	125,921,993
Operating income	10,690,318	28.3%	8,333,052
Investment income	1,317,182	–6.0%	1,401,179
Increase in unrestricted net assets	$ 12,007,500	23.4%	$ 9,734,231

The liquidity indicators lead to the conclusion that Sample Hospital has sufficient current assets to pay off the currently maturing liabilities during the next twelve months. The quick ratio indicates that even if no further services are performed, and the organization is forced to live off of their cash and accounts receivable collections, they could still pay their current liabilities. The days cash on hand ratio indicates that a slowdown in the collection of accounts receivable could cause difficulties. It is important to remember that a slowdown in collections could come about for any number of reasons—change in payer mix, increasing average length of stay, clerical staffing problems, a nursing strike, a postal strike, change in

Exhibit 11–6B
Sample Hospital
Statement of Operations
for the year Jan 1 thru Dec 31
Vertical analysis

	19X9		19X8	
Unrestricted revenues, gains, and other support:				
Net patient service revenue	147,651,713	98.7%	132,376,986	98.6%
Other operating revenues	1,907,390	1.3%	1,878,059	1.4%
Total revenues, gains, and other support	149,559,103	100.0%	134,255,045	100.0%
Operating expenses				
Salaries and wages	71,188,228	47.6%	65,662,968	48.9%
Employee benefits	11,520,087	7.7%	9,300,574	6.9%
Physician and other professional fees	3,893,032	2.6%	3,364,884	2.5%
Supplies	24,285,494	16.2%	22,810,454	17.0%
Repairs and maintenance	2,249,573	1.5%	2,136,898	1.7%
Utilities	2,302,258	1.5%	2,218,834	1.7%
Insurance	2,869,367	1.9%	2,644,094	2.0%
Provision for bad debts	1,955,000	1.3%	1,530,000	1.1%
Interest	1,277,678	0.9%	1,404,279	1.0%
Depreciation	8,495,806	5.7%	7,706,048	5.7%
Other	8,832,262	5.9%	7,142,982	5.3%
Total operating expense	138,868,785	92.8%	125,921,993	93.8%
Operating income	10,690,318	7.2%	8,333,052	6.2%
Investment income	1,317,182	0.8%	1,401,179	1.0%
Increase in unrestricted net assets	$ 12,007,500	8.0%	$ 9,734,231	7.2%

Federal Medicare policies, Federal cash flow difficulties, etc. The days cash on hand indicator may indicate potential problems for Sample Hospital, and perhaps should be lengthened. Since the current ratio has decreased while the quick ratio has increased from 19x8 to 19x9, this would indicate that the composition of the current assets has changed, and should be examined.

The second column presented with the financial data presents the composition ratios, or proportions of different categories making up the whole. For example, the composition ratios for current assets are as follows:

	19X9	19X8
Cash	4.08%	5.02%
Accounts receivable, net	76.05%	66.11%
Inventories	7.87%	9.60%
Prepaid expenses	5.52%	8.48%
Current portion of assets whose use is limited	6.48%	10.79%
	100.00%	100.00%

These proportions add up to 100 percent and indicate the distribution of current assets among the different current asset accounts. The conclusions developed previously regarding the liquidity position are supported by the significant increase in the proportion of current assets comprising accounts receivable. The increase in accounts receivable on a per bed basis is even more significant. Examination of the composition ratios also indicates that the proportion of total assets made up of current assets increased from 18.54 percent in 19x8 to 25.69 percent in 19x9, with almost all of the increase coming from accounts receivable. This is an area that definitely needs further examination by the organization.

Profitability indicators for Sample Hospital:

1. $Return\ on\ Net\ Assets = \dfrac{increase\ in\ unrestricted\ net\ assets}{unrestricted\ net\ assets}$

   $= \dfrac{\$12,007,500}{\$91,768,250} = 13.1\%\ (11.3\%)$

2. $Return\ on\ Assets = \dfrac{increase\ in\ unrestricted\ net\ assets}{total\ assets}$

   $= \dfrac{\$12,007,500}{\$126,121,456} = 9.5\%\ (8.5\%)$

3. $Operating\ Margin = \dfrac{operating\ income}{total\ revenues} = \dfrac{\$10,690,318}{\$149,559,103} = 7.1\%\ (6.2\%)$

4. $Profit\ Margin = \dfrac{increase\ in\ unrestricted\ net\ assets}{total\ revenues} = \dfrac{\$12,007,500}{\$149,559,103} = 8.1\%\ (7.3\%)$

5. *Prefinancing Return on Assets*

   $= \dfrac{increase\ in\ unrestricted\ net\ assets + interest\ (1 - tax\ rate)}{total\ assets}$

   $= \dfrac{\$13,285,178}{\$126,121,456} = 10.5\%\ (9.7\%)$

The profitability ratios indicate what appears to be a high level of profitability. A return of almost 14 percent is being realized by the organization as a return on net assets, while each dollar of invested assets is generating a 9.5 percent increase in net assets. The difference between the operating margin of 7.1 percent, and the profit margin of 8.0 percent is attributed to nonoperating income. This indicates that while Sample Hospital generates some nonoperating income, it is not dependent on those funds to remain in operation. The prefinancing return on assets indicates what the return on assets figure would be in the absence of debt. Sample Hospital appears to be operating at a satisfactory level of profitability. All profitability indicators have increased from 19x8 to 19x9.

The capital composition ratios for Sample Hospital are:

Current liabilities	(19,253,206 / 126,121,456)	=	15.2%	(10.4%)
Long-term debt	(15,100,000 / 126,121,456)	=	12.0%	(15.0%)
Net assets	(91,768,250 / 126,121,456)	=	72.8%	(74.6%)
Total			100%	(100%)

1. *Debt to Unrestricted Net Assets* $= \dfrac{total\ debt}{unrestricted\ net\ assets}$

$$= \frac{\$34,353,206}{\$91,768,250} = 37.4\% \ (34.0\%)$$

2. *Unrestricted Net Assets to Total Assets* $= \dfrac{unrestricted\ net\ assets}{total\ assets}$

$$= \frac{\$91,768,250}{\$126,121,456} = 72.8\% \ (74.6\%)$$

3. *Debt to Total Assets* $= \dfrac{total\ debt}{total\ assets} = \dfrac{\$34,353,206}{\$126,121,456} = 27.2\% \ (25.4\%)$

4. *Times Interest Earned* $= \dfrac{increase\ in\ net\ assets + interest\ expense}{interest\ expense}$

$$= \frac{\$13,285,178}{\$1,277,678} = 10.4\ times\ (7.9)$$

5. *Fixed Charges Coverage*

$= \dfrac{interest\ payments + principal\ payments + other\ fixed\ charges}{cash\ provided\ by\ operating\ activities}$

$$= \frac{\$16,577,474}{\$3,577,678} = 4.6\ times\ (5.3)$$

6. *Cash Flow to Total Debt* $= \dfrac{cash\ provided\ by\ operating\ activities}{total\ debt}$

$$= \frac{\$16,577,474}{\$34,353,206} = 0.48\ (.68)$$

7. *Cash Return on Assets* $= \dfrac{cash\ provided\ by\ operating\ activities + interest\ expense}{total\ assets}$

$$= \frac{\$16,577,474 + \$1,277,678}{\$126,121,456} = \frac{\$17,855,152}{\$126,121,456} = .14\ (.18)$$

8. *Quality of Income* $= \dfrac{cash\ provided\ by\ operating\ activities}{increase\ in\ unrestricted\ net\ assets}$

$$= \frac{\$16,577,474}{\$12,007,500} = 1.38\ (2.03)$$

9. $Quality\ of\ Revenue = \dfrac{cash\ received\ from\ patients\ and\ providers}{total\ revenues}$

$$= \dfrac{\$138,890,327}{\$149,559,103} = .93\ (.98)$$

The second and third ratios indicate that 27.2 percent of the organization's assets are financed with debt. Conversely, 72.8 percent was financed by unrestricted net assets. Note that current liabilities have almost doubled between 19x8 and 19x9. Times interest earned indicates that Sample Hospital has a substantial margin over and above its ability to repay its interest expense and therefore faces little risk of being unable to repay interest on the debt. The fixed charges coverage provides a sufficient margin of safety. Comparison of these indicators becomes important in cases where the organization is leasing equipment, in cases where the organization is paying interest only, or in any other situation where the numbers may diverge more than anticipated. The cash flow to total debt indicates that sufficient cash flow was generated so that if the need arose, just less than 50 percent of the debt could have been retired, or it would take two years of this cash flow to pay off all of the debt. This is primarily a safety measure and indicates a secure position for Sample Hospital. From 19x8 to 19x9 total debt has increased while long-term debt has decreased, relative to net assets. This means the increase in total debt has been made up primarily of current liabilities. This premise is supported by the decrease in the current ratio over this same period. Some coverage and cash flow indicators have increased, consistent with the improved profitability position, while others have decreased. For example, the cash return on assets shows a decrease consistent with the other cash-based ratios. Similarly, both quality of income and quality of revenue ratios have also slightly decreased. These results are all based primarily on the decline in cash.

Activity/efficiency indicators for Sample Hospital:

1. $Total\ Asset\ Turnover = \dfrac{total\ revenues}{total\ assets} = \dfrac{\$149,559,103}{\$126,121,456} = 1.19\ (1.17)$

2. $Fixed\ Asset\ Turnover = \dfrac{total\ revenues}{fixed\ assets} = \dfrac{\$149,559,103}{\$74,397,879} = 2.01\ (2.02)$

3. $Days\ in\ Accounts\ Receivable = \dfrac{accounts\ receivable}{total\ revenues/365}$

$$= \dfrac{\$24,645,297}{\$409,751} = 60.2\ days\ (38.3)$$

4. $Days\ Inventory\ on\ Hand = \dfrac{inventory}{supplies\ expense/365}$

$$= \dfrac{\$2,549,676}{\$66,536} = 38.3\ days\ (32.7)$$

The first two ratios indicate that Sample Hospital is generating $1.19 for each dollar invested in assets, and is generating $2.01 in revenues for every dollar of noncurrent assets. Days in accounts receivable indicates that almost sixty-one days worth of facility services have been provided for which payment has not been received. This ratio has increased significantly. The last ratio indicates that Sample Hospital has thirty-eight days worth of inventory that needs to be further examined. This does not, however, mean that the level of inventory is inappropriate for this particular organization at this time and in this place. Total asset turnover and fixed asset turnover have remained relatively stable over this time period, while there has been an increase in the amount of inventory on hand relative to its daily usage rate. The substantial increase in the accounts receivable collection period would need to be examined by management at Sample Hospital.

Because of increases in the price of fixed assets over time, it is useful to adjust the operating margin ratio to reflect the estimated replacement costs of fixed assets. This is accomplished by substituting price-level depreciation for the hospital depreciation expenses shown on the income statement.

Other indicators for Sample Hospital:

1. $Average\ Age\ of\ Plant = \dfrac{accumulated\ depreciation}{depreciation\ expense}$

$$= \dfrac{\$44,304,068}{\$8,495,806} = 5.2\ years\ (5.4)$$

2. $Price\text{-}Level\ Adjusted\ Operating\ Margin$

$$= \dfrac{price\text{-}level\ adjusted\ increase\ in\ net\ assets}{total\ revenues}$$

$$= \dfrac{\$9,076,115^*}{\$149,559,103} = 6.1\%\ (5.1\%)$$

$^*[\$10,690,318 - (8,495,806 \times .19)] = 10,690,318 - 1,614,203) = 9,076,115$

3. $Replacement\ Viability = \dfrac{resources\ available\ for\ plant\ replacement}{PLA\ accumulated\ depreciation \times .5^{**}}$

$$= \dfrac{\$14,378,162}{\$26,360,920^*} = .54\ (.83)$$

$^*(44,304,068 \times .19 + 44,304,068) \div 2$
**Assume .5 is the "desired" debt-asset ratio.

These ratios indicate that the financial age of the fixed assets has decreased from 5.4 to 5.2 years. Therefore, new fixed assets must have been acquired. The price level adjusted (PLA) operating margin is less than the operating margin calculated in the profitability indicators (7.2 percent), but is a more accurate measure of the true rate of return from operations, since it considers an estimate for the replacement cost of assets. The replacement viability indicates that for each dollar Sample Hospital needs for plant replacement, it already has fifty-four cents. The average age of the plant has decreased slightly, indicating that Sample Hospital is continuing to make capital expenditures to maintain the plant and the equipment. The improvement in the PLA operating margin is consistent with the improved profitability. Replacement viability indicates that additional funds have been made available for plant replacement. The improved profitability position makes this possible.

Notice that a complete evaluation of Sample Hospital would include a comparison of the calculated indicators with comparable ratios from similar institutions, with the same indicators calculated for other years for Sample Hospital, and with norms or standards established by the management of the organization.

A statement of cash flows has been provided for Sample Hospital as *Exhibits 11–7A* and *B*. This statement shows a declining trend in cash provided from operating activities (e.g., from 19,800,749 to 16,577,474). It also shows slightly reduced cash outflows for financing activities (e.g., from 8,858,673 to 7,636,252). The statement further shows significant fluctuations in cash provided or used by investing activities. The statement shows that cash balances have increased very slightly in each of the two years shown.

Cash from operations does seem to be "sustainable" at a level of 15 to 20 million dollars per year. However, the other sources and uses of cash are much more erratic and do not indicate a clear trend or clear strategies. In other words, this example illustrates some vacillation and variation in cash provided or used for investing and financing activities. In order to get a clearer picture of the impact of these activities on liquidity, other sources and ratios must be used. Changes in resources listed as assets whose use is limited would bear significant examination and discussion.

Relationship between financial ratios—The Dupont Chart

Interpretation of any of the ratios listed above is very subjective and highly dependent on other information. No individual ratio should be interpreted without examining other related ratios. For example, the total asset turnover rate, listed under activity ratios, is a valuable indicator of the extent to which assets are being used to provide health services and generate the associated revenues. However, as the age of the assets becomes older (a greater amount has been depreciated) the book value of the assets decreases, and the total asset turnover rate increases. Thus, caution must be taken when interpreting individual indicators. Likewise, it is important for the manager to recognize that every one of the financial indicators are related to the bottom line indicator—return on net assets.

Starting with the first profitability ratio, return on net assets, the relationships between the financial indicators can be diagramed. The first

Exhibit 11–7A
Sample Hospital
Statement of Cash Flows
for the year Jan 1 thru Dec 31
Horizontal analysis

	19X9		19X8
Cash flows from operating activities:			
Cash received from patients and third-party payers	$ 138,890,327	5.5%	$ 131,705,045
Cash paid to employees and suppliers	(121,500,142)	9.9%	(110,566,928)
Interest received	52,170	37.7%	37,901
Receipts from other operating activities	1,776,797	0.3%	1,771,010
Malpractice settlements paid	(1,364,000)	−21.7%	(1,742,000)
Interest paid	(1,277,678)	−9.0%	(1,404,279)
Net cash provided by operating activities	16,577,474	−17.0%	19,800,749
Cash flows from investing activities:			
Additions to property and equipment, net	(16,269,970)	11.6%	(14,578,694)
Donations restricted for purchase of hospice supplies	38,410	0.3%	38,289
Computer software acquired	(442,396)	−38.4%	(718,037)
Transfer of assets limited as to use	7,984,458	64.6%	4,845,403
Net cash used in investing activities	(8,689,498)	−16.6%	(10,413,039)
Financing activities:			
Payment on long-term debt	(2,300,000)	0.0%	(2,300,000)
Transfer to affiliates	(5,356,252)	−19.9%	(6,558,673)
Net cash used in financing activities	(7,636,252)	−13.8%	(8,858,673)
Net increase in cash and cash equivalents	251,724	−52.4%	529,037
Cash and cash equivalents, beginning of year	1,070,600	97.7%	541,563
Cash and cash equivalents, end of year	$ 1,322,324	23.5%	$ 1,070,600

Exhibit 11–7B
Sample Hospital
Statement of Cash Flows (Direct Method)
for the year Jan 1 thru Dec 31
Vertical analysis

	19X9		19X8	
Cash flows from operating activities:				
Cash received from patients and third-party payers	$ 138,890,327	837.8%	$ 131,705,045	665.2%
Cash paid to employees and suppliers	(121,500,142)	–732.9%	(110,566,928)	–558.4%
Interest received	52,170	0.3%	37,901	0.2%
Receipts from other operating activities	1,776,797	10.7%	1,771,010	8.9%
Malpractice settlements paid	(1,364,000)	–8.2%	(1,742,000)	–8.8%
Interest paid	(1,277,678)	–7.7%	(1,404,279)	–7.1%
Net cash provided by operating activities	16,577,474	100.0%	19,800,749	100.0%
Cash flows from investing activities:				
Additions to property and equipment, net	(16,269,970)	187.2%	(14,578,694)	140.0%
Donations restricted for purchase of hospice supplies	38,410	–0.4%	38,289	–0.4%
Computer software acquired	(442,396)	5.1%	(718,037)	6.9%
Transfer of assets limited as to use	7,984,458	–91.9%	4,845,403	–46.5%
Net cash used in investing activities:	(8,689,498)	100.0%	(10,413,039)	100.0%
Financing activities:				
Payment of long-term debt	(2,300,000)	30.1%	(2,300,000)	26.0%
Transfers to affiliates	(5,356,252)	68.8%	(6,558,673)	74.0%
Net cash used in financing activities:	(7,636,252)	100.0%	(8,858,673)	100.0%
Net increase in cash and cash equivalents	251,724	19.0%	529,037	49.4%
Cash and cash equivalents, beginning of year	1,070,600	81.0%	541,563	50.6%
Cash and cash equivalents, end of year	$ 1,322,324	100.0%	$ 1,070,600	100.0%

relationship is between return on assets and the net assets financing ratio, as follows:

$$Return\ on\ Net\ Assets = return\ on\ assets \div net\ assets\ financing\ ratio*$$

$$Return\ on\ Net\ Assets = return\ on\ assets \div equity\ financing\ ratio*$$

$$\frac{increase\ in\ unrestricted\ net\ assets}{unrestricted\ net\ assets} =$$

$$\frac{increase\ in\ unrestricted\ net\ assets}{total\ assets} \div \frac{unrestricted\ net\ assets}{total\ assets}$$

*The net assets financing ratio or equity financing ratio is equal to [1 – (debt to total assets ratio)].

The return on assets is also a function of two other ratios—the total asset turnover rate and the profit margin:

$$Return\ on\ Assets = total\ asset\ turnover \times profit\ margin$$

$$\frac{increase\ in\ unrestricted\ net\ assets}{total\ assets} = \frac{total\ revenues}{total\ assets} \times \frac{increase\ in\ unrestricted\ net\ assets}{total\ revenues}$$

For an investor-owned organization, the Dupont ratios are:

$$\frac{net\ income}{total\ assets} = \frac{total\ revenues}{total\ assets} \times \frac{net\ income}{total\ revenues}$$

Given the preceding two relationships we can now adjust our decision making to include these relationships. In order to increase the return on net assets we can either increase the return on assets or decrease the net asset financing ratio. In order to increase the return on assets we can either increase the total asset turnover rate or increase the profit margin. In order to increase the total asset turnover ratio we need to either increase revenues or decrease total assets. In order to increase the profit margin we need to either increase revenues or decrease expenses. The net result of increasing these ratios will be an increased return to the owners of the organization, i.e., the shareholders or the community.

Summary

This chapter has identified several categories of ratios that are useful from the perspective of the various stakeholders. Comparative evaluation, across different healthcare organizations, or across years, will permit stakeholders to evaluate critical areas of concern. Trend analysis is an essential component of ratio analysis. An even more important component is the manager's assessment of future financial performance based on the result of this period's ratio analysis.

Various other user's guides may be acquired that explain each ratio in terms of how it is calculated and how it can be interpreted. Such calculations should be based on audited financial statements, and should identify median ratios for a variety of possible peer group comparisons. The financial manager who wants to avoid some computational drudgery and/or wants to obtain additional data from similar hospitals and long-term care organizations should consider subscribing to the CHIPS service. Similar information, for managed care organizations, is available through the results of the annual survey of the Group Health Association of America (GHAA).

Questions and problems

1. How can ratio analysis help the healthcare organization's financial manager?

2. What are the first steps to take before computing any particular financial ratio?

3. Define the following categories of financial ratios:
   a. Liquidity
   b. Turnover or activity or efficiency
   c. Performance or profitability
   d. Capitalization or leverage

4. Why should consolidated financial statements be made before financial ratios are computed?

5. When should year-end financial statements' amounts be used to compute financial ratios?

6. What ratios would you compute as an aid in determining:
   a. the financial solvency of a healthcare organization?
   b. the management of the use of resources?
   c. the relationship of revenue and expenses and total investment?
   d. the financial structure of the healthcare organization and the relative risk involved?

7. The Navajo Mission Hospital financial statements indicate the following amounts:

| | *Dec. 31 (in thousands)* | | |
	19X1	*19X2*	*19X3*
Net patient services revenue	$18,859	$20,742	$23,890
Patient accounts receivable	3,813	4,266	4,760

   a. Calculate the number of days charges in receivables (average collection period) and the accounts receivable turnover.
   b. What judgment would you make about the management of patient receivables?

8. The financial statements for Castile Laboratories, Inc. are given below:

Castile Laboratories, Inc.
Balance sheet
May 31, 19X1

Assets		Liabilities and Stockholders' Equity		
Current assets:		Liabilities:		
Cash	$ 6,500	Current liabilities		$ 50,000
Accounts receivable,		Bonds payable, 10%		80,000
net	35,000	Total liabilities		130,000
Inventory	70,000	Stockholders' equity:		
Prepaid expenses	3,500	Common stock,		
Total current assets	115,000	$5 par value	$ 30,000	
Property and		Retained earnings	140,000	
equipment, net	185,000	Total stockholders'		
		equity		170,000
Total assets	$300,000	Total liabilities		
		and equity		$300,000

Castile Laboratories, Inc.
Income statement
for the year ended May 31, 19X1

Revenues	$420,000
Less cost of materials	292,500
Gross margin	127,500
Less operating expense	84,500
Net operating income	43,000
Interest expense	8,000
Net income before taxes	35,000
Income taxes (40%)	14,000
Net income	$ 21,000

Account balances on June 30, 19X1, were: accounts receivable $25,000; inventory $60,000. All sales were on account.

a. Compute the following:
   1. current ratio
   2. net working capital
   3. capital structure (composition)
   4. accounts receivable turnover
   5. inventory turnover
   6. times interest earned
   7. total asset turnover
   8. profit margin
b. Write a brief (two paragraphs) evaluation of Castile Laboratories.

9. a. Using the data that follows, calculate each of the following requirements for No Name Hospital:

   1. liquidity ratios
   2. activity ratios
   3. profitability ratios
   4. capitalization ratios

   b. What assessment would you make of the financial condition?

No Name Hospital
Anywhere USA
December 31, 19X2
Balance Sheet

Assets		Liabilities and Net Assets	
Current assets:		Current liabilities	
Cash and savings	$ 28,000	Accounts payable	$ 404,000
Investment	60,000	Notes payable	123,000
Net accounts receivable	1,895,000	Accrued expenses	37,000
Inventory	450,000	Mortgage payable -	
Prepaid expenses	21,000	current portion	40,000
Total current assets	$2,454,000	Total current liabilities	$ 604,000
Long-term assets		Long-term liabilities	
Plant and equipment	4,200,000	Notes payable	460,000
		Mortgage payable	1,600,000
		Total long-term liabilities	$2,060,000
		Net assets	3,990,000
		Total liabilities	
Total assets	$6,654,000	and net assets	$6,654,000

No Name Hospital
Anywhere USA
for the period Jan. 1, 19X2 to Dec. 31, 19X2
Statement of Operations

Patient services revenue	$3,700,000
Professional services revenue	1,300,000
Total operating revenues	$5,000,000
Operating expenses	
Nursing services	$1,855,000
Professional services	1,050,000
Dietary	320,000
Interest	265,000
Administrative and general	250,000
Depreciation	125,000
Provision for bad debts	625,000
Total expenses	$4,490,000
Increase in net assets	$ 510,000

No Name Hospital
Anywhere USA
December 31, 19X2
Statement of Cash Flows (indirect method)

Cash flows from operating activities:	
Increase in net assets	$ 510,000
Adjustments to change net assets to cash basis:	
Provision for bad debts	625,000
Depreciation	125,000
Cash provided by operating activities	1,260,000
Cash flow from financing activities:	
Principal payment on long-term debt	($ 40,000)
Donations	200,000
Purchase of marketable securities	(60,000)
Cash flow from financing activities	100,000
Cash flows from investing activities:	
Purchase of equipment	(1,450,000)
Sale of equipment	100,000
Cash provided (used) by investing activities	(1,350,000)
Net increase in cash	10,000
Beginning cash balance	18,000
Ending cash balance	28,000
Cash paid during the year	
For interest	$ 265,000

10. You have been recently hired as the controller of the Manchester County Hospital. The administrator has asked you to review the financial statements for the organization (*Exhibits A to D*). She is particularly interested in determining any problem areas that might be identified in the financial management area. Using the information contained in the financial statements, write a report to the administrator about the financial condition of the Manchester County Hospital.

Exhibit A

Manchester County Hospital
Assets

Assets	1999	1998
Current assets:		
Cash and cash equivalents	$ 391,767	$ 1,125,628
Accounts receivable net allowance for uncollectable acccounts and contractual allowances of $3,393,361 in 1999 and $2,367,641 in 1998.	8,399,210	7,524,313
Other accounts receivable	477,274	554,433
Reimbursement settlements receivable	72,601	80,668
Inventory of supplies	356,798	373,901
Prepaid expenses	53,251	80,714
Assets whose use is limited that are required for current liabilities	1,624,400	1,689,400
Total current assets	11,375,301	11,429,057
Assets whose use is limited by Board-designation		
Cash and cash equivalents	614,423	1,063,749
Short-term investments	6,348,645	2,966,819
Investment in Corporation pooled funds	1,842,483	2,551,979
Accrued interest receivable	31,628	10,079
Total assets whose use is limited	8,837,179	6,592,626
Less - current portion	(1,624,400)	(1,689,400)
Net assets whose use is limited	7,212,779	4,903,226
Property, plant, and equipment, at cost Hospital operations —		
Land and improvements	1,358,809	1,342,397
Buildings and leasehold improvements	16,607,453	15,556,408
Fixed equipment	14,206,950	14,209,592
Movable equipment	10,401,089	9,769,731
Construction in progress	80,170	768,910
Total property, plant and equipment	42,654,471	41,647,038
Less - accumulated depreciation	(19,645,445)	(17,143,693)
Net property, plant and equipment	23,009,026	24,503,345
Deferred liability costs		164,000
Deferred financing costs	533,517	587,313
Total assets	$ 42,130,623	$ 41,586,941

Exhibit B

Manchester County Hospital
Liabilities and net assets

	1999	1998
Liabilities and Net Assets		
Current liabilities:		
Accounts payable and accrued expenses	$ 2,326,397	$ 1,953,484
Accrued payroll, payroll taxes and employee benefits	2,000,348	1,900,659
Accrued interest payable	—	40,895
Other current liabilities	385,821	480,596
Reimbursement settlement payable	665,623	521,561
Payable to related division	630,000	—
Current portion of long-term debt	1,624,400	1,689,400
Total current liabilities	7,632,589	6,586,595
Other liabilities and deferred revenue:		
Deferred revenue	70,560	72,240
Reserve for professional liability costs	82,000	164,000
Total other liabilities and deferred revenue	152,560	236,240
Long-term debt		
Notes payable to Corporation	13,949,900	16,354,300
Total long-term debt	13,949,900	16,354,300
Less - current portion	(1,624,400)	(1,689,400)
Net long-term debt	12,325,500	14,664,900
Commitments and contingent liabilities		
Net assets	—	—
Unrestricted	21,762,926	20,020,776
Temporarily restricted	257,048	78,430
Total net assets	22,019,974	20,099,206
Total liabilities and net assets	$42,130,623	$41,586,941

Exhibit C

Manchester County Hospital
Statements of revenues and expenses
for the years ended June 30, 1999 and 1998

	1999	1998
Patient service revenue:		
Inpatient	$32,810,632	$31,678,226
Outpatient	12,160,684	10,300,583
Net patient service revenue	44,971,316	41,978,809
Other operating revenue	1,131,716	1,085,983
Total operating revenues	46,103,032	43,064,792
Operating expenses:		
Salaries and wages	18,417,626	16,742,397
Employee benefits	3,422,329	2,992,994
Professional fees	2,161,173	1,811,640
Supplies and other expenses	13,572,313	12,686,302
Depreciation	2,852,235	2,814,982
Interest and amortization	1,574,605	1,819,874
Provision for bad debts	2,424,088	1,903,053
Total operating expenses	44,424,369	40,771,242
Income from operations	1,678,663	2,293,550
Nonoperating revenues (expenses):		
Investment income, net	693,487	567,292
Other expenses	—	(90,000)
Total nonoperating revenues	693,487	477,292
Excess of revenues over expenses	$ 2,372,150	$ 2,770,842

Exhibit D

Manchester County Hospital
Statement of cash flows

	1999	1998
Cash flows from operating activities:		
Increase in unrestricted net assets	$ 2,372,150	$ 2,770,842
Adjustments		
Depreciation and amortization	2,906,031	2,867,525
Provision for bad debts	2,424,088	1,903,053
Less write offs	(1,398,368)	(1,672,864)
(Gain) Loss on sale of property, plant, and		
equipment	36,162	(19,346)
Restricted donations and grants	210,240	11,929
Expenditure of restricted donations and grants:	(31,622)	(57,345)
Changes in operating assets and liabilities:		
(Increase) Decrease in:		
Accounts receivable	(1,900,617)	(1,808,847)
Other accounts receivable	77,159	33,131
Reimbursement settlement receivable	8,067	7,318
Inventory of supplies	17,103	(90,284)
Prepaid expenses	27,463	126,828
Deferred professional liabilities costs	164,000	(164,000)
Increase (decrease) in:		
Accounts payable	372,913	(303,320)
Accrued payroll, payroll taxes,		
and employee benefits	99,689	(33,391)
Accrued interest payable	(40,895)	(3,466)
Other current liabilities	(94,775)	(28,864)
Reimbursement settlement payable	144,062	521,561
Other liabilities and deferred revenues	(83,680)	162,320
Net cash provided by operating activities	5,309,170	4,222,780
Cash flows from investing activities:		
Purchase of property	(1,506,819)	(2,814,626)
Proceeds from sale of property,		
plant, and equipment	112,741	29,499
Increase in assets whose use is limited	(2,244,553)	(337,626)
Net cash provided by investing activities	(3,638,631)	(3,122,753)
Cash flow from financing activities:		
Principal payments on long-term debt	(2,404,400)	(1,285,400)
Increase in deferred financing costs	—	(17,550)
Net cash used in financing activities	(2,404,400)	(1,302,950)
Net decrease in cash and cash equivalents	(733,861)	(202,923)
Cash and cash equivalents, beginning of year	1,125,628	1,328,551
Cash and cash equivalents, end of year	$ 391,767	$ 1,125,628

11. Conduct a comprehensive analysis of the financial statements of Completecare Health Services, Inc. Pay particular attention to the Notes. As appropriate, calculate the necessary ratios described in chapter 11, and, then, make adjustments to reflect any unusual or non-recurring circumstances.

12. Based on your analysis in problem 11, write a one to two page memo to the CFO summarizing your concerns and recommendations.

Exhibit 1

Completecare Health Services, Inc.
Financial Statements

Report of Independent Public Accountants

To the Board of Directors of
Completecare Health Services, Inc.:

We have audited the accompanying balance sheets of Completecare Health Services, Inc. (a Colorado corporation) as of December 31, 1999 and 1998, and the related statements of income and changes in stockholder's equity and cash flows for the years then ended. These financial statements are the responsibility of the Company's management. Our responsibility is to express an opinion on these financial statements based on our audits.

We conducted our audits in accordance with generally accepted auditing standards. Those standards require that we plan and perform the audit to obtain reasonable assurance about whether the financial statements are free of material misstatement. An audit includes examining, on a test basis, evidence supporting the amounts and disclosures in the financial statements. An audit also includes assessing the accounting principles used and significant estimates made by management, as well as evaluating the overall financial statement presentation. We believe that our audits provide a reasonable basis for our opinion.

In our opinion, the financial statements referred to above present fairly, in all material respects, the financial position of Completecare Health Services, Inc. as of December 31, 1999 and 1998, and the results of its operations and its cash flows for the years then ended in conformity with generally accepted accounting principles.

Denver, Colorado
February 8, 2000 (except with respect to
  the matter discussed in Note 10 as to
  which the date is March 12, 2001)

Exhibit 2

Completecare Health Services, Inc.
Balance Sheets (in thousands, except share data)

As of December 31,	1999	1998
Assets		
Current Assets:		
Cash and cash equivalents	$25,015	$22,822
Premium revenue receivable, net of allowances of $732		
in 1999 and $850 in 1998 for doubtful accounts	6,846	5,729
Receivable from related parties (Notes 1 and 3)	570	678
Reinsurance claims receivable	0	100
Prepaid expenses and other current assets	58	75
Total current assets	32,489	29,404
Property and Equipment (Note 6)		
Property and equipment, at cost	10,713	9,234
Less - accumulated depreciation	(4,409)	(1,128)
Net property and equipment	6,304	8,106
Other Assets		
Goodwill, net of accumulated amortization		
of $1,327 in 1999 and $1,135 in 1998 (Note 2)	1,136	1,328
Cash investment escrow - State (Notes 2 and 7)	1,029	900
Deferred receivable from related party (Note 4)	472	0
Total other assets	2,637	2,228
Total Assets	$41,430	$39,738
Liabilities and Stockholders' Equity		
Current liabilities:		
Hospital claims payable	$10,452	$11,493
Payable to related parties (Notes 1 and 3)	13,636	6,215
Other accounts payable and accrued expenses	297	1,383
Unearned premium revenue	2,881	2,224
Current portion of capital lease obligations	576	1,179
Total current liabilities	27,842	22,494
Capital Lease Obligations,		
net of current portion (Note 8)	723	408
Deferred Payable to Related Party (Note 3)	1,300	0
Total liabilities	29,865	22,902
Commitments and Contingencies (Note 8)		
Stockholder's Equity (Notes 1 and 5)		
Common stock		
$.10 par value; 50,000 shares authorized;		
1,000 shares issued and outstanding	—	—
Paid-in capital	11,565	16,836
Retained earnings	0	0
Total stockholder's equity	11,565	16,836
Total Liabilities and Stockholder's Equity	$41,430	$39,738

The accompanying notes are an integral part of these balance sheets.

Exhibit 3

Completecare Health Services, Inc.
Statements of Income (in thousands)

For the years ended December 31,	1999	1998
Premium Revenue	$231,928	$205,466
Expenses:		
Medical care costs	99,151	89,097
Hospital and other healthcare costs	92,252	81,067
	191,403	170,164
Management fees (Note 3)	26,195	23,341
Administrative expense	62	163
Profit share (Note 3)	6,892	4,953
Depreciation expense	3,285	1,169
Amortization of goodwill	192	192
	36,626	29,818
Income Before Non-Operating Items	3,899	5,484
Interest income, net	567	983
Income Before Income Taxes	4,466	6,467
Income Tax Provision (Note 4)	(1,737)	(2,000)
Net Income	$ 2,729	$ 4,467

The accompanying notes are an integral part of these statements.

Exhibit 4

Completecare Health Services, Inc.
Statement of Changes in Stockholder's Equity
(in thousands except share data)

For the years ended December 31, 1999 and 1998

	Common Stock		Paid-in	Retained	
	Shares	Amount	Capital	Earnings	Total
Balances, December 31, 1997	1,000	$—	$10,487	$ 9,937	$ 20,424
Transfer of property and equipment from parent	0	0	7,304	0	7,304
Income tax liability contributed by parent	0	0	2,000	0	2,000
Dividends paid to parent (Note 5)	0	0	(2,955)	(14,404)	(17,359)
Net income	0	0	0	4,467	4,467
Balances, December 31, 1998	1,000	—	16,836	0	16,836
Dividends paid to parent (Note 5)	0	0	(5,271)	(2,729)	(8,000)
Net income	0	0	0	2,729	2,729
Balances, December 31, 1999	1,000	$—	$11,565	$ 0	$ 11,565

The accompanying notes are an integral part of these statements.

Exhibit 5

Completecare Health Services, Inc.
Statements of Cash Flows (direct method)
(in thousands)

For the years ended December 31,	1999	1998
Cash flows from operating activities:		
Cash received from customers	$ 230,768	$ 205,795
Cash paid to suppliers	(93,668)	(80,925)
Net cash paid to related parties	(102,698)	(105,411)
Cash paid for administrative expenses	(22,922)	(163)
Interest received	725	1,060
Interest paid	(112)	(45)
Net cash provided by operating activities	12,093	20,311
Cash flows from investing activities:		
Purchases of property and equipment	(1,170)	(111)
Receipts from sale of equipment	7	254
Payments to increase investment escrow	(129)	(150)
Net cash used in investing activities	(1,292)	(7)
Cash flows from financing activities:		
Cash dividends paid to parent	(8,000)	(17,359)
Principal payments on capital lease obligations	(608)	(503)
Net cash used in financing activities	(8,608)	(17,862)
Net change in cash and cash equivalents	2,193	2,442
Cash and cash equivalents at beginning of year	22,822	20,380
Cash and cash equivalents at end of year	$ 25,015	$ 22,822
Cash flows from operating activities		
Net income	$ 2,729	$ 4,467
Adjustments to reconcile net income to		
net cash provided by operating activities:		
Amortization of goodwill	192	192
Depreciation expense	3,285	1,169
Income tax provision contributed by parent	0	2,000
Deferred receivable from related party	(472)	0
Deferred payable to related party	1,300	0
Gain on disposal of property and equipment	0	(25)
Decrease/(increase) in current assets other		
than cash and cash equivalents	(892)	7,656
Increase in current liabilities other than		
current portion of capital lease obligations	5,951	4,852
Total adjustments	9,364	15,844
Net cash provided by operating activities	$ 12,093	$ 20,311

Exhibit 5 (cont.)

Supplemental disclosure of non-cash investing and financing activities:

In 1999, CHSI refinanced certain capital lease obligations resulting in an approximate $320 increase in the property and capital lease obligation accounts. In 1998, the Company received property and equipment totaling $7,304 from its parent, and acquired property and equipment totaling $2,090 through capital lease obligations.

The accompanying notes are an integral part of these statements.

Exhibit 6

Completecare Health Services, Inc.
Notes to Financial Statements
December 31, 1999 and 1998

1. Corporate Organization

Completecare Health Services, Inc. ("CHSI" OR "Company"), a Colorado corporation incorporated on August 30, 1985, is a wholly owned subsidiary of Completecare Management Services, Inc. ("CMSI"). CHSI was licensed on January 2, 1986, by the Division of Insurance, State of Colorado to operate under the state statutes as a health maintenance organization ("HMO"). On March 7, 1986, CHSI also received federal qualification status as an HMO from the Department of Health and Human Service ("DHHS") under Title XIII of the Public Service Act.

The medical component of health plan benefits is provided by Columbia Medical Group, Inc. ("CMG"), an individual practice association, under a Medical Services Agreement (Note 3). The cost of this provider contract is based on a negotiated capitation rate (a fixed amount per health plan member per month) in lieu of customary fees for services performed. The pharmacy component of health plan benefits is also provided to subscribers who are supplied under a capitated payment arrangement. The hospital component of health plan benefits is provided to subscribers primarily by participating hospitals under provider contracts, most of which have established fixed per-diem rates. All contracts, referred to above, contain "hold harmless" clauses. This clause precludes contracted providers from billing individual members for covered services rendered.

A description of the major subscriber contracts follows:

a. Completecare Conventional HMO Plan

Completecare, the conventional HMO plan, is the Company's most popular plan, with approximately 14,300 members. The conventional HMO plan may be customized for the specific requirement of an employer group. This plan included approximately 490 employer groups, including private and public entities. Premium revenue earned by CHSI under this program, and included in the accompanying statements of income, totaled approximately $186.7 million and $167.4 million for 1999 and 1998 respectively.

b. Completecare Plus Plan

Completecare Plus, a point-of-service ("POS") or open-ended HMO plan with approximately 15,000 members, combines the features of a conventional HMO plan with those of an indemnity plan. As a POS plan, Completecare

Exhibit 6 (cont.)

Plus allows members at the "point-of-service" to choose a non-participating provider or facility at an additional cost. Colorado laws require that the indemnity portion of the POS plan be underwritten by a licensed accident and health carrier. The company satisfies this requirement through Completecare Insurance Company ("CIC"), a wholly owned subsidiary of CMSI. Premiums for these policies were allocated between 85 percent and 90 percent to CHSI, and between 15 percent and 10 percent to CIC based on actuarial estimates of utilization of HMO and non-HMO services. Premium revenue earned by CHSI under this program and included in the accompanying statements of income, totaled approximately $16.5 million and $12.6 million for 1999 and 1998, respectively. CHSI had a receivable from CIC of approximately $570,000 at December 31, 1999, for amounts paid on CIC's behalf, and a payable to CIC of approximately $129,000 at December 31, 1998, for amounts received on CIC's behalf.

c. Medicare Plans

Completecare offers two plans for the Medicare population, the largest of which is Medicare Risk with approximately 7,000 members. The Medicare Risk plan substitutes an HMO format for a Medicare recipient's Medicare benefits, with the federal government paying the larger portion of the monthly HMO premium. The Medicare Risk plan is marketed directly to Medicare recipients and through group plans, following annual approval and contract negotiations with the federal government's office of Health Care Finance and Administration ("HCFA"). Effective June 1, 1986, CHSI entered into a contract with HCFA. Monthly premium revenues are determined on a per member basis adjusted for demographic characteristics of the member. Medicare Risk members can withdraw from the plan at the end of any month. Premium revenue earned by CHSI under these plans totaled approximately $28.1 million in 1999 and $25.3 million in 1998. The medical and hospital benefits are provided to subscribers under similar contractual arrangements as those described above. One employer group represented approximately 24 percent of CHSI's total premium revenue for each of the years, 1999 and 1998.

2. Summary of Significant Accounting Policies

a. Cash and Cash Equivalents

Short-term investments with a maturity of three months or less at the time of purchase are reported as cash equivalents.

b. Property and Equipment

Property and equipment are recorded at cost. Property and equipment, except for software costs, are depreciated on the straight-line basis over the estimated useful lives of three to seven years. Amortization expense on software is calculated under a double declining balance methodology over a five year life. Upon asset retirement or disposal, the cost and accumulated depreciation accounts are adjusted, and the resulting gain or loss is reflected in operations.

c. Goodwill

Goodwill of approximately $2.5 million is being amortized on a straight-line basis at $16,000 per month, which approximated the average 13 year life assigned to goodwill based upon external valuation analysis.

d. Hospital Claims Payable

CHSI provides a liability for non-capitated claims which have been received and are unpaid at year end, and for those claims which are estimated to have

Exhibit 6 (cont.)

been incurred but not reported ("IBNR") as of year end, based on past experience and accumulated statistical data. Any differences between estimates and actual claims incurred are reflected in subsequent periods. Claims payable also includes certain contract settlements which are paid outside of the claims system.

CHSI follows Statement of Position 89-5, "Financial Accounting and Reporting by Providers of Prepaid Health Care Services." Statement of Position 89-5 provides for accrual of services to specific members the company is obligated to beyond the premium period. CHSI has therefore estimated and accrued the expense associated with its members confined to an inpatient facility at year end through discharge.

e. Revenue Recognition

Premium revenue from members is recorded as revenue in the applicable period of service. Premium revenue received in advance is deferred.

f. Reclassifications

Certain reclassifications were made to the prior year's financial statements to conform to the current year's presentation.

3. Related Party Transaction

a. Medical Services Agreement

CHSI has an exclusive contract with CMG for the provision of medical services (the "Medical Services Agreement"). The Medical Services Agreement is effective through December 31, 1999. The physicians who contract with CMG to provide services to CHSI subscribers have a "hold harmless" clause in their individual contracts with CMG. This clause precluded the contracted physicians from billing the individual members for covered medical services rendered. In the event CMG is unable to perform its contractual obligations, CHSI does reserve the right to contract with other medical providers for medical care. CMG is represented on the CHSI Board of Directors. CMSI provides claims administration and related services for CMG, and shares claims records information with CMG at no charge.

The cost of the Medical Services Agreement is based on a negotiated capitation rate per health plan member per month for commercial members and a percentage of Medicare premiums for Medicare members. Amounts paid under such agreements totaled approximately $99.2 million and $89.1 million for the years ended December 31, 1999 and 1998, respectively.

CHSI accrued approximately $6.9 million and $5.0 million in profit shares to CMG in 1999 and 1998 respectively, in accordance with the Medical Services Agreement. The profit shares represent 50 percent of CMSI's consolidated cash flow, as defined, in excess of $6.5 million for the years ended December 31, 1999 and 1998. The profit share arrangement ended in December 31, 1998.

CHSI and CMG have established a per member per month target for certain healthcare expenses beginning in January, 2000. This target, which will be renegotiated annually, is for certain healthcare expenses, consisting principally of inpatient and outpatient in area hospitalization costs and certain radiology, laboratory, physical therapy, and home healthcare costs. If the actual annual expenses for these services meet the agreed target, CHSI will pay CMG an incentive bonus payment (which at current membership levels would approximate $1.5 million in 2000). If actual expenses exceed the target, the

Exhibit 6 (cont.)

bonus payment will be reduced by the amount of the excess. If the excess expenses are greater than the amount of the bonus payment, CMG will be obligated to reimburse CHSI for 50 percent of such amount. If, however, actual expenses are less than the target, CHSI will be obligated to pay CMG 50 percent of the savings.

b. Management Agreement

CHSI and CMG were parties to a 20-year term management agreement (assumed by CMSI August 30, 1998—see Note 1) whereby CMSI agreed to provide all administrative and management functions for CHSI for a fee of 11.25 percent in 1999 and 1998 of all revenue received by CHSI. CHSI incurred management fees of approximately $26.2 million and $23.2 million for the years ended December 31, 1999 and 1998, respectively.

c. Indemnification Agreement

CHSI indemnifies CMG for physician claims incurred during the contract year on members in excess of $15,000 for a charge of $.10 per member per month. Net reimbursements to CMG, which are included in Note 3(a), amounted to approximately $2.0 million and $1.3 million for the years ended December 31, 1999 and 1998 respectively. The parties have orally agreed that, beginning in 2000, reimbursement under the above arrangement will be restricted to Medicare members. Fees and reimbursements are included in medical care costs in the accompanying statements of income.

d. Receivable from and Payable to Related Parties

CHSI has recurring receivable and payable with CMG, CMSI and CIC. The balances consist of normal operating transactions, such as medical care costs and management fees, and are reimbursed monthly with no interest accrued. At December 31, 1999, CHSI had a net payable to CMG of $9.4 million of which $1.3 million is classified as a long-term liability in the accompanying 1999 balance sheet. At December 31, 1998, CHSI had a net payable to CMG of $6.1 million. CHSI had a payable to CMSI of $5.5 million at December 31, 1999. At December 31, 1998, CHSI had a receivable from CMSI of $678,000. Refer to Note 1(b) for a discussion of related party transaction with CIC.

e. Premium Revenue Earned from Affiliates

Premium revenue received by CHSI on behalf of CMSI employees amounted to $829,000 and $881,000 for the years ended December 31, 1999 and 1998, respectively.

4. Income Taxes

In February 1992, the Financial Accounting Standard Board issued Statement of Financial Accounting Standards No. 109 ("SFAS 109, 'Accounting for Income Taxes'") established accounting and reporting standards for recording the tax effects of differences between the tax basis of assets and liabilities and their reported amounts in the financial statements. CHSI's parent adopted the provisions of SFAS 109 effective January 1, 1992.

Effective January 1, 1999, income taxes were paid by CHSI's parent and allocated to CHSI by applying the provisions of SFAS 109 as if CHSI were a separate taxpayer. The provision for income taxes includes the following (in thousands):

Exhibit 6 (cont.)

December 31, 1999

Currently payable to related party	$2,055
Deferred	(318)
Provision	$1,737

CHSI's effective income tax rate was different than the statutory federal and state income tax rates due to amortization of non-deductible goodwill.

Deferred taxes are determined based on estimated future tax effects of differences between the amounts reflected in the financial statements and the tax basis of assets and liabilities given the provisions of the enacted tax laws. The deferred receivable from related party, which arose due to deferred tax assets, is comprised of the following (in thousands):

December 31, 1999

Depreciation	$ (36)
Software amortization	508
Total deferred receivable from related party	$472

5. Stockholder's Equity

During 1999, CHSI paid CMSI dividends totaling $8.0 million. During 1999 CHSI paid dividends totaling $17.4 million of which $11.5 million was paid to CMSI. As retained earnings of CHSI were insufficient to pay the dividends declared to CMSI, $5.3 million and $3.0 million were treated as a return of capital and deducted from paid-in capital in the accompanying 1999 and 1998 financial statements, respectively.

Property and equipment of $7.3 million was transferred at predecessor cost from CMSI to CHSI in July, 1998, resulting in an increase in paid-in capital. At that time, CHSI also assumed lease obligations relating to certain of the transferred assets. In connection with the change in ownership, $1.7 million in lease obligations was subsequently capitalized.

6. Property and Equipment

CHSI's property, equipment and related accumulated depreciation balances for December 31, 1999 and 1998 are as follows (in thousands):

CLASSIFICATION	1999	1998
Capitalized Total:		
Leasehold improvements	$ 124	$ 124
Equipment and fixtures	3,706	2,296
Software	6,883	6,814
Totals	$10,713	$9,234
Accumulated Depreciation		
Leasehold improvements	$ 33	$ 8
Equipment and fixtures	1,092	214
Software	3,284	906
Totals	$ 4,409	$1,128

Exhibit 6 (cont.)

7. Statutory Net Worth Requirement

Pursuant to Colorado law, CHSI is required to maintain a deposit in an account held jointly with the State Commissioner of Insurance. At December 31, 1999 and 1998, this deposit totaled $1.029 million and $900,000, respectively. The deposit is required for protection of subscribers in the event CHSI is unable to satisfactorily meet its contractual obligations.

Under the laws of the State of Colorado, CHSI is required to maintain a contingency reserve of net worth based upon a percentage of premium revenue. CHSI reported statutory net worth in excess of the requirement as of December 31, 1999 and 1998. In connection with the most recent Colorado Insurance Commission examination, which is still in process, the net worth reported by CHSI was decreased such that CHSI no longer met the contingency reserve requirement. This reduction is a result of the non-admission of certain assets due to investment in excess of statutory limitations.

In January, 2000, CHSI restructured its investment portfolio as a result of this examination and currently meets statutory net worth requirements.

8. Commitment and Contingencies

a. Claims and Assessments

In the normal course of business, the Company is involved in various asserted and unasserted claims. In management's opinion, these matters will not have a material adverse impact on the financial statements.

b. Capital Lease Obligations

CHSI leases computer hardware and software under a capital lease arrangement. Future minimum rental payments required under these leases continue through 2003 as follows (in thousands):

	2000	2001	2002	2003	Total
Computer hardware and software	$576	$575	$123	$25	$1,299

Interest expense was $114,000 and $45,000 for 1999 and 1998, respectively.

CMSI, under the terms of the lease obligation, has pledged a one-year certificate of deposit in the amount of $100,000 as collateral. This collateral expires in June, 2000. The leases are also collateralized by the leased hardware and software.

9. Reinsurance

CHSI annually purchases, on a premium basis, reinsurance coverage from an insurance company which limits CHSI's exposure on claims for an individual in excess of $150,000. For 2000, this deductible will increase to $300,000. Such claims are covered by the reinsurance agreement in varying amounts up to a maximum of $2 million per member per lifetime.

Premiums paid, net of amounts recovered, are included in other direct costs in the accompanying statement of income. A summary of reinsurance recoveries and premiums follows (in thousands):

For the year ended December 31,	1999	1998
Recoveries	$ 21	$100
Premiums	$231	$223

Exhibit 6 (cont.)

10. Subsequent Event

    On March 12, 2001, Completecare, Inc. signed a letter of intent to merge with TakeCharge, Inc. The merger is expected to be consummated in mid-2001.

13. Conduct a comprehensive analysis of the financial statements of Provident Health Partners, Inc. Pay particular attention to the Notes. As appropriate, calculate the necessary ratios described in chapter 11, and, then, make adjustments to reflect any unusual or non-recurring circumstances.

14. Based on your analysis in problem 13, write a one to two page memo to the CFO summarizing your concerns and recommendations.

Exhibit 1

Provident Health Partners
Report of Independent Auditors

Board of Trustees
Health Care Systems, Inc.

We have audited the accompanying consolidated balance sheets of Provident Health Partners and subsidiaries (the Corporation) as of June 30, 1999 and 1998, and the related consolidated statements of income and changes in net assets and cash flows for the years then ended. These financial statements are the responsibility of the Corporation's management. Our responsibility is to express an opinion on these financial statements based on our audits.

We conducted our audits in accordance with generally accepted auditing standards. Those standards require that we plan and perform the audit to obtain reasonable assurance about whether the financial statements are free of material misstatement. An audit includes examining, on a test basis, evidence supporting the amounts and disclosures in the financial statements. An audit also includes assessing the accounting principles used and significant estimates made by management, as well as evaluating the overall financial statement presentation. We believe that our audits provide a reasonable basis for our opinion.

In our opinion, the financial statements referred to above present fairly, in all material respects, the consolidated financial position of Provident Health Partners and subsidiaries at June 30, 1999 and 1998, and the consolidated results of their operations and their cash flows for the years then ended in conformity with generally accepted accounting principles.

Bailey & Smart

August 16, 1999

Exhibit 2

Provident Health Partners
Consolidated Balance Sheets

| | June 30, | |
	1999	1998
Assets		
Current assets:		
Cash and cash equivalents	$ 1,625,098	$ 11,904,719
Short-term investments	27,259,026	25,015,361
Accounts receivable (Note 3)	31,922,328	29,184,452
Inventories	2,540,985	3,266,578
Current portion of assets whose use is limited	6,382,311	1,072,547
Prepaid expenses	3,470,198	3,202,029
Interest	236,752	305,630
Total current assets	73,436,698	73,951,316
Assets whose use is limited (Note 4)		
By board for future capital purposes	17,191,961	14,691,486
By trustees under bond agreements	15,124,844	2,802,882
By donors—restricted net assets	871,191	838,063
	33,187,996	18,332,431
Property and equipment, net (Notes 5 and 6)	114,488,860	103,945,728
Other assets	8,644,018	6,298,047
Deferred financing costs, net	3,088,251	2,300,708
Total assets	$232,845,823	$204,828,230
Liabilities and Net Assets		
Current liabilities:		
Accounts payable	$ 14,842,921	$ 13,805,259
Accrued expenses	29,911,516	28,544,858
Accrued interest	810,602	1,165,788
Current portion of long-term debt	3,941,629	3,952,384
Total current liabilities	49,506,668	47,468,289
Other liabilities	1,420,159	900,986
Insurance reserves and claims	2,875,872	3,632,490
Long-term debt	115,584,209	95,930,761
Unrestricted net assets	63,458,915	56,895,704
Total liabilities and net assets	$232,845,823	$204,828,230

See accompanying notes.

Exhibit 3

Provident Health Partners
Consolidated Statement of Operations

| | Year ended June 30, | |
	1999	1998
Net patient service revenues (Note 2)	$243,631,506	$226,877,359
Other operating revenues	7,014,582	6,388,748
Total operating revenues	250,646,088	233,266,107
Operating expenses:		
Salaries and wages	102,744,316	96,439,738
Employee benefits	17,403,217	17,397,353
Supplies, utilities, and other	92,822,491	80,323,402
Depreciation and amortization	14,089,126	13,553,178
Interest	6,745,350	7,951,057
Provision for bad debts	10,531,705	11,914,312
Total operating expense	244,336,205	227,579,040
Income from operations	6,309,883	5,687,067
Non-operating gains, net (Note 8)	1,433,721	1,189,924
Income before extraordinary item	7,743,604	6,876,991
Extraordinary item—loss on refinancing (Note 6)	(1,435,112)	(746,000)
Increase in unrestricted net assets	6,308,492	6,130,991

See accompanying notes.

Exhibit 4

Provident Health Partners
Consolidated Statement of Cash Flows

	Year ended June 30,	
	1999	1998
Cash flows from operating activities		
Increase in unrestricted net assets	$ 6,308,492	$ 6,130,991
Noncash items included above:		
Depreciation, amortization, and other	18,534,651	16,321,929
Extraordinary item	1,435,112	746,000
Net changes in current assets and liabilities:		
Accounts receivable	(2,737,876)	13,274,937
Other current assets	526,302	635,261
Accounts payable	1,037,662	672,187
Other current liabilities	1,011,472	4,280,105
Decrease in other liabilities	(237,445)	(470,000)
Other changes		(228,758)
Net cash provided by operating activities	25,878,370	41,362,652
Cash flows from investing activities		
Additions to property and equipment	(28,383,654)	(13,699,312)
Proceeds from sale of property and equipment	655,955	343,700
Net change in assets whose use is limited	(20,165,329)	(13,678,563)
Net change in other assets	(3,512,704)	92,671
Net cash used in investing activities	(51,405,732)	(26,941,504)
Cash flows from financing activities		
Proceeds from long-term debt	55,555,012	7,355,000
Payment of long-term debt	(37,347,431)	(11,871,290)
Increase in deferred financing costs	(970,894)	(284,046)
Other changes	254,719	620,541
Net cash provided by (used in) financing activities	17,491,406	(4,179,795)
Net (decrease) increase in cash and short-term investment	(8,035,956)	10,241,353
Cash and short-term investments at beginning of year	36,920,080	26,678,727
Cash and short-term investments at end of year	$ 28,884,124	$ 36,920,080

See accompanying notes.

Exhibit 5

Provident Health Partners
Notes to Consolidated Financial Statements
June 30, 1999

1. Summary of Significant Accounting Policies
   a. Organization
      Provident Health Partners (the Corporation) is a tax-exempt Colorado corporation that serves as the parent holding company of St. Andrew Hospitals, Marcy Medical Center, and several other affiliated healthcare-related organizations. The Corporation is a member of a larger Health Care Systems, Inc. (HCS), a tax-exempt Delaware corporation, which supervises and conducts the healthcare activities of the HCS in Ohio and Delaware.
   b. Mission Statement
      The Corporation's mission includes providing healthcare and related services through its inpatient, outpatient, and community-based facilities and programs. Those activities which are directly related to the furtherance of this purpose are considered to be operating activities.
   c. Nonoperating Gains and Losses
      Activities that result in gains or losses which are indirectly related to the Corporation's primary mission are considered to be nonoperating. Nonoperating gains and losses include interest and similar earnings on investments (other than trustee-held investments related to borrowed funds). A majority of fund-raising activities and general donations are solicited by an affiliate of the Corporation, the Provident Health Foundation. Unrestricted gifts and bequests received directly by the Corporation or its affiliates are recorded as nonoperating items.
   d. Basis of Presentation
      The accompanying consolidated financial statements include the accounts of the following entities: Provident Health Partners, St. Andrew Hospitals, Marcy Medical Center, Provident Senior Care Services, Provident Health Foundation, Provident Home Health Services, and Provident Care Services, Inc. All significant balances and transactions between entities have been eliminated.
   e. Net Patient Service Revenues
      Patient service revenues are recorded net of all deductions from revenue. Accordingly, gross revenues have been reduced to reflect contractually agreed-upon allowances and other allowances or deductions whereby the services rendered are paid at less than the Corporation's established billing rates. Accounts receivable for patient services and revenues that have been adjusted to the estimated amounts are subject to further adjustment upon review by the third-party payers. The settlements related to these third-party payers, $11.8 million and $7.8 million at June 30, 1999 and 1998, respectively, are included in accrued expenses. Management believes that adequate provision has been made for any adjustments that may result from review by the third-party payers.
   f. Charity Care
      In accord with the mission and philosophy of the Corporation, the Corporation accepts and treats patients without regard to their ability to pay. A patient is

Exhibit 5 (cont.)

classified as a charity patient in accordance with criteria defined in established policies of the Hospital. Charity care is the recognition of services rendered for which no payment is expected. Charity care is measured in gross patient service charges and is not included in net patient service revenue. Charity care provided in 1999 and 1998, measured at the Corporation's established rates, totaled $6,103,799 and $5,429,209, respectively.

g. Cash and Cash Equivalents

All certificates of deposit, debt instruments purchased, cash on deposit and other cash equivalents with a maturity of 90 days or less are included in the category of cash and cash equivalents; those with a maturity of 91 days to one year are included in the category of short-term investments. The carrying value of these assets approximates market value.

h. Inventories

Inventories are stated at the lower of cost or market, with cost determined on a first-in, first-out basis.

i. Assets Whose Use is Limited

Assets whose use is limited are stated at the lower of cost or market value. The market values of investments traded on a national exchange are based on the last reported sales price on the last business day of the year; market values of investments traded in the over-the-counter market are based on the average of the last recorded bid and ask prices. The market values of pooled investment trusts are based on the Corporation's pro rata portion of the market value of the trusts.

j. Property and Equipment

Property and equipment are stated at historical cost or, if donated, at fair market value at date of receipt. Depreciation is calculated using the straight-line method over the estimated useful lives of the assets and includes amortization of assets held under capital leases.

k. Deferred Financing Costs

Issuance costs of long-term debt are capitalized and amortized using the interest method over the outstanding term of the related debt.

l. Unrestricted Net Assets

Donor-restricted funds included in net assets are for purposes designated by donors or grantors and are not available for general operating purposes. Donor-restricted funds were $871,191 and $838,063, respectively, as of June 30, 1999 and 1998. All remaining net assets are available for general operating purposes.

m. Liability Insurance

The Corporation's professional and general liability insurance is underwritten primarily through MSJ Insurance Company (MSJ), a wholly owned, captive insurance company of HCS. Professional liability coverage is provided up to $3 million per occurrence with an annual aggregate of $20 million. Excess insurance of $30 million for professional and general liability risks is maintained through coverage with Consolidated Casualty Risk Retention Group (CCRRG). In addition, the Corporation participated in a group risk sharing pool, on a claims-made basis, offered by a commercial insurance company. Under the terms of the risk sharing pool, which terminated in May 1997, the

Exhibit 5 (cont.)

Corporation is responsible for paid losses, subject to an established maximum, and shares in group losses determined on a retrospective basis. Premiums charged for all insurance coverage purchased through MSJ were $2,442,710 and $2,241,609 in 1999 and 1998, respectively, and include retrospective adjustment based upon the claims experience of MSJ.

n. Tax Status

The Corporation and its affiliates, except for Care Service, Inc., are exempt from federal income taxes under Section 501 (c) (3) of the Internal Revenue Code. Care Services, Inc. is a for-profit taxable entity.

o. Reclassifications

Certain reclassifications have been made to the 1998 financial statements in order to conform with the 1999 presentation.

2. Net Patient Service Revenues

A summary of gross and net patient service revenues for the years ended June 30, 1999 and 1998 follows:

	1999	*1998*
Inpatient revenues	$ 297,548,299	$ 275,338,747
Outpatient revenues	89,499,747	81,833,097
Long-term care revenues:		
Skilled nursing care	1,318,810	2,770,982
Independent living care	3,193,917	2,886,557
Gross patient service revenues	391,560,773	362,829,383
Less provision for:		
Contractual adjustments and allowance	$(141,825,468)	$(130,522,815)
Provisions for charity care	(6,103,799)	(5,429,209)
Net patient service revenues	$ 243,631,506	$ 226,877,359

3. Accounts Receivable

A summary of total accounts receivable at June 30, 1999 and 1998 follows:

	1999	*1998*
Patient accounts receivable	$ 41,862,427	$ 39,814,316
Less allowance for doubtful accounts	(11,228,597)	(11,656,265)
Net patient accounts receivable	30,633,830	28,157,871
Other receivables	1,288,498	1,026,581
Total accounts receivable	$ 31,922,328	$ 29,184,452

The carrying value of accounts receivable approximates fair value.

4. Assets Whose Use is Limited

Assets whose use is limited include amounts designated for capital improvements and debt retirement purposes by the Board of Trustees. Also included are assets

Exhibit 5 (cont.)

held according to bond indenture requirements. As of June 30, 1999 and 1998, assets whose use is limited consisted of:

	1999 Market Value	1999 Carrying Value	1998 Carrying Value
Cash and equivalents	$ 2,330,096	$ 2,330,096	$ 1,503,529
Interest receivable	144,537	144,537	142,500
Investments:			
U.S. Government securities	10,364,928	10,315,210	10,581,377
Corporate debt securities	1,087,000	1,087,000	4,489,572
HCS Investment Pool (HIP)	2,741,441	2,688,000	2,688,000
HCS Venture Investment Pool (VIP)	1,500,000	1,500,000	
HCS 1998B Funds	21,505,464	21,505,464	
Total assets whose use is limited	$39,673,466	$39,570,307	$19,404,978

HIP, VIP, and 1998B Funds are pooled investment trusts administered by HCS. Investments in the trusts are comprised of cash equivalents, U.S. Government and other fixed income securities, and loans to HCS member institutions.

The market value of assets whose use is limited approximates cost at June 30, 1998.

5. Property and Equipment

At June 30, 1999 and 1998, property and equipment consisted of:

	1999	1998
Land improvements	$ 3,313,690	$ 3,112,474
Buildings and improvements	123,574,703	118,747,680
Equipment	61,913,416	61,583,965
Assets held under capital leases	7,010,841	8,731,708
	195,812,650	192,175,827
Less accumulated depreciation and amortization	(108,514,133)	(100,590,700)
	87,298,517	91,585,127
Land	5,365,870	5,513,870
Construction in progress	21,824,473	6,846,731
Property and equipment, net	$ 114,488,860	$ 103,945,728

Exhibit 5 (cont.)

6. Capital Structure

At June 30, 1999 and 1998, long-term debt consisted of the following:

Series	Interest Rates	1999	1998
Fixed Interest Rate Bond Issues 1988A	6.40% to 7.75%	$ 48,075,000	$ 49,050,000
Variable Interest Rate Bond Issues 1985A (refunded with 1998 issue)	Weekly rates		22,065,000
		48,070,000	71,115,000
Other borrowing under the HCS master trust indenture:			
Series 1991A Note Payable to HCS	4.75% to 8.50%	6,831,194	7,297,059
Colorado Health Facilities Authority Note, Series 1980, bearing interest at 7.75%, due in increasing annual installments through 2010		$ 1,315,408	$ 1,453,868
Colorado Health Facilities Authority Revenue Bonds, Series 1986A, bearing interest at rates ranging from 5.75% to 7.375%, due in increasing annual installments through 2014			10,510,000
Series 1998A Note Payable to HCS	3.10% to 6.25%	12,020,000	
Series 1998B Note Payable to HCS	4.30% to 6.25%	23,055,000	
Series 1992C Note Payable to HCS	Variable	21,770,000	
Other		4,062,929	4,215,176
Total Obligated Group debt		117,129,531	94,591,103
Capital lease obligations		3,668,983	5,372,822
Other long-term debt		168,772	237,918
		120,967,286	100,201,843
Less:			
Unamortized bond discount		(1,441,448)	(318,698)
Current portion		(3,941,629)	(3,952,384)
Total long-term debt		$115,584,209	$ 95,930,761

Exhibit 5 (cont.)

7. Nonoperating Gains, Net
Nonoperating gains, net consists of the following for the years ended June 30, 1999 and 1998:

	1999	1998
Income on investments	$1,827,820	$1,885,268
Unrestricted contribution, net		(12,187)
Rental properties	(10,516)	(49,271)
Loss on sale of assets	(287,174)	(522,270)
Other, net	(96,409)	(111,616)
	$1,433,721	$1,189,924

8. Related Party Transactions
HCS provides certain administrative and biomedical services to the Corporation. During the years ended June 30, 1999 and 1998, the Corporation incurred expenses of $1,967,724 and $1,879,836, respectively, for services provided by HCS.

9. Commitments
The Corporation has commenced certain construction expansion projects. These expansion projects include a parking garage and major renovation at St. Andrew Central and are expected to be completed in 1999. These projects are financed by operations and revenue bonds issued in 1998 (see Note 6). Construction in progress related to the projects through June 30, 1999 was approximately $8,600,000. Estimated cost to complete at June 30, 1999 is approximately $32,600,000.

15. International HOMECARE, Inc. reported the following results for 1998, as summarized below:

	1998	1997
Revenues:		
Net sales	$228,051,236	$221,725,771
Service fees	50,626,542	46,933,304
Franchise sales (fees)	7,010,918	7,194,566
Property management	9,984,184	11,308,381
Other	1,436,944	1,661,352
	297,109,824	288,823,374
Costs and expenses:		
Supplies and materials	204,649,409	197,713,547
Property management expenses	9,357,375	10,677,337
Selling, general and administrative	35,472,375	35,210,686
Interest expense (income)	316,316	(179,471)
	249,795,156	243,422,099
Income before income taxes	47,314,668	45,401,275
Income taxes	27,220,000	17,480,000
Net income	$ 20,094,668	$ 27,921,275
Earnings per common share	$1.12	$1.05

International HOMECARE's Consolidated Balance Sheet is summarized below:

Assets		
Current assets:		
Cash and cash equivalents	$ 32,243,394	$ 32,748,307
Marketable securities	7,072,786	—
Notes receivable, net	5,852,112	5,076,813
Accounts receivable, net	21,393,559	19,283,001
Inventories	4,373,280	5,511,885
Prepaid expenses	1,225,901	1,453,522
Miscellaneous	935,745	534,652
Total current assets	72,096,777	64,608,180
Other assets:		
Notes receivable, net	14,282,384	14,922,966
Miscellaneous	2,226,970	2,179,963
Total other assets	16,509,354	17,102,929
Other revenue producing assets:		
Franchise rights, net	84,954,847	86,298,940
Rental properties, net	2,381,828	2,565,880
Miscellaneous	70,227	132,125
Total other assets	87,406,902	88,996,945
Property, plant, and equipment, net	3,466,675	4,243,307
	$179,479,708	$174,951,361

Liabilities and Stockholders' Equity		
Current liabilities:		
Drafts and accounts payable	$ 16,799,022	$ 17,330,549
Committed advertising	1,603,745	31,476
Other liabilities	5,996,213	6,282,776
Income taxes payable	87,743	2,020,140
Current maturities (L-T Debt)	12,040,373	2,261,396
Total current liabilities	36,527,096	27,926,337
Deferred franchise income	394,245	580,518
Deferred income taxes	4,280,000	3,660,000
Long-term debt	25,819,558	46,011,431
Contingencies and commitments (see notes)		
Stockholders' equity:		
Class A common stock	164,011	169,157
Class B common stock	91,751	93,289
Paid-in capital	4,099,358	4,088,861
Retained earnings	109,430,867	92,147,342
Equity adjustments	(1,327,178)	274,426
Total stockholders' equity	112,458,809	96,773,075
	$179,479,708	$174,951,361

A summary of HOMECARE's cash flow statement shows:

Net cash provided by operating activities	$ 19,133,570	$ 26,302,458
Net cash provided by (used in) investing activities	2,802,752	(11,239,423)
Net cash used in financing activities	(22,865,102)	(11,174,581)
Other adjustments	(576,133)	86,363
Net (decrease) increase in cash	$ (1,504,913)	$ 3,974,817
Cash payments for income taxes	$ 19,989,926	$ 17,153,932
Cash payments for interest	$ 4,052,302	$ 3,703,994

    a. Identify any unusual terms in International HOMECARE's summarized financial statements.

    b. Identify any unusual trends or events.

16. With regard to the preceding financial statements from International HOMECARE, Inc., prepare a horizontal analysis of the income statement.

17. With regard to the preceding financial statements from International HOMECARE, Inc., prepare a vertical analysis of the income statement.

18. With regard to the preceding financial statements from International HOMECARE, Inc., calculate the appropriate liquidity ratios.

19. With regard to the preceding financial statements from International HOMECARE, Inc., conduct a profitability analysis.

20. With regard to the preceding financial statements from International HOMECARE, Inc., conduct a capital structure analysis.

21. With regard to your analysis of International HOMECARE, Inc., write a short memo summarizing your conclusions. Indicate why this firm might be facing financial threats or opportunities. Also, indicate what additional data you might need to refine your analyses or conclusions.

22. General Hospital Corporation reported the following results for 1998, as summarized below:

Years Ended October 31,	1998	1997
Revenues	$3,716,918	$3,587,777
Costs applicable to revenues	2,355,424	2,391,310
Selling, general and administrative expenses	1,076,848	1,209,433
Corporate expenses	43,560	42,169
Merger and restructuring charges		72,777
Operating earnings (loss)	241,086	(127,912)
Investment income	23,716	129,120
Interest expense	(86,097)	(349,061)
Other income (expense), net	8,341	(15,171)
Earnings (loss) before income taxes, extraordinary gain, and other adjustments	187,046	(363,024)
Income tax expense (benefit)	72,947	(69,902)
Earnings (loss) before extraordinary gain and other adjustments	114,099	(293,122)
Extraordinary gain on elimination of debt, net	419,557	—
Other adjustments	(39,196)	—
Net earnings (loss)	$ 494,460	$ (293,122)
Amounts applicable to common shareholders:		
Earnings (loss) before extraordinary gain and other adjustments	$ 1.44	$ (3.88)
Extraordinary gain, net	5.30	—
Other adjustments, net	(.49)	—
Net earnings (loss)	$ 6.25	$ (3.88)

General Hospital's cash flow statement is summarized below:

Year ended October 31,	1998	1997
Net cash provided by operations	$ 237,137	$ 206,385
Net cash used by investment activities	(493,355)	(485,832)
Net cash (used) provided by financing transactions	(932,022)	262,230
Net decrease in cash during the year	(1,188,240)	(17,217)
Supplemental schedule of cash flow information		
Cash paid for interest	$ 109,944	$ 232,856
Cash paid for income taxes	$ 59,192	$ 64,350

General Hospital's consolidated balance sheet is summarized below:

October 31,	1998	1997
Assets		
Current assets		
Cash and equivalents	$ 430,728	$1,618,968
Accounts receivable, net	399,265	340,265
Inventories	411,093	417,585
Other current assets	52,874	176,428
Total current assets	1,293,960	2,553,246
Property and equipment		
Land, buildings & improvements	683,081	621,092
Fixtures and equipment	470,080	427,148
Radiology plates and films	354,280	364,875
	1,507,441	1,413,115
Less accumulated depreciation and amortization	655,870	584,306
Total property and equipment, net	851,571	828,809
Other assets		
Goodwill and other intangibles	415,072	427,991
Other	115,359	98,284
Total other assets	530,431	526,275
Insurance assets		
Fixed maturity securities, commercial paper, cash, and other investments	2,361,598	2,070,007
Other assets	249,523	229,011
Total insurance assets	2,611,121	2,300,018
	$5,287,083	$6,208,348

Liabilities

Current liabilities

Notes payable	$ 18,369	$1,827,116
Accounts payable	258,936	241,324
Accrued liabilities	385,280	377,152
Taxes payable	24,281	28,455
Other current liabilities	58,765	80,022
Total current liabilities	745,631	2,554,069
Long-term liabilities		
Notes and debentures	902,295	860,147
Other long-term liabilities	183,758	120,077
Total long-term liabilities	1,086,053	980,224
Deferred income taxes	205,600	138,983
Insurance liabilities	2,325,358	2,062,318
Commitments and contingencies	—	—
Shareholders' equity		
Preferred stock		
Cumulative convertible	2,890	3,855
Common stock		
Class B stock	21,951	24,819
Common stock	54,341	50,341
Paid-in capital	860,133	854,240
Other adjustments	(3,409)	4,598
Retained earnings (deficit)	(11,465)	(465,099)
Total shareholders' equity	924,441	472,754
	$5,287,083	$6,208,348

23. With regard to the preceding financial statements from General Hospital Corporation, prepare a horizontal analysis of the income statement.

24. With regard to the preceding financial statements from General Hospital Corporation, prepare a vertical analysis of the income statement.

25. With regard to the preceding financial statements from General Hospital Corporation, calculate the appropriate liquidity ratios.

26. With regard to the preceding financial statements from General Hospital Corporation, conduct a profitability analysis.

27. With regard to the preceding financial statements from General Hospital Corporation, conduct a capital structure analysis.

28. With regard to your analysis of General Hospital Corporation, write a short memo summarizing your conclusions. Indicate why General Hospital might be facing financial threats or opportunities. Also, indicate what additional data you might need to refine your analyses or conclusions.

29. EDSYS is a world leader in developing healthcare informatics technology for other healthcare providers. EDSYS reported the following results for 1998, as summarized below:

Year Ended December 31 (in millions)	1998	1997
Revenues		
Contractual revenues and fees	$8,507.3	$8,155.2
Interest and other income	54.5	63.7
Total revenues	8,561.8	8,218.9
Costs and expenses		
Cost of revenues	6,390.6	6,205.8
Selling, general and administrative	1,005.4	969.3
Interest	34.5	43.0
Total costs and expenses	7,430.5	7,218.1
Income before income taxes	1,131.3	1,000.8
Provision for income taxes	407.3	365.3
Separate consolidated net income	$ 724.0	$ 635.5

EDSYS reported the following consolidated balance sheets, as summarized below:

December 31 (in millions)	1998	1997
Assets		
Current assets		
Cash and cash equivalents	$ 383.4	$ 421.9
Marketable securities	224.1	166.0
Accounts receivable	1,412.5	1,214.0
Accounts receivable (subsidiaries)	112.6	41.1
Inventories	130.7	88.5
Prepaids and others	243.5	225.5
Total current assets	2,506.8	2,157.0
Property and equipment, net		
Land	121.6	84.7
Buildings and facilities	532.0	534.6
Computer equipment	1,275.5	916.2
Other equipment and furniture	185.6	185.2
Total property and equipment, net	2,114.7	1,720.7
Operating and other assets		
Land held for development, at cost	94.4	148.1
Investment in leases and other	1,159.9	1,231.4
Software, goodwill, and other intangibles, net		
Total operating and other assets	1,066.3	866.3
Total Assets	$6,942.1	$6,123.5
Liabilities and Stockholders' Equity		
Current liabilities		
Accounts payable	$ 359.8	$ 348.0
Accrued liabilities	996.0	918.4
Deferred revenues	429.7	295.8
Income taxes	202.2	66.0
Notes payable	172.7	274.9
Total current liabilities	2,160.4	1,903.1
Deferred income taxes	641.5	595.9
Notes payable	522.8	561.1
Commitments and contingencies	—	—
Stockholders' equity		
Common stock, without par value	421.2	365.9
Retained earnings	3,196.2	2,697.5
Total stockholders' equity	3,617.4	3,063.4
Total Liabilities and Stockholders' Equity	$6,942.1	$6,123.5

EDSYS's consolidated statements of cash flow disclosed the following summary information:

Net cash provided by operating activities	$ 1,395.0	$1,135.8
Net cash used in investing activities	(1,049.7)	(813.6)
Net cash used in financing activities	(370.2)	(153.0)
Effect of exchange rate changes	(13.6)	(7.9)
Net increase (decrease) in cash	$ (38.5)	$ 161.3
Cash paid for:		
Income taxes, net of refunds	$ 183.8	$ 252.6
Interest, net	$ 40.2	$ 46.8

30. With regard to the preceding financial statements from EDSYS, prepare a horizontal analysis of the income statement.

31. With regard to the preceding financial statements from EDSYS, prepare a vertical analysis of the income statement.

32. With regard to the preceding financial statements from EDSYS, calculate the appropriate liquidity ratios.

33. With regard to the preceding financial statements from EDSYS, conduct a profitability analysis.

34. With regard to the preceding financial statements from EDSYS, conduct a capital structure analysis.

35. With regard to your analysis of EDSYS, write a short memo summarizing your conclusions. Indicate why EDSYS might be facing financial threats or opportunities. Also, indicate what additional data you might need to refine your analyses or conclusions.

36. In your library, find several recent articles that discuss financial statement analysis, which may also be called financial analysis.
    a. Compare and contrast the ratios presented in this text with those in the articles you selected.
    b. Discuss the advantages and disadvantages of any new ratios that were consistent across several of these articles. In other words, if the authors of these articles are in agreement about several ratios, focus your attention on these new ratios where there is commonality.
    c. Apply these new (part b) ratios to the text's discussion of Sample Hospital in chapter 11. Compare the results of using these new ratios with the results obtained using the ratios described in this text.

37. In your library, find several recent articles that discuss financial statement analysis, which may also be called financial analysis.
    a. Compare and contrast the ratios presented in this text with those in the articles you selected.
    b. Discuss the advantages and disadvantages of any new ratios that were consistent across several of these articles. In other words, if the authors of these articles are in agreement about several ratios, focus your attention on these new ratios where there is commonality.
    c. Apply these new (part b) ratios to an analysis of a real healthcare organization. Your instructor will probably determine which organization on which to focus. Compare the results of using these new ratios with the results obtained using the ratios described in this text.

38. Obtain the audited financial statements of a local healthcare provider. Apply the financial analysis framework described in chapter 11, as appropriate, to this firm. Write a short report describing your conclusions regarding this firm's performance. Indicate why you would, or would not, be concerned about the long-term success of this firm.

References

Abbey, Duane C., and L. Lamar Blount. "Assessing the Financial Implications of APGs." *Healthcare Financial Management* (October 1996): 50–55.

AICPA. *Audit and Accounting Guide: Health Care Organizations, 1996.* New York, NY: AICPA, 1996.

Altman, Edward. "Financial Ratios, Discriminant Analysis and the Predictions of Corporate Bankruptcy." *The Journal of Finance* (September 1988): 589–608.

Black, C. "Use and Abuse of Net Working Capital." *Accountants' Journal* 72, no. 3 (1993): 76–78.

Boles, Keith E. "Stategic Financial Analysis for Long-Term Care Facilities." *The Journal of Long-Term Care Administration* 16, no. 3 (fall 1988): 10–15.

Broyles, Robert W., and Michael D. Rosko. *Fiscal Management of Healthcare Institutions.* Owings Mills, MD: National Health Publishing, 1990, chapter 13.

Cheramy, Shirley J., and Martha Garner. "Guidelines Clarify Managed Care Accounting Procedures." *Healthcare Financial Management* (August 1989): 45–56.

Choate, Marc G. "Financial Ratio Analysis." *Hospital Progress* (January 1974): 49–57, 67.

Choate, Marc G., and Kazuaka Tanaka. "Using Financial Ratio Analysis to Compare Hospital's Performance." *Hospital Progress* 60, no. 12 (December 1979).

Cleverley, William O., PhD., CPA. "1996 Hospital Finance Almanac." *Healthcare Financial Management* (1996).

————. "Financial Flexibility: A Measure of Financial Position for Hospital Managers." *Hospital & Health Services Administration* 29, no. 1 (January–February 1984): 23–37.

———. "Strategic Operating Indicators Point to Equity Growth." *Healthcare Financial Management* (July 1988): 54–64.

———. "Trends in the Hospital Financial Picture." *Healthcare Financial Management* (February 1994): 57.

Coffey, R.S. "Retroactive Reimbursement Under HCFA's PPS for Capital." *Healthcare Financial Management* (October 1993): 60–66.

Counte, Michael E., Gerald L. Glandon, and Karen Holloman. "Using Ratios to Measure Hospital Financial Performance: Can the Process Be Simplified?" *Health Services Management Research* 1, no. 3 (November 1988): 173–180.

Coyne, Joseph S. "Measuring Hospital Performance in Multi-Institutional Organizations Using Financial Ratios." *Health Care Management Review* (fall 1985): 35–42.

Foster, George. *Financial Statement Analysis.* Englewood Cliffs: Prentice Hall, 1986.

Gallinger G.W., and P.B. Healey. *Liquidity Analysis and Management.* Reading, MA: Addison-Wesley Publishing, 1987.

Gapenski, Louis C. *Understanding Health Care Financial Management: Text, Cases, and Models.* Ann Arbor, MI: AUPHA Press and Health Administration Press, 1993.

Glandon, Gerald L., Michael Counte, and Karen Holloway. "An Analytical Review of Hospital Financial Performance Measures." *Hospital & Health Services Administration* (November 1987): 439–455.

Gombola, Michael J., Mark E. Haskins, J. Edward Ketz, and David D. Williams. "Cash Flow in Bankruptcy Prediction." *Financial Management* (winter 1987): 55–65.

Granof, M.H., P.W. Bell, and B.R. Neumann. *Accounting for Managers and Investors.* Englewood Cliffs, NJ: Prentice Hall, 1993.

Hay, L.E., and J.H. Engstrom. *Essentials of Accounting for Governmental and Not-for-Profit Organizations.* Homewood, IL: Irwin, 1987.

Karpinski, Joseph P. "Designing a Successful Investment Program." *Healthcare Financial Management* (February 1997): 58–63.

Long, H.W. "Valuation as a Criterion in Not-for-Profit Decision-Making." *Health Care Management Review* (summer 1976): 34–46.

Luecke, Randall W., David T. Meeting, and William G. Stotzer. "Implementing SFAS No. 121: Accounting for Impaired Assets." *Healthcare Financial Management* (October 1996): 56–62.

Lynch, Janet, and Michael McCue. "The Effects of the For-Profit Multihospital Ownership on Hospital Financial and Operating Performance." *Health Services Management Research* 3, no. 3. (November 1990): 182–92.

McCue, Michael J. "The Use of Cash Flow to Analyze Financial Distress in California Hospitals." *Hospital & Health Administration* 36, no. 2 (summer 1991): 223–241.

McCue, Michael J., Steven T. Renn, and Geoge D. Pillari. "Factors Affecting Credit Rating Downgrades of Hospital Revenue Bonds." *Inquiry* 27 (fall 1990): 242–254.

Mieling, Terence M., and John O. Keshner. "Accessing Capital for Integrated Delivery Systems." *Healthcare Financial Management* (January 1996): 32–35.

Mullner, Ross, Robert Rydman, David Whiteis, and Robert Rich. "Rural Community Hospitals and Factors Correlated With Their Closing." *Public Health Reports* 104, no. 4 (July–August 1989): 315–325.

Murray, Dennis, Bruce R. Neumann, and Pieter Elgers. *Using Financial Accounting: An Introduction.* Cincinnati, Ohio: South-Western College Publishing, 1997.

Nelson, Bruce. "Improving Cash Flow Through Benchmarking." *Healthcare Financial Management* (September 1994): 74–78.

Neumann, Bruce R., Jan P. Clement, and Jean C. Cooper. *Financial Management: Concepts and Applications for Health Care Organizations.* Dubuque: Kendall/ Hunt, 1997.

Ryan, J. Bruce, and Scott B. Clay. "How to Determine Financial Reserves for Capitated Contracts." *Healthcare Financial Management* (March 1995): 18.

Saccurato, F. "The Study of Working Capital." *Business Credit* 96, no. 1 (1994): 36–37.

Smith, Larry J., Jeannie Frazier, and W. Seth Crone. "Strategic Considerations for Capital Formation and Development." *Healthcare Financial Management* (March 1994): 30–36.

Soenen, L.A. "Cash Conversion Cycle and Corporate Profitability." *Journal of Cash Management* 13, no. 4 (1993): 53–57.

Sterns, Jay B., and Todd K. Majidzadeh. "A Framework for Evaluating Capital Structure." *Journal of Health Care Finance* (winter 1995): 80–85.

Stickney, Clyde P. *Financial Statement Analysis: A Strategic Perspective.* New York: Harcourt, Brace, Jovanovich, 1996.

Sylvestre, Joanne, and Frank R. Urbanic. "Effective Methods for Cash Flow Analysis." *Healthcare Financial Management* (July 1994): 62–72.

Titera, W. "FASB Proposes Changes in Not-for-Profit Reporting." *Healthcare Financial Management* (April 1993): 39–49.

Varwig, David, and Ronald Barkley. "Capital Financing Along the Integration Highway." *Journal of Health Care Finance* (summer 1995): 60–75.

West, Joan, Sandee Glickman, and Alan G. Seidner. "Investing: Reducing Risks to Enhance Returns." *Healthcare Financial Management* (September 1996): 48–51.

Comparative Data Sources:

1. Dun & Bradstreet Information Services, *Industry Norms and Key Business Ratios,* Murray Hill, NJ.
2. Robert Morris Associates, *Annual Statement Studies,* Philadelphia, PA.
3. Standard & Poor's Corporation, *Ratings Handbook and Industry Surveys,* New York, NY.
4. Gale Research Inc., *Manufacturing U.S.A. Industry Analyses,* Detroit, MI.
5. Medical Group Management Association, *Cost Survey,* Denver, CO.
6. Center for Research in Ambulatory Health Care Administration, *Performance Efficiency Evaluation Report* (PEER), Denver, CO.
7. Prentice Hall, *Almanac of Business and Industrial Financial Ratios*
8. Medical Economics, *Practice Expenses Survey.*
9. American Medical Association, *Socioeconomic Characteristics of Medical Practice.*
10. American Medical Association, *Physician Marketplace Statistics.*
11. Medical Group Management Association, *Management Compensation Survey.*
12. Hoechst Marion Roussel, Inc., *Managed Care Digest,* HMO, Medical Group Practice, Nursing Home editions, also information on PPOs, Home Health, and Pharmacies, K.C., MO.

13. Missouri Department of Health, *Missouri Hospital Revenues,* Jefferson City, MO.
14. U.S. Department of Health and Human Services, *Health United States 1993,* Washington, DC.
15. U.S. Department of Health and Human Services, *Vital and Health Statistics, Current Estimates From the National Health Interview Survey,* published annually, Washington, DC.
16. U.S. Department of Health and Human Services, *Vital and Health Statistics: National Ambulatory Medical Care Survey:* Annual Summary, Washington, DC.
17. Billian Publishing, *Hospital Blue Book,* Atlanta, GA.
18. Billian Publishing, *Healthcare Blue Book,* Atlanta, GA
19. Group Health Association of America, HMO Industry Profile, Washington, DC.
20. Health Care Investment Analysis, 207 East Redwood St., Suite 400, Baltimore, MD 21202, 301-576-9600 (HCIA).
    —*HCIA, Comparative Performance of U.S. Hospitals: The Sourcebook*
    —*The GUIDE to the Nursing Home Industry*
    —*Medicare DRG Handbook:* Comparative Clinical and Financial Standards, Baltimore, MD.
    —*Directory of U.S. Hospitals.*
    —*Distressed Hospital Quarterly.*
    —*Directory of Nursing Homes.*
    —*Directory of Retirement Facilities.*
    —*Directory of Medical Rehabilitation Programs.*
    —*Directory of Alzheimer's Disease Treatment Facilities and Home Health Programs.*
21. The Center for Healthcare Industry Performance Studies (CHIPS), Columbus, OH.
    —*The 1994 Almanac of Hospital Financial & Operating Indicators.*
    —*Facility & Activity Center Tracking (FACT) Service.*
    —*Clinical Assessment Profiles (CAPS) Service.*
    —*Financial Analysis Service (FAS).*
    —*Strategic Operating Indicator Service (SOI).*
    —*Medicare Cost Report Service (MCR).*
    —*Physician Practice Acquisition Resource Book.*
    —*Healthcare Bottom Line. (Newsletter)*

APPENDIX 11–1

Sample reports from the following professional association are included in this appendix. For additional information refer to:

The Almanac of Hospital Financial and Operating Indicators, 1996–1997
   The Center for Healthcare Industry Performance Standards (CHIPS)

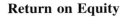

Return on Equity

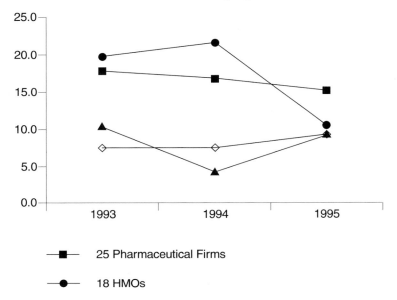

- ■— 25 Pharmaceutical Firms
- ●— 18 HMOs
- ▲— 11 For-Profit Hospital Chains
- ◇— Voluntary Non-Profit Hospitals

Key Financial Indicators

	Small Urban Hospital Median	U.S. Hospital Median
Total Margin	1.7%	4.7%
Days Cash on Hand, All Sources	45.4	92.1
Total Debt to Total Assets	51.6%	45.1%
Average Age of Plant	8.9	8.7

Source: The Center for Healthcare Industry Performance Standards (CHIPS),
The Almanac of Hospital Financial & Operating Indicators 1996–1997 Edition p.5

Composite Average Balance Sheet*
U.S. Hospital Industry, 1991–1995

	1991	1995	Annual Growth Rate
Assets			
Cash & Short-Term Investments	$ 4,424	$ 8,696	18.4%
Accounts Receivable	11,339	12,417	2.3%
Inventory	831	1,021	5.3%
Other Current Assets	1,504	2,872	17.6%
Total Current Assets	18,098	25,006	8.4%
Net Fixed Assets	30,608	39,886	6.8%
Replacement Funds	10,570	16,833	12.3%
Other Assets	5,865	8,349	9.2%
Total Assets	$65,141	$90,074	8.4%
Liabilities & Equity			
Current Liabilities	$ 9,822	$13,080	7.4%
Long-Term Debt	21,517	26,666	5.5%
Other Liabilities	2,280	4,184	16.4%
Equity	31,522	46,144	10.0%
Total Liabilities & Equity	$65,141	$90,074	8.4%

*Data in thousands

Source: The Center for Healthcare Industry Performance Standards (CHIPS), The Almanac of Hospital Financial & Operating Indicators 1996–1997 Edition p.6

Composite Average Income Statement*
U.S. Hospital Industry, 1991–1995

	1991	1995	Annual Growth Rate
Revenues			
Net Patient Revenue	$56,746	$74,678	7.1%
Other Operating Revenue	3,236	4,719	9.9%
Total Operating Revenue	59,982	79,397	7.3%
Operating Expenses			
Interest Expense	1,532	1,689	2.5%
Depreciation Expense	3,132	4,441	9.1%
Other Operating Expense	53,722	70,121	6.9%
Total Operating Expense	58,386	76,251	6.9%
Operating Income	1,146	3,146	28.7%
Nonoperating Revenue	1,177	1,443	5.2%
Extraordinary Items	357	(50)	NM
Excess or Revenues over Expenses	$ 2,680	$ 4,539	14.1%

*Data in thousands

Source: The Center for Healthcare Industry Performance Standards (CHIPS), The Almanac of Hospital Financial & Operating Indicators 1996–1997 Edition p.7

Total Margin

Definition

Total Margin is defined as the excess of revenues over expenses divided by total revenues net of allowances and uncollectibles. This ratio therefore reflects profits from both operations and nonoperations. Total Margin can also be expressed as the sum of the Operating Margin plus the Nonoperating Gain Ratio.

Trends

• Total Margin increased significantly in 1995 to 4.9 percent from 4.0 percent in 1994. This increase was in sharp contrast to the relative stability of Total Margins during the last four years. The improvement in Total Margins was a result of increases in Operating Margins and also increases in Nonoperating Gains. Also contributing was a decline in extraordinary losses that resulted from advance refundings of tax exempt debt and declines in charges for post retirement health care benefits. Data from Medicare Cost Reports show a Total Margin of 4.1 percent which is up from 3.2 percent in 1994. Medicare Cost Report measures of profitability are usually lower than the Financial Analysis Service (FAS) audited database values because FAS subscribers are often larger and more profitable.

Performance Implications

• Hospitals in the high-performance group realized significant improvements in their Total Margin,

All U.S. Quartiles (CSS)

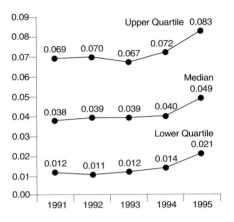

Performance Medians (CSS)

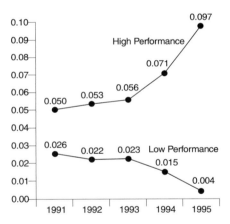

while those in the low-performance group slid further downhill. The gap between these two groups appears to be widening and causes some concern for the long-term viability of many low-performance hospitals. Improving Operating Margins has been the factor contributing most to the increase in Total Margin for the high-performance hospitals, and declines in Operating Margin have caused the decline in Total Margin for the low-performance hospitals. High-performing hospitals have a substantial advantage over low-performing hospitals in their price structures and realize $716 more per case mix adjusted discharge than low-performing hospitals.

Source: The Center for Healthcare Industry Performance Standards (CHIPS), The Almanac of Hospital Financial & Operating Indicators 1996–1997 Edition p.16 and p.17

Operating Margin

Definition

Operating Margin is defined as the proportion of total revenue that has been realized in income from operations. This measure is used by many analysts as the primary measure of hospital profitability. While this measure is valuable, we believe that income must ultimately be related to investment to provide a meaningful measure of profitability.

Trends

- Median values for the Operating Margin have been increasing each year during most of the last five years and increased to 3.2 percent in 1995 from 3.0 percent in 1994. The primary reason for increasing Operating Margins has been the continuous drive to reduce costs. Hospitals actually reduced their Cost per Discharge (Adjusted for Case Mix and Wage Index) to $5,174 from $5,194 in 1994. This was the first reduction in cost during the entire 18 year period that CHIPS has been collecting data. We expect that future price increases will be minimal as further pressure by government payers and large managed care

All U.S. Quartiles (CSS)

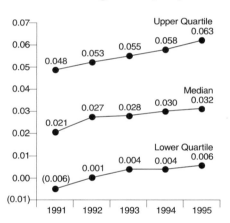

Performance Medians (CSS)

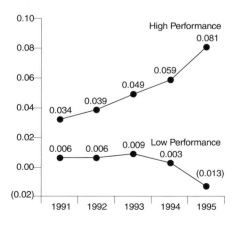

programs keeps realized price increases to minimal levels. The hospital industry must therefore further expand its efforts to cut costs and keep them lower than price increases.

Performance Implications

- The high-performance group of hospitals experienced an improvement in Operating Margin during the five-year period. This is in sharp contrast to the low-performance hospitals, who saw their Operating Margins drop sharply in both 1994 and 1995. Further erosion in Operating Margin will have grave consequences for hospitals in the low-performance group.
- High-performing hospitals may be vulnerable in the near future if significant price pressure is forthcoming. At present, these hospitals have median values for Net Price per Discharge (Adjusted for Case Mix and Wage Index) that are $716 higher than low-performing hospitals and $434 higher than the U.S. median.

Source: The Center for Healthcare Industry Performance Standards (CHIPS), The Almanac of Hospital Financial & Operating Indicators 1996–1997 Edition p.20 and p.21

Profitability Ratios—Return on Total Assets

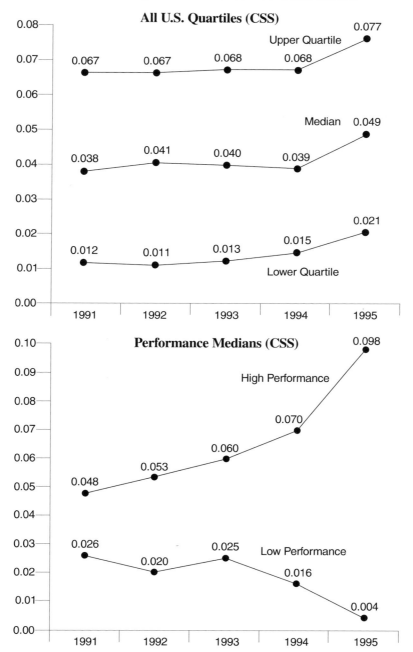

All U.S. Quartiles (CSS)

Upper Quartile

0.067   0.067   0.068   0.068   0.077

Median   0.049

0.038   0.041   0.040   0.039

0.012   0.011   0.013   0.015   0.021

Lower Quartile

1991   1992   1993   1994   1995

Performance Medians (CSS)

0.098

High Performance

0.070

0.060

0.053

0.048

0.026   0.025   Low Performance

0.020   0.016

0.004

1991   1992   1993   1994   1995

Source: The Center for Healthcare Industry Performance Standards (CHIPS), The Almanac of Hospital Financial & Operating Indicators 1996–1997 Edition p.37

Profitability Ratios—Return on Equity

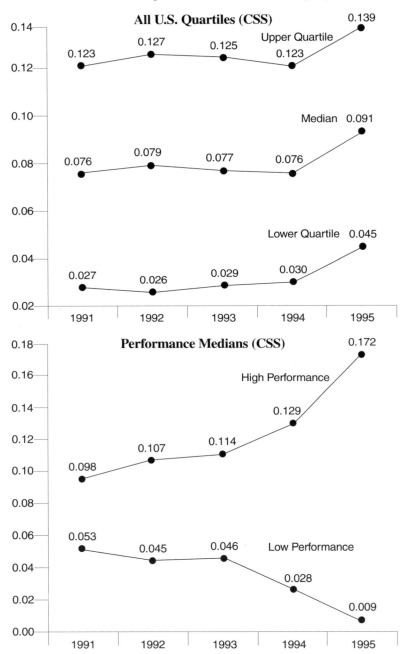

Source: The Center for Healthcare Industry Performance Standards (CHIPS), The Almanac of Hospital Financial & Operating Indicators 1996–1997 Edition p.45

Liquidity Ratios—Current Ratio

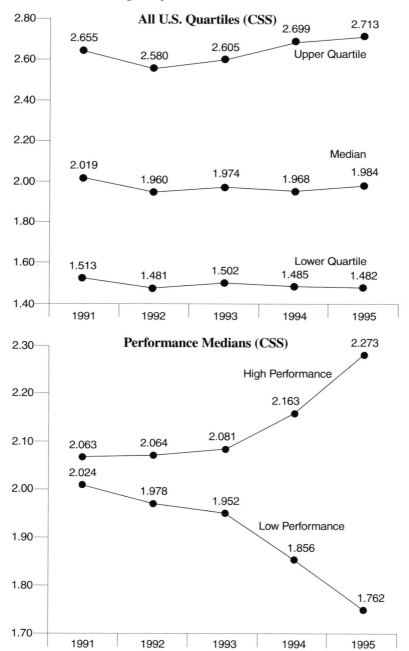

Source: The Center for Healthcare Industry Performance Standards (CHIPS), The Almanac of Hospital Financial & Operating Indicators 1996–1997 Edition p.55

Liquidity Ratios—Days Cash on Hand, Short-Term Sources

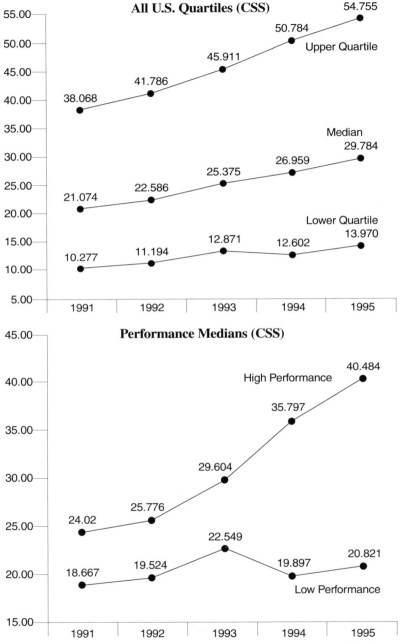

Source: The Center for Healthcare Industry Performance Standards (CHIPS), The Almanac of Hospital Financial & Operating Indicators 1996–1997 Edition p.69

Liquidity Ratios—Days in Patient Accounts Receivable

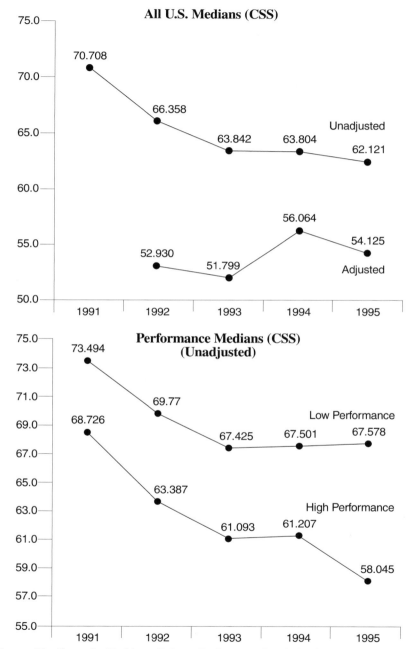

All U.S. Medians (CSS)

- 70.708
- 66.358
- 63.842
- 63.804
- 62.121

Unadjusted

- 56.064
- 52.930
- 51.799
- 54.125

Adjusted

1991 1992 1993 1994 1995

Performance Medians (CSS)
(Unadjusted)

- 73.494
- 69.77
- 67.425
- 67.501
- 67.578

Low Performance

- 68.726
- 63.387
- 61.093
- 61.207
- 58.045

High Performance

1991 1992 1993 1994 1995

Source: The Center for Healthcare Industry Performance Standards (CHIPS), The Almanac of Hospital Financial & Operating Indicators 1996–1997 Edition p.59

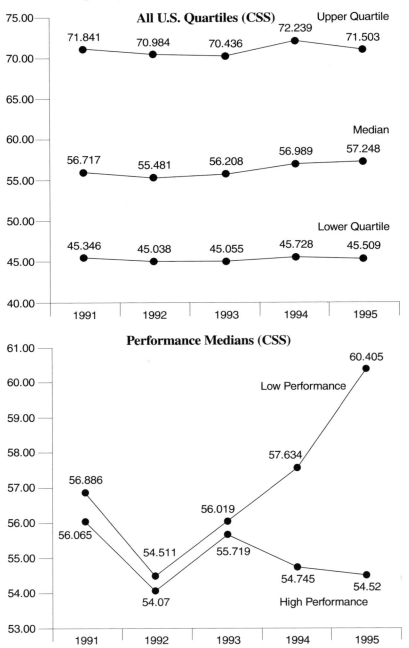

Source: The Center for Healthcare Industry Performance Standards (CHIPS), The Almanac of Hospital Financial & Operating Indicators 1996–1997 Edition p.65

Capital Structure Ratios—Equity Financing Ratio

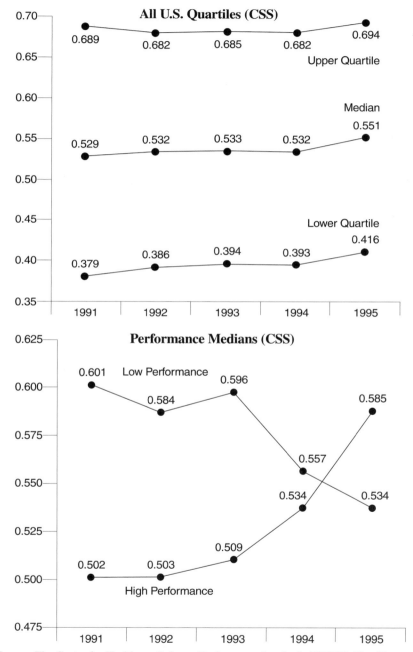

Source: The Center for Healthcare Industry Performance Standards (CHIPS), The Almanac of
Hospital Financial & Operating Indicators 1996–1997 Edition p.79

Capital Structure Ratios—Cash Flow to Total Debt

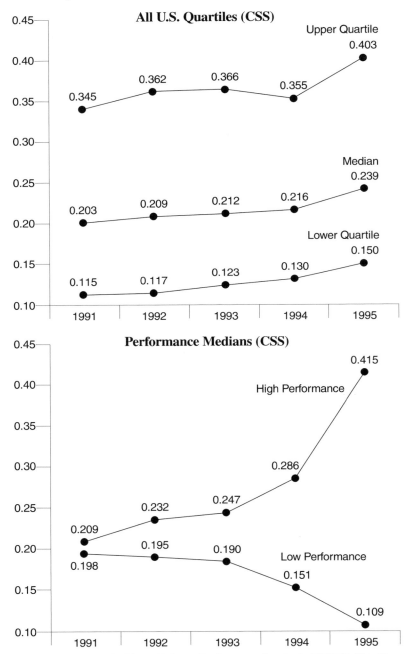

All U.S. Quartiles (CSS)

Upper Quartile
0.403

0.345   0.362   0.366   0.355

Median
0.239

0.203   0.209   0.212   0.216

Lower Quartile
0.150

0.115   0.117   0.123   0.130

Performance Medians (CSS)

0.415

High Performance

0.286

0.232   0.247

0.209

0.195   0.190   Low Performance

0.198

0.151

0.109

Source: The Center for Healthcare Industry Performance Standards (CHIPS), The Almanac of
Hospital Financial & Operating Indicators 1996–1997 Edition p.91

Definition of Financial Indicators

Indicator	Definition	Desired Position	
		Trend	Relative to Median*
Liquidity Ratios			
Current Ratio	$\dfrac{\text{Current Assets}}{\text{Current Liabilities}}$	Up	Above
Days in Patient Account Receivable (Including Due From) (Days)	$\dfrac{\substack{\text{Net Patient Accounts Receivable} \\ \text{(Including Due From)}}}{\text{Net Patient Service Revenues} / 365}$	Down	Below
Days in Accounts Receivable w/all Third Party Settlements (Days)	$\dfrac{\substack{\text{Net Patient Accounts Receivable} \\ \text{(Including Third Party Due To/From)}}}{\text{Net Patient Service Revenues} / 365}$	Down	Below
Average Payment Period	$\dfrac{\text{Current Liabilities}}{(\text{Total Expenses} - \text{Depreciation}) / 365}$	Down	Below
Days Cash on Hand, Short-Term Sources (Days)	$\dfrac{\text{Cash} + \text{Marketable Securities}}{(\text{Total Expenses} - \text{Depreciation}) / 365}$	Up	Above
Days Cash on Hand, All Sources	$\dfrac{\substack{\text{Short-Term Cash} + \text{Marketable} \\ \text{Securities} + \text{Unrestricted Investments} \\ + \text{Construction Funds}}}{(\text{Total Expenses} - \text{Depreciation}) / 365}$	Up	Above

*Desired position is categorized with respect to the relationship between the trend and median values. The desired position only identifies whether increasing or decreasing values are desirable with respect to trend, or whether values above or below the median values are desirable. In summary, if larger values of the indicator are favorable, they will be designated as *up* and *above* in the desired position columns, whereas indicators for which smaller values are favorable will be designated as *down* and *below.*

Source: The Center for Healthcare Industry Performance Standards (CHIPS), The Almanac of Hospital Financial & Operating Indicators 1996–1997 Edition. p.502–503

APPENDIX 11–2

Long-Term Care Performance Ratios for Freestanding or Hospital-based Facilities

Summary Measure
Intermed Care Occupancy
Skilled Length of Stay
Operating Ratio
Total Expense per Patient Day
FTE Employees per Bed
Percent Medicaid Revenue
Percent Other Payers Revenue

Overall Occupancy Ratio
Overall Length of Stay
Intermediate Length of Stay
Operating Expense per Patient Day
Total Expense per Patient Day
Percent Medicare Revenue
Percent Private Pay Revenue
Percent Skilled Revenue

Special Services or Department
Direct Expense per Patient Day
Other Direct Expense per Patient Day
Paid Hours per Patient Day

Salary Expense per Patient Day
Average Hourly Salary

Food services
Direct Expense per 100 Meals
Purchased Services Expense per 100 Meals
Paid Hour per 100 Meals
Direct Expense per Patient Day
Patient Meals per Patient Day

Salary Expense per 100 Meals
Other Direct Expense per 100 Meals
Average Hourly Salary
Total Meals per Patient Day

Total Nursing Services
Overall Percent RN Staff
Overall Percent Aide Staff
LPN Average Hourly Salary
RN Paid Hours per Patient Day
Aide Paid Hours per Patient Day
LPN Salary Expense per Patient Day
RN Purchased Services Expense per Patient Day
Salary Expense per Patient Day
Purchased Services Expense per Patient Day

Overall Percent LPN Staff
RN Average Hourly Salary
Aide Average Hourly Salary
LPN Paid Hours per Patient Day
RN Salary Expense per Patient Day
Aide Salary Expense per Patient Day
Direct Expense per Patient Day
Other Direct Expense per Patient Day
Paid Hours per Patient Day

Nursing Administration
Total Expense per Patient Day
Purchased Services Expense per Patient Day

Salary Expense per Patient Day
Paid Hours per Patient Day

Pharmacy
Revenue per Patient Day
Salary Expense per Patient Day
Purchased Services Expense per Patient Day

Direct Expense per Patient Day
Other Direct Expense per Patient Day
Average Hourly Salary

Laundry & Linen
Total Pounds per Patient Day
Total Direct Expense per 100 Pounds
In-house Salary Expense per 100 Pounds
Contract Expense per 100 Pounds
Total Laundry Direct Expense Percent
In-house Average Hourly Salary
Contract Pounds per Patient Day

In-house Direct Expense per 100
  Pounds
In-house Other Direct Expense per
  100 Pounds
Purchased Services Expense as a
  Percent of Salaries
In-house Paid Hours per 100 Pounds

Housekeeping
Housekeeping Square Feet per Bed
Salary Expense per 1,000 Square Feet
Other Direct Expense per 1,000 Square Feet
Average Hourly Salary

Direct Expense per 1,000 Square Feet
Purchased Services Expense per 1,000
  Square Feet
Paid Hours per 1,000 Square Feet

Plant Operations & Maintenance
Building Square Feet per Bed
Salary Expense per 1,000 Square Feet
Paid Hours per Discharge
Direct Expense per 1,000 Square Feet

Purchased Services Expense per 1,000
  Square Feet
Average Hourly Salary

Source: Division of Data Services, American Hospital Association, 1991.

APPENDIX 11–3

Sample reports from the following professional association are included in this appendix. For additional information refer to:

Medical Group Management Association Cost Survey: 1996 Report Based on 1995 Data
  The Medical Group Management Association
  104 Inverness Terrace East
  Englewood, CO 80112-5306
  (303) 799-1111

Mean Gross and Adjusted Fee-for-Service Collection Percentages for Multispecialty Practices 1980 through 1995

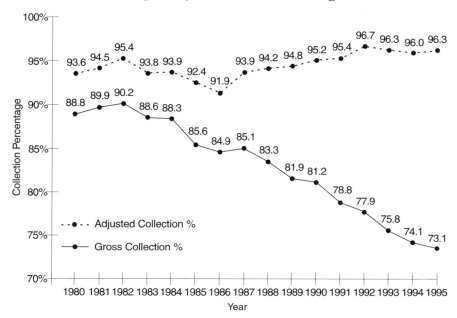

Source: Medical Group Management Association Cost Survey: 1996 Report Based on 1995 Data p.16

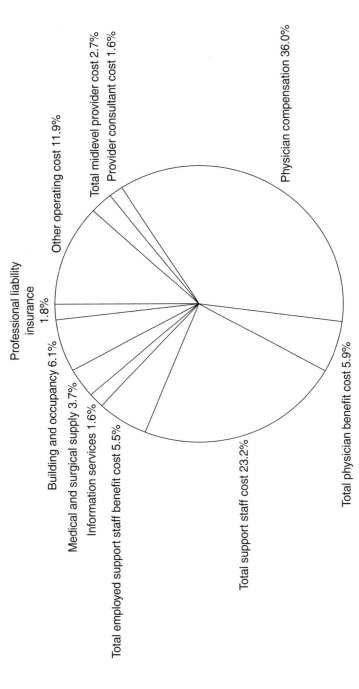

Median Cost Categories as a Percentage of Total Cost for Multispecialty Practices—1995

Physician compensation 36.0%

Total midlevel provider cost 2.7%

Provider consultant cost 1.6%

Other operating cost 11.9%

Professional liability insurance 1.8%

Building and occupancy 6.1%

Medical and surgical supply 3.7%

Information services 1.6%

Total employed support staff benefit cost 5.5%

Total support staff cost 23.2%

Total physician benefit cost 5.9%

Source: Medical Group Management Association Cost Survey: 1996 Report Based on 1995 Data p.16

Staffing and Practice Data for Multispecialty Practices

Staffing and Practice Data	Practice type					
	Multispecialty					
	Count	Mean	Std. Dev.	10th %tile	Median	90th %tile
Total FTE providers	271	87.78	318.33	10.10	35.64	143.70
Total number of FTE physicians	353	55.33	189.32	6.10	25.40	106.56
Total FTE midlevel providers	271	21.42	112.36	1.00	4.90	32.20
Total FTE support staff	353	263.74	834.26	23.50	117.00	586.00
Total at-risk man care revenue %	245	27.26	27.70	2.00	16.50	69.50
Capitation contract revenue %	226	22.43	25.58	1.00	13.10	60.00
At-risk FFS contract revenue %	134	15.48	18.57	1.00	10.00	34.00
Number of satellite clinics	251	7.07	7.78	1.00	4.00	18.00
Square ft of all facilities	254	103,928.01	327,423.93	10,000.00	48,000.00	220,000.00
Total oper cost to total cost ratio	353	.54	.09	.44		.64
Total prov cost to total cost ratio	353	.46	.09	.36		.56

Source: Medical Group Management Association Cost Survey: 1996 Report Based on 1995 Data *adapted from (p. 48)*

Accounts Receivable Data, Collection Percentages, and Financial Ratios for Multispecialty Practices

Accounts Receivable Data, Collection Percentages, and Financial Ratios	Practice type					
	Multispecialty					
	Count	Mean	Std. Dev.	10th %tile	Median	90th %tile
Total accounts rec ($/phy)	275	117,481.27	75,848.73	40,402.37	104,741.87	193,144.72
Total accounts rec ($/prov)	214	100,145.32	65,137.61	43,825.61	87,302.32	169,285.82
0 to 30 days % of total A/R	241	37.83	14.90	20.11	35.96	57.60
31 to 60 days % of total A/R	241	17.14	6.49	9.36	16.59	25.31
61 to 90 days % of total A/R	241	9.52	3.48	5.27	9.18	13.88
91 to 120 days % of total A/R	241	6.77	4.05	3.83	6.03	9.51
Over 120 days % of total A/R	241	28.62	13.34	11.63	27.85	43.86
Months gross FFS charges in A/R	243	2.66	1.04	1.72	2.53	3.79
Gross FFS collection %	275	73.13	11.56	60.36	74.02	86.02
Adjusted FFS collection %	251	96.28	6.12	90.88	97.60	100.00
Net cap rev % of gross cap chrg	142	95.01	41.04	54.23	91.04	140.24
Gross FFS+cap collection %	171	77.55	14.82	62.56	76.07	93.89
FFS collect % for unins pat	43	56.46	26.90	20.00	55.00	90.00
Total net med revenue/total asset ratio	262	13.03	44.42	1.39	3.37	22.08
Return on total assets	270	.05	3.31	-.58	.00	.28
Total debt to total asset ratio	259	.93	1.47	.31	.77	1.28
Current ratio	244	6.17	43.43	.38	1.38	5.09
Return on equity	259	-11.37	354.47	-1.03	.08	1.22
Debt to worth ratio	249	672.87	10,102.15	-5.05	1.22	8.70

Source: Medical Group Management Association Cost Survey: 1996 Report Based on 1995 Data *adapted from (p. 48)*

Staffing, RBRVS RVUs, Patients, and Square Footage per FTE Physician for Multispecialty Practices

Staffing, RBRVS RVU, Patient, and Square Footage Data	Practice type Multispecialty					
	Count	Mean	Std. Dev.	10th %tile	Median	90th %tile
Total FTE providers per FTE phy	271	1.25	.28	1.05	1.18	1.48
FTE prim care phy per FTE phy	286	.67	.26	.32	.67	1.00
FTE nons spec phy per FTE phy	194	.30	.20	.08	.28	.53
FTE sur spec phy per FTE phy	188	.22	.15	.07	.20	.38
Total FTE MLP per FTE phy	271	.25	.28	.05	.18	.48
FTE prim care MLP per FTE phy	203	.15	.14	.02	.10	.31
FTE nons spec MLP per FTE phy	117	.14	.16	.02	.09	.33
FTE sur spec MLP per FTE phy	75	.08	.08	.01	.06	.16
Total FTE sup staff per FTE phy	353	4.72	1.69	2.81	4.63	6.37
General administrative	276	.34	.47	.10	.23	.61
Business office	260	.75	.42	.32	.67	1.17
Managed care administrative	92	.17	.18	.03	.12	.38
Information services	175	.16	.12	.04	.14	.29
Housekeeping/maint/security	184	.17	.15	.04	.14	.32
Other admin support	139	.17	.32	.02	.09	.33
Registered Nurses	250	.56	.47	.14	.44	1.06
LPNs, medical assistants, etc.	262	.96	.49	.42	.91	1.62
Medical receptionists	260	.74	.37	.30	.70	1.20
Med secretaries/transcribers	239	.30	.22	.10	.26	.51
Medical records	229	.39	.19	.17	.37	.64
Clinical laboratory	220	.36	.18	.14	.34	.59
Radiology/imaging	220	.25	.18	.09	.23	.40
Physical therapy	54	.15	.26	.01	.08	.30
Optical	76	.08	.07	.02	.05	.17
Ambulatory surgery unit	25	.15	.08	.05	.16	.28
Other medical support serv	148	.37	.58	.04	.16	.80
Total RBRVS RVUs per FTE phy	36	8,737.78	3,185.23	5,151.50	8,478.81	12,389.05
Total patients per FTE physician	63	2,212.22	1,526.96	841.96	1,672.52	4,293.29
Square feet per FTE physician	254	1,969.98	748.29	1,142.86	1,883.70	2,877.32

Source: Medical Group Management Association Cost Survey: 1996 Report Based on 1995 Data *adapted from* (p. 49)

Charges and Revenue per FTE Physician for Multispecialty Practices

Charges and Revenue Data	Practice type					
	Multispecialty					
	Count	Mean	Std. Dev.	10th %tile	Median	90th %tile
Net fee-for-service revenue	342	$369,310	$166,374	$153,021	$366,054	$549,453
Gross fee-for-service charges	275	$519,832	$250,679	$214,500	$507,022	$800,109
Adjustments	257	$134,798	$103,320	$38,576	$114,761	$248,500
Adjusted fee-for-serv charges	251	$388,071	$177,492	$165,537	$387,500	$607,120
Bad debts	211	$14,157	$16,939	$1,705	$9,649	$30,337
Uninsured patient care charges	69	$46,230	$54,570	$7,193	$29,748	$86,980
Net capitation revenue	222	$126,610	$200,693	$4,843	$50,489	$355,724
Gross capitation charges	142	$136,158	$172,468	$6,114	$64,768	$358,562
Capitation revenue	157	$173,259	$295,495	$4,893	$60,000	$500,332
Other capitation contract rev	66	$40,958	$64,531	$879	$23,237	$91,385
Pur serv for cap patients	70	$117,954	$170,791	$3,662	$56,165	$300,049
Net other medical revenue	187	$31,585	$68,072	$1,152	$9,376	$89,652
Gross rev from other activity	134	$37,030	$57,502	$2,409	$15,511	$108,377
Subsidies and grants	52	$60,188	$106,524	$317	$8,534	$205,922
Rev from sale of goods/serv	110	$22,034	$25,381	$1,566	$13,994	$53,637
Cost of sales	74	$15,166	$20,168	$1,048	$7,367	$41,802
Total gross charges	279	$591,262	$244,767	$299,696	$577,471	$840,018
Physician gross charges	220	$478,730	$205,148	$271,210	$453,332	$752,580
MLP gross charges	157	$42,123	$51,515	$5,169	$26,403	$103,191
Other gross charges	147	$130,675	$96,334	$16,947	$123,909	$240,187
Total net medical revenue	353	$463,384	$180,783	$268,758	$451,423	$662,156

Source: Medical Group Management Association Cost Survey: 1996 Report Based on 1995 Data adapted from (p. 49)

Operating Cost per FTE Physician for Multispecialty Practices

Operating Cost Data	Practice type				
	Multispecialty				
	Count	Mean	Std. Dev.	10th %tile	Median	90th %tile
Total support staff cost	353	$109,872	$48,966	$62,461	$103,448	$157,057
General administrative	263	$14,256	$11,312	$5,542	$10,720	$28,893
Business office	254	$15,816	$9,258	$7,802	$14,189	$24,392
Managed care administrative	82	$4,368	$4,453	$767	$2,822	$9,193
Information services	170	$4,057	$2,657	$1,039	$3,532	$7,154
Housekeeping/maint/security	195	$3,487	$3,020	$1,019	$2,784	$6,576
Other admin support	109	$3,170	$5,400	$267	$1,548	$8,602
Registered Nurses	232	$17,781	$15,822	$4,667	$13,787	$34,444
LPNs, medical assistants, etc	243	$20,169	$11,083	$7,402	$18,948	$32,599
Medical receptionists	240	$13,679	$7,310	$5,484	$12,544	$22,722
Med secretaries/transcribers	225	$6,669	$4,771	$2,333	$5,942	$11,040
Medical records	216	$6,359	$3,339	$2,692	$6,088	$10,508
Clinical laboratory	215	$9,306	$4,545	$4,073	$8,933	$15,882
Radiology/imaging	217	$6,627	$5,181	$2,300	$5,800	$11,384
Physical therapy	55	$4,329	$8,267	$214	$1,733	$8,380
Optical	68	$1,779	$1,639	$296	$1,293	$4,264
Ambulatory surgery unit	24	$4,783	$3,957	$870	$3,431	$10,738
Other medical support services	155	$12,345	$20,708	$616	$4,058	$31,914
Total emp sup staff benefit cost	351	$25,906	$12,633	$12,546	$24,344	$38,333
Total nonsupport staff oper cost	353	$125,177	$58,720	$69,004	$117,048	$189,291
Information services	258	$8,166	$5,024	$2,415	$7,360	$14,314
Clinical laboratory	248	$12,410	$9,174	$1,665	$11,903	$21,215
Radiology/imaging	236	$7,245	$7,171	$1,036	$4,618	$17,721
Physical therapy	56	$2,007	$3,979	$55	$862	$4,080
Optical	66	$1,637	$2,089	$32	$866	$4,379
Ambulatory surgery unit	24	$7,546	$6,732	$1,059	$6,173	$20,393
Medical and surgical supply	288	$20,959	$17,689	$4,359	$16,481	$36,906
Building and occupancy	294	$28,957	$15,296	$13,320	$27,199	$45,950
Furniture/equipment	267	$8,022	$7,096	$1,756	$6,667	$15,564
Admin supplies and services	284	$9,495	$8,891	$3,554	$7,564	$15,991
Prof liability insurance	284	$9,612	$7,503	$3,490	$7,857	$17,321
Other insurance premiums	231	$1,190	$1,804	$196	$725	$2,385
Outside professional fees	274	$6,238	$10,431	$667	$3,560	$12,431
Promotion and marketing	268	$2,338	$2,066	$389	$1,854	$4,891
Other interest	190	$3,679	$5,580	$124	$1,411	$10,960
Health/business/property taxes	231	$3,892	$5,381	$326	$2,129	$10,226
Recruiting	239	$1,450	$2,263	$95	$869	$3,246
Other operating cost	270	$9,551	$15,008	$699	$4,013	$23,871
Total operating cost	353	$260,852	$109,356	$150,430	$245,632	$363,639

Source: Medical Group Management Association Cost Survey: 1996 Report Based on 1995 Data *adapted from (p. 50)*

Assets and Liabilities per FTE Physician for Multispecialty Practices

Asset and Liability Data	Practice type				
	Multispecialty				
	Count	Mean	Std. Dev.	10th %tile	90th %tile
Total assets	262	$171,822	$205,483	$21,464	$363,552
Current assets	248	$83,777	$75,160	$6,778	$183,857
Noncurrent/other assets	250	$95,786	$173,794	$8,858	$229,008
Total liabilities	260	$126,843	$130,365	$13,769	$305,986
Current liabilities	253	$59,854	$68,671	$5,577	$130,071
Noncurrent/other liabilities	203	$87,728	$111,173	$3,528	$219,862
Working capital	244	$23,171	$68,988	-$25,873	$98,849
Total net worth	251	$45,848	$137,902	-$17,130	$148,819

Source: Medical Group Management Association Cost Survey: 1996 Report Based on 1995 Data *adapted from (p. 51)*

Charges, Revenue, and Cost per FTE Provider for Multispecialty Practices

| Charges, Revenue, and Cost Data | | Practice type | | | | |
| | | Multispecialty | | | | |
	Count	Mean	Std. Dev.	10th %tile	Median	90th %tile
Net fee-for-service revenue	263	$304,788	$139,068	$127,756	$296,862	$474,227
Net capitation revenue	181	$109,250	$156,388	$4,950	$52,289	$293,437
Net other medical revenue	157	$23,285	$43,361	$954	$8,402	$64,514
Total gross charges	222	$494,281	$187,816	$279,727	$483,682	$719,286
Physician gross charges	172	$393,992	$159,908	$222,644	$366,964	$611,709
Total net medical revenue	271	$388,783	$131,835	$241,957	$383,330	$524,299
Total support staff cost	271	$92,515	$32,286	$59,222	$89,670	$133,053
Total emp sup staff benefit cost	269	$21,766	$8,956	$11,871	$20,599	$31,461
Total nonsupport staff oper cost	271	$104,354	$41,335	$60,012	$99,375	$158,014
Total operating cost	271	$218,483	$73,811	$136,993	$209,781	$301,242
Net med rev before distribution	271	$170,965	$83,088	$74,093	$166,565	$268,573
Total midlevel provider cost	253	$11,469	$8,347	$2,720	$9,867	$21,358
Provider consultant cost	133	$13,251	$46,175	$379	$5,856	$23,061
Total physician cost	271	$164,625	$59,425	$95,922	$159,522	$245,142
Physician compensation	253	$143,020	$54,050	$84,089	$136,141	$221,196
Total physician benefit cost	245	$22,700	$10,719	$9,179	$21,884	$36,161
Total provider cost	271	$182,618	$69,920	$114,337	$174,584	$268,870
Total cost (oper cost+prov cost)	271	$401,101	$121,305	$264,983	$396,977	$535,029
Net nonmedical income	196	$5,361	$9,511	-$69	$2,484	$14,078
Net practice income (or loss)	271	-$7,805	$42,671	-$67,464	$150	$18,638

Source: Medical Group Management Association Cost Survey: 1996 Report Based on 1995 Data *adapted from (p. 54)*

Charges, Revenue, and Cost per RBRVS RVU for Multispecialty Practices

| Charges, Revenue, and Cost Data | Practice type | | | | | |
| | Multispecialty | | | | | |
	Count	Mean	Std. Dev.	10th %tile	Median	90th %tile
Net fee-for-service revenue	36	$46.90	$21.54	$27.57	$40.21	$65.71
Net capitation revenue	26	$10.71	$9.39	$.87	$8.37	$23.90
Net other medical revenue	22	$3.61	$9.02	$.16	$.80	$10.06
Total gross charges	34	$74.76	$36.26	$40.92	$68.90	$106.88
Physician gross charges	27	$52.86	$17.67	$31.08	$50.01	$80.25
Total net medical revenue	36	$56.84	$23.89	$33.75	$54.41	$82.32
Total support staff cost	36	$13.74	$6.81	$7.40	$12.23	$20.70
Total emp sup staff benefit cost	36	$3.28	$2.11	$1.43	$2.77	$4.94
Total nonsupport staff oper cost	36	$17.11	$8.76	$8.25	$15.30	$27.46
Total operating cost	36	$34.13	$16.48	$17.39	$31.73	$50.95
Net med rev before distribution	36	$23.21	$9.99	$12.96	$21.24	$33.81
Total midlevel provider cost	30	$1.73	$1.50	$.46	$1.06	$3.51
Provider consultant cost	16	$1.00	$.83	$.05	$.78	$2.06
Total physician cost	36	$24.60	$10.59	$12.39	$22.05	$45.43
Physician compensation	32	$22.18	$8.93	$14.16	$19.57	$36.20
Total physician benefit cost	31	$3.58	$1.81	$2.31	$3.32	$4.71
Total provider cost	36	$26.50	$11.11	$14.83	$24.05	$46.97
Total cost (oper cost+prov cost)	36	$60.62	$25.20	$34.43	$55.84	$93.56
Net nonmedical income	21	$.72	$.98	-$.10	$.19	$2.05
Net practice income (or loss)	36	-$2.87	$9.03	-$17.38	$.01	$3.54

Source: Medical Group Management Association Cost Survey: 1996 Report Based on 1995 Data *adapted from* (p. 56)

Charges, Revenue, and Cost per Patient for Multispecialty Practices

| Charges, Revenue, and Cost Data | Practice type | | | | | |
| | Multispecialty | | | | | |
	Count	Mean	Std. Dev.	10th %tile	Median	90th %tile
Net fee-for-service revenue	62	$221.59	$164.06	$66.44	$163.42	$490.73
Net capitation revenue	47	$111.74	$202.86	$.90	$34.85	$321.18
Net other medical revenue	40	$31.30	$61.20	$.68	$6.25	$115.03
Total gross charges	60	$385.27	$291.06	$104.22	$282.30	$760.39
Physician gross charges	49	$281.38	$188.83	$70.22	$247.53	$581.33
Total net medical revenue	63	$321.35	$246.57	$81.80	$254.00	$551.52
Total support staff cost	63	$77.68	$58.05	$21.50	$65.63	$152.97
Total emp sup staff benefit cost	62	$18.78	$15.81	$4.16	$16.13	$38.38
Total nonsupport staff oper cost	63	$88.89	$64.48	$24.04	$74.04	$164.16
Total operating cost	63	$185.06	$132.43	$46.95	$165.41	$325.56
Net med rev before distribution	63	$137.40	$126.60	$32.67	$108.31	$275.73
Total midlevel provider cost	51	$11.24	$12.26	$1.09	$5.04	$29.84
Provider consultant cost	29	$27.11	$102.27	$.08	$4.65	$28.74
Total physician cost	63	$122.00	$84.60	$34.67	$96.40	$232.63
Physician compensation	61	$105.35	$72.61	$29.30	$82.31	$200.67
Total physician benefit cost	60	$18.58	$14.57	$4.91	$15.09	$41.66
Total provider cost	63	$143.63	$120.99	$39.70	$112.02	$274.93
Total cost (oper cost+prov cost)	63	$328.68	$241.70	$85.27	$264.61	$546.63
Net nonmedical income	39	$6.30	$8.39	$.13	$2.92	$21.00
Net practice income (or loss)	63	–$2.33	$37.98	–$18.57	$1.32	$28.91

Source: Medical Group Management Association Cost Survey: 1996 Report Based on 1995 Data adapted from (p. 57)

MGMA Ratios

The Section 1 formulas include:

1. Total FTE providers =

> Total number of FTE physicians (#131) +
> Total number of FTE midlevel providers (#135)

If either #131 or #135 is a missing value, then the sum is also a missing value. In this formula, and most other formulas described in this report, missing values are not recoded to zero. Thus, if any component of a formula is missing for a given case, the result of that formula is also a missing value.

The Section 2 formulas include:

1. Months of gross fee-for-service charges in accounts receivable =

$$\frac{\text{Total accounts receivable (#98)}}{(1/12)\text{ Gross fee-for-service charges (#7)}}$$

Note that this is a change from 1995 when this ratio was called "Months of adjusted fee-for-service charges in accounts receivable" and the denominator consisted of "Adjusted fee-for-service charges" (#9) instead of "Gross fee-for-service charges" (#7).

2. Gross fee-for-service collection percentage =

$$\frac{\text{Net fee-for-service revenue (#11)} \times (100)}{\text{Gross fee-for-service charges (#7)}}$$

3. Adjusted fee-for-service collection percentage =

$$\frac{\text{Net fee-for-service revenue (#11)} \times (100)}{\text{Adjusted fee-for-service charges (#9)}}$$

4. Net capitation revenue percentage of gross capitation charges =

$$\frac{\text{Net capitation revenue (#16)} \times (100)}{\text{Gross capitation charges (#12)}}$$

5. Gross fee-for-service plus capitation collection percentage =

$$\frac{(\text{Net fee for service revenue (#11)} + \text{Net capitation revenue (#16)}) \times (100)}{\text{Total gross charges (#22)}}$$

6. Total net medical revenue to total asset ratio =

$$\frac{\text{Total net medical revenue (#23)}}{\text{Total assets (#88)}}$$

7. Return on total assets =

$$\frac{\text{Net practice income (or loss) (\#85)}}{\text{Total assets (\#88)}}$$

8. Total debt to total asset ratio =

$$\frac{\text{Total liabilities (\#91)}}{\text{Total assets (\#88)}}$$

9. Current ratio =

$$\frac{\text{Current assets (\#86)}}{\text{Current liabilities (\#89)}}$$

10. Return on equity =

$$\frac{\text{Net practice income (or loss) (\#85)}}{\text{Total net worth (\#92)}}$$

11. Debt to worth ratio =

$$\frac{\text{Total liabilities (\#91)}}{\text{Total net worth (\#92)}}$$

Source: Medical Group Management Association Cost Survey: 1996 Report Based on 1995 Data p.11 and p.12

The Cost Allocation Model

In any production process, whether it be durable manufacturing or health-care delivery, inputs are utilized and/or consumed by the production process to produce the outputs of the process. In the durable manufacturing of automobiles, inputs such as steel, plastic, rubber, and labor are combined to produce the output, which is an automobile. In healthcare delivery, while the inputs to the production process are easily identified—land (the medical office building), labor (physicians, midlevel providers, and support staff), and capital (computers, radiology and laboratory equipment, surgical supplies, etc.)—the outputs of the healthcare delivery process are not as easily identified as in the case of durable manufacturing.

In healthcare delivery, the outputs could be a nonsurgical encounter, a surgical case, a laboratory procedure, or the care of a covered life under contract for a year, regardless of services required. For the purpose of the 1996 cost survey, MGMA has aggregated all activity in the medical practice into eight categories of output, as listed on questions #111 to #118 of the questionnaire. These eight activities or outputs of the medical practice are:

1. Nonsurgical encounters inside the practice's facilities
2. Nonsurgical encounters outside the practice's facilities
3. Surgery/anesthesia cases inside the practice's facilities

4. Surgery/anesthesia cases outside the practice's facilities
5. Diagnostic radiology/imaging procedures inside the practice's facilities
6. Diagnostic radiology/imaging procedures outside the practice's facilities
7. Clinical laboratory/pathology procedures inside the practice's facilities
8. Clinical laboratory/pathology procedures outside the practice's facilities

Historically, the cost survey has standardized medical practice cost data in terms of cost per FTE physician or cost per FTE provider. In other words, cost data has been standardized in terms of cost per unit of input. Although apparently useful in comparing the performance of medical practices in a traditional fee-for-service environment where the medical practice objective might be to maximize physician compensation, such cost per unit of input data may have less utility when the medical practice operates in a capitated environment where the objective focuses more on minimizing cost per covered life. In capitated and at-risk managed care environments, it may be more useful to look at cost data in terms of cost per unit of output.

Therefore, this year's report presents refinements in the model that develops cost data on a per unit of output basis. The primary difference between the 1995 cost model and the 1996 cost model, is that this year's model utilizes eight activities instead of six activities as used last year. In 1995, the model did not explicitly distinguish between activities conducted inside the practice's facilities and activities conducted outside the practice's facilities. This year's model does explicitly address these distinctions and does a better job in accurately assigning practice costs to each of the eight activities.

In order to assign expenses to each of the eight medical practice outputs, MGMA developed a cost allocation model which is graphically illustrated by the Cost Allocation Input-Output Matrix on page 8. Each row on the cost allocation matrix represents a cost item. Row 1, for example, "General administrative support staff cost," represents the cost for variable #24 from the cost survey questionnaire. Each column in the matrix represents one of the eight medical practice activities or outputs. The column labeled "Nonsurgical encounters inside the practice's facilities" represents cost survey variable #111.

Wherever a number one through seven appears in a cell of the matrix, that signifies that some of the cost for the given row should be allocated to the activity in the given column in order to develop a total cost per activity variable. The costs are allocated to each activity based upon the ratio of charges for the given activity to the gross charges for a given allocation pattern. The numbers one through seven signify one of the seven cost allocation patterns utilized in this model.

Source: Medical Group Management Association Cost Survey: 1996 Report Based on 1995 Data p.7 and p.9

Cost Allocation Input-Output Matrix

Variable Label	Variable #	Nonsurgical encounters inside the practice's facilities #111	Nonsurgical encounters outside the practice's facilities #112	Surgery/anesthesia cases inside the practice's facilities #113	Surgery/anesthesia cases outside the practice's facilities #114	Radiology/imaging procedures inside the practice's facilities #115	Radiology/imaging procedures outside the practice's facilities #116	Clinical laboratory/pathology procedures inside the practice's facilities #117	Clinical laboratory/pathology procedures outside the practice's facilities #118
Gen admin support staff cost	#24	1	1	1	1	1	1	1	1
Bus office support staff cost	#25	1	1	1	1	1	1	1	1
Man care admin support staff cost	#26	1	1	1	1	1	1	1	1
Info serv support staff cost	#27	1	1	1	1	1	1	1	1
House/maint support staff cost	#28	2		2		2		2	
Other admin support staff cost	#29	2		2		2		2	
RNs support staff cost	#30	3		3					
LPNs support staff cost	#31	3		3					
Med recep support staff cost	#32	2		2		2		2	
Med secr support staff cost	#33	1	1	1	1	1	1	1	1
Med records support staff cost	#34	1	1	1	1	1	1	1	1
Clin lab support staff cost	#35							4	
Rad/imag support staff cost	#36					5			
Physical therapy support staff cost	#37	6							
Optical support staff cost	#38	6							
Amb surg unit support staff cost	#39			7					
Other med support staff cost	#40	2		2		2		2	
Total emp support staff benefit cost	#46	1	1	1	1	1	1	1	1
Info serv oper cost	#47	1	1	1	1	1	1	1	1
Clin lab oper cost	#48							4	
Rad/imag oper cost	#49					5			
Physical therapy oper cost	#50	6							
Optical oper cost	#51	6							
Amb surg unit oper cost	#52			7					
Med/surg supply oper cost	#53	3		3					
Building oper cost	#54	2		2		2		2	
Furn/equip oper cost	#55	3		3					
Admin supply/serv oper cost	#56	1	1	1	1	1	1	1	1
Liability insurance oper cost	#57	1	1	1	1	1	1	1	1
Other insurance oper cost	#58	1	1	1	1	1	1	1	1
Outside prof fee oper cost	#59	1	1	1	1	1	1	1	1
Promotion oper cost	#60	1	1	1	1	1	1	1	1
Other interest oper cost	#61	1	1	1	1	1	1	1	1
Health/bus/prop tax oper cost	#62	1	1	1	1	1	1	1	1
Recruiting oper cost	#63	1	1	1	1	1	1	1	1
Other oper cost	#64	1	1	1	1	1	1	1	1
Total mid prov cost	#70	3		3					
Prov consultant cost	#71	1	1	1	1	1	1	1	1
Total physician cost	#80	1	1	1	1	1	1	1	1
Purchased serv for capitation	#15								
Cost of sales	#20								
Nonmedical cost	#83								

Source: Medical Group Management Association Cost Survey: 1996 Report Based on 1995 Data p.8

Hints for Interpreting the Cost Allocation Model

The *Cost Survey: 1996 Report Based on 1995 Data* utilizes a unique cost allocation input-output matrix to assign practice costs to eight activities or outputs. As described on page 9, costs are allocated to each activity based on the ratio of gross charges for the activity compared to the gross charges of activities for a given allocation pattern. The cost allocation input-output matrix on page 8 describes the seven different patterns used to allocate cost.

Users of the *Cost Survey: 1996 Report Based on 1995 Data* need to understand that the gross charges attributable to any given activity have an impact on the allocation of costs to the other seven activities. For example, if a large proportion of a practice's total gross charges are produced by its clinical laboratory, then a proportionally large amount of cost will be allocated to the clinical laboratory, thereby reducing the cost available to be allocated to the other activities. Thus, this practice may exhibit a low "Operating cost per nonsurgical encounter inside the practice's facilities," not as a result of any unique operational efficiencies, but simply because a small proportion of cost is allocated to nonsurgical encounters.

MGMA has other sources of information on medical practice revenue and costs besides the data presented in this report. *The Academic Practice Management Survey: 1996 Report Based on 1995 Data* presents similar types of data for academic practices. *The Performance Efficiency Evaluation Report* provides participating medical practices with a custom report comparing the practice's performance to that of similar type practices on a quarterly and/or annual basis. If you have a question concerning the survey results or the survey questionnaire, contact the Survey Operations Department at (303) 397-7895 or by e-mail at "survey@mgma.com."

Source: Medical Group Management Association Cost Survey: 1996 Report Based on 1995 Data p.14

Price level adjustment calculations

Determination of a price level adjusted figure requires the calculation of the average age of plant. A price index is also needed in order to calculate an approximate replacement cost figure. Although a healthcare specific cost index would be most appropriate, the Consumer Price Index series is commonly available and convention has resulted in its use. A sample Consumer Price Index series is provided in *Figure 1*.

Figure 1

Consumer Price Index 19x1–19x9	
19x1	0.909
19x2	0.965
19x3	0.996
19x4	1.039
19x5	1.076
19x6	1.096
19x7	1.136
19x8	1.183
19x9	1.240

Given the year being considered is 19x9, and the average age of plant is 5.2 years, the assumption is made that the average plant asset was purchased in 19x4. This means that there are approximately five years of historical cost depreciation included in the accumulated depreciation figure reported on the Balance Sheet. As indicated by *Figure 1* the Consumer Price Index (CPI) for 19x4 was 1.039, while the CPI for 19x9 was

1.24. This means that something which cost $1.04 in 19x4 would cost $1.24 in 19x9. The percentage increase in price over this time amounts to:

$$\frac{1.24 - 1.04}{1.04} = 19\%$$

Prices have increased by 19 percent over this time period. Therefore, in order to recognize what it would cost to replace the equipment in terms of today's (19x9) dollars, depreciation expense must be increased by 19 percent. In a similar manner, to determine the total replacement cost of assets indicated by accumulated depreciation, that figure must also be increased by 19 percent as illustrated below.

PLA depreciation expense = ($8,495,806 × .19) + $8,495,806 = $10,393,297.

PLA net income = net income − (depreciation expense × price level adjusted
         factors)
         (1,614,203) = $12,007,500 − ($8,495,806 × .19) = $10,393,297

PLA accumulated depreciation = ($44,304,068 × .19) + $44,304,068
         = $52,721,841

CHAPTER 12

Capital investment decisions

"I just don't know what to do. We have so many good projects and only so much money. How do we decide where to put our capital investment funds?"

"This project looks good, but isn't there some way we can account for the fact that we have to wait so long to start making a profit?

"If we don't get our money back within three years, I don't care what rate of return it gives us."

"If we purchase the new infusion pumps then we are stuck with the risk of obsolescence, however, if we lease them the manufacturer is stuck with the risk. What are the cost implications of each alternative?"

Introduction

A major factor in ensuring the long run viability of a healthcare organization is its capital investment decisions. Capital investment decisions typically involve the investment of large sums of money for long periods of time. A poor capital investment process can lead an organization toward an over-investment in the wrong kind of facilities, create an inability to maintain up-to-date technology, generate a high fixed cost environment, and therefore limit the opportunity to adapt to a changing environment.

It is clear to many healthcare decision makers, providers, insurers, and governments, that one way to control healthcare costs in the long run is to control capital investment decisions. Although the emphasis has shifted from capital investment as a control mechanism to an overall comprehensive approach, the importance of the capital investment decision cannot be denied. Attempts to control capital investment decisions include the decision of the Congress to integrate capital-related costs (called capital pass-through costs) into the prospective payment system.

Effective for cost reporting periods after September 30, 1991, Medicare will pay for inpatient capital costs on a per discharge basis rather than aggregate reasonable cost basis. The new rule applies to all prospective payment system (PPS) hospitals and PPS-exempt distinct part units. Non-PPS hospitals will continue to be paid on a cost-related basis along with rural primary care hospitals. The new payment system will be phased in over a ten year period and provides for PPS hospitals to be paid under a "hold harmless" or "fully prospective" basis depending on whether they are "high cost" (hospital-specific capital rate exceeds its adjusted standard federal capital rate per Medicare discharge) or "low cost" (hospital-specific capital rate is below the federal capital rate per Medicare discharge). "Low cost" hospitals will be paid on a fully prospective basis on a blended basis (80 percent hospital-specific rate and 10 percent federal rate for FY92) with the mix changing by 10 percent each year until 2001 when the hospital will be 100 percent federal rate. The "high cost" hospitals will be paid the higher of two options:

Option 1: 85 percent of its FY92 actual incurred reasonable cost for *old* capital plus an amount for new capital based on the federal capital rate.

Option 2: 100 percent of the Federal capital rate.

The actual amounts to be paid to each hospital will require detailed calculations and will vary significantly between hospitals depending on when the assets were put into use and method of financing.[1] For capital investment decisions, the financial management staff must calculate the amounts to be received each year and any potential delays in the receipt of reimbursement from the intermediary as they implement the new rules. In this chapter, we will assume that all cash flows in the examples have been adjusted for the new PPS amounts.

What is a capital expenditure?

A capital expenditure is generally considered to be an expenditure that, under generally acceptable accounting principles (GAAP), is not properly chargeable as an expense of the current year. In other words, the expense is expected to provide benefits to the organization over a period of more than one year. In application, most organizations also place a dollar limit on the projects that will be considered as a capital expenditure. Since operating expenses do not receive the same depth of examination and analysis as is true of capital expenditures, a large expense item, which might normally not be considered to be a capital investment, is included in the analysis process because of the significant dollar amounts involved. No dollar figure limit can be given here, since $50,000 might be a significant expenditure for one organization, while anything under $250,000 might not be considered significant to another.

In theory, capital investment requirements should primarily flow from the institution's objectives. These objectives should be reflected in the healthcare organization's comprehensive strategic or master plan, which should be based on such factors as community needs, the competitive market, technological advances, the medical staff, and demographic characteristics and forecasted changes.

---

[1] For a detailed explanation of the new rules for paying for Medicare inpatient costs, see Grimaldi, Paul L., "Capital PPS: Trekking through the Labyrinth," *Healthcare Financial Management*, November 1991, pp. 72–87.

The capital budgeting process

Most capital investment needs should flow from the healthcare professionals providing patient services. However, due to the number of dollars involved and the time period over which most capital investment decisions have an impact on the organization, an effective capital budgeting system would involve all levels of management in the process. Such a system should include a standardized set of worksheets to help in the identification and justification of financially feasible projects, a timetable for the submission, review, and approval process, and follow up procedures to monitor and compare results with the plan.

The healthcare professional who identifies the need for capital investment should be able to request the help of qualified staff personnel in completing the forms. For example, the purchasing agent can help in identifying the capabilities and relative costs of equipment alternatives. The maintenance engineer can assist in estimating modification and installation costs; the fiscal officer can help in preparing cost estimates and completing the evaluation process. The completed capital budgeting documents should represent the best expert advice available to assist in preparing the proposal.

A framework for analysis

As is true of most analyses which take place, the application of the scientific approach provides an appropriate framework for the analysis. The steps in the capital budgeting process consist of the following:

1. Identification of the capital investment needs.
2. Identification of alternatives.
3. Evaluation of the alternatives.
4. Screening and ranking of competing proposals.
5. The recommended decision.
6. Re-evaluation of previous investment decisions.

Identification of the capital investment needs

As noted earlier, capital investment decisions should be based on the institutional objectives. However, most organizational objectives do not provide enough specific guidance to develop all the needed proposals. Capital investment proposals should include a broad spectrum of types of projects, such as:

a. plant or equipment replacement;
b. expansion of product line;

c. geographic expansion;
d. research and development;
e. upgrades in technology;
f. mandated (by either OSHA, EPA, etc.);
g. cost containment.

Capital investment proposals should be solicited and accepted from all levels of the organization. Departmental and responsibility center needs can be best identified by managers and care givers. Strategic capital investment proposals will more often be generated at the higher levels of the organization.

Identification of alternatives

Once a need has been identified, it is important that alternative methods to meet these needs be identified. Typically, the individual identifying the need will also have a suggested approach to meeting this need. However, other alternatives to meet this need should be considered which may involve other members of the organization. A formal capital budgeting committee composed of clinical and administrative personnel can be useful in identifying alternatives.

There will always be both qualitative and quantitative aspects in the analysis of capital investment proposals. The first and most important will be qualitative issues. Such factors as quality of care, improved employee morale, and other intangible benefits are decided on subjective grounds. However, most proposals also have a quantitative side. It is the analysis of the quantitative factors that is beginning to play a more important role in the evaluation of capital projects. There will never be one absolutely right decision where qualitative issues are involved. Experience, training, and political factors can all play roles in the decision. The quantitative analysis also requires some subjectivity in estimating the numbers involved, but the analysis can be fairly objective. Therefore, it is important to complete the qualitative analysis first to provide the foundation for the quantitative analysis.

Evaluation of the alternatives

Every capital investment proposal should require information on four quantitative factors:

1. *Cash Outflows*

The cash outflows consist of the original investment amount or purchase cost, installation costs, and any other out-of-pocket costs which must be made in order to acquire or initiate the investment proposal. They also include any periodic and continuing operating and maintenance costs.

2. *Cash Inflows*

The cash inflows consist of the incremental revenues or expense reductions (on a cash basis) associated with the capital project. (It is important to stress that only cash flows are used, not accrual-based data, in the analysis). Periodic cash inflows are generally subtracted from the periodic cash outflows; only the net difference each year needs to be entered into the subsequent analysis.

3. *Economic Life*

The economic life of the proposal should be consistent with the timing of the cash inflows and cash outflows. The economic life can be defined as the period of time during which the initiating organization is expected to receive the benefits and/or incur the costs. It should not be confused with the physical life of the project or the depreciation period established by the Internal Revenue Service or third-party payers. However, either of these two periods may set the upper limit on how long the project will continue.

4. *Discount Rate*

To compensate for the different timing of cash flows, all cash flows need to be adjusted to a common reference point, usually the starting point of the project (although any point in time could be used). This technique, called discounting, requires the determination of the discount rate to be used. The most commonly used approach requires an estimate of the required returns to suppliers of capital (creditors and equity owners). This required rate of return is the cost of capital to the organization, and is discussed in more detail later in this chapter.

Before leaving this section it is important to note that the cash flow estimates must be calculated very carefully in order to consider only the incremental cash flows (those which arise strictly due to the proposal) on an after-tax basis where appropriate (since this represents what the organization gets to keep). To the extent that interest and depreciation expense has an impact on the cash flows under cost-based reimbursement it must also be taken into consideration. Interest and depreciation expense are lumped together by Medicare as capital related costs and reimbursed on a cost basis. For capital investment analysis purposes, interest expense (a cash outflow) and depreciation expense (a noncash outflow) are treated separately. Interest expense reimbursement is included in determining the net cost of interest to the healthcare provider. It is important to recognize that depreciation expense is a noncash expense and, therefore, is not reflected in the cash outflows. For taxable healthcare organizations, since depreciation is tax deductible, changes in depreciation expense must be considered in terms of the overall impact on the organization's tax liability.

Exhibit 12–1 illustrates a graphic portrayal of the four factors discussed earlier. It is useful in visualizing the future cash flows, when they occur and the impact on economic life. The table for calculations can be used

Exhibit 12–1
A capital investment decision model

Cash flows (end of year)

	Inflows						
+							
0	1	2	3	4	5		6
−	Outflows						

Economic life

Time	Net Cash flow	Discount** factor	Present value
0	_____	_____	_____
1	_____	_____	_____
2	_____	_____	_____
3	_____	_____	_____
4	_____	_____	_____
5	_____	_____	_____
		Net present value***	_____

*adjusted for tax rates

**calculated from $\dfrac{1}{(1 + i)^n}$

***1. If NPV is positive (greater than zero) the investment returns a rate greater than the discount rate used.
  2. If NPV is negative (less than zero) the investment returns a rate less than the discount rate used.
  3. If NPV is zero, the investment returns the same rate as the discount rate used; this is called the internal rate of return.

to portray the impact of time and the sensitivity of the discount rate selected on the dollars received.

Time value of money techniques

Before we can discuss the next step, the process of evaluation, we must first introduce one of the primary tools in the evaluation process—discounted cash flow.

A. Tools of Analysis

The concept of discounted cash flow is based on the idea of the time value of money. The time value of money is explicit recognition that a dollar received at some time in the future does not have the same value as a dollar received today. The process referred to as *discounted cash flow (DCF)* analysis provides a method of placing all cash flows at the same point in time.

1. Future value of a present amount

The discounted cash flow process may be more easily understood if we first consider the compounding of interest with which most individuals are familiar. Money placed in a savings account earns interest at a given rate for some period of time. For example, assume you place $1,000 into a savings account paying 6 percent interest per year, compounded annually. At the end of one year, the savings account has a balance of $1,060; the original (principal) amount of $1,000 plus interest on the $1,000 at the rate of 6 percent, or $60. During the second year the total $1,060 earns interest at the rate of 6 percent, resulting in a balance after two years of $1,123.60. During the third year, this $1,123.60 earns interest at the rate of 6 percent, for an ending balance of $1,191. This would continue indefinitely until we withdraw some or all of our account balance. The mathematics of calculating the balance in the savings account is represented by the following formula:

$$\text{original deposit } (1 + \text{interest rate})^n;$$
where n equals the period of time the money is left on deposit.

For managers who do not want to actually compute these values, tables are available which solve the compounding equation, assuming an original deposit of $1. This table, and several additional tables to be discussed, are included in *Appendix 12–1*. Most financial calculators perform this function, and it is also very easy to have the calculations performed with any type of spreadsheet program.

2. Present value of a future amount (PV) (discounted cash flow)

The relationship of compounding to discounting can be illustrated in the following manner. Assume that management wants to replace a piece of equipment in four years that will cost $1,000. They would like to determine how much would have to be deposited into a savings account today in order to have the full $1,000 balance in three years. The problem is very similar to the previous problem except that now we want to know how much must be deposited in a savings account today.

End of year		
1	$BA(1.10)^1$	= Balance end of year 1 (B1)
2	$BA(1.10)^2$	= Balance end of year 2 (B2)
3	$BA(1.10)^3$	= $1,000
where: $BA = Beginning Amount		

In this case we are interested in the *present value of a future amount* and would need to solve for $BA indicated above. This problem is the complement to the first problem where the manager wanted to know the *future value of a present amount*. Mathematically, we can perform this calculation by using the formula developed for the first calculation, since the discounted cash flow amount is the reciprocal of the compounded amount:

$$Future\ Value = \$BA\ (1 + i)^n \text{ (from the preceding section)}$$

By rearranging terms we can solve for the original deposit:

$$Original\ Deposit = Future\ Value * \frac{1}{(1 + i)^n}$$

Tables have also been constructed to facilitate this type of computation and are included in the *Appendix 1. Exhibit 12–2* illustrates the solution to this type of problem.

3. Annuities

In most capital investment decisions, the decision to commit resources today is for the right to receive cash inflows in the future. When these cash inflows consist of equal amounts at fixed intervals, you have what is commonly called an annuity. You can have future value annuities such as equal payments into a sinking fund to retire a bond issue or to provide a retirement pension to a current employee. In capital investment decisions, you have a present value annuity in which you want to know what a stream of cash inflows in the future is worth today. Annuity problems can be solved in the same manner as discussed earlier as you can use an annuity table factor. *Exhibit 12–3* illustrates the future value of an annuity and *12–4* shows the present value calculations for the same annuity. Both use a 6 percent rate for compounding and discounting respectively.

The concept of discounting and compounding is important to the capital budgeting evaluation process, with the present value concept being used most often.

B. Screening and Ranking of Competing Proposals

There are two problems in evaluating capital investment cash flows. The first is a screening problem: Does the investment meet the minimum return on investment criterion of the organization? The minimum return is usually defined as the cost of capital. The second is a problem of ranking: Given the number of investment proposals, how do we set priorities for them? This is a particularly sensitive area, especially when there are more projects than the available funds can support. Evaluation of the cash flows

Exhibit 12–2
Present value of a future amount

Amount needed at end of the 4th year $1,464
Present value factor, 10%, 4 years
(from *Appendix 1, Table 1*) .683
Present amount that must be invested today
$1,464/.683 = $1,000

Exhibit 12–3
Future value of an annuity

Amount	Year	Compound interest factor	Future value
$2,500	1	1.19102	$ 2,977.54
$2,500	2	1.12360	$ 2,809.00
$2,500	3	1.06000	$ 2,650.00
$2,500	4	1.00000	$ 2,500.00
Totals		4.37462*	$10,936.54**

*Notice that the total of the compound interest factors is equal to the amounts factor.
**Since the annual payments are equal (2,500) it would also be possible to calculate the future value by using the future value annuity factor for four years at 6 percent or 4.37462.
2,500(4.37462) = $10,936.54

Exhibit 12–4
Present value of an annuity

Amount	Year	Discount interest factor	Future value
$2,500	1	0.94340	$2,358.49
$2,500	2	0.89000	$2,224.99
$2,500	3	0.83962	$2,099.05
$2,500	4	0.79209	$1,980.23
Totals		3.46511*	$8,662.76**

*Notice that the total of the discount interest factors is equal to the annuity factor.
**Using the PV annuity for four years at 6 percent or 3.46511 would give you the same result.
2,500(3.46511) = $8,662.76

requires the application of the tools presented above. However, there are also techniques for evaluation which do not make use of the discounted cash flow tools presented. This disadvantage, however, is sometimes outweighed by the ease of use of the technique even though the resulting answer does not consider the time value of money. The methods of evaluation include the following:

Evaluation techniques—*not* adjusted for the time value of money:

1. accounting rate of return (ARR);
2. payback method (PB).

Evaluation techniques—adjusted for the time value of money:

3. net present value method (NPV);
4. internal rate of return (IRR);
5. profitability index (benefit/cost ratio).

Each of these techniques have different strengths and weaknesses, and should be thoroughly understood in order to be used effectively.

1. The accounting rate of return

The accounting rate of return has been used extensively in the past because it relies on information that normally appears in the financial statements. The net income from the project (as reported on the statement of revenues and expenses) is divided by the average book investment required for the project. The resulting rate of return is compared with the desired rate of return to decide whether to accept the investment. This technique is very easy to compute and is very easy to understand. However, it violates several of the criteria necessary to provide for an appropriate evaluation of capital investment projects. First, it does not consider the time value of money in assuming that a dollar at some point in the future is considered to represent the same economic value as a dollar today. Secondly, it uses accounting expenses rather than cash flows from the project. Accounting expenses include depreciation which is not a cash outflow to the organization. The accounting rate of return can be calculated as follows:

$$ARR = \frac{\text{Average Annual Change in Income}}{\text{Average Investment of Project}} = \frac{\Delta I_a}{O/2}$$

The average investment (O/2) is equal to the initial outflow (project cost) divided by two since depreciation expense is subtracted from net income each year. This is a noncash outflow but serves to reduce the initial outflow each year by the amount of the depreciation. The average amount of the initial outflow over the life of the project would occur at the midpoint.

For example, if we assume that a new X-ray machine for radiology has an initial cost of $10,000, is expected to reduce total labor costs by $1,500 per year, and is expected to have a useful life of ten years, we would determine the ARR as follows:

Change in operating expenses:

Labor expense	($1,500)
Additional depreciation expense	$1,000
Change in net income	$ 500
Average investment = $10,000/2 = $5,000	
ARR = $500/$5,000 = 10%	

This example has assumed that there are no reimbursement or tax implications. Appropriate and separate calculations would have to be made for the payment of tax liability or for outflows from third-party payers.

2. The payback method

The payback method refers to the amount of time it takes to recover the initial cash outflow for the investment from the future cash inflows. This method is quite easy to compute and to understand, but it has several weaknesses. The first is that it disregards any cash flows which occur after the payback period. The second is that it typically does not consider the time value of money. The payback period is calculated as follows:

$$Payback\ Period = \frac{Initial\ Investment}{Average\ Annual\ Cash\ Inflow} = \frac{O_o}{CF_a}$$

Continuing with the previous example, the payback period for the X-ray machine would be calculated as follows:

Cash flow per year = $1,500 (the labor cost savings)
Initial investment = $10,000
Payback period = $10,000 / $1,500 = 6 2/3 years.

The major objection to the first two methods is that they tend to ignore the time value of money. This can have a significant impact on the evaluation of the cash flows when there is a long time period involved, when there are very uneven cash flows over the life of the project, or the discount rate used in the calculation is relatively high. (In *Appendix 12–2*, the use of discounted cash flows to determine the payback period is illustrated.) An interested reader could explore this issue further in a financial management textbook, or a book on capital budgeting.

3. Net present value (NPV)

The net present value (NPV) approach to evaluating capital investment projects computes the difference between the discounted cash inflows and the discounted cash outflows arising from the project. This amount can be either positive or negative. A positive net present value indicates that investment in the project exceeds the desired or criterion discount rate (required rate of return), and would be an acceptable use of funds from a financial sense. A net present value of zero would indicate that the project meets the required rate of return and is acceptable from a financial sense. A negative net present value indicates the opposite, and the project is rejected as unacceptable from a financial sense. Examples of both acceptable and unacceptable projects are provided later in this chapter. The calculations for NPV are provided by using the following:

$$Net\ Present\ Value = \Sigma \frac{CF_t}{(1 + i)^t}$$

where: CF_t = Cash flow during period t
$(1+i)^t$ = Discount factor at interest rate i for cash received during t.

Application of this equation is demonstrated in the following example. This problem is fairly straightforward since all the annual cash inflows were assumed to be the same. In reality, equal cash flows will not be the case. In this instance, each of the annual cash flows will have to be considered separately in the present value calculation. This process is now shown for the same figures as *Exhibit 12–5.*

Exhibit 12–5
Net present value technique

Initital cash outflow	$20,000
Annual cash outflows for 10 years	$3,500
Opportunity cost for organization	15%

0	Outflow $20,000 × 1.0	=	<$20,000>
1–10	Inflows $3,500 × 5.018	=	$17,563
	Net present value	=	<$2,437>

In this case the present value of the cash inflows are less than the present value of the initial cash outflow, giving a negative net present value. This indicates that the project is not acceptable for financial reasons since it will not provide the required 15 percent rate of return.[2] If, however, the cash inflows can be increased to $4,500 per year for the project, we can see that the net present value of the project becomes positive and the project is acceptable from a financial perspective.[3] (See *Exhibits 12–6* and *12–7.*)

4. Internal rate of return

An alternative discounted cash flow method is the internal rate of return method. This method is conceptually similar to the net present value technique, except that it calculates a rate of return for each capital investment project. The internal rate of return is defined to be that rate of return at which the net present value is equal to zero. The following formula is solved for r, where r is defined to be the internal rate of return.

$$Net\ Present\ Value = \Sigma \frac{CF_t}{(1+r)^t} = 0$$

where: CF_t = cash flow during period t
The summation takes place over the economic life of the project.

---

[2] The internal rate of return (IRR) for this project (presented in the following section) is 11.73 percent. This was determined using the @IRR function of the spreadsheet programs.

[3] The internal rate of return (IRR) for this project is 18.31 percent, using the spreadsheet programs.

Exhibit 12–6
Net present value technique revisited

Initial cash outflow		$20,000			
Annual cash inflows for 10 years		$3,500			
Opportunity cost for organization		15%			

Year	Cash	Amount	×	Factor	= Present value
0	Outflow	$20,000	×	1	($20,000)
1	Inflow	$ 3,500	×	0.869565	$ 3,043
2	Inflow	$ 3,500	×	0.756144	$ 2,647
3	Inflow	$ 3,500	×	0.657516	$ 2,301
4	Inflow	$ 3,500	×	0.571753	$ 2,001
5	Inflow	$ 3,500	×	0.497177	$ 1,740
6	Inflow	$ 3,500	×	0.432328	$ 1,513
7	Inflow	$ 3,500	×	0.375937	$ 1,316
8	Inflow	$ 3,500	×	0.326902	$ 1,144
9	Inflow	$ 3,500	×	0.284262	$ 995
10	Inflow	$ 3,500	×	0.247185	$ 865
					($ 2,434)

Exhibit 12–7
Continuation of net present value technique example

Initial cash outflow		$20,000			
Annual cash inflows		$4,500			
Opportunity cost for the organization		15%			

Year	Cash	Amount	×	Factor	=	Present value
0	Outflow	$20,000	×	1.0	=	$20,000
1–10	Inflows	$ 4,500	×	5.018	=	$22,581
						$ 2,581

A simpler way to make this computation is demonstrated in *Exhibit 12–8.*

In *Exhibit 12–8* we need to solve for the interest rate which will equate the future cash inflows to a present value of $20,000. This can be accomplished (in this case) by dividing the initial investment ($20,000) by the future annual cash inflow ($3,500) to give a factor of 5.714. This is the factor which would be calculated from the formula for the present value of an annuity. That is, the problem can be reworded by stating that we are looking for that interest rate which makes the present value of a ten year annuity of $3,500 equal to $20,000. It is now necessary to examine *Table 2* (present value of an annuity of $1 per period) in *Appendix 12–1*. Look-

Exhibit 12–8
Computation of internal rate of return

Initial cash outflow				$20,000		
Annual cash inflows				$3,500		

Year	Cash	Amount	×	Factor	=	Present value
0	Outflow	$20,000	×	1.0	=	<$20,000>
1–10	Inflows	$ 3,500	×	?	=	$20,000
Net present value (inflows - outflows)					=	-0-

The factor is equal to $20,000/$3,500 or 5.714.

ing at 10 time periods, we then search for a factor having a value close to 5.714. Once we have found that factor, we then identify the interest rate which provided that factor—in this case 12 percent.

This example was very simplistic in that it was assumed that each annual cash inflow was identical. In cases when the cash flows are not equal, the process is somewhat less precise and more complex. The method to be used is an iterative process of choosing a discount rate and calculating the present value of the cash flows for each rate. The process of changing discount rate continues until a net present value close to zero has been found.

The financial decision rule for acceptance or rejection of a project using the net present value technique is to accept the project if the net present value is greater than zero and to reject the project if the net present value is negative. A project having a negative net present value indicates that the rate of return is less than the required rate of return that was used to discount the cash flows. With the internal rate of return method, the discount rate calculated is compared to the required rate of return. If the internal rate of return is greater than the required rate of return the project is acceptable for financial reasons. If the internal rate of return is less than the required rate of return, the project is rejected as unacceptable for financial reasons.

Both the net present value method and the internal rate of return method incorporate the time value of money concept. Both are effective as screening devices when the required rate of return is known. However, when ranking of priorities becomes of major concern, the internal rate of return method becomes the more commonly used method. This is primarily due to the fact that decision makers find it easier to rank investments according to a rate of return criterion because interest rates are more understandable than present value amounts. Net present value and IRR will always give the same decision regarding the acceptability of a project, although they will occasionally rank projects differently because of some of the assumptions made by the IRR approach. These assumptions are beyond the scope of this text, but the interested reader is referred to any basic financial management text for a more detailed approach.

5. Profitability index (benefit-cost ratio)

One additional technique which is used to assist in the capital investment decision is the profitability index. This technique does not require any new calculations from those already introduced, but uses the net present value calculations in a different way. The ratio of the present value of cash inflows to the present value of cash outlays indicates a value centered around one. If the value is greater than one, the project is acceptable since it earns more than one dollar for each dollar of investment, while if the value is less than one, the project is rejected because it earns less than one dollar for each dollar of investment benefits. A profitability index of one means the project IRR is equal to the discount rate used in the discounting (an example is provided in *Exhibit 12–9*).

Exhibit 12–9
Profitability index

$$\text{Profitability index} = \frac{\text{Present value of cash inflows}}{\text{Present value of cash outlfows}}$$

$$\frac{17,563}{20,000} = .88 \qquad \frac{22,581}{20,000} = 1.13$$

Sample problem

Let's assume that a CEO is confronted with two capital investment proposals, only one of which can be accepted. Each project is described in *Exhibit 12–10*.

For convenience we will assume that straight line depreciation will be used, although for income tax purposes the accelerated capital recovery system (ACRS) method would be used. (This method is discussed in *Appendix 12–3*). In the example above, the CFO has estimated that the opportunity cost for alternative investments is 16 percent. The five methods

Exhibit 12–10
Two capital investment projects

Diagnostic equipment	Project A	Project B
Cost, including installation	$60,000	$55,000
Estimated annual labor cost savings	$20,000	$16,000
Estimated economic life	5 years	5 years

Exhibit 12–11
Five methods of evaluating capital projects

	Project A	Project B
Cost of capital	15.00%	15.00%
Initial investment	$60,000	$55,000
Additional cash receipts	$20,000	$16,000
Depreciation expense	$12,000	$11,000
Net income from investment	$8,000	$5,000
Accounting rate of return	26.67%	18.18%
Payback	3	3.4375
Net present value		
Year 0 cash outflow	$60,000	$55,000
Years 1–5 inflows	$20,000	$16,000
Factor for inflows	3.352	3.352
Present value of inflows	$67,040	$53,632
Profitability index	1.12	0.975
Internal rate of return	19.86%	13.95%

of analysis are applied to these two situations and presented in *Exhibit 12–11*.

In *Exhibit 12–11*, Project A is ranked better than B, since the accounting rate of return, net present value, profitability index, and internal rate of return is higher for A than for B, and the payback period for A is shorter than for B. None of these measures, however, have told us whether or not B should be accepted. In order to make this decision a hurdle rate should be determined. The required rate of return, the opportunity cost, and the required payback period are all legitimate criteria to be considered for the acceptance or rejection of projects. In the following section we examine several methods designed to help establish the hurdle rate.

The issue of rationing was mentioned as a portion of this step in the capital budgeting process. Rationing of capital budgeting funds arise in the situation where there is a greater dollar volume of capital investment opportunities than there are capital resources. The decision as to which projects should be implemented will then depend on the relative values of the alternative investment opportunities, from both a financial and an organizational mission standpoint. Additional information on this topic can be gained through examination of the references listed at the end of the chapter.

Re-evaluation of past capital investment decisions

This step is extremely important, but also most often neglected. After a decision has been made to implement capital investment projects, based on projected costs, revenues, demographic, and technological forecasts, and after a period of time has passed during which experience has occurred, a comparison of the forecasted results with the actual results must be made. These comparisons provide data for improving future forecasts, adjusting past decisions, and provide needed information with which to update forecasts regarding the behavior of capital investment projects.

Cost of capital

In order to evaluate capital investment projects using the time value of money concept, it is necessary to establish a discount rate or minimum required rate of return. This criterion has been variously referred to as: required rate of return, discount rate, cost of capital, opportunity cost, hurdle rate, or any number of additional terms. Regardless of what it is called, the concept is the same. The financial management literature presents the arguments for the development of the appropriate interest rate to be used in this evaluation process, but basically it determines the return that must be earned to meet the suppliers' required return on capital.

The "cost of capital" for any organization is considered to be the opportunity cost for the various sources of funds available for capital investment. The approach used to calculate the cost of capital is to determine the weighted average cost of all funds provided to the organization, or expected to be needed by the organization. The concept is relatively easy to understand, but determining the specific numbers is exceedingly difficult. To do so the financial manager must make the following estimates for the firm:

1. An optimum capital structure for the welfare of the organization and its various stakeholders.[4] Capital structure refers to the amount of debt

---

[4]The theory of valuation in financial management has determined that different combinations of debt and equity financing for an organization result in different "cost of capital." This is due to the fact that debt creates a legal liability for an organization and a fixed interest expense. In the event of financial difficulty, an inability to pay interest and principal on the debt can result in bankruptcy. Therefore, as more debt is used, the risk of bankruptcy is increased. Equity financing has no similar risk characteristics, since nonpayment of dividends cannot force an organization into bankruptcy. On the other hand, under normal circumstances, the use of some debt is useful if it can be used to increase the profits of the organization. This happens when the interest rate being paid on the debt is less than the return that can be earned with the borrowed money. This tradeoff between profitability and bankruptcy risk results in some capital structures which are better than others—some debt is used to increase profits, but not so much as to make the risk of bankruptcy too high.

relative to the amount of equity funds which are used by the organization.[5] The relationship between the two sources of capital funds determines the cost of acquiring each source of funds. For example, a board may decide that 40 percent is the maximum amount of funds that should come from debt sources of capital; the remaining 60 percent needs to come from other sources available to the organization. The capital structure of the organization would thus be: 40 percent debt financing and 60 percent equity (or fund balance) financing. This means that an organization with $1,000,000 of assets will have borrowed $400,000 in the debt markets and acquired the remaining $600,000 in forms which did not have a legal liability for repayment associated with it. Even though the current capital structure may not be 40 percent debt and 60 percent equity, these are the weights that should be used to determine the cost of capital since over a long enough period of time, debt and equity of funds will be acquired in these approximate proportions. For any specific project, or year, one or the other source of funds may be used to finance capital projects but the firm has to balance the total amount of funds available through its capital structure from both debt and equity sources.

2. The cost of the various sources of capital. The cost of debt poses no particular problem since this can be determined by examining the current capital markets and predicting the rates for varying amounts of debt in the financial structure. The cost of capital is determined by looking at what rate of return needs to be earned in the future, not what has happened in the past. Thus, the interest rate on currently existing debt is not necessarily a good measure of what the long-term average cost of debt will be. Current rates of interest, forecasts of future interest rates, in addition to historical interest rates, should be used to determine the appropriate cost of debt financing to be used in the cost of capital calculation. To the extent that interest expense is reimbursed on a cost basis by Medicare, the effective cost of interest expense is less than the stated rate. For example, a 10 percent interest rate on $1,000 in debt would cost $100. In a provider with a 40 percent Medicare payer mix, Medicare would reimburse the provider for 40 percent of this interest cost or $40. The actual interest cost would

---

[5] Nonprofit organizations do not generally refer to equity funds, but instead refer to the "fund balance" or "net assets." The fund balance for a tax exempt organization refers to funds which have not been borrowed. Since they have not been borrowed, they do not have to be paid back, similar to stock for an investor-owned organization. The source of these funds are donations, grants, endowments, tax receipts, and earned profits (excess of revenues over expenses). However, while stockholders expect to receive dividends and are able to sell their ownership position, for tax exempt entities, there can be no distribution of funds to any of the fund balance (equity) sources. Organizations which have been granted tax exempt status, however, are expected to provide communities with free care, education, and other community service activities. This becomes the dividend to the community of permitting the organization to have tax exempt status.

be \$60 (\$100–40) which would equate to an effective interest rate of 6 percent (\$60/1000). The Medicare policy of reimbursement for interest expense has the effect of debt being a relatively cheap alternative to other sources of capital. The same impact on the cost of debt can be observed through the federal government allowance of interest expense as an allowable deduction to income before the income tax liability is determined. It is much more difficult to estimate the cost of the other sources of funds—the equity sources. If the organization has stockholders, their required rate of return determines the cost of these other sources of funds. Stock price, risk considerations, and corporate growth rates can be used to estimate the cost of this equity capital, using the "Gordon Growth Model" discussed in financial management textbooks. The cost of equity funds for a tax exempt entity has been much debated in the literature. An argument could be made that tax exempt equity funds should earn the same rate of return as taxable funds. One point needs to be stressed — the cost of equity or fund balance funds will always be higher than the cost of debt due to the increased risk associated with being last in the priority to receive any disbursements. While this is true for both profit and nonprofit organizations, it is often misunderstood. Interested readers can explore this issue further through the articles listed at the end of the chapter.

Estimates of the cost of capital using debt and equity sources can be calculated as shown below.

	Balance Sheet	
Given:	Debt $w_d = 40\%$ $k_d = 8\%$	
	Equity $w_e = 60\%$ $k_e = 12\%$	
Where:	w_d = proportion of debt financing	
	k_d = cost of debt financing	
	w_e = proportion of equity financing	
	k_e = cost of equity financing	

The weighted average cost of capital is calculated as follows:

$w_d \times k_d + w_e \times k_e$ = cost of capital = k

Proportion	Cost	Relative cost
40%	8%	3.2%
60%	12%	7.2%
100%	Average cost of capital	10.4%

This computation indicates the organization would need to earn at least a 10.4 percent rate of return on its capital investment projects. If this rate could not be earned on the investments, it means the investment is not returning the required rate of return to its suppliers of capital. The following example indicates that all the sources of capital are satisfied if the cost of capital (10.4 percent) is earned on a capital investment of

$20,000,000 (of which $8,000,000 was borrowed and $12,000,000 came from other sources).

Assets	=	$20,000,000
Rate of return	=	.104
Returns	=	$ 2,080,000

Of this $2,080,000, $640,000 ($8,000,000 × 8%) is paid to the debt capital as interest payments, leaving $1,440,000 for all other sources. This provides a rate of return to all other sources of:

$$\frac{\$1,440,000}{\$12,000,000} = 12\%$$

It is easily seen that all sources of funds have received their required rate of return. The weighted average cost of capital requires that the financing decision (the source of the funds) should be separated from the investment decision (how the funds are used). Although it may be possible to obtain 100 percent debt financing for some projects, this high proportion of debt financing is available only because equity or other sources of funds have been used or will be used in the future for other projects. It should be clear that using all debt financing for one project will require that some other project must obtain all of its financing from other sources. Unless the distinction between sources of capital and uses of capital is maintained, capital investment decisions will not hinge on the relative merits of each proposal, but would be dependent on the specific type of financing available at a specific point in time. When cheap money is available, poor projects would be accepted, while essential projects might be bypassed due to the lack of available debt funds in the future.

Lease versus purchase decision

Leasing as an alternative to purchasing has grown in importance in the health services industry. This is due to the increasing risk associated with the industry, the reduced profitability, and the rate of technological advancements and lack of available funds for investment purposes. But before going further we need to discuss the concept of leasing.

In general, a lease consists of a contractual agreement between two parties—one who owns a piece of equipment or property (called the lessor) and one who wishes to utilize the piece of equipment or property (called the lessee). The contract determines the amount of payment for the use of the item and the specific time period involved, responsibilities for maintenance, insurance, and other necessary determinations which must be made.

In general, there are two types of leases—operating and financial. An operating lease is not financial in structure and is generally written for a short period of time—hours, days, weeks, or months. This time period is always shorter than the asset's useful life. With an operating lease, the owner (lessor) generally assumes all of the responsibilities associated with ownership, including maintenance, service, insurance, liability, property and sales taxes. Both the lessor and the lessee have the right to cancel this contract with short notice.

From this description it may appear that the lessee receives many benefits while the lessor retains all the responsibilities and risks. However, the lessor is able to depreciate the equipment for tax and reimbursement purposes, and if it was purchased with borrowed funds (a leveraged lease) is also able to reduce the taxes of the organization, due to the interest expense. There are additional reasons as to why a corporation or individual prefers to be a lessor of equipment which provides a benefit to both the lessor and the lessee. These will be discussed as they arise.

The second type of lease is called a capital or financial lease. In this case, the contract is primarily financial in nature. The lessee agrees to pay the lessor a fixed sum of money for a period of time. The sum of money typically equals or exceeds the purchase price of the asset, and the time period generally is equal to at least 75 percent of the useful life of the asset. From the standpoint of the lessor, the sum of the cash flows over the term of the lease payments, the tax savings, and the equipment's residual value is sufficient to pay back the lessor's investment and provide a reasonable rate of return. Accountants and reimbursers use the requirements of FASB 13 to classify the lease. [6]

Most financial leases are called "net" leases in that all the fundamental responsibilities associated with ownership of the asset are transferred to the lessee. The financial lease is normally not cancelable by either party. At the time of termination of the lease, the equipment may be returned to the lessor, while in some cases, the lessee is given the option of purchasing the asset, often for a nominal amount.

Benefits of leasing

There are several real or imagined benefits associated with leasing a piece of equipment as opposed to borrowing and/or buying the asset. Likewise, some of these benefits are applicable to tax paying entities while others are benefits regardless of tax status.

---

[6] FASB stands for the Financial Accounting Standards Board, an organization which provides guidelines for specific accounting activities. FASB 13 provides guidance for the classification of leases as either capital or operating according to specific lease characteristics.

1. Improved Cash Flow. With leasing there is no required down payment, although the first lease payment is usually made at the beginning of the term. Likewise, other associated initial cash flow items—taxes, installation, etc., are all included in the equal periodic payments. In addition, the lease payment period may be longer than the available borrowing period, thereby slowing the rate of cash disbursement necessary to gain the use of the asset. An asset which is currently owned by the lessee, but has been fully depreciated, can be sold and leased back. This *sale and leaseback* arrangement provides cash to the organization. Both operating and capital leases can qualify for Medicare capital reimbursement.

2. Obsolescence Risk. In the healthcare industry there has been a rapid rate of technological advancement. This has presented a risk to organizations which acquire the latest technology only to find it to be outdated within a relatively short period of time. In the current environment where capital funds for equipment acquisition purposes is increasingly scarce, the risk of obsolescence provides a significant cost to the organization. An organization which acquires the equipment for leasing purposes is able to spread this obsolescence risk among a variety of clients, some of whom are not ready for the latest technology. The lessor becomes, in effect, a broker of items to a variety of firms within the healthcare industry.

3. Lower Cost to the Lessee. There are several reasons why a lease may cost less, in present value terms, than borrowing and purchasing the piece of equipment. There are underwriting and associated costs of floating new issues of stocks and/or bonds; it takes less time to acquire a contract to lease than it does to float a new issue; the total amount of the lease payment can be tax deductible—if the period of the lease is shorter than the allowed depreciation schedule, there would be tax benefits relative to ownership of the asset.

4. Lower Cost to the Lessor. Advantages to the lessor consist of the ability to acquire a depreciable asset. This is especially important to organizations which may have a great deal of cash but very little in the way of depreciable assets. Financial organizations, banks, insurance companies, etc., can acquire assets to lease while retaining the depreciation tax shield.

5. Flexibility. As mentioned previously, a leasing contract takes less time to consummate than does the acquisition of financing and purchase of the asset; leasing does not often provide the same type and level of constraints often included as covenants when funds are borrowed for acquisition purposes; while a financial lease provides the same financial obligation as does a borrowing instrument, the lessor is often willing to take back the asset as opposed to forcing the organization into bankruptcy.

6. Tax Benefits to a Tax Exempt Entity. This provides a case where the Internal Revenue Service oversees the leasing activities of tax exempt organizations. Since tax exempt healthcare organizations do not have the tax benefits associated with depreciation and interest deductibility, situ-

ations may exist where a lessor can lease a piece of equipment to a tax exempt organization at a lower cost than the healthcare organization could purchase the asset. The Internal Revenue Service does not permit this type of activity when it can be identified. On the other side of the coin, as long as depreciation and interest expense has been a cost reimbursable to Medicare, there has been little incentive for healthcare organizations to examine the leasing alternative.

7. Medicare reimbursement payment may be increased, if the organization is an "excess borrower" according to Medicare definitions. An "excess borrower" is one who borrows money before exhausting its unrestricted funds. Doing this creates unnecessary interest charges that Medicare will not pay as allowable interest charges. Since lease payments are not subject to this restriction, using leasing instead of debt financing may provide additional reimbursement to the organization if they are able to recover the indirect interest charges in the lease payment.

There has been a great deal of confusion and disagreement regarding the handling of lease decisions relative to the alternative. Indeed, there has been disagreement as to the relevant alternative. The financial management experts insist on the importance of separating the investment decision from the financing decision. In most instances this is very easy to do, and the net present value techniques discussed previously follow this requirement. In the case of leasing, however, it appears this is not the case. Leasing a piece of equipment or property includes both the financing and use of the asset in one decision. However, the authors believe that two decisions need to be made:

1. *Whether to acquire the asset*—this is the normal capital budgeting decision, using the calculated cost of capital and net present value or internal rate of return techniques.

2. *How to finance the acquisition*—leasing is an approach to financing the capital investment, providing an alternative method of trying to find the lowest net cost to the purchaser. There may be special circumstances which endow lease financing with particular tax savings not available with ordinary debt or equity financing arrangements. These factors are part of the financing decision, not the investment decision. The options are debt and/or equity, consistent with the long-term capital structure decisions of the organization, as opposed to leasing.

The healthcare industry is unique when it comes time to evaluate a leasing decision. The rate of technological change is extremely rapid, and the integration of the latest technology into a healthcare organization is primarily a function of factors other than cost—physician and patient demands. While technological change may be as rapid in other industries, a major difference between healthcare and other industries is the nature of the consumer and the output. Care givers play a major role in the importance of acquiring the latest technology available for their patients. In the healthcare industry, different players must make a conscious decision regarding where they will stand in terms of technology—leading edge, competitive edge, or trailing edge. The leading edge users consist of the initial users of a new technology. They acquire high-tech equipment early in its product life and tend to have a short, useful life for the equipment (before the next generation of equipment is available). These users have a great deal of brand loyalty and seldom purchase used equipment. The competitive edge users generally wait until the technology is proven both technologically and economically, and will sometimes consider the purchase of used equipment (from the leading edge users). Finally, the trailing edge users acquire stripped down versions and bargain hard with vendors. For them, prestige takes a back seat to cost; they often consider used equipment as a cost-effective strategy. Behind all these strategies stands the nature of the patient. What do they need?

To the extent that these "after-markets" exist for high-tech equipment, there is an active market for the leasing of healthcare organization equipment. This active market provides a situation where a healthcare organization can save money through the leasing of equipment and increase its flexibility in gaining access to the latest technology. The existence of this second and third market (competitive edge and trailing edge users) drives the evaluation technique to consider the residual value of the piece of equipment at the end of its useful life. The useful life varies greatly depending on the type of user, and is always shorter for the leading edge user. The useful life must be compared with the product life, where the product life is the length of time over which the asset has value to anyone. The greater the difference between the useful life and the product life, the more attractive the leasing option will become. This is due to the fact that a leasing organization can earn a profit on the equipment while still charging the lessee a rate less than the lessee would have to pay if they were to borrow and purchase the equipment, or even pay cash for it.

Summary

Capital investment decisions are a vital part of the management function in most organizations. Only by properly evaluating alternative proposals and selecting those that meet the qualitative and quantitative objectives of the organization will the leadership of the organization provide those services which it is designed to provide in a manner consistent with the needs of its various stakeholders.

Various methods of evaluating capital investment projects have been provided. These methods provide information relative to the acceptability of the projects from a quantifiable objective standpoint. We have not explored ways of handling capital investments where there are more projects available than there are sources of financing with which to pay for them. Nor have we explored many of the arguments for or against the various methods. Those methods which are the more difficult to calculate (the discounted cash flow techniques) are also the most correct to use.

Due to the increasing competitive nature of healthcare and the diminishing importance of cost-basis reimbursement, leasing will become an increasingly attractive option relative to the purchase of certain capital investment projects. This is due to qualitative factors as well as quantitative factors.

Questions and problems

1. Define a capital investment decision for a healthcare organization.

2. Define the capital screening problem.

3. Define the capital ranking problem.

4. What four factors must be considered in the capital budgeting process?

5. Define the cash inflows for a healthcare investment decision.

6. Define the cash outflows for a healthcare investment decision.

7. What is the cost of capital concept as it pertains to a healthcare organization?

8. Name and explain the four basic quantitative methods for evaluating capital investment decisions.

9. Compute the net present value of the following capital investment decisions (assume a 15 percent discount factor).

Project	Outflow	Inflows by year			
		1	*2*	*3*	*4*
A	$2,000	$1,150	0	$1,150	0
B	2,000	1,150	0	0	$1,150
C	2,000	0	$1,150	1,150	0

10. Compute the internal rate of return for each of the following independent investments.

Project	Outflow	Inflows by year		
		1	*2*	*3*
A	$3,000	$1,575	0	$1,735
B	$3,000	1,500	$1,780	0
C	$3,000	0	1,700	1,690

11. Community Hospital is considering the purchase of a new piece of diagnostic equipment costing $100,000 for its nuclear medicine laboratory. It is anticipated that the new asset will bring an incremental increase in cash flow of $35,000 for each of the next four years. At the end of the four years the machine will be obsolete and discarded. The opportunity cost of funds for Community Hospital has been computed to be 15 percent. Ignore taxes and the impact of reimbursement. Community Hospital uses straight line depreciation.
    a. Compute the payback period.
    b. Compute the accounting rate of return.
    c. Compute the net present value of the investment.
    d. Compute the internal rate of return on the investment.

12. Using the data from the previous problem, assume that 60 percent of patient care is delivered to Medicare patients, which are reimbursed for capital expenses on a straight line basis.
    a. Compute the payback period.
    b. Compute the accounting rate of return.
    c. Compute the net present value of the investment.
    d. Compute the internal rate of return of the investment.

13. The Central City Medical Center has recently learned of a new gamma computer which can be purchased for $60,000 cash. This new computer can be added to the camera the center now owns for an additional cost of $40,000. This adaptation will not affect the remaining four-year useful life of the camera or its estimated salvage value of $10,000. Variable costs of using the equipment would increase by 10 cents per test.

    The current income statement for the camera operations is as follows:

Revenues (100,000 tests @ $4)		$400,000
Variable costs	$180,000	
Fixed costs*	120,000	
Total costs		300,000
Excess of revenues over expenses before taxes		$100,000
Income taxes		40,000
Net income		$ 60,000

*All fixed costs are directly allowable to the processing of the tests and include depreciation on equipment of $20,000 calculated on a straight line basis of ten years.

Market research has disclosed three important findings relating to the new computer. First, the local nonprofit hospital will certainly purchase the computer if the center does not. If this were to happen, the medical center's demand for tests would fall to 70,000 per year. Second, if no increase in the selling price is made, Central City Medical Center could expect to accomplish 90,000 additional tests per year with the new computer. Third, it is anticipated that because of rapid technology changes in the area, the new computer will be obsolete at the end of four years.

a. Prepare a schedule which shows the after-tax cash flows for the two alternatives. Assume that Central City Medical Center will use the straight line method for depreciating the costs of the computer.

b. Using present value techniques, should Central City buy the new computer? Assume the cost of capital is 20 percent and there are no cost-based payers for this test.

14. The Rocky Mountain Institute is a nonprofit healthcare organization which engages in research projects to advance medical science. It is entirely supported by donations and earnings on endowment funds. The director is confronted with the purchase of a small scientific computer which costs $800,000 and will reduce administrative costs by $150,000 per year. The computer will cost $20,000 per year to operate and will last ten years before it is obsolete.

a. What rate of return is earned by the computer?

b. It may be possible to use some endowment earnings to buy the computer which have been invested in 15 percent securities. Assume the computer must be acquired: would it be better to buy the computer outright and use $20,000 per year for the operating costs, or to make annual payments out of the endowment of $150,000 for the ten years?

15. Rainbow Pharmacy is investigating the purchase of a new drug dispensing machine that is capable of dispensing several different types of medication/drugs at one time. The machine costs $20,000. It will have an eight-year useful life and a $2,000 salvage value. The machine falls in the five-year property class. The company will use straight line depreciation. The following annual operating results are expected if the machine is purchased:

Increase in annual revenues		$14,000
Increase in expenses:		
Cash operating expenses	$7,000	
Depreciation	4,000	11,000
Increase in net income before taxes		3,000
Increase in income taxes (30%)		900
Increase in net income		$ 2,100

Rainbow Pharmacy expects an after-tax return of 20 percent on all equipment purchases.

a. What is the after-tax payback period on the new machine? If the company has a required payback period of three years or less, should the machine be purchased?

b. What is the after-tax accounting rate of return on the new machine? Is it an acceptable investment?

c. The president is uneasy about the results obtained by the simple rate of return, and would like some further analysis done:

1. What is the net annual cash inflow before taxes promised by the new machine?

2. Using discounted cash flows, determine whether the machine will provide the minimum 20 percent after-tax return required by the company.

*3. Compute the new machine's internal rate of return.

* To be assigned at the option of the instructor.

16. The Sweetwater Clinic would like to buy a new machine that would automatically "dip" film as it is taken in the development process. The "dipping" operation is presently largely done by hand. The machine the company is considering costs $115,000 new. It would last the company 12 years, but would require a $4,500 overhaul at the end of the 7th year. After 12 years, the machine could be sold for $8,000.

The company estimates that it will cost $12,000 per year to operate the new machine. The present method of developing costs $30,000 per year. In addition to reducing operating costs, the new machine will increase output by 6,000 films per year. The company realizes a contribution margin of $1.50 per film. The company requires a 20 percent return on all investments.

a. What are the annual cash inflows that will be provided by the new dipping machine?

b. Compute the new machine's net present value.

c. Compute the internal rate of return for the new machine.

17. On January 1, 19X1, Belleview Hospital purchased a new machine for $200,000 with an estimated useful life of five years and no salvage value. The straight line method of depreciation will be used for both tax and book purposes. The machine is expected to produce annual cash flows from operations, before taxes, of $40,000. Belleview uses a time adjusted rate of 12 percent and assumes its income rate is 40 percent for all years.

a. What is the net present value of the machine?

18. Jackson Clinic purchased new X-ray equipment on July 1, 19X2. The cost of the equipment was $150,000 and is to be depreciated using the straight line method over five years, with a salvage value of $10,000. The equipment is expected to produce cash flow from operations of $42,500 in each of the next five years. Assume a full year's depreciation is taken in the year of purchase. Jackson Clinic uses a cost of capital of 20 percent.
    a. What is the payback period?

19. Southside Hospital is considering the purchase of new emergency room equipment. The cost of the equipment is $450,000 and will be depreciated over six years using the straight line method. Assume a full year's depreciation is taken during the year of acquisition. It is expected that the equipment will produce cash flows (net of income taxes) of $112,500 a year over each of the next six years.
    a. What is the accounting rate of return on the initial investment?

20. Woodside Nursing Homes purchased heart monitor equipment which will be depreciated on the straight line basis over seven years. Woodside believes the appropriate discount rate to use for evaluation purposes is 12 percent. The equipment is expected to generate cash flows of $95,000 in each of the following seven years. Assuming a negative net present value of $16,860, what is the cost of the equipment?

21. Marcus Hospital purchased equipment for $950,000 with a useful life of eight years and no salvage value. Expected cash flows from the equipment are estimated at $200,000 while the equipment is being depreciated on the straight line basis. Assume Marcus uses a time adjusted rate of return of 12 percent. Ignoring income taxes, what is the net present value?

22. Greendale Hospital currently owns ventilation equipment that was purchased three years ago for $85,000. The equipment has a remaining useful life of six years, however, it will require a major overhaul at the end of three years at a cost of $15,000. The disposal value is currently $25,000 and in six years its disposal value is expected to be $12,000, assuming the $15,000 major overhaul is done on schedule. Cash operating costs of the equipment are expected to be $45,000 annually.

    The hospital has recently been approached by a local electrical contractor offering to sell the hospital new ventilation equipment. The new equipment will cost $64,000 or $44,000 plus the old equipment. The new machine will reduce operating costs by $15,000 annually, will have a useful life of six years, will have a salvage value of $3,000 (after six years) and will not require any major overhauls.

a. Assuming a required rate of return of 10 percent, determine which alternative should be chosen using the net present value method.

23. The board of trustees has decided that Memorial Trust Hospital must have a computer if it is to render the best possible service. The only decision facing the board is whether to purchase or rent. The useful life of the computer is estimated to be ten years. Because of the newness of this type of machine and its complexities, it is essential that a factory maintenance and inspection contract be in effect. Such a contract costs $200 per year. However, this contract is included in the rental fee. Data for the alternative actions are as follows:

Rental, including maintenance and inspection:

Year	Rental expense
1	$5,000
2	5,000
3	4,000
4	4,000
5	3,000
6	3,000
7	2,000
8	2,000
9	1,000
10	1,000

The annual rental can be paid in twelve equal monthly installments.

Because of lack of sufficient funds, it will be necessary to purchase the computer on an extended payment basis. The best terms that can be arranged are:

Down payment = $5,600
Each year thereafter = $1,600 for nine years
Interest at the rate of 6 percent on the unpaid balance must be added to the principal payment.

a. Prepare a schedule which compares the effect on operating expenses and on cash requirements under the rental plan with the effect under the purchase plan for each of the ten years of the computer's life. The hospital uses straight line depreciation. In this case, the rate would be 10 percent. Indicate comparative costs under the rental and purchase options. Both the lease and the purchase options would be treated the same for reimbursement purposes. The administrator would also like to know which of the options would be best for the long-range financial condition of the hospital. The cost of capital for the hospital has been estimated at 10 percent by the controller.

24. Healthcare Plan, Inc. (HP, Inc.) has accepted a global capitation contract to provide a full range of healthcare services to a defined pop-

ulation group. One of the services it does not currently provide is women's health services. Use the following information to determine if HP, Inc. should provide such services, or should subcontract with Women's Health, Inc. to provide these services. Women's Health, Inc. has submitted a bid of $55,000. To produce such services internally, HP, Inc. would have to hire clinicians on a part-time basis. No new equipment is needed. The following projected costs pertain to the internal option:

Costs	Amount
Clinicians	$45,000
Supplies	850
Depreciation	2,100
Administration	2,400
Pharmacy	500
Telephone, Office Supplies	1,600
Computer Services	

Pharmacy includes a 20 percent markup on all pharmaceuticals for indirect costs.

Should HP, Inc. make or buy the services? Why?

25. A hospital is evaluating potential contracts with two emergency physician groups. Both groups would bill and collect for all physician services. The hospital will pay nothing and will incur no additional billing costs. The full costs associated with the hospital's Emergency Room were:

Expense	Amount
Administration	$ 75,000
Other Hospital Admin.	50,000
Depreciation	110,000
Supplies	48,000
Labor	290,000

One physician group (A) would also like the hospital to purchase $60,000 of new equipment for its use. Another group (B) has promised to increase non-ER hospital net revenues by $95,000, but would require a rebate of $27,000 in supply expenses beyond those required by Group A.

With which group should the hospital contract? Why?

26. Should a provider necessarily drop out of the Medicaid program if its payment only covers 75 percent of the average cost of a Medicaid patient day? Use differential, fixed, and variable cost concepts in responding.

27. The managers of Raleigh, Durham, and Chapel Hell, Inc. (RDCHI) are considering self-insuring their employee medical expenses. For claims processing services, they could either contract with BRN, Inc. or handle the processing within RDCHI. Meghan Wizard, head of the Management Information Systems (MIS) Department, projects the following claims processing costs (RDCHI):

Labor	$120,000
Computer services	35,000
Supplies	75,000
Travel	12,000
Training	37,000

The MIS Dept. owns all of its computer equipment and pays no fees for computer usage. Meghan estimates that only one new employee would have to be hired at a cost of $70,000. In addition, existing personnel would take on new responsibilities. She plans to spend 10 percent of her time on the project. However, she feels that no additional training costs and conferences will be needed to upgrade existing personnel's skills.

BRN, Inc. has submitted a bid of $190,000 for the project.

Should RDCHI contract with BRN, Inc. for the claims processing services? Why?

28. Alex's Hospital must evaluate whether to contract with PHysicians Over & Out Extra Yes, Inc. (PHOOEY) for $300,000 to eliminate projected staff shortages. An estimated 3,800 physician visits at an average of $50 per visit would be provided under the contract. Current staffing is at a level of 6,500 visits. Alex's Hospital expects an additional $95,000 in inpatient revenue.

The extra visits will require an additional $60,000 of supplies. Senior management will spend approximately 7 percent of their time, costing $35,000, on the project. Billing costs are expected to increase by $8,000, and depreciation expenses are expected to be $46,000. The hospital's corporate overhead allocated to these visits is $35,000.

Should Alex's Hospital contract with PHOOEY? Why?

29. The Radiology Center is trying to decide whether to continue offering staff training programs or to contract with SelfTaughtUni (STU) to provide such training. Currently, training is conducted or coordinated by a staff member whose annual salary and benefits total $80,000. The Director of Nursing also typically spends 10 percent of his time, amounting to $8,000, on educational programs. Other administrative staff costs $18,000. In addition, materials are $5,000, depreciation is

$8,500, and utilities are estimated at $2,000 per year. STU's contract price is $75,000.

Should the Radiology Center contract with STU? Why?

> **Keywords:** accounting rate of return; ACRS; cost of capital; internal rate of return; lease; net present value; payback period; profitability index; time value of money.

References

Ayers, D.H., and T.J. Kincaid. "Avoiding Potential Problems When Selling Accounts Receivable." *Healthcare Financial Management* (May 1996): 50–55.

Blake, J.W. "Financing Medical Office Buildings." *Journal of Health Care Finance* 22, no. 1 (1995): 43–48.

Boles, Keith E. "Implications of the Methods of Capital Cost Payment on the Weighted Average Cost of Capital." *Health Services Research* 21, no. 2 (June 1986): Part I.

Brigham, E.F., and L.C. Gapenski. *Financial Management.* Chicago, IL: The Dryden Press, 1991.

Brown, J.B. *Health Capital Financing.* Ann Arbor, MI: Health Administration Press, 1988.

Capettini, Robert, Chee W. Chow, and James E. Williamson. "Breakdown Approach Helps Managers Select Projects." *Healthcare Financial Management* (November 1990): 48–56.

Carpenter, C.E., L.C. Weitzel, N.E. Johnson, and D.B. Nash. "Cost Accounting Supports Clinical Evaluations." *Healthcare Financial Management* (April 1994): 40–42.

Cerne, F. "Capital Decisions—Where is the Smart Money Being Invested?" *Hospitals & Health Networks* (June 5, 1995): 33–42.

Fallon, Robert O. "Not-for-Profit = No-Profit: Profitability Planning in Not-For-Profit Organizations." *Health Care Management Review* 16, no. 3 (summer 1991).

Ferconio, S., and M.R. Lane. "Financing Maneuvers." *Healthcare Financial Management* (October 1991): 74–78.

Gallinger, G.W., and P.B. Healy. *Liquidity Analysis and Management.* Reading, MA: Addison-Wesley Publishing, 1987.

Gapenski, L.C. *Healthcare Finance for the Non-Financial Manager.* Chicago, IL: Probus Pulishing, 1994.

Gapenski, L.C. *Understanding Health Care Financial Management.* Ann Arbor, MI: AUPHA Press/Health Administration Press, 1991.

Gapenski, L.C. "Using MVA and EVA to Measure Financial Performance." *Healthcare Financial Management* (March 1996): 56–60.

Gapenski, L.C., and Barbara Langland-Orban. "Leasing Capital Assets and Durable Goods: Opinions and Practices in Florida Hospitals." *Health Care Management Review* 16, no. 3 (summer 1991): 73–81.

Gordon, David C., and Douglas F. Londal. "Guidelines to Capital Investment." *Topics in Health Care Financing,* 15, no. 4, (summer 1989): 9–17.

Grant, Larry, and Dianne O'Donnell. "Watch for Pitfalls When Analyzing Lease Options." *Healthcare Financial Management* (July 1990): 36–43.

Herr, Wendy W., and R.R. Kovener. "The Troubled History of Medicare Capital Payments." *Healthcare Financial Management* (August 1990): 60–64.

Kamath, Ravindra R., and Julie Elmer. "Capital Investment Decisions." *Topics in Health Care Financing* 14, no. 2 (spring 1989): 45–56.

Karpinski, Joseph P. "Designing a Successful Investment Program." *Healthcare Financial Management* (February 1997): 58–63.

Kelly, V.K. "Banks as a Source of Capital." *Topics in Health Care Financing* 19, no. 4 (1993): 21–34.

Kincaid, T.J. "Purchase of Receivables—Healthcare Providers." *Credit World* 82, no. 4 (1994): 14–17.

Long, Hugh W. "Valuation as a Criterion in Not-For-Profit Decision-Making." *Health Care Management Review* (summer 1976).

Lutz, S. "Doc Companies Dominate Top IPOs." *Modern Healthcare* (January 22, 1996): 42–44.

McCormack, E.J. "The Hidden Costs of Accounts Receivable." *Healthcare Financial Management* (November 1993): 80.

McCue, Michael J., Steven C. Renn, and George D. Pilari. "Factors Affecting Credit Rating Downgrades of Hospital Revenue Bonds." *Inquiry* 27, no. 3 (fall 1990): 242–254.

Mieling, T.M., and J.O. Keshner. "Accessing Capital for Integrated Delivery Systems." *Healthcare Financial Management* (January 1996): 32–35.

Murray, Dennis, Bruce R. Neumann, and Pieter Elgers. *Using Financial Accounting: An Introduction.* Cincinnati, Ohio: South-Western College Publishing, 1997.

Nadler, Michael R., and Victor E. Schimmel. "Evaluating Financial Capability." *Topics in Health Care Financing* 17, no. 3 (spring 1991): 74–88.

Neumann, Bruce R., and Joyce Kelly. *Prospective Reimbursement for Hospital Costs.* Oakbrook, IL: Healthcare Financial Management Association, 1984.

Pauly, Mark. "Returns on Equity for Not-For-Profit Hospitals." *Health Services Research* 21, no. 1 (April 1986): 1–16.

Pierce, E. "Financing of Integrated Delivery Systems." *Topics in Health Care Financing* 20, no. 3 (1994): 28–36.

Ponton, K.T. "Medical Accounts Receivable—An Underused Asset for Hospitals." *Trustee* 46, no. 6 (1993): 24–25.

Sen, S., and J.P. Lawler. "Securitizing Receivables Offers Low-Cost Financing Option." *Healthcare Financial Management* (May 1995): 32–37.

Sherman, Barnet. "How Investors Evaluate the Creditworthiness of Hospitals." *Healthcare Financial Management* (March 1990).

Sutton, H.L., Jr., and A.J. Sorbo. *Actuarial Issues in the Fee-For-Service/Prepaid Medical Group.* Englewood, CO: Center for Research in Ambulatory Health Care Administration, 1993.

Teschke, Deborah A. "Program Offers Help for Capital Expenditures." *Healthcare Financial Management* (February 1991): 100.

Topics in Health Care Financing: Equity Financing for Health Care Enterprises 18, no. 1 (fall 1991).

Valentine, Steven T., ed. "Financially Troubled Hospitals." *Topics in Health Care Financing* 17, no. 2 (winter 1990): 1–86.

Varwig, D., and R. Barkley. "Capital Financing Along the Integration Highway." *Journal of Health Care Finance* (summer 1995): 60–75.

West, Joan, Sandee Glickman, and Alan G. Seidner. "Investing: Reducing Risks to Enhance Returns." *Healthcare Financial Management* (September 1996): 48–51.

Present value and compound interest tables

Table 1
Present value of $1:

$$P_{n,i} = \frac{1}{(1+i)^n}$$

n	1.0	1.5	2.0	5.0	6.0	8.0	10.0	15.0	20.0	25.0	30.0
					Rate of interest, i%						
1	.990	.985	.980	.952	.943	.925	.909	.869	.833	.800	.769
2	.980	.970	.961	.907	.890	.857	.826	.756	.694	.640	.592
3	.970	.956	.942	.863	.839	.793	.751	.657	.578	.512	.455
4	.961	.942	.923	.822	.792	.735	.683	.571	.482	.409	.350
5	.951	.928	.905	.783	.747	.680	.620	.497	.401	.327	.269
6	.942	.914	.888	.746	.705	.630	.564	.432	.334	.262	.207
7	.932	.901	.870	.710	.665	.583	.513	.375	.279	.209	.159
8	.923	.887	.853	.676	.627	.540	.466	.326	.232	.167	.123
9	.914	.874	.836	.644	.591	.500	.424	.284	.193	.134	.094
10	.905	.861	.820	.613	.558	.463	.385	.247	.161	.107	.073
11	.896	.848	.804	.584	.526	.428	.350	.214	.134	.085	.056
12	.887	.836	.788	.556	.497	.397	.318	.186	.112	.068	.043
13	.878	.824	.773	.530	.468	.367	.289	.162	.093	.055	.033
14	.870	.811	.757	.505	.442	.340	.263	.141	.077	.044	.025
15	.861	.799	.743	.481	.417	.315	.239	.122	.064	.035	.020

(cont.)

Table 1 (cont.)

n	Rate of interest, i%										
	1.0	1.5	2.0	5.0	6.0	8.0	10.0	15.0	20.0	25.0	30.0
16	.852	.788	.728	.458	.393	.291	.217	.106	.051	.028	.015
17	.844	.776	.714	.436	.371	.270	.197	.092	.045	.022	.012
18	.836	.764	.700	.415	.350	.250	.179	.080	.037	.018	.009
19	.827	.753	.686	.395	.330	.231	.163	.070	.031	.014	.007
20	.819	.742	.673	.376	.311	.214	.148	.061	.026	.011	.005
21	.811	.731	.659	.358	.294	.198	.135	.053	.021	.009	.004
22	.803	.720	.646	.341	.277	.183	.122	.046	.018	.007	.003
23	.795	.710	.634	.325	.261	.170	.111	.040	.015	.005	.002
24	.787	.699	.621	.310	.247	.157	.101	.034	.012	.004	.002
25	.779	.689	.609	.295	.233	.146	.092	.030	.010	.003	.001
26	.772	.679	.597	.281	.219	.135	.083	.026	.008	.003	.001
27	.764	.669	.585	.267	.207	.125	.076	.023	.007	.002	.001
28	.756	.659	.574	.255	.195	.115	.069	.020	.006	.001	.001
29	.749	.649	.563	.242	.184	.107	.063	.017	.005	.001	.001
30	.741	.639	.552	.231	.174	.099	.057	.015	.004	.001	.000
35	.705	.593	.500	.181	.130	.067	.035	.007	.001	.000	.001
40	.671	.551	.452	.142	.097	.046	.022	.003	.000	.000	.000
45	.639	.511	.410	.111	.072	.031	.013	.001	.000	.000	.000
50	.608	.475	.371	.087	.054	.021	.008	.000	.000	.000	.000

Table 2
Present value of an annuity of $1 per period:

$$P_{n,i} = 1 - \left[\frac{1}{(1+i)n} \right]$$
$$\frac{}{i}$$

Rate of interest, i%

n	1.0	1.5	2.0	5.0	6.0	8.0	10.0	15.0	20.0	25.0	30.0
1	.990	.985	.980	.952	.943	.925	.909	.869	.833	.800	.769
2	1.970	1.955	1.941	1.859	1.833	1.783	1.735	1.625	1.527	1.440	1.361
3	2.911	2.912	2.883	2.723	2.673	2.577	2.486	2.283	2.106	1.952	1.816
4	3.902	3.854	3.807	3.546	3.465	3.312	3.169	2.855	2.588	2.361	2.106
5	4.853	4.782	4.713	4.329	4.212	3.992	3.796	3.352	2.990	2.689	2.436
6	5.795	5.697	5.601	5.075	4.917	4.622	4.355	3.784	3.325	2.951	2.643
7	6.728	6.598	6.472	5.786	5.582	5.206	4.868	4.160	3.604	3.161	2.802
8	7.651	7.485	7.325	6.463	6.209	5.746	5.334	4.487	3.837	3.328	2.925
9	8.566	8.360	8.162	7.107	6.801	6.246	5.759	4.771	4.031	3.463	3.019
10	9.471	9.222	8.982	7.721	7.360	6.710	6.144	5.018	4.192	3.570	3.092
11	10.367	10.071	9.786	8.306	7.886	7.139	6.495	5.233	4.327	3.656	3.147
12	11.255	10.907	10.575	8.863	8.383	7.536	6.813	5.420	4.439	3.725	3.190
13	12.133	11.731	11.348	9.393	8.852	7.903	7.103	5.583	4.532	3.780	3.223
14	13.003	12.543	12.106	9.898	9.295	8.244	7.366	5.724	4.610	3.824	3.249
15	13.865	13.343	12.849	10.379	9.712	8.559	7.606	5.847	4.675	3.859	3.268

(cont.)

Table 2 (cont.)

n	Rate of interest, i%										
	1.0	1.5	2.0	5.0	6.0	8.0	10.0	15.0	20.0	25.0	30.0
16	14.717	14.131	13.577	10.837	10.105	8.851	7.823	5.951	4.729	3.887	3.283
17	15.562	14.907	14.291	11.274	10.477	9.121	8.021	6.047	4.774	3.090	3.295
18	16.398	15.672	14.992	11.689	10.827	9.371	8.201	6.128	4.812	3.927	3.304
19	17.226	16.426	15.678	12.085	11.158	9.603	8.361	6.198	4.843	3.942	3.311
20	18.015	17.168	16.351	12.462	11.469	9.818	8.513	6.259	4.869	3.953	3.316
21	18.857	17.900	17.011	12.821	11.764	10.016	8.648	6.312	4.891	3.963	3.320
22	19.660	18.620	17.658	13.163	12.041	10.200	8.771	6.358	4.909	3.970	3.323
23	20.455	19.330	18.292	13.488	12.303	10.371	8.883	6.398	4.924	3.976	3.325
24	21.243	20.030	18.913	13.798	12.550	10.528	8.984	6.433	4.937	3.981	3.327
25	22.023	20.719	19.523	14.093	12.783	10.674	9.077	6.464	4.947	3.984	3.328
26	22.795	21.398	20.121	14.375	13.003	10.810	9.160	6.490	4.956	3.987	3.330
27	23.559	22.067	20.706	14.643	13.210	10.935	9.237	6.513	4.963	3.990	3.330
28	24.316	22.726	21.281	14.898	13.406	11.051	9.306	6.533	4.969	3.992	3.330
29	25.065	23.376	21.844	15.141	13.590	11.158	9.369	6.550	4.974	3.933	3.331
30	25.807	24.015	22.396	15.372	13.764	11.257	9.426	6.566	4.978	3.995	3.331
35	29.408	27.075	24.998	16.374	14.498	11.651	9.614	6.616	4.991	3.998	3.331
40	32.834	29.915	27.355	17.159	15.046	11.924	9.779	6.641	4.996	3.999	3.331
45	36.094	32.552	29.490	17.774	15.455	12.108	9.862	6.654	4.998	3.999	3.331
50	39.196	34.999	31.423	18.255	15.761	12.233	9.914	6.660	4.999	3.999	3.331

Table 3
Compounded value of $1: $A_{n,i} = (1 + i)^n$

n	Rate of interest, $i\%$							
	1.0	1.5	2.0	3.0	4.0	6.0	8.0	10.0
1	1.010	1.015	1.020	1.030	1.040	1.060	1.080	1.100
2	1.020	1.030	1.040	1.060	1.081	1.123	1.166	1.210
3	1.030	1.045	1.061	1.092	1.124	1.191	1.259	1.331
4	1.040	1.061	1.082	1.125	1.169	1.262	1.360	1.464
5	1.051	1.077	1.104	1.159	1.216	1.338	1.469	1.610
6	1.061	1.093	1.126	1.194	1.265	1.418	1.586	1.771
7	1.072	1.109	1.148	1.229	1.315	1.503	1.713	1.948
8	1.082	1.126	1.171	1.266	1.368	1.593	1.850	2.143
9	1.093	1.143	1.195	1.304	1.423	1.689	1.999	2.357
10	1.104	1.160	1.219	1.343	1.480	1.790	2.158	2.593
11	1.115	1.177	1.243	1.384	1.539	1.898	2.331	2.853
12	1.126	1.195	1.268	1.425	1.601	2.012	2.518	3.138
13	1.138	1.213	1.293	1.468	1.665	2.132	2.719	3.452
14	1.149	1.231	1.319	1.512	1.731	2.260	2.937	3.797
15	1.161	1.250	1.345	1.558	1.800	2.396	3.172	4.177
16	1.172	1.269	1.372	1.604	1.873	2.540	3.425	4.595
17	1.184	1.288	1.400	1.652	1.947	2.692	3.700	5.054
18	1.196	1.307	1.428	1.702	2.025	2.854	3.996	5.559
19	1.208	1.327	1.456	1.753	2.106	3.025	4.315	6.115
20	1.220	1.346	1.485	1.806	2.191	3.207	4.661	6.727
21	1.232	1.367	1.515	1.860	2.278	3.399	5.033	7.400
30	1.347	1.563	1.811	2.427	3.243	5.743	10.062	17.449
40	1.488	1.814	2.208	3.262	4.801	10.285	21.724	45.259

Table 4
Compounded amount of an annuity of $1 per period:

$$A_{n,i} = \frac{(1+i)^n - 1}{i}$$

Rate of interest, i%

n	1.0	1.5	2.0	3.0	4.0	6.0	8.0	10.0
1	1.000	1.000	1.000	1.000	1.000	1.000	1.000	1.000
2	2.010	2.015	2.020	2.030	2.040	2.060	2.080	2.100
3	3.030	3.045	3.060	3.090	3.121	3.183	3.246	3.310
4	4.060	4.090	4.121	4.183	4.246	4.374	4.506	4.641
5	5.101	5.152	5.204	5.309	5.416	5.637	5.866	6.105
6	6.152	6.229	6.308	6.468	6.633	6.975	7.335	7.715
7	7.213	7.323	7.434	7.662	7.898	8.393	8.922	9.487
8	8.285	8.432	8.583	8.892	9.214	9.897	10.636	11.435
9	9.368	9.559	9.754	10.159	10.582	11.491	12.487	13.579
10	10.462	10.702	10.949	11.463	12.006	13.180	14.486	15.937
11	11.566	11.863	12.168	12.807	13.486	14.971	16.645	18.531
12	12.682	13.041	13.412	14.192	15.025	16.869	18.977	21.381
13	13.809	14.236	14.680	15.617	16.626	18.882	21.495	24.522
14	14.947	15.450	15.973	17.086	18.291	21.015	24.214	27.975
15	16.096	16.682	17.293	18.598	20.023	23.276	27.152	31.772

(cont.)

Table 4 (cont)

n	\multicolumn{8}{c}{Rate of interest, i%}
	1.0	1.5	2.0	3.0	4.0	6.0	8.0	10.0
16	17.257	17.932	18.639	20.156	21.824	25.672	30.324	35.949
17	18.430	19.201	20.012	21.761	23.697	28.212	33.750	40.544
18	19.614	20.489	21.412	23.414	25.645	30.905	37.450	45.599
19	20.810	21.796	22.840	25.116	27.671	33.760	41.446	51.159
20	22.019	23.123	24.297	26.870	29.778	36.785	45.762	57.275
21	23.239	24.470	25.783	28.676	31.969	39.992	50.422	64.002
22	24.471	25.837	27.299	30.536	34.248	43.392	55.456	71.402
23	25.716	27.225	28.845	32.452	36.617	46.995	60.893	79.543
24	26.973	28.633	30.421	34.426	39.082	50.815	66.764	88.497
25	28.243	30.063	32.030	36.459	41.645	54.864	73.105	98.347
26	29.525	31.514	33.670	38.553	44.311	59.156	79.954	109.181
27	30.820	32.986	35.344	40.709	47.084	63.705	87.350	121.099
28	32.129	34.481	37.051	42.930	49.967	68.528	95.338	134.208
29	33.450	35.998	38.792	45.218	52.966	73.639	103.965	148.630
30	34.784	37.538	40.568	47.575	56.084	79.058	113.283	164.494
35	41.660	45.592	49.994	60.462	73.652	111.434	172.316	271.024
40	48.886	54.267	60.402	75.401	95.025	154.762	259.056	442.592
45	56.481	63.614	71.892	92.719	121.029	212.743	386.505	718.904
50	64.463	73.682	84.579	112.796	152.667	290.335	573.770	1163.908

APPENDIX 12–2

Discounted pay back period

Using Project A from the sample problem for this chapter, the method of using discounted cash flow techniques for the payback period can be demonstrated.

Cost, including installation	$60,000
Estimated annual labor cost savings	$15,000
Estimated economic life	5 years

Using the given data, we develop the following table of present values:

Year	Cash flow	P.V. factor (15%)	P.V. cash flows
1	$15,000	.869	$13,035
2	$15,000	.756	11,340
3	$15,000	.657	9,855
4	$15,000	.571	8,565
5	$15,000	.497	7,455

	Determination of payback period:	
Cash flow	Contribution	Investment balance
($60,000)		($60,000)
13,035	1	(46,965)
11,340	2	(35,625)
9,855	3	(25,770)
8,565	4	(17,205)
7,455	5	(9,750)

It should be noted that the payback period for this project is longer than the economic life of the project, making it an unacceptable investment.

APPENDIX 12–3

Accelerated capital recovery system (ACRS)

The ACRS method is a recognition by the Internal Revenue Service (IRS) that straight line depreciation techniques do not adequately compensate for the impact of inflation on depreciation. The methods discussed in financial accounting include double declining balance, sum of the years digits, and production related rates. In order to provide for more consistency across organizations (and to reduce the amount of income tax fraud) the IRS has established specific rules to control how depreciation is used for income tax purposes.

The IRS determines the number of years over which a specific asset can be depreciated and then provides a table of depreciation factors. The normal approach of the IRS is to permit double declining balance depreciation (200 percent of the straight line depreciation rate), with the assumption that an asset is placed in service for only six months during the year of acquisition. For example, assume that the IRS permits the use of a five year life for a specific project. On a straight line basis, the depreciation rate would be 20 percent per year. Using the double declining balance method, the applicable percentage is 40 percent per year of the book value of the asset. This is the percentage to be applied to the remaining book value of the asset. However, for the year of acquisition of the asset, a depreciation rate of 20 percent will be applied (40 percent for one-half a year), then the final depreciation will be taken during year 6 (also for six months).

This concept and application can be more easily understood through the use of a table. Assume an asset having a value of $500,000. For income tax purposes it is defined to be a five year asset. Thus, it can be depreciated for five years, dispersed as follows:

Year	Depreciation use	Depreciation rate applied to book Value
1	Six months	20%
2	Twelve months	40%
3	Twelve months	40%
4	Twelve months	40%

After year 4, straight line depreciation gives more depreciation in year five, therefore, straight line is accepted for year five and the six months of year 6.

		Proportion of original cost
5	Twelve months	11.5%
6	Six months	5.8%

	Beginning Balance	*DDB%*	*Depreciation*	*Ending balance*	*%[1]*
1	$500,000	20%	$100,000	$400,000	20%
2	$400,000	40%	$160,000	$240,000	32%
3	$240,000	40%	$ 96,000	$144,000	19.2%
4	$144,000	40%	$ 57,600	$ 86,400	11.5%
5	$ 86,400	*	$ 57,600	$ 28,800	11.5%
6	$ 28,800	*	$ 28,800	$ -0-	5.8%

[1] This percentage represents ACRS depreciation expense as a proportion of the original acquisition cost of the asset. This is the percentage quoted by the IRS in their ACRS tables. For example, applying 40 percent to the book value at the end of year 2 of $400,000, results in a depreciation expense of $160,000. This same $160,000 can be determined applying the ACRS percentage (32%) to the initial cost of the item ($500,000).

* At the end of year 4, the depreciation method is switched to straight line, since this provides more depreciation in year 4 than under the double declining balance method. At the end of year 4, there is $86,400 of book value that has not been depreciated and 18 months of life remaining. Consider the straight line method of depreciation, that equates to a monthly charge of $4,800 (86,400/18) and an annual depreciation charge of $57,600 (4,800 × 12) from year 5. In year 6, there is 6 months remaining or $28,000 (4,800 × 6).

The final column is the percentage of the depreciable amount which is depreciated each year. These figures are published by the IRS.

CHAPTER 13

Total quality management (TQM) and its potential impact on the management accounting function

"Why is it we never have time to do it right the first time but always have time to do it over?"

Anonymous

Introduction

Total quality management (TQM) is appearing in almost every organization as a new way of thinking, as a catalyst for organizational change, and as the "sine qua non" for success in meeting the challenges of a competitive world in an uncertain future. Total quality management (TQM) is rapidly becoming the major focus of senior managers in the healthcare field. Under TQM a different behavioral focus and climate is created such that the *team* is responsible for quality improvement and the *team* shares responsibility for the defects and deficiencies that may occur. The primary purpose of this chapter is to introduce the TQM concept and its potential impact on the management accounting function in healthcare organizations.

Total quality management (TQM)

TQM can be defined as a philosophy (and actions) of an organization which is dedicated to *continuous quality improvement* (CQI) throughout the organization. A hospital with total quality management will, for example, set specific quality goals, choose a number of high priority *quality improvement projects* (QIPs), make quality improvement part of job descriptions throughout the organization, legitimize time spent on quality improvement, provide necessary resources (financial and otherwise), provide essential training, and formally recognize quality improvement efforts.

The emphasis on quality in healthcare organizations is not a new phenomenon. Given the nature of the output of healthcare organizations, it is logical that quality be a prime concern of management. Quality in healthcare organizations has been difficult to define exactly. The typical approach has been on process and conformance to established requirements. The emerging forms of quality under TQM have been on meeting customer needs and expectations. The ultimate customer is, of course, the patient, but other internal customers such as the physician, allied health personnel, and other departments in the health services organization are also customers under the TQM approach. In addition, other external users such as payers and families are also important. This full range of customers has not always been recognized. It should also be recognized that the healthcare environment in the past may not have been receptive to the amount of change needed to implement a TQM approach. It is important to recognize that TQM represents a paradigm shift in organizational values and should pervade every aspect of the healthcare provider's activities. It cannot be bounded by departments or responsibility centers or professional specialties. When a physician, a nurse, an allied health professional, or any nonclinical personnel observe a quality detracting activity or a delay or a breakdown in communication, their efforts to improve that aspect of the system must be viewed as having benefit to the entire organization and should be rewarded accordingly. McLaughlin and Kaluzny identified a potential problem in the shift to TQM type of management: natural tension between the organizational models of professionalism and TQM as illustrated in *Exhibit 13–1*.

Exhibit 13–1
Areas of conflict between professional and TQM organization models

Professional		TQM
Individual responsibilities		Collective responsibilities
Professional leadership		Managerial leadership
Autonomy		Accountability
Administrative authority		Participation
Professional authority	Versus	Participation
Goal expectations	↔	Performance and process expectations
Rigid planning		Flexible planning
Response to complaints		Benchmarking
Retrospective performance appraisal		Concurrent performance appraisal
Quality assurance		Continuous improvement

Source: McLaughlin, Curtis P., and Arnold D. Kaluzny, "Total Quality Management in Health: Making It Work," *Health Care Management Review,* Aspen Publishers, Inc., 15(3), 1990, pp. 7–14.

TQM can lead to "turf battles" and conflicts between different professional norms and role models. In healthcare, this potential is exacerbated because physicians and other professionals are often not full-time employees of the healthcare provider. However, their somewhat external perspective is an untapped source of improvement in quality because they are often able to view the particular relationships from fresh perspectives. Unfortunately, such suggestions or observations are often ignored because someone on the inside feels that their professional reputation is at stake when an "outsider" makes suggestions that will improve patient care. Of course the same conclusions could be drawn regarding suggestions made by nurses about physicians' behaviors and medical practice or vice versa. To be effective, TQM requires all healthcare professionals to recognize that potential quality improvement ideas can emerge from nonclinical sources and not to view such suggestions as impinging or impugning on professional identities. Accomplishing this can be a crucial role of senior management.

Total quality management requires commitment and personal involvement of senior management. It should be emphasized that *quality control* (prevention of *unwanted change* in quality) must be maintained in parallel with quality improvement. An essential feature of TQM is the concept of continuously seeking improvement in quality and the elimination of all activities that do not add value to the process of providing quality healthcare. Nonvalue activities (NVA) include checking, filing, sorting, moving, copying, waiting, rework, retesting, etc. Nonvalue activities are considered "waste" under the TQM concept and are candidates for elimination.

To stress again, one of the most important requirements of TQM is the total focus on the customer or client. Under previous management styles, organizational changes were evaluated from the perspective of the employee or the organization itself. Under TQM the meeting of the client's or user needs is paramount. In healthcare settings, the client is usually said to typically be the focus of the process. However, many healthcare systems are often designed for the convenience of the provider. Waiting times, lack of input, conflicting or missing records, piece-meal approaches, and inadequate discharge planning are often a function of professional domains and roles, lack of time, no requirement to design comprehensive services, inattention, or a culture that says, "it's just not my problem" and shift the blame. TQM shifts this emphasis on oneself to the user of the services you are providing whether the user is the patient, another health professional in the organization, or external parties.

Quality assurance

It is important to understand the impact of the quality assurance function on the implementation of TQM. Given the personal nature of many health services provided (physician/patient) and the lack of valid process/

outcome measures, the management of quality fell under the general label of quality assurance (QA) activities. In the 1970s the establishment of Professional Standards Review Organizations (PSRO), (now called Peer Review Organization—PRO), and the initiatives of the Joint Commission on Accreditation of Healthcare Organizations (JCAHO) led to an increased emphasis on the quality assurance function. For example, the review of medical charts was now mandated on a periodic basis and an attempt to identify problem patterns was made and followup studies initiated. To summarize, the quality assurance function became "the sum of all the activities, wherever performed, through which the hospital achieves the *quality of care* it provides. This usage is comparable to speaking of the "fiscal function," which is the sum of the activities, wherever performed, through which the hospital achieves fiscal soundness. The term "quality function" covers all quality-enhancing activities.

Several aspects of quality assurance activities limited the impact on improving quality in healthcare organizations. First, they were generally imposed by external agencies and the QA department in the organization was viewed with suspicion by some of the care givers. This might be compared to the reception given to the internal audit function of the hospital accounting department. Basically they were outsiders, second guessing the care givers in the performance of their duties. Secondly, the QA process primarily focused on the medical staff in contrast to other activities that also were involved in the provision of care. Thirdly, most of the QA activities focused on care that had already been given or "an after the fact approach." Finally, the increasing emphasis on cost control led to the identification of QA with the pressures to reduce costs and further reduced the cooperation between QA staff and patient care givers.

Continuous quality improvement

TQM may logically be considered an expansion of continuous quality improvement (CQI), which applies management theories of quality to a healthcare setting. The management theory of quality is based upon principles developed by W. Edwards Deming and Joseph M. Juran. While traditional "quality control" theories seek out "fault" and attempt improvement by exhorting people to change their behavior, continuous improvement seeks to understand processes and revise them on the basis of data about the processes themselves. CQI sees "problems" as opportunities for improvement. The CQI process involves a project-by-project approach to systematically improve quality.

Many organizations set quality targets, or standard defect rates, and when those rates are achieved, the affected departments are rewarded. TQM takes a different view in that improvements are continuously sought. There is no acceptable level of quality—it can always be improved. The search for continuous process improvements requires a change in mind away from traditional thinking about quality goals and standards.

The references to Deming and Juran are important because they are generally recognized as the leading gurus of quality management. Deming's fourteen points are often quoted as the foundations of continuous quality improvement and need to be understood to more fully recognize their impact on existing management control systems (Deming's fourteen points are listed in *Appendix 13–1*). The concepts of Deming, Juran, and others will be discussed in the next section.

In summary, TQM offers significant opportunities to healthcare providers, and yet also creates potential for significant conflicts between professional norms, traditional behaviors, and expectations, and crosses boundaries between job responsibilities and functions. Resolving these issues is a major challenge to the senior managers of all functional areas.

This concludes a brief overview of TQM and the references should be consulted for more detailed information. Fully understanding the TQM concept is crucial for a successful implementation. *It is not an overnight implementation. Careful planning is a must.*

The TQM movement

Drs. W. Edwards Deming, Joseph M. Juran, and Philip Crosby were generally considered to be the leading innovators and proponents of TQM in the United States today. Deming, through his experiences in quality improvement in Japan after World War II, believed it is not the employees who lead to poor quality, but rather poor design of systems and procedures. More than 90 percent of all errors are system errors and not employee errors. Poor quality is institutionalized and reinforced by traditional management methods. Current accounting reports do not permit the effects of declining quality to be recognized or valued. Many traditional management accounting reports serve to fix blame or find the culprit for higher costs.

His basic philosophy centers around preventing defects before they occur by improving the process of providing the service. This requires the involvement of all employees of the organization, from the individual providing the service to the manager directing the activities. The elimination of waste through a reduction in work delays and unneeded services will increase productivity as well as quality.[1]

Dr. Joseph Juran, developed the quality trilogy of "quality planning, quality control and quality improvements." Quality planning involves identifying the needs of internal and external customers. Quality control determines the quality characteristics that must be measured and the

---

[1] Sahney, U.K., and G.L. Warden, "The Quest for Quality and Productivity in Health Services," *Frontiers of Health Services Management*, Vol. 7, No. 4, Summer 1991, pp. 4–7.

establishment of control limits for the factors. Quality improvements focus on selecting well defined projects to move to new heights of quality improvement through the use of knowledgeable teams and focused efforts.[2]

The third leading expert in quality management is Philip Crosby. He has considerable hands-on experience in quality improvement and the implementation of TQM in health service organizations. Crosby developed fourteen steps for quality improvement which are also listed in *Appendix 13–1* for comparison with Deming's fourteen points.[3]

Finally, an important concept of TQM is the use of a scientific approach to process improvement. The PDCA methodology (Plan/Do/Check/Act) developed by Shewhart was modified into FOCUS-PDCA (TM) by Paul Batalden and Associates at Hospital Corporation of America.[4] FOCUS-PDCA stands for:

*F*ind a process to improve
*O*rganize a team that knows the process
*C*larify current knowledge of the process
*U*nderstand sources of process variation
*S*elect the process improvement
*P*lan a change or test
*D*o carry out the change
*C*heck and observe the effects of the change
*A*ct, adopt or modify the plan[5]

The typical PDCA cycle is illustrated as shown in *Exhibit 13–2*.

To summarize, many of the concepts discussed so far in this chapter are being implemented in many different types of health service providers. Modifications must be and are being made to meet the needs of the specific organization. However, there are several key concepts that need to be stressed.

1. *Identification of the customer*

To stress again, it is important to recognize that the customers or clients of healthcare systems include more than just the direct recipients of care. In many cases, physicians are the clients as they are the source of referrals and they are the source of "ordering" patient services. Often the patient's

---

[2] Ibid, p. 2.

[3] For an excellent discussion of the philosophy of Deming, Juran, and Crosby, see U.K. Sahney and G.L. Warden, "The Quest for Quality and Productivity in Health Services," in *Frontiers of Health Services Management*, Vol. 7, No. 4, Summer 1991, pp. 4–7.

[4] Ibid, p. 11.

[5] McEachern, E., and D. Neuhauser, "The Continuous Improvement of Quality of the Hospital Corporation of America," *Health Matrix*, Fall 1989, pp. 5–11.

Exhibit 13–2
The PDCA Cycle

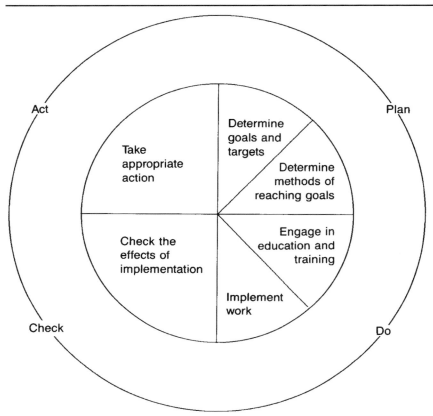

Source: Merry, Martin D., *Healthcare Executive,* March/April 1991, pg. 20 adapted from Walton M. The Deming Management Method, New York: The Putnam Publishing Company 1986, p. 87.

family or friends are the important clients who cannot be ignored. In almost every situation, the payer is also a client. Most patients will have multiple payers that include insurance companies, government agencies, and personal resources. Employees and suppliers are also important clients who will have valuable TQM inputs and perspectives to share. Different departments may be viewed as clients. For example, the business office is a consumer and user of the outputs of medical records. Medical-surgical wings or floors are consumers of ancillary services including radiology, laboratory, housekeeping, and laundry services.

In other words, the customer orientation is broad and includes almost every person or relationship that is affected by the process of providing healthcare. For a healthcare provider, this customer orientation will produce more conflicts than are typical in most organizational settings. Professional identities and bureaucracies can be threatened and severely impacted. Conflicts between the patient as client and family or payer as client are inevitable. But the point of TQM is not to minimize these conflicts, but to recognize the acceptability and necessity of differing views and needs. Organizational problems are no longer solved from a single perspective—whether it is to minimize the risks of malpractice liability or to maximize the patient's or family's satisfaction. All perspectives will have value in the TQM process. Finding ways to meet the needs of one client or client group without sacrificing the needs of other constituencies is the goal of a TQM process. In its broadest sense, the TQM customer approach would define quality as doing the *right task,* the *right way,* the *first time* to meet the needs and expectations of the customers.

2. *Define quality in measurable terms*

Quality has been a difficult term to define in almost all industries but especially in a healthcare setting. However, one caveat seems to pervade all industries. The customer knows when they are receiving a quality product or service. Even though they can't define it exactly, they know what quality is. In healthcare organizations, the definition of what is quality care has been left to the clinician. However, under the customer definition of TQM, there is more than one customer and quality may be defined differently by the clinician and the patient. Omachonu defines the two definitions as "quality in fact" and "quality in perception" respectively.[6] To be useful for managerial decision making, quality must be expressed in terms that can be measured and presented to management on a timely basis. To be effective, quality must be defined more in terms of the strategic mission of the organization rather than just from a clinical perspective. For example, TQM requires new measures of organizational quality. Healthcare providers must get beyond clinical definitions of quality. The expressions of quality must be understood and shared by all key participants in the organization and they must all believe that increases in such measures will enhance values for the relevant clients. Generally, the measures of quality should meet or exceed client expectations. *In all respects, these new quality measures should be tangible and concrete.* Some of the statistical reporting tools that the management accountant should be familiar with are illustrated in *Appendix 13–2.*

3. *Focus on process relationships*

In many service settings, the management focus is on outputs. Many budgeting and costing systems are driven by output measures (i.e., bottom line, number of DRGs). Under TQM, the focus shifts away from these

---

[6]Omachonu, Vincent K., *Total Quality Productivity Management in Health Care Organizations*, Norcross, GA: Institute of Industrial Engineers, 1991, pp. 31–59.

types of outputs towards a continuous review and analysis of all of the activities necessary to produce specified outputs. The focus is not on the services, but on the activities necessary to produce the services and how they relate to each other. Does an activity add value to the service or expectations of the client? Or does a particular activity cause waste, i.e., what would happen to quality if this activity was eliminated? In other words, the focus of TQM is on redesigning processes and relationships in order to achieve the desired outcomes the first time, without waste or rework or repetition. Nonvalue added steps are removed and the remaining processes are streamlined.

4. *Involve employees*
   TQM cannot work if only managers are involved. Employee *involvement* and *empowerment* is essential. Employees have the knowledge and skills to find and fix problems, remove barriers to improved customer service, and make appropriate process decisions. Creativity and innovations can rarely be achieved without the involvement of employees. Management controls must be refined or eliminated under TQM. Many accounting functions that focus on control of employees must be revised. In many cases, the existing system of effective financial reports must be completely revised. These demands on the accounting function will be more fully covered in the next section.

Total cost management

The emphasis on a *total cost management* system is a natural outgrowth of a *total quality management (TQM)* approach. An effective cost management system should provide the necessary information through effective reporting that enables managers to make better decisions. To accomplish this goal, the emphasis on cost accounting which is basically a reactive system based on past financial results must be changed to a proactive system which includes incorporating information or impact assessment of the organizational environment and operational technology. For example, the organizational environment would include employee reactions to financial reports and the failure of most current accounting systems to fully capture the hidden costs of quality has understated the significance of the amount of costs involved. Finally, TQM requires a continuing improvement of the processes used to provide the services which make historical data even more suspect for management decisions. McIlhattan identified (*Exhibit 13–3*) the strengths and attributes of a total cost management system in the following way.[7]

---

[7] McIlhattan, Robert D., "The Path to Total Cost Management", in *Journal of Cost Management for the Manufacturing Industry,* Warren, Gorham and Lamont, Inc., Vol. 1, No. 2, 1987, p. 5. Extracted with permission.

Exhibit 13–3
Total cost management

Attributes	Strengths
• Management as well as systems integration	• Links operating position to strategic goals
• An uncompromising attitude to match process to cost information	• Includes all business functions
• Captures strategic measures in addition to financial measures	• Focuses on only important product cost elements from procurement through distribution
• Shifts from variable to fixed cost focus	• Adapts to changing technology
• Links technology, human behavior, and information systems	• Coordinates human resources, technology, cost, and planning elements of business
• Reflects total product life cycle costs for comparison with competition	• Associates business cost to value creation
• Focus on profitability and cash flow as opposed to cost only	• Supports customer demands on business
	• Serves as a catalyst for organizational improvements

Under his concept, total cost management becomes an extension of the planning process (and TQM) and requires both financial and nonfinancial indicators to support decision making.

Costs of quality

The standard theme of TQM is that poor quality is expensive and high quality does not have to be expensive. The challenge of TQM is to re-orient employees to think about the high cost of nonvalue added activities. Quality improvements can result in improved revenues or in reduced costs, and both result in an improved bottom line. As client needs are better satisfied, revenues will increase. For example, new services, or revisions of existing services, will result in more revenue dollars. As waste is eliminated, costs will be reduced. Elimination of scheduling gaps or testing errors in ancillary departments will help reduce costs. Similarly, producing any service without errors, the first time, will result in lower costs. Since cost data has typically been the domain of the management accountant, it is crucial to fully understand the nature of quality costs.

The American Society for Quality Control defines quality costs as:

> Quality costs are a measure of costs specifically associated with the achievement or non-achievement of product or service quality— as defined by all product or service requirements established by the company and its contracts with customers and society. More spe-

cifically, quality costs are the total of the costs incurred by (a) investing in the prevention of non-conformance to requirements; (b) appraising a product or service for conformance to requirements; and (c) failure to meet requirements.[8]

A slightly more concise definition of quality costs would be "all costs incurred to help the employee do the right job every time and the cost of determining if the output is acceptable, plus any cost incurred by the organization and the customer because the output does not meet specifications and/or customer expectations."[9]

The traditional view of quality costs is that at least 20 percent of any organization's revenues are involved in achieving and not achieving quality. In many service organizations, quality costs exceed 40 percent of total revenues. However, these costs are not explicitly reported in financial reports because quality costs are not categorized in the chart of accounts. Traditional financial reports bury the quality costs in overhead and labor cost categories. They do not permit a convenient and timely analysis of the costs of low quality, nor of the benefits that could be achieved with higher quality levels.

To expand on this concept Milakovich separates poor quality costs into two areas: direct (visible) and indirect (hidden). *Exhibit 13–4* indicates the nature of these two cost of quality categories.

In both of these categories, quality costs can be separated into three areas: prevention costs, appraisal costs, and failure costs. Prevention costs are incurred at the front-end of any process and are designed to prevent errors and defects. Prevention costs also include the design costs necessary to incorporate quality into the service delivery process. Prevention costs are prospective in nature and include:

identification of client needs;
education and training;
quality monitoring and reporting systems;
quality administration;
quality planning and design.

These costs are incurred before any services are provided. The effective and different design of healthcare delivery systems will have a major effect on the resultant quality costs of actual services. At some level of appraisal costs, it will be impossible to achieve further quality improve-

---

[8] J.T. Hagan, *Principles of Quality Costs,* Milwaukee: American Society for Quality Control, 1986, p. 3.

[9] James H. Harrington, *Poor-Quality Cost,* Milwaukee: ASQC Quality Press, 1987, p. 5.

Exhibit 13–4
Hidden costs of poor quality

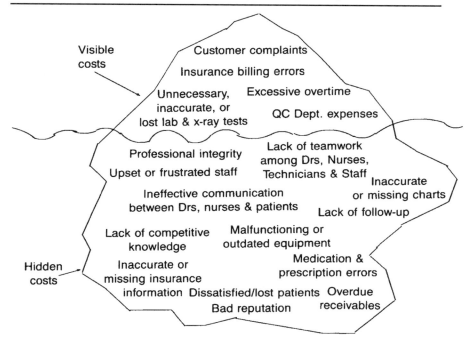

Source: Milkavoich, M.E., "Creating a Total Quality Health Care Environment," *Health Care Management Review,* Aspen Publications, 16(2), p. 13.

ments without increasing design and prevention efforts. It should also be noted that every aspect of prevention costs results in additional outlay costs by the healthcare provider.

Appraisal costs represent the costs of inspecting and evaluating the extent to which the service delivery process meets customer requirements. Appraisal costs are usually incurred at the completion of a process and are retrospective in nature. Appraisal costs include:

     quality audits, accreditation, state surveys and other licensure or certifications;
     calibration and maintenance of equipment;
     inspection and testing of purchased items;
     service or process documentation;
     service or process inspection or evaluation.

Any audit of patient services, e.g., medical records, billing, or PRO activation, represents appraisal costs. Flow charting and industrial engineering reviews of processes or services are also appraisal costs. Under new systems of materials management (just-in-time [JIT], etc.), the costs of incoming inspections should be minimized. In each case, appraisal costs are incurred at the completion of some identifiable service or activity. Preventive and appraisal costs also fall in the category of control costs.

Failure costs can be separated into internal and external failures. Internal failure costs are the costs associated with correcting or replacing defective products or services before they reach the client. Internal failures typically occur during the service delivery process and include:

waste of any kind, e.g., wasted tests or supplies;
investigation of defective tests or other errors;
repeated tests, or any other unnecessary repetition;
idle time, or any other wasted time;
reinspection and correction time.

Internal failures represent costs that could be avoided. These costs are buried in administrative overhead and in the labor costs or provider departments. The costs of labor for time wasted are rarely identified in financial reports.

The second type of failure costs are the costs of external failure which are triggered or identified after the services have been performed and are recognized primarily by the client. External failure costs are generally discovered by the client and the resulting negative feelings can lead to lost revenue in the future. Typical external failure costs include:

client complaints;
liability costs or exposure to malpractice risk;
loss of client goodwill, referrals;
lost revenue due to word of mouth complaints.

These last two categories represent opportunity costs that are not usually included in financial reports and are not included in the estimated costs of quality noted above. However, these lost opportunities may be the most significant of any quality costs in terms of long-term effects on the provider's quality and ability to sustain itself in a competitive market. *Exhibit 13–5* is a graphic portrayal of the trade offs between the quality cost components.

As illustrated, preventive and appraisal costs have the same impact on failure costs, i.e., the more preventive costs incurred, the fewer failures will be incurred. In a similar manner, the more appraisal costs incurred, the fewer failures will be incurred.

It should be stressed, however, that preventive costs also reduce appraisal costs as the more steps that are taken to reduce the potential

Exhibit 13–5
Traditional trade-off in costs of quality

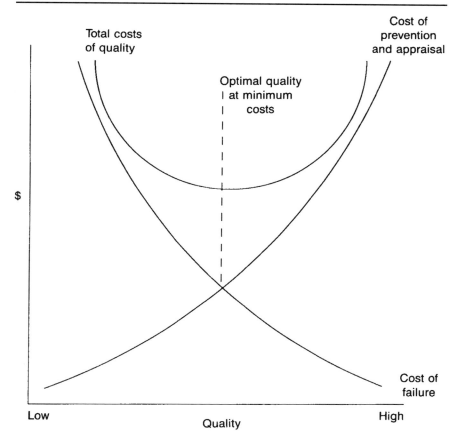

Source: Atkinson, John H., Jr., et al, *Current Trends in Cost of Quality,* NJ: NAA Study, 1991, p. 12.

for failures (i.e., improved design, employee training) the less need there is for appraisal costs. TQM methods focus on the use of preventive costs rather than appraisal costs to prevent failures. Appraisal costs fall into the nonvalue added category and should be eliminated whenever possible.[10]

In many organizations the costs of failure far exceed the other costs of quality. One estimate puts the costs of external failure at 30 percent, the

[10] Muthler, David L., and James B. Simpson, "Quality Costs: Facilitating the Quality Initiative," *Journal of Cost Management for the Manufacturing Industry,* Warren, Gorham and Lamont, Inc., Vol. 1, No. 1, 1987.

costs of internal failure at 45 percent, the costs of appraisal at 20 percent, and the costs of prevention at 5 percent.[11]

Ideally, the commitment of any healthcare provider should be to reduce the total costs of quality through process improvements primarily achieved through design efforts. Preventive costs should replace failure costs. The biggest improvement in quality will be achieved by preventing errors or defects before they occur. Preventive activities will reduce or eliminate appraisal and failure costs and should result in a reduction of the total costs of quality.

There are several methods available to calculate the cost of quality for a healthcare provider. *Exhibit 13–6* illustrates a cost of quality worksheet that encompasses all of the preventive, appraisal, and failure costs discussed before. Some of the data for this worksheet will be obtained from activity reports or graphs, some will be obtained from accounting records, and some must be estimated on the basis of observation and intuition. Process flow charts might also be used to develop estimates of nonvalue added time or waste time. The key ingredient to the assessment of costs of quality will be time spent in various activities and these time measures may not be readily available. But developing some formal process for identifying quality costs will facilitate the TQM process and will lead to the potential improvements noted earlier.[12] An example of an actual calculation of the cost of quality is illustrated in *Exhibit 13–7*.

Reporting the cost of quality

As noted earlier, in many organizations, the costs of quality are not reported in the financial statements because the information was not readily available from the accounting systems. In particular the hidden costs of lost customers would only show up in reduced revenues and profit margins and loss of market share. This weakness of financial reporting made it very difficult to sustain top management interest in the costs of quality unless they buy into TQM. TQM has as its primary focus the identification and elimination of poor quality and the related costs of poor quality. Reporting on the implementation and progress of TQM has had a significant impact on the accounting information reported for management decision making in the area of quality costs. The importance of monitoring and reporting the costs of quality is illustrated in *Exhibit 13–8*.

---

[11] Harrington, James H., *Poor-Quality Cost*, Milwaukee: ASQC Quality Press, 1987, p. 121.

[12] Anderson, Craig A., and Robin D. Daigh, "Quality Mind-Set Overcomes Barriers to Success," *Health Care Financial Management*, February 1991, p. 31.

Exhibit 13–6
Cost of quality worksheet

Department: _____   Date: _____

Internal Failure Costs

Description	No. Hours per Month	$ Rate per Hour	$ Labor per Month	$ Supply per Month	$ Oth exp per Month	$ Qual cost per Month	$ Qual cost per Year
(1)	(2)	(3)	(4) $(2)\times(3)$	(5)	(6)	(7) $(4)+(5)+(6)$	(8) $(7)\times 12$
Total							

External Failure Costs

Description	No. Hours per Month	$ Rate per Hour	$ Labor per Month	$ Supply per Month	$ Oth exp per Month	$ Qual cost per Month	$ Qual cost per Year
(1)	(2)	(3)	(4) $(2)\times(3)$	(5)	(6)	(7) $(4)+(5)+(6)$	(8) $(7)\times 12$
Total							

Department: _____   Date: _____

Prevention Costs

Description	No. Hours per Month	$ Rate per Hour	$ Labor per Month	$ Supply per Month	$ Oth exp per Month	$ Qual cost per Month	$ Qual cost per Year
(1)	(2)	(3)	(4) $(2)\times(3)$	(5)	(6)	(7) $(4)+(5)+(6)$	(8) $(7)\times 12$
Total							

Appraisal Costs

Description	No. Hours per Month	$ Rate per Hour	$ Labor per Month	$ Supply per Month	$ Oth exp per Month	$ Qual cost per Month	$ Qual cost per Year
(1)	(2)	(3)	(4) $(2)\times(3)$	(5)	(6)	(7) $(4)+(5)+(6)$	(8) $(7)\times 12$
Total							

Source: Daigh, Robin D., "Financial Implications of a Quality Improvement Process," *Topics in Health Care Financing*, Vol. 17(3), 1991, pp. 47–48.

Exhibit 13–7
Sample cost of quality calculation

Type	Description	Estimated volume	Annual volume	Position type	Minutes per occurrence	Annual hours	Average wage rate	Salary expense	Benefits (20 percent)	Estimated cost of quality
Prevention	Train technicians on equipment	8 hours per year × 20 technicians	160	Diagnostic imaging technician	—	160	$12.75	$ 2,040	$ 408	$ 2,448
Appraisal	Check registration for proper information	100 percent of 50,000 inpatient and outpatient visits	50,000	Diagnostic imaging technician	1	833	12.75	10,621	2,124	12,744
Internal failure	Locate master jacket not in file room	22.5 per day × 365 days	8,213	Diagnostic imaging file clerk	22.5	3,080	7.05	21,714	4,343	26,057
External failure	Retake film	4 percent of 70,000 exams	2,800	Film plus labor cost per exam	—	—	10.00[a]	28,000	—	28,000

a. Estimated cost of labor and materials for retaking an exam, per industry figures provided by imaging department director.

Source: Anderson, Craig A., and Robin D. Daigh, "Quality Mind-Set Overcomes Barriers to Success," *Healthcare Financial Management*, February 1991, p. 31.

Exhibit 13–8
Cost of quality guides the continuous improvement process

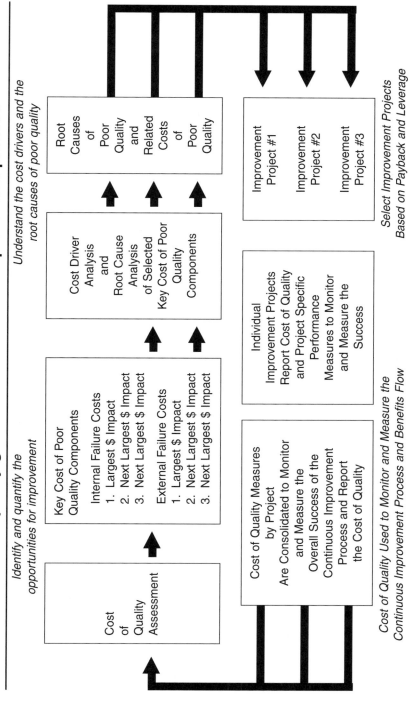

Identify and quantify the opportunities for improvement

Understand the cost drivers and the root causes of poor quality

Select Improvement Projects Based on Payback and Leverage

Cost of Quality Assessment

Key Cost of Poor Quality Components

Internal Failure Costs
1. Largest $ Impact
2. Next Largest $ Impact
3. Next Largest $ Impact

External Failure Costs
1. Largest $ Impact
2. Next Largest $ Impact
3. Next Largest $ Impact

Cost Driver Analysis and Root Cause Analysis of Selected Key Cost of Poor Quality Components

Root Causes of Poor Quality and Related Costs of Poor Quality

Improvement Project #1

Improvement Project #2

Improvement Project #3

Individual Improvement Projects Report Cost of Quality and Project Specific Performance Measures to Monitor and Measure the Success

Cost of Quality Measures by Project Are Consolidated to Monitor and Measure the Overall Success of the Continuous Improvement Process and Report the Cost of Quality

Cost of Quality Used to Monitor and Measure the Continuous Improvement Process and Benefits Flow

Source: Atkinson, John Hawley Jr., et al, *Current Trends in Cost of Quality;* NJ: NAA Study, 1991, p. 87.

As noted earlier, quality costs are typically not collected and reported separately under most management accounting systems. Special studies and special reports are often needed to identify and track quality costs. Quality costs are often viewed as a percentage of some underlying expenses, labor hours, or volume of services. Reports encompassing the entire organization are often based on percentages of revenues, while departmental reports are based on expenses or labor hours or volume measures. Another base used in tracking quality costs are percentages of per unit costs, but since per unit costs can be distorted by volume changes or by fixed costs allocations, this method may not be sufficiently accurate for decision making.

Quality cost reports should be simple and straightforward. The purpose of a quality cost report is to help in planning quality improvements and in evaluating their effectiveness. They should not be used as a barrier to improvements. One of the TQM gurus, Philip Crosby, warns "Don't get so involved with the techniques of calculating the costs of quality that you forget what it should be used for: to call attention to the problems and identify those areas needing corrective action."[13]

Cost drivers

Total cost management requires the identification of "cost drivers." Cost drivers are the activities that cause the incurrence of the cost. Basically, the characteristics of these activities include the complexity of the service being performed and the environment in which it is being provided. Complexity would include the type of equipment being used, number of setups required, number of reworks or bad outputs. The environment would include number of vendors, number of direct and indirect staff, number of material moves, and number of schedule changes. In most cases, the number of transactions add to the costs of providing the service. Many of the transactions involved nonvalue added activities such as movement from one area to another, waiting time due to inefficient scheduling (i.e., copying and filing time).

By properly identifying the cost drivers and resulting costs, the elimination of NVA in a TQM system becomes more feasible as cost drivers are identified and reported in terms of costs avoided.

The importance of determining the costs of quality should not be underestimated. For the management accountant, determining the best estimates of these costs and reporting them in a meaningful fashion is crucial to the successful implementation of a total quality management (TQM) and total cost management (TCM) systems.

---

[13] Crosby, Philip B., *Quality is Free: The Art of Making Quality Certain*, New York: Mentor, 1979, p. 181.

Standard cost systems

The introduction of standard cost systems in healthcare organizations was facilitated by management's desire to know the cost of a specific product line or service. This resulted in the identification of cost elements such as labor, material, and overhead. As the standard costs systems became more complex, overhead was segregated into direct categories (similar to manufacturing's overhead) and indirect for general administration functions. The direct and indirect overhead costs had to be allocated to the specific services or product lines in order to obtain the full cost of offering the service.

Since direct labor was routinely collected by services or product line, in many systems direct labor hours were used as the allocation activity. Under the cost driver approach, it became clear that direct labor hours were not the prime reason for the incurrence of the overhead costs and therefore, overhead was misapplied resulting in erroneous costing of the service. For example, in pharmacy, the number of prescriptions filled may be a more valid indicator of a cost driver than the labor hours of the pharmacy staff. In a like manner, the number of meals served would be an appropriate cost driver for cafeteria costs. In *Exhibit 13–9,* an example of some of the possible cost drivers for services provided in a healthcare setting are compared to the typical measures used in a standard cost accounting system. In the rush to adapt cost accounting systems, many healthcare providers no longer used the activity bases suggested by the Medicare cost report. It is possible that the activity bases used by Medicare will be used again under an activity-based accounting system as the appropriate allocation choices.

In selecting activity measures, many healthcare providers only use macromeasures which do not adequately reflect the intensity of services offered. The micromeasures allow for more precise identification of the cost drivers.

Variance Analysis

The use of a standard cost system also facilitated the use of variance analysis. Variance analysis consists of analyzing the difference between standards and actual costs and attempting to fix responsibility for the variance through the calculations of spending, wage, and efficiency variances. Under the TQM approach, the use of standards for performance measurement can result in dysfunctional behavior. For example: lower per unit costs result from long production runs, i.e., batch all of a certain type of procedures to be done at the same time. This usually results in patient wait time, physicians not receiving test results on a timely basis, and other NVA costs.

Exhibit 13–9
Sample activity bases and cost drivers
for costing techniques

Department	(Macro)	(Micro)
Operating Room	Surgical case	Operating room minutes
Anesthesiology	Anesthesia case	Anesthesia care minutes
Postoperative Rooms	Postoperative case	Postoperating room minutes
Radiology	Exams	RVUs
Laboratory	Tests	RVUs
Physical Therapy	Modalities	Person minutes
Isotopes	Treatments	RVUs
Blood Bank	Transfusions	RVUs
Delivery Room	Deliveries	Person minutes
Social Services	Visits	Person hours or fractions of hours
Emergency Room	Visits	Person minutes
Routine Services	Charges	RBRVS
Ambulatory Care	Visits	AVGs
Per procedure or per case	DRG	Intensity of care or activity levels being developed

Standard cost bases

Cost components	Allocation bases
Direct labor	N/A
Direct materials	N/A
Direct overhead	Direct labor hours
Indirect overhead	
General expenses	Direct labor hours
Administrative expenses	Direct labor hours

Another potential problem is that basing performance measurement on the achievement of a standard can result in managers/employees relaxing when that standard is reached. This is the antithesis in the TQM approach which focuses on the continuing pursuit of increasing quality. The quality staircase is typically used to emphasize this approach. Assuming the standard achieved is a level one, the goal of the TQM process would be to continue to maintain this level while attempting to move up the staircase to the next higher step. This is illustrated in *Exhibit 13–10*.

For example, strict reliance on nurse staffing based on estimated acuity levels and standard hours can cause dysfunctional behavior as the standard hours can be accepted as appropriate quality and cost of care. TQM requires a continuous evaluation of the standards and seeks for ways to reduce NVA activities included in the standard.

An organization implementing TQM must insure that the employees understand how to identify potential problems, how they can be analyzed, and how the results are presented. Since the accounting department is usually tasked with the number collecting and crunching function, the

Exhibit 13–10

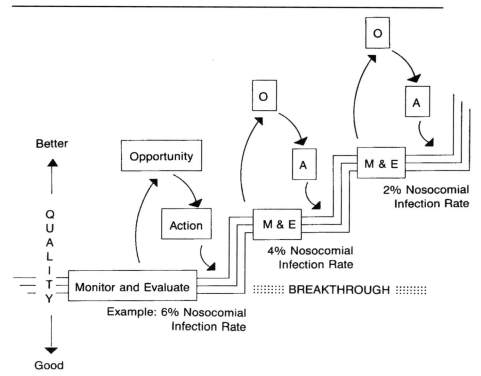

Adapted from: Slee, Vergil N., and Debora A., *Health Care Terms,* 2nd ed., St. Paul, MN: Tringa Press, 1991.

accountants must understand the work processes of the care givers and the needs of management for decision making. The inclusion of members of the accounting department in the quality circle groups and the total quality management task force is crucial to this development.

Finally, it is also important that accountants have a full understanding of the statistical tools available and the most appropriate reporting formats that can be used in presenting the data. The goal should be to present the data in an easy to understand format which allows problems to be identified and results checked against the planned effort. *Appendix 13–2* illustrates some examples of the most commonly used reporting tools which have met with success in quality management efforts.

Achievement under TQM

Many healthcare providers have had positive and well-documented successes under TQM. This chapter cannot provide an exhaustive compendium of such successes. However, it may be instructive to look at several such achievements.

Rush-Presbyterian-St. Luke's Medical Center in Chicago has achieved the following departmental improvements under TQM:

- decreased X-ray repeat rates in diagnostic radiology
- decreased employee absentee rate by 22.7 percent (1987–88)
- reduced laboratory turn-around time by 25 percent
- reduced hand-drawn checks by 25 percent
- improved patient transport by adding eight FTEs
- consolidated nine prescription forms into three forms
- increased patient education about refill procedures
- identified why many prescriptions were unfilled

In this case, TQM was in the early stages and many staff were still participating in educational programs. TQM would extend to the larger context of the university and in various managed care programs. The bottom-line view was that "ultimately, the feedback in the TQM process can take virtually any operation ahead in its quest for customer satisfaction."[14]

Parkview Episcopal Medical Center in Pueblo, Colorado, is an HCA role model for the TQM quality improvement process. After an intensive educational effort involving many senior managers, a quality improvement council was established and advisors were designated for quality improvement teams. These teams study various service delivery processes to detect where breakdowns occur, chart data to discover trends, suggest solutions, and monitor results. A monthly newsletter has been established to keep all employees informed of quality improvement efforts. Results include:

- reducing employee turnover from 15 to 18 percent per year
- saving at least $10,000 per year in food service delivery
- reducing late surgeries from 48 to 8 percent per month
- reducing medication cart filling errors by 80 percent

The behavioral effects accompanying TQM have been enormous at Parkview. Managerial roles have changed from being responsible for generating good ideas to being able to recognize and accept good ideas that come from employees. "Our belief is that employees really know what they're doing. As managers we should be listening to them instead of them listening to us. Our job now is to manage the process."[15]

---

[14] Koska, Mary T., "Case Study: Quality Improvement in a Diversified Health Center," *Hospitals,* December 5, 1990, pp. 38–39.

[15] Koska, Mary T., "Adopting Deming's Quality Improvement Ideas: A Case Study," *Hospitals,* July 5, 1990, pp. 58–64.

In another example, in the 257-bed Bellin Memorial Hospital in Green Bay, Wisconsin, an expert member quality improvement team analyzed incident reports from the previous thirty-two months to identify the number and types of medication errors in three hospital units. There were a total of 1,149 drug errors reported categorized by the following types:

Medication not administered	(282)	25%
Wrong dose	(175)	15%
Wrong medications	(174)	15%
Wrong time	(121)	10%
Wrong IV flow	(103)	9%
Other	(294)	26%

An analysis of the causes for wrong medication was completed which indicated over 70 percent of the errors were due to storage and dispensing problems. Implementing a variety of changes in the labeling of drugs and dispensing processes led to an 80 percent reduction in wrong medications in eight months and also resulted in a labor savings of $15,000 on an annual basis.[16]

Summary

Total quality management is a way of life. It is not the fad of the month, but a philosophy that becomes embedded in the fabric and culture of the organization. It is hard to implement and it will result in major changes in the organization and in its management accounting processes. In many respects, these changes are yet evolutionary and not well-known. Perhaps in future editions the entire contents of a text such as this will be different as management reporting and decision making processes have adapted to TQM.

Questions and problems

1. Define quality in a healthcare organization.

2. Define the quality assurance function in a healthcare organization.

3. What is CQI?

4. Define total quality management.

5. Who were Deming, Juran, and Crosby?

---

[16] Burda, David, "Hospital Teams Find Solutions Savings through Quality Management Techniques," *Modern Health Care*, November 12, 1990, p. 44.

6. What was Deming's basic philosophy?

7. What does PDCA stand for in a TQM environment?

8. What is the role of senior managers in a TQM environment?

9. Define nonvalue-added activities.

10. What are the costs of quality?

11. Can all quality costs be eliminated?

12. What is total cost management?

13. What are "cost drivers"?

14. What are some of the disadvantages of using standard costs in a TQM environment?

15. Why should management accountants and healthcare managers fully understand the use of statistical tools and reporting methods in the TQM environment?

References

Anderson, Craig A., and Robin D. Daigh. "Quality Mind-Set Overcomes Barriers to Success." *Healthcare Financial Management* (February 1991): 21–32.

Beloff, Jerome. "What is Quality, and How is it Measured." *Physician Executive* 17, no. 3 (May/June 1991): 20–24.

Berliner, Callie, and James A. Brimson, eds. *Cost Management for Today's Advanced Manufacturing, The CAM-I Conceptual Design.* Boston, MA: Harvard Business School Press, 1988.

Borok, Lawrence, S. "The Use of Relational Databases in Health Care Information Systems." *Journal of Health Care Finance* (summer 1995): 6–12.

Burda, David. "R.I. Hospital Group Acts as Quality Catalyst." *Modern Healthcare* (October 1, 1990): 42.

———. "Total Quality Management Becomes Big Business." *Modern Healthcare* (January 28, 1991): 25–29.

Cooke, David J., and Kathleen L. Iannacchino. "The Deming Method for Problem Solving in Group Practice." *MGM Journal* (March/April 1991): 52, 53, 61.

Couch, James B., ed. *Health Care Quality Management for the 21st Century.* Tampa, FL: The American College of Physician Executives, 1991.

Crosby, Philip B. *Quality Without Tears: The Art of Hassle-Free Management.* New York, NY: New American Library, 1984.

Czarnecki, Mark T. "Benchmarking Can Add Up for Healthcare Accounting." *Healthcare Financial Management* (September 1994): 62–67.

Daigh, Robin D. "Financial Implications of a Quality Improvement Process." *Topics in Health Care Financing* 17, no. 3 (spring 1991): 42–52.

Gapenski, L.C. *Understanding Health Care Financial Management.* Ann Arbor, MI: AUPHA Press/Health Administration Press, 1991.

Geigle, Ron, and Stanley B. Jones. "Outcomes Measurement: A Report from the Front." *Inquiry* 27, no. 1 (spring 1990): 7–13.

Haedicke, Jack, and David Feil. "In a DOD Environment Hughes Aircraft Sets the Standard for ABC." *Management Accounting* (February 1991): 29–33.

Horngren, Charles T., George Foster, and Srikant M. Datar. *Cost Accounting: A Managerial Emphasis.* Englewood Cliffs, NJ: Prentice Hall, 1994.

Howell, Robert A., and Stephen Soucy. *Factory 2000+ Management Accounting's Changing Role.* Montvale, NJ: National Association of Accountants, 1988.

Kanatsu, Takashi. *TQM for Accounting a New Role in Company-Wide Improvement.* Cambridge, MA: Productivity Press, 1990.

Koska, Mary T. "Case Study: Quality Improvement in a Diversified Health Center." *Hospitals* (December 5, 1990): 38–39.

Longo, Daniel R., and Deborah Bohr. *Quantitative Methods in Quality Management, A Guide for Practitioners.* Chicago, IL: American Hospital Association, 1990.

Lynn, Monty L., and David P. Osborn. "Deming's Quality Principles: A Health Care Application." *Hospitals & Health Services Administration* 36, no. 2 (spring 1991): 111–19.

McLaughlin, Curtis P., and Arnold D. Kaluzny. "Total Quality Management in Health: Making it Work." *Health Care Management Review* 5, no. 3 (summer 1990): 7–14.

Merry, Martin D. "Illusion vs. Reality TQM Beyond the Yellow Brick Road." *Healthcare Executive* (March/April 1991): 18–21.

Milakovich, Michael E. "Creating a Total Quality Health Care Environment." *Health Care Management Review* 16, no. 2 (1991): 9–20.

Omachonu, Vincent K. *Total Quality Productivity Management in Health Care Organizations.* Norcross, GA: Institute of Industrial Engineers, 1991.

Palmer, R. Heather, et al. *Striving for Quality in Health Care.* Ann Arbor, MI: Health Administration Press, 1991.

Smith, L.J., J. Frazier, and W.S. Crone. "Strategic Considerations for Capital Formation and Development." *Healthcare Financial Management* (March 1994): 30–36.

Steiner, Thomas E. "Activity-Based Accounting for Total Quality: Analyzing Activities Means Better Service to the Customer." *Management Accounting* (October 1990): 39–42.

Topics in Health Care Financing: Measuring Quality of Care 18, no. 2 (winter 1991).

Tyler, Russell D. "From QA to TQM." *Physician Executive* 17, no. 3 (May/June 1991): 25–28.

A brief summary of Deming's and Crosby's fourteen points for quality management

W. Edwards Deming's fourteen points are:[1]

1. Create constancy of purpose for the improvement of product and service
2. Adopt the New Philosophy
3. Cease dependence on mass inspection
4. End the practice of awarding business on price tag alone
5. Improve constantly and forever the system of production and service
6. Institute training
7. Institute leadership
8. Drive out fear
9. Break down barriers between staff areas
10. Eliminate slogans, exhortations, and targets for the work force
11. Eliminate numerical quotas
12. Remove barriers to pride of workmanship
13. Institute a vigorous program of education and retraining
14. Take action to accomplish the transformation

---

[1] Reprinted with permission of The Putnam Publishing Group from *The Deming Management Method* by Mary Walton, copyright 1986.

Philip Crosby's fourteen steps to quality improvement:[2]

1. Management commitment
2. Quality improvement team
3. Quality measurement
4. Cost of quality evaluation
5. Quality awareness
6. Corrective action
7. Establish an ad hoc committee
8. Supervisor training
9. Zero defects day
10. Goal setting
11. Removal of error causes
12. Recognition
13. Quality councils
14. Do it again

All of the approaches have a consistent theme of quality teams of workers involved, an awareness that quality depends on them, and management's commitment to allowing knowledgeable individuals to change the process.

---

[2] Reprinted with permission from Philip B. Crosby's *Quality Without Tears: The Art of Hassle-Free Management,* McGraw-Hill, Inc., 1984, p. 99.

Statistical reporting tools for TQM

One of the major goals of a change in the reporting system to meet TQM requirements must be in the area of simplification. The care givers and the management must be able to understand the reports presented by the accounting department. Some reporting tools that fit these needs are:

- PARETO diagrams
- Cause and effect diagrams
- Run charts
- Control charts
- Flow charts

A brief description of the tools follows:[1]

• PARETO analysis focuses on the major causes of a problem area and displays them in descending order or frequency of occurrence. The graph helps to determine which factors to concentrate on first.

Exhibit 1
PARETO analysis

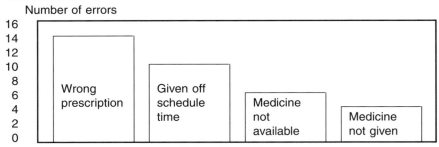

---

[1] For an excellent discussion of statistical tools in a healthcare setting see *The Memory Jogger: A Pocket Guide of Tools for Continuous Improvement,* Methuen, MA: GOAL/QPC, 1985 and 1988.

• Cause and effect (typically called the fishbone diagram) diagrams are used to show the relationship between some outcome and all the causes influencing it. The key is to identify the possible causes that will impact on the outcome and analyze them accordingly.

Exhibit 2
Cause and effect diagrams

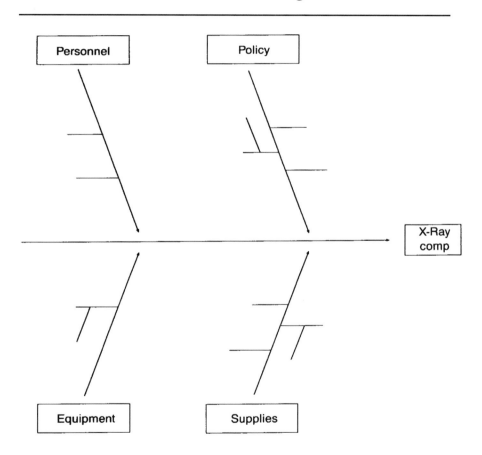

• Run charts are useful to monitor a process to detect changes over time through visual means and observe if the average measurement is changing.

Exhibit 3
Run charts

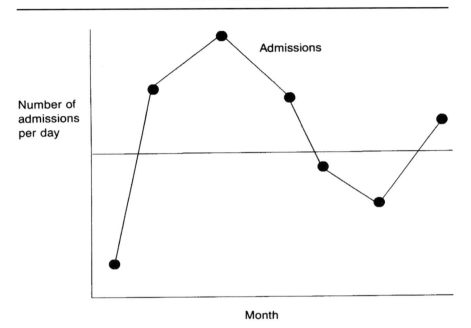

Number of admissions per day

Admissions

Month

• Control charts are very similar to run charts with statistically determined control limits drawn on either side of the average or desired level of activity. There are two types of variations that can occur, *common* or expected deviations from the average due to causes inside the system by design, or other controllable factors and *special* deviations which come from unplanned activities outside the system. The special deviations must be removed from the control chart before control activities can take place.

Exhibit 4
Control charts

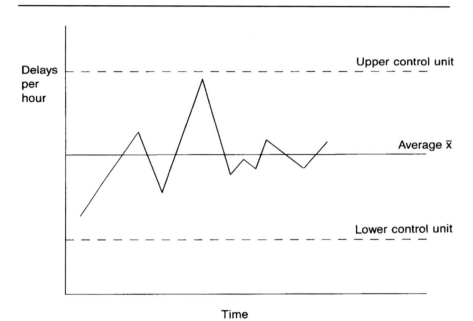

• Flow charts illustrate the steps a process takes from beginning to end. They can be very useful in identifying where decisions are made, potential problem areas and the path the process follows in achieving output.

Exhibit 5
Flow chart

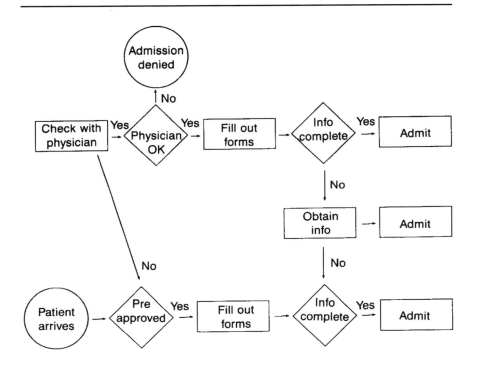

Index